A HISTORY OF JAPAN

DURING THE CENTURY OF EARLY FOREIGN INTERCOURSE (1542–1651).

BY

JAMES MURDOCH, M.A.,

IN COLLABORATION WITH

ISOH YAMAGATA.

WITH MAPS.

KOBE, JAPAN:

PUBLISHED AT THE OFFICE OF THE "CHRONICLE."

1903

A HISTORY OF JAPAN.

PREFACE.

I HAVE to thank Professor B. H. Chamberlain and Sir E. M. Satow, K.C.M.G., for putting many exceedingly valuable books and documents at my disposal, and H.E. Lieutenant-General Baron Terauchi, Minister for War, for permission to re-produce the maps and plans in the *Nihon Senshi* and to utilise that excellent and most painstaking work. Mr. Ozaki Yukio, M.P., very kindly read the rough draft of this work and furnished me with many hints, and valuable assistance in various ways; while Mr. J. C. Hall, H.B.M.'s Consul at Kobe, has also placed me under obligation by going through the book. To Mr. Y. Iwasaki, Director of the Kago-shima High School, I am indebted for a translation of an important passage from the *Seihan-Yashi* and for information about some points in the history of Satsuma. Mr. Murakawa, *Bungakushi*, has ren-dered sterling service by his researches among the historical manuscripts in the Imperial University of Tokyo.

But to none am I under greater obligations than to my collaborator, Mr. Isoh Yamagata. Besides being responsible for the maps, he has supplied me with thousands of pages of excellent translations from standard Japanese authorities and from hitherto unpublished manuscripts. Without his assistance the book could not have been written.

The heavy task of seeing the work through the press has fallen upon Mr. Robert Young, Editor of the *Kobe Chronicle*.

JAMES MURDOCH.

November, 1903.

CONTENTS.

—·→⊕←·—

CONTENTS.

HISTORY OF JAPAN.

———◦⟩✦⟨◦———

CHAPTER I.

INTRODUCTORY.

THIS volume does not purport to be a History of Japan, but a History of Japan merely from the date (1543?) when Europeans first appeared in the Archipelago down to a date some dozen years subsequent to the expulsion of the Portuguese in 1639 and the virtual imprisonment of the Dutch traders in the artificial islet of Deshima in Nagasaki Harbour in 1641. It assumes to deal with nothing beyond the century of early European intercourse, at the end of which the timid Tokugawa Bureaucracy thought fit to foist upon the Empire the luxury of a retirement from all the duties and all the worries and responsibilities of active international life. The nine hundred odd years of authentic Japanese history before 1543 A.D. do not fall within the scope of this work, properly speaking, in any way whatsoever.

Yet, inasmuch as not every one is familiar with the state of affairs which prevailed in the Japanese islands at the time Europeans first made their shores, it may be well to set forth a brief and compendious review of the salient circumstances which led to the rise and development of that feudal system the Portuguese found established in Japan in the middle of the sixteenth century.

When in 793 A.D.—seven years before Charlemagne's coronation in Rome—Kyōto was made the permanent capital of the realm by Kwammu Tennō, the fiftieth Emperor, the country was a monarchy, which was really ruled by the central administration. The machinery through which the sovereign acted had been borrowed from China about a century and a quarter before Kwammu's time, and consisted of a Council of

B

State of three members—sometimes fewer—under which were
the Eight Boards charged with the details of departmental
executive and judicial work.[1]

At various times Japan had been portioned out into provinces; and about the beginning of the seventh century we
hear of as many as one hundred and eighty provincial governors.
However, if not before the time of Kwammu, at all events
within a century after his death, we meet with that division
of the Empire into sixty-six provinces and two islands, which
continued down to the date of the Revolution of 1868.[2] At
the date of the first appearance of Europeans in Japan these
provinces were mostly mere geographical expressions. Originally,

---

[1] This Council of State, called the *Daijō-kwan*, consisted of—
    1. The Chancellor of the Empire (*Daijō-daijin*);
    2. The Minister of the Left (*Sa-daijin*);
    3. The Minister of the Right (*U-daijin*);
while the First Adviser of State (*Dai-nagon*) took part in advising, and the
Minister of the *Nakatsukasa-sho* (one of the Eight Boards) inspected and affixed
his seal to Imperial Rescripts. Much later on, in addition to these three great
Ministers, another, somewhat inferior in rank, was created. This was:—
    4. The Interior Great Minister (*Nai-daijin*).
Only once—namely, in the reign of the Emperor Juntoku (1211-1227)—were
these four Ministries all filled at the same time. The rank attached to the last
three was but slightly different, and they were of equal authority.
In 888 the office of *Kwanbaku* was instituted. Through the *Kwanbaku* the
affairs of State were brought to the knowledge of the Emperor. "This office
was usually combined in the person of either the Chancellor of the Empire,
the Minister of the Left, the Minister of the Right, or the Lord Keeper
of the Privy Seal. The *Kwanbaku* was the highest of the official positions, and
consequently when the Minister of the Left, or the Minister of the Right, or
the Lord Keeper of the Privy Seal was appointed to this post, he took precedence
over the Chancellor of the Empire."
For details of the functions of the Eight Boards, see Marquis Ito's *Commentaries
on the Constitution of the Empire of Japan*, pp. 86-88.

  [2] It is perfectly hopeless to expect to attain any mastery over the history of
Japan without a close study of the map of the Empire in provinces and in circuits.
The sixty-six Provinces were portioned out among seven circuits or *do*, in addition
to the five Home Provinces, which formed the *Go-kinai*.
    1.—The *Go-kinai* (August Home Provinces, because they had been the Imperial
domain), appearing in the missionary writings as the *Tenka* and the *Tenshi*, consisted of the five provinces of Yamashiro, Yamato, Kawachi, Idzumi, and Settsu.
This region was the seat of the Imperial family for more than 2,000 years; at
nearly all times (until 1868) it has been the chief seat of Japanese culture. In
mediæval times it was the most densely-peopled part of the Empire, and even to-
day, with its great cities of Kyōto, Osaka, and Kōbe it can claim to be the industrial
centre of the Empire.
    2.—The Tōkaidō, or East Sea Circuit, extending from the eastern frontiers of
the Home Provinces along the Pacific coast on to a point some hundred and
twenty miles north of Cape King. This region embraced fifteen provinces, viz.,
Iga, Ise, Shima, Owari, Mikawa, Tōtōmi, Suruga, Idzu, Kai (which is wholly
inland), Sagami, Musashi, Awa, Kadzusa, Shimōsa, and Hitachi. To the north of
No. 2 ran Circuit
    3.—The Tōsandō, or East Mountain Circuit, which embraced the eight provinces
of Omi, Mino, Hida, Shinano, Kōdzuke, Shimotsuke (all inland), and the vast
stretches of Mutsu (or Oshiu) and Dewa. To the north of Omi, Mino, Hida, and
Shinano lay Circuit
    4.—The Hokurikudō, North Land Circuit, which consisted of six provinces—
Wakasa, Echizen, Kaga, Noto, Etchū, Echigo, and the Island of Sado. It was only

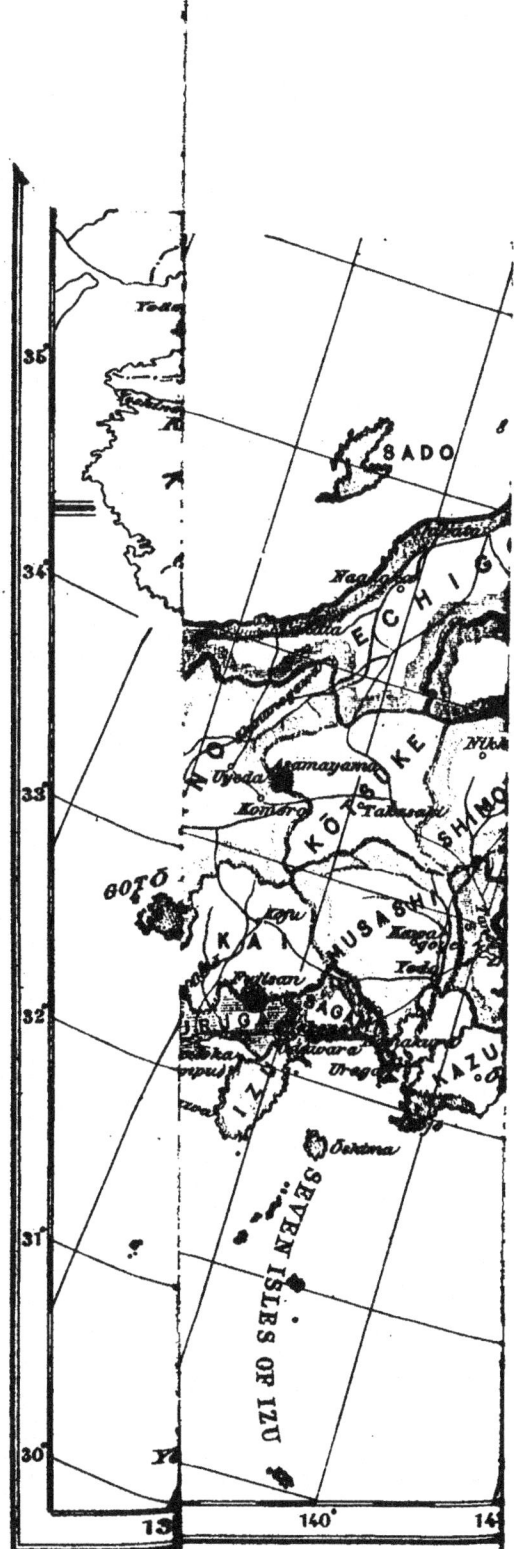

however, they had been administrative units, and as such they continued to be down to the thirteenth century. Each of them was in charge of a Governor appointed by the Central Imperial authorities for a term of four (at one time six) years, whose chief duties were the maintenance of order and the collection of the various taxes paid in kind or in textures or in money. It was mainly on the revenue thus collected from the provinces that the real power of the Emperor and of the central administration, composed exclusively of *Kugé*, or Court nobles, was based. However, it is to be noted that until as late as the eleventh century. the hold that the Kyōto Government had upon the Northern and Eastern provinces was the reverse of a strong one. In some of these quarters the *Emishi*, or aborigines, had not been brought to subjection, and in others revolts were not infrequent. But from the eighth century the reduction of the country between Fuji-san and the Straits of Tsugaru had been proceeding, with one result, among others, that large tracts of cultivable land became available for settlement. This result was a most important one, for it very soon helped to revolutionise the system of land-tenure in Japan. So long as the Imperial authority had been confined mainly to the *Go-kinai*, or Home Provinces, especial care had been taken to prevent anything in the shape of *latifundia*.[3] Yet even so, already by the

at a comparatively late date that these latter two circuits were brought under the sway of the Kyōto Government. To the west of the Home Provinces the main island was partitioned into two more Circuits. That on the Sea of Japan (5), called the Sanindō, Mountain-back Circuit, comprised Tamba (wholly inland), Tango, Tajima, Inaba, Hōki, Idzumo, Iwami, with the Island of Oki, while (6), the Sanyodō, or Mountain-front Circuit, fringing the northern shores of the Inland Sea, was made up of Harima, Mimasaka (wholly inland), Bizen, Bitchū, Bingo, Aki, Suwō, and Nagato. So far, with the five Home Provinces, we have accounted for fifty-one provinces in the Circuits of the main island with which we have so far been dealing.

Of the remaining fifteen, eleven belong to (7) the Saikaidō, or Western Sea Circuit, nearly synonymous with the Island of Kyūshū. These were Chikuzen, Chikugo, Buzen, Bungo, Hizen, Higo, Hiūga, Satsuma, and Ōsumi, together with the Iwo Islands—Iki, off the Hizen coast, and Tsushima, half-way between Japan and Korea. In (8) the Nankaidō, or Southern Sea Circuit, were the four provinces of the Island of Shikoku—Awa, Tosa, Iyo, and Sanuki—together with the Island of Awaji, and the province of Kii across the channel in the main island.

[3] "A piece of land shall be given to each person in the district where he lives. Even when the boundaries of a district are changed, one does not lose one's title to land which thereby falls within a different district. Every six years an investigation shall be made, and the number of those who have died shall be ascertained. Their land will then be given to those who have reached the proper age, or have immigrated since the last distribution. Every male of five years or over is to receive two *tan*, and each female of that age one-third of the amount; but according to the size of the district the quantity may vary. Slaves under public authority shall receive two *tan*, and those belonging to individuals shall receive one-third of this amount"—Code of Taihō, 702 A.D. A *tan* was then equal to 1,500 square yards, roughly speaking.

beginning of the eighth century evasions of the Imperial land regulations in the old settled districts had become frequent; and as the conquest of the north and east proceeded, the regulations in question lost all their force. In the recently conquered districts certain individuals brought large stretches of *Shin-den*, or new land, under cultivation, most probably by colonies of slaves; and as land of this description was at once hereditary and tax-free, the Kyōto Government drew no advantage from it whatsoever. In fact, such tax-free estates very soon sapped the financial resources of the central administration. The peasants on the adjacent tax-paying lands, finding that by removing to these *Shin-den* they would have to pay a rent much less than the amount of their annual taxes on ordinary land, hastened to become tenants of these great landlords, and so the tax-paying land was often left untilled. In addition to that, the occupants of the public estate evaded the payment of taxes by conveying their farms to the owners of *Shin-den*—or of the other species of *Shōyen*[4]—and so taking refuge under the immunity of the latter, deprived the Central Government of its legitimate revenue.

However, it may perhaps be questioned whether this development was at first so pregnant with disaster to the influence of the central administration as might appear. From the organisation of that administration towards the end of the seventh century down to the beginning of the eleventh, nearly all its offices had been filled by members of one single family of Court nobles—by the Fujiwaras. It was also from them that the provincial governors and their staffs were chiefly appointed, and in the extension of the *Shōyen* these officials found their opportunity. After their four years' tenure of office they usually returned to the capital large landholders and rich men, while they had not neglected to look after the interests of their kinsmen wielding authority in Kyōto. Hence the revenues of the provinces that had flowed into the Imperial Treasury now flowed into the private coffers of the Councillors and Ministers of State and of the officials of the Eight Boards. But so

---

[4] "*Shōyen*, so-called, arose in several ways. It originally meant land apportioned to members of the Imperial Family, or given to some one as reward for meritorious deeds in war or peace, or offered to a temple (for all such paid no taxes). But the largest part of the *Shōyen* consisted of waste land reclaimed and owned by persons of high rank or great power."—Simmons' and Wigmore's *Land-tenure and Local Institutions*, footnote 86.

long as the central administration and the Fujiwaras were synonymous terms, the Kyōto Government did not fail to find means to make its power felt in the older settled districts of the Empire. In those centuries the provincial governor was also commander of the militia when its services were required, and at first the Fujiwara prefects had taken part in the campaigns against the *Emishi* from time to time. But with lapse of years they had found that risking their lives against savages was not the easiest road to advancement, and accordingly they abandoned the conduct of punitive expeditions to the two military families (both descended from Emperors) of Taira and of Minamoto that had been founded in the ninth and tenth centuries respectively. This abandonment of the camp by the Fujiwaras was at once the cause of their own ruin, and of the overthrow of the centralised Kyōto Government administered by *Kuge* (Court nobles) in the name of the Emperor.

The younger family of Minamoto, after two generations of fighting, contrived to reduce the eight or ten provinces around what is now the capital of Japan (Tōkyō) to tranquillity and to professed obedience to the Kyōto Government. This they had been able to effect by enlisting the services of what was then called the "warrior class." At the date of the organisation of the central administration on Chinese models—towards the end of the seventh century—a class of generals had been created, and commanders of the "Six Guards" or household troops appointed, while the War Office had been made one of the Eight Boards. The able-bodied males of each province had been divided into three parts, one of which was set aside for military service, and a regiment of 1,000 men organised in each of the outlying provinces. Some time later on the authorities ordered that all useless soldiers should be dismissed, and those among the rich peasants who had sufficient capacity for archery and horsemanship and who were most skilled in military exercises should be called out when need be, and that the bodily feeble should apply themselves to agriculture or industry exclusively. This regulation really amounted to the institution of a separate military class—a class that found most employment in Dewa, Mutsu, and the Kwantō. Although the services these rendered in the field would have entitled many of them to enter the ranks of the Six Guards, or to become Court pages in Kyōto, they mostly remained

in their native provinces, where they contrived to be appointed
heads of *mura* or administrative districts, or in the newly-
conquered territories, where they either obtained grants of, or
seized upon, tracts of *Shōyen*, or untaxed land.   In the former
case they not infrequently extended their influence over adjacent
mura, and in course of time emerged as territorial lords, after
purchasing a title from the Kyōto administration.[5]   In the
latter case they occasionally emerged as territorial lords also,
although they more usually, by a sort of commendation, became
the vassals of the great military leaders of the time.   What
gave a great impulse to this movement in North-eastern Japan
was the short-sightedness of the civilian Fujiwara administration in Kyōto.   The two Minamotos, Yoriyoshi and his son
Yoshiiye, had conquered and kept all the north-east of the main
island in peace for fifteen years at their own expense, and when
they petitioned the Court to reward their soldiers they were left
without the Imperial commission, while their conquests were
contemptuously characterised as "private feuds."   The Minamotos,
well aware that the military class would not continue to risk
their lives and to spill their blood for naught, thereupon took
upon themselves the responsibility of conferring upon their
followers grants of *Shōyen* in the conquered territories in their
own names.   And the older house of Taira that meanwhile
had been suppressing piracy and revolts in the South and the
West was not slow to follow the example of the Minamoto in
these quarters.   Too late the Fujiwara awakened to two truths—
first, that a special military class had arisen in Japan, and,
secondly, that over that class they themselves exercised no
control whatsoever.   Its allegiance was divided between the
rival military houses of Taira and of Minamoto; and for the
civilian Fujiwaras and their fortunes it cared not one straw.
At the beginning of the twelfth century they induced the
seventy-fourth Emperor, Toba Tennō (1108–1123), to issue a
decree forbidding the warrior class in the various provinces to
constitute themselves vassals of the Taira or of the Minamoto;
and in the following reign, in 1127, an Imperial decree forbade
any further increase of the *Shōyen*, or tax-free estates.   The
language of this latter decree is worthy of attention.   It sets

---

[5] More will be said about these *Goshi* in Vol. II.

forth that "the *Shōji* (officers put in charge of *Shōyen* by the owners) are earnestly inviting holders of public land to become tenants of the *Shōyen*," and that "those who have become tenants in *Shōyen* never return to their former status: the *Shōyen* are all filled with farmers, while the public land is left wild and uncultivated." Fifty years before this date the central administration (Fujiwara) had tried to confiscate all the *Shōyen* that had any irregularity in their titles, a measure doubtless chiefly directed against the Minamotos in the East and the North. By this time (1127) nearly the whole revenue of the country went, not to the central administration, but to the holders of *Shōyen*. It was this lack of revenue that was the chief immediate cause of the decline of the Emperor's power. From an early date it affected the sovereign himself; but for some centuries, the Fujiwaras being the chief holders of *Shōyen* and also the Ministers of the Crown, it had not seriously affected the power of the Kyōto administration. But now that the bulk of the cultivated land in Japan was passing into the hands of the adherents of the military houses of the Taira and of the Minamoto, the civilian Fujiwaras and the Kyōto Government alike were threatened with the complete loss of power and of prestige.

By the middle of the twelfth century the two warlike houses were nearly as powerful in the capital itself as the Fujiwaras were. Then, in 1156, a disputed succession to the throne was actually decided—not by Fujiwara intrigue, as such disputes had been settled for centuries,—but by the clash of arms. The seventy-sixth Emperor, Konoye Tennō, died in 1155, and his eldest brother, Shutoku Tennō, who had abdicated in 1141, then wished to re-ascend the throne, while yet another brother, Go-Shirakawa, aspired to the sovereignty. The latter was supported by the Taira, the former by the Minamoto: and in the armed debate that followed, the Minamoto were routed and driven from Kyōto. This was the beginning of an inter-necine strife between the two great military houses that, with various pauses, went on for nine-and-twenty years. Before a decade had gone, the Minamoto seemed to have been utterly crushed and all but exterminated, and Taira Kiyomori had become the real ruler of Japan. In 1167 he had been made Daijō-daijin, or Chancellor of the Empire; sixty of his men then

held high office at Court, and the revenues of some thirty
provinces were the private property of the family. This was
really the beginning of military rule in Japan. From this
date the civilian *Kugé*, or Court nobles, who had manipulated
the administrative machinery of the centralised monarchy for
nearly five centuries, were stripped of their wealth, banished,
depressed in countless ways, and relegated to an impotent
obscurity from which they were not destined to emerge until a
time yet within the memory of the living.

However, it was not Taira Kiyōmori who organised that
system of administration which made the military class the rulers
of the Empire for some seven centuries. Just as Kiyōmori died,
in 1181, the Minamoto, under Yoritomo and his relations, were
again raising their heads in the East, where they had made
Kamakura, in Sagami, their stronghold. After four or five
years' desperate fighting the Taira were ultimately virtually
annihilated in the great sea-fight of Dannoūra, in the Straits of
Shimonoseki, in 1185; and then, in their turn, the Minamotos
became the real masters of the Empire. Luckily for the
Minamoto, their chief, Yoritomo, was not only a good soldier, but
also a great statesman who had the good fortune to command the
services of advisers of administrative genius. Unlike Taira
Kiyōmori, when he became master of the Empire, Yoritomo did
not take up his quarters in the Imperial capital of Kyōto, but
continued to reside at Kamakura, where he had already organised
a Council of State, tribunals, and a system of administration which enabled him to exercise control over all the surrounding provinces, and, in fact, over the greater portion of North-
eastern Japan. The problem was how to extend his authority
over the rest of the Empire without removing from his own
capital of Kamakura. The solution found for this problem was
an astute one, and says much for the genius of Oye-no-Hiromoto,
who seems to have devised it. Down to this date all the
governors and vice-governors of provinces, whose chief duties had
been the maintenance of order and the collection of the revenue,
had been civilians. After the victory of Dannoūra (1185)
Yoritomo memorialised the Emperor, praying that five men of
his own family name might be made *Kami* or governors of as
many provinces in the South and West of Japan; and among the
five, Yoshitsune, Yoritomo's own illustrious brother, was made

Governor of Iyo in Shikoku by a special decree. But this was only the first step. A little later Oye-no-Hiromoto advocated a still more important innovation. " The universal commotion has now been allayed, and the Kwantō reposes in tranquillity under the administration of its military chief. But abandoned ruffians lurk in every circuit ; and no sooner are they put down than they rise again. The trouble and expense of mobilising the Eastern forces against them are incalculable, and the people groan under the burdens laid upon them in consequence of so doing. The best plan which could be adopted in this emergency would be to place *Shiugo* (military protectors) with the *Kokushiu* (civilian governors of provinces) and *Jito* in the *Shōyen*. Then the Empire will be at rest with no stirring on your part."

When this plan was laid before the Emperor by Hōjō Tokimasa (Yoritomo's father-in-law), when he appeared in Kyōto to take command of the garrison there, it was at once sanctioned. The *Shiugo*, or provincial military protector, who was a nominee of Yoritomo's, and who had one-fiftieth of the assessed yearly rental of *all* the lands in the province at his disposal, besides a military force behind him, in course of time usurped all the authority, and reduced the *Kokushiu*, or civilian prefect, appointed for four years, to comparative insignificance. The only duty now left to the civilian provincial governor was the collection of the taxes, and as by this time most of the cultivated soil of Japan had become *Shōyen*, or tax-free land, the duties of the civilian governor were not very onerous. And by placing *Jito* in the *Shōyen* (with which the *Kokushiu* had nothing whatsoever to do), Yoritomo contrived to acquire a strong control over all the untaxed estates in the Empire. " He also asked leave to levy a tax of 5 *sho* per *tan* (*i.e.* 2 per cent. of the produce) throughout the Home Provinces and in the four Western and Southern Circuits to provide food for the troops quartered there. Now these provinces and circuits made up the Kwansei, or West of the Barrier, and Yoritomo had already the actual possession of the Kwantō, which in those days meant the whole country east of the Barrier near Zeze in the province of Ōmi."

It is to be noted that Yoritomo had thus rivetted the fetters of military government upon Japan before he formerly instituted, or revived, the Shōgunate. After a victorious campaign in the extreme north of Japan in 1190 he betook himself to Kyōto,·

and (1192) the "Emperor sent a dignitary of the Court to
confer upon him the title of *Sei-i-tai-Shōgun* (Barbarian-subduing-
great-general)," a title by which the head, or the nominal head,
of the military class and of the government by the military
class continued to be known in Japan down to the year 1867.[a]

With the overthrow of the civilian centralised administration conducted by the Fujiwaras and the ascendency of the
military Tairas, the fortunes of the Imperial line of the Emperors
of Japan had been brought low indeed. With the exception
of the ex-Emperor Go-Shirakawa (1156 to 1158), who had
abdicated and ostensibly retired from the world to a cloister (like
Charles V.), but who really continued to exercise an important
influence in the government down to his death in 1192, the
occupants of the throne from 1156 to 1186 had been merely children
and puppets. During this short space of thirty years there had
been no fewer than five Emperors! With the rise of Yoritomo
to supremacy the position of the Imperial line had been vastly
bettered. For every important step that he took—for the
appointment of provincial governors, for example—Yoritomo was
careful to obtain the Imperial sanction, and his administration
from first to last was carried on in the Emperor's name and as the
Imperial deputy. During the last decade of the twelfth century
Japan enjoyed the blessings of a strong central administration;
but this administration, while resembling that of the civilian
government of the Fujiwaras and the other Court nobles in the
matter of acting by the Emperor's authority and of carrying
out the Imperial will, differed from the administration of
670–1150 A.D. in being essentially a military one, and in being
conducted, not from the Emperor's place of residence, but from
Kamakura, some three hundred miles distant therefrom. The
old form of government, with its Chancellor, its Ministers of the

---

[a] This title of *Sei-i-tai-Shōgun* was not a new one. In the reign of the
fiftieth Emperor, Kwammu Tennō, who permanently established the capital in
Kyōto seven years before Charlemagne was crowned in Rome (in 800 A.D.),
"it had been bestowed [for the first time] on Ōtomo-Ota-Marō and then on
Sakano-uye-no-Tamura-Marō. This title was not given to anyone during the
following reign [806–810]. Under the next Emperor [Saga, 810–824],
Bunya-no-Waia-Marō was invested with it. During the numerous years that
followed there was no nomination of this kind till the time of Minamoto
Yoshinaka, who was killed [1156] shortly after his investiture with the title.
Yoritomo then [1192] became the new *titulaire* in his family." It was a principle subsequently observed that no one of non-Minamoto stock could aspire
to this title of *Sei-i-tai-Shōgun*.

Shōguns there had been in plenty,—for a *Shōgun* was simply a general in
command of a brigade of three *dan*, or regiments, of 1,000 men each.

Right and of the Left, and its Eight Boards, still continued to subsist in Kyōto, but although the ranks and titles of its officials were eagerly sought after, they had ceased to carry with them any real duties or any real power.

Yoritomo's attitude towards the Imperial house had been a correct one; his successors in the Kamakura Government acted in quite a different fashion. On the great statesman's death in 1198 (a few months before that of Richard I. of England), the actual power passed into the hands of his widow Masago, her father Hōjō Tokimasa, and his family. Yoritomo's two sons were indeed successively made nominal heads of the military protectors and administrators stationed in the provinces, and invested with the title of *Sei-i-tai-Shōgun*; but both were *fainéants*, and in 1219 the line of Yoritomo became extinct. The Hōjō, who, under the title of *Shikken* or Regents, were the real heads of the Kamakura Government and the actual rulers of Japan from 1199 to 1334, then set up a succession of puppet or "shadow" Shōguns, taken partly from the house of Fujiwara and partly from among the Imperial princes, and deposed them whenever they showed the slightest inclination to assert themselves.[7]

And even towards the Emperors themselves the Hōjō behaved in no less cavalierly a manner. The eighty-second Emperor, Go-Toba, who had invested Yoritomo with the title of *Sei-i-tai-Shōgun*, had either abdicated or had been forced to abdicate, in 1199, the year after Yoritomo's death. At his abdication he was no more than twenty years of age, and his successor, Tsuchimikado, was a child of five, who in turn, at the age of sixteen or seventeen, had to make way for Juntoku (1211), then a boy of fifteen. Juntoku was largely under the influence of Go-Toba; and Go-Toba, restive under the domination of the Hōjō, plotted against them and mustered a force to overthrow them. The Hōjō were victorious in the subsequent struggle (1221), and

---

[7] A glance at the list will at once reveal how things then stood:—

1.—Fujiwara Yoritsune, nine years old at appointment in 1220; deposed by Hōjō Tsunetoki in 1243.

2.—Fujiwara Yoritsugu, seven years old at appointment in 1244; deposed in 1251.

3.—Munetaka Shinnō, eleven years old at appointment in 1252; deposed in 1265.

4.—Koreyasu Shinnō, three years of age at appointment in 1266; deposed in 1289.

5.—Hira-akira Shinnō, sixteen years old at appointment in 1289; deposed in 1307.

6.—Morikuni Shinnō, seven years old at appointment in 1308; deposed in 1333.

did not scruple to depose Juntoku and to banish him to the Island of Sado, to make one ex-Emperor, Go-Toba, become a priest and to banish him to Oki, and to exile the other ex-Emperor and the two princes of the blood to Awa, Tajima, and Bizen respectively. This was indeed carrying things with a high hand ![8] But this was not all. Wholesale confiscation immediately followed. "The whole of the confiscations amounted to more than 3,000 fiefs! Hōjō Yoshitoki divided them all among his officers who had distinguished themselves on the field of battle, and he did not keep even one for himself. So the power and dignity of the Hōjō family increased day by day. Yasutoki having now destroyed the loyal army [*i.e.* the Imperial forces], stopped at the capital [Kyōto] with Tokifusa and governed it and the surrounding country in conjunction with him."

This means that at this date the whole administration of Japan was openly and undisguisedly in the hands of the military class. This wholesale confiscation of fiefs, many of them belonging to Court nobles, and their distribution among the captains of the victorious Kamakura army as a reward for service in the field, must be regarded as a very important incident in the development of Japanese feudalism. And what made the military government of the Hōjō so fatal to the old civilian central administration was its high efficiency—an efficiency that was maintained for at least a century after its inception in 1198. It is the fashion to declaim upon the miseries of Japan under the rule of the Hōjō; but as a sober matter of fact, the administration of the Hōjō during the first century of their unobtrusive yet vigorous supremacy was one of the best that Japan has ever known. With a fine contempt for the empty titles and honours and dignities so dear to the little soul of the superior flunkey, the best men among their seven successive generations just quietly

[8] As serving to indicate the policy of the Hōjō towards the Imperial house, the following list of Emperors (only one of whom died in actual possession of the throne, Go-Nijō, 1308, *ætat* 24) is instructive:—

85.	Chukyō	1221–1221	5 years of age at accession.		
86.	Go-Horikawa	1221–1232	10	" " "
87.	Yojō	1232–1242	2	" " "
88.	Go-Saga	1242–1246	23	" " "
89.	Go-Fukakusa	1246–1259	4	" " "
90.	Kameyama	1259–1274	11	" " "
91.	Go-Uda	1274–1288	8	" " "
92.	Fushimi	1288–1298	24	" " "
93.	Go-Fushimi	1298–1301	11	" " "
94.	Go-Nijyō	1301–1308	17	" " "
95.	Hanazono	1308–1318	4	" " "

but resolutely went on doing their best endeavour to promote the general interests and welfare of the Empire. Hōjō Yasutoki (1225–1242), on becoming Regent, divided all his property among his brothers, and devoted all his attention to administrative work. He was evidently a man who could, and did, "toil terribly." He perfected Yoritomo's system of government; and this system, in capable hands, maintained in the empire that peace and order of which it stood so sorely in need. Besides, the code of laws (*Joei Shiki-moku*) he drew up was really enforced. His second successor, Tokiyori (1246–56), after retiring in favour of his son Tokimune, wandered over Japan in disguise like another Haroun-al-Raschid, seeing for himself the reality of things in the political and social life of the nation. Tokimune (1257–1284) was able to organise a most efficient defence against the descents of the Mongols, and in 1281 the complete rout of an invading host of 100,000 men indicated that at that date Japan was indeed united. The truth is that, during the thirteenth century, the Hōjō exercised far more real authority over the feudatories of Japan than the central authorities in England, in France, in the Holy Roman Empire, or in any European country where a feudal polity then prevailed, did over those of the West.

However, by the early years of the fourteenth century the character of the Regents had changed sadly for the worse. Instead of Yasutoki and Tokiyori, who worked from sunrise to sunset without intermission, and who led the simplest of simple lives, we now usually find the Regent a young profligate, squandering the national treasures and the national income in unseemly riot, degrading debauchery, and empty pomp and show, and paying but little heed to the hard and thankless work of administration. In this state of affairs the Imperial Court and the Emperor Go-Daigo (1318–1339) very rightly saw a possible chance to emancipate themselves from the thraldom of the Rokuhara, the fortress in Kyōto from which Kamakura dominated the Imperial capital. A first revolt near Kyōto was put down in 1322; a second one in 1324; in 1331 Go-Daigo escaped from Kyōto and called his partisans to arms, but was captured and banished to the Island of Oki. However, his partisans still kept the field, and defections among the vassals of the Hōjō were preparing. In fact, Go-Daigo had scarcely escaped from Oki before both the Rokuhara in Kyōto, and Kamakura itself, had been captured and fired and the family of the Hōjō virtually exterminated (1333). The Roku-hara had fallen before the assault of Ashikaga Takauji, while Kamakura had been captured by Nitta, both former partisans of the Hojō, and both of Minamoto stock, and, therefore, both eligible for the Shōgunate. But at first neither one nor the other was invested with this office; it was bestowed upon the Imperial Prince, Morinaga, who, together with Kusunoki Masa-shige, had borne the brunt of the strife before the defection of Ashikaga and of Nitta.

The period from 1334 to 1336 is usually called the Temporary Mikadoate, from the circumstance that during these years the Emperor (Go-Daigo) was ostensibly what the Em-peror had been in the early ages—the real ruler of Japan. However, any revival of the centralised civilian government was found to be impossible; and the Emperor was constrained to reward those who had fought for him in the same manner as Hōjō Yasutoki had recompensed his supporters (in 1222) more than a century before; for to the system of feudal administration devised by Yoritomo, and under which Japan had enjoyed a very large measure of peace and prosperity for nearly a century and a half, the nation had become so habituated that the system could not now be set aside. So all the Emperor's partisans were rewarded with fiefs,—among others, Kusunoki received the provinces of Settsu and Kawachi in fee, Nitta those of Kōdzuke and Harima, and Ashikaga those of Hitachi, Shimōsa, and Musashi. From this it will be seen that the provinces were ceasing to be ad-ministrative units, and even at this comparatively early date were becoming not much more than mere geographical expressions.

The distribution of rewards—or of spoils—by the Emperor Go-Daigo failed to give satisfaction to many of those who had fought for the Imperial cause more out of hatred for the degenerate Hōjō than from any real love for the Emperor. "Should such a partial administration continue," said they, "then we are simply the slaves of concubines and of dancing-girls and Court favourites. Rather than be the puppets of the Emperor's amusers it would be well to have a Shōgun and to become his vassals." Of this widespread and deep-seated discontent Ashikaga was swift to avail himself and to turn it to his own advantage. By a clever but dastardly intrigue he contrived to have the Shōgun, Prince Morinaga, accused of harbouring rebellious projects, arrested and murdered at Kamakura (1335), which was then being rebuilt, and where Ashikaga had established himself. Too late the Emperor Go-Daigo became aware of the plot; and an Imperial army was launched against Ashikaga, who, however, proved strong enough to break it utterly, to advance upon and occupy Kyōto, and to drive Go-Daigo to take refuge in the wilds of Yoshino. Having failed to retain possession of the person of the rightful Emperor, whom he would doubtless have compelled to abdicate, Ashikaga set up a prince of the blood as sovereign in Kyōto, and from him obtained his own investiture as *Sei-i-tai-Shōgun*. From this date, 1336, down to 1392 Japan had two rival Emperors: one called the Northern Emperor, residing in Kyōto; the other the Southern, in the mountain fastnesses of Yamato.

The effect of this was to divide Japan into two warring camps; and in the course of the strife the feudatories passed almost entirely out of the control of the central authorities, and Japanese feudalism became very similar to the chaotic feudal welter that prevailed in France from 950 to 1100 A.D. Even when the difference between the Northern and the Southern dynasties was composed by the pact of 1392, and Go-Komatsu was acknowledged as sole Emperor, the country enjoyed but a brief term of repose. It was Yoshimitsu, the third Ashikaga Shōgun, and the ablest of all the fourteen successors of Ashikaga Takauji, the founder of the line, that had succeeded in effecting this arrangement; and in addition to this service he contrived to reduce Kyūshū and the West of Japan to some brief semblance of order, and to project a new scheme of feudal administration. In terms of this it is stated that he made the military magistracies hereditary in the families of his own nominees—a step of some importance in the history of Japanese feudalism, inasmuch as these magistrates founded some of the great feudal families of Japan. The Rokuhara in Kyōto was the chief seat of the Ashikaga Shōguns, although the descendants of Ashikaga Takauji's second son had become hereditary rulers of Kamakura and the Kwantō, and on more than one occasion claimed to be the true *Sei-i-tai-Shōgun*. This was the occasion of wars between Kamakura and the Ashikaga of Kyōto; while in 1467, in consequence of a disputed succession to the office in the older Kyōto

branch of the house, the war of *Onin* broke out between the two
parties of its retainers and went on for a score of years with the
most disastrous results, among which even the burning of the
capital was far from being the most calamitous. Then, later on,
as the result of another series of civil wars, Yoshitane, the tenth
of the Ashikaga line, was deposed in 1493, restored as the
twelfth of that line in 1508, and yet once again deposed in
1520; while at one time there were no fewer than five rival
Shōguns, most of them children, used merely as counters by the
rival retainers of the house and the feudatories allied with them,
all really fighting for their own hands in spite of all their fine
and plausible professions. The chief Minister of the Ashikaga
Shōguns—known as the *Kwanryō*—had, as a rule, been the real
governing power, so far as there was one; and for this office the
struggles at the beginning of, and during, the first two-thirds of
the sixteenth century were exceedingly bitter and fierce. These
Ministers had mostly been of the house of Hosokawa, who held
large estates in Shikoku besides the whole island of Awaji; but in
1508, Ōuchi, the feudal chief of Suwō and Nagato in the extreme
west of the main island, entered Kyōto with an army, drove out
Hosokawa and his puppet, the eleventh Ashikaga Shōgun, restored
the tenth Shōgun, Yoshitane, to nominal power, and obtained his
own appointment as Kwanryō. On Ōuchi's retreat to his fief in
1520, the Hosokawa reappeared upon the scene to dispute the
position of Minister with the Miyoshi, an offshoot of their own
family, who had meanwhile dispossessed them of Awaji, of about
half their estates in Shikoku, and who had also seized upon the
seaboard tract of Settsu and Idzùmi on the opposite main island.
Of these Miyoshi and of their ally, Matsunaga, Lord of Nara, we
hear much from the early Jesuits in Japan.

Kyōto was thus the seat of continual conflicts; the Shōgun
was a nonentity—a mere puppet, not even supreme within the
narrow precincts of his own Rokuhara—while as for the Emperors
and their Court, their position was deplorable. Under the third
Ashikaga Shōgun (Yoshimitsu) a handsome civil list had been
apportioned for the support of the Imperial House; but as the
constant wars in Kyōto and its neighbourhood had made all
agriculture and mostly all industry impossible, the domains
charged with the support of the Court now returned no revenue
whatsoever. Most of the Court nobles had withdrawn and sought

shelter with one or other of the feudal chiefs who no longer recognised the authority of the Shōgun—except when it suited them to do so. How it fared with the rightful sovereigns of Japan at this time may be inferred from the fact that on the death of the 104th Emperor, Go-Tsuchi-Mikado, the corpse was kept for forty days because the means for the usual funeral expenses were not available! With the Emperor in the most abject poverty; with his deputy, the Barbarian-subduing-great-General, a mere puppet in the hands of his *Kwanryō* or Minister; and with this *Kwanryō* (except for a possible brief hour in Kyōto itself) utterly impotent beyond the limits of the estates he had succeeded in purloining in the general game of land-thievery, all central government had ceased to exist.

And how was it in the provinces? How was it in feudal England under Stephen; in France under the early Capets; in Germany during the Interregnum in the second half of the thirteenth century; in Lowland Scotland under the weakest of the Stuarts? All over the face of the empire it was one grand game of land-thieving—comparatively respectable but not very lucrative from the circumstance that the great bulk of the land had gone out of cultivation,—while in most of the landward portions of the country brigandage of the more vulgar kinds was prevalent, and along whole stretches of the sea-board piracy was rife. One effect of this state of things, however, was to break up in many sections that system of serfdom that had prevailed in Japan for more than a thousand years, for any able-bodied and courageous man now readily found service either as a soldier with the land-thieving feudatories, or as a foot-pad with the less aspiring robber chiefs who were content to limit their attentions to moveable property. In the early half of that sixteenth century which witnessed the Protestant revolt in Central and Northern Europe and the destruction of the monasteries in England (1539), and during which the centrifugal forces, having proved altogether too strong for the central authorities, had turned the feudal map of Japan into a constantly-shifting kaleidoscope, the greatest power, if not in Japan, at all events in Kyōto, was—the Church. And this too at a time when the ignorance of its priests was crass and colossal; when their morality—sexually and otherwise—had not only sunk to the lowest ebb, but had become a vanished (not

c

a vanishing) quantity; when the commandments of the Buddhist canon were regarded as so many puritanical and pedantic injunctions to be more honoured in the breach than in the observance.

The indigenous cult of Japan had been Shintō, the Way of the (autochthonous) Gods—a species of ancestor and nature worship. About the fifth century of the Christian era a few of the higher classes in the empire had acquired some slight knowledge of Chinese literature and thought, and, in the sixth, Buddhism had been introduced into Japan *via* Korea. But for generations the exotic religion had been but a sickly plant, and, in spite of the adhesion of the Sovereigns and of certain members of their Courts, it acquired no really firm foothold in the country until early in the ninth century, when in the monastery of Hiyei-san, founded by Kwammu Tennō (782–806) on the mountain-range behind his new capital of Kyōto, Dengyō Daishi proclaimed that the deities in the national pantheon of Japan were simply so many incarnations of. Buddha—an announcement that was incessantly reiterated by Kōbō Daishi, the founder of the Shingon sect, and of the monastery of Kōya-san, a few decades later on. From that date the progress of the foreign cult among the higher classes in Japan was rapid. Kwammu Tennō, however, although favouring Buddhism, seems to have looked upon it with a certain degree of suspicion, for in his reign (782–805 A.D.) we meet with an edict against mortmain.[9] Yet before the end of that ninth century bequests of land to the various temples had become very common. One deed of this time runs:—"This land was transferred to me by Arata-Kimi-ina when he was dying, with the injunction to transfer it to the temple Tōdaiji; and I now do so in obedience to his behest. Now Arata will obtain happiness in the other world and I and my descendants will also be blessed for ever." By 1000 A.D. many of the temples had acquired considerable landed estates; and these kept on increasing during the succeeding centuries. These estates were acquired not only as pious bequests, but in two other ways at least. All temple lands, like other *Shōyen*, were tax-free; and so it became

---

9 "His Majesty forbade private individuals to have chapels in their houses, or to present or sell land or immoveables to the priests."

exceedingly common for the occupants of the public land (in their own financial interests) to bestow their holdings upon some temple, and to become its tenants. And in the great game of land-thieving that prevailed in the fifteenth and in the early sixteenth centuries the Buddhist clergy joined to much purpose. Ages before this the large monasteries had taken soldiers into their service for the defence of their estates; many of the monks themselves had been warriors before becoming priests; while the acolytes often paid a good deal more attention to the art of war than to the precepts and mysteries of the faith. Then, in Kyōto itself, it became a common practice for the Emperor to abdicate while still in the vigour of manhood, to shave his head, and to enter the cloister, where the atmosphere soon became more political than religious; for in not a few cases it was these "cloistered" Emperors who really chiefly directed the affairs of the Court, if not of the State. It was also common for such of the Court nobles and high-placed officials as not infrequently fell into disgrace, to retire to one or other of the fanes in or around Kyōto; and so it came to pass that the hot-beds of intrigue and of cabal were the very temples of the priests whose constant texts were the vanity of wealth and pomp, and the uncertainty of all mundane things!

How rapidly the Buddhist priesthood had developed into a political factor may be inferred from certain incidents in the reign of the seventy-second Emperor, Shirakawa, who, according to the accepted accounts, was really a man of mettle and of ability, and with a will of his own strong enough to dominate the Fujiwara ring of Ministers that usually kept the Sovereign in thraldom. "In this reign [1073–1086, contemporary with that of William the Conqueror in England] the priests of Enriaku-ji [Hiyei-san], having a protest to make to the Government, descended to address the Emperor with arms in their hands. His Majesty ordered the police to repel them by force. For a long time even before this the priests of the various temples had been accustomed to decide their differences by arms, and had even finished by taking troops into their service. On several occasions the capital had been the theatre of bloody frays caused by them. Shirakawa Tennō reduced the family of Fujiwara to silence, and really governed himself; it may be said that during the

forty years that followed his abdication he still held the reins
of government. Unfortunately, he was very devout, and
erected more than fifty pagodas and statues of Buddha. The
result of this extreme devotion was that the priests became so
arrogant that it became almost impossible to constrain them
to obedience, the Emperor wittily remarking that 'there are
three things over which I have no power—the waters of the
Kamogawa [a river that often flooded Kyōto], the fall of
the dice, and the monks of Buddha.'" In 1184 we find
Yoritomo petitioning the Emperor to "entrust to your servant
the duty of prohibiting the priests from wearing arms, and
of confiscating the weapons of such as offend therein." Yet
although Yoritomo was resolute in his suppression of an armed
priesthood, he did not venture to deal with the abuse in a
truly radical fashion. He was anxious to secure the support
of the monks, to whom his rivals the Tairas had been bitterly
hostile, and as a means of conciliating them he exempted
the ecclesiastical manors from the taxation which he imposed
upon all the other *Shōyen*, while he does not appear to have
done anything to check mortmain. The wealth of the monasteries consequently kept on increasing, and they thus
acquired abundant resources for reappearing as armed feudal
powers whenever the central administration lost its vigour.
Down to this, however, Buddhism had been the religion of the
Court and of the upper classes only; by the great missionary
efforts of Hōnen, of Shinran, and of Nichiren in the following (thirteenth) century it became the cult of the common
people as well. Notwithstanding its rapid increase of power
in this century, the priests were kept in their right place by
the strong central government of the Hōjō. But, on the
overthrow of the Kamakura Administration in 1333, the
monks, who had been among the Emperor Go-Daigo's most
strenuous supporters, and who had rendered him the most important services in the struggle, again got entirely out of
hand, and once more became fighting men. In the incessant
turmoils of the next two centuries many of the monasteries
became castles and arsenals, with strong garrisons composed
partly of the ecclesiastics themselves and partly of hired
troops, while the broad domains they owned became fiefs,—
mostly portioned out among retainers who paid their rents by

military service, and who were most efficient agents in the prosecution of the craft of land-thieving. The whole of Hiyei-san behind Kyōto was simply one great feudal fortress in the hands of ecclesiastics. On its heights and in its thirteen valleys there were at one time as many as three thousand so-called monasteries, and the garrisons of these—for their in-mates were nearly all fighting men—dominated the capital, and in the strife between rival Ministers (with their rival puppet Shōguns) in the early sixteenth century these mailed men-of-God almost invariably proved the arbiters. The judge-ments they rendered in these quarrels were usually very ex-pensive ones for the city of Kyōto, for not infrequently in the course of the combats in its streets it was fired and pillaged, and experienced all the horrors of a captured town. Even inter-necine quarrels between the sects themselves now and then proved disastrous to the capital—for instance, in 1537 the Nichiren sect and the Tendai sect had a difference over some knotty point of doctrine, and in the course of the debate not merely the Nichiren temple, but half the metropolis of Japan was reduced to ashes. Five years before this date these Nichiren monks, who then got the worst of it, had attacked, captured, and burnt the chief seat of the Monto sect (the Protestants of Japan) at Yamashina (five miles from Kyōto) and had driven them to take refuge in the provinces, where they were exceedingly powerful. On the coast of the Sea of Japan these Protestants held a certain portion of Echizen; while of the whole province of Kaga successive abbots of the Monto sect continued to be feudal lords for a century. In what is now Ōsaka, they had, from 1536 onward, the strongest fortress in contemporary Japan; in Ise their estates were extensive; and in the Kwantō their influence was nearly as great as the most powerful feudatory in that quarter. In the stretch of country between the Inland Sea and the Gulf of Owari stood the two great monasteries of Kōya-san (of the Shingon sect) and of Negoro;— these two institutions were really first-class feudal powers in the district. We shall find that it was a priest of the latter (Negoro) who shared with a merchant of the great mart of Sakai the somewhat questionable honour of introducing fire-arms into Central Japan, and that, until reduced by

Hideyoshi in 1585, the monastery of Negoro as a fighting-power was much more formidable than that of any feudal chief within a similar distance from the capital.

However, although banished from the neighbourhood of the capital, it was the. Monto sect that was the greatest political force among the Buddhists at this time, inasmuch as from its very foundation in the thirteenth century its chief doctrine had been an easy justification by faith in Amida, which made all penances and works, as well as all theological metaphysics, unnecessary; while its priests, allowed to eat meat, to marry, to found families, and to transmit their offices to their sons, had ever been men of the world, mingling actively in its affairs and taking full part in all the social and political life of the time. It was at once an aristocratic and a popular body; for while its founder and its chief priests belonged to the Fujiwara, one of the proudest lines in Japan, it spared no effort to sweep the commonest of the people within its fold. Renniō, the chief Monto priest after the year 1500, wrote out the creed and most important doctrines of the cult in the common script—in the *hiragana* writing—which in those, the veritable dark ages of Japanese literature, was the only thing even the middle classes could read. Thus it came to pass that the Monto priests got in touch with, and acquired a strong influence over, all classes in the provinces. Driven as they had been from Kyōto in 1532, yet over the *samurai* and the lower classes in Satsuma in the extreme south they had a strong hold; and from there, all over the country districts of Japan, right on to the Straits of Tsugaru, they could count their adherents in thousands. As has been said, Abbots of the sect continued to be feudal lords of the great and fertile province of Kaga for a century; while their *shōyen*, their manors, in other parts of the Empire were at once numerous, well-administered, and populous. After their expulsion from Yamashina, near Kyōto, in 1532, what is now Ōsaka became their headquarters. Here between 1570 and 1580 we shall find Kenniō, the eleventh head of the sect, laughing to scorn all the efforts of Nobunaga (then the greatest soldier in Japan), with his army of nearly 60,000 men, to capture the monastery-fortress. This Kenniō, according to certain speeches of Hideyoshi (who

succeeded in again consolidating a central power in Japan),
aimed at nothing less than the *real* sovereignty of the
country; and according to this same Hideyoshi, this un-
speakable Kennio was at one time in a fair way towards
success in his project. It is no exaggeration to say that at
the date of the first arrival of Europeans in Japan the
greatest political power in the empire was that of the Buddhist priesthood, foremost among which stood that Monto
sect which had been harried and hunted from the neighbourhood of the capital only ten years before. The crying
need of the time in Japan was the re-establishment of a
strong central government; and before any such government
could be re-established the feudal and military power of the
Buddhist priests had to be broken.

Long before this date, it is needless to say, the provinces
had ceased to be administrative units, and in most cases had
become mere geographical expressions. In some of them there
might be as many as half-a-score or a dozen small barons
with their sub-feudatories at constant strife with each other;
often a mere chief of banditti would hastily raise a castle
of his own and set up as a respectable titled, if not
chartered, land-thief. Then a retainer in charge of a frontier
castle would make little scruple about shaking off his
allegiance to his lord, and becoming his rival instead of
his servant. These border castles were constantly changing
owners; for an inconsiderable bribe it was common for their
custodians to pass over with their whole garrisons to the
enemy of their feudal superior. In many of the provinces
no accurate feudal map could be made, simply because of
the constant changes in the extent, the boundaries, and the
ownership of the fiefs. On the other hand, in certain quarters
of the islands some great families had been able to extend
their rule to whole provinces,—in some rare cases over two,
three, or four provinces. Al that the ordinary feudal chief
thought of was to extend the immediate confines of his
possessions. However, there *were* men in Japan who saw
clearly enough that so long as feudal chiefs had no aims
beyond that, the general strife and confusion of the previous
two centuries might very well continue for ever. The only
hope for the peace and general welfare of the country was

the re-appearance of a man like Yoritomo, who could repeat Yoritomo's work with the modifications demanded by the lapse of some three hundred years. Both in Kyōto and at Kamakura the Ashikaga rulers had shown themselves impotent to control the feudatories. In Kyōto itself the quarters of their Ministers, the Hosokawa and Miyoshi, in which the very unclerical clerics of Hiyei-san usually acted as umpires (with the sword), rendered both Hosokawa and Miyoshi powerless to repeat the work of the great Yoritomo, although their large landed estates within easy reach of the capital furnished them with a better base than any other feudal chieftain could boast. Something indeed might have been expected from Ōuchi, who held the provinces of Aki, Iwami, Suwō, and Nagato, together with portions of Buzen and Chikuzen in Kyūshū. On several occasions he had made his influence felt in Kyōto; in 1508 he had restored the banished Shōgun, Yoshitane, and had acted for several years as his *Kwanryō* or Minister, and in 1536 we find him defraying the expenses of the Emperor and his Court. But between the capital and Ōuchi's domains were several powerful rivals, and from the North-east he was threatened by Amako in Idzumo, and from the South by Ōtomo in Kyūshū, and all these would have to be effectually dealt with before Ōuchi could set to work to restore a centralised administration.

Still less could anything be expected from any of the Daimyō in Kyūshū. The chief of these were Shimadzu, with the province of Satsuma; Itō, with the great but wild province of Hiūga; Ōtomo in Bungō rapidly extending his power over Higo; while Riūzōji had just established himself on the frontiers of Chikugo and of Hizen. In the island of Shikoku, Chōsokabe in Tosa was the most powerful feudatory; but his resources were as yet altogether unequal to mastering his neighbours and all those that lay between him and the capital and the rivals he would have to encounter there. As for the Daimyō in the main island, in the year 1540 it would have been hard to discover who of them could be expected to succeed in that task of reducing the whole empire to order which was actually accomplished within half a century from that date. Amako in Idzumo was powerless to move because of Ōuchi; the lords within a radius of sixty miles around Kyōto ruled over comparatively limited domains, and were too

weak to effect anything, besides being all occupied with purely
local squabbles. Beyond the Gulf of Owari, however, there
were (in 1540) four of the greatest feudatories in Japan; and
provided any one of these could reduce the other three, that one
might not unreasonably have been expected to march on Kyōto,
and to obtain the Emperor's mandate for the reduction of all
the country to his sway. The one of these nearest to Kyōto,
Imagawa, who held Mikawa, Tōtōmi, and Suruga, did indeed
cherish such a design while the other three were embroiled
in strife among themselves; and he was baffled in his
attempt, defeated and killed at Okehazama (1560) by the men
who really finally accomplished the project on which Imagawa
was bent. What may have stimulated Imagawa to action in
1560 was the fact that the great and powerful Daimyō of
Echigo had in the previous year (1559) actually proceeded to
Kyōto to pay his respects to the Emperor, and to claim his
investiture with the office of *Kwanryō*, or Minister of the
Shōgun, who was then regarded as a puppet. This Daimyo
of Echigo (1559) now received the name of Uyesugi Terutora,
Uyesugi being the name of the Ministers of the Kamakura
Shōgun. In 1510 Nagao, a retainer and relative of one of
these, had revolted against him, had seized upon that
Uyesugi's possessions in Echigo, and had rapidly extended
their frontiers. By this date (1559) in mere superficial extent
the rebel Nagao's (now known as Uyesugi's) Echigo fief had
become the greatest in Japan. In pressing onwards towards
the South, Nagao (or Uyesugi) had come into conflict with
two other great families, who, however, were frequently at
strife with each other. The origin of one of these is worthy
of note, inasmuch as the founder of the house of the later
Hōjōs was no descendant of the former Regents of Kamakura.
In 1476 an Ise *samurai*, Shinkwio by name, had set out for the
Kwantō with no more than six followers. With the support
of his brother-in-law, Imagawa of Suruga, he soon collected
a powerful body of partisans, and, having established himself
as Lord of Nirayama in Idzu, he seized the castle of Odawara by a *coup-de-main* in 1495 and made it his headquarters. On his death, at the age of 88, in 1519, he was
succeeded by his highly capable son Ujitsuna, and he in
turn by his equally capable son Ujiyasu, who defeated the

Uyesugi badly in 1551, and successfully maintained Odawara against a siege by Uyesugi Kenshin nine years later on. Shortly afterwards the Hōjōs were masters of most of the Kwantō, where Kamakura, the capital of the Ashikagas, had meanwhile dwindled to a fishing-village. Even by 1540 the Hōjōs were in a position to maintain themselves against such formidable rivals as Imagawa, Uyesugi, and Satomi, who then was all-powerful in the peninsular stretch between the Gulf of Yedo and the Pacific Ocean. But in the mountainous province of Kai, immediately behind Fuji-san, the Hōjō had to deal with an antagonist more to be dreaded than any of these. There the Takeda stock had been settled for centuries, and in 1538, when the old Daimyō's second son, who under the name of Shingen had been made a Buddhist acolyte sorely against his will, escaped from the monastery, deposed his father, and set aside his elder brother, the fief passed into the hands of a ruler and a soldier of consummate ability. If the contest had lain between the Hōjō and him alone it would have gone but ill with the merchant-lords of Odawara. But fortunately for them, Takeda " Shingen" during nearly the whole of his thirty-four years of rule was at strife either with his neighbours in the south or with Uyesugi in the north. As commanders, both these chiefs, Takeda Shingen and Uyesugi Kenshin, appear to have been possessed of something like real military genius; and in the campaigns of the equal war they waged against each other for years for the possession of Shinano the strategy and the general conduct of operations have commanded the admiration of successive generations of military critics. But if they were equals in soldiership Takeda was far superior to Uyesugi as an administrator. Among the peasants of Echigo there is now no remembrance of Uyesugi Kenshin whatsoever; to the present day the farmers of Kai speak of Takeda—" Shingen-Kō," Prince Shingen, they call him—with affectionate respect and reverence. The system of administration he devised for his fief was so excellent that it is said to have been minutely studied by Iyeyasu, the founder of the Tokugawa Shōgunate, to have served him as a model for his own domains, and to have been carefully preserved within the limits of Kai even down to the Revolution of 1868. It is perhaps possible that if there had been no Uyesugi Kenshin to fall upon his rear whenever he essayed to deal with Imagawa and Hōjō,

Takeda Shingen might have proved not unequal to the task of unifying and pacifying the Empire. And of all the four great feudatories in Central and Eastern Japan from whom some such effort might have been expected shortly after 1540 A.D., he, and he alone, had the combination of qualities such a gigantic undertaking demanded. That Imagawa who set out for Kyōto with a force of some 40,000 men and was overthrown by Nobunaga at Okehazama in 1560, was no great captain and no great statesman. Hōjō Ujiyasa was a bold captain, and a man of no small political ability; but there is nothing recorded of him to justify the belief that he was capable of the work Nobunaga achieved. Uyesugi of Echigo was a dashing soldier, indeed— possibly even a great captain; but for the task of the permanent reorganisation of the distracted Empire his talents were unequal, for that task was one demanding the exercise of something much higher than mere military talent.

Withal, however, to any Japanese patriot with sufficient insight to perceive the only remedy that could save the Empire from anarchy, if not from dissolution, the prospect in this year of 1540 A.D. must have been a gloomy one. But the darkest hour precedes the dawn. Already seven years before, Oda Nobunaga, who was to bear the burden and the heat of the day as the pioneer in the herculean task of unifying the Empire, had been born; two years later Hideyoshi, who was to carry the work to completion, saw the light; and in two years from that date Tokugawa Iyeyasu, who was destined to consolidate the results of the efforts of his two illustrious predecessors, came into the world.

The first and third of these great men, although of ancient and honourable lineage, were certainly neither of those who were born great nor who had greatness thrust upon them. Oda Nobunaga was the son of a small baron in Owari, who, with his roughly-built castle of Kiyōsu, was lord of no more than four small districts in that province; while Tokugawa Iyeyasu was merely a comparatively insignificant sub-feudatory of that Imagawa, Daimyō of Mikawa, Tōtōmi, and Suruga, who in 1560 had his march upon Kyōto so summarily arrested by Nobunaga not far from Okehazama. As regards Nobunaga, he was of old Taira stock, being able to trace his lineage back for some four or five centuries; while Iyeyasu, as a descendant of the great

rival warlike house of Minamoto, was by birth eligible for the
Shōgunate, provided by achievement he could ever conquer all
that stood between him and the office. The second, and the
greatest of this great trio, Hideyoshi, was merely a peasant's son.
When he attained to a complete mastery over the Empire,
fantastic genealogies were devised for him in plenty, and within
thirty years after his death the purveyal of the most wonderful
of apocryphal bib-and-porringer biographies for his early and
mysterious years was proving a rich source of wealth to im-
pecunious penmen blessed with an unscrupulous conscience and
a picturesque and popular style.

In 1540 A.D., then, the Empire of Japan was mostly a
weltering chaos of warring feudal atoms—atoms in certain
quarters, however, integrated into not inconsiderable masses
which could boast of a fair amount of cohesion and stability.
The feudatories and the warrior-class in general had passed
completely out of the control of the Shōgun, who was supposed
to be their head as well as the protector and the servant of the
Emperor. That Shōgun had become a mere puppet; and if he
was not summarily and unceremoniously brushed aside, it was
merely because the striving feudatories around the capital aimed
at legitimising their wars with their neighbours and their
conquests by obtaining his (the Shōgun's) commission. With
the Emperor's " protector " brought to such low estate, it fared
but ill with the Sovereign himself. For years the lands appropriated to defray the civil list had produced nothing, and on more
than one occasion the Court had found itself face to face with
virtual starvation. Most of the Court nobles had withdrawn and
accepted hospitality from one or other of the provincial territorial
lords; in several cases, like that of Kitabatake in Ise, of Ichijō
in South-west Shikoku, and of Anenokōji in Hida, they had
become territorial lords themselves. Yet during all this time,
though powerless, poverty-stricken, and utterly secluded from the
world—between 1521 and 1587 the Sovereign made not one
single public appearance—the Emperor still continued to be the
fountain of honour. When the centralised civil administration
had been established in the seventh century, every official—from
the Ministers down to the lowest clerks—obtained a certain
rank, and it was in accordance with this rank that all questions
of precedence at Court were settled. Although the Cabinet with

its eight subordinate Boards had centuries before lost every
vestige of its power, yet its ranks and titles still existed, and it
was a prime object among the feudatories to obtain these empty
honours. As a matter of fact, it was still upon the *Kugé* or
Court nobles that they were bestowed; and the poorest Court
noble invested with one of them would look upon most of the
greatest feudatories with contempt. Certain of the feudatories,
indeed, had possessed this Court rank for generations—ever since
the provincial administration had passed out of the hands of
civilians appointed from Kyōto. The military men who had
thrust the civilians aside assumed the official titles which were
attached to their posts, holding them at first merely during their
tenure of office. But as time went on the duties of these posts
became nominal merely, just as was the case with all the offices
in the old civil centralised government), the military governor
became a feudal lord, and the titles were transmitted to his
heirs.[10]

---

[10] These Court titles, which were objects of the eager ambition of even the
most powerful of the Daimyō or great feudatories, must be sharply distinguished
from the territorial titles which the Daimyō assumed themselves and even
bestowed upon their retainers without any reference to the Emperor whatsoever.
These territorial titles consisted of the word *Kâmi* (Warden) joined to the name
of a province, and originally, as was the case with many family names, referred
to the territory which its bearer actually held. But by the middle of the
sixteenth century we find retainers of a Daimyō who owned no more than a
portion of the province of Mino bearing the titles of Iyo-no-kami and Iga-no-
kami (Warden of Iyo and Warden of Iga)—provinces with the lordship or
administration of which they had no more to do than they had with those of
the moon. At this time there may have been some score or two of similar
"Wardens of Iyo" and "Wardens of Iga" to be found in the various fiefs in
Japan.

All Daimyō had some such territorial title, and some Daimyō had a Court
title besides. In such cases, if the two titles were used, the Court title always
came first; in many instances it alone was used, and the territorial title virtually
suppressed.

In the use of these titles to designate their holders, the foreign student of
Japanese history finds a great—though not the greatest—source of confusion.
A man known at first by a territorial title might attain a Court title, and
henceforth be generally referred to under it. Nor is this all. Besides Court
titles there were Court ranks—thirty of them, twenty-nine for the living and
one for the dead. Promotions in these ranks were not infrequent; and hence,
unless the student keeps keenly on the alert, he is apt to imagine that a new
character has been introduced upon the stage, whereas he is dealing merely with
an old character with a new name.

But even this is by no means the whole of the difficulty. Men of the
warrior class, apart from titles, bore two names—a family and a personal, of
which, contrary to Western usage, the family name comes first. Thus "Tokugawa Iyeyasu" according to the European fashion would appear as Iyeyasu
Tokugawa. In Japanese histories, after a first mention of the two names in
full, it is common to make use of the personal name only subsequently; although,
indeed, sometimes the family name alone crops up in lieu of the personal.
And then in the course of his life a *samurai* would change possibly his personal
name three or four times; possibly his family name, or possibly both his
personal *and* his family as often or even oftener!

The case of Hideyoshi may serve as an illustration of the difficulty, or rather

However, it must never be forgotten that the most powerless
and the most poverty-stricken *Kugé* or Court nobles (the great
majority of whom, by the way, could have met an armed foot-pad
at any hour with the greatest of equanimity),[11] by far out-
ranked a Daimyō with three or even half-a-score of provinces in
fee, if he were destitute of a title and of rank conferred by

---

of these difficulties. When he first appears upon the scene he has no family
name—only a personal one, Tokichiro. By-and-bye he assumes a family name,
and becomes Kinoshita Tokichiro. At the age of 26 he changes his personal
name of Tokichiro to Hideyoshi, and it is by this personal name that he is
best known. Later on he altered his family name of Kinoshita to Hashiba,
and in 1585 he obtained from the Emperor a patent of the family name of
Toyotomi. Henceforth his plain name (or names) was (or were) Toyotomi
Hideyoshi. But from 1585 to 1592 he appears in history as the *Kwanbaku*
(Cambacundono of the Jesuits) or Regent, a Court title he had then extorted
from the Emperor; and from 1592 down to his death in 1598 as the Taikō or
Taikōsama, an honorary title given to a retired *Kwanbaku* (Regent). As if all
this were not enough, for nearly a dozen years previous to 1585 he was also
known by his territorial title of Chikuzen-no-kami (Warden of Chikuzen), a
province in which he never had set foot at the time.
  In this volume, what is aimed at before all things is to keep the identity of the
chief actors perfectly clear and distinct. Titles have indeed been used where they
would be likely to occasion no confusion. But in most cases the simplest *personal*
name—Nobunaga, Hideyoshi, Iyeyasu; in some cases the *family* name—Ishida,
Konishi, Ukida; in others both names combined—Katō Yoshiaki—have been
adopted. Clearness must count for more than a pedantic accuracy where the
claims of both cannot be satisfied. Such a course has been deliberately—and
perhaps perversely and sinfully—adopted as the result of a somewhat dour
experience. In the missionary letters between 1590 and 1618 we meet with
frequent mention of a mysterious "Jecundono." Who could detect, under this
odd guise, that Hosokawa who played such an important part just before the
great battle of Sekigahara in 1600 A.D.? Yet the "Jecundono" and Hosokawa
are identical, for Hosokawa's territorial title was Etchiu-no-kami, and the Jesuits
often use "tono" or "dono" instead of *kami*, while "Etchiu-no" appears as
"Jecun" or "Yetsun." To establish this very simple identification took some
little time, which might have been more profitably employed otherwise.
  Again, this very word *kami* is also a source of confusion. Besides its use as a
mere territorial title, it is used as a Court title in three different senses (see
Dickson's *Japan*, pp. 292–3).
  As regards the representation of the sounds of Japanese names by Roman
letters, nothing beyond an approximate accuracy can be attained. The common
system of the *Romaji Kai* (Roman Alphabet Association) has been followed, and
according to it the consonants are to be pronounced as in English, the vowels as in
Italian. To the general rule that there are no silent vowels in Japanese trans-
literated according to this system, the only exception is that a short final "u" is
often so very short that it is almost inaudible. "Iyeyasu," for example, might
almost be written "Iyeyas" or "Iyeyass." Of course "Date," the family name
of the Daimyō of Sendai, must not be pronounced as the English word "date" is
pronounced, but as a dissyllable, "Dah-tay." As regards Japanese nouns appearing in the text, when plural, they have sometimes got the additional "s" and
sometimes they have not. What has been aimed at above all things is mere
clearness. The spelling of Elizabethan and Jacobean times was not altogether
quite consistent with itself; yet such a writer as Saris, for example, cannot be
accused of the exasperating vices of obscurity and confusion.
  Perhaps it may be well here to advert to another seeming piece of carelessness
to be met with in the subsequent chapters. "Prince" in Japanese history means
usually a Prince of the Imperial House. However, in this volume the term
Prince when used is invariably convertible with Daimyō or the heir of a
Daimyō, the Daimyōs being those chiefs of fiefs whom the missionary writers
dignify with the royal title of "King." No confusion can possibly result from
this, however, inasmuch as during the whole century the volume treats of no
Prince of the Blood played any conspicuous part in the history of the Empire.

11 " *Cantabit vacuus coram latrone viator.*"

Imperial patent. And many of the Daimyō had no Court rank at all; few of them stood higher than the first sub-division of the fourth grade; while the Shōgun himself, the head of the *Buké* or military class, was elevated from one rank to another by favour of the Emperor, at times not rising higher than the first sub-division of the second class (for the living). The Shōgun, it must be remarked, was commonly called "Emperor" by the missionaries, and by the Dutch and English merchants in Japan in the early years of the sixteenth century; while the real Emperor they styled the "Dairi," and to the Dairi they sometimes referred contemptuously enough as "this Prince"! It cannot be too strongly insisted upon that to the poorest and the most abject and wretched of the Court nobles, every one not invested with Court rank or a Court title was merely so much indiscriminate common clay.

Yet one other point must be dwelt upon with some slight emphasis. In 1540 A.D. the demarcation between the *samurai*, or the warrior-class, and the farmer, or between the *samurai* and the artisan or the merchant, was by no means a strict one. Any plebeian that could prove himself a first-class fighting-man was then willingly received into the armed *comitatus* which every feudal potentate was eager to attach to himself and to his flag. It is common to regard the "two-sworded class" as a caste of hoary antiquity. As a sober matter of historical fact, it was only in the sixteenth century that the wearing of two swords was confined to the select and privileged class of the *samurai*! Down to the death of Iyeyasu in 1616, in Japan there was *la carrière ouverte aux talents*; and any man of ability and of mettle could then carve out a career for himself. A modern Japanese statesman has remarked that there has been no age so prolific (not to say so prodigal) in talent as the latter half of the sixteenth century; and he has explained this fact by pointing out that the real rulers of the Empire then were men of real genius, who insisted that the promotion of their subordinates should depend upon nothing but upon native ability and devotion to duty. In those days the rings and cliques, from the ascendency of which it has been the almost constant ill-fortune of Japan to suffer, were ruthlessly and remorselessly broken up whenever they made their loathsome appearance. It was only with the full re-establishment of a central military government

in Japan that the caste system, which is commonly but
erroneously regarded as having existed at all times in Japan,
was, if not devised, at all events organised, by the astute and
self-seeking Yedo bureaucracy.

As regards this special volume, the clues to its structure
are very simple and should be tolerably easy to follow. There
are only two of them. The first is the re-centralisation of Japan
under a military rule, while the second is the history of early
foreign—*i.e.* European—intercourse with the Island Empire of
the Far East. On the re-establishment of this central military
government foreign intercourse exercised no great influence; on
the progress of this foreign intercourse with Japan, the influence
exercised by the re-establishment of the Shōgunate with stronger
powers than it had had in the days of Yoritomo, was at once
strong, decisive, and—fatal. So much, one may venture to
believe, will appear from what is set forth in the following
chapters.

CHAPTER II.

THE PORTUGUESE DISCOVERY OF JAPAN.

THE year of the birth of Mary Queen of Scots (1542) was an important one in the history of Japan. It was then that Iyeyasu, who was destined to put the coping-stone to the centralising work of his predecessors, Nobunaga and Hideyoshi, and to give the whole of the country a government under which it should be at peace for two centuries and a half, was born. And it was probably in this year that Europeans made their first appearance in Japan.

About the exact circumstances of this European discovery of Japan there is unfortunately a good deal of confusion and obscurity, and various dates ranging from 1534 to 1545 have been assigned for it. However, it appears that that given by Antonio Galvão (1542) was generally accepted by the missionaries subsequently in Japan as the correct one. In the library of Ajuda in Lisbon is the unpublished manuscript of the *History of the Church of Japan, composed by the Religieux of the Company of Jesus who have been resident in that Country from the year 1575 to the present year of 1634.* One of the authors of that work, as quoted by Father Cros, writes thus :—

The first among Europeans to discover these islands were the Portuguese. After Albuquerque had taken Malacca in 1511, Andrade went to China as Ambassador from King Emmanuel in 1518. He then had knowledge of the Lûchû Islands, which are a continuation of those of Japan, are very near to them, and, to speak correctly, belong to Japan, for the Kings of Japan come from them. But as Galvão's book *Dos varios descubrimentos* proves, it was only in 1542 that an acquaintance with the islands of Japan themselves was obtained. In this year Martin Alphonso de Sousa being Governor of India, and Francis Xavier arriving there, Antonio Da Motta, Francisco Zeimotto, and Antonio Peixotto went in a *junco* from Siam to China, when a great tempest called *Tufao* (from the Chinese *Tay-fum*, or the Japanese *Tai-fu*, great wind) drove their *junco* for twenty-four hours on the open sea, and brought them among the islands of Japan : they landed on one of those islands, called Tanegashima, in the Sea of Satsuma. The Portuguese taught the inhabitants of the island how to make arquebuses (*espingardas*), an art which quickly spread through the whole of Japan. A recollection of these three Portuguese, of their names, and of the service they rendered, is still preserved at Tanegashima. Fernão Mendez Pinto in his book *Fingimentos* represents himself as one of the

three of the *junco*; but that is false, as are many other things in his
book, which seems to have been composed rather to amuse than to set
forth truths. Later, another Portuguese vessel went to Bungo, as our
Brother Yiofoken Paulo, a Japanese, writes in his *Monogatari*
(*Dialogues*); and he himself has told me of the fact verbally. In
Bungo they traded with these Portuguese without a word passing; the
scales and the weights served as words. The Duke of Bungo at that
time, the father of the Duke Francis Ōtomo (Yoshishige), who became
a Christian, seeing the riches of the vessel, was minded to kill the
Portuguese in order to appropriate the cargo; his son dissuaded him
from doing so, saying that such an act would dishonour him, being
contrary to reason and to the sentiments of respect and benevolence
always due to strangers.

As Pinto is frequently spoken of as the discoverer of Japan,
it may be advisable to give the briefest of outlines of his story
here. Finding himself stranded at Lampaçāo, and wishing to
get to Malacca, in default of finding any vessel proceeding
thither, he, in company with Diego Zeimoto and Christofero
Borello, took service with a Chinese corsair, Samipocheca by
name, one of whose vessels with three Portuguese on board
being afterwards disabled in a fight with another piratical
flotilla was constrained to make for the Lūchūs, with which the
corsair was familiar. However, a tempest drove the junk
considerably north of the Lūchūs, and she made the land at
what Pinto calls the isle of Tanukima. By this he means Tanegashima, the long low island, whose extreme northerly point
lies some five-and-twenty miles off the southern coast of the
province of Ōsumi. Here the adventurers were welcomed with
the greatest cordiality, the princelet of the islet according them
honours that might almost be described as extravagant. Borello
especially was overwhelmed with marks of distinction—a
circumstance to be attributed to the fact that he was the
possessor of a wonderful arquebus whose performances excited
universal amazement and admiration. This weapon, to his
intense delight, was presented to the prince, who at once set his
armourers to work with it as a model, and within six months,
according to Pinto, 600 arquebuses were made in the island.
In consequence of their original seat of manufacture in Japan,
fire-arms became known throughout the archipelago as Tanegashima.

Reports of these new wonders in the little island spread
fast and spread far. The hypochondriac Prince of Bungo, who
was the uncle, father-in-law, and feudal superior of the ruler

of Tanegashima, sent for one of the Portuguese; and as the princelet was utterly averse to parting with Borello, Pinto, with his own consent, was selected to go, as being of a " more lively humour " than was Zeimoto. Pinto's reception at the Court of Bungo was most flattering, and the ultimate results of the visit substantial. His Highness had, for some time, to the great anxiety of his retainers, been the victim of a seemingly incurable depression of spirits. Pinto very soon succeeded in banishing the Prince's melancholy, and at the same time in curing him of the gout. This of course served to procure the adventurer great credit. But his smattering of medical knowledge rendered him a still greater service. He had brought a matchlock with him, and his feats with that weapon excited as much sensation as Borello's had in Tanegashima. A son of the prince, some seventeen years of age, got infatuated with shooting, and one day, all unknown to Pinto, he set to practising on his own account. An extra charge of powder produced a disastrous explosion, with unpleasant results to the young prince, and Pinto's life was in danger for having been the occasion of the mishap. But he was given a chance of binding up the wounds and curing the victim, with the result that the young prince quickly recovered, and Pinto's fame as a leech got bruited all over the principality. "So that," writes Pinto, " after this sort I received in recompense of this my cure above 1,500 ducats, which I carried with me from this place."

Meanwhile the Chinese corsair had disposed of his lading at Tanegashima; and thither Pinto proceeded to take passage with his two companions for Ningpo. In this settlement the liveliest commotion was excited by the news of the discovery of Japan and the intelligence that a cargo bought for 2,500 taels had been disposed of for twelve times that value there.[1] Nine vessels were hastily fitted out and dispatched; but of these nine eight foundered with the loss of 700 men, of whom 140

---

[1] At this time it is to be noted that the Spanish and Portuguese ratio of gold to silver was 13¼ to 1. In Japan gold and silver were then said to be of equal value, weight for weight. These metals were not currency at that date; although there were indeed some gold and silver coins in existence, they were not in circulation. Copper coin was almost the sole medium of exchange; if gold and silver were used in payments they were weighed out in small quantities. In Japan, then, the precious metals were chiefly used to ornament temples and idols, for small ornaments, and to decorate saddles and harness, helmets, armour and sword hilts, and for similar purposes. It was only from 1586 that gold and silver began to be coined on an extensive scale, and it seems to have been the exigencies of foreign trade which occasioned the new mintage.

were Portuguese, while the remaining one with Pinto on board reached the Lūchūs only to be wrecked on a shoal there. From the Lūchūs Pinto after numerous stirring adventures succeeded in making his way to Malacca, whence he again proceeded to Japan on board a vessel commanded by Captain George Alvarez (1547).

Apart from the express assurance of the Jesuit priest just quoted that Pinto was not one of the three of the *junco*, and that there are many falsities in his narrative, this tale of his must be rejected for various considerations. He tells us that the princelet of Tanegashima was then a feudatory of the "King" of Bungo, who was also his uncle and his father-in-law. Now as far as we can discover, Tanegashima was never subject to the House of Ōtomo of Bungo; and at that date, as it had been for long, it acknowledged Shimadzu of Satsuma as its feudal superior. Then the "King" of Bungo's letter to the island chief is certainly peculiar in more than one respect. "Origendono, King of Bungo, and of Hakata, lord of the great House of Fianzima, of Tosa, and of Bandō (*i.e.* the *Kwantō*), Sovereign of the small Kings of the Gotō Islands and of Shimonoseki." When Pinto appeared at the Court of Bungo as Ambassador from the Viceroy of India in 1556, the Daimyō of Bungo (Ōtomo Yoshishige) had indeed conquered most of Chikuzen, and Hakata was then held by him. But even then beyond the island of Kyūshū he had no footing; and the Gotōs were not subject to him. But between 1542 and 1556 there had been a great expansion of the Bungo domains. In 1542, the year of the Portuguese discovery of Japan, the "King" of Bungo was "King" of nothing but the one single province of that name in the north-eastern corner of Kyūshū. Again, it is tolerably safe to conclude that Pinto's account of the mishap to the young prince, and his part in the affair, is not altogether correct, for in 1577 Ōtomo Yoshishige wrote to Cabral, the Jesuit Vice-Provincial, that "at the beginning of the navigation from China to Japan he had had a Portuguese with him *for more than three years*, who cured his brother the King of Yamaguchi of an arquebus wound." Then the account of the hundreds of Chinese trading-vessels that hurried to the Gulf of Kagoshima after the "discovery" of Japan is absurd. At that date, as there had been for years before, there was a regular traffic between China and Ōuchi's fief of Yamaguchi at least, and probably with Kyūshū as well. The Chinese had been more or less acquainted with the existence of Japan for some considerable time before Pinto " discovered " it for them. It is rather strange to find Charlevoix, who devotes twenty-two pages to these fairy tales, remarking that it seems very difficult to regard all Pinto here says as entirely fabulous, especially if we consider he wrote at a time when several persons could have contradicted him. Now the " Peregriniçāo," written of course before Pinto's death in 1583, was published in 1614—that is, seventy-two years after Pinto's alleged " discovery " of Japan. And then, almost immediately, we do find him contradicted by the Jesuit historian already cited. This unknown author arrived in Japan in 1577, and enjoyed several years of intimacy with many of Xavier's converts and with others who remembered the first coming of the foreigners perfectly well. Elsewhere, speaking of the "Peregriniçāo," Charlevoix says: " Pinto there gives us to understand that he had been three times in Japan, and he claims even to have discovered it. It is certain that he was with Xavier at the Court of the King of Bungo (September to November 1551), and it is partly from him that we learn what passed there. He was one of the witnesses in the *Proofs* of the Canonisation of the Apostle, and it is this which gives a great weight to his memoirs, in which he makes no mention of his last adventure in Japan." It is to be feared that Pinto's claim to be the discoverer of the Island Empire of the Far East must be dismissed as one of his "figments." He was doubtless acquainted with the circumstances of its discovery by his fellow-countrymen and with certain incidents in the earliest European intercourse with the Japanese; but that he himself was in any way either their hero or their veracious chronicler cannot be admitted by any one who takes the trouble to scrutinise his romance at all narrowly.

When news of the discovery of the new islands reached the Portuguese settlements in China, the Straits, and elsewhere, expeditions were promptly fitted out to proceed to them from various bases—from Malacca among the rest. How many of these were set on foot during the next decade we are not aware; probably enough there were many of them, but of seven we know for certain. In 1543, we learn from Japanese sources, the Lusitanians came to Bungo, and some of them were sent on

by the Daimyō to Kyōto accompanied by an officer named Saitō.
From a letter of Xavier's (November 5th, 1549), among other
things urging the establishment of a Portuguese factory at Sakai,
we learn that before that date two Portuguese had seen Kyōto,
which they reported to be a city of 96,000 houses, larger than
Lisbon; and in an earlier epistle of his we are told that a certain
Portuguese had lived " a long time " in Satsuma previous to 1548.
We hear of Captain da Gama's vessel at Hiji in Bungo in 1551,
of Portuguese ships at Hirado in Hizen in 1549 and 1550, while
before 1549 there had been at least three separate voyages to
Kagoshima, or at all events to Satsuma.

These ventures have come to our knowledge mainly because
they were all intimately connected with the introduction of
Christianity into Japan, and so have all been referred to in the
early missionary letters,[2] and put on record by the historians of
the Church. The story of the introduction of the new faith
into the Island Empire is an interesting one; but Crasset and
Charlevoix alike have sought to make it still more enthralling
by reading between the lines of their original authorities in a
somewhat liberal fashion, while in Japanese hands the tale of
Anjiro has developed or degenerated into the legendary, if not
the fabulous. Those who desire nothing beyond a plain un-
varnished edition of the matter will find all they need in the
latter part of the first and in the opening two hundred pages of
the second volume of Father Cros's excellent book.

As every one is supposed to know, it was Francis Xavier
and his companions who were the pioneers of the many hundred
Christian missionaries who laboured in Japan. The earliest
mention we meet with of Japan in Xavier's letters is in the
long one written from Cochin on January 20th, 1548. There he
says :—

While at Malacca I learned great news from some Portuguese
merchants, very trustworthy people. They spoke to me of certain
great islands discovered some time ago; they are called the islands of
Japan. Our Holy Faith, they say, could there be more profitably

2 In this connection the new documents in Father Cros's *Saint François de
Xavier, Sa Vie et ses Lettres* (Toulouse and Paris, 1900) are of great value to the
historian. Besides the original letters of Xavier faithfully translated from the
Portuguese or Spanish, Father Cros gives several other pieces of high interest.
His extracts from Froez's unpublished *History of Japan*, from the unpublished
work of the writer whom he calls the "Annalist of Macao," and from
Valegnani's two works on early Christianity in Japan serve to excite a keen
regret that the whole of these pieces are not available in print.

propagated than in any other part of the Indies, because the Japanese are very desirous of being instructed, which our Gentiles of India are not. With these merchants came a Japanese called Angero who was in quest of me; so that these merchants spoke of me to him. Angero came with the desire of confessing to me, because having told the Portuguese of certain sins of his youth and asked them how he could obtain pardon from God for such serious sins, the Portuguese counselled him to proceed with them to Malacca, where he would find me, and he did so; but when he reached Malacca.I had departed for Maluco; so that he re-embarked to return to Japan. When they were in sight of these islands (Japan) a great tempest, in which they were like to perish, drove them back; he then resumed the way to Malacca and found me there. His joy was great, and afterwards he came again and again to be instructed. As he spoke Portuguese tolerably well, we could understand—I the questions he asked, and he the answers I returned. If all the Japanese are as eager to learn as Angero is, they are of all nations newly discovered the most curious. . . . All the Portuguese merchants who have been to Japan tell me that if I go there more will be done there for the service of the Lord than among the Gentiles of India, the Japanese being a people of great sense (*da mucha razon*). What I feel in my soul makes me think that I, or another of the Company, will go to Japan before two years, although the voyage is full of perils.

. This Anjiro, or Yajiro,[3] a Satsuma man of some thirty-five years of age, tells his own story in a letter (November 29th, 1548) from Goa to Ignatius Loyola:—"When I lay plunged in the blind fog of superstitions in Japan," he writes, "fearing the hostile attempts of some upon my life, I had by chance fled for refuge to a monastery of the *bonzes* as to an asylum. A Portuguese vessel had put in to the same place to trade. Among these merchants was Alvarez Vaz, who was already known to me; and he on learning of my situation at first freely offered his services out of friendship, if I wished to depart with him. Then as his departure was likely to be delayed for some time by reason of his business not being completed, and as there would be danger for me in delay, he recommended me by letter to a friend of his, anchored in a neighbouring port, who was making ready to start. This letter I took there at once in the dead of night; and in the haste and confusion I mistakenly delivered it not to *Ferdinand*, to whom it was addressed, but to Captain *George* Alvarez." His tale from this point onward has just been succinctly given by Xavier, the only points of interest therein omitted being that on Anjiro's

---

[3] Writes Valegnani:—"This Japanese is commonly called Angero; his true name was Yajiro. He then took the name of Anxey when, in Japan, in token of renunciation of the world, he cut his hair and beard, and finally at baptism he received the name of Paul of the Holy Faith."

first visit to Malacca he was refused baptism on the grounds that he purposed to return to Japan to live with a pagan wife, and that after being driven back to China by the tempest he there met Alvarez Vaz, "who had been the first, in Japan, to encourage him to proceed to Malacca," and that with Vaz he made his second visit to that settlement. On arriving there, the first man he met was George Alvarez; and Alvarez at once conducted him to Xavier, who was then celebrating a marriage in the church. Eight days afterwards he was dispatched in Alvarez's ship to the College of St. Paul in Goa, where he arrived at the beginning of March 1548, five days before Xavier, who had come overland from Cape Comorin. Anjiro was attended by his Japanese servant, while Xavier had sent still another Japanese with them from Malacca to be instructed in the College. There they were put under the special care of Cosme de Torres, who after ten years' roving in America and elsewhere had entered the Company of Jesus shortly before. Of Anjiro in Goa, Froez, who had just then arrived there, writes:—" Anjiro had a fine intelligence; besides, he already spoke Portuguese,— at all events he made himself understood, and what was taught him he learned. When the things of the Faith were explained to him, he reduced to writing what had been said. His memory was of the happiest, so that after he had twice listened to Father Torres's commentary on St. Matthew, he knew the text of that evangelist by heart from the first chapter to the last, as Father Torres himself records in one of his letters. Six months of his sojourn at the College sufficed for him to learn to read and write Portuguese, and there were few pupils in the house more capable than he." On the Pentecost Day of 1548, Anjiro, together with his companions, was baptized in the Cathedral by the Bishop of Goa.

Xavier thus had the means ready to hand for prosecuting the mission to Japan on which he had been meditating so earnestly. From his own letters it appears that he regarded this enterprise as an escape from the discouraging condition of things in the Portuguese Indies. At all events he wrote at great length to John III. about the conduct of his deputies and officers in the colonies, declaring to him that he was *escaping* to Japan, and that one of the chief reasons for his flight was, the disgust and despair which the sight of the maladministra-"

tion of the Indies caused him. In addition to this, Xavier's opinion of the people he had so far worked among was the reverse of a high one. In a letter to Loyola (January 14th, 1548) he asserts that "all these Indian nations are very barbarous, vicious, and without inclination to virtue, no constancy of character, no frankness." All this considered, it is perhaps not surprising that he pushed his Japanese project with so much earnestness and vigour that he was ready to depart on it well within the space of the two years he had allowed for the preparations. On the last day of May 1549 he arrived at Malacca in company with Father Torres and Juan Fernandez, a lay-brother of the Company, both Spaniards like himself, while besides the Japanese converts there were also a Chinese and a Malabar servant and a Portuguese friend of Xavier's in the little band. Before following Xavier and his companions on their adventurous mission, however, it is well for us to obtain a clear conception of the general position of the Portuguese in the Far East, and especially of their position in relation to the recently founded and organised "Company of Jesus."

The collation of Japanese authorities with the letters of the Jesuits and other contemporary European documents serves to show that native writers are far from accurate in the data they give regarding early foreign intercourse. In the matter of dates even such a careful and painstaking writer as Arai Hakuseki makes serious blunders. As regards the date of the Portuguese discovery of Japan, Japanese authors present us with a bountiful variety of choice. Some authorities assign 1545 as the date of the occurrences at Tanegashima, while others say that Europeans had reached Japan in 1534. One Japanese statement is that in the 12th year of Tembun, which would be 1543 A.D., Portuguese who came to the island of Také, in the province of Satsuma, taught the Japanese the use of fire-arms. In the reign of Oki-machi Tenno (1558–1586) they imported cannon. We append three other Japanese accounts of this important event about which there are so many conflicting assertions :—

(a.) "In the 10th year of Tembun (1541) a Portuguese merchant-ship drifted to the island of Tanegashima, belonging to the province of Osumi. The ship then entered the harbour of Kagoshima and at last reached Bungo. Otomo, the prince of the Province, gave the Portuguese a lodging-house in a temple called Jinguji. From this time the Portuguese came every year to various ports in Kyūshū, bringing with them various commodities. The natives were charmed by the novelty of the commodities, and so eagerly welcomed the foreigners in their ports that, if they did not come, they complained bitterly.

"Tokitaka, lord of Tanegashima, was struck with wonder on seeing the Portuguese firing muskets, and was taught their use by the latter. The next year the Portuguese were accompanied by some blacksmiths, and they taught him how to manufacture fire-arms. Suginobo, a priest of Negoro, in the province of Kii, and Tachibanaya Matasaburo, a merchant of Sakai, came to the island and were instructed in the use and manufacture of the fire-arms. In a few years after the weapon was diffused throughout the country. The Portuguese also taught the manufacture of ordnance to Ôtomo."

(b.) Professor Tsuboi says in the *Shigaku Zasshi* (Historical Magazine):—"Among the Japanese books describing the first importation of fire-arms, one written in the Keicho period (1596–1615) by Dairyuji Fumiyuki, entitled *Nanpo-Bunshiu*, may be considered to be the most trustworthy. In it is found the following account :-

"'On the 25th of the 8th month of the 12th year of Tembun (Sept. 23rd, 1543 A.D.) a big ship arrived at the bay of Nishimura in the island of Tanegashima. The crew consisted of about one hundred persons, who were quite different to the natives in their appearance and language. The natives regarded them with wonder and curiosity. There was one Chinese scholar called Goho among the crew. With this Chinese the headman of the village, named Ori-be-nojo, held a conversation, writing with sticks on the sand, and learned from him that they were merchants from Western countries. Ori-be-nojo then directed them to steer their ship to a port called Akaogi, 13 *ri* distant from the place. At the same time he informed my grandfather and my old father Tokitaka of the arrival of the strange ship. In consequence Tokitaka dispatched many small boats to tow the foreign ship to Akaogi, where she arrived on the 27th. The crew were given lodging at a Buddhist temple at the port. All the time the Chinese Goho acted the part of interpreter. There were two chiefs of the foreign merchants, one being called Francisco and the other Kirishita da Mota. They had one article in their possession which was about two or three *shaku* in length. It was straight, heavy, and hollow. One end, however, was closed, and near it there was a small hole, through which fire was to be lighted. The article was used in this way : some mysterious medicine was put into it with a small round piece of lead, and when one lit the medicine through that hole, the lead piece was discharged and hit everything. When it was discharged, light like lightning was seen and noise like thunder was heard, so that bystanders invariably closed their ears with their hands. On seeing this article, Tokitaka regarded it as a most extraordinary thing, but did not know its name or its use. Afterwards people called it "teppô," but I am not sure whether the name is of Chinese or of native origin. One day Tokitaka asked the two foreigners to teach him its use, and he soon became so skilful that he could nearly hit a white object placed at the distance of a hundred steps. He then bought two pieces, regardless of the very high price asked for them, and kept them as the most precious treasures of his house. He continued to practice shooting incessantly, and at last made himself so skilful that he never missed his aim. As for the manufacture of the mysterious medicine, Tokitaka had his retainer Sasakawa Koshiro instructed in it. He also ordered some blacksmiths to manufacture the tube, and after much labour they so far succeeded in their work that they could produce almost similar articles, but they did not know how to close one end. Next year the foreign merchants again came to Kumano-ichi-ura in Tanegashima. Among them there was one blacksmith. Tokitaka was filled with joy, and at once sent one of his retainers, Kimbeinojo Kiyosada, to learn from him how to close the end. In this way the manufacture of fire-arms was learnt, and in a year or so sixty or seventy muskets were manufactured,'"

Professor Tsuboi concludes that "although there are various opinions concerning the exact date, September 23rd, 1543 A.D., as given in this book, is the most trustworthy."

In connection with this it is to be noted (1) that the *Nanpo-Bunshiu* was no contemporary record, it having been written more than half-a-century after the first arrival of the foreigners, and (2) that 1542 seems to have been the date generally accepted by the missionary writers, who were as a rule exceedingly particular about the accuracy of their dates.

(*c.*) "The first importation of fire-arms to this country was made in the 12th year of Tembun (1543 A.D.). Before this time it is recorded in an old chronicle (*Intoku-taiheiki*), that in the 1st year of Bunki (1501 A.D.) muskets were presented by foreigners. But as powder and bullets were not presented with the fire-arms, and besides, none knew how to use them, the arms were abandoned and left to decay."—Prof. KUROKAWA, in his *Kokushi-an.*

[Since this chapter was written the first volume of Herr Haas' *Geschichte des Christentums in Japan* has been published. In this painstaking work will be found the most thorough collation of Japanese and foreign authorities for the date of the Portuguese discovery of Japan that has yet appeared. Herr Haas arrives at substantially the same conclusion as Professor Tsuboi. But he takes no account of the fact that 1542, the date given by Galvao, was accepted by the " Annalist of Macao," who had opportunities of sifting the evidence of living Japanese who were already young men in 1542 or 1543. Although the event itself is important, and although it would be highly interesting to say exactly when it occurred, the exact date is of no very great practical consequence, for the matter of a few months backwards or forwards exercised no influence upon the subsequent course of events whatsoever.]

CHAPTER III.

THE PORTUGUESE IN THE ORIENT AND THE JESUITS.

THE position of Portugal in the comity of civilised nations is now so insignificant that it is somewhat hard to credit the assertion that some four centuries ago the little kingdom stood in the very forefront of European progress and enterprise. Yet such is an undoubted fact—in certain spheres of activity at least. In the all-important matter of maritime discovery, the Portuguese led the way with indomitable courage and perseverance for the greater part of two centuries. The chief impulse to their early activity in facing the mystery and lifting the veil of the unknown that shrouded the African coast came from the lonely and wave-buffetted promontory of Sagres, on whose inhospitable and windy height the half-English Prince, Henry the Navigator, had reared his observatory and established the school whence proceeded the most daring and the most skilful seamen of the age. During the Prince's lifetime (1394–1460) the successive captains he had sent out had league by league groped their way southwards along the African coast as far as the Gambia; while twenty-six years after his death, Dias, with two ships of 50 tons burthen each, actually reached the extreme southerly point of the continent. This point he called Cabo Tormentoso, but King John II., foreseeing the realisation of the long-sought passage to India, changed this name of sinister import to the euphemistic and enduring one of the Cape of Good Hope. In a little less than two years the King's prescience was fully justified, for on May 20th, 1498, Da Gama anchored before Calicut. Seven years thereafter the first Viceroy of the Indies was sent out in the person of Almeida, shortly to be followed by the great Albuquerque. In 1510 Goa was captured and made the capital of the Eastern possessions of Portugal; shortly after Malacca was taken after a stout fight; while in 1512 the Moluccas were reached. Five years after this the Lusitanians opened up communication with China, Andrada with a squadron of eight ships being sent as royal Ambassador to the Chinese capital, where he received Imperial sanction for the opening of trade at Canton,—a privilege,

by the way, the English got only 117 years afterwards (1634).
There the traders' headquarters were at first on the islands of
Lampaçáo and Sanchoan; it was not till 1557 that they were
permitted to erect factories at Macáo. They also established
themselves at Ningpo in 1522; and in 1549, when the Chinese
fell upon the settlement and massacred two-thirds of the
Portuguese in it, yet as many as four hundred escaped. The
Lusitanians were also at Amoy in 1544, and we have incidental
evidence of their driving a trade at other Chinese ports not
specified in the Imperial sanction obtained by Andrada.

At the date of the discovery of Japan (1542), from the Red
Sea and the Cape of Good Hope on to a line 17° eastward of
the Moluccas the Portuguese held an absolute and undisputed
monopoly of maritime trade. On all that vast expanse of water
no other European flag was to be seen. It was in the following
year (1543) that the Spaniard Villalobos, sailing with five ships
and 370 men from Navidad in Mexico, endeavoured to establish
a settlement on the Philippines, where Magellan had lost his
life in 1521. However, this attempt was abortive; it was only
from the arrival of Legaspi in 1565, and the foundation of
Manila six years later on, in 1571, that the Spaniards evinced any
serious determination to make themselves masters of Luzon and
the surrounding archipelago. This foundation of Manila was
really an event of importance; the new city within a quarter of a
century proved a rival to Macáo, which had hitherto been the
chief European base for the prosecution of the trade with Japan.
As it was not till 1592 that the first quarrel between the Spaniards
and the Portuguese over this Japanese trade commenced, it will be
seen that the Portuguese held an undisputed monopoly of it for
just fifty years. Although this first tradal difficulty between the
rival merchants[1] was smoothed over for the time being, yet
within the next decade Manila was at serious variance with
Macáo over the prosecution of the commerce interdicted to the
former, an interdict which the Spanish traders paid but scant
heed to. There is no doubt that this tradal quarrel between
Spaniards and Portuguese did much to impair the position the
Lusitanians had acquired in Japan, for the jealousy between the

---

[1] Not rival Powers, for Philip II. of Spain had become King of Portugal in
1580, and the two Crowns remained united until 1640, the year after the expulsion
of the Portuguese traders from Japan.

Peninsulars led to systematic mutual slandering and back-biting which cannot have done much to raise the reputation of the foreigners in the opinion of the Japanese.

But this was after all a comparatively small matter in itself; it was the importation of sectarian bitterness into the question that ultimately proved so fatal to the continuance of European intercourse with Japan. Of course the Spaniards had brought their priests with them to the Philippines; the Agustino Calzados had come with Legaspi in 1565, the Franciscans had established themselves there in 1577, while the Dominicans had appeared ten years later on, in 1587 (the very year in which Hideyoshi issued his first edict against Christianity in Japan). Now, in 1592, a Dominican had been dispatched from Manila to Japan; and in 1593 several Franciscans were sent in the quality of "Ambassadors." The conduct of these latter led to serious misunderstandings with the Jesuits, who down to that date had been the sole and only missionaries at work in the country. From 1542 to 1592 the Portuguese monopoly of the Japanese trade had been absolute and undisputed; for the forty-four years following the arrival of Xavier at Kagoshima in 1549—that is, down to 1593—the Jesuit monopoly of religious propagandism in Dai Nippon had been, if possible, still more unquestioned. This propaganda of theirs had been carried on in Japan, as it had been throughout all the East, under Portuguese auspices. Hence the invasion of Japan by merchants and priests from Manila led to an embittered and a complex jealousy—a jealousy at once tradal, religious, and national.

In these last paragraphs we have somewhat anticipated events; the excuse for so doing is that it is all-important to grasp the fact that down to 1592—possibly down to 1598—the only foreign traders in Japan were Portuguese, and down to 1593 the only foreign *religieux* there were Jesuits. To explain how it was that these latter came to occupy the privileged position in the country they did, it is necessary to advert briefly to the origin of that famous Society, as well as to a very remarkable characteristic of all early Portuguese colonial effort.

The long contest she had had to wage with the Moors for her existence left an indelible impress upon the national character of Portugal—at least upon the Portugal of the fifteenth and sixteenth centuries. In spite of the undoubted possession of great practical ability, the best Portuguese of these two centuries were above all things knights-errant and crusaders, who looked upon every pagan as an enemy at once of Portugal and of Christ. Such at least is the conclusion forced upon any one who has made a study of the records of Portuguese maritime enterprise from the days of Prince Henry the Navigator downwards. For example, in 1438 Pope Eugene IV. issued a Bull applauding the past efforts of the Portuguese, exhorting them to proceed on the laudable career on which they had entered, and granting them an exclusive right to all the countries they might discover from Cape Nun to the continent of India. It was in consequence of the representations of Prince Henry the Navigator himself that this Bull was obtained. The language of the Prince's application to the Pope is indeed remarkable. After dwelling on the unwearied zeal with which for twenty years he had devoted himself to discovering unknown countries, the wretched inhabitants of which were utter strangers to true religion, wandering in heathen darkness or led astray by the delusions of Mahomet, he besought His Holiness, to whom, as the Vicar of Christ, all the kingdoms of the earth were subject, to confer on the Crown of Portugal a right to all the countries possessed by infidels which should be discovered by the industry of its subjects and subdued by its force of arms, and entreated the Holy Father to forbid all Christian Powers, under the highest penalties, to molest Portugal while engaged in this laudable enterprise, or to settle in any of the countries the Portuguese might discover. In return the Prince promised that in all their expeditions it should be the chief object of his countrymen to spread the knowledge of the Christian religion, to establish the authority of the Holy See, and to increase the flock of the universal Pastor. The Bull issued in response to this application was merely the first of a long series that had the effect of making the Kings of Portugal omnipotent politically and ecclesiastically in the East so far as Europeans were concerned. In the sixteenth century, without the consent of the Portuguese monarch no bishop could be appointed there, no episcopal see created, no vacancy in any see filled up. Furthermore, no European missionary could proceed to the East without His Majesty's sanction, and even with that only in a Portuguese vessel; while no Bull or Brief from the Holy See was of any effect in the East unless it had received his approbation. In return His Majesty was solemnly pledged to protect and support the Holy Church in his Oriental possessions. This Protectorate of the Crown of Portugal, as it was termed, was annually confirmed by Papal Bulls, in which stood a clause which annulled beforehand every Bull which might be issued by any succeeding Pope to the contrary.

It must ever be borne in mind that after the discovery of India by Da Gama in 1498, the Eastern trade was always maintained as a royal monopoly, and that the early Portuguese discoverers were not, as were the English afterwards, mere traders or private adventurers, but admirals with a royal commission to conquer territory and to promote the spread of what was called Christianity. So much appears, for example, in the case of Cabral, who was in command of the fleet of thirteen sail that left the Tagus for India in 1500. " The sum of his instructions was to begin with preaching, and, if that failed, to proceed to the sharp determination of the sword." As for Da Gama and his method of propagating " the true religion," in spite of his well-deserved and undying fame as a discoverer, his career is a record of brutal atrocities that make one blush for civilisation, for religion, and for humanity alike. And these atrocities were all committed in the name not merely of religion, but of the *only true religion*. Indeed, generally speaking, of all these adventurers, with the honourable exception of Albuquerque, it has been truly remarked that it is impossible for any one who has not read the contemporary narratives of their discoveries and conquests to conceive the grossness of the superstition and the cruelty with which the whole history of the exploration and subjugation of the Indies is stained. But at the same time it is well to be on our guard against stigmatising these chartered pirates as hypocrites, the most opprobrious of epithets that can possibly be applied to any of the sons of men. These pious ruffians seem to have been thoroughly convinced that it was not only their right, but their duty, to conquer and convert the heathen by any and every means whatsoever. Possibly when the keen-witted Japanese came to grasp the import of this fact— as there are grounds to believe they did—in the early seventeenth century, their expulsion of the foreign missionaries and their stern and ruthless suppression of Christianity in the country became merely matters of course. But of this more in the sequel.

Just at the time his subjects first appeared in Japan, Portugal was governed by one of the most bigoted kings that ever sat upon her throne. The zeal of John III. (1521–1557) had introduced the Inquisition into his kingdom in 1536,[2] and his zeal prompted him to push on the conversion of his Oriental subjects and their neighbours in the most vigorous fashion. To effect that purpose a strong, dauntless, and efficient missionary organisation was necessary. Not much was to be hoped for from the older monastic orders; they had become so effete and such a scandal to Christendom that in 1538 a committee of four cardinals, deputed to investigate and report upon them, had expressed to the Pope its opinion that they should all be abolished. Now it was at this very juncture that Ignatius Loyola presented to the Pope the draft of his regulations for his proposed " Company (or Society) of Jesus." So, although on perusing this document His Holiness is reported to have exclaimed " The finger of God is here," yet there was a strong opposition to the formation of any new organisation at all similar to the orders of the monastic system that many regarded as hopelessly broken down, if not actually mischievous. However, on hearing of the projected Company, the King of Portugal instructed his Ambassador at the Vatican to press it on the Pope, and at the same time to ask Loyola himself for some priests of his Society for work in Portugal and its Indian possessions. The latter request was attended to at once; in March 1540 Rodriguez, the only Portuguese in the original company of seven that took the vow in the crypt of Nôtre Dame de Montmartre in Paris in 1534, and the Spaniard Xavier were sent to the King. Six months later, on September 27th, 1540, the Bull *Regimini militantis ecclesiæ* was published, confirming the new Order, but limiting its members to sixty, a restriction which was removed by a later Bull of March, 1543. In 1542 the earliest College of the Society was founded at Coimbra by the Portuguese king, Rodriguez being appointed rector. This establishment was designed as a training-school to feed the Indian mission, while, as a matter of fact, a seminary at Goa was the second institution founded out of Rome in connection with the Company. This latter foundation was one of the

2 The first Grand Inquisitor in the Portuguese dominions, the Bishop of Ceuta, was soon succeeded by the King's own brother, the Cardinal Henry, who was afterwards King of Portugal from 1578 to 1580.

earliest works of the "Apostle of the Indies," to whose career it may now be well to direct our special attention.

On reaching the Court of Lisbon, Xavier speedily succeeded in winning the entire confidence of the King, and was very soon requested to assume the oversight and direction of the Indian mission that was so great a solicitude to His Portuguese Majesty. Xavier was not slow to comply with the request, and with four briefs from the Pope, one of them appointing him Papal Nuncio in the Indies, he set sail from the Tagus on his thirty-fifth birthday—April 7th, 1541. The voyage was long and tedious; it was not till the 6th May, 1542, that Goa was reached—the very time, by the way, that Charlevoix will have it Mendez Pinto was on his way from Tanegashima to the Court of Bungo to cure His Highness the Prince of despondency and of the gout, and to astonish him and his subjects with the potentialities of the matchlock. Xavier remained in India, with a visit to Ceylon, till the autumn of 1545 ; on the 25th September of that year he arrived at Malacca. Here he remained about four months, but his efforts were attended with comparatively little success, and just a few days before the refugee Japanese Anjiro appeared in the port in quest of him, he had abandoned the place as intractable, and set forth on a missionary expedition to Amboyna and the Moluccas. During his first stay in Malacca Xavier took what his sincerest admirers cannot but now deplore as a regrettable step. He then addressed a letter to the King of Portugal urging him to set up the Inquisition in Goa. The request was readily listened to, although the actual erection of the tribunal there did not take place till 1560, eight years after Xavier's death, and three years after that of the King. A knowledge of the functions and methods of the Holy Office would go far to prejudice intelligent Japanese against Christianity, intolerance being especially distasteful to them, and there is reason to believe that Iyeyasu and his successor Hidetada, who dealt so drastically with the foreign priests in Japan, came to have no inaccurate notion of the functions and methods in question. Xavier was absent from Malacca some eighteen months. Some time after his return there in July 1547, Anjiro, under the conduct of Alvarez Vaz, arrived in the settlement for a second time on the renewed quest for the Apostle of the Indies. How Xavier received him has already been narrated.

CHAPTER IV.

XAVIER IN JAPAN.

WHILE at Malacca Xavier was gladdened by the news that a Japanese "King" had dispatched a request to the Viceroy of the Indies at Goa for "priests of his nation" to serve in the "King's" dominions. Who this "King" was is unfortunately not stated, and, indeed, there are several other points of obscurity in the story. Most probably the "King" in question was the Prince of Bungo. His Highness is said to have been induced to prefer his request on grounds that this irreverent and incredulous age cannot fail to regard as amusing. Some Portuguese traders arriving in one of his harbours, had asked to be allowed to lodge ashore, and all unknown to themselves had, by the orders of the Prince, been installed in a house reputed to be haunted by demons of a most malignant type. For the first night or two the Portuguese had very unpleasant experiences, the demons making them the victims of very rough horse-play. However, the pious traders invoked the Saints, and had recourse to the use of the Cross, and thereupon they were left undisturbed, and the reputation of the house was redeemed. Asked about the matter by the officials, they told what had happened and what they had done, and the marvel their story excited ultimately led the "King" to endeavour to obtain the services of some of the priests of this new religion, so potent to cope with the spirits of mischief and of darkness. The story at all events would serve to show that Portuguese traders had not been slow to make their way to the new El Dorado.

However, Xavier at Malacca could then find no Portuguese vessel bound direct to Japan. But a Chinese junk was about to sail there soon, and in this junk Xavier and his companions took passage. This craft was owned and commanded by a certain Neceda, who had the reputation of being one of the most daring corsairs then making an honest living by piracy in the Far Eastern seas. It must be remembered that at that time the condition of things in those waters,—and, in fact, in

E 2

most waters elsewhere,—was very similar to what Thucydides assures us prevailed among " the Greeks in the old time," when piracy was " an employment that involved no disgrace, but rather brought with it something of honour." Accordingly, the Governor of Malacca thought it prudent to detain Neceda's wife as a hostage for his good behaviour. It was perhaps well the Governor did so, for on the seven weeks' voyage to Japan the honest corsair on more than one occasion behaved in a way that was the reverse of amiable. However, he did the missionaries no real bodily harm, and on August 15th, 1549, Xavier and his friends stepped ashore at Kago-shima.

Here Anjiro quickly appeared at the Prince's Court, where he was questioned closely and exhaustively about his wanderings abroad and the state of affairs in the various countries he had visited in the course of his travels, the Prince evincing special curiosity in the matter of the commerce and power of the Portuguese in India and of the re-ligion they had established there. This intelligent interest in foreign countries and their affairs then displayed by his Highness is a trait of Japanese character that is especially marked. Almost every one of the priests and of the early traders who have left us records of their experiences in the country has either dwelt upon, or at least adverted to, the fact.

Xavier had his audience at the Court of Satsuma on the 29th September, six weeks after his landing. His reception was highly satisfactory, full permission being accorded him to preach in the dominions of the Prince. But the language was a difficulty; and over this Xavier's complaint is piteous. It is to be remarked that nowhere during his ten years' sojourn in the East did Xavier show any special aptitude for the acquisition of Oriental languages. His biographers indeed speak of his receiving the gift of tongues at Yamaguchi in 1551, but, apart from the fact that Xavier nowhere makes any such claim himself, the assertion may be dismissed with a smile as one of those pious and well-intentioned frauds concocted *ad majorem gloriam Dei* and the spiritual edification of the credu-lous. As a matter of fact, his two companions, Torres and Fernandez (and especially Fernandez), were much more proficient in Japanese than he. At the time Anjiro was sent to Goa,

Anjiro could speak Portuguese tolerably well, and his preceptors there could consequently gather real profit from his instructions in his native tongue whilst Xavier had his hands more than full elsewhere.

However, be that as it may, there were no more than 150 baptisms during Xavier's stay in Satsuma, and for these the efforts of Anjiro and his two companions were mainly responsible. At Heshandono's fortress [Froez tells us Heshandono was Niiro, Ise-no-kami, and that his castle was not far from Ichiku], some eighteen miles from Kagoshima, Christianity was accepted by the steward and some of the upper retainers; but apart from these, nearly all the converts were peasants or workmen. One of the latter, Barnabas, the first man baptized in the principality, became a sort of body-servant to Xavier, and seems to have accompanied him in nearly all his future wanderings in Japan.

The propaganda in Satsuma, meagre in results as it had so far proved, received an abrupt check in the summer of 1550, when the Prince issued an edict making it a capital offence for any of his subjects to embrace Christianity from that date. So Xavier and his two companions deemed it advisable to withdraw from the principality, leaving Anjiro in charge of the converts there. On their way they called at Heshan's fortress and left with him a copy of the catechism translated into Japanese. From Satsuma they proceeded to Hirado in the north-west of Hizen, and here Xavier made as many converts in a few days as he had done in Satsuma in the course of a year. This circumstance, taken with all its concomitants, was highly significant, and its import, if not understood by Xavier at the moment, was soon fully grasped by his fellow-workers and successors.

The simple fact was that in matters of religion the average intelligent Japanese among the upper class was an indifferentist —a Laodicean, or a Gallio who cared for none of these things. To him a new religion was of far less consequence or interest than a new sauce would have been to an Englishman of the time of Voltaire. His attitude towards it, in fact, is exceedingly well indicated by Nobunaga's reply to those who questioned him about the advisability of admitting Christianity into his dominions, —that the establishment of one more sect in a country counting some thirty odd sects already could not be a matter of any real consequence. On the other hand, to any new product or new notion in the sphere of practical utility and to the advantage the country might draw from it, the Japanese mind was then, as it is now, keenly alive and alert. Hence every Japanese princelet was eager to see the Portuguese ships in his harbours, but he wished them to bring him guns and gunpowder, not crosses and missals—merchants and not priests, unless these latter could teach his subjects something of real practical consequence.

Now, as has been remarked, before the arrival of Xavier in 1549 there had been several Portuguese trading ventures to Kagoshima, and the Prince had Anjiro's assurances that the presence of the missionaries would surely attract the foreign ships to his ports. Accordingly, when he learned that one of the expected vessels had gone to Hirado in 1549 and two in 1550, and that the hospitality he had extended to the priests from over-sea had been profitless, his disappointment was keen, and the Church historians accuse him of allowing his resentment to disclose itself in the issue of the edict that practically put a stop to Xavier's efforts within the Satsuma confines. On the other hand, the arrival of Xavier at Hirado was honoured by the Portuguese merchantmen in harbour there with salvoes of artillery, and by other marks of profound respect from the traders. Now all this was not lost upon the keen-witted young princelet, Matsuura Takanobu, who doubtless was also perfectly well informed of what had passed in Satsuma. He promptly gave orders that the missionaries were to be listened to with the utmost respect, and during the ten days Xavier remained there he and his companions baptized over a hundred converts.

So, to use the language of Charlevoix, Xavier, " conceiving that if the favour of such a small prince was so potent for the conversion of his subjects, it would be still quite another thing if he (Xavier) could have the protection of the Emperors," determined to push on to the capital. Leaving Torres in charge of the neophytes, he passed on through Hakata to Shimonoseki, and thence to Yamaguchi, then the capital of Ouchi (Oxindono), with whom he had an interview. As the town was a large one—in fact, although now with its 15,000 inhabitants it is only one of those gossipy villages where every

one knows all about his neighbour and his business better than
his neighbour himself, it was then one of the most considerable cities in Japan—Xavier resolved to stay there and work.
A month's sojourn produced little result, however, and so he resumed his intention of proceeding to Kyōto. Starting just before
Christmas, accompanied by Fernandez and a servant, Xavier
found the two months' journey a terrible one. On more than
one occasion the Papal Nuncio had to hire himself out as a
baggage-bearer to mounted merchants, who kept him mercilessly
on the trot, tearing his feet and the calves of his legs to ribbons
with briars and bamboo-grass, while he was frequently denied
admission to hotels and had to pass the freezing nights in
outhouses or under the open sky. At Sakai he and his companions had to build themselves huts with branches in a
neighbouring pine-wood, and the city urchins came and pelted
them with stones. In these circumstances Xavier's impressions
of the capital when he reached it were after all no great matter
for astonishment. As regards Kyōto, over which Japanese
writers have ever been wont to fall into enthusiastic raptures,
and in which the stranger from afar has time and again found
a subject for brilliant but illusive word-painting, Xavier and
his companion found that its situation had nothing fine; that it
was far from the sea, built on a sterile plain, with high ruin-
covered mountains behind it from which a snowy north wind
blew ever cheerless and chill.[1] In spite of the fact that the
subjective element enters largely into the picture, it is to be
confessed that at the time it yet carried in it a substantial
amount of objective accuracy. It was then the month of
January, when at the best of times, with its penetrating cold,
Kyōto is the reverse of inviting, and in the January of 1551
the times at Kyōto and its neighbourhood were the very worst.
Five years before, the Japanese records tell us, the city
had been reduced by war and fires to such a state that it was
impossible to live in it; whoever did attempt to live there ran

---

[1] Yet even then the city was one of some 500,000 inhabitants. Writes
Xavier: "Meacus (Kyōto) urbs olim fuit amplissima, nunc propter assiduas
bellorum calamitates magna ex parte eversa atque vastata est. Quondam (ut
aiunt) tectectorum millibus CLXXX constabat. Id sane mihi verisimile videtur.
Murorum enim circuitus longe maximam fuisse urbem declarat. Nunc etsi
magna ex parte eversa est, tamen domorum millia continet amplius centum."
Of Yamaguchi he says: "Ea urbs familiarum amplius decem millibus con-
tinetur." This would indicate that the common assertion that it then contained
half-a-million of inhabitants cannot be taken seriously.

the risk of being burnt, slain, or starved. The Court nobles had left, and had generally settled under the protection of some feudal chief in the provinces. Since that year the Shōgun had been ignominiously hunted from the city; the Hosokawas and Miyoshis had all the time been assiduously engaged in slaughtering each other, aided from time to time by the turbulent priests of Hiyei-san; and a few months before Xavier's arrival Miyoshi had fired the monastery of Higashi-yama and made a fell slaughter of its cowled inmates, ever ready to don mail. In such a condition of affairs Xavier found he could make no headway in the capital. Besides, his poverty here rendered him contemptible; he could get no audience either with the Emperor or with the Shōgun, and when he essayed street-preaching nobody would listen to him. After a fortnight, " having learned that the Dairi was only a monarch in name, and that the Cubosama (*i.e.* the Shōgun) commanded absolutely only in the Gokinai, he (Xavier) saw it would be useless to obtain from him (the Cubo) at great expense permission to preach through the whole of Japan, since he (the Cubo) was not master of it." So, bitterly disappointed in the expectations he had formed at Hirado, Xavier made haste to shake the dust of Kyōto from off his shoes;—as he and Fernandez passed down the Yodo in an open boat they chanted *In exitu Israel*.

Nine more years were to pass before the missionaries were to obtain any foothold in the Japanese capital. As a matter of fact, Kyōto and the Gokinai at this time were in a state of utter anarchy. The Shōgun by no manner of means commanded absolutely in the Gokinai, as Xavier says he did. The Gokinai then was nothing but one wild, wallowing welter of confusion, presenting a marked contrast to the condition of affairs in Kyūshū, where the local princes mostly contrived to maintain a fairly strong and stable administration. If regard is had to the all-important matter of authority, the little princelet of Hirado was much more of a " king" than either the Shōgun or the " Dairi" then was, while the two great Princes of Satsuma and of Bungo were infinitely more so. Beyond the Straits of Shimonoseki, too, there was a vigorous administration in Yamaguchi, where the family of Ōuchi, descended from a Korean prince that had settled in Japan in the seventh century, had been all-powerful for two hundred years. As already stated, Xavier had spent a month in Yamaguchi on his way to the capital, and to Yamaguchi he and Fernandez now returned.

On his previous visit Xavier had thought to make headway by placing his reliance upon the primitive simplicity of the early apostles, as he had done everywhere else down to this time. But his former experiences in Yamaguchi and his late experiences in Kyōto had sufficed to convince him that Japan was different from the Indies, or at all events from those parts of them frequented by Portuguese merchantmen and traders. Apostolic simplicity could not fail to impress the native mind when the natives perceived the extreme respect, not to say reverence, evinced by the most highly-placed Portuguese officials and the richest foreign traders for the poor and self-denying missionary. We have seen that the princelet of Hirado was very quick to grasp the significance of the honours with which the Portuguese traders had welcomed the arrival of Xavier at his capital in the preceding year. But so far at Yamaguchi, and still less at Sakai and at Kyōto, there had been no such object-lesson to smooth the way for the missionaries, and as a consequence the harvest so far reaped in these quarters had been but scanty. Having grasped the import of these facts, Xavier now condescended to make a sacrifice to the exigencies of the situation. He returned to Hirado for better clothes and for some foreign novelties to be presented to the Court of Yamaguchi, and when he again arrived there he tendered these as presents from the Viceroy of India and the Governor of Malacca, at the same time producing letters of credence from the former and from the Bishop of Goa. Amongst the presents were a clock and a harpsichord, which, though of little value, were highly appreciated by the Prince, as nothing of the kind had ever before been seen in his dominions. A considerable sum of gold and silver was offered in return for the presents, but Xavier declined to receive it, and begged instead for permission to preach Christianity. The request was readily granted, and a proclamation was issued declaring that the Prince approved of the introduction of the new religion, and granting to his subjects perfect liberty to embrace it, while an empty Buddhist monastery was assigned as a residence for the foreign priests. Their operations were now crowned with considerable success; among the numerous converts they made in the next few months were some of "high distinction" in the principality.

All this was in marked contrast to the ill-success that had attended Xavier's first effort in Yamaguchi. In connection with this, it may be not improper to point out that the Prince of Yamaguchi was eager in his efforts to encourage over-sea trade. In 1523 he had sent ships over to Ningpo, and obtained a patent from the Chinese authorities authorising commerce between China and his dominions.[2] Knowing of the visits of the Portuguese traders to harbours of Kyūshū, Ōuchi would naturally be anxious to attract them to his ports also, and now, perceiving that by these traders the missionaries were held in the highest consideration, he would be all the more ready to give the latter and the religion they professed a hospitable welcome in his domains.

The most valuable convert made in Yamaguchi was a young man destined for the Buddhist priesthood, who, under the name of Laurence, was received into the "Company of Jesus," and who, down to his death in 1592, bore his full share of the burden and heat of the day in introducing the new religion into Japan. He was the first of the many Japanese that became Jesuits, for it must ever be borne in mind that the success of the propaganda in Japan was in no small measure to be attributed to the zeal of the numerous natives among the *ouvriers apostoliques* in the country.

In the autumn of 1551 Xavier felt that his presence was desirable in the Indies, and having received a letter from Captain da Gama, then in the harbour of Hiji, in Bungo, he resolved to take passage with him. So, summoning Torres from Hirado, and leaving him and Fernandez in charge of the Church in Yamaguchi, he passed over to Bungo, with four companions, and, carrying his valise on his shoulder, was met by da Gama some distance out of Hiji. While in Yamaguchi he had received an invitation to visit the Court of Bungo, and thither he now repaired, escorted by the Portuguese in all their bravery, and made his entrance into Funai (the capital) with almost regal pomp.

At the date of Xavier's visit to Funai, the House of Ōtomo had been seated in Bungo for more than three centuries and a half. Its founder had been one of those Governors established in

---

2 In the revolution of 1551, when Ōuchi was killed, this patent was lost, and the Chinese trade came to an end.

the provinces by Yoritomo after he had been invested with the Shōgunate in 1192, and was indeed an illegitimate son of this Yoritomo himself. In 1193 Ōtomo Yoshinao, who had taken the name of his maternal grandfather, was appointed Governor of Bungo and Buzen, with the title of Sakon Shōgen, and in the same year another illegitimate son of Yoritomo's was made Governor of Satsuma, and founded the great House of Shimadzu in that province. It was not until the close of the fourteenth century, however, that the Ōtomo began to be really formidable to their neighbours. At that epoch, Chikāo, the ruling chief, was a man of administrative ability and military genius, and under him Buzen, Chikugo, and Chikuzen were constrained to acknowledge the supremacy of Bungo. On the death of Chikāo a succession of commonplace men administered, or rather mismanaged, the Bungo dominions, and the chief vassals in Chikuzen, Chikugo, and even Buzen threw off their allegiance to the Court of Funai. Thus by the beginning of the sixteenth century the Ōtomō domains and the single province of Bungo were synonymous. What had contributed to the decay, if not to the ruin, of the House of Ōtomo had been the fierce contentions regarding the succession to the headship by which it had been racked from time to time. On two occasions the father had perished at the hands of the son, and just the year before Xavier's appearance the ruling Ōtomo had been done to death by some conspirators because he was endeavouring to deflect the succession from Yoshishige, the rightful heir, to a son by a favourite concubine. This murdered Daimyō was the prince Pinto would have us believe he cured of the gout and of hypochondria, and Yoshishige it was who now received the Apostle of the Indies with such extraordinary tokens of deference and respect. This young Daimyō (he was then twenty-three years of age) was the ablest chief the House had had since the famous Chikāo. Even in the lifetime of his hypochondriac father his energy and ability had been of great service to the clan, whose boundaries he had extended by some successful campaigns in Higo. He had been quick to perceive the immense advantage of the arquebus and of artillery, and from several indications it may be inferred that the Bungo troops were soon well equipped with firearms. Young Ōtomo was exceedingly anxious to attract the Portuguese merchantmen to his ports, and exerted every effort to cement amicable relations with them. In the lifetime of his father he had prevented the confiscation of a richly-laden Portuguese ship, and in gratitude for this the merchants, and especially one of them called Diego Vaz, had spared no pains in teaching him all the Western science they knew.[3] Shortly after his accession to the headship of the House we find Yoshishige writing to the King of Portugal, and later on sending him handsome presents, while an envoy of his to the Viceroy of India set sail with Xavier on da Gama's vessel. Now, since his appearing in the character of envoy from the Viceroy of India at the Court of Ōuchi in Yamaguchi, Xavier had been a much-talked-of personage in Kyūshū and Western Japan, and Yoshishige had made a point of ascertaining the truth about him from his Portuguese acquaintances. And be it noted that Xavier was one of those exceptional prophets who are not without honour in their own country or among their fellow-countrymen. By the Portuguese, at that time the most priest-ridden people on the face of the earth, he was more than reverenced,—he was all but worshipped. To the devout it may sound impious to assert that Christ's entry into Jerusalem was a small thing to Xavier's entrance into Funai, but a reference to the Gospels on the one hand and to Charlevoix on the other will show that the impious assertion is but the simple and unadorned truth. After such an object-lesson it would have indeed been strange if the astute young Ōtomo, eagerly bent on conciliating the good-will of the Lusitanian traders, should have failed in courtesy towards the grey-headed apostle of forty-five. Xavier, of course, put out every effort to convert his host, but the young politician was too keen-witted to compromise his position by embracing a "law"

---

3 Charlevoix identifies Yoshishige with the young prince who was nearly killed by the bursting of Pinto's arquebus. From the summary of a letter of Yoshishige's to Cabral given by Froes (1577) it becomes clear that this is a mistake. "At the beginning of the navigation from China to Japan he had a Portuguese with him for more than three years who cured his brother, the King of Yamaguchi, of an arquebus wound. From this man he had kept on always cunningly inquiring about the things of the Portuguese and of India; and, above all, about the condition, the manner, and the mode of living of the *religieux*. This moved him so much that, in order to ascertain the truth, he purposely sent a gentleman to India twenty-six years before [*i.e.* in 1551]. The gentleman was converted there, and came back a Christian, and from him he learned that what that Portuguese had told him fell far short of the actual truth." The King of Yamaguchi was Yoshishige's younger brother, Hachirō. This passage would seem to indicate that Pinto's account of his first visit to Bungo needs to be taken with caution. However, we know that Pinto was again at Funai during Xavier's visit there.

which was as yet regarded with contempt and aversion by the gentry and the educated classes in Japan. There was no lack of polite and flattering speeches on his part; but it is tolerably clear that at the bottom of his heart he had not at that time the appreciation for the foreign religion he undoubtedly had for foreign fire-arms. Some seven-and-twenty years were to pass before this Ōtomo was to abandon his "false gods" and embrace "religion." Nor does it seem that Xavier made any very great impression upon the Prince's subjects, for although we hear of him preaching in Funai, we hear of but few baptisms there.

As regards the actual number of professed converts made by Xavier it is well to have accurate ideas. In Satsuma, where he tells us three times he remained for more than a year, he baptized about one hundred persons.[4] Apart from Anjiro's own relatives and the few converts made at Heshan's castle, these all belonged to the lower strata of society, with little or no education to boast of. The people in Heshan's fortress, as appears from a subsequent letter of Almeyda's (1562), looked upon the crosses, the rosaries, and the scourge left with them by Xavier as so many magic charms for safeguarding their bodily health, and for keeping the devils at a distance. If one has regard to the claims of reason, to which Xavier and his successors keep on appealing even to the extent of being tiresome, the value of such converts as most of these Satsuma proselytes were cannot be placed very high. Yet these Satsuma Christians were of far greater worth than the batch of one hundred proselytes baptized at Hirado during Xavier's short stay there in September 1550. In Satsuma the missionaries commanded the services of a competent interpreter in the person of Anjiro. His earliest work had been to memorise the Gospel of St. Matthew and to turn it into Japanese, and during the first year after his return to Japan he was much occupied in translating a compilation by Xavier which it would be interesting to unearth. This was an account of the creation of the world, of the fall of man, of the doctrine of the redemption, and the other chief points of the Catholic faith. One copy of this was written, not in Japanese characters, but in

---

4 In his unpublished *History of Japan* Froez writes:—" I found at Hirado some papers in which Brother John Fernandez noted what passed at Kagoshima during the ten months they lived there, and I see that they baptized about 150 persons." Father Cros makes it tolerably clear that Xavier was in Kagoshima from August 1549 to September 1550, making, however, a journey to Hirado to get and to dispatch letters in 1549.

Roman letters.[5]   When the three missionaries left Satsuma their interpreter, Anjiro, was left there in charge of the neophytes, and as none of the three could yet speak Japanese it may well be wondered how it was they contrived to make about a hundred converts in a few days at Hirado.   Writes Xavier:—" None of us knew Japanese; yet by reciting that semi-Japanese volume, and by delivering sermons (!), we brought several over to the Christian cult."   Now, without probing into the honesty of these conversions, a cold-blooded critic may very justifiably question whether the converts taxed their reasoning powers to any headache-producing extent before they accepted the foreign religion.   During his first stay in Yamaguchi the apostle had little or no success, while in Kyōto he had absolutely none whatsoever.   On his return to Yamaguchi, when he was forced to make himself respectable and to appear as the envoy of the Viceroy of the Indies, he had a much better record. During this special period he made as many as five hundred converts, some of whom were *samurai* undoubtedly.   These constituted the most valuable of his scanty gleanings in Japan; for by this date Fernandez had begun to acquire considerable command over Japanese, and, prompted by Xavier, could engage in doctrinal discussions with the *bonzes* to some purpose.   Of the three original Jesuits in Japan, this Fernandez was by far and away the best linguist; when Torres went to Yamaguchi in September 1551 he composed the homilies, and Fernandez rendered them into Japanese, while it was Fernandez who invariably had to interpret for the new missionaries.   As has been remarked, Xavier evidently never exhibited the slightest aptitude for the acquisition of Japanese, or indeed of any other Oriental language, and it is perhaps to smooth over this serious defect in a missionary that his biographers have trumped up the silly fudge about his receiving the " gift of tongues " during his second stay at Yamaguchi.   During his sojourn in Bungo he is represented as having had numerous public debates with the *bonzes*; to a debate with one Fucarandono, reputed to be the ablest priest in Japan, which is said to have extended over six days, Charlevoix devotes as many as eighteen pages.   Now it may well be asked who acted as Xavier's interpreter on this occasion?

---

5 See Letter vii. of Bk. IV. in the collection of Tursellinus.

Fernandez was then in Yamaguchi, and Xavier had with him
only two Yamaguchi *samurai* and two ignorant body-servants
whom he was about to send to Europe. If he spoke without the
aid of any interpreter, it is much to be feared that he was but
poorly equipped for discussing the most perplexing metaphysical
subtleties with one of the first scholars in Japan in that
scholar's own language. It may be surmised that in this special
encounter the apostle's appeal to reason was attended by
anything but the brilliant results some Church historians would
have us believe it was.

What really caused Xavier to be taken seriously by the
Japanese was his knowledge of astronomy. This knowledge would
now be regarded with an indulgent smile of pity; the apostle
no doubt plumed himself on being able to prove to the benighted
Japanese that the world was round, and to give them a more or
less plausible account of " the causes of comets, thunderbolts,
and showers." But to Xavier this little pea of an earth of
ours was the centre of the Universe, with the sun and the
other greater worlds all circling round it for the express
benefit of homunculus more especially. Copernicus's treatise
on the *Revolutions of the Heavenly Bodies* had appeared in 1543,
two years after Xavier had sailed for the Indies; and for
venturing to question the old and orthodox Ptolemaic theory
Galileo was to be haled before the Inquisition ninety years
later on (1633), and there condemned to abjure his deadly error !
However, Xavier's astronomical lore, such as it was, commended
itself to the Japanese as superior to their own; and, admitting
this much, several of them reasoned that a scholar of such high
scientific attainments would not be likely to be seriously at
fault in the sphere of religion. On the other hand, many
possible converts were repelled by the humane and gentle
doctrine that whosoever had not worshipped the true God during
his terrestrial life would surely burn in Hell eternally and
for ever. This thesis was a terrible shock to the ancestor-
reverencing if not ancestor-worshipping Japanese, and it was
only a few of them that could be satisfied but not consoled by a
revamping of the sophisms of Aquinas on the matter. "However," writes Xavier, after informing us of the pitiful distress of
the neophytes about this, " in this evil there is this good, that
there is hope that they will labour all the more on behalf of

their own safety, lest they too should be damned to eternal
punishments like their ancestors"! This special doctrine was
a much more serious matter than was the contention that the
Japanese should be contented with one wife—a contention for
which the missionaries were pelted by the Yamaguchi urchins
and hobbledehoys with stones and clods and sand and several
other unconsidered trifles.

Yet another impediment to the ready acceptance of the new
religion by the educated was that the Chinese had evidently
heard nothing about a creation of the world, or about a personal
Creator. "If there were really any one first Cause of all
things, surely the Chinese, from whom they had adopted their
religious systems, would not have been ignorant of it. For the
Japanese defer to the Chinese as being first in wisdom and
knowledge in all things, whether pertaining to religion or to
the civil administration. Accordingly they made many inquiries
about this first Cause, as to whether it was good or bad, and
whether the first Cause of good and of evil were one and the
same."[6] This objection doubtless had not a little to do with
Xavier's resolve to quit Japan and make an assault upon the
Middle Kingdom. "I trust to pass thither this year (1552) and
to penetrate to the Chinese King. . . . And if the Chinese adopt
the Christian religion the Japanese also will abandon the
religions they have introduced from China."[7] Accordingly, on
his return to Goa in February 1552, he set out (April 25th) on
that futile mission to China, which was to be wrecked by
Ataide, Governor of Malacca, and by Xavier's own death on the
island of Chang-chuang, not far from Canton, on December 2nd
of that same year.

Yet a third thing militated still more strongly against the
success of the apostle's efforts in Japan. As remarked in the
introductory chapter, the monks in certain quarters at this

---

[6] In certain quarters in Japan there was still a more or less superficial
acquaintance, not, indeed, with Chinese philosophy, but with the works and
doctrines of Confucius and Mencius. Three centuries before this there had been
a great development of thought in China, doing for Confucius and Mencius
something analagous to what the contemporary schoolmen in Europe were doing
for the Vulgate—expanding and elaborating them into a full and rounded
system of philosophy. But with the Teishū philosophy of the Sung schoolmen,
which was to dominate the intellect of Japan during the seventeenth and
eighteenth centuries, the Japanese as yet had no acquaintance, and did not have
any until forty years after Xavier's death.

[7] Of the Chinese, Xavier in the same letter says:—" Magnitudine autem
ingenii etiam Japones ipsos facile vincunt."

time held large fiefs and counted as something like first-class feudal Powers. Even in the ordinary secular fiefs their political influence was very great, for it had long been customary for the ruling families to make all the younger sons enter the priesthood, in order to lessen the chances of those disputed successions which so often involved the greatest and most illustrious houses in disastrous ruin. The hostility of such a body would be a very serious matter, and this hostility Xavier wittingly and deliberately excited, in spite of his early resolve "to enter into no rash contests with the *bonzes*." On arriving at Kagoshima in 1549 the first foreign missionaries had been well received by the Buddhist priests. This was nothing to be wondered at, for, with the exception of the *Nichirenshiu*, none of the great Buddhist sects were intolerant. Teachers of new religious doctrines had often come from China and Korea before this, and had always been listened to with respectful attention, as Xavier was himself by the Abbot of the Shinshiu monastery in Kagoshima. This abbot and the other priests of the city are said to have spoken of the newcomers in the most favourable terms during the first few weeks or months of their stay in the place. However, when it gradually became apparent that the foreigners were fiercely exclusive in the honour they claimed for their own God and his Saints, and were inclined to be at once aggressive and bitterly intolerant, these first sentiments of kindly regard and respect began to give place to others of a different stamp. From the letters of the missionaries we can infer that their interpreter, Anjiro, was something of a fanatic, and, all things considered, it is not strange to find that shortly after Xavier left Kagoshima the Satsuma men thought it well for the peace and quiet of the clan that Anjiro[8] should also

---

[8] Anjiro's subsequent career has been somewhat carelessly dealt with by the Church historians. Bartoli makes him die six months after Xavier's withdrawal from Satsuma. Charlevoix writes:—"Francis charged Paul (Anjiro) with the superintendence of this nascent Church. Paul felt himself infinitely honoured by this trust, and gave up everything to devote himself solely to so holy a ministry; but God had not laden this fervent neophyte with so many favours in order to make an ordinary Christian of him. The *bonzes* excited so many troubles that they obliged him to withdraw voluntarily from his country." This is very well turned, indeed; but let us hear what Froez says in his unpublished *History of Japan*:—"Anjiro, driven to this by misery, entered upon the *métier* of a *Bahan* along the coasts of China. The *Bahan* is only a pirate, who joins to outrage on the sea outrages along the coasts at the expense of groups of fishers or other poor people who have their dwellings there. Having set out with others on one of those expeditions he was killed. We hope that before dying he had contrition for his sins. Nothing else is known of his end."

F

betake himself elsewhere. Then, too, Xavier began to assail
the morals, or rather the immorality, of the monks, and to
denounce their superstitions and their chicaneries in the most
scathing terms. In none of his letters does he say that he
did so at Kagoshima, but at Yamaguchi it seems to have been
his chief occupation and pleasure. At all events, the failure of
the Portuguese vessels to appear at Kagoshima in 1550 was only
one of the reasons which led to the proscription of Christianity
in Satsuma. The *bonzes*, who had at first been so favourably
disposed towards the missionaries, had gone to the Prince and
clearly given him to understand that any further continuance of
the Christian propaganda would be prejudicial to the domestic
peace of his principality. At Yamaguchi we hear of Xavier
"confounding" *bonzes* over and over again. From the converts
he made he ascertained the weak points of the various sects, and
devoted much effort to equipping these neophytes with arguments
to employ against their former pastors and teachers. The town
was soon a scene of confusion, and it is small wonder to hear of
the Daimyō punishing some of the new-made Christians for
their aggressive and disorderly conduct. The Buddhist monks
might very well be forgiven for evincing no great amount of
pleasure at this turn of affairs. What would have happened to
a Buddhist missionary pursuing a line of action in contemporary
Spain or Portugal analogous to that which Xavier pursued at
Yamaguchi, and which most of the Jesuits pursued in Japan till
Hideyoshi taught them to be cautious? As regards the morals of
the *bonzes*, there is no doubt that in many monasteries flagrant
vices were rife. But then had contemporary European monasticism any cleaner record to show? The Jesuits never tired of
denouncing what they called the superstitious practices of the
Japanese. Any one who attempts to plod through the missionary
letters very soon perceives, on the Jesuits' own showing, that this
is merely a glaring case of the pot calling the kettle black.

While Xavier was at Funai there had been a revolution at
Yamaguchi. Suye Harukata, the chief vassal of Ōuchi, had been
driven to rise against his lord, with the result that Ōuchi was
killed. The town was fired, and "overflowed with blood for the
space of eight days," during which the missionaries, Torres and
Fernandez, had to go into hiding. Suye, however, did not
presume to establish himself as lord of the fief. He threw the

blame of what had happened upon Sugi, one of his own confederates, and put him to death; and, to disarm all hostility on the part of possible rebels, he became a monk. Still he continued in reality to retain all his power as chief councillor of the clan, and in that capacity he sent an envoy to Bungo to request Ōtomo to allow his younger brother to accept the succession of the Ōuchi family, and to be installed as Daimyō at Yamaguchi. Ōtomo at first, for prudential reasons, refused his consent, but Hachirō insisted on going. Xavier, still at Funai, now made a point of obtaining a promise from Ōtomo that he would request his brother, the new Daimyō of Yamaguchi, to take Torres and Fernandez under his special protection. Ōtomo kept his word, and, before starting, Hachirō himself promised Xavier and the Portuguese that "he would do so as soon as ever he set foot in his kingdom." After getting settled in Yamaguchi, Hachirō, or, as he was now styled, Ōuchi Yoshinaga, established the two missionaries in a Buddhist monastery, and furnished them with title-deeds to paste upon the gate. This document is noteworthy as being the oldest of its kind, and also for another reason. It runs :—" With respect to Daijōji in Yamaguchi Agata, Yoshiki Department, Province of Suwō. This deed witnesseth that I have given permission to the priests who have come to this country from the Western regions, in accordance with their request and their desire that they may found and erect a monastery and house in order to develop the Law of Buddha." It appears from the last half-dozen words of this translation, and also from the application of the term *Sō* to the missionaries, that the new religion was regarded merely as a superior kind of Buddhism. The misconception was no unnatural one; the two cults were exceedingly like each other in ritual,—the flowers on the altars, the candles, the incense, the rosaries, the images, the processions were common to both,— while the shaven-headed missionaries from over sea approved of every one of the ordinary five Buddhist commandments, and made a point of copying the *bonzes* closely in their manners and way of living. Yet this misconception caused the foreigners no small annoyance. In Bungo, in 1553, we learn from a letter of Sylva's that the *bonzes*, after being worsted in public controversies, " having no other resource, loaded the people with a notorious falsehood, to the effect, namely, that Christianity differed in no way from the Japanese religion. That was indeed dangerous. Accordingly our people, fired with zeal for the divine glory, addressed themselves at this time to teaching the people nothing but the great difference between these two religions; that the Japanese law was based on nothing but fables and falsehoods, whereas Christianity clearly rested upon the most certain principles." (Again it may be asked how Buddhist propagandists preaching in a similar strain would have fared in contemporary Portugal or Spain?) Some years later on (December 1561), Almeyda, on a visit to Satsuma, conciliated the good-will of some Kagoshima *bonzes*, and they offered to accept baptism on the condition that they should still be free to officiate at the funerals of the princes and chief men of Satsuma. Great was their astonishment to find that the exclusiveness of Christianity could accept of no such harmless condition!

In addition to bespeaking the favourable regard of the new Daimyō for Torres and Fernandez in Yamaguchi, Xavier also sought an undertaking from Ōtomo that missionaries should have free scope for their activity within the bounds of the Bungo domains. The young ruler not only gave such an undertaking eagerly, but he also sent an envoy along with Xavier to assure the Viceroy of India that priests and merchants alike would meet with the warmest of receptions in Bungo, while he also at the same time sent a letter and presents to the King of Portugal. When Xavier left Japan on November 20th, 1551, besides Ōtomo's envoy, he was accompanied by his two body-servants, Matthew and Bernard the Satsuma man. The former died at Goa, but the latter reached Lisbon safely, whence he was sent on to Rome. He shortly returned to Portugal, when he entered the "Society of Jesus," and ended his days at the College of Coimbra. This was most likely the first Japanese who ever set foot in Europe. Xavier was prompted to send these men to Europe by the fact that he found the Japanese fancied themselves vastly superior to all other peoples, and that he wished to give some of them an opportunity of seeing for themselves "the difference between the resources of the Christians and of Japan." He had endeavoured to send two scholarly *bonzes*, in order that Europeans might make acquaintance with a specimen of the Japanese intellect (" nihil enim illis acutius aut prudentius "), but, strange to say, he found that well-to-do Japanese of good family " had no desire to visit foreign lands." He had been able to prevail upon four of some quality, however (two of them *bonzes*), to go as far as India to examine the state of Christianity there for themselves, and these four were all baptized at Malacca.[9] Accompanied, then, by Ōtomo's envoy and his own two Japanese servants, Xavier left Japan in November 1551, after a sojourn of twenty-seven months in the country.

---

[9] In the letter to Rodriguez, Rector of the College of Coimbra, recommending Matthew and Bernard to his care, there is a somewhat remarkable passage about the Spaniards and Japan. Xavier there requests Rodriguez to ask the King and Queen of Portugal to inform the Emperor Charles V. (also King of Spain) that he (Xavier) had heard from Portuguese in Japan that the Spanish ships making for the Moluccas from Mexico were wont to coast Japan, and that such of their ships as attempt to reach Japan perish on the way, foundering upon the shoals which fringe the Japanese coast opposite to New Spain. The Emperor was to be warned of this, "lest ships should be sent from New Spain to seize upon the 'Silver Islands,' for the ships will all infallibly perish. For if they do reach the islands in safety, if they attempt to conquer them by force of arms, they will have to do with a people no less covetous than warlike, who seem likely to capture any hostile fleet, however strong. Besides, this land is so waste and barren that foreign forces can be reduced by famine without any difficulty. Further, round these islands there are such tempests that the Spanish vessels are threatened with certain destruction if they have no friendly harbour to retreat to. Again, I say, the Japanese are so eager for arms, that from the mere desire of possessing their arms they will slaughter the Spaniards to a man. I wrote as much to the King some time ago, but perhaps, from press of affairs, the whole thing may have slipped from his mind. But to clear my conscience on this point, I would have you remind the King of it; for it would indeed be sad to hear that many fleets from New Spain had perished in the quest for the 'Silver Islands.' For besides the islands of Japan there are no islands in that part of the Orient with silver mines."

CHAPTER V.

KYŪSHŪ AND CHRISTIANITY IN KYŪSHŪ (1552–1582).

MERITORIOUS as Charlevoix's History of Japan undoubtedly is in many respects, it is still exceedingly difficult to obtain from it any clear and crisp notion of the precise amount of progress made by Christianity in the Island Empire from time to time. In some respects his record reminds us of those earlier Books of Livy, where the Romans are continually winning battles against the Volsci and conquering and annexing their territories, without apparently advancing their own boundaries a single mile. For example, he speaks of Xavier having made 3,000 converts in Yamaguchi before he left it in September 1551. Now, between that time and 1554 great progress was made, and yet we learn from a missionary letter of that year that there were about 1,500 Christians in the fief, while when Torres was driven from it in 1556 the number had not got beyond 2,000. From many of the missionary letters written during the next quarter of a century a casual reader might readily gather the impression that the foreign priests had really converted a very considerable proportion of the population of Japan. Now, it may be just as well here to make some endeavour to obtain a bird's-eye view of the general situation, and to arrive at some definite conception of the actual relation of things to each other. What the total population of Japan was at this time cannot be stated accurately, for there was no such thing as a census in those days. But working backwards from the figures of the Tokugawa epoch, and availing ourselves of certain data we obtain under Hideyoshi, and remembering that we have very clear indications that at this time population was pressing upon the limits of subsistence, we cannot be far wrong in estimating it at something between 15,000,000 and 20,000,000 souls. As regards contemporary Europe, we find that in 1580 the population of the dominions of the House of Austria is estimated at 16,500,000; of France at 14,300,000; of Spain at 8,150,000; and of England at 4,600,000. Thus Japan was fully as populous as the greatest European Powers of the time. At this date it is also somewhat difficult to say precisely how many fiefs there were in Japan, for the feudal map of Japan was then somewhat kaleidoscopic. However, at the death of Hideyoshi in 1598 these fiefs were one hundred and ninety-seven in number; and they were certainly not less numerous during the preceding half-century. Now of all these 15,000,000 or 20,000,000, it is questionable whether Xavier baptized as many as 1,000, while of the two hundred fiefs in the Empire he made converts in no more than four—Satsuma, Hirado, Yamaguchi, and Bungo, in the latter of which, by the way, there appear to have been less than a score of baptisms.

Now let us see how things stood a generation after this. In 1582 the Annual Letter of the Jesuits was sent by the vessel that left Nagasaki with the four Japanese envoys to the Pope. This letter, written by Coelho, is dated February 13th, 1582, and refers to the state of things prevalent about the end of 1581—that is, exactly thirty years after Xavier's departure from Japan. This letter is unusually accurate, inasmuch as Valegnani, the Visitor-General then in Japan, had spent three years in a minute investigation of the actual state of affairs. Writes Coelho:—

"The number of all the Christians in Japan in this year, according to the Father Visitor's information, amounts to 150,000, a little more or less, of whom many are nobles, since besides the Kings of Bungo, of Arima, and of Ōmura, there are also many lords of different lands, who, together with their relatives and vassals, are Christians. The majority of these live in Kyūshū, on the lands of Arima, Ōmura, Hirado, and Amakusa, where, with the others in the lands of Gotō, there are 115,000 Christians. In the kingdom of Bungo there are 10,000; in the Kyōto district, with those who are scattered in the home provinces and Yamaguchi, there will be 25,000. The churches we have in those kingdoms where there are Christians, between great and small, are 200 in number."

Now, taking the inhabitants of the Empire at 15,000,000, we see from this that after a generation of missionary effort, no more than one per cent. of the population had been converted to Christianity. And with the exception of Bungo all the converts were in petty fiefs; over 100,000, or more of them, indeed, concentrated in two very petty fiefs, for later on out of the 18,000,000 odd koku of rice representing the total assessed revenue of the Empire, Arima was rated at 40,000 and Ōmura at no more than 25,000 koku. Hirado, where there were some

3,000 or 4,000 believers, was assessed at 63,000 *koku*; and Gotō, where there were 200, at 12,000 *koku*.. Before 1579 the Bungo fief, extending over five provinces, had been one of the most considerable in Japan, but since the conversion and baptism of the old Daimyō in 1578, it had been stripped of all his former conquests and was now restricted to but a single province. The population of this province might amount to some 250,000 or 300,000, but of these only 10,000 were Christians, and of these 8,000 had given in their adhesion to the faith since 1578.

Yet, even so, 150,000 converts in thirty years constituted a wonderful record when we consider the small number of missionaries engaged in the work. In this year of 1582 there were indeed as many as seventy-five members of the "Company of Jesus" in Japan. But down to the year 1577 there had never been more than eighteen of them, and down to 1563 no more than nine! The great increase took place between 1577 and 1579, when the numbers advanced from eighteen to fifty-five. Most of the new members came from India; but a good many Portuguese who came on the Great Ship from Macao turned their backs upon commerce in order to enter the "Company of Jesus" in Japan. Of the twenty-six Japanese admitted before 1580, only a few had been received as Brothers, for at that special period the Jesuit Vice-Provincial was very chary about entrusting the converts with any real authority.

Having thus obtained a general notion of the measure of success that attended the Christian propaganda during the thirty years subsequent to the date of Xavier's departure from Japan in November 1551, we will now address ourselves to tracing the course of events during that period somewhat in detail. When Xavier left the Empire, Torres and Fernandez were the only missionaries in Japan, and both of these were established in Yamaguchi. On reaching India, Xavier had arranged to send a reinforcement to his former companions, and on August 13th, 1552, Father Gago and the Brothers Alcaçeva and da Sylva arrived at Kagoshima. Here they were very well received by the Prince of Satsuma, whom they found eager for trade; but they stayed only eight days in the Prince's capital, pushing on to Funai, where they arrived on September 21st. They were immediately received in audience by Ōtomo, and delivered the presents they had been charged with by the Viceroy of India, Fernandez meanwhile having arrived to interpret for them. In October they set out for Yamaguchi, where they were received with great rejoicings by Torres and his congregation. After celebrating Christmas Day with great pomp, Father Gago returned to Bungo, taking Fernandez with him to serve as his medium of communication, while da Sylva was left to learn Japanese and assist Torres in Yamaguchi, it being arranged that Alcaçeva should return to Goa to urge the dispatch of more missionaries to Japan. The messenger carried with him another letter from Ōtomo to the Viceroy of India, assuring him that "he would take good care of the Fathers who were with him, that he greatly rejoiced in Gago's presence, that he would do anything to pleasure the King of Portugal, and that he eagerly desired that missionaries should be sent, in order that as many of his subjects as possible should become Christians.". The Jesuits offered up many fervent prayers for the speedy conversion of Ōtomo, for they assured themselves that on that depended in great measure the prompt success of their efforts in the Empire. Yet, much as he favoured the foreign priests for the sake of his intercourse with the Portuguese, when it came to the matter of the religion they inculcated, Ōtomo showed himself exceedingly cautious. Prompted by the representations of Alcaçeva, and urged on by the Viceroy of India, who was charmed with Ōtomo's letter, Father Nugnez Barretto, the Jesuit Vice-Provincial, accompanied by Mendez Pinto in the quality of envoy, set out for Japan in 1554. It was only in the summer of 1556 that he reached Bungo, however, where he and the envoy met with a very honourable reception. Writes Barretto:—

"When I reached Bungo I took care to see the King, and endeavoured to bring him over to Christ by many arguments. But in vain; partly because from dread of his enemies he had betaken himself to a fortress for protection; partly also because he understood that if he accepted Christianity there must be a change in his morals. In addition to this there was the suspicion that his subjects would not tolerate a Christian king and that they would kill him. But what chiefly held back the man was that he was given over to the Devil in that heresy which says that the soul perishes with the body, that there is no spirit, and nothing beyond what we perceive by sense."

Barretto requested Ōtomo to arrange a public debate between him and the most learned *bonzes* in the principality. "Which he verbally promised us he would do; in reality, although we repeatedly asked for it, he did not keep his word. The *bonzes* are all related by marriage to the chief men in the kingdom, and are most hostile to us because we expose their crimes and their frauds to the common people; and they lade the people with such lies that in these quarters there seems to be no greater obstacle to the Gospel." Seeing that Ōtomo had just before this put down a rebellion in blood, that he was still apprehensive of secret disaffection, and that this sedition had been the second if not the third one he had had to face since Xavier's visit, it is not hard to understand why he was not so very eager for public discussions on religion in his recently burned capital.

At this moment, in 1556, all the Jesuits in Japan were then in Bungo, for Bungo was then the only place where they had a church. Earlier in that year there had been a revolt in Yamaguchi against the new Daimyō, Ōtomo's brother, in the course of which the town had been burned. Torres had escaped with his life, but a few days afterwards his flock urged him to withdraw, and he passed over to Bungo. Not long after this, in the same year, Mōri Motonari defeated and killed the Daimyō of Yamaguchi, and assumed the headship of the fief himself. One of his earliest acts was to proscribe the foreign religion within his domains, and, with the exception of a visit of Cabral in 1574, the Christians of Yamaguchi saw no missionaries till after the submission of Mōri to Hideyoshi in 1585 or 1586.[1] The Jesuits now in Japan, assembled in Bungo, were, exclusive of Barretto, eight in number.[2] These were Father Torres and Fernandez, who had come with Xavier; Father Gago and da Sylva, who had arrived in 1552; Father Vilela, who had just come with Barretto, who during his stay admitted three

[1] Torres during his stay of five or six years had had to put up with a fair amount of annoyance. "Even within the walls of his own house he was stoned and spat upon by the *bonzes*, and treated with contumely by them, while he scarcely could put his foot beyond the door. . . . So that it might with the very best reason be said that he was crucified to the world, and the world to him in turn. . . . Finally he told me that he had never in his life felt so much joy and pleasure as he had during that time at Yamaguchi, *plane ut existimem illum e lacrymarum mira suavitate et copia magna ex parte oculorum aciem perdidisse.*"— BARRETTO, January 1558.

[2] There were indeed nine, for at this time Mendez Pinto was actually a member of the Company. This singular episode does not appear in his own memoirs, but Charlevoix, who writes a lengthy account of it, says that there can be no doubt about it. At all events, most of Pinto's immense wealth went to support the Jesuit Mission in Japan.

Portuguese into the Company. One of these, Almeyda by name, was a valuable capture. He was a Portuguese trader some thirty years of age, not particularly proficient in theology, but with no mean skill in surgery and medicine. Like several other Portuguese admitted into the Society in Japan, he was wealthy, for Charlevoix's assertion that he employed 5,000 crowns, *in which consisted all his property*, in erecting hospitals at Funai is contradicted by a subsequent assertion that he also invested 4,000 ducats in trade for the benefit of the Jesuits. In addition to this he was exceedingly energetic and a man of rare tact, and down to his death in 1582 he was to render the best of service as the pioneer in breaking new ground and as the ordinary emissary in missions of extreme difficulty and hardship. Be his theological attainments what they may have been, Almeyda at all events was a keen and accurate observer, and he writes with a clearness and a crispness which are sadly non-apparent in the letters of some of his more erudite but terribly long-winded *confrères*.

The two hospitals founded in Bungo by Almeyda are interesting not merely as an instance of one of those little ironies in which the Jesuits would have us believe God sometimes indulges, but as casting some light upon certain phases of contemporary sociology. At the present day there are certain villages in Bungo notorious for the prevalence of syphilis, and one of these hospitals of Almeyda's, opened three centuries and a half ago, was for the reception of patients suffering from this disease and from leprosy. Whether syphilis was prevalent in Japan before the arrival of the Portuguese we have not so far been able to discover. The Portuguese had frequented the harbours of Bungo for the previous fourteen years, and as sexual morality in Bungo was then notoriously loose, the disease may very well have obtained a footing in the principality during that period. At all events, this effectually disposes of the assertion that syphilis first appeared in Japan at Nagasaki between 1624 and 1644. The Jesuit account of the circumstances which prompted the foundation of Almeyda's second hospital is still more instructive. Says Barretto :—

"When Almeyda came to Japan (he is exceedingly well known in these regions) in 1554, and met Gago in Bungo and heard from him of the custom the Japanese women had of killing with the utmost barbarity those new-born children whom they fancied they could not rear on account of poverty, he arranged with Gago that the latter should treat with the King for the abolition of this most iniquitous custom somehow or other, he [Almeyda] undertaking to contribute as much money of his own for the purpose as might be necessary. The King approved of his proposal, and promised to furnish nurses to rear the children. Accordingly Almeyda remained in Bungo for that purpose, and with great popular approval is erecting a house into which the children may be conveyed to be reared and baptized, and which may also serve as a refuge for the poor Christians in the city."

It must not be supposed that this custom was confined to Bungo, or that this is the only passage in the missionary letters in which it is referred to. Over and over again the Jesuits allude to it, and in Cocks also we meet with mention of it. Says Vilela, speaking of an anticipated famine :—" For it wrings the heart to see the multitude of children perishing at the hands of their parents; if they are not spared now in a season of low prices, what are we to expect in a dearth ?" And many other similar passages might be easily quoted. Even at the present day the lower classes in Japan are remarkable for the fewness of their wants rather than for the abundance of their possessions, but in the brave old days of the sixteenth century few of them could indulge in the luxury of having any wants at all—beyond those of the birds or of the rabbits. The poverty of the country-people at this time was clearly grinding. So much becomes evident from numberless details given by the missionaries, who had the amplest opportunities for becoming accurately acquainted with the general condition of the toiling millions. Even towards the end of this century and the beginning of the next they record several cases of cannibalism occasioned by sheer want in time of famine.

These hospitals of Almeyda's had been erected with great popular approval, we are told. Yet, strange as it may appear, these institutions did more to impede the spread of Christianity in Bungo than all the hostile efforts of the *bonzes* or any other cause. As we find no hint of this in Church histories—(in Charlevoix at all events),—and as the bare assertion may sound utterly incredible, we deem it well to let the original authorities here speak for themselves. For more than a quarter of a century the Jesuits had failed to convert either Ōtomo himself or any member of his family. Then at last, in 1576, they succeeded in capturing Ōtomo's second son, an impressionable lad of fifteen or·

sixteen years of age, who was baptized as Sebastian by Vice-Provincial Cabral. In his letter of September 9th, 1576, to Acquaviva, the Vice-Provincial gives a full account of this incident, and in the course of it he says :—

"I leave Your Paternity to imagine the jubilation of all this Christianity of Funai at seeing the son of the KING a Christian, together with so many other persons of quality, since down to this hour the Christians have been so abject and vile, that they have shown no desire to acknowledge themselves, partly from being so few in the midst of so many Gentiles, partly because the said Christianity began in the hospital where we cure the people of low condition, and those suffering from contagious diseases, like the French evil, and such others. Whence the Gospel came to be of such little reputation in Funai that no man of position would dare to accept it (although it seemed good and true to him) merely lest he should be confounded *con quella plebe*. And although we gave much edification with such works, this thing nevertheless was a great obstacle to the spread of the holy faith.[3] And thus during the twenty years we have had a residence in Funai one gentleman became a Christian, and this after he had been cured of the said evil in his house; but as soon as he was cured he afterwards thought it shame to acknowledge his Christianity in the presence of others. Now, praise be to God, seeing that the KING [Ōtomo] evinces such respect for the Christians, all the past sadness is converted into joy, and the Gentiles, who before would not deign to speak to a Christian, even although a relative, now begin to do them honour, and to speak well of the law of God, and many are converted, and even some who at first were our greatest enemies."

Two years after this, in 1578, Ōtomo himself at last became a Christian, and this event is dealt with in the newly-instituted Annual Letter of the following year (1579). We are told there that "it is Ōtomo, next to God, whom the Jesuits have to thank for their success in Japan." It was on account of his letters that the Fathers had been received at Kyōto and "in many other kingdoms," and on account of them that many persecutions excited by the *bonzes* against Christianity and the Fathers had been allayed.

"And although from the beginning he gave his subjects free permission to become Christians, yet, since he himself was one of the wisest men in Japan, inasmuch as his vassals saw that he did not become a Christian, they made so little account of our law and of our Fathers that during the twenty-five years or more the Fathers were in Bungo *they scarcely made two thousand Christians altogether* in that country, and these commonly were of very low condition—the poor and the sick who came to be cured in a hospital

---

3 The actual words are—" nondimeno la cosa era di gran disturbo all dilatatione di santa fede."

the Fathers had there. So that our law was despised and held in contempt by all the Gentiles, who kept saying that it was a law merely for the diseased and the poor; and the Fathers every day had to suffer a thousand affronts and insults."[4]

As has been said, this extract is from the first of the official reports to the Jesuit-General in Rome, known as the Annual Letters. These were instituted by Valegnani during his first visit to Japan in this year of 1579, " in order that many letters may not occasion confusion rather than clearness," and Valegnani took much pains to find the man best fitted to write them. Most of those between 1583 and 1597 were penned by Froez, who not infrequently writes with the insight and breadth of view of a statesman, while he exhibits rare ability in his mastery over details and in his subordination of them to the great questions and main issues he has to treat of from time to time. This first letter by Carrion is no very brilliant production, for Carrion clearly had no great appreciation of pithy terseness. Yet his assertions are no doubt correct, for Valegnani was not the man to put up with slipshod inaccuracy, and so this, the official summary of the history of missionary effort in Bungo down to 1579, is to be taken as authoritative. As has been remarked, a casual perusal of Charlevoix gives the unsuspicious reader the impression that during all this time Christianity in Bungo was advancing by leaps and bounds. We do not mean actually to accuse the worthy old Father of the heinous crimes of *suppressio veri* and *suggestio falsi*. But after carefully plodding through most of the original authorities he manifestly used, we have no hesitation in saying that he sometimes handles the truth rather carelessly, and at others doles it out with sparing economy.

Yet meagre and mangy as was the spiritual harvest the Jesuits gleaned among the rank tares and darnel of the sin-sodden heathendom of Bungo, it was in Bungo that they chiefly laboured, and it was Bungo that was their base of operations from 1556 to 1562. Mission work was also attempted in Hakata and Hirado, but it was the Lord of Bungo the priests had to thank for admission to the former town. Immediately

---

4 More than a century afterwards Kämpfer tells us the Japanese called the fifty Christians then (1692) in the various prisons of Nagasaki *Bungojos*, or the *canaille* of Bungo. The reason was most likely not because they had been brought from Bungo. The origin of the term may be inferred from the above extracts.

oh the death of his brother, the Daimyō of Yamaguchi, Ōtomo had levied war against Mōri, the new Daimyō of the fief, and by the end of 1557 had ousted the latter's vassal chiefs from Chikuzen, of which Hakata was the capital.   Ōtomo at once gave the missionaries a residence in the suburbs of this city, and Gago and a Portuguese Brother were at work here when the place was temporarily recovered by Mōri's supporters.   The Jesuits then had a very trying experience, for after being captured, stripped naked, bound and starved, and repeatedly menaced with swords, they escaped only with the greatest difficulty. This experience shattered Gago's nerve so badly that he became all but useless for work in Japan, and Torres found himself reluctantly constrained to order him to return to India, together with one of the Brothers who had also broken down.   This was in November 1560, and Torres found himself with but one priest and four Brothers in the whole Empire.   This priest, however, was a host in himself, for few of the early Jesuits were so indefatigable, so aggressive, so versatile, and withal so successful in their methods as Vilela was.   In these years Portuguese ships came pretty frequently to Hirado, and early in 1557 the captain of one of these sent to Bungo for a priest to hear confessions.   Gago and Fernandez had at once hurried over ; and after satisfying the Portuguese, they addressed themselves to missionary work, and in September Vilela was dispatched to join them.   At the time of his arrival there were two more Portuguese vessels in the harbour, and the three Jesuits made adroit and unstinted use of their compliments to give the heathen a due idea of the pomp and circumstance of Christianity, and of the honours that were justly due to themselves as ministers of the Gospel from the laymen compounded of common clay.   From 1587 onwards the missionaries frequently make complaint about the scandalous conduct of the Portuguese merchants and seamen in Japan, contrasting them in bitter terms with the early traders of the 'fifties, 'sixties, and 'seventies.   It must certainly be admitted that letters such as those of Vilela's of November 1557, and of Froez of October 1564, clearly indicate that the *religieux* of those days had the laymen completely at their beck and call, and that it needed no very lusty ecclesiastical blast to whistle them humbly and crouchingly to heel.   On Gago's leaving for

Hakata, Vilela took supreme charge in Hirado. He made every effort to attract the children to the church, sending out one of the Brothers through the streets with a bell, singing parts of the Church service. Then the boys were organised in bands to sing through the town what they had been taught at church, and also to repeat it in their homes so as to arouse the interest and curiosity of their parents. Near the town Vilela erected a model of Mount Calvary, and thither the converts betook themselves to pray and also to scourge themselves, for the Jesuits never tired of extolling the merits of bodily "discipline" to their converts.[5] Among others the zealous missionary converted a brother of the Daimyō who held the neighbouring islets of Takashima and Ikutsushiki as a sub-feudatory of the family chief. This noble neophyte, baptized as Anthony, became so infected with Vilela's zeal that he turned preacher and missionary himself, and began that temple-razing and idol-breaking which were presently seen in all quarters where the Jesuits obtained the upper hand. As might have been expected, this iconoclasm caused a great and sudden commotion. The *bonzes*, who had been already irritated by the uncourteous and uncourtly things said about their cult and their own morals, were roused to action when they saw the temples of their gods going to the ground, and in Hirado itself, where the Christians were as yet weak, a cross in the cemetery was thrown down by way of retaliation. Thereupon some of the

---

5 In 1562 Almeyda visited Heshan's Castle in Satsuma, where Xavier had baptized about a dozen people in 1550. Writes Almeyda:—" The little book with the Litanies and other forms of prayer written down by Xavier's own hand, as well as the sacred relics, were kept with most religious care as a remedy of proved virtue. For when the booklet had been placed upon the bodies of several of them who had fallen ill—among them being Heshandono, who was already despaired of—it had cured them. Nor was it with less care that the old man kept the scourge also given by Xavier, with which they had been accustomed to beat themselves sometimes (for he would not permit them to do so too often lest it should be consumed and worn away with too much use), because they divinely understood that this thing benefited not merely their souls, but their bodies as well. Accordingly the woman herself, of whom we have spoken, having fallen into a very serious illness, and having tried various remedies in vain, finally had recourse to the scourge, and was forthwith restored to her pristine health by the merits of Francis Xavier, as must be supposed." Such passages in the letters are far from uncommon. In this same letter of Almeyda's (1562) we are told that the Church of Bungo was now the greatest in Japan, and that it was increasing greatly every day! "No night passes without scourging in the church, and almost always all those present scourge themselves at the same time. Those who cannot do so in the church, scourge themselves with their whole household within their own walls." The little children were organised into bands, who went through the streets "disciplining" themselves. On certain occasions Nagasaki might well have been mistaken for a fourteenth-century Italian town in the temporary possession of an army of crazed and frenzied flagellants. In one letter it is noted as a point in favour of Japanese dress that it is much more convenient for "discipline" than European clothes are.

converts set fire to a temple in the town, and a riot ensued. The Daimyō was appealed to, and he requested Vilela to withdraw for a time, informing him he might return when order had been restored and the excitement had abated.   Just about this time the Lord of Hirado was threatened by Ōtomo, inasmuch as he had secretly furnished help to a relation of his whose estates had been overrun by the Bungo troops.   Ōtomo had previously written to Vilela advising him to withdraw from Hirado for a time, but whether Matsuura the Daimyō got to know of this does not appear.   At all events Matsuura had good reasons for being displeased with the foreign priests, and he likely enough continued to give them fair words merely because, like all the other princes of Kyūshū, he was eager for foreign trade, and because he had had occular demonstration that these priests were all-powerful with the foreign traders.   Meanwhile he was resolved that they should depart from his territories, and events showed that he really intended their withdrawal to be permanent.   This affair in Hirado took place about the same time as the expulsion of Gago and his companion from Hakata, and thus in 1559 the Jesuits were once more all thrown together in Bungo.   Some time before a Hiyeisan *bonze* had written to Torres asking for information about Christianity, and requesting him to send one of his *religieux* to Kyōto, and Torres now deemed this a proper time to dispatch Vilela to the capital of the Empire, where Xavier had failed so utterly some eight years before.   At this date the Jesuits had five Japanese interpreters or coadjutors, none of whom had as yet been formally admitted into the Company; and with one of these, Laurence, converted by Xavier in Yamaguchi, and with letters of recommendation from Ōtomo, Vilela set forth for Kyōto in September 1559.

All the other Jesuits remained in Bungo for the next three years except Almeyda, who made a visit to Hakata and Hirado in 1560–61, and another to Hakata, Hirado, and Satsuma in 1561–62.   On the former visit to Hirado he took delivery of some church furniture from a Portuguese vessel then in the port.   One passage in his letter is noteworthy:—" And since there was no church in Hirado, the captain asked the King for permission to build one on our site, so that the Portuguese, who were there to the number of ninety, might betake themselves to

G

it for the sake of religion, and that the Hirado Christians might make use of it in turn." From this it is evident that the foreign traders had not ceased to frequent Matsuura's little port.

Matsuura's neighbours were uncharitably envious of his good fortune, and one of them now took astute advantage of his strained relations with the foreign priests. To the south of the Hirado domains lay the petty fief of Ōmura, which consisted of the territory round the Gulf of the same name, and round what is now Nagasaki haven, and between it and the open sea on both sides. The chief of this, Ōmura Sumitada, was a younger son of the Lord of Arima, who then held the Shimabara peninsula. If we are to believe Charlevoix, this young man had come across "a book composed by Father Vilela in which the Christian religion was clearly explained and solidly proved. Not to act too precipitately in an affair of such importance, he wished to confer with one of the European *religieux*; and as he did not wish to disclose his purpose, he proposed to his councillors to attract the Portuguese vessels to his harbours. He exaggerated the advantages his States could draw from this commerce, and added that the best means of inducing the merchants to give him the preference over all the other princes of Japan would be to offer them greater advantages than were accorded them elsewhere, and above all to assign the ministers of their religion an establishment in his lands." This, be it remarked, lends countenance to the Japanese account that Sumitada "pretended to lean towards the foreign religion for the sake of inducing the Portuguese to visit his dominions exclusively, and thereby debarring other chieftains from obtaining fire-arms," etc. At all events, Ōmura now made one of his councillors write to Torres in Bungo that the harbour of Yokoseura (25 miles south of Hirado) would be open to the Portuguese vessels, that the Portuguese would be free from all dues for ten years, that the port and all the adjoining land within a radius of two leagues would be ceded to them, that there would be a house for the missionaries, and that no idolater might establish himself there without their consent. Torres, of course, jumped at this overture with the greatest eagerness, and Almeyda was at once recalled from Satsuma and dispatched to Ōmura to arrange matters definitely. Meanwhile Matsuura of Hirado got some hint of what was toward, and he now wrote to Torres asking him to forget the past; it was only the necessities of the situation that had constrained him to dissimulate his friendly feelings towards the missionaries for a time, and that he trusted Torres would once more send priests to Hirado. Soon things had got so far in Ōmura that Ōmura's very slight "religious doubts" had all been satisfied, and the house for the Jesuits at Yokoseura had been finished. When Matsuura was beginning to fancy that things were going sorely against him, a Portuguese merchantman entered Hirado harbour. Thereupon Matsuura repented of his late advances to Torres, and said publicly that there was no need to conciliate the priests in order to attract the foreigners to his ports; and that to the merchants it did not matter much how he treated the Christians. When this speech was reported to Torres in Bungo, it roused the infirm old man to sudden and vigorous action. Despite his bodily frailty, he at once hurried to Hirado, where he was welcomed by the Portuguese with no less circumstance than the Shōgun would have been received by Matsuura himself. "The King of Firando was astonished at the honours rendered by the captain to the missionary when he boarded the ship; but he was still more astonished when he learned that the vessel had got up her anchors, and that the captain had declared in leaving that he could not remain in a country where they maltreated those who professed the same religion as himself." Before that year of 1562 was out Ōmura Sumitada had been baptized, and Yokoseura was rapidly becoming a flourishing town where none but Christians were allowed to settle. Ōmura proved a most zealous proselyte, and addressed himself with vigour to the suppression of ancestor worship and "idolatry" within his domains. This excited such discontent that a series of revolts followed, during which Torres, as well as Ōmura himself, had to flee for their lives, while the new Christian town of Yokoseura was attacked, fired, and reduced to ashes. Before the close of the year 1564, however, Ōmura had retrieved his position, and had not merely stamped out domestic rebellion in blood, but had repelled an attack of his more powerful neighbour, Matsuura of Hirado. In the same year he was the proud recipient of a letter from King Sebastian of Portugal (then of the mature age of ten years), who congratulated him upon his

conversion to Christianity and upon his zeal in procuring the
same happiness for his subjects, and who swore an eternal
friendship with him. Meanwhile Matsuura of Hirado had
received another lesson from the missionaries. In 1564 Torres
was joined by three new priests, while in the previous year
Fathers Froez and Monti had arrived in Japan. After the
burning of Yokoseura Torres had removed to Takase in Higo,
then part of Ōtomo's domains, while Froez had settled with
Matsuura's converted brother, Anthony, in his islet of Takashima. Access to Hirado itself was still denied the priests—
at least for the purpose of holding services in the town.
After Froez had been the best part of a year in Takashima,
two Portuguese vessels arrived at Hirado; and " as the
captains of these refused to enter Hirado without my order,
the King, constrained by the desire of gain, excused himself to
me through one of his servants, because, distracted by military
affairs, he had not yet sent to greet me, and earnestly begged
me that I would not hinder the Portuguese from entering
the port, and promising that he would at once arrange
with the captains for my introduction into the town.
Therefore they put into the harbour with my permission,
and asked the King to make good his promises, undertaking
to erect a church at their own expense." However, Matsuura
began to tergiversate, and while he was casting about for
still more plausible excuses another vessel appeared in the
offing. This was the *Santa Cruz*, commanded by Peter
Almeyda, a great friend of Froez's in particular and of the
Jesuits in general, three of whom (all priests) he had actually
brought to reinforce the mission in Japan. Froez at once
put out and boarded her, and on his explaining the situation,
the captain at once took in sail and came to anchor six miles
outside the harbour. At Froez's request he sent word to
Matsuura that unless the priests were readmitted to Hirado he
would certainly go elsewhere. After delaying a few days
Matsuura surrendered, and a church was soon re-erected in
Hirado, and Fernandez and Cabral (one of the new missionaries)
were left for work there.[6]

---

[6] A judgement of Heaven overtook some of the Portuguese who dared to
disobey the man of God. "The merchants, whether from the nausea and tedium
of the voyage, or from some other cause, could be dissuaded by no arguments from

In 1566 Matsuura was roused to ill-advised action by a still more provoking incident. Shortly after the restoration of the missionaries to his capital, he learned of the arrival of a Portuguese, accompanied by four Ōmura Christians, who brought letters to his brother Anthony from the Daimyō of Ōmura. As the relations between the two fiefs were then anything but amicable, Matsuura saw fit to regard these four Ōmura Christians as spies or hostile emissaries, and so he had them seized and executed. Some time before, the Hirado Christians had dispatched a vessel to India to buy all the ornaments and furniture necessary for their new church, and the Gentiles of the town, learning of this, dispatched some craft to intercept the vessel on her return. They seized her, and threw most of the church ornaments into the sea; but they reserved a picture of the Virgin and sent that to Matsuura's son. He and one of his friends "disfigured the countenance of the Virgin in a manner to excite horror, and then exposed the picture to the derision of the infidels." This caused the Christians to arm, and Matsuura, who had already banished some of the *bonzes* to placate the converts, had great difficulty in preventing an outbreak of civil strife. Shortly afterwards a Portuguese ship, commanded by Pereyra, the Governor of Macao, appeared in the offing. But instead of entering, she put about, and made off to Fukuda, in Ōmura, just outside the harbour of Nagasaki, Pereyra sending word to Matsuura that he would have no dealings with a place where Christianity was wantonly outraged and its professors maltreated. Angered by this, Matsuura secretly equipped a flotilla of fifty craft and dispatched it to burn all the Portuguese vessels in the ports of Ōmura. Its attack upon Pereyra was a failure, however, and it had to beat a precipitate retreat beyond the range of the Portuguese artillery, after losing several of its chief officers.

For the next year or two Fukuda was much frequented by the Portuguese traders. Meanwhile, however, they had explored the neighbouring fiord, and had been much impressed by the facilities offered. On the site of what is now the busy town of Nagasaki there were then only a few fishermen's huts. But here

proceeding to the town and exposing their wares there. Their landing cost them dear; for their stores were fired by thieves, and a great part of their goods was consumed by raging wind-driven flames, or carried off by the thieves in the midst of the confusion, and they incurred a loss of about 12,000 gold *scudi*."

the early history of Yokoseura was to repeat itself. Ōmura Sumitada now (1567) wrote to Torres, then at Kuchinotsu, offering to build a church at Fukaye, or Nagasaki, in order that it might become the centre of the Portuguese commerce and an assured asylum for the Christians when they were persecuted. Torres at once accepted the offer, and Vilela, then in Kamishima, in Amakusa, was sent to take charge of the city that was to be. Several Portuguese traders also established themselves there, and from this time Nagasaki Haven became the chief resort of the merchantmen from Macao, which had been founded some ten years before. About this time Ōmura had spoken of his intention of making his fief a purely Christian one, and expelling all his subjects who refused to abandon the national cults. But it was not until 1573 or 1574 that he found himself in a position to venture upon this step. In the former year he had been assailed by his neighbours, the Lord of Isahaya and Matsuura of Hirado, and after a sharp struggle he had succeeded not merely in beating them out of Ōmura, but even in annexing some of the Isahaya territory. Then towards the end of 1574 Ōmura " fully resolved to remove all impediments to the propagation of the Gospel in his States, saying that till then, from fear of men and from the dread of a popular rising, he had refrained from breaking the idols and casting their temples to the ground; but now, as it was clear that it was God alone who protected and preserved his States, he meant to execute his purpose, and so he publicly proclaimed that all who would not accept the law of God, whether *bonzes* or laymen, should quit his lands, inasmuch as they especially were traitors and adversaries of the law of God." At this date there were no priests in his territories; but a Jesuit Father and a Brother hurried to him at once, and " these, accompanied by a strong guard, but yet not without danger of their lives, went round causing the churches of the Gentiles, with their idols, to be thrown to the ground, while three Japanese Christians went preaching the law of God everywhere. Those of us who were in the neighbouring kingdoms all withdrew therefrom to work in this abundant harvest, and in the space of seven months 20,000 persons were baptized, and the *bonzes* of about sixty monasteries, except a few who quitted this State." [7]

[7] This passage is from a letter of Francis Cabral, who arrived as Vice-Provincial in 1570, just a little before the death of the Superior Torres in the same year. In this letter (September 1573) he exults at seeing the *bonzes* abased,—

In the Annual Letter of 1579 we are told that there were then no Gentiles among Sumitada's subjects, and that the population of his fief amounted to between 50,000 and 60,000 souls. After this the only baptisms we hear of in Ōmura were those of children and of outside Gentiles who were anxious to settle in the fief in order to participate in the benefits of the foreign trade. From this Annual Letter of 1579 it appears that if we take the population of Ōmura at 60,000, there were 104,000 or 105,000 Christians in the Empire in that year. In Satsuma, where Xavier had begun operations in Japan, there were still a few believers—sometimes given at fifty, sometimes at a hundred. In Hirado, the second scene of his efforts in the Empire, there were now 3,000, and in Yamaguchi 500. In Kyōto, where he had failed so utterly, there were as yet but 200, but in the surrounding home provinces there were as many as 15,000, while in Bungo there were only 2,000. That means that of the 105,000 Christians in Japan in 1579 fully four-fifths were in quarters where Xavier had never set foot. There were now 12,000 converts in the Shimabara peninsula and 11,000 in Amakusa, and these had mostly been made under pressure from their rulers, who, like Sumitada, were all eager to see the Portuguese vessels in their harbours.[8] About 1567 the petty princelet of Kamishima (part of Amakusa) had accepted Christianity and had induced his vassals to accept it, in order, as the missionaries plainly and unequivocally assert, to attract the foreign traders. When they did not come he not only abjured the new religion himself, but he even insisted upon all his subjects returning to their ancient

"who, most perverse in their errors, lead the people with them to Hell, and who eat the best in the land, from being relatives of the principal lords of these parts where only the first-born succeeds to the State, and the other brothers enter monasteries, with great endowments, and are generally made Superiors, whence they are filled with an arrogance and a pride which are intolerable. And that these should now come to such a humility that they throw themselves on the ground before two ragged members of the Company is one of the miracles worked by the Divine Majesty." Later on in the same letter he rejoices at seeing "the very men who formerly regarded us as viler than slaves, and scarcely deigned to look at us, haughty as they were beyond measure naturally, and also by the prompting of the Devil, now with hands and forehead on the ground in token of submission according to the usage of the country, humble before every one of us; and those who a short time ago held themselves as masters of the world now like children in the presence of every one of our Brothers teaching them the Christian doctrine and how to make the sign of the Holy Cross."

8 There were also three hundred converts in Hakata. In the Gotō Islands there had once been 1,000 Christians. Christianity was proscribed there after the death of Prince Louis, the apostle of the Gotōs, in 1579, and the 1,000 Christians dwindled to 200. If we take the population of the Ōmura fief at 50,000, there would have been about 95,000 Christians in Japan in 1579.

gods, and forced the missionaries to withdraw. No fewer than 60,000 out of the whole body of 105,000 Christians then in Japan were in the Ōmura territories, where there were as many as forty churches.

To read the character of Sumitada of Ōmura clearly is no easy task. How far he would have been influenced by the casual perusal of a missionary tract if there had been no Portuguese trade to attract to his ports may well be matter for speculation. But it must be frankly and fully conceded that from his conversion in 1562 down to his death on May 24th, 1587, of swerving or backsliding in his allegiance to the new faith there was none. In truth, such accusation as can be brought against him rests upon diametrically opposite grounds—upon those of fanaticism and persecuting intolerance. His early zeal for Christianity and his hostility to the old cults all but cost him his fief and his life on more than one occasion. Yet he was not without his reward. We have it on high authority that we cannot serve both God and Mammon. The career of Sumitada does not indeed utterly tend to falsify this deliverance, but it must be noted that his zeal in the service of the "True God" was undoubtedly exceedingly profitable to him from a worldly and temporal point of view. By reason of his friendship with the missionaries, and through them with the Portuguese traders, he contrived to become, not indeed one of the most powerful, but one of the richest of the princelets of Kyūshū. The sudden growth of Nagasaki, which numbered nearly 30,000 inhabitants as early as 1583, is in itself very indicative of the supreme value of the Portuguese commerce to Sumitada and his subjects, the number of whom the commerce in question did much to augment. Doubtless it was the hostility of his neighbours, especially of Hirado, whither the foreign ships were proceeding, that chiefly prompted the princelet of Ōmura to cast about for devices to deflect these Portuguese vessels to his own ports. In his strife with Hirado he no doubt reckoned that, other things equal, it would be the advantages arising from the friendship of the Lusitanian merchants with their imports of firearms and ordnance that would prove the deciding and decisive factor. And if, indeed, such was his forecast, it was amply borne out by the course of events, for he was able to extend the boundaries of his circumscribed domains at the expense of Hirado, as well as of his

neighbour of Isahaya. Thus Sumitada contrived to draw an
accession of territory as well as of wealth from the over-sea trade.
And, apart from profit in pelf and lands, he must have found
the letters and presents from the Portuguese king extremely
flattering to his *amour propre*, while the magnificent reception in
Europe of the embassy he in common with Bungo and Arima
dispatched to the Pope in 1582 must have afforded him the
liveliest satisfaction. It is true that he died three years before
the return of the ambassadors in 1590, but as they assisted at the
coronation of Sixtus V. in the quality of *Royal* Ambassadors
in 1585, and had been previously received as such by Philip II.
of Spain and Portugal, the greatest European potentate of his
times, Sumitada had had plenty of time to learn of the great
consideration he was held in at the central points of Christendom.
Altogether, in making the best of both worlds, Sumitada, with
the worthy missionaries as henchmen, attained a larger measure
of success than has fallen to the majority of the sinful sons of
men who have essayed the practice of the art.

But apart from all question of the sincerity of Sumitada's
own conversion, what has especially to be noted here is that from
the Jesuits' own letters we can see that the majority of the
60,000 Christians in the Ōmura fief had become converts not
from conviction of the truth of the new doctrines, but merely
from self-interest or from necessity. About this time in another
quarter the new religion was also imposed by the arbitrary fiat
of the ruler upon vassals who were really indifferent to it.
Across the water from the Ōmura fief, and directly south of
Arima, lay the large and hilly island of Amakusa. At this
time it was portioned out among five petty rulers, all of whom
acknowledged the suzerainty of Ōtomo of Bungo. One of these
was the apostate Lord of Kamishima, on whose grounds no
missionaries were now allowed, although there were still about
one thousand converts there. Of the other four island chiefs,
the most considerable had been captured by Almeyda about
1570. Popular opposition to the new religion was almost as
strong in Amakusa as it had been in Ōmura, and Ōtomo of
Bungo had first to write (at the request of Almeyda) and then to
send troops, while Almeyda had to take shelter at Kuchinotsu
for some time. The princelet's wife was something of a blue-
stocking and a theologian, for we are told that the grave doctors

of the law of Buddha frequently consulted her about disputed
points of doctrine, and, being a strong-willed woman to boot, she
pretty effectually blocked the progress of the religion her
husband had embraced in order to obtain a share in the
lucrative foreign trade. Naturally the Jesuits exerted themselves
to capture her, and they succeeded in doing so in 1576 or 1577.[9]
No sooner was the worthy lady baptized than at the instigation
of the Jesuits she prompted her husband to offer his subjects the
choice of conversion or exile, to leave their revenues to such of
the *bonzes* as became Christians, and to confiscate all the
property of the others and hunt them from the fief.[10] Here
again, perhaps, some eighty per cent. of the general population
had to accept a cult to which they were either adverse or
indifferent, or to abandon the homesteads their families had held
for generations. Xavier and his successors often praise the
Japanese for yielding to the arguments of reason ; but here in
Amakusa, as in Ōmura, the appeal to pure abstract reason had
exceedingly little to do with the conversion of the great bulk of
the people. Later on, when Hideyoshi proscribed Christianity
on political grounds, we shall find the missionaries heartily
applauding the Japanese who appealed to the great principle
of liberty of conscience and freedom of religious belief and
profession. They then quote with huge approval the assertion
of their converts that " at all times every Japanese had been
free to adopt whatsoever religion he chose." Their own account
of their work in Japan, however, clearly shows that whenever
they had the slightest opportunity, none were more ready
to trample upon these principles, for which Japan had always
been honourably distinguished, than themselves.

During the next two years, between the end of 1579 and
the beginning of 1581, there was a great increase of the
Christians in Kyūshū—of 30,000 if we take the population of
Ōmura at 60,000 in 1579, and of as many as 40,000 if we
estimate the inhabitants of that fief at 50,000 in that year.

---

9 Cabral says that before baptizing her he made her return all the wealth she
had wrung out of her vassals by usury, in accordance with the practice of the time.
He also made her return all the numerous female slaves she held to their husbands,
for any wife was then free to desert her husband by taking refuge in the lord's
castle and becoming a slave there.

10 Cabral again exults over the humiliation to which some of these, " old men
of sixty, and of a very venerable presence," were put in having to submit to
being instructed in the true faith by a stripling of twenty years of age.

Of these 30,000 or 40,000 new converts there were 8,000 in Bungo, a few hundreds in other places, and all the rest in the single fief of Arima, where the population did not exceed that of Ōmura in number. The history of the Christianisation of this principality is at bottom the same as that of Ōmura and Amakusa, although it is a little more complicated.

As has been said, at the date of the conversion of Ōmura Sumitada (1562), his elder brother was the ruling Lord of Arima, the old prince, the father of two brothers, being still alive and living in retirement, however. Ōmura evidently gave his brother of Arima an inkling of his intentions, for in the year of Sumitada's baptism we find the Lord of Arima inviting the missionaries to his fief and giving them an establishment at Kuchinotsu, a fine harbour and a "great port for commerce," while they also obtained a footing in the town of Shimabara at the same time. Shortly after this we hear of Portuguese vessels at Kuchinotsu quite frequently. Christianity was making headway in the Arima fief when the anti-Christian rebellion broke out in Ōmura. The Ōmura rebels, to prevent Sumitada from receiving any help from Arima, had engaged Riūzōji of Saga, then beginning to rise to a first place among the chieftains of Kyūshū, to attack the Arima territories. He did so with such vigour that the young prince's position became desperate, and his father had to leave his retirement and reassume the direction of affairs. After a fierce struggle he managed to rescue part of the fief from Riūzōji's clutches, and to make terms with him. As he held Sumitada's Christianity to have been the primary cause of all the trouble in the two fiefs, he set himself to repress the new religion, and when Torres had to flee for his life from Yokoseura he could find no refuge in Arima, and had to pass on to Takase in Higo, then under the rule of Ōtomo of Bungo. However, the old prince died in 1564; and thereupon Torres hurried over to Kuchinotsu,[11] which now became his headquarters for the rest of his life, as it was also those of

<hr/>

[11] Writes Almeyda (October 1564):—"The Prince of Arima showed me other marks of kindness, and welcomed me at supper. Having asked many questions about the King of Bungo, as regards Torres he replied that the port of Kuchinotsu was entirely Christian (there are about four hundred and fifty neophytes there), and that Torres might betake himself thither until the war was finished; that he would furnish a guide to take me there, and assign me a site and a house for the use of Torres."

Cabral, his successor in the headship of the mission. This town itself was soon entirely Christian, while in 1571, after a seven years' repression, Christianity also obtained free course in Shimabara, but down to 1576 it made little or no headway in any other quarter of the peninsula. In 1573–74 Arima had even been a party to the league of Isahaya and Hirado against his uncle Sumitada of Ōmura; but after the decisive victory of the latter (which was ascribed to the favour of the Christian God), Arima began to think that it was really worth while to listen to his uncle's advice, and to make open profession of allegiance to that God who had rewarded Sumitada's devotion so richly and munificently. Besides, elsewhere Christianity was now becoming respectable; not in Kyōto itself, indeed, but in the neighbourhood of Kyōto several notable personages had embraced it, while in Bungo, where it had been regarded with contempt by the upper classes as a cult only for the poor and the diseased, Ōtomo's second son had just been baptized with great pomp and with his father's approval. Accordingly Arima sent for Almeyda, then at Kuchinotsu, and after having "his doubts satisfied," he himself, his wife, a brother, a sister, three of his nephews, and a great number of gentlemen and lords were baptized on April 8th, 1576. "The first thing Prince Andrew of Arima did after his baptism was to convert the chief temple in his capital into a church, its revenues being assigned for the maintenance of the building and the support of the missionaries. He then took measures to have the same thing done in the other towns of his fief, and he seconded the preachers of the Gospel so well in everything else that he could flatter himself that he soon would have not one single idolater in his States." Prince Andrew, however, died in less than two years after his conversion (November 30th, 1577), by which time as many as 20,000 of his subjects had become Christians. His heir and successor had made great efforts to make his father abjure the foreign religion, and he now kept the missionaries aloof and had the funeral conducted by the *bonzes*. The old prince had scarcely drawn his last breath before his son issued an edict ordering all the foreign doctors to quit his States at once, and the Christians to return to the cult of the gods of the country; all the holy places were destroyed and the crosses thrown down.

The Christians of Kuchinotsu showed a bold front, however,

and threatened that they would withdraw *en masse* rather than abandon their faith, and Arima, no doubt remembering the episodes at Hirado, thought it well to mitigate the rigour of his decree. A Jesuit was allowed to return to Kuchinotsu, and the converts there were not interfered with. Elsewhere not a few of the new Christians apostatized; at all events, at the end of 1579 there were not more than 12,000 converts in the whole of the fief. In this year Valegnani, the Visitor-General, arrived in Japan, in the Great Ship from Macao, and he induced her captain to proceed to Kuchinotsu. This gave great satisfaction to Arima, who at once hastened to call upon the Visitor-General, "making him great compliments." Later on, Valegnani returned the visit at the capital of the fief, "where he was received with great tokens of love," and here Arima offered to accept baptism and to allow his subjects to do so also. This did not satisfy Valegnani, however, for Arima told him that it was not possible for him to do anything with his uncles or the *bonzes*; and the Jesuit, determined to capture the whole principality, refused to baptize him unless in company with them. Just at this time Riūzōji of Saga, who had got all the Daimyō of Hizen to acknowledge his suzerainty except Arima, gained a great victory over Ōtomo's troops, which made him master of the whole province of Chikugo, and he now addressed himself to the reduction of Arima. Several of Arima's frontier fortresses were betrayed to Riūzōji, who, a zealous Buddhist himself, was regarded with less aversion by the *bonzes* of Arima than that foreign religion the young Daimyō was seeking to impose upon them. Only one of the prince's uncles remained staunch to him at this crisis, and the uncle was a Christian. Meanwhile, from the Annual Letter of 1580 it appears that the wily Jesuit, sure of his prey, kept playing with young Arima pretty much as a cat plays with a mouse. "The whole country came into such danger that it was regarded as lost. The good youth seeing himself in such a state, and it appearing to him that there was no other remedy but to unite with the Church and with Ōmura by becoming Christian, used great diligence in order that the Father should baptize him; to this he was also urged by an old *bonze*, the principal one in the whole kingdom, who, having always been like a father to that house, and now eighty years of age, told him with great grief in his heart that although he was so old a Gentile, he could not, on account of the great love he bore him, refrain from counselling him to become a Christian, because he saw no other remedy and no other hope of saving his territory. And so potent was the counsel of this unfortunate old man (he died a Gentile a few days afterwards) that the youth made haste to become a Christian, together with some of the said *bonzes.*" Still Valegnani continued to make difficulties; but after a great many *pourparlers* over the affair, Arima was baptized, together with his wife, in April 1580. Finally all the city was made Christian; they burned their idols, the *Kami* and the *Hotoke*, and destroyed forty temples, reserving some materials to build churches. " Besides this nine or ten thousand Christians were reconciled who had returned to their vomit by reason of the great persecutions of the previous years."

In perusing the eleven pages of this Annual Letter of 1580 dealing with the affairs of Arima, one cannot help feeling that the whole story is not told there, and that there is no small need to read between the lines. We do learn from it that Valegnani provisioned some of Arima's threatened fortresses, and that he caused the Christians of Kuchinotsu and of Nagasaki to fortify these ports. But of any reference to Portuguese activity there is nothing. Charlevoix, however, who may have had access to other documents besides the Annual Letters, asserts that the " Portuguese who had brought Father Valegnani to Japan, had promised, at the instigations of this Father, to serve Arima with their munitions and even with their persons. Finally the Father Visitor, convinced that Riūzōji only looked for a fine door to get out of Arima, went to meet him, represented the obligations he was under to the House of Arima, made him understand that the Prince of Ōmura would not see his nephew crushed with indifference, especially since he had become his brother in Jesus Christ; and that in obstinately running after an uncertain conquest, he exposed himself to being stripped of what he possessed and of all his glory. He then made him very advantageous propositions on the part of the Prince of Arima, and they were accepted; Riūzōji led his troops into Chikugo, and, after having established order and tranquillity there by his presence, he resolved to invade Higo, a course which embroiled him with the King of Satsuma." Be all this as it may (and it is probably correct), one thing becomes abundantly plain from these letters, and that is that the ascendency of Valegnani and of the priests over this comparatively weak-minded youth of twenty was complete. In 1583 some slaves had been stolen from a Christian who had bought them from the Portuguese, and some converts still kept concubines. The Rector of the Seminary ordered the Prince to rectify these two matters, and also to remedy the insolence of the *bonzes* and the sorcerers. As this was not done soon enough to satisfy him, he threatened to withdraw from the fief, and had actually got as far as Kuchinotsu when the Prince hurriedly sent his uncle with some gentlemen to give him satisfaction, and at the same time informed the *bonzes* that they had either to become Christians or to quit his estates at once.

"These made answer that they would surrender all their books, their robes, and the idols themselves and would not go any more with that pomp provided they were allowed to remain in the country. The offer was rejected; and finally three of the chief and the most obstinate of them changed their country. The others yielded, and the keepers of concubines were also put into a proper state to the great edification of all. Then Don Protasius (Arima) went in person with many nobles to Kuchinotsu, and brought back the Father to Arima with great general rejoicing. A few days ago the said Lord having fallen into a troublesome fever, and not wishing to take medicine from any other quarter, a little holy water was sent him from the church, and, having placed a reliquary he wore about his neck in it, and making the sign of the cross on the cup, he drank it, and immediately he recovered entirely."

At this date he had not yet proceeded to the lengths of his uncle Sumitada in forbidding his fief to all non-Christians, but he was indeed rapidly advancing in that direction. In Froez's letter of September 1584 we are told that "his intention is in conformity with a spontaneous and solemn promise he has already made to the Lord God not to permit idolatry of any sort whatsoever in the whole of his State." By 1582 the great majority of Arima's vassals had accepted, or had been forced to accept, the foreign religion.

In 1582, as has been said, the total number of Christians in Kyūshū amounted to 125,000. Of these as many as 110,000 were subjects of Sumitada of Ōmura, of Protasius of Arima, and of Michael of Amakusa. In all these petty fiefs Christianity had been imposed upon the overwhelming majority of the population by the arbitrary fiat of their rulers, who were all

eager to participate in the blessings of the Portuguese trade as
well as in the blessings of the Christian religion. Outside of
these fiefs there were 3,000 Christians in Hirado, 1,000 in
Kamishima of Amakusa, a few hundreds in Chikuzen, 200 in
the Gotōs, and a very few in Satsuma. The remaining
10,000 were to be found in Bungo, where the number had been
quintupled since the conversion of Ōtomo in 1578.

In Bungo the general feeling towards Christianity had been
exceedingly hostile from the very first. How it fared with the
priests there has already been stated. It was entirely owing to
the good-will of Ōtomo himself that they had been able to
remain in Funai. Time and again Ōtomo had been urged by
his most influential advisers to expel them and their converts.
But as he regarded them as something in the nature of mascottes,
he remained unshaken in his resolve to accord them the hospitality
of his domains. Almeyda, in referring to Ōtomo's edict to be
posted on the church door of Takase and Kawajiri in Higo,
informs us that " it gave full permission to all his subjects, from
the highest to the lowest, to become Christians; that it
threatened with pains and penalties any one who either hindered
or injured the preachers of the Gospel, and that it declared that
it was his pleasure that the Gospel should be preached throughout all his fiefs *in perpetuum*," and then goes on :—

"And indeed, it is wonderful how greatly he favours the Christian
religion, although he has not yet accepted it. To certain individuals
making request in the name of the *bonzes* that he should exterminate
us, since it was inconsistent with his dignity that he should put up
with those who reviled his gods, who were infamous because they ate
human flesh (for they are not ashamed of accusing us of that), and
who, wherever they went, brought tumults and destruction with
them,—when, I say, they laded us with these and six hundred other
enormities, he made answer : ' It is now fourteen years since these men
came into these parts to my own very great good ; for inasmuch as I
was then Lord of three kingdoms, I now possess five. Before I was
hampered by want of money ; now I surpass all the kings of Japan in
wealth, and this benefit extends also to my subjects. Finally, in
consequence of the hospitality I accord them, all my undertakings turn
out happily. Nay, more, when I had no son before, I am now blessed
with one—a thing which I passionately desired. I now ask you, what
advantage has my protection of *your* religion brought me ? Wherefore
be careful not to make speeches of that sort in future.'"

The probability that Ōtomo really did then hold language
of this description is confirmed by what Froez says in a letter of
1577, thirteen years later on. He there tells us that the
missionaries had been no more favoured by Ōtomo himself than

they had been hated and molested by his Princess, who was
commonly called Jezebel, and who had often urged her husband
to drive out the Fathers of the Company and all their
Christians with them as a noxious and abominable sect. "But
the King, confuting her, rebutted her arguments easily, and was
wont to say to her: 'Before the Fathers came here I was lord
of no more than of this single kingdom of Bungo; and now I
wear the crown of five kingdoms. And as for you, who were at
first barren, you have now six or seven sons and daughters, and
riches in abundance. Therefore, while I live I will never cease
to favour all the Christians.' "

The only notable discrepancy between the remarks of
Ōtomo, as reported by Almeyda in 1564, and as given by
Froez in 1577, is with respect to the extent of his dominions
in 1551. According to the latter statement, at that date he
held no more than the province of Bungo, while Almeyda
quotes him as saying that he was then lord of three provinces.
The fact was that by 1551 he had conquered considerable
portions of Higo and Chikugo. Within the next few years he
succeeded in completing the reduction of these two provinces.
Then after the death of his brother Hachirō, who as Ōuchi
Yoshinaga had been installed as Daimyō in Yamaguchi, he
began a contest with Mōri Motonari, who had seized the fief
of Yamaguchi in 1556. The result of this struggle was that
Ōtomo overran Buzen and Chikuzen, which had formed part
of the Ōuchi domains, and he was confirmed in the possession
of these provinces by the treaty of 1563. In that year the
Shōgun sent down a Court noble (*Kugé*) to arrange matters
between Mōri and Ōtomo, the latter of whom paid the im-
pecunious grandee 30,000 *scudi* for his kindly services, if we
are to believe Froez. Six years later Mōri's forces again invaded
the two provinces; but Ōtomo not only made successful head
against the invaders in Kyūshū, but he even lent a scion of the
Ōuchi line such substantial aid that he was able to seize and
hold Mōri's capital of Yamaguchi for a time, although the
venture ultimately cost him his life. This was the last direct
attempt made by Mōri to assert his claims to Buzen and
Chikuzen, and for the next ten years Bungo continued to be
incontestably the greatest feudal power in Kyūshū. Of the
16,000 square miles of the island, fully 7,000 owned the

H

supremacy of Ōtomo. What the population of his estates amounted to we cannot say, but the Jesuits assure us, not in one passage, but in several, that he could readily muster 100,000 fighting men in case of need, while on one occasion they tell us he actually had 60,000 troops in the field, and in 1569 as many as 80,000. These assertions are by no means so improbable as they seem, for down to the time of Hideyoshi, at least, not merely *samurai*, but many peasants and craftsmen also kept arms, and could use them with effect. Besides, when the chief right to possession was the power to hold, the inducements to adopt settled occupations were not great, and it is probable that the *samurai* in those times formed a much larger proportion of the population than they did at the downfall of feudalism in 1871. The Bungo troops were formidable not merely from their numbers, but also from their equipment, for a considerable proportion of them were furnished with fire-arms. We hear of Portuguese teaching Ōtomo's people to cast artillery; and although the reference to this is vague and unsatisfactory, yet what is certain is that Ōtomo had artillery, for we know on the best authority that he presented several pieces to Nobunaga.

At this point it may be well to take a general survey of the feudal map of Kyūshū as it stood in 1578, the year before Ōtomo's swift and sudden fall, and his loss of the hegemony in the island. At that date the five provinces of Bungo, Buzen, Chikugo, Chikuzen, and Higo acknowledged his supremacy. Of Hizen, the sixth province, a good deal has already been said. Its sea-board from the north, round by Nagasaki to the Gulf of Shimabara, was occupied by the three petty fiefs of Hirado, Ōmura, and Arima. The two former, together with the still pettier inland princelets, had by this year been compelled to acknowledge the suzerainty of that Riūzōji Masanobu, Lord of Saga, of whom mention has been made in connection with Arima's conversion to Christianity. This Riūzōji had been by birth a vassal of Arima's, and by profession a priest, but at an early age he had exchanged the cassock for the cuirass, and had obtained high honours and ample rewards in the Bungo service. When he quitted this he set to work to carve out a principality for himself in North-eastern Hizen, and his rapid success in swallowing up his lesser neighbours and his defiant attitude towards his former suzerain provoked the hostility of Ōtomo.

Yet even against the attack of Ōtomo Riūzōji contrived to maintain himself, and once before this year of 1578 he had baffled a Bungo force of nearly 80,000 men. From the circumstance that he was always surrounded by *bonzes* and that he was the sworn foe of Christianity, the missionaries have not too many good words for this " Gentile Lord," and it is with much more grudging than grace that Froez admits that he was exceedingly capable both as a captain and as a politician. Perhaps it was his experience in the Bungo service that led him to set such high store upon the match-lock as a weapon ; at all events, we find that of the 25,000 men he captained at the battle of Shimabara (1584) no fewer than 9,000 were equipped with fire-arms. Although not yet entirely master of the resources of a single province, his undoubted abilities as a leader of men rendered him formidable even to Ōtomo with his five provinces.

Immediately to the south of Bungo itself lay Hiūga, the most extensive but the most sparsely-peopled of all the nine provinces of Kyūshū. Here the Itō family had settled in the times of Yoritomo, almost at the date when the first Ōtomo had been established in Bungo and the first Shimadzu in Satsuma, and at this time an Itō still held it, or at all events laid claim to it. The relations between Ōtomo and Itō had always been friendly, and some years before this one of Ōtomo's four daughters had become Itō's wife. With his neighbour to the south Itō's relations were not quite so happy. For the previous two decades there had been a wasting, wearing warfare between Hiūga and Satsuma, and in 1578, on the death of Itō, the Satsuma troops had poured into Hiūga, and Itō's widow, with her two infant sons, had to flee to Bungo to take refuge with her father.

Satsuma and Ōsumi, the two remaining provinces of Kyūshū, were then held by Shimadzu Yoshihisa, the invader of Hiūga. If there is one thing more than another for which the Satsuma clan is generally regarded as having been remarkable, it is the unity and cohesion of its units, their ready obedience to their chiefs, and the solid and united front they have always presented to external foes. It may thus come as something of a surprise to not a few to be assured that down to the date of the arrival of the Portuguese in Japan the chief thing for which Satsuma had been remarkable had been internal discord and incessant civil strife. The question

of the succession to the headship of the Shimadzu family
had occasionally given rise to bitter feuds, but even when
there was no succession in dispute the local chieftains
had found no difficulty in devising specious and plausible
pretexts to justify themselves in cutting each other's throats
and stealing each other's lands. It was just about the
time Xavier was in Kagoshima that two chieftains of the
neighbourhood of that town[12] persuaded their fellows to agree
upon and to submit to one sole and single chief. During
the previous ten years Shimadzu Takahisa, an adopted son
of the fourteenth Daimyō of Satsuma, had acquired a great
local reputation for sagacity and ability in administration
and military affairs in the course of his warfare with his
neighbours in the centre of the principality. Accordingly
it was Takahisa, then thirty-one years of age, who was invited
to assume the direction of the general affairs of the clan.
To allay the internal strife that had previously paralysed
the fief he saw it was necessary to find some external
foe against whom all the hitherto discordant and clashing
energies of the clan could be combined in a single and
harmonious effort. As certain of the chieftains of Ōsumi at first
refused to submit to his suzerainty, he found sufficient occupation for his restless subjects to keep them fully employed there
for some five or six years. Then when Ōsumi was at last completely reduced in 1556, Takahisa had to look about for some one
else to pick a quarrel with, and so Itō in Hiūga was then
assailed. For all the remaining fifteen years of Takahisa's life
the border warfare between Satsuma and Hiūga went on, without
any very decisive result. At the death of Takahisa in 1571, his
frontier had been only a little advanced. But this was the
slightest of the benefits that had meanwhile accrued to Satsuma.
It was then that the fiery Satsuma men, with their superb
physique and magnificent *élan*, were broken in and habituated to
that prompt and ready obedience to their chiefs for which the clan
has ever since been famous. During the last three centuries of
Japanese feudalism there was perhaps no fief in the whole
Empire where devotion to their chief and the general interests of

---

12 Kagoshima was not then the residence of the Prince of Satsuma. Xavier
had to go six leagues from Kagoshima to get his audience on September 29th,
1549. It was only after 1600 A.D. that the so-called "castle" of Kagoshima was
built. At the date of Xavier's arrival the Satsuma Court resided at Kokubu.

the clan was so strong as it was among the *samurai* of Kagoshima. If there was such a thing as *esprit-de-corps* anywhere in Japan it was to be found in the *sha*[13] or sections of the capital of the Satsuma clan. It was to its discipline, its unity and its *esprit-de-corps* that the Satsuma clan owed all its greatness, and for the establishment of the traditions which made it great it is to Shimadzu Takahisa that its thanks are due.

On the death of Takahisa in 1571 he was succeeded by his capable and mettlesome son, Yoshihisa, who followed his father in sparing no effort to increase the military strength and spirit of the clan. The war with Itō of Hiūga was now prosecuted with still greater vigour, every year seeing an extension of the Satsuma territory, and at last in 1578, as has been said, the Satsumese swept Hiūga from their own up to the Bungo frontier. Naturally and in ordinary circumstances the annexation of Hiūga by Shimadzu Yoshihisa would have been the preliminary of a struggle between Satsuma and Bungo for the hegemony of Kyūshū. But in addition there was the fact that Itō's dispossessed widow was Ōtomo's daughter, and her infant children his grandsons. The great patron of the Jesuits had associated his eldest son with himself in the administration two years before, in 1576, and this son, Yoshimune, eager to wield undivided sway, now arranged with the fugitive Hiūga princess, his sister, that she should cede her children's claims to Hiūga to him in return for certain lands in his own fief, his purpose being that his father should withdraw from Bungo and devote himself to the government of Hiūga exclusively. A force of 60,000 Bungo troops was launched against Shimadzu, and the Satsuma garrisons left in the conquered province were soon captured or driven over the southern frontier. Old Ōtomo now proceeded to his new province and chose a site for the new capital he purposed to call into existence, and then returned to Bungo to make a final settlement of affairs there. In the autumn of that very same year, however, the Satsuma men had again burst into Hiūga and stormed most of its strongholds. This once more caused a muster of the Bungo levies, and 40,000 men were at

---

13 When these *sha* were really organised is not exactly known. Some refer their origin to the age of Shimadzu Yoshihisa, who was conquered by Hideyoshi, while other authorities maintain that they date only from the eighteenth century. But the warlike spirit and the rigorous discipline which they fostered had been first effectually inculcated by Takahisa.

once hurried to the front under old Ōtomo, while Yoshimune, his son, took up his headquarters near the borders to superintend the dispatch of reinforcements. But before dealing with this fateful struggle it is well to say something of the strange events that had passed in Bungo during the three preceding years.

As has been mentioned, the Jesuits had captured Ōtomo's second son, then sixteen years of age, in 1576. This had a great effect upon his fourteen-year-old friend, the adopted son of Tawara Tsugitada, the Chief Councillor of the fief, and the brother of Ōtomo's wife; and this lad, in spite of all the restraint his adopted father and aunt put upon him, was also baptized in 1577. Jezebel was so furious in her wrath at this that she forbade the ceremony to proceed unless the prospective bridegroom apostatized. When he refused to do so Jezebel induced her brother to disinherit him. This affair excited a great commotion among the Bungo *samurai*, and Tawara was said to have ordered his vassals to kill the Vice-Provincial and the other priests, and to slaughter their congregations. For twenty days the church at Usuki was thronged with an excited crowd, praying, fasting, scourging themselves, and making ready to meet the martyrdom they fancied to be imminent. It was solely to the intervention of Ōtomo that the priests then owed their lives. The old Prince sent word to Cabral by a Christian that "all this trouble had been excited by the machinations of his wife [Jezebel]; and that for this he would have been minded to repudiate her and drive her from his house without fail were it not that she had been his spouse for thirty years and had borne him seven children, and that he greatly feared his doing so would excite serious tumults at a time when things were far from quiet." From the Jesuits' own letters it is clear that their capture of these two boys, the Chief Councillor's heir and Ōtomo's second son, who now made common cause with his friend, created great discontent and disaffection among the upper classes in Bungo. Between the foreign priests and Jezebel it was war to the knife. Ōtomo had returned from Hiūga to attend the wedding of the Councillor's heir with his daughter, and the coolness with which he regarded the breaking-off of the match by his wife and the disinheriting of the bridegroom was only assumed. He now, says the Annual Letter of 1579, " determined, according to the usage of the country, to repudiate

his wife and take another"; and his new choice was a lady who
was already a catechumen of the priests. After this second
marriage Ōtomo was continually present when the Japanese
Jesuit was instructing his new spouse; and one day he sent word
to Cabral that he himself was ready to receive baptism at his
hands, that he had esteemed Christianity from the first, and that
if he had not embraced it, it was because he wished to be first
thoroughly persuaded of the falsity of Buddhism, and also because it was not convenient for him to do so until he himself had
retired from the administration of his States. So at last Ōtomo
was baptized with his new wife on August 28th, 1578, and early
in October, five weeks after this baptism, he and his spouse, his
second Christian son, the Chief Councillor's disinherited heir, Vice-
Provincial Cabral, Almeyda, and the young Japanese Jesuit who
had instructed Jezebel's successor, set out by sea for the new town
Ōtomo had ordered to be built in Hiūga. "They were accompanied by a great number of Christians of all ages and conditions, Ōtomo having declared that he would suffer no idolater
in his new city."

It was just a few weeks after this that the Satsumese again
poured into Hiūga, carrying all before them. Shimadzu Yoshihisa seems to have withdrawn the bulk of his troops quickly,
however; at all events, the initial Bungo force of 40,000 men
met with little opposition till they had advanced a good way
beyond the frontiers. This force, nominally commanded by old
Ōtomo, was really directed by the Chief Councillor, Jezebel's
brother, for Ōtomo followed more than a day's march behind the
army. The old prince was accompanied by Cabral, Almeyda,
and seven Jesuit brothers. Says the Annual Letter of 1579:—

"And thus as he took possession, he went on burning and wrecking
the temples of the *Kami* and *Hotoke*, and frequently said to Father
Cabral that he wished to plant such a good Christianity in this
kingdom that the fame of it would go to Rome, and that he meant it
to be governed according to the laws of the Christians. He at once
assigned the revenues of two Buddhist monasteries to make a house for
us, and for the maintenance of some Fathers, promising to give what
was necessary for residences. He at once ordered the erection of a
church in a fortress of great importance, and early every morning in
the month of November, a season of great cold, he came from his house
a considerable distance to hear Mass in a church which had been
erected in a trice. He confessed and communicated and said his
prayers; and he acted towards us as familiarly as if he had been a
Brother of the house. He urged his attendants to appear to learn the
things of our faith in such a way that one Brother had much to do in

catechising so many. Although they are occupied with the affairs of the war, and although we are far from the army, as much as a day and a half, there are no catechisings at which the King is not always present."

Such a state of affairs at the Bungo headquarters was doubtless a very fortunate thing for the Satsuma commanders. And at the Bungo base near the borders matters were in a very similar condition. There Ōtomo's eldest son, the new Daimyō Yoshimune, was supposed to be wholly engaged in mustering and dispatching fresh troops and in forwarding supplies. If one had nothing but the Jesuit letters to judge him from, it would be hard indeed to arrive at any definite estimate of Yoshimune's character. He first appears in a letter of Almeyda's of November 1562:— "*Puer ille quidem, ac pœne infans (annum quippe agit quintum) sed in quo sensus animi ac ratio longe prœcurrat œtatem.*" Generally there is the note of sincerity in Almeyda's letters; but this sounds suspiciously like a sample of the nauseous conventional trash which constitutes a portion of the stock-in-trade of that toadyism and flunkeyism ever ready to discover bib-and-porringer prodigies in the families of the great or the wealthy from whom favours may be expected. Later on, after 1580, the missionaries have many hard things to say of him; they find him *borné*, of limited capacity—or rather of no capacity at all,—of a light and inconstant spirit, and so on and so forth. In these years of 1578 and 1579 he appears as "this good young man," "this worthy young prince," and altogether the priests become unpleasantly nasal in cataloguing his virtues and his merits. The reason for this was that he and his wife were then Jesuit catechumens, that he himself was clamouring to be baptized, and that besides he had been showering very substantial favours upon the missionaries. Father Froez was now specially attached to his person to supervise his spiritual progress, which was certainly remarkable. One day, after a discussion on the seventh commandment, " he said in a loud voice to all, ' I am a young man, and know well and am well assured that there is only one God, that the soul is immortal, that there is eternal glory for the good and hell for the guilty. Therefore I am resolved to make no more account of the body, but to give diligent heed to my soul, quitting all looseness, and contenting myself with a single wife. . . . And thus I command you all to refrain from similar things [*i.e.* loose conduct], for when I hear of any one being loose, I will have him exceedingly

well chastised.' . . . Once tempted by the Devil with brutish
thoughts, he not only drove them from him, but remaining with
scruples he said to Father Froez, ' Now since I am a Gentile and
cannot confess, at least give me some penance, that I may make
satisfaction with that.' On other occasions when the temptations
were very troublesome, to free himself from them he cast cold
water upon his back, it being the middle of winter, and in this
way he mortified his sensuality, and made resistance against it.
On other occasions, while praising the law of God, he said that
whoever maliciously refrained from becoming a Christian, merited
death. With these and similar speeches, and the favours he
shows to the converts and the disfavour with which he regards
such as oppose the law of God, such an extraordinary fervour has
appeared among his vassals and the country people that all come
with the utmost diligence to learn the things pertaining to their
safety. And one Brother giving three or four lessons a day does not
suffice to answer the questions they ask and to catechise so many.
It is of great edification to see many nobles as if they were so
many boys walking in the streets learning the Pater Noster, the
Ave Maria, and the rest of the Christian doctrine. And in a
short time there has been such a change that where a little ago
the law of God and we were despised and contemned and held
for naught, we are respected and obeyed, and our law held in
such high regard, that our travails and sufferings of the past year
seem to have been well bestowed."

All this, though pleasing enough to the priests, gave but
scant satisfaction to those engaged in the turmoil of the Hiūga
campaign. Some of Yoshimune's vassals proceeding to the front
remonstrated warmly with him, and counselled him that " he
would be better occupied in matters of greater importance
pertaining to the war and the good government of his fiefs. To
these (as they were persons of great quality) he made answer that
they saw very well that it was to attend to the war that he
had left his Court and come there with such discomforts, and
that he was providing with all possible diligence for what was
necessary in the war. As to his devotion to the law of God,
that caused no hindrance or trouble, and as it seemed to them
that this holy law was of little importance, it would have
been better for them to hear what it contained so as to be
able to pronounce judgement on it with better foundation,

Not very well contented with such an answer, they pursued their way towards Hiūga." In Hiūga meanwhile the campaign had gone very well for Bungo. The castles in the extreme north of the province had been quickly reduced by the Chief Councillor's force, and Nobeoka and two other considerable fortresses had been carried without any great difficulty. When this news was conveyed to Yoshimune his behaviour was somewhat theatrical. " He received the letter while on horseback, and as he read the good news, before finishing it, he dismounted, knelt down, and with uplifted hands rendered thanks to Our Lord for so great a victory without any loss on the part of his own troops. As his attendants marvelled at what they saw, not knowing what was in the letter, he read the whole of it to them, and, turning to the Christians who were present, he ordered them to thank God for so great a blessing. And he at once dispatched a servant to bear the news to our House and to thank us, saying that he regarded it as very certain that this victory had been gained through the sacrifices and prayers of our Fathers and Brothers." Before this many of the Bungo *samurai* had kept saying that their enterprise would surely miscarry as a just punishment for the late outrageous treatment of the national gods, and some of them still kept saying so, although the Jesuits now laughed them and their idols to scorn. The national gods had probably just as much or as little to do with the success or failure of the campaign as the God preached by the Jesuits had, but in a few days such of the religious conservatives of Bungo as survived had the melancholy satisfaction of seeing the worst of their ominous forebodings more than fully realised.

The Bungo army, now swelled by successive reinforcements and the adhesion of many of the Hiūga *samurai* to as many as 70,000 men, had advanced beyond the Mimikawa before it found its progress at all seriously impeded. Seventeen miles south of this stream Iyehisa, the third son of Yoshihisa, the Satsuma prince, had thrown himself into the castle of Taki, with a body of 3,000 picked troops, and showed no inclination either to surrender or to evacuate the place, as the Satsuma captains had done further north. Judging it unsafe to leave this stronghold unreduced, so exposing himself to the risk of having his communications cut, the Bungo commander sat down to the leaguer of the fortress. Meanwhile the war-beacons were ablaze on all the hills of Satsuma, Ōsumi, and Southern Hiūga, where Shimadzu Yoshihisa had ordered a general levy of everything in the clan capable of bearing arms and marching. It was no mere undisciplined mob, however, that now hurried to the relief of the gallant Iyehisa. The Bungo host, flushed with a cheap and almost bloodless success, and looking upon the fall of Taki as but a question of a few days, had become over-confident and reckless. Their chief had neglected his intelligence department, and the advance of any relieving force large enough to give serious trouble to his army of 70,000 men was what he had never reckoned with. As it was, it was only a division of the Satsuma force that appeared; the remainder lay beyond the hills safe from observation. So much is inferable from Father Carrion's account of the battle, written shortly afterwards, and there is nothing in the Jesuits' narrative which is at all inconsistent with the details given in the *Seihan-yashi*, a history of the House of Shimadzu compiled by a Kagoshima *samurai* from authentic records towards the end of the eighteenth century. On reaching Sadowara, Yoshihisa's onward swoop had been checked by a terrific storm which raged for several days, and meanwhile his brother Tadahira, advancing from Northern Ōsumi, had come into contact with a fairly strong body of Bungo troops operating in that direction. By clever tactics Tadahira succeeded in ambushing them and routing them with a loss of five hundred killed, and then he kept hot upon the traces of the fugitives as they made for Matsuyama. The smoke of the burning houses fired by the victorious Satsumese was visible at Sadowara, and Yoshihisa at once dispatched a column under Ijuin, which helped Tadahira to storm Matsuyama while Yoshihisa himself pushed on to Takikawara, within a few miles of the vast Bungo host beleaguering Iyehisa and his three thousand men in Taki. Exasperated by the reverse at Matsuyama, the Bungo commander determined to seek Yoshihisa and offer him battle at once. Yoshihisa marshalled his troops in five divisions. Two of these, forming the centre, were thrown well forward under Honda and Hongō; the right and left wings, commanded by Yukihisa and Tadanaga respectively, occupied strong positions some distance to the rear of the centre; while Yoshihisa himself took charge of the reserves posted behind on the route over which the centre had advanced. The whole of the huge Bungo army hurled itself with such force upon the Satsuma centre that the Southerners staggered under the shock; they lost both their commanders, and were driven back upon the reserves. These, however, animated by Yoshihisa's voice and example, stood firm against the charge of the Bungo men, who, holding their foe all too cheaply, had penetrated well within the Satsuma wings. These now came into action, and fell fiercely upon the flanks of the Northerners. Checked in front, and thus assailed on the right and left, these began to waver, and their commander's chief aim was now to extricate them from this critical position. But just at this moment Iyehisa with his garrison sallied out of the leaguered fortress, sweeping the brigades left to mask Taki before him like thistledown, and fell like a thunderbolt upon the rear of Ōtomo's men, already reeling under the onset of the Satsuma troops, who had caught them in a veritable cul-de-sac. It soon became a case of *sauve qui peut*; the *débâcle* was utter and complete. That night there were thousands of women in the Bungo domains who had been widowed since the morning.[14]

When fugitives from the stricken field appeared at old Ōtomo's headquarters, " the fear and confusion among the followers of the King was such that, although Father Cabral did everything possible—advising the King not to depart so soon or with such haste, but to wait to collect and rally the *débris* of his

14 In Bungo the contest was regarded not merely as a trial of strength against Satsuma, but as a struggle between the national gods and the Deus of the foreign priests. The Satsumese, at all events, had no slight reason for supposing that the *Kami* and *Hotoke* were fighting on their side. Says the *Seihan-yashi*: " At last the great host of Ōtomo advanced to the leaguer of Taki. Then came a hard time for the defenders, not only from the numbers of the enemy, but also from the scarcity of drinking water in the fortress. The garrison endeavoured to fetch a supply from a stream outside the wall, but they were prevented from doing so by the besiegers. Strange to say, however, it one day happened that from under an old wall within the castle pure sparkling water gushed out in great abundance, and the stream proved to be constant. All the men in the castle jumped for joy, saying that Heaven was thus to bless the family of Shimadzu. . . . Just on the night Yoshihisa arrived in Hiūga he composed a poem in a dream: 'The enemy's defeated host is as the maple leaves of Autumn floating on the waters of the Tatsuta stream.' The army of the prince hailed it as an omen of victory. . . . In the vicinity of the battle-field were two large ponds, each about twenty-five feet deep, and over a thousand feet in length as well as in breadth. Several hundred of the beaten troops lost their lives in these ponds, and the men, horses, and flags floating there appeared pretty much like the fallen leaves of Autumn on the surface of a stream. Then the soldiers of the Shimadzu clan said one to another that the prince's dream had been realised, and that it was nothing but the power of Heaven which had given them such a glorious victory over their foes. Thus their strength and valour increased a hundredfold, and they pressed the pursuit vigorously. The seventeen miles between the fortress of Taki and the Mimikawa were strewn with the corpses of fallen foes." In the grounds of the Prince of Satsuma's mansion at Iso, near Kagoshima, are two fine pieces of bronze ordnance, the spoils of the battle of the Mimikawa.

army; all the more so as the place he was in was a strong one and the enemy could not come so soon as was said; perhaps the number of the fallen was exaggerated as was usual in such cases,—the Father had the utmost difficulty in persuading the King to wait by these and similar arguments. Nor did he abide long by this decision (on which, morally speaking, the restoration of his people and of his States depended); but the clamour and the appeals of his attendants were so loud, and the terror with which they inspired him was so great, that he allowed himself to be overcome by them, and with the greatest haste and confusion they put themselves on the route for Bungo. That same night he sent a message to the Father urging him with the Brothers to start also, as it was no longer time to wait. The anxiety and the confusion of that night was such that the King's Ministers and attendants forgot to take provisions for the way with them, and, being three or four days distant from Bungo, all suffered much hunger and travail—even the King and the Queen, who went with him with great inconveniences." Cabral and the seven or eight Jesuits he had with him, after firing the church to prevent its being put to profane uses by the enemy, had also to start on what was a terrible journey back to Bungo. They were in deadly peril of their lives, for they and their new-fangled aggressive religion were almost universally regarded as the real and undoubted source of the fell disaster that had stripped Bungo of all her prestige and plunged almost every family in her into mourning. Then when they did reach Funai after the cold, the hunger, and the exhaustion of a four days' journey on foot, during which they had to sleep out in the nipping frost of winter, to ford many icy-cold streams, and to sustain themselves on one miserable meal of rice, they found themselves in no pleasant position. Of course the *bonzes* now were fierce and bitter against them. But "the wicked Jezebel, with her brother and many other lords who had each lost father or son or brothers or relatives in this war, were attributing the whole calamity to us, saying that it all proceeded from our presence in Bungo and the destruction of the *Kami* and *Hotoke*. And so they resolved to make every effort to kill us, or at least to expel us from all these kingdoms. And as the fallen in that war had been so numerous, great part of the city was in affliction, and resentful on this account; and we could not

appear in the streets in consequence of the numberless outrages
and affronts and insults and the abusive epithets they hurled at
us." It surely argued no small restraint on the part of the
general population in such circumstances that these worthy
gentlemen who had just been breaking the idols and wrecking
the temples of the national gods, and jeering and scoffing at
their impotence to protect themselves, did not now find a shower
of something a good deal harder and more solid than mere
abusive epithets flying about their ears. However, the two
Princes, the father more especially, still retained authority
enough to protect the Jesuits. Of their goodwill, about which
Cabral had been so terribly anxious during the four days of his
flight from Hiūga, there had been no alienation. Ōtomo had
forgotten to provide himself with provisions for his retreat, but
he had not forgotten to go to fetch a much-prized crucifix from
the church. "When Cabral arrived in the church the King
knelt down, and with uplifted hands returned thanks to God for
the trials and afflictions he suffered"; and later on he said to
the Vice-Provincial in private that "the loss of the battle really
seemed to him to be a divine ordination for the better progress
of the conversion of his people; for the principal lords and
captains of his States, who were cruel enemies of our holy law,
and who most opposed and impeded the promulgation of the
Holy Gospel, had fallen there. If they had remained alive,
even if he had obtained the victory, they would always have
opposed this good work, so that neither he nor his son would
have been able freely to carry out their intentions regarding
Christianity." Thus to Ōtomo the reappearance of his Chief
Councillor, who for a whole month was supposed to have fallen
in the battle he had lost, may have been a genuine disappointment. Shortly after his return the latter proposed to his fellow
councillors that the foreign priests should be killed, or at least
expelled, all the churches razed, and Christianity proscribed.
The Jesuits in Usuki again prepared for martyrdom, and wrote
touching farewell letters to their brethren in Funai. But
nothing happened either to them or their church. They accused
Jezebel of having been the prompter of her brother's proposal.
Jezebel, it may be remarked, was now fighting a tolerably even
fight with the priests. Yoshimune, generally thoroughly under
her influence, had cut the Japanese equivalent for the apron-

string a few months before the rout of the Mimikawa. A great contest then went on between him and the Jesuits on the one side, and Jezebel on the other, regarding the religion of Yoshimune's young princess, and Jezebel had been victorious not at the eleventh hour, but just on the very stroke of twelve, for when Froez had everything ready for the baptismal service, instead of baptizing the princess he had to rest ill content with "singing a solemn mass *in musica con diacono e sudiacono* in the newly-reared chapel in the palace." Jezebel, not satisfied with this, now exerted herself to regain her ascendency over Yoshimune, and here again she proved more than a match for Ōtomo and the priests combined. Yoshimune did not, indeed, begin to persecute his former friends and their converts; but he became politely indifferent to them, and returned to the cult of the ancestral gods. And in the meantime, while the limited intelligence of Yoshimune was wholly occupied in giving a practical decision upon the relative merits of what Hideyoshi held to be two elaborately organised rival systems of kindred superstition, the young man had lost four of his five provinces.

Yoshihisa of Satsuma, being something more than a mere soldier, had been doing something in addition to counting his musters at the time the war-beacons were aflare on the grass-topped hills of his provinces. Even after one crushing defeat in Hiūga, Ōtomo, he told himself, might still prove more than a match for him when he had time to bring up his distant Chikuzen and Chikugo levies. To prevent their appearance in Hiūga something had to be devised to give them abundant occupation at home. Accordingly emissaries were dispatched to induce Riūzōji of Saga to assail Chikugo. Riūzōji needed no great urging to do so, and, as we have already seen, in 1579 a great victory over the Bungo vassals there had made him so decisively master of that province that he felt he could devote his undivided attention to reducing his original lord, Arima, to subjection, and thus completing the reduction of Hizen. In Chikuzen a certain Akidzuki, a vassal of Ōtomo's, had long been waiting for a favourable opportunity to cast off his allegiance, and now, assured of the indirect support of Satsuma and Riūzōji, he rose, stormed Hakata, the capital of the province, beat the supporters of Bungo in the rest of the province to their knees, and speedily overran a great section of Buzen. Yoshihisa of Satsuma in the meantime had been reducing the strongholds of Southern and Central Higo, where he met with no check to his progress till Riūzōji, deflected from Arima by Valegnani's diplomacy, bethought himself that in the general break-up of the Ōtomo power the number and marksmanship of his arquebusiers entitled him to something more than the single province of Chikugo. In addition to all this there was sedition in Bungo itself. One of the Chief Councillor's colleagues, whom the missionaries call Cicafiro, had blocked his project of massacring the Jesuits, not from any affection he bore them, but merely because the proposal was of the Chief Councillor's making. Cicafiro now withdrew to his castle, mustered his men, and threatened to march on Funai unless the Chief Councillor restored certain lands to him he had been forced to cede by Ōtomo's orders some time before. The lands were restored, but Cicafiro died that same year, and his son openly revolted, and was only reduced after a sharp struggle, during which two other feudatories rebelled and had to be crushed. Many of the Bungo vassals in the four outlying provinces, who would otherwise have remained perfectly staunch, sent word that they would not fight if Yoshimune continued to favour the foreign priests. Then, in 1580, the Bungo councillors appealed to old Ōtomo to reassume the direction of affairs, and when he did so he ordered the destruction of the temples and shrines wherever he led his forces. In the Annual Letter of 1582 we hear of a success he gained over the combined forces of Riūzōji and Akidzuki on the Chikuzen border with very slight loss on his own side, after which "he captured a very strong place [probably Hikōsan], where there was one of the chief pagodas and the most frequented in these parts, which had around it three thousand houses of the *bonzes*, and he at once gave orders to burn all the houses, and the Venerable Pagoda was turned into ashes. After this victory the King wrote a very humble and Christian letter to the Father Visitor, in which he confessed that it had been achieved solely by God and the prayers of the Fathers, and not by his own skill or might, and that he was so grateful to God for the mercies vouchsafed him that it seemed to him that he could never thank Him duly if he did not put forth every effort to have His divine Majesty for ever acknowledged and adored in his States." Such devout temple-wrecking could have done little to conciliate the good-will of the former vassals of Bungo in the four lost provinces, in not one of whom there had ever been more than three hundred Christians. We may take it as almost certain that those Higo *samurai* who sent word to Yoshimune that they would not budge on his behalf if he continued to favour the foreign priests and their religion were by no means singular in the attitude they assumed. It is little marvel, then, that with the iconoclastic old prince at the head of affairs, but few of the *samurai* in Higo, Chikugo, Chikuzen, or Buzen rallied to the Ōtomo standard. All things considered, the marvel is not that the old daimyō failed to recover his lost provinces, but that he even contrived to retain his ancestral and original fief of Bungo. In one passage the Jesuits clearly and distinctly say that he neglected his own interests and those of his States to serve theirs, and the statement is nothing but the truth. Even in this year of 1581, when there were as many as 5,000 baptisms in Bungo, no more than 10,000 of Ōtomo's 250,000 or 300,000 subjects were Christians. Many of these were women and children, and nearly all belonged to the lowest strata of society. It is extremely questionable whether there were as many as five hundred *samurai* among them. The vast majority of the military class were not so much indifferent as bitterly hostile to the foreign religion. The deity most worshipped by them was Hachiman, the War-God, whose great temple "so famous, so wealthy, and so resorted to by pilgrims," stood in Buzen, just beyond the Bungo frontier, and "the King did not cease until he had set fire to this also and burned it completely." Just before this passage in the Annual Letter of 1583 (February 13th) we read: "The destruction of the monasteries in this kingdom proceeds. Their revenues are given to soldiers. The *bonzes* are quitting their robes; some marry, some go to the wars and to seek their fortunes, some here and some there. The chief monastery of Funai, which had long been regarded as the ornament of the whole of this kingdom, was fired shortly after the departure of the Father Visitor, and burned so that not a palm of it remains." The spoils of the monasteries might indeed placate the more needy of Ōtomo's retainers, but the fact remained that the religious persecution— for such it really was—was regarded with sullen disfavour by his chief vassals and the best men in the clan. Besides, the *bonzes* who had to seek refuge elsewhere, mostly in the four lost

I

provinces, spared no effort to inspire the people among whom they settled with their own feelings.

It was with no great pleasure that the generality of the Bungo *samurai* witnessed their old chief lavishly spending his money upon the erection of magnificent churches at Usuki and elsewhere, all the more so as the late war and its results had reduced the clan to the greatest indigence. Valegnani, the Jesuit Visitor-General, on his way to Funai from Arima was waylaid by some of the discontented vassals ; and it was only the prompt dispatch of a considerable force by Ōtomo that enabled the Father Visitor to reach his destination in safety. When he arrived at Usuki he immediately took in hand the establishment of a Novitiate there, and the organisation of a college in Funai for the training of would-be members of the Company. He was strongly in favour of utilising the services of Japanese, and on this point he came into collision with Cabral, the Vice-Provincial. The latter, who had been at the head of the mission during the preceding ten years, held strongly to the belief " that the Japanese, being naturally haughty and of an overweening spirit, and of an excellent wit, would, if cultivated by the study of all sciences human and divine, quickly abuse them, and soon come to despise Europeans"; and so he had merely instructed them so far as was necessary for the occupation of the lowest posts in the service of the Mission. The difference of opinion between him and Valegnani over this matter was so acute that the Visitor-General found it advisable to send him to Macāo and to instal Father Coelho in his position. Valegnani later on wrote to Acquaviva, the Jesuit General in Rome, to the effect that " the most austere Order in the Church has no Novitiate so severe as is the apprenticeship to good breeding that is necessary in Japan." At the same time he had to admit that there was something to be said for Cabral's contention, for one of the avowed motives that prompted him to organise the famous embassy from the Christian princes of Kyūshū to the Pope was his desire to open the eyes of the Japanese to the fact that there were States in Europe superior to their own in might and resources and more advanced in civilisation. In his letters to the King of Spain, to the Pope, and to Acquaviva on the subject, he said that the people of " this nation, haughty by nature, were ready to believe that any deference shown to them was simply their due; that they fancied themselves superior to those who accorded them any marks of distinction; and that it was advisable to inspire the youthful envoys with a great idea of the magnificence of our churches and the might of the princes of Christendom." We meet with frequent mention in the missionary letters of the contempt of the *samurai* for the foreign priests and for Europeans, Cabral in one passage bitterly remarking that " there are many in these parts with whom there is no dealing until they have been humiliated and abased." [15]

Experience had taught the Jesuits that if Japan was ever to be thoroughly Christianised, the new religion would have to be imposed upon the general population from above. In those quarters where they had failed to capture the Daimyō or the princelet, Christianity had either languished or disappeared. This had been the case in Satsuma, in Yamaguchi, and in the Gotō islands. In Hirado there were scarcely any converts beyond the islets of Takashima and Ikutsushikishima, which belonged to the Daimyō's Christian brother Anthony, who, like

---

[15] The famous Japanese embassy to the Pope consisted of four youths of fifteen or sixteen years of age. Two of these, Julian Nakaura and Martin de Hara, from Ōmura, were the attachés of the two envoys. These latter were Michael de Chiji-iwa (cousin of the Prince of Arima), representing Arima and Ōmura combined, and Mancio Itō, cousin of the dispossessed Daimyō of Hiūga, acting for old Ōtomo of Bungo. Itō was specially charged to urge the beatification of Francis Xavier. Accompanied by Valegnani and two other members of the Company, the envoys left Nagasaki in Feburary 1582, and reached Goa in September 1583, where Valegnani remained behind. They arrived at Lisbon in August 1584, where the highest Church dignitaries at once took charge of them and provided them liberally with money, as did also the Duke of Braganza on their way to Madrid. At the Spanish Court they met with a reception of extraordinary magnificence, all the great ladies of Madrid crowding eagerly to see them. They passed on from Madrid to Alicante, and, sailing from there, and providentially escaping capture by an Algerine pirate, they landed at Leghorn, whence they passed on to Rome by way of Pisa, Florence, and Sienna. At Rome their arrival caused a great commotion. They were received in solemn audience by Gregory XIII. just five days before his death, and at the subsequent coronation of Sixtus V. they assisted as " Royal Ambassadors," His Holiness a little later on creating them Knights of the Golden Spur, while the Senator and Conservators of the City admitted them as Patricians in the Capitol, when they had to listen to a very beautiful discourse in Latin, in reply to which young Itō gave evidence that the Japanese were past-masters in the art of turning graceful compliments. Then, liberally furnished with funds by His Holiness, they set out on their return, passing through Bologna, Venice, Milan, and other cities of Northern Italy, where their appearance was attended by commotions scarcely less remarkable than it had produced in the Holy City. At Genoa they embarked for Spain. They had a second magnificent audience with Philip II. (at Monzon), and then, proceeding to Lisbon, they embarked for Japan, together with seventeen Jesuits, on April 13th, 1586. On reaching Goa they were rejoined by Valegnani, with whom they were there associated in an embassy from the Viceroy of India to Hideyoshi, and the whole party ultimately reached Nagasaki in July 1590, after an absence of eight years and a half. Two years later, in 1592, all four youths, now young men of twenty-five or twenty-six, were admitted into the Company of Jesus.

12

Philip II. of Spain, would have preferred to rule over a desert rather than over non-Christian subjects. Even in Bungo, where the foreign cult had always been tolerated, it was only since the baptism of Ōtomo himself that Christianity had made any headway. Between 1578 and the end of 1581 the number of converts, although even then standing at no more than 10,000, had quintupled. In Ōmura, Arima, and Amakusa only did Christianity flourish ; and there, after the capture of the chiefs, the general population had been ordered to choose between conversion or exile. And in these States the princelets had accepted the foreign religion mainly because their doing so brought the foreign ships into their harbours. To obtain a share in this foreign trade even the chief non-Christian princes of Kyūshū were ready to make concessions to the Jesuits. Akidzuki, after seizing Chikuzen, made overtures to them ; and it was only when he failed to get definite assurances about the visits of Portuguese traders that he proscribed Christianity in Hakata. Riūzōji of Saga had invited Valegnani to visit him, and had entertained the Visitor-General in the most courteous manner. He requested the Jesuit to induce the foreign ships to go to Karatsu, and his third son actually offered to accept baptism. It was only because Valegnani then endeavoured to drive too hard a bargain that Riūzōji forbade any foreign priest to enter his domains.

Now let us see how it stood with the remaining great fief in the island. The Church historians represent the Prince of Satsuma as having been generally hostile to Christianity. However, the " Prince of Satsuma " was not the single evergreen Methusaleh they evidently regard him to have been. Seeing that the present head of the Shimadzu stock is the thirtieth of his line, that the family was founded in 1193, and that the average rule of a prince has thus covered no more than fourteen years, it would indeed be strange if the prince Xavier met in 1549 was the one who commanded the clansmen at the battle of Sekigahara in 1600. As a matter of fact, the latter was the grandson of the former. Takahisa, who died in 1571, was followed by his son Yoshihisa, who was compelled to retire from the headship of the clan by Hideyoshi in 1587 in favour of. his son Yoshihiro. Of these three only Takahisa could in any way be accused of being at all hostile to Christianity, and even.

Takahisa was no very bitter foe of the foreign religion. He had been chosen prince for the especial purpose of establishing peace and unity among its discordant factions. Now, when the *bonzes*, who had at first extended a hospitable welcome to Xavier, began to take serious offence at having their religion stigmatised as lies and fables and themselves denounced as impostors and tricksters, they took their complaints to the new ruler, threatening to withdraw if he could not or would not remedy the matter. Takahisa's special commission being to establish peace and order, he not unnaturally dealt very promptly with what bade fair to be the source of deadly and disastrous internal discord, and issued an edict threatening all future converts with death. It is no doubt true that disappointment at learning that the expected Portuguese merchantmen had gone to Hirado had also something to do with his vigorous action. It was eleven years after Xavier's departure before any other missionary appeared at Kagoshima.[16] Meanwhile Portuguese traders had visited Satsuma, for in a letter of Takahisa's to the Viceroy of India, written in December 1561, he apologises for Alvarez Vaz's ship having been mistakenly treated as a pirate some time before, while Almeyda in this year tells us he induced a Portuguese whom he found living with a concubine and two children at Akune to marry the woman. Furthermore, the reason of this visit of Almeyda's to the principality was to confess Captain Mendoza and seven other Portuguese who had put in to the harbour of Tomari. During this journey the missionary made three visits to the town of Kagoshima, on the first of which he met Takahisa, and was entrusted by him with two letters to hand to Mendoza, who was to take them to Goa. One was to the Viceroy of India, assuring him that Portuguese, whether traders or priests, would always receive a hospitable welcome in Satsuma, while the other was to the Provincial of the Jesuits, asking him to send priests, and also informing him that traders would also be well received. On this occasion Almeyda spent several weeks at Heshan's fortress, where he baptized seventy people, while there were thirty-five baptisms in Kagoshima itself, among whom were two of the chief men of

---

16 The two Brothers sent by Xavier from Goa to reinforce the Japan Mission had indeed landed at Kagoshima, but they stayed only eight days there and engaged in no missionary work.

the clan, relatives of Takahisa himself.[17] On the death of
Takahisa in 1571 his son and successor Yoshihisa showed himself
equally friendly towards the Jesuits.   Writes Cabral in
September 1576 :—"During the last three years the King of
Satsuma has constantly urged us by letters and with presents to
send him preachers of the law of God, and now afresh two *bonzes*
have come from him to press the same request." Five years
later, in the Annual Letter of February 1582, we read :—" The
King of Satsuma, designing that the Portuguese ships should go
to his ports, and judging that if there were churches and
Christians in his lands the Portuguese would be induced to go
there more readily, treated of this matter with the Father Visitor
[Valegnani] and the Vice-Provincial [Coelho].   Afterwards,
when the Father Visitor was returning from Bungo, he passed
through his lands, and the King sent to greet him, and at the
same time sent a rich present of a horse and a sword to be
presented to the Viceroy of India in his name, showing great
desire to have friendship with the Fathers and with the
Portuguese.   And afterwards, when the Father Visitor was
about to embark, the King sent other envoys to him offering to
assign a site for churches and houses in the principal city of his
kingdom, and promising permission for all within his land to
become Christians."   The truth would seem to be that Yoshihisa

---

17 In view of these facts Charlevoix's account of the matter needs to be
taken with caution. At the instigation of Heshan's wife, Almeyda had urged
Heshan to accept baptism himself. "Tum ille Deum testatus Christianam
religionem sibi plane probari, secus permissurum se nequaquam fuisse, ut eam
familia sua tota susciperet; una re quominus eos imitaretur, impediri se dixit,
quod vereretur, ne gravius animum Regis offenderet; sperare se Deo propitio
fore aliquando, ut Rege ipso libente, Christum, quem intimis sensibus adorabat,
palam ac libere profiteri posset." In Charlevoix this becomes:—"The God of
Heaven whom you preach, and whom I recognise as the only true God, is witness
that my heart adores him, and that his Law is graven thereon; otherwise would
I have allowed my family or even the least of my subjects to embrace it? But
you do not know the measures I am obliged to take with the Court of Satsuma.
You fancy, because the King shows you a pleasant countenance, that he regards
the progress of your doctrine with a favourable eye. You are mistaken. This
Prince does not concern himself much about what the people do, because their
actions are of no consequence, and because their attachment to your religion may
attract the Portuguese to his harbours: thus he tolerates it, and even pretends to
be pleased that it should be established among the common people; but he is far
from being of the same disposition with regard to the nobility [i.e. *samurai*].
However, I hope that the Divine kindness will bring round the favourable
moment when I can without risk cease to disguise my real sentiments in any
way." It is to be noted that the Father needs quite a deal of French to render
" ne gravius animum Regis offenderet," and that Heshan's two sons, and the "two
chief men, relatives of the King himself," were just as noble as Heshan himself
was. Charlevoix is rather fond of expansions of this sort, and now and then
reads between the lines of his original documents with an ingenuity that almost
amounts to inspiration.

was very favourably disposed towards the Jesuits, and that his efforts to attract them to his fief—of course as decoys for the foreign traders—were thwarted by the *bonzes*. These were then exceedingly powerful in Satsuma; and their hostility to Christianity was all the more determined because it was in Satsuma that most of the Buddhist priests, driven from Ōmura, Arima, and Amakusa by the persecuting, temple-wrecking iconoclastic princelets, had settled. When, after a good deal of negotiation between the Prince and the Vice-Provincial, Almeyda went to Kagoshima (he now made two journeys) to make the necessary arrangements, the *bonzes* tumultuously demanded his expulsion. "Further these ministers of the Devil, together with some principal lords, pressed the King expressly to order every one of the nobles to swear by their idols and promise in their own handwriting never to become Christians or to allow their vassals to do so." One of the Prince's favourites who supported Almeyda and went to hear him was actually murdered by the *bonzes*; and Yoshihisa, seeing the Buddhist priests prepared to go to extremities in their opposition to the introduction of Christianity, was obliged to admit that it was best for Almeyda to retire.

The sole hope for the conversion of the Empire, as has been said, was to capture the rulers of the fiefs, to get them to impose the new religion upon their subjects, and to introduce it into all the territories they might conquer. To extend the Jesuit influence with the governing class in Kyūshū, Valegnani founded a seminary in Arima for the education of youths of noble birth. The care expended upon this institution was immense. In every one of the Annual Letters full reports are made of its condition. The subjects taught were the Japanese, Portuguese, and Latin languages, painting, drawing, carving, vocal and instrumental music, and above all the doctrines of the Catholic faith. All the four youths who went on the embassy to the Pope had passed rather more than a year in this school.

At this point we will take leave of Kyūshū and Christianity in Kyūshū for the present. It only remains to add that Yoshihisa of Satsuma had invoked the arbitration of Nobunaga to establish peace between him and Bungo in 1581; that war still went on between Yoshimune and Riūzōji, supported by Akidzuki, in which, though Yoshimune had the worst of it,

Bungo itself was not invaded; and that Riūzōji was now fighting fiercely with Satsuma for the possession of Northern Higo. It was this pre-occupation alone which prevented him from swallowing up Arima. As for Ōmura, its Christian princelet had already had to acknowledge himself a vassal of pagan Riūzōji and to send his sons as hostages to Saga, thus causing the Jesuits much anxiety lest their faith should be perverted. The hegemony of Kyūshū had for ever passed from the House of Ōtomo, and was now disputed in no unequal strife between Satsuma and Riūzōji, although the missionaries seem to have inclined to the opinion that the prize would probably fall to the latter. We shall now pass to a consideration of affairs in the main island of the Archipelago, resuming the narrative of the Introductory Chapter.

CHAPTER VI.

NOBUNAGA AND HIS CONTEMPORARIES.

IN the Introductory Chapter it was remarked that in this volume there are two main threads of narrative—one being the course of the events in the re-establishment of a strong central military government in, and the other the progress of European intercourse with, Japan. So far we have been occupied in following the second of these almost exclusively. It is now time to devote some little attention to the first, and the more important of the two.

It has been already remarked that the prime object with the greatest and most ambitious feudal chiefs was to conquer their way to Kyōto, and there, making themselves masters of the Shōgun's person, to legalise their wars of conquest against their fellow-feudatories by conducting them in the Shōgun's name and with his commission. About 1540 A.D. some four great chiefs in Central and Eastern Japan might have aspired to achieve this project—namely, Uyesugi in Echigo; Takeda in Kai; Imagawa in Tōtōmi, Mikawa, and Suruga; and Hōjō of Odawara in the Kwantō. The first of these actually to set forth on such an undertaking was Imagawa, who with the levies of his three provinces, some 46,000 strong, began his march in the year 1560. But almost immediately on passing beyond the western frontiers of his own possessions his host was routed and he himself slain in an encounter with the vastly inferior forces of a comparatively insignificant baron. This was Oda Nobunaga, who at the age of sixteen had succeeded to the estates of his father, Oda Nobuhide, on his death in 1549—the year in which Xavier landed at Kagoshima. These estates were not very extensive, since they embraced no more than four small cantons in the province of Ōwari. The young chief's prospects at that date were the reverse of brilliant, for on every side he was surrounded by powerful foes, while he himself gave such scant signs of promise that he was usually referred to by the nickname of "Baka-dono," or "Lord Fool,"

However, he was not long in proving that retainers and foes
alike were holding him all too cheaply; for he not only maintained his position, but he even contrived to improve it, and
before a decade had gone by he found himself surrounded by
liegemen of real ability, while other able men were eager to enter
his service.   Among these latter was a certain Tōkichirō, three
years younger than himself, scarcely sixty inches in height,
with a face as wizened as an aged and sapless apple or a
septuagenarian ape, but with a supple and sinewy frame of
the wiriest, that never seemed to know what fatigue was.   Even
at this date this peasant Tōkichirō was perhaps the keenest
judge of character in Japan ; and the common story has it that
after passing in review all the great feudatories in the land,
he came to the deliberate conclusion that this small baron, Oda
Nobunaga, formerly cleped " Lord Fool " by the undiscerning,
was really the "coming man " in the Empire, and that if he
himself were ever to rise to mastery—as he was firmly bent on
doing—the best means of achieving his purpose would be by
finding employment with Nobunaga.   This he was able to
do in 1558, and from the date of Hideyoshi's (for it is by that
name that this Tōkichirō became best known in Japanese
history) entry into his service, Nobunaga's rise was rapid.   By
the end of 1559 he had brought the whole of Owari under his
sway and beaten back a formidable attack from the province of
Ise on the south.   In the following year (1560) he astonished
Japan by overthrowing Imagawa's huge host at Okehazama.
According to the commonly accepted popular account, on this
occasion Hideyoshi had no small share in devising the excellent
strategy of the brief campaign, and took a leading part in
the execution of the daring and brilliant tactics which decided
the battle ; but the results of modern research indicate that
this account must be regarded with the gravest suspicion.
This fight of Okehazama had important ulterior results upon
the history of the country.   Among Imagawa's sub-feudatories
was Tokugawa Iyeyasu, then eighteen years of age ; and
almost immediately after the death of old Imagawa at
Okehazama his son and successor mortally offended Iyeyasu,
who thereupon promptly accepted the overtures he had
just received from the victorious Nobunaga.   A defensive
and offensive alliance was arranged between them ; each

was to make what conquests he could, while the one of them who should first succeed in reaching Kyōto and there obtain the Shōgun's commission was to claim the subjection of the other. From this date we find Nobunaga and Iyeyasu (and of course Hideyoshi, then Nobunaga's captain) always acting in concert. In the following year Nobunaga proceeded to Kyōto, made report of what he had done, and received the Shōgun's official sanction for the conquests he had made. Meanwhile he had assailed Saitō, who held the neighbouring province of Mino, and on thoroughly reducing this foe he removed from his castle of Kiyosu in Owari to Saitō's former stronghold of Inabayama, afterwards known as Gifu in Mino. Then by 1568 he had effected the conquest of the northern cantons of Ise, and was in the full tide of success there when a chance offered elsewhere that could not be neglected.

In the following chapter fuller reference will be made to the assassination of the fourteenth Ashikaga Shōgun, Yoshiteru, by his Ministers Miyoshi and Matsunaga in 1565. The assassins set up a puppet Shōgun of their own; but the younger brother of Yoshiteru, Yoshiaki, escaped from the monastery where he had been immured as a priest, and betook himself to the provinces to engage some of the powerful feudatories in support of his rightful claims. The first of these he appealed to—Sasaki, who held Southern Ōmi—was an ally of Miyoshi's; and on his appearance in that fief Yoshiaki not only received no assistance, but had actually to flee for his life. He next had recourse to Takeda, the Daimyō of Wakasa; but this daimyō, after feeding him on hopes for more than a year, finally told him that he was powerless to stir in his behalf. Thereupon Yoshiaki fared on to Asakura, the powerful lord of Echizen, whom he also found disinclined to support him materially. Then, finally, he sent a messenger to Nobunaga to solicit aid; and by Nobunaga not merely promise of support, but real substantial support, was promptly accorded.[1] On this occasion Hideyoshi is said to have

---

1 To reconcile Charlevoix's account of the matter with the native authorities has not been easy, for he attributes everything to Wada (Vatodono). A reference to Froes's letter makes things plain, however. Writes he:—"Frater demortui Cubi, Cavadonus Voyacata (i.e. Yoshiaki) elapsus e conjuratorum custodiá, ad Vatadonum (Dynastam in regno Vomi) opis implorandæ causá confugit supplex, quem ille non modo benigné exceptum ingenti sumtu et munificentiá plus

insisted that "Nobunaga could do nothing without a name; and that if by then espousing Yoshiaki's cause he could maintain that all his subsequent wars were waged in obedience to his command, he (Nobunaga) could conquer the whole Empire."

Between the western frontiers of Mino and the capital the road ran through the province of Ōmi. The northern portion of this province was then held by Asai, whose stronghold was on one of the heights on the eastern shore of Lake Biwa, while in the south all the territory round the exit of the Yodo from the lake was dominated by some score of castles and stockades held by Sasaki. This Sasaki, as has been said, was hand-in-glove with Miyoshi, and accordingly he would have to be fought with and reduced. But Asai might be conciliated and won over to support the cause of Nobunaga's protégé. The usual device of a political marriage was resorted to; Nobunaga's younger sister became Asai's wife, and Asai became Nobunaga's confederate.[2] Before the year (1568) was out, Sasaki's castles had all been reduced, and Nobunaga and his confederate had occupied Kyōto, and there installed Yoshiaki as the fifteenth (and last) Ashikaga Shōgun. This accomplished, and invested with the office of Vice-Shōgun himself, Nobunaga resumed his interrupted operations in Ise, and by the end of 1569 the whole of that province had been subjugated. Master now of the three provinces of Owari, Mino, and Ise, with the south of Ōmi and the capital itself garrisoned by his troops,—Vice-Shōgun himself, and with the Shōgun merely his puppet, Nobunaga now thought fit to push his conquests farther afield.

Here it may well be asked how, while making himself master of Kyōto, had Nobunaga been able to secure himself from all attack on the rear. As has been said, there were then four

---

annum in arce sua Ooca (Kōka) fovit atque custodiit, magno ob idipsum aere alieno conflato: sed etiam ut in fraternum imperium restitueret finitimos Reges nationesque circumire atque omni ratione sollicitare non desiit, quoad Nobunanga, Rex Voaris armatorum quinquaginta millium exercitu comparato et Mioxindoni et Dajandoni, qui conjurationis principes fuerant, repressa audaciâ, quem dixi exulem in fraternis opibus et gradu honoris amplissimi collocavit."

[2] On being subsequently stripped of his fief by his quondam ally this Asai became a Christian. By Nobunaga's sister he had several daughters, one of whom, Yodogimi, became one of Hideyoshi's secondary wives, and (in 1592) the mother of Hideyori. Yodogimi was no Christian, but her younger sister, the Maria Kiogocou of the Jesuits, and the Jōkōin of Japanese history, was not only a Christian, but a most ardent Christian propagandist.

great feudatories in Central and Eastern Japan each in command of greater resources than those of Nobunaga. Nobunaga's safety lay principally in the mutual jealousy of these great chiefs and in his alliance with young Tokugawa Iyeyasu shortly after the battle of Okehazama in 1560. Iyeyasu had soon tried conclusions with Imagawa, his former feudal superior, and within a decade had stripped the Imagawa family of two-thirds of their possessions. Thus master of the provinces of Mikawa and Tōtōmi, and the ally of Nobunaga, Iyeyasu rendered the Hōjō powerless to afford any trouble. Accordingly only Takeda Shingen of Kai and Uyesugi Kenshin of Echigo had to be considered. These two great chieftains were ever at strife with each other. Hostilities had first broken out between them in 1553, when Uyesugi responded to the appeal of the daimyō Murakami, whom Takeda had driven from North-eastern Shinano. In the November of that year Uyesugi raided Shinano with 8,000 troops, and in the following month Takeda met him with 20,000 men, and the first of the four famous indecisive engagements of the Kawanakajima war was then fought. In 1557 a peace had been patched up, and during the next three years Uyesugi bent all his powers against Hōjō of Odawara, whose territories he once completely over-ran, and whom he actually blockaded in Odawara Castle in 1560. In this latter year Takeda broke the truce of 1557, and invaded Echigo, whither Uyesugi hurried back to fight more indecisive actions with him. As these were deemed unsatisfactory by both parties, it was at last arranged that matters should be settled by single combat between representative champions, and as in this encounter Uyesugi's man had the best of it, Takeda made over four districts in Shinano to Murakami, the evicted daimyō. For the next dozen years, although jealously watching each other, the two rival chieftains were busily occupied elsewhere, Uyesugi being engaged in hostilities with the Hōjō while Takeda was pushing his conquests southwards through Suruga to the Pacific seaboard. Thus down to 1572 Nobunaga's rear remained safe from any great risk either from Uyesugi or from Takeda. In the case of the former the road to Kyōto was blocked by Takeda or by other intervening feudatories, while as for Takeda, whose expanding possessions now marched with Nobunaga's north-eastern confines, apart from the fact that Uyesugi would have at once taken advantage of any such movement on his part, any attack from the Lord of Kai would have immediately invited an assault on the south from Iyeyasu, who not only kept true to the terms of the alliance he had struck with his western neighbour in 1560 or 1561, but who was far from being on good terms with Takeda even at the best of times. So for several years at least Nobunaga's rear remained safe from all attempts on the part whether of Hōjō or of Uyesugi or of Takeda, while Iyeyasu in his provinces not only protected it, but even carried reinforcements into Ōmi and Echizen to aid his ally in his struggles there.

There, indeed, such help was sorely needed, for early in 1570 Nobunaga, by his assault on the powerful Daimyō of Echizen (Asakura) for failing to recognise the new Shōgun, soon embroiled himself in a contest with a confederacy that bade fair to prove a hopeless over-match for him. Although the details are differently given in the missionaries' letters and in Japanese histories, yet both missionaries and Japanese writers are at one in indicating that at this crisis on more than one occasion Nobunaga's fortunes seemed to be almost hopeless. Asakura of Echizen and Nobunaga's brother-in-law, Asai, were close friends; and Asai's troops had taken umbrage at the overbearing conduct of Nobunaga's men in Kyōto in 1568. So, when pressing the attack (now accompanied by Iyeyasu) upon the Echizen frontier, Nobunaga was suddenly assailed upon the rear by Asai, his former ally. He did indeed manage to extricate himself from a difficult position; but on retreating to the capital he found that not only were Asakura and Asai marching upon him in conjunction, but that Sasaki, who had been evicted from Southern Ōmi in 1568, was also threatening him with a large force. However, a pitched battle at the Anegawa, in which Nobunaga and Iyeyasu broke Asai and Asakura's vastly superior numerical forces, relieved the situation for the time being. Shortly afterwards Miyoshi and some confederates in Settsu, supported by the Buddhist priests in what is now Ōsaka, threatened Kyōto, and Nobunaga marched upon them, and—was worsted. Thereupon Asai and Asakura— to be reinforced by Sasaki—fancied they saw their opportunity to seize the capital, and had actually reached its suburbs when Nobunaga succeeded in checking their advance. They

thereupon established themselves on Hiyei-san, where the priests
welcomed them with eagerness, and the blockade instituted
by Nobunaga was raised only at the request of the Shōgun.
Next year (1571) the cowled warriors of Hiyei-san paid dearly
for thus aiding and abetting the Vice-Shōgun's enemies. By the
cunning of Hideyoshi, Asai was provoked into resuming the
strife with Nobunaga in 1572, and before the end of the
following year Asai had been forced to surrender all his
domains, which (180,000 koku) were conferred on Hideyoshi
in addition to his former possessions (40,000 koku), while
Asakura, to avoid capture, had been driven to commit suicide,
and his vast estates bestowed upon Shibata, Hideyoshi's fellow-
councillor in the service of Nobunaga, and—his own dearest
foe, with whom he contrived to settle accounts of long
standing in a final and very effective manner eleven years
later on (1583).   These conquests were really the turning-
points in the careers of both Nobunaga and of Hideyoshi. On
the one hand they enabled other captains of Nobunaga to
push their way to the north-east to wrest the rich province
of Kaga from the Monto sect of priests, to seize upon parts
of Noto and Etchiu, and to threaten the great Uyesugi of
Echigo himself. However, although Nobunaga had dealt the
Monto priests a serious blow by the conquest of Kaga,
where his councillor, Sakuma, was installed as feudal lord,
their power was yet far from broken. The head of the sect,
Kenniō Kōsa, entrenched in his fortress-monastery of Ōsaka,
continued to bid defiance to all the assaults delivered against
him, while in 1575 an insurrection fomented by Kenniō's
adherents in Nobunaga's natal province of Owari proved
really a serious affair. And so far, down to 1572, the
Vice-Shōgun had established no foothold in Western Japan
whatsoever.

In Kyōto itself, Nobunaga's power began to be seriously
threatened in this year of 1572. His protégé, the Shōgun
Yoshiaki, was a man of dissolute life, and Nobunaga had seen
fit to remonstrate with him about his conduct. The Shōgun
resented this, and opened up a secret correspondence with Takeda,
with Uyesugi, and with Mōri of Aki, inviting them to march on
Kyōto and free him from the thraldom of his protector. The
only one of the three who responded to the appeal was Takeda, and

Takeda never reached Kyōto.[3]   Early in 1573 the Shōgun threw
up two forts at Ishiyama and Katata commanding Nobunaga's
route to and from the capital, and Nobunaga promptly sent a
force to reduce them, and in April he himself marched into
Kyōto from Gifu, and made the Shōgun express regret for his
action and promise obedience for the future.   On Nobunaga's
return to Gifu, the Shōgun once more rose against him, in
August, and this time, on marching to Kyōto and storming the
upper town held by Yoshiaki's men, the Vice-Shogun went so far
as to depose his protégé, although he did not actually strip him
of his title.[4]   Meanwhile Takeda had mustered a strong force in
January 1572, and had set out for the West.   At this point,
however, Iyeyasu proved his worth as an ally, and, secretly
reinforced by Nobunaga, threw himself in the way of Takeda's
advance.   The result was the great battle of Mikatagahara, in
which Takeda fell tempestuously upon Iyeyasu's force, broke it,
and swept it across the river Tenriu back upon Hamamatsu in
disorderly rout.   If he had pressed on, Iyeyasu's chief fortress
would have fallen, but his officers urged that a delay of twenty
days in carrying Hamamatsu would surely see Nobunaga on the
scene with a numerous relieving force, that a contest with him
would not be decided before the end of the winter, when
Uyesugi, free to move, would raid Shinano in their absence,
and that a withdrawal to meet him then would be construed
as a confession of inferiority to Nobunaga, whereupon the
resulting loss of prestige would be serious.   Takeda accordingly
withdrew till the snows of the following winter should render

---

3 In Charlevoix, Takeda is a very shadowy figure.   That Takeda was in
communication with the Shōgun is tolerably clear from a letter of Nobunaga to
Daté, reproduced in the *Daté Seisan Kō Chiku Kiroku* :—" I having followed the
Shōgun in his journey to the capital and having securely installed him in the Government, peace has been established for some years.   But Takeda of Kai, Asakura,
and some other wicked daimyōs have schemed and instigated the Shōgun to rise
against me.   It is a very unfortunate affair, and I regret it exceedingly."   This is
further confirmed by the following extract from the *Hosokawa-ke-no-ki* (*Record
of the House of Hosokawa*) :—" The Kubosama [*i.e.* the Shōgun] was angry because
of this remonstrance, and Nobunaga also felt unpleasant.   Previous to this
there had been some friction in the relations between Lord Yoshiaki and
Nobunaga owing to the schemes of Takeda Shingen."

4 Yoshiaki was first banished to Wakaye in Kawachi, and afterwards
wandered about for some time in Idzumi, Kii, and Harima, until in 1573 he
went to Tomonotsu in Bingo to invoke the help of Mōri to recover his
position.   In 1584 he was again back in Kyōto, and as Hideyoshi at that
time was anxious to become Sei-i-tai-Shōgun himself, he asked Yoshiaki to adopt
him.   The latter, however, was still proud enough to refuse the request.   He
died (61) in 1597, the year before Hideyoshi.   Thus during all Hideyoshi's
sway there *was* a Sei-i-tai-Shōgun in Japan.

his rear safe from Uyesugi's assault. He was now bitterly
incensed against Nobunaga, however, in spite of all the latter's
efforts to placate him. In the late battle one of Nobunaga's
general officers had been killed, and his head had been taken
to Takeda. Consequently Nobunaga's professions of goodwill
were futile; Takeda sent him the grisly trophy as a proof of
his breach of faith, and refused to have any further peaceful
relations with him. In January 1573 he again invaded
Iyeyasu's territories, and at the castle of Noda he was hit by
a sharpshooter. Upon this he retreated, but by April his
wound was so far cured that he was once again on the route
at the head of 30,000 men, vowing that on this occasion
he would reach Kyōto in good earnest. Nobunaga advanced
to meet him with an inferior force, but instead of offering
battle, he endeavoured to make peace. Takeda declined the
overture, and pushed onward into Mikawa. However, just
at this point his wound re-opened, and he suddenly died
(*ætat.* 53).

Among the five ablest men in Japan at this time this
Takeda must be accorded a foremost place. In Hideyoshi he
would have doubtless found more than his match; but in
soldiership he was certainly the equal either of Nobunaga or of
Uyesugi, while he was greatly superior to either of them as an
administrator. What Iyeyasu thought of Takeda's administrative system is abundantly shown by the fact that he made
a most careful and exhaustive study of it; that when Takeda's
former fief passed into his hands that system was not only
maintained intact in Kai, but many of its features were actually
introduced into the government of the Tokugawa family
domains. The death of Takeda Shingen at this critical juncture
was a stroke of the most consummate good luck for Nobunaga.
The great Takeda fiefs then passed into the hands of a man
of a very different stamp. Katsuyori, Shingen's second son,
owed his succession to the headship of the family to the
success of a dastardly intrigue by which he had done his
elder brother, a man of sterling ability, to death. The only
good quality he himself had inherited from his father was his
intrepid courage. Of his tact, of his statesmanship he
possessed extremely little. Before five years had gone he had
succeeded in alienating the goodwill of all the men of worth

in the clan; and ringed round as it was on all sides by the most formidable foes, in such a case its downfall became merely a question of time.

Thus providentially freed from the dire menace of Takeda Shingen, Nobunaga soon found himself confronted by an antagonist that bade fair to prove well-nigh as formidable. In 1574 Uyesugi Kenshin of Echigo, at the head of 30,000 men, had over-run the two provinces of Kaga and Noto in a brief campaign, and seemed to be on the point of forcing his way through to Kyōto as soon as the snows should melt. To check him, Nobunaga reared his famous new castle of Azuchi on the shores of Lake Biwa (March 1576), and leaving his son Nobutada in Gifu to observe Takeda Katsuyori, he took up his quarters in his new capital. Next year the storm broke. Uyesugi had arranged with Matsunaga Hisahide and Tsutsui Junkei in Yamato to fall upon Nobunaga himself from the south, while he assailed his captains in the north and drove them before him towards Kyōto. The operations in the south miscarried; but in the north Nobunaga's lieutenants tried to hold their ground in vain; and even when he appeared there in person, he judged a retreat to be advisable, and from his celerity in accomplishing it he drew a sarcastic compliment to his powers as a runner from Uyesugi. Next spring Uyesugi had levied another great force, and was just on the point of beginning his march when he was suddenly taken ill, and died (*ætat.* 49) soon after. His death was welcome news to Nobunaga. When he heard it he involuntarily dropped the object he was holding in his hand, and exclaimed with a sigh of mingled relief and exultation :—"Now the whole country is on the way to peace !"

Meanwhile by this date Takeda Katsuyori had had time to display his incompetence as a leader of men. During the first years of his rule he had been regarded as formidable by his neighbours, and an invasion of Mikawa by him in 1575 had really put Iyeyasu into very great straits, so much so that he had been constrained to send to Nobunaga for urgent succour. Nobunaga, accompanied by Hideyoshi, appeared on the scene in time to relieve Nagashino, the key to the province, gallantly held by Okudaira, one of Iyeyasu's captains who has immortalised himself by conducting one of the three classic

sieges of Japanese history.[5] In the subsequent operations
Katsuyori was hopelessly outwitted and outmanœuvred, and had
to make a precipitate retreat after losing the flower of his troops
and many of his veteran captains. This blow he tried to
retrieve by a marriage alliance with the Hōjō; but Iyeyasu
and Nobunaga, in spite of this alliance, kept eating into
his territories, and his officers began to desert. At last in 1581
Nobunaga made arrangements for the complete overthrow of
the House of Takeda. Katsuyori's father-in-law, Hōjō Ujimasa,
so far from now lending him aid, had actually entered into an
alliance with Iyeyasu, while his brother-in-law, one Kiso, had
entered Nobunaga's service, and had beaten one of his generals
at Torii-toge. With all this, it is hard to understand why the
confederates deemed such large forces necessary for the conquest
of a fief already falling asunder. Nobutada advanced from
Gifu with an army of 50,000; he was followed by his father,
Nobunaga, with 70,000 more; Iyeyasu was marching from
Suruga with 30,000 troops; and Hōjō with as many more from
the Kwantō; while a petty princelet moved 3,000 men from
Hida in support of all these! Katsuyori had mustered a matter
of 20,000 men to oppose Nobutada at Suwa; but by the time
Nobutada's columns had appeared there this force had melted
away like the snow off a dyke in April, and while Nobutada
entered Kōfu, the capital of the fief, unopposed, Katsuyori had to
flee to Tenmoku-san and there go into hiding. Here an expeditionary force surprised him with no more than forty followers,
and all that was left for the last of the stock of the Takedas was
to die a soldier's death (April 1582). In the distribution of the
four provinces that had belonged to Takeda, Suruga fell to
Iyeyasu, while such portions of the rest of the territory as were
not left in the hands of those officers of Takeda who had made a
timely surrender were parcelled out among captains of Nobunaga.

Meanwhile Nobunaga had been pushing his conquests in
Western Japan. He had at last disposed of his old foe Miyoshi,
and in 1577 Miyoshi's ally, Matsunaga, was defeated and slain
by Hideyoshi, who promptly pushed on into Harima and reduced
Araki and that province to subjection, whereupon Harima was

---

[5] The other two are Kusunoki Masatsura's defence of Kongo-san somewhere
about 1340, and Sanada's stand in Uyeda against Hidetada in the course of the
great Sekigahara campaign of 1600.

then bestowed upon Hideyoshi as a reward for his services. He had just laid a plan for the conquest of the whole of the Chūgoku before Nobunaga, and the project was at once approved. In the Chūgoku, by which is meant the sixteen western provinces of the main island, a new great feudal power had arisen. To that power some slight reference has been made in a preceding chapter; but inasmuch as the story of the rise of the Mōri family suffices to shed no small amount of light upon the feudal polity of the time, it is not unprofitable to enter into details at some little length.

Although it was that Mōri Motonari who avenged the death of Ōuchi, the Lord of Yamaguchi, and occupied (1556) his former fief, who is regarded as the founder of the House of Chōshiu, so famous in modern Japanese history, the Mōris could yet trace their lineage back to Ōye-no-Hiromoto, the great Minister of the great Yoritomo, towards the end of the twelfth century. The Mōris had settled in the province of Aki in the fourteenth century; but, to quote Sir Ernest Satow, "had occupied a very unimportant position amongst the local chieftains until a few years previously. Mōri Motonari was the son of a family which possessed about 2,500 acres, and as no provision for him could be carved out of the hereditary domain, he was given in adoption to a *samurai* who owned a little over 60 acres of land. To this small fief Mōri added about 6,600 acres more, the property of the High Constable of Aki, who had rebelled against the Shōgun and who was overthrown chiefly by Motonari's efforts. By the death of another relation without heirs he came into a third property of about 8,000 acres. In 1523, on the failure of heirs in the direct line of the Mōri family, he was chosen by the chief retainers to succeed to the headship, and thus obtained a larger field for the development of his talents as a soldier and a statesman. During the first few years after he obtained possession of the hereditary fief of his family he was a dependent of the Amako, then lords of the province of Idzumo, but he subsequently quarrelled with them and went over to the side of the Ōuchi [of Yamaguchi], whose chief, Yoshitaka, had given him aid in an unequal contest against his former suzerain. In that period of Japanese history the holders of small fiefs were nominally vassals of the Shōgun, but they usually found it convenient to attach themselves to some local chief of greater power than themselves, who was also in theory a vassal of the Shōgun. There were instances of this also in Chikuzen, where some of the less powerful *samurai* acknowledged fealty to Ōtomo, Lord of Bungo, though the whole of the province [of Chikuzen] was nominally under the sway of the Ōuchi of Yamaguchi.

"Just before he committed suicide [1551] Ōuchi Yóshitaka wrote a letter to Mōri Motonari entrusting to him the task of avenging his death. Motonari shed tears on reading it, and vowed to punish the treason, but for the moment was afraid to attack the successful rebel (Suye Harukata), then at the height of his power. By the advice of his officers he turned his attention to increasing his own military resources, whilst contriving to let it appear as if he were too weak for an enterprise of any importance. In 1553 he began to lay plans for an attack on Harukata, and called a council of his chief adherents. His son, Kobayakawa Takakage, advised that the Emperor should be requested to issue a commission for the punishment of the traitor because that would justify the war and conciliate public opinion. A memorial was therefore addressed to the Court dwelling upon the services of the Ōuchi family during successive generations and its unswerving loyalty to the throne, declaring Mōri Motonari's desire to punish the rebel who had murdered his lord, and begging that a commission might be granted to strengthen the avenger's arm. This was exactly what the Court desired. It had already, upon hearing of Ōuchi's death, given orders to the Shōgun and his lieutenants to march against Harukata (his murderer), but they had either refused or neglected to execute the mandate, and Mōri Motonari's petition was therefore granted with readiness."

On receiving his commission Mōri Motonari circulated copies of it far and wide, and at last, in June 1554, he and his sons put their forces in motion and began operations by capturing several fortresses in the west of Aki, which still belonged to the Ōuchi family. In the first engagement with Suye's troops, Mōri was victorious; but as the former soon appeared in the field at the head of 30,000 men, against whom Mōri could muster no more than a sixth of that number, Mōri thought it well, like Lysander, "to eke out the shortage in the lion's skin with the fox's."

Much against the advice of his officers he began to fortify the island of Miyajima off the coast of Aki, renowned throughout the Empire as one of the *san-kei*, or three famous landscapes of Japan. The fortress, with its redoubts on the opposite shore and on the islet of Niō, was completed and manned by the end of May 1555. Mōri now pretended to regret that he had wasted effort in fortifying a place that could be so easily taken, the fall of which must immediately be followed by the loss of

all his other fortresses, and he took care to spread about a report
to this effect in such a manner that it came to the ears of
the enemy. Suye fell into the trap. Towards the end of
September he marched down to Iwakuni with 20,000 men,
and, embarking his army in junks, easily made himself master
of Miyajima. He then dispatched a defiant message to Mōri,
who responded by at once occupying Kusatsu on the mainland,
just over against the island, thus cutting off Suye's retreat.
Most of the *samurai* of the province, holding Mōri's defeat to
be a certainty, held aloof from him, but he received an unexpected reinforcement from two chiefs of Iyo in Shikoku,
who placed 300 men at his disposal. Then under cover of
the darkness of a wild and tempestuous October night, Mōri
embarked his men and stood over to the island. On reaching
it he sent back his boats, thus leaving his followers the
simple choice of " do or die." Suye, fancying that no attack
was possible in such a terrible evening, had neglected to post
sentries ; and so when just as day broke the conches of Mōri
sounded the onset the confusion in the overcrowded camp was
overwhelming. The works were carried with a rush. All Suye's
efforts to rally his men were vain ; they fled wildly to their
junks, and thousands were drowned in trying to get on board.
Suye was extremely corpulent, and consequently unable to walk
fast. With a few followers he made his way to the strand,
hoping to find the means of escape ; but there was no boat to
be had, and so he committed *hara-kiri*, " according to custom."
Early in 1556 Iwakuni was assaulted and captured ; in May,
Yamaguchi was in Mōri's hands ; and after that his work
was easy.

By the year 1556 Mōri Motonari (then sixty years of age)
was master of Ōuchi's former provinces of Aki, Suwō, Nagato, and
Iwami in the main island, with more or less well-founded claims
to Chikuzen and Buzen across the water in Kyūshū. However,
when he endeavoured to enforce these claims he discovered that
the line of least resistance did not lie towards the south. In the
two campaigns of 1563 and 1569 especially he found that the
matchlock-equipped troops of Ōtomo of Bungo were really
formidable. In the latter year, while Mōri's main force was
prosecuting operations in Chikuzen, the Bungo men actually
invaded the Mōri domains, captured the capital, Yamaguchi,

and held it for some little time. But this ill-success in Kyūshū was amply atoned for by the brilliance of his achievements on his eastern frontiers. Before he died, at the age of seventy-five, in 1571, Mōri Motonari had not only fully settled accounts with his former suzerain, Amako, but he had overrun and added to the original provinces of Ōuchi those of Idzumo, Hōki, Oki, Inaba, Mimasaka, Bingo, Bitchiu, and Bizen. In this year (1571), when Mōri Motonari died lord of no fewer than eleven provinces and the island of Oki, even Nobunaga was undisputed master of no more than three! Mōri Motonari's successor was Mōri Terumoto, the son of Motonari's eldest son, who had died in 1563; and although the young chief was inferior to his grandfather in ability, he had the inestimable advantage of the counsel and support of Mōri Motonari's second and third sons, one of whom (Motoharu) had become the head of the House of Kikkawa, and the other (Takakage) chief of the Kobayakawa family. The death of the founder of the House did not serve to check the course of the Mōri conquests; within the next few years the eastern frontiers of the family were not inconsiderably advanced towards Kyōto and a footing established in Tango, Tajima, Tamba, and Harima, as well as on the north coast of Shikoku, while attempts had also been made on Miyoshi's former possession, the island of Awaji.

From all this it will readily appear what Hideyoshi's project of a conquest of the Chūgoku really signified. Yet the peasant commander contrived to prove that he had not over-estimated his capacities. Between 1578, when he had set forth on his first expedition against Mōri, and 1582, when Nobunaga was assassinated, besides overrunning Awaji he had driven Mōri from all foothold in Tamba, Tajima, Tango, and Inaba, had stripped him of Mimasaka and Bizen, and just at the very moment of the death of Nobunaga (20th June, 1582) he was on the point of receiving the surrender of the castle of Takamatsu, the key to the whole province of Bitchiu.

By the date of his death in 1582 Nobunaga had succeeded in extending his sway over thirty-two of the sixty-eight provinces of Japan. What made these provinces especially important was that they all lay compactly either immediately around the capital or within an extreme radius of some one hundred and fifty miles distance from it. Then Iyeyasu, Nobunaga's ally, had possessed himself of three provinces at least. Mōri Terumoto was still suzerain of nine; while the Hōjō domain in Eastern Japan covered five provinces. Down to 1579 the House of Ōtomo in Kyūshū had held as many. In the south of that island the Satsuma men had meanwhile added Hiūga to their two provinces of Ōsumi and Satsuma, and were rapidly over-running Ōtomo's domains. In Shikoku, also, something like a first-class feudal power had just been consolidated by Chōsokabe of Tosa. This Chōsokabe family, like the Ōuchi stock of Yamaguchi, who were the descendants of a Korean prince, was of continental origin, being reputedly of the lineage of Shikotei, who built the Great Wall of China. Certain incidents in its history during the fifteenth century are, like those just quoted in connection with the rise of the Mōri family, very instructive. During the wars of 1467–1489 most of the Court nobles found it advisable to withdraw from Kyōto; and one of them, Ichijō Kazubusa, went into hiding in Hyōgo. The Chōsokabe of that time, hearing of this, went to see him and invited him to return with him to Tosa, on the ground that Ichijō's father had once taught him certain necessary rules of Court etiquette while he was on a visit to Kyōto. What Chōsokabe really aimed at, however, was to strengthen himself by means of an alliance with a Court noble of high rank—as, indeed, all the warring feudal lords of Japan, most of whom were mere nobodies at Kyōto, were very eager to do. These Ichijō were nominated *Kokushiu* (Provincial Civilian Governor) of Tosa, and the family acquired a small fief in the extreme south-western horn of the island. In the latter half of the sixteenth century one of the Ichijō became a Christian, and was banished to Usuki in Bungo, where he contracted a matrimonial alliance with the House of Ōtomo; and it is to him the missionaries refer as the very virtuous exiled "King" of Tosa. Then the Chōsokabe (Motochika), contemporary with Nobunaga, made an end of the Ichijō as a feudal house; seized upon the former possessions of the Hosokawas, who had been the chief Ministers of the Ashikaga Shōguns; and, forcing the remaining chiefs to recognise him as suzerain, made himself acknowledged master of all the 7,029 square miles of Shikoku, except an odd 600 in the north-eastern province of Sanuki. Against this rapidly rising power Nobunaga had organised and dispatched an expedition under

Niwa, and it had got as far as Kishiu, whence it was to embark for Sanuki, when it was arrested by the news that Akechi Mitsuhide had revolted and murdered Nobunaga.[6]

Although this assassination is one of those commonplaces of Japanese history with which every schoolboy is familiar, it is questionable whether in the commonly accepted account we meet with the whole truth and nothing but the truth. About a year before, Hideyoshi, after four years' fighting in the West, had returned to see Nobunaga, and after a short rest he had been again summoned to take the field on receipt of the intelligence that Mōri had made a formidable irruption into the conquered provinces on the coast of the Sea of Japan, and had invested the castle of Tottori in Inaba. Instead of marching directly to the relief of that fortress, Hideyoshi made a sudden swoop on Awaji, which Mōri claimed, and then, hurrying on along the northern shores of the Inland Sea, quickly reduced two considerable fortresses in Bitchiu, and assaulted the castle of Takamatsu, the key to that province, and indeed to Mōri's position in the south. This strategy had the expected effect of relieving Tottori and of forcing Mōri to concentrate all his forces to raise the siege of Takamatsu, which, by clever military engineering, Hideyoshi soon brought to its last gasp. But feeling assured that his capture of this key to Mōri's domains would excite Nobunaga's jealousy if it were accomplished without his aid, Hideyoshi dispatched a courier to inform him of the situation, and to beg him to come to superintend the capture of Takamatsu and the repulse of the large relieving force that was now threatening the beleaguerers.[7] Nobunaga at once issued orders to his feudatories and officers, among whom were Hori, Tsutsui (afterwards one of the architects of Ōsaka castle), Ikeda, Akechi Mitsuhide, and Takayama Yūsho (Don Justo Ucondono of the Jesuits), to muster

---

[6] This took place on the 2nd of the sixth month of 1582, the year in which the Gregorian calendar was adopted in Italy, Spain, and Portugal. Froez gives the early morning of June 21st as the exact date of the occurrence.

[7] Such is the account given in most Japanese histories. Froez, however, writes:—"The King of Amangucci (i.e. Mōri), seeing himself so pressed, made a last effort and collected a very great army against Faxiba (Hideyoshi). He not having more than 20,000 to 25,000 troops, wrote to Nobunaga to send him help, *without coming in person*, because with 30,000 men more he could within a few days accomplish his design of chasing Mōri from his State, taking his life, and presenting his head to Nobunaga. But Nobunaga designed to go first to Kyōto and thence to Sakai, and then to finish the subjugation of Mōri and the other princes, and thus being supreme lord of the sixty-six kingdoms of Japan, to pass with a great armament to the conquest of China, leaving the kingdoms of Japan divided among his three sons."

their troops and advance at once, while he himself, accompanied
by Iyeyasu, purposed to follow in a day or two. Thus when
Nobunaga with a slender train of about a hundred men (instead
of the bodyguard of 2,000 with which he was usually
surrounded) entered Kyōto and took up his quarters in the
Honnōji, he found the capital entirely denuded of troops. As
Akechi was to march from his castle of Kameyama, which lay to
the west of Kyōto, there was no reason for him to enter the city ;
but on reaching the Katsura-gawa, instead of heading for the
west, he suddenly wheeled round, exclaiming, " The enemy is
in the Honnōji," entered Kyōto in the grey of morning, and
assailed Nobunaga in his quarters. The latter with his slender
train made a gallant but hopeless defence, and after receiving a
severe wound Nobunaga committed *hara-kiri* and was buried in
the wreck of the blazing temple. At the same time his eldest
son, Nobutada (the great friend of the Jesuits), who had
accompanied him, but who was quartered in another temple,
also fell in the general massacre.

As regards the motives by which Akechi was really actuated
on this occasion, there has been much speculation. The current
Japanese account of the matter is that Akechi suspected that
Nobunaga intended to deprive him of his fiefs in order to bestow
them on one Rammaru, a favourite page of his, who now
perished with him in Kyōto. What tended to strengthen
Akechi's suspicions was a series of insults offered to him by
Nobunaga just a little before. Iyeyasu had been coming to
visit Nobunaga, and Akechi had been charged with the duty
of furnishing forth the feasts in honour of the guest, and
after having been put to great expense, he found all his efforts
wasted by reason of Iyeyasu's · non-appearance. When this
happened a second time, Akechi went to Nobunaga and
expostulated, and Nobunaga being then, if not in his cups,
at all events in a roughly playful mood, seized Akechi, put his
head " in Chancery," and beat a tattoo on it with his heavy iron
fan ! Naturally enough, to the outraged feelings of a proud and
high-spirited man an apology of such a description would not be
very soothing, and Akechi may possibly have there and then
made up his mind to have a full settlement of accounts at the
earliest opportunity. However, it is possible that this revolt was
prompted by something more than mere personal resentment.

A distinguished writer has seen in this the indications of a widely-ramified conspiracy, of which Hideyoshi was not altogether ignorant, and in which Iyeyasu was most likely compromised,—chiefly on the ground that at that time he was close at hand with his troops in Sakai, and yet made no movement. But when it is stated that Iyeyasu had only a small body of men with him in Sakai, whither he had gone to wait for Nobunaga; that immediately on the murder of Nobunaga, troops had begun to surround Sakai in order to capture Iyeyasu; and that it was only by the friendly warning of a tea-grower of Uji that Iyeyasu was able to escape in time, it will be found somewhat difficult to accept Siebold's theory of Iyeyasu's complicity in the plot.[8]

The Jesuits' explanation of the matter is a comparatively simple one. Akechi they characterise as a man of an ambition out of all due proportion to his ability, although the measure of ability they attribute to him is the reverse of insignificant. They tell us that he was perhaps the cleverest draughtsman and engineer of the time; that as an officer he stood high, and that in counsel he had the reputation of being at once penetrating and adroit. That all this is most probably correct may be inferred from Akechi's rapid advancement in the service of Nobunaga. He had entered it when a *rōnin*, or lordless man, some time after Hideyoshi; and now in 1579–1582 we find him in possession of a fief reputed to be rated at 500,000 *koku*—as great as that of Hideyoshi's in Harima or of Shibata's in Echizen. Now it was not Nobunaga's use and wont to bestow fiefs of

8 We are told that Kamba Eshi, the tea-grower in question, and a great admirer of Iyeyasu, on hearing of the murder of Nobunaga, determined to get to Iyeyasu to inform him, but that he found it impossible to penetrate the cordon then being drawn around Sakai. So he dressed himself as a woman, pretended to be crazy, and, dancing fantastic dances, gradually worked his way through the guards. When he at last reached Hirakata, where Iyeyasu then was, he did not address him, but kept dancing and singing a song of warning, the purport of which Iyeyasu was not slow to seize, and so immediately got off in disguise. The way was infested by foot-pads; but the assistance of a friendly farmer enabled Iyeyasu to reach Ise, and from there he contrived to make his own province of Mikawa in safety.

From Froez we gather that Akechi and Iyeyasu were on very bad terms with each other. It had been originally intended that Iyeyasu should lodge with the Jesuits, and the latter assert that it was only his absence in Sakai that saved their premises from destruction. When Akechi wheeled round upon Kyōto his followers believed that it was Iyeyasu that was to be the object of their attack. The Jesuit church stood midway between the quarters of Nobunaga and those of his son, and a priest in it saw most of the fighting. After the death of Akechi the heads of the rebels were piled up in such heaps where Nobunaga fell that when the wind blew from that direction the stench drove the priests to close their doors.

500,000 *koku* upon *ci-devant* lordless men unless for very good consideration received. The missionaries will have it, then, that Akechi was consumed with a lust for power and supremacy, that he had an overweening belief in his own capacities, and that in the situation of affairs in June 1582 he discerned the psychological moment for the achievement of his most cherished desires. In Japan the possession of the capital, and more especially of the person of the Emperor, counted for more than much; and by his daring *coup de main* Akechi had not only secured this, but by a rapid dash on Azuchi he had made himself master of all Nobunaga's treasures. As for Nobunaga's two surviving sons, little was to be feared from them, for both were dullards and *fainéants*, while his brother officers were at this moment on the extreme confines of Nobunaga's dominions, busily occupied with formidable adversaries who might reasonably enough be expected to claim their whole attention, and so prevent them moving against him. Shibata in Echizen and Sakuma in Kaga were both hotly engaged with the great Uyesugi of Echigo, while Hideyoshi, who was on notoriously bad terms with Shibata and Sakuma, could not very well withdraw from the contest with Mōri. However, he *might* be able to do so, for Hideyoshi was a man of infinite resource; and so Akechi devised a scheme for the assassination of Hideyoshi in the course of his not impossible return to the capital which miscarried only by a hair's-breadth. As for Iyeyasu, Akechi seems to have made arrangements for surprising and entrapping him in Sakai. All things considered, and due attention being paid to the records of previous Japanese history, Akechi's attempt was by no means the mad one it is generally represented to be. It was simply one of those notorious attempts which can be justified (?) by nothing but success; and unfortunately for the ambitious Akechi, there was in Japan at that moment another man quite as ambitious as himself, and infinitely more able— Hideyoshi, to wit.

Meanwhile at Takamatsu, on hearing that Nobunaga was to march upon him with a *corps d'armée* of 30,000 men, Mōri sent an envoy to Hideyoshi to negotiate a peace. In most Japanese histories we are told that Hideyoshi declined the overture; but on the day after he heard of Nobunaga's death the castle fell, and on Mōri sending another envoy Hideyoshi informed Mōri of what had happened, and told him that he now had his choice of peace or a continuance of the strife. At a council of war Mōri's uncle, Kobayakawa Takakage, who if not actually a man of genius, seems to have been something very nearly akin to one, found himself the sole advocate of coming to an immediate understanding with Hideyoshi, whom he declared to be much more formidable now than Nobunaga ever could have proved. His arguments prevailed, peace was concluded, and Mōri actually lent Hideyoshi a body of troops when he set off towards the capital to deal with Akechi. However, there is strong reason for believing that this account is seriously incorrect. Professors Shigeno, Hoshino, and Kumé have adduced documents going to show that Hideyoshi was careful to conceal the death of Nobunaga from Mōri, while Froez expressly states that before divulging the death of Nobunaga to Mōri, Hideyoshi "concluded a very advantageous truce with him." In the following year (1583) there were some difficulties between Mōri and Hideyoshi; but they were smoothed over by the efforts of Kuroda, Hideyoshi's chief-of-staff, and Mōri's favourite, the priest Ankokuji Yekei. In the reduction of Kyūshū (1587) Mōri and Kobayakawa rendered Hideyoshi the greatest services, and at the death of Hideyoshi (1598) we find Mōri in possession of ten provinces with an assessment of 1,205,000 *koku*, Kobayakawa in Chikuzen with 522,500 *koku*, and two other members of the Mōri family with estates rated at 190,000 *koku* in Chikugo and Buzen—all, of course, owning Hideyoshi's supremacy.

Akechi, thirteen days after the murder of Nobunaga, was overthrown by Hideyoshi (with whom served Nobutada, Nobunaga's third son, and Takayama) at Yamazaki, and was killed by a peasant as he fled from the field. Shortly after (July 22nd, 1582) Nobunaga's captains assembled at Gifu to arrange for the succession to the headship of the House, and there after a stormy debate it was agreed that the infant Sambōshi (whose cause was espoused by Hideyoshi), the son of Nobutada, who had fallen with Nobunaga, should be acknowledged as the heir, under the guardianship of his uncles Nobuo and Nobutaka (each of whom had claimed the succession), and that the administration of affairs should be entrusted to a council composed of Shibata, Ikeda, Niwa, and Hideyoshi. However, the arrangement was a hollow one; and a bitter civil war between Nobunaga's three descendants, or rather between the rival captains who were merely using them as puppets, was felt to be inevitable. In the following spring it broke out. Nobutaka in Gifu in Mino, in league with Takigawa, the Daimyō of Ise, rose against Hideyoshi, who in the name of his ward Sambōshi was now carrying things with a high hand in the capital. When Hideyoshi marched upon and laid siege to Gifu he suddenly found his rear threatened by the advance of an overwhelming force of Shibata's from Echizen, supported by the levies of Sakuma of Kaga. Wheeling round quickly, Hideyoshi, by desperate efforts, was able to meet them at Shizugatake, on the Ōmi-Echizen frontier, and to defeat them so disastrously there that Echizen and Kaga almost at once passed into his hands, Shibata committing suicide and Sakuma being captured and executed in Kyōto. Shortly afterwards Nobutaka also committed the " happy dispatch."

Meanwhile, from all this imbroglio among the descendants and former captains of Nobunaga, Iyeyasu had been careful to hold himself aloof. On returning to his estates in June 1582 he had directed all his efforts to incorporate with them the adjacent fragments in the wreck of the fortunes of the House of Takeda. Suruga on the east was now annexed, while the Tokugawa frontier was pushed northward well on into the heart of Shinano. During 1582 and 1583 the power of Iyeyasu had increased tremendously. Then at the beginning of 1584 Nobuo, now the only surviving son of Nobunaga, seeing plainly from the fashion in which Hideyoshi was treating Sambōshi that he meant to sweep the House of Nobunaga aside and rule the country himself, took up arms and engaged Iyeyasu in his cause. Hideyoshi sent his nephew Hidetsugu to deal with them; and Hidetsugu was thoroughly beaten. Then when Hideyoshi took the field in person, he found, not indeed his over-match, but his equal in Iyeyasu; and as both had other pressing interests to attend to they thought it better to come to terms (November 1584) than to prolong this resultless Komakiyama war, as it is usually termed. Eighteen months later Hideyoshi's younger sister was given to Iyeyasu in marriage, Iyeyasu's son, Hideyasu, having been previously given in adoption to Hideyoshi; and shortly afterwards—but not till Hideyoshi's mother had been sent to him as a hostage—Iyeyasu proceeded to Kyōto, where Hideyoshi was now (1586) all-powerful. His attitude towards both Mōri and Iyeyasu, also towards Shimadzu and Uyesugi about the same time, or not much later, indicates that Hideyoshi was sometimes—in fact generally—more eager to conciliate than to crush. And in this respect, at least, he did not "copy" Nobunaga, as several of the missionaries assert he invariably did. Hideyoshi had fully recognised what Nobunaga never had perceived—that while the mailed fist may on occasion prove a very powerful and a very convincing argument, it is one, after all, that belongs to a comparatively primitive stage of culture. Hideyoshi was a genius; that Nobunaga who favoured the Christian priests, and who as a consequence reaped his reward in being committed by them to the pages of history as "this great prince," was at bottom and essentially merely a magnificent savage.

CHAPTER VII.

THE JESUITS, THE BONZES, AND NOBUNAGA: CHRISTIANITY IN KYŌTO—1559-1582.

IN the fourth chapter it was stated that when the *émeute* at Hakata and the riots in Hirado had thrown all the Jesuits together in Bungo, Torres, the Superior, at last found himself in a position to re-open missionary operations in Kyōto, the capital of the Empire. Some time before an aged *bonze* of Hiyei-san had written requesting him to send one of his *religieux*, if he could not come himself, to instruct him in the principles of the new religion. Accordingly Vilela was dispatched thither in the autumn of 1559, accompanied by Laurence, whom Xavier had baptized in Yamaguchi. On arriving at Sakamoto on Lake Biwa, at the foot of Hiyei-san, Vilela sent Laurence with a letter to a *bonze* " named Daizembo, who, on reading it, answered that his master, one of the chiefs of his Order, who had summoned us from Bungo, had died in the previous year, and that he himself having been left with limited means and no authority in the monastery, could be of no service to us. However, on the following day Vilela and I [Laurence's letter of June 4th, 1560] returned to him, and since he and ten *bonzes*, his disciples, seemed eager to hear us, we preached to them; and as we learned from them that no cult could be introduced into those places without the permission of the chief *bonze*, we made every effort to meet him. But as we could not do this, we finally begged the prefect of the town to be kind enough to introduce us to him. His reply was: 'If you have come to argue, you will be excluded; if for the purpose of seeing the buildings, that privilege must be bought with money and gifts.'" Thus repulsed, the two missionaries withdrew to Kyōto, where they went into lodgings. Twenty-five days after their arrival, "under the conduct of a *bonze*, one of the most respected men in the city, Vilela visited the Shōgun, by whom he was so amicably received, that as a mark of honour and friendship he drank out of the same cup

with him." Here, no doubt, the hand of Ōtomo had been at
work. Twenty years later we learn from a missionary letter that
it was " through Ōtomo's favours and letters that the Fathers
had been received in Kyōto," while we hear of him furnishing
valuable presents to priests proceeding to the capital " to be
offered to Nobunaga, according to the custom of the country."
The Shōgun assigned his visitors a house in a more frequented
part of the city, and soon all conditions of men crowded to
their quarters, to listen to them or to argue with them ; but " at
first with such obdurate hearts that they blasphemed the Word
of God when they heard it ; and partly even derided and made
mock of us." Two *Kugé* or Court nobles, like Nicodemus
of old, came stealthily under cover of night to hear of the new
doctrines, and were pleased to express their approbation of them,
while "one of the chief men of the town of Yamashina who
dwells in Kyōto and ten others became Christians." Shortly afterwards Vilela was conducted to Miyoshi by one of the chief men
of Kyōto to " ask for help," and the result was that the prefect
of the city sent notice to the various wards that the missionaries
were not to be molested. Meanwhile the *bonzes* had begun to
show hostility, probably not without reason, for Vilela was
nothing if not aggressive and delightfully free in his language,
and he and his companion had become so unpopular that their
landlord respectfully begged them to find other quarters. The
Buddhist priests were soon stigmatising their interloping rivals
as monkeys, foxes, possessed of the devil, and eaters of human
flesh, while the small boys also forgot all their good manners
and presented them with little-appreciated gifts of Japanese real
estate in the shape of mud and sand and stones. Yet with all
this, by the April of 1560 they had succeeded in making about
a hundred converts, among them being a noted monk of the
Shingon sect, whose example was soon followed by fifteen of
his fellows. Vilela's attacks upon the loose conduct of the
bonzes produced a salutary effect in one direction at least, for
the Superior of one of the Nichiren-shiu monasteries was
deposed by his sect because he kept concubines, took money
for teaching his "law," and ate flesh and fish in violation of his
vows.

In the summer of 1560 Vilela had another interview with
Yoshiteru, the Ashikaga Shōgun, and obtained from him the

issue of a decree threatening such as injured the missionaries or obstructed them in their work with death. Before the end of the year Vilela found it necessary to hire more commodious premises. Then the *bonzes*—stirred up by the Devil, he would have us believe, but more likely provoked by his own bitter tongue—again made themselves unpleasant. They raised a great amount of money by a general contribution, bribed the city officers, and induced them to order the slaughter of the two missionaries. This they proposed to do without referring the matter to the Shōgun, but one of his courtiers friendly to Vilela heard of the matter, and on the night before the projected attack on the church he got the missionaries to take refuge in a castle of his own six miles out of the city. Here they remained four days, and meanwhile it was arranged that before a final decision was reached as to whether they were to be expelled or not they should be allowed four months' grace. Before the end of this period the Shōgun was informed of what was passing, and he evinced so much resentment at the disregard of his former edict that the missionaries were left in possession of their church and in comparative peace. Shortly afterwards Vilela received orders from Torres to begin operations in the great mart of Sakai, and hither he betook himself in August 1561.

To-day Sakai with its 50,000 inhabitants is little more than a suburb of Ōsaka with its population of over 900,000 souls. But in those times the relations between the two places were vastly different, for Ōsaka, although not unimportant as the seat of the great fortress monastery of the Monto priests, was merely a small country town with little or no sea-borne trade at all. Sakai was then the great harbour and distributing centre for this section of Japan. The city, originally known as Sakai-no-Tsu, or the "boundary seaport," from its position on the confines of the three provinces of Idzumi, Kawachi, and Settsu, was not a particularly ancient one. Until the end of the fourteenth century, when a fortress was built there by Yamana Ujikiyo, it had been a mere village. For years after this, although it increased in wealth and population, it was in no way distinguished from the ordinary Japanese towns of the time, all clustering round the stronghold of some feudal lord, by whom they were governed and on whom they were wholly dependent. However, in time the people of Sakai had developed all the spirit and self-reliance of a mediæval Italian republic; they had expelled the feudal lord and had organised a municipal administration of their own which was entirely unique in the Empire. Says Vilela:—"From all the inconveniences of that war (1561) the city of Sakai was immune, as it is the most strongly fortified against hostile attacks of all the cities of Japan. For on the west it is washed by the sea, and in all other directions it is surrounded by exceedingly deep moats, always filled with water. It is totally free from all intestine tumults, and broils are scarcely ever heard of. All the streets have gates and guards, and the gates are immediately shut in case of need, so that criminals having no escape are at once arrested and haled to the tribunals. Yet if those who are at enmity with each other meet a stone's cast beyond the wall, they receive each other very badly." In a previous letter he tells us that "the city of Sakai is very extensive, exceedingly thronged with very many rich merchants, and governed by its own laws and customs in the fashion of Venice." In this great, busy, and law-abiding emporium the harvest reaped by Vilela was but scanty. "The people are affluent, and especially avid of dignities, and the Devil easily deters them by setting before them the insults and contumelies to which Christians are almost always exposed in this life if they wish to imitate their Lord and Saviour. Hence it is with great difficulty they come to be baptized, although in the midst of these difficulties about forty have been baptized." This was written in 1562, and in his letter of April 1563 he says:—"In this city of Sakai I have now indeed no hope of a speedy harvest. For the pride and levity of the inhabitants is such that they are unwilling to purchase heaven with the loss of honour and reputation."

Shortly after Vilela's arrival in Sakai, Kyōto and all the surrounding country became convulsed with a war which lasted a full year. The Shōgun was compelled to abandon the capital to the insurgents and to take refuge in his citadel. His uncle advanced to his relief with a strong force, but he was beaten in a series of engagements, and was ultimately held blockaded in a fortress some miles out of Kyōto. This was one of the many occasions when the arquebus-equipped monks

L 2

of Negoro, whose constitution Vilela found analogous to that
of the Knights of Rhodes, gave an earnest of their prowess
in the field, for it was they who had foiled the Shōgun's
uncle.

"The camps being pitched between Kyōto and Sakai, many
battles were fought, with the result that the *bonzes* always had the
best of it. At last, on the twentieth day, when it came to a general
engagement, the Shōgun's uncle was beaten and took refuge in a
fortress. The Shōgun in Kyōto, hearing of this, betook himself to
his citadel, abandoning the city, which was taken and fired and
pillaged by the enemy. And they, following up their victory,
advanced against the Shōgun's uncle and prepared to destroy his
forces utterly, when the Shōgun, collecting an army of 20,000 men
with the utmost secrecy, and passing a great river, suddenly and
unexpectedly fell upon the enemy with such vigour that, although
30,000 strong, they were beaten and routed. The Shōgun, then
joining his uncle, followed the fugitives to Kyōto and recovered
the city with such a slaughter of the foe that it is supposed that
by that victory matters have been decided for many years. The
opposing faction, fearing their utter destruction, begged the Shōgun
for peace, and obtained it through the interposition of the Vo
[*i.e.* Emperor]."

On the cessation of hostilities Vilela once more proceeded
to Kyōto, where the *bonzes* soon began to concert measures
against him. Pursuing the tactics he had adopted in Hirado,
he paid especial attention to the young converts, urging them
on to assail the doctrines and the immorality of the *bonzes* at
all times and seasons. Certain of them he charged with a
special study of one or other of the several sects, and some of
the brightest boys in Almeyda's Foundling Hospital in Bungo
were summoned to act as his instruments in this method of
warfare. The *bonzes* now appealed to Matsunaga Hisahide,
the Daihanji or Chief Judge of the city, requesting him to
proscribe the new doctrines. His reply was that before doing
so he wished to have accurate information about their nature
and general tendency. Two commissioners were appointed to
report upon them. As these were two *bonzes* who were supposed
to be bitterly hostile to Christianity, and as riots then broke
out in Kyōto, Vilela was urged to retire to Sakai. Within a
few months, however, he was recalled to the capital to—baptize
the two commissioners ! At the same time one of Miyoshi's
chief retainers also became a convert, while the Shōgun continued to show himself no less friendly than before. Vilela
had received letters from Yamaguchi telling him of Mōri's harsh

treatment of the converts there, and he now succeeded in getting
the Shōgun to write to Mōri informing him that he would be
pleased if he (Mōri) protected the Christians and help them
to restore their demolished church.   As it was just about this
time that his Highness, in response to their appeal, had sent down
a *Kugé* or Court noble to arrange matters between Mōri and
Ōtomo, this letter might have been expected to produce some
effect.   Before this, when Miyoshi's Christian retainer had gone to
Imori in Izumi, he sent for Laurence, and the latter baptized
sixty of the five thousand *samurai* then in or about the fortress.
Subsequently Vilela visited Miyoshi himself there, obtained the
promise of his protection for the converts, and made thirteen
baptisms.   By September 1564 churches had been established in
five walled towns, all within a distance of fifty miles from Kyōto.
Sakai and Imori were two of these, and Nara was a third.   In
none of these, however, did Christianity ever come to be of
much consequence.   But in another quarter, where it had
just been planted, it was to strike root and flourish vigorously.
A certain *samurai*, Takayama by name, had undertaken to
confute Vilela in public.   But the missionary had the best of the
discussion, and Takayama not merely admitted as much, but he
even insisted on carrying off the priest to his fortress some
dozen miles or so from Kyōto, and there received baptism
at his hands, together with his wife and all his children.   The
eldest of these, a boy of ten years, was destined to do more
for Christianity than any man in the Kyōto district,—than any
man in the whole of Japan, perhaps.   This lad, baptized
as Justus, is presently to appear as the famous Don Justo
Ucondono of the missionaries.   To anticipate matters somewhat,
we find that when in 1582 the total number of Christians
in Central and Eastern Japan stood at 24,500, no fewer than
18,000 of these were living in Don Justo's fief of Takatsuki.
Takayama's brother (Don Justo's uncle), the Lord of Sawa, fifty
miles east of Kyōto, was also converted in 1564, and in the
following year we find him imposing the foreign religion upon
all his dependents.

From 1559 down to the beginning of 1565, Vilela and
Laurence had been the only missionaries in the Kyōto district.
Then at last, in the January of that latter year, Froez and
Almeyda arrived in Sakai, the former to stay and assist Vilela,

the latter merely to report on the condition and prospects of
Christianity in the Home Provinces.[1]

Froez tells us that Vilela had had several interviews with
the Shōgun in previous years, and that he himself and Vilela
were admitted to a New Year's audience with his Highness in
1565. Those who then presented their respects filled a long suite
of waiting-rooms, and when admitted to the Shōgun's presence

[1] Almeyda and Froez were the two great letter-writers of that time. Both
were keen observers, and both were exceedingly careful and accurate. Almeyda,
who remained behind in Sakai for two months, in his long letter of October 1565
gives us an interesting account of a *Cha-no-yu* function in that city, an exhaustive
description of the temples and chief sights of Nara, and full details about the new
fortress Matsunaga Hisahide was then rearing there. This fortress is said by some
to have been the first of the Japanese castles in the new style which owed something to Portuguese ideas. Others maintain that Azuchiyama, built by Nobunaga
twelve years later, was the earliest of them. (See Prof. CHAMBERLAIN's *Things
Japanese*, 4th Edition, p. 150.) Matsunaga Hisahide was no Catholic, however,
but a devout follower of Nichiren. Vilela had been invited to Nara in
1563, and he was not quite sure about the reasons of the invitation. Possibly the
castle architects may have been anxious to consult him.

During 1565 Froez wrote a series of valuable letters. In one of these he tells
us that " silver mines abound in the district, which is sterile not so much through
the fault of Nature as the negligence of the inhabitants. . . . The Japanese are
in appearance bland and affable, but proud and haughty in reality. . . . A
merchant, however wealthy, is contemned; patricians [i.e. *samurai*], though of
slender means, retain their honour. They cling to their dignity with the utmost
tenacity, and vie with each other in empty ceremonies and verbal honours. Any
negligence in this respect often earns a man enemies for trifling cause. Poverty
(from which most of them suffer) they detest; so much so that in households
of scanty means, cruelly pitying the new-born children, especially females, they
do not hesitate to suffocate them by trampling on their necks. They almost all
have one wife each, and the highest as well as the lowest generally repudiate their
spouses for the very slightest cause, such as conceiving a child; and the wives
likewise (though more rarely) abandon their husbands and marry others. Among
relatives the right of marriage extends to those of the second degree. . . . In
Kyōto and Sakai the use of litters is very prevalent. [This use was later on
interdicted by Hideyoshi.] As for the education of their children, they correct
their faults with words only; and boys of six or seven are admonished no less
considerately and gravely than if they were adults or old men. They take great
delight in meeting strangers, and question them with the greatest curiosity
about foreign manners and observances even in the smallest matters. . . . They
hate all kinds of theft. If any one is detected in that crime, he is killed by
anybody with impunity. There are no public prisons, no jailers, no executioners
of the law. The heads of households take cognizance of capital offences
privately at home, and inflict capital punishment for the more serious offences
without the least delay. And by the resulting dread, the people are kept in
the path of duty."

After describing and praising a sermon by a *bonze* he heard in a Kyōto temple,
Froez tells us that he ceased to wonder how it was that the Buddhist priests were
held in so much respect and reverence by the people. " And as I reflected on
this it occurred to me that it was not without the strong prompting of the Holy
Spirit that Francis Xavier's mind was so eagerly bent upon this long journey to
Japan. For in truth these people, both in goodness of nature and excellence of
wit, surpass many nations of our Europe (be it said without offence to them). And
if the Portuguese merchants entertain a less exalted opinion, or express themselves
less enthusiastically about the Japanese, it is merely because their intercourse is
confined to the people of the ports, who are so far removed from the culture and
refined manners of those of the interior that they seem little short of rustics to the
latter. Accordingly the people of Kyōto generally term them savages in contempt,
although, indeed, the people of the sea-coast are very far from being destitute of
courtesy and good-breeding."

" he makes no reply to their words or their salutations. Only certain illustrious *bonzes* are so far honoured that he makes a slight inclination of the fan he holds in his hand. And in this way the men of the chief nobility are introduced, for to men of lower rank, no matter how rich, or how precious the gifts they bring, admission is absolutely denied. And since to pave the way for the Gospel, and to acquire reputation with the ruder people ignorant of true virtue and glory, it seemed highly expedient that the messengers of the Gospel should not be excluded, Vilela exerted himself that he also should be admitted to his presence at this season of the year. In former years he had been several times introduced through the kindness of a certain powerful man, well disposed towards the Christian religion ; and now through the services of the same, I [Froez] also obtained access." What was peculiar in this and similar functions at the Shōgun's Court at this time was that his Highness's mother and consort fully participated in the honour and respect then paid him. After their audience with Yoshiteru himself, the missionaries presented their respects to his spouse, and then, proceeding to another palace, to his mother. By her they were received with much courtesy and attention, and Froez, after lauding the "wonderful quiet, the wonderful modesty, and the wonderful domestic training" he saw around her, writes that "it is matter for poignant grief to see such a fine nature overpowered by such frauds of the Devil."

It was in the summer of this year of 1565 that the Shōgun Yoshiteru was murdered by Miyoshi and Matsunaga. If we are to believe Froez, this attack upon the Shōgun was an exceedingly treacherous one, for Miyoshi had just been the recipient of distinguished favours from his victim, by whom he was implicitly trusted. The conspirators moved 12,000 picked men to the neighbourhood of Kyōto, a thing Miyoshi could do without exciting any suspicion or alarm from the fact that he was Minister of War and commander of the Shōgun's levies. An invitation was then sent to Yoshiteru to meet Miyoshi and Matsunaga in a suburban monastery, but as the Shōgun just at this point had his apprehensions excited, he not only refused to go, but even prepared for flight. Unhappily for him, some of his courtiers dissuaded him from this step. Miyoshi now brought his troops close up to the city, and sent

a messenger to Yoshiteru to inform him that it was not his
life that was aimed at. What Miyoshi could not endure was
the predominance of certain of his relatives and friends in his
councils, and if the execution of a certain number of these
mentioned by name in a list the envoy carried was ordered,
everything would be well. The old courtier who met the envoy,
threw the list upon the ground, and after informing Yoshiteru
of the demand, committed *harakiri* in his presence, while four
of his fellows followed his example in the fore-court of the
palace. The conspirators now advanced upon the palace and
fired it, and Yoshiteru met his end fighting like a gallant
soldier. The hundred courtiers he had about him made a
most determined struggle; among them a boy of fourteen
astounded the assailants by his wonderful audacity, and they
all shouted "to take him alive. But he, seeing the fall of the
Shōgun, and holding it for foul disgrace to survive his king
and lord, at once threw away his sword, drew his dagger, and
first cutting his throat with it, drove it into his vitals."
Yoshiteru's mother and his youngest brother, who had become
a monk, were now slaughtered, as was also his consort, who
had at first made her escape to a monastery in the suburbs.
From this and other circumstances it is inferable that Miyoshi
and Matsunaga had regarded the ascendency of the two
ladies in Yoshiteru's Court and counsels with anything but
satisfaction.[2] The Shōgun's two daughters escaped, thanks to
the good offices of a Christian; his two sisters, both Buddhist
nuns, were not killed, though they were harshly treated; while
the elder of his two younger brothers, being at the time at Nara,
was not involved in the general slaughter. This brother, then
twenty-nine years of age, only a year younger than Yoshiteru,
had also become a *bonze*, like the youngest brother who was
then killed, and after some time he was taken from his
monastery and set up as puppet Shōgun by the conspirators.
However, somewhere in 1566 seemingly, their tool slipped out

[2] It is difficult to reconcile the very circumstantial details given in Froez's
letter of August 1565 with some statements in the *Miyoshi-Ki*. According to that
chronicle, Miyoshi Chōkei, the Shōgun's Prime Minister, died in 1564, after con-
fiding his adopted son, Miyoshi Yoshitsugu, to the care of his vassal Matsunaga.
The latter attempted to set his ward aside, and claimed the post of Prime Minister.
Because the Shōgun protested against this, Matsunaga rose against him and killed
him. On the other hand, Froez expressly makes Miyoshi himself the ringleader
of the revolt, and Matsunaga " cum alio quodam dynasta " merely an abettor and
participator in it.

of the hands of the conspirators, and, as has been already said, kept leading a fugitive life, appealing vainly to various territorial chiefs for assistance, until Nobunaga was approached. During all this time he owed much to the petty Lord of Kōka in Ōmi, Wada Iga-no-kami, who appears in the Jesuit letters and Church histories as Vatadono. "The brother of the deceased Cubo," says Froez, "escaping from the ward of the conspirators, fled, as a suppliant asking help, to Vatadono (a dynast in the kingdom of Ōmi); and the latter not only welcomed him kindly, maintaining him for more than a year in his citadel of Coca with great expense and munificence, loading himself with a great debt in consequence, but he did not cease to go round among the neighbouring princes soliciting them by every argument to restore the fugitive to his brother's position, until Nobunaga, the King of Voary, raising an army of 50,000 men and repressing the audacity of Mioxindono [Miyoshi] and Dajondono [Matsunaga], who had been the chiefs of the conspiracy, established the said exile in his brother's state and degree of most ample honour." As this Wada, or Vatadono, was an elder brother of that Takayama who had proved such an indefatigable propagandist since his conversion by Vilela in 1564, this turn of affairs was to prove exceedingly advantageous to the missionaries.

When the Shōgun was murdered in 1565, the two priests in Kyōto had been in imminent peril of their lives, for the *bonzes* who had been in sympathy with Miyoshi, and with Matsunaga more especially, had then urged them to kill the Jesuits. Thanks, however, to the good offices of Miyoshi's Christian secretary, they were permitted to retire, and shortly after the Emperor, at the instigation of Matsunaga and the *bonzes*, issued an edict proscribing the Christian religion and declaring it abominable. For nearly three years the missionaries were to see nothing of Kyōto. After a stay of more than a year in Sakai, Vilela went back to Kyūshū, and in 1568 we hear of him baptizing nearly everybody in the lately-founded town of Nagasaki, while Froez remained behind in the great emporium of Central Japan, busied not so much with its citizens as with the numerous strangers that resorted to it from time to time.[3] In the campaign that had established Yoshiaki as Shōgun, Wada, or Vatadono, had rendered substantial services to Nobunaga, for he had fought two stubborn actions with Miyoshi and Matsunaga near Sakai, in the latter of which he had routed them, while he had also maintained the castle of Akutagawa against all hostile attacks. At the instance of his brother Takayama he took advantage of his influence with Nobunaga to urge the recall of the foreign priests to Kyōto, and on March 26th, 1568, Takayama appeared in Sakai to conduct Froez to the capital. When the missionary reappeared there, a *bonze* went to Nobunaga and assured him in the tone of prophet that if the Doctor of the Christians was not expelled at once great calamities would ensue, and that the capital would be destroyed. Nobunaga coolly turned his back upon the priest, without vouchsafing him a word in reply, and merely remarked to the bystanders: " The fool! Does he take Kyōto for a village that could be destroyed by one unarmed stranger?" Shortly afterwards Vatadono took Froez to pay his respects to Nobunaga and to the Shōgun, but both of them declined to meet him—the former because he was listening to a

---

[3] While in Sakai the two missionaries had been invited to the University of Bandoue, by which is meant the school of Ashikaga in Bandō or the Kwantō. Writes Xavier (1549):—" Besides that of Kyōto, the five other chief Academies in Japan are the Coyana, the Negruensis, the Fissonia and the Homiana, which are all within moderate distances of Kyōto, and each of which is frequented by about 3,500 students, and the Banduensis, which is by far the greatest and most celebrated in all Japan, and the most remote from Kyōto." By the first two are meant Kōya-san and its off-shoot Negoro, both in Kii, and both belonging to the Shingon sect. The Fissonia was Hiyei-san, and the Homiana the Shinshin monastery of Kibe in Ōmi. The "University of Bandoue" at Ashikaga seems to have been originally founded as one of the numerous provincial schools established in Japan about the time of Charlemagne in Europe, and by the middle of the fifteenth century it had become the sole survivor of all these establishments. In the course of that century three successive heads of the Uyesugi family contributed to its funds and to its library, and under the patronage of that powerful House it soon attained a national reputation. About 1460 the priest Kaigen became its rector, and from that date onward it remained under the control of ecclesiastics of the Zen sect. One reason why we hear so much about it in the Jesuit letters is that one of the most important and intelligent of the converts Xavier had baptized in Yamaguchi had received his early training in it.

Froez wrote a History of Japan (1549-1579), which is still in manuscript in the library of Ajuda, and which has never been printed. Among the extracts from that manuscript given by Father Cros is the following:—"When the *universities* of Japan are spoken of, it must not be imagined that they resemble the universities of Europe. Most of the students are *bonzes*, or study to become *bonzes*, and the principal end of their work is to learn the Chinese and Japanese characters. They endeavour also to master the teachings of the different sects (that is, their theology); some little astronomy, some little medicine; but in the method of teaching and learning there is nothing of the strict system which characterises the schools of Europe. Furthermore, in Japan there is but one single University with a semblance of *United Faculties*; it is in the region of Bandou, in the place called Axicanga [Ashikaga]."

concert, and the latter on the plea of indisposition. Nobunaga
afterwards said that his refusal to meet the missionary was
because he did not know what compliment to make to a
stranger who had come so far. Vatadono, however, pressed
his point, and a little later on went with a train of thirty
men to fetch Froez, and this time conducted him into
Nobunaga's presence. The latter was on the drawbridge of
the new castle he was rearing, surrounded by a numerous
Court, and with 7,000 men under arms about him. Froez
saluted him in the Japanese fashion, but Nobunaga requested
him to rise, and to cover himself because the sun was hot,
and then asked him his age, how many years he had passed in
study, how long he had been in Japan, whether he counted
upon ever seeing his native land again, and whether, supposing
the Japanese did not become Christians, he would return to
India. Froez satisfied these queries in a few brief words;
only in reply to the last he said that if there were only one single
Christian in Japan he would remain to instruct and to fortify
him in the faith, but that he was not yet reduced to that, as
the number of believers in the Empire was very considerable.
"But why have you no house or church in Kyōto?" asked
Nobunaga. "Your Highness," answered Froez, "it is because
of the *bonzes* who have driven us out of those we had."

Now this reply served to disclose that the foreign priests
and Nobunaga had at least one thing in common—an enemy, to
wit. In this year of 1568 it was not as yet open and avowed
war between Nobunaga and the whole priesthood of Buddha.
But the strife had nevertheless begun. The monks, especially
those of the Nichiren-shiu, to which Matsunaga belonged,
had lent substantial support to the murderers of the Shōgun
Yoshiteru, and for this Nobunaga bore them a grudge. When
after his occupation of Kyōto he set to work to rebuild the
Shōgun's and the Emperor's palaces, he demolished several
neighbouring monasteries and made use of their materials in
the new structures, and when the supply of stone ran short
he ordered all the stone idols in Kyōto and the neighbourhood
to be broken up and utilised. It was then a common sight
to see the erstwhile tutelary divinities of the capital dragged
through the mud of the streets with ropes round their necks,
while Nobunaga made mock of all the futile clamour of the

bonzes. Then when he began his own new citadel in Kyōto he stripped some of the most famous temples of their woodwork and wainscoting for the benefit of his own palace. All the time that work on these buildings proceeded the only bell that was allowed to be sounded in the capital was the one in the citadel that summoned the workmen.[4] Froez's answer struck a sympathetic chord in Nobunaga, who then delivered himself of an invective against the *bonzes,* although there were several of them beside him at the time, among them some of the Monzeki, or abbots of the Imperial stock. Froez took advantage of this to commend his own religion, remarking that one must indeed be well convinced of the truth of his faith if he ventured to the very extremities of the earth to preach it. He further begged Nobunaga to assemble all the most famous and most learned *bonzes* in the Empire to meet him in a public discussion, offering to be punished as an impostor if vanquished, and expecting to have Nobunaga's protection for his cult if victorious. Thereupon Nobunaga turned to his courtiers and remarked that it was only a great country that could produce such a great mind, and then he said to Froez himself that he feared the *bonzes* would be readier to fight with the cold steel than to join issue with one who knew more than they. Froez now ventured to beg Nobunaga for letters-patent authorising the preaching of Christianity in Kyōto, but Nobunaga, although seeming to be favourably inclined, would give no definite answer to the request. He ordered Vatadono to conduct the missionary through all the apartments of the palace and over all the works, and when Froez repassed him on the drawbridge he inquired of him if he was pleased with what he had seen.

---

[4] In this work, by the way, discipline of the sternest was maintained. The only access to the place was by drawbridge; and here Nobunaga was usually to be found, clad in a tiger-skin, with scimitar in hand and thousands of armed men around him. There were sometimes as many as 25,000, and never fewer than 14,000, men at work, and among these there was not even the semblance of disorder. Once Nobunaga observed a soldier offer some slight incivility to a woman; he at once strode over to the man, struck off his head with his sword, and coolly and without saying a word returned to his position, and resumed the conversation that had been interrupted for a moment, as if nothing had happened. Even at that date the former petty Owari lordling had inspired those he met with a most wholesome dread of him. On this occasion we are told "even princes and lords did not disdain to put their hands to the work, and to mingle with the crowd of workers, by way of paying court to Nobunaga, and were only too happy when he deigned to favour them with a look."

Of course Froez would have been no Jesuit if he had failed to return a courtier's answer to the query. When he said that he had as yet seen nothing in the whole world which had impressed him so much, his compliment was well received, and Nobunaga was flattered to find that a European admired what he was doing.

This first interview of a Jesuit, or indeed of a European, with Nobunaga has been dealt with at what may seem disproportionate length, to the neglect of weightier matters. But it must be remembered that the fortunes of Christianity in the Kyōto district owed much to the favourable regard of Nobunaga, and that it was Froez who did the most of all his fellows to conciliate the goodwill of the all-powerful ruler. As has been remarked, this interview on the drawbridge took place in the summer of 1568, and during the remaining fourteen years of his life Nobunaga kept up an intimate intercourse with the few foreigners in Kyōto. Here, again, it may be well to have precise ideas about the actual numbers of the Jesuits then in these regions, for many worthy writers seem to imagine that they were to be counted by scores. On this occasion Froez's stay in Kyōto extended from 1568 to the beginning of 1576, and for more than the first three years of that term he was the sole European in the capital of Japan. He had, however, a right trusty and able henchman in the person of the Japanese Brother, Laurence. About 1572 he was joined by Father Organtino Gnecchi (or Soldi), and from this date there were usually two Jesuit Fathers and as many Brothers in Kyōto and the Home Provinces. Then in 1579 these numbers were doubled, while in 1582, the year of the death of Nobunaga, there were five Fathers and nine Brothers in this section of the Empire distributed among four Residencies. Now, the Jesuits who chiefly came in contact with Nobunaga were Froez and Organtino Gnecchi; Cabral, the Vice-Provincial, was entertained by him in his castle of Gifu when on a visit to Central Japan in 1572; while Valegnani, the Visitor-General, was hospitably welcomed at Azuchi and had several other interviews with Nobunaga in 1581. As it was from Froez that Nobunaga got his first impressions of Europeans and of Christianity, as for more than three years Froez was the only European priest he saw, and as the impressions he gleaned at this time counted for much in determining his subsequent general attitude towards the Jesuits and their converts, Froez's movements and proceedings at this time are really of some considerable importance.

Two days after his interview with Nobunaga on the draw-bridge the Jesuit was conducted by Vatadono to an audience with the new Shōgun, Yoshiaki. Before the end of the year he had the satisfaction of obtaining "Patents for the Safety of the Father of the Christian Religion in the Chapel of the True Doctrine, as it is called." The *bonzes*, however, made every effort to get the document cancelled and Christianity once more proscribed ; and, failing to impress Nobunaga with their arguments, they appealed to the Emperor (the Dairi). The latter had already once proscribed the foreign religion (1565), and he now signed another decree against it shortly after Nobunaga had left Kyōto for his own domains at the beginning of the autumn of 1568. The chief agent employed by the monks in accomplishing their purpose on this occasion was a certain Nichijo Shonin, who, after being first a soldier and then a brigand, and, according to the Church historians, after having earned a unique reputation for scoundrelism by the commission of every conceivable kind of crime, had sought respectability·by accepting the tonsure. In person he was insignificant and deformed even to the verge of monstrosity ; "but the beauty and vivacity of his mind amply indemnified him for the deformity of his body ; above all he possessed in sovereign degree that courtierly address and dexterity of which princes are so frequently the dupes. He was not learned ; but a happy memory, a wonderful facility in expressing himself, and a boldness which amounted to impudence served him in lieu of study, and he spoke of everything with as much assurance as if he had grown pale by reason of a lifetime spent over his books. The Dairi [Emperor] had employed him in arranging certain matters with Nobunaga, and the latter took a liking to him, and made him his favourite, or rather his buffoon." The truth was that in this age, when Japanese scholarship was at a very low ebb, and mere high birth counted for little, any able man who could make himself interesting had little difficulty in making his way. This sketch of Nichi the *bonze*, as Froez calls him, might well have served for a portrait of Hideyoshi, with the change of a very few of its strokes. On learning of what the *bonzes* were aiming at, Vatadono had urged Froez to see Nobunaga before he left Kyōto for his own fiefs. The missionary, who was accompanied by Laurence, was very well received by Nobunaga, who was found surrounded by a brilliant Court, and Froez then made request that Vatadono should be charged to protect the Christians during Nobunaga's absence. Nichi (Nichijo Shonin), who down to this date was unknown to Froez, was present, and Nobunaga, wishing to amuse himself by pitting the two priests against each other, inquired of Froez why the *bonzes* hated the Portuguese doctors so bitterly. "Because we expose the errors of their doctrine to the great and the learned, and the corruption of their morals to the people," was the reply. Nobunaga then went on to ask a series of innocent-looking questions which he knew perfectly well would lead to a lively scene, and Nichi soon took a part in the discussion. Presently it became very hot, and it was not long before the *bonze* was shouting with all the strength of his lungs that this "European *canaille* that seduced the people with its tricks ought to be hunted from the Empire." Nobunaga made him calm himself, and then raised a discussion on the immortality of the soul, in the course of which the monk seized a sword hanging on the wall with the intention of cutting off Laurence's head in order to see a soul living after the death of the body it animated. This scene is interesting, as it is here that Hideyoshi makes his first appearance in the Jesuits' letters. He was then present, and he it was (together with Vatadono) who seized Nichi and disarmed him before he did any damage.[5]

---

[5] In the famous interview between the Vice-Provincial Coelho (then accompanied by Froes and Laurence) and Hideyoshi in Ōsaka Castle eighteen years later (May 4th, 1586) this incident was alluded to by the latter. "And recalling here a discussion which Froes and Laurence had had in Kyōto in Nobunaga's presence with a *bonze* called Nici Tozomiri, in which the *bonze*, seeing himself vanquished, became so furious that he laid hands on a scimitar of Nobunaga's to kill Brother Laurence, he [Hideyoshi] said with reference to it: 'I was present then, and I was of the same opinion as you.' And getting up, he approached Brother Laurence, who was already an old man, and placing his hand on his head, he said, 'He knows all that I say very well: and if that is so, why do you keep silence and not speak?' He then added that if such a thing were to take place in these times of his, a similar discourtesy would have to be paid for with life."

The incident in question is also remarkable from the fact that three of the chief participants in it were perhaps the ugliest men in Japan. Of the *bonze's* personal appearance something has just been said. Hideyoshi, little better than a dwarf, was a bye-word among his fellows for his monkey-like physiognomy.

On Nobunaga's return to Gifu, Vatadono seems to have been left as his lieutenant in Kyōto and the Home Provinces; at all events, we know from Japanese authorities that when the Miyoshi partisans assailed the new Shōgun Yoshiaki in his temporary residence in the Hongokuji it was Wada Iga-no-kami who fell upon and routed them in Kyōto.[6] Between him and the *bonzes'* representative, Nichi (Nichijo Shonin), there was now a sharp contest about Froez. The monk succeeded in obtaining letters of proscription against the two missionaries from the Emperor (Dairi) soon after Nobunaga had left the capital, and the Emperor had furthermore written to Nobunaga that it was neither his province nor that of the Shōgun to authorise a foreign religion by patent. Nobunaga took no offence at this communication, but on Vatadono communicating its purport to the Shōgun, Yoshiaki sent word to the Emperor that the foreigner was under his protection, and that whoever molested him would have to answer to him (the Shōgun). The Emperor pressed the matter, but Yoshiaki stood firm; and Nichi then publishing it abroad that he had asked and obtained permission from the Dairi to kill Froez, Vatadono sent word to Froez's neighbours that they would be held answerable with their lives for

---

Charlevoix tells us that he "was of very diminutive stature, pretty fat, and extremely strong; he had six fingers on one of his hands and something hideous in his presence and in the traits of his countenance He had no beard, and his eyes stood out from his head in such an ugly fashion that it was painful to look at him." Froes, in his unprinted History of Japan (1549–79), tells us that Laurence "had a very comical face" (*de muy ridiculosa fisionomia*). He was more than half blind, for he had lost the use of one eye entirely, and was very badly served by the other. He was a native of Hizen, and when Xavier met him at Yamaguchi he was earning his living by going round among the houses of the *samurai* amusing them by chanting ballads to the viola—a Japanese edition, if not of Homer, at all events of an old rhapsodist.

6 Charlevoix calls Vatadono Viceroy or Governor of Kyōto. But this is a mistake, for Murai, who appears as Moraidono, or Muraidono, in the missionary letters, was the first Governor of Kyōto appointed by Nobunaga, and Murai did not assume office before 1577. We get an idea of the Kyōto Murai administered from the unpublished manuscript of an unnamed Jesuit whom Father Cros cites as the "Annalist of Macao." "When we went to Japan in 1577 we found Kyōto very wretched. There were two quarters (*barrios*) formed by a single street running north and south, with a few transverse lanes. The best houses, those of the *kugé*, were of very poor exterior, and the *kugé* themselves were indigent and poorly clad. What remained of the palace of the Shōgun, after the fire and sack of 1565, was protected only by an *enceinte* made of earth and reeds, which had already fallen into ruins. . . . The town properly so called (without speaking of four immense suburbs) formed a square, with a side of 2,764 geometric paces. . . . As to the number of houses, a popular proverb spoke of the "98,000 fires of Kyōto," without comprising the number of fires in the four suburbs,—108,000, —in all 206,000 fires (or houses)." This would mean a population of between 900,000 and 1,000,000.

any mishap that might befall him. However, as Nichi's influence was increasing so much with Nobunaga that the Shōgun as well as Vatadono was becoming jealous of him, Froez did not feel altogether at his ease. A little later, on Vatadono's retiring to his fief of- Takatsuki, Nichi resumed his efforts to get the Shōgun to consent to the publication of the edict of proscription already signed by the Emperor. Vatadono, learning of this from Froez, wrote a very civil letter to the monk requesting him to accept the situation and to desist from his efforts. Some sentences in Nichi's reply to this communication are noteworthy. " Five years ago," he wrote, " the Dairi expelled Father Froez from Japan; to oppose such a weighty decree is a crime, of which there has been no example till you were in the post you now hold. From the beginning of the world the word of the Dairi has been as the sweat of the body, which never goes back. It has been reserved for you to commit a crime like this."

On Vatadono's advice, Froez now hurried off to appeal to Nobunaga in Gifu, armed with a letter of introduction to Vatadono's friend Shibata, Nobunaga's Chief Councillor and right-hand man at this time. Froez has left us a long account of all that befell him and of all he saw or was shown on this visit of his to the new citadel of Gifu. The kindness and courtesy with which he was welcomed by the haughty and ruthless Nobunaga were indeed remarkable, " every one being vastly surprised at his treating a poor foreigner without character as he never treated any prince, for never was there ruler in Japan who made himself less familiar than Nobunaga, or took more pleasure in humiliating people of the highest distinction." Froez stayed four or five days in Gifu, during which he had several long interviews with Nobunaga. He was shown over all the apartments of the palace and all the works of the citadel, Nobunaga standing two hours beside him on the highest point of the donjon, pointing out all that was remarkable in the landscape beneath and before them. But what was most to the purpose was that Nobunaga, not content with the very mildly worded memoir Froez had drawn up for presentation to the Shōgun, at once ordered his secretary to write two others of much greater force—one for the Shōgun and the other for the Emperor—and delivered these to Froez, while he told him not to trouble himself about what was going on in their Courts, as it was with himself alone that the missionary would henceforth have to deal. On Froez's returning to Kyōto and making report to Vatadono, the latter penned another polite note to Nichi. "The Father of the Christians," it ran, "proceeded a few days ago to the Court of Nobunaga, who received him with a truly remarkable distinction, and has requested me to favour him in every way I can. This is the reason of my writing you these few lines to beg you to advocate his interests with the Dairi, and you may count upon my being duly grateful for your kindness in so doing." Stung to fury by this, Nichi wrote a rude and haughty reply, and posted off to Nobunaga himself. Here, however, Vatadono had been beforehand with him, and had written to Shibata and others explaining the situation, and Nichi found himself roughly and brusquely repulsed. On returning to Kyōto in high dudgeon, in concert with some of the monks of Hiyei-san he concerted a most ingenious plot against Vatadono, with the result that the latter lost all credit with Nobunaga for the time, was stripped of his offices, deprived of most of his revenues, and had one of his castles razed. Within a few months, however, before the end of 1569, his friends succeeded in unravelling the intrigue and placing the facts before Nobunaga, who was not slow to re-admit Vatadono into his favour, and shortly after his return to Kyōto he ordered Nichi to be put to death. The Emperor interceded for him, however, and his life was spared, although he was left with little or nothing to support it. Under the protection of Vatadono, and favoured by Nobunaga himself, Froez could now live in Kyōto with less anxiety than before. Early in 1571, however, Vatadono was killed in a quarrel with a local chief not far from his own castle of Takatsuki. It is questionable whether this event was really such a serious blow to Christianity as it seemed. Vatadono, although exerting himself strenuously on Froez's behalf, had never been baptized, but his younger brother Takayama was not only a convert, but a most zealous propagandist, and it was Takayama who now succeeded to the Takatsuki estates. During the five years he continued to administer them he spared no legitimate effort to induce his subjects to embrace the foreign religion. It is to be noted and imputed to Takayama for righteousness that his methods of making proselytes were thoroughly legitimate and very different from those adopted by the princelets of Ōmura, Arima, and Amakusa, and later on by his own son, the famous Don Justo Ucondono. In 1576 Takayama handed over his fief to this Don Justo (then twenty-two years of age), and devoted all his time to preaching the Gospel to his subjects and to attaching them to the faith by the exercise of a humane and whole-hearted charity which extended to believer and non-believer alike. The result was that in 1579, when the aggregate number of Christians in the main island of Japan stood at 15,000, more than 8,000 of these were living on the Takatsuki fief. And that there had been little or no persecution there down to that date may be inferred from the fact that 17,000 of the Takatsuki vassals and peasants still adhered to the national cults.

Although Nobunaga had had difficulties with the Buddhist priests before 1570, it was in that year, shortly after Nichi's disgrace, that they began to evince a determined and organised hostility against him. At this date Miyoshi and Matsunaga, who had been merely scotched in 1567-68, again appeared in force in the provinces of Idzumi and Settsu.[7] In the latter year the Monto sect of Buddhists had established their headquarters at what is now the city of Ōsaka in 1532, and the monastery had assumed the nature of a fortress. Kennio Kosa, who was more of a soldier than of a priest, now made common cause with Miyoshi and Matsunaga, and contributed in no small measure to foiling Nobunaga by provisioning two of the fortresses he assailed. Whereupon Nobunaga vowed the extermination of the sect, high-priest and all. Among Nobunaga's own followers were many who held the Monto creed, and two of them secretly betrayed his designs to Kennio, who promptly proceeded to make his monastery-fortress impregnable. This he was able to do at considerable leisure, as Nobunaga's foes, Asakura of Echizen and Asai of Ōmi, had just marched upon the capital, purposing to occupy it in his absence. When Nobunaga wheeled round upon them

---

[7] It ought to be stated that according to Japanese authorities there was a quarrel and a war between Matsunaga and Miyoshi between 1565 and 1567. The matter is not important, as it had no effect upon the general contemporary history of the Empire.

they retired to Hiyei-san, and here, provisioned and supported
by the priests, they were beyond his reach, and he had to
spend some fruitless months in blockading them. When they at
last sued for peace, and obtained it through the intercession
of the Shōgun Yoshiaki, Nobunaga was fully determined that
the monks of Hiyei-san should never baulk him again. This
time, however, he kept his own counsel, and during the next
nine months or so he seemed to be thinking of anything but
the priests. Then in the September of that year he advanced
with a strong army from Gifu in Mino towards Kyōto,
ostensibly to reduce the province of Settsu. However, on
arriving at Seta he summoned his officers and informed them
that Hiyei-san was their objective. When some of them
ventured to remonstrate against the sacrilege of destroying
the most famous monasteries in Japan, which had an unbroken
history of nearly seven hundred years, Nobunaga informed
them that so long as these monasteries existed his projects
would be continually thwarted, and that they were a prime
source of the national disorder and anarchy he was striving
so hard to suppress. " If I do not take them away now, this
great trouble will be everlasting. Moreover, these priests
violate their vows; they eat fish and stinking vegetables,
keep concubines, and never unroll the sacred books. How can
they be vigilant against evil, or maintain the right? Surround
their dens and burn them, and suffer none within them
to live ! "

Thus taken suddenly and by surprise, the *bonzes* saw that
they were lost if they could not agree with the adversary at
their gates at once. They offered Nobunaga a huge ransom,
while they at the same time engaged the Emperor and the
Shōgun to write to him on their behalf. But all was vain ;
Sakamoto, on the lake shore at the foot of the hill, was at
once fired, and the assailants then stormed and burnt the
monasteries on the lower slopes of Hiyei-san. If we are to
believe Froez, however, the fighting farther up and on the
higher scarps and spurs of the mountain was severe and
protracted, the *bonzes* making a most vigorous defence of some
of the exceedingly strong positions on the rocks and in the
defiles. The final assault, delivered on September 29th, 1571,
ended in the extermination of every occupant of the three

thousand monasteries that had studded the faces of the mountain and its thirteen valleys a week or so before.

How many priests actually perished in this grim massacre cannot be stated with accuracy; at the lowest computation there must have been several thousands,—possibly many thousands of them. It was indeed a terrible blow to Buddhist monasticism; but to imagine that it sufficed to crush the *bonzes* as a political force would be perilously wrong. Hiyei-san, it must be conceded, from its proximity to the capital, from its long history, its traditional fame as the cradle of all the most important sects in Japan (the Shingon alone excepted), its vast wealth, and the ability of its abbots and chief priests, appealed to the imagination of the religious as no other holy place in the Empire did. But at this date there were seven thousand monks in the Shingon monastery of Kōya-san, and besides these it sheltered a still greater number of armed retainers. Its offshoot at Negoro, not far off, was now as powerful as it had been in 1561–62, when it had assumed the offensive against the forces of the Shōgun, and worsted them in the open field. Then the Monto priests, as has been said in the introductory chapter, constituted a first-class feudal power. The whole of the province of Kaga, and parts of Echizen, Noto and Etchiu belonged to them, while their head, Kennio Kosa, had just turned his monastery at Ōsaka into one of the strongest, if not indeed the strongest, fortress in the home provinces. It was against this stronghold that Nobunaga purposed to direct all his powers; but for the next three years he had too many other foes upon his hands to be able to invest Kennio, who meantime actually assumed the offensive, supported by Miyoshi and Matsunaga.

In 1574 Nobunaga at last advanced upon Ōsaka, but all that passed on this occasion was—two months. In 1576 another attempt was made, but the fortress was found to be impregnable, and Nobunaga had to convert the siege into a blockade, hoping to reduce his foe by starvation. Two years later (1578) Nobutada, Nobunaga's eldest son, led a great force to the storm of Ōsaka, but he was repulsed with terrible slaughter. Next year Kennio had the assistance of Araki of Settsu, and Mōri of Nagato, but by this time Nobunaga had no other enemies to meet, and so Mōri was repulsed and Araki driven to take refuge with

Kennio in Ōsaka, while Nobunaga's army of sixty thousand
men sat down outside the *enceinte*, within which, crowded
in the five connecting fortresses, were thousands of women
and children, besides the priests and their retainers.
Provisions were none too plentiful among the besieged, and
to reduce the number of mouths to be fed several thousands
of useless old men, women, and children attempted to
escape from one of the forts under cover of a pitchy night
when a furious storm was raging. Next morning a junk
with a gruesome load of human ears and noses that
dropped down stream past the besieged informed them of
the fate of the escapees. Shortly after, the beleaguered
made a desperate sortie, but it was beaten back, although
with severe loss to the investing troops, and not long after
the assailants were in possession of three of the five connecting
strongholds. The slaughter had been immense, and the stench
of burning flesh poisoned the air for miles around. Just at
this point the Emperor sent three Court nobles and a priest
of another sect to arrange a surrender before things were
pushed to the very last extremity. Even then Nobunaga was
by no means certain that the fall of the remaining forts would
be speedy; Kennio, who had escaped from the beleaguered
stronghold four months before (May, 1580), would probably soon
appear with a relieving force, while Nobunaga's own troops
were now pinched for supplies. Accordingly it was not
difficult to come to terms; in exchange for certain lands elsewhere Kiō-nio (Kennio's son), who now commanded in Ōsaka,
was to surrender it to Nobunaga, and to march out with
all the survivors of the siege. All that fell to the victors,
however, was a fine strategical position and a heap of
blackened ruins, for Kiō-nio had fired the monastery before
he evacuated it. This contest, which had gone on (sometimes indeed in a desultory fashion) for fully ten years, had
seriously impeded Nobunaga in the general subjugation of
the Empire. Seven years later (1587) we find Hideyoshi asserting that Kennio had given Nobunaga more trouble than all his
other enemies combined.

In the previous year (1579) Nobunaga had been enabled to
deal another Buddhist sect a staggering blow. For some time
there had been a bitter strife between the Jōdō priests and those

of the Nichirenshiu, and they had been so ill advised as to appeal to Nobunaga to pronounce judgement on the matter after it had been fully debated in his presence. He accepted the office, with the proviso that the champions of the losing side should be scourged and decapitated. The discussion, famous as the *Azuchi Ron*, took place in Nobunaga's new castle of Azuchi. The Nichirenshiu advocates had to confess that they had had the worst of the debate, and thereupon Nobunaga not only exacted the full penalty from them, but he furthermore seized most of the other leading priests of the sect and deported them to a desert island, while such swingeing mulcts were imposed on the sect that its members, finding payment impossible, had to seek refuge in quarters where the heavy hand of Nobunaga was not as yet felt. This incident caused the greatest rejoicing among the Jesuits and their converts,[8] who began to regard Nobunaga as the chosen but unconscious instrument of God. Says Coelho (Annual Letter of 1582):—

"This man seems to have been chosen by God to open and prepare the way for our holy faith, without understanding what he is doing, because he not only has little respect for the *Kami* and the *Hotoke*, whom the Japanese worship with such devotion, but he is furthermore the capital enemy and persecutor of the *bonzes*, inasmuch as among the various sects many are rich and powerful and lords of great fortresses and rich territories, and by their opposition they have often put him into great straits; and if it had not been for the *bonzes* he would now be lord of the whole of Japan. For this reason he is so hostile to them that he aims at their total ruin. . . . On the other hand, in proportion to the intensity of his enmity to the *bonzes* and their sects, is his good will towards our Fathers who preach the law of God, whence he has shown them so many favours that his subjects are amazed, and unable to divine what he is aiming at in this."

It may be well to dwell at some further length upon Nobunaga's intercourse with the Jesuits. The Vice-Provincial Cabral, as has been mentioned, came up to Kyōto on his first visit at the

---

[8] In the Annual Letter of 1579 we are informed that "all the temples and monasteries of this sect in the four kingdoms around Kyōto were promptly ruined, destroyed, and burned; and the *bonzes* were much persecuted and dishonoured even in Kyōto. Nobunaga had resolved either to abolish this sect utterly, or to condemn them to pay so much that it would either be impossible for them to pay it, or that the payment of it would annihilate them, or reduce them to abject poverty. This was of no small importance in facilitating the sowing of our holy faith in these parts; because these *bonzes* were numerous and rich and proud, and opposed to the Christian law in the highest degree. Thus in future we shall have fewer enemies. The number of the monasteries and *bonzes* seems incredible; although the temples ruined formerly and during the last few days by Nobunaga appear infinite, yet with all that they do not come to an end."

end of 1571. Early in the following year, accompanied by
Froez and Laurence, he went to present his respects to Nobunaga
at Gifu. The latter was then about to give audience to certain
envoys and lords, but he told them to wait as soon as he heard
of the arrival of the missionaries, and ordered the priests to
be introduced at once. After a long discussion on religion
Nobunaga turned to his courtiers and said :—"There are the
men whom I like,—upright, sincere, and who tell me solid things,
while the *bonzes*, with their *Kami* and their *Hotoke*, regale us
with fables, and are real hypocrites." Shortly afterwards he
dismissed all the attendants, except a lord of Kyōto who had
come as envoy from the Shōgun, and sat down to dinner with the
Jesuits and this lord. As chance would have it, the latter was
a bitter enemy of the missionaries, and Nobunaga now told him
that a change of attitude in this matter was expected from him.
After being shown over the castle the Jesuits were dispatched to
Kyōto under the protection of a cavalry escort, while Laurence
was expressly ordered to inform Nobunaga of anything the
foreigners might stand in need of. During the next four years
(1572–76) Froez continued to stand very high in Nobunaga's
good graces, and was frequently received by him, and by the
time Froez left Kyōto for Bungo, Organtino Gnecchi, who had
arrived in the capital in 1572, had succeeded in winning a large
measure of the Vice-Shōgun's favour. This Gnecchi was a
determined temple-wrecker and iconoclast, and this in itself
would have been a sure passport to Nobunaga's regard. But in
addition to this Gnecchi had been able to render Nobunaga a
considerable political service in 1579. In that year Araki, the
Lord of Settsu, had combined with Mōri of Nagato and Abbot
Kennio of Ōsaka against the Vice-Shōgun. Now, it was from
Araki that Don Justo Ucondono held the castle of Takatsuki.
In accordance with the general custom of the times Araki had
exacted hostages as a guarantee of fidelity of his vassal,
and Don Justo's sister, as well as his only son, was now in
Araki's hands. Inasmuch as Takatsuki was the key to Araki's
fief on the side of Kyōto, it would be against it that Nobunaga
would launch his first assault. Don Justo thus stood in a very
difficult position. He was a Christian himself, while Nobunaga
was the great patron of the Christian priests and also Araki's
over-lord. On the other hand, Araki was hostile to Christianity,

was leagued with its bitterest foes, but he was Justo's immediate feudal superior, and, what was still more to the purpose, he had Justo's sister and his son in his power. In his dilemma Don Justo wrote to Gnecchi in Kyōto for counsel. The Father's reply might easily be divined; Justo was informed that it was his duty to espouse the cause of Nobunaga, as Nobunaga was Araki's suzerain. Araki was only a rebel, and besides, he had leagued himself with the bitterest enemies Christianity had. This reply could scarcely have reached its destination before Nobunaga had taken resolute action. He seized the Jesuits in the capital, interned one half in a fortress, and ordered the other half into his presence, and told Gnecchi that if he influenced his convert Justo to side with him, he would continue to favour the Christians in every way, but if not, he would forthwith suppress the new religion utterly. Gnecchi informed him of what he had already done, and added that neither because of threats nor promises would he have given any counsel which was not in conformity with his holy law. Thereupon the Father was sent to Takatsuki to make sure that his advice was adopted. His counsel may have been in conformity with the Christian law, but it was certainly not in conformity with the unwritten feudal law of Japan, and Justo's father (old Takayama), mother, wife, and retainers all urged him to bid defiance to Nobunaga, and to detain Gnecchi in order to prevent the sacrifice of his life for returning *re infectâ.* However, his ghostly counsellor had more weight with Justo than all his relatives and retainers and the feudal law of Japan combined; he shaved his head as a sign that he had renounced the world, and, setting out with the priest, placed himself at Nobunaga's disposal, while the castle of Takatsuki was handed over a few days later. Old Takayama, Justo's father, meanwhile went to Araki and cast in his lot with him, and, on being captured in Ōsaka after Araki's overthrow, he was first imprisoned and then banished to Echizen, where he devoted himself to the life and work of a Christian missionary. At Nobunaga's special request Justo allowed his hair to grow again; he was replaced in Takatsuki with an increased revenue, and was soon entrusted with important commands by Nobunaga. Although the sequel was to show that it was to prove of but questionable advantage to the best interests of Christianity in Japan, this incident did not a little to enhance the Vice-Shōgun's consideration for the Jesuits In the Annual Letter of 1580 Father Mexia writes :—

"I will only say that (humanly speaking) what has above all given great credit and reputation to the Fathers is the great favour Nobunaga has shown for the Company. Father Organtino and others of us have paid several visits to him, and he has always shown them great kindness, treating them very differently from the *bonzes*—a circumstance that is the marvel of all. Among others, on one occasion he was pleased to enter into a serious discussion of the matters of our holy law, propounding many doubts to Father Organtino and Brother Laurence in the presence of many barons. And he ordered the doors to be thrown open so that those in the ante-room might hear and see everything. And besides the things of our faith, he caused a globe or sphere to be brought, and, after asking many questions, he was greatly satisfied with the replies, saying that the Fathers surpassed all the *bonzes* in learning. For all that he cannot be convinced of the immortality of the soul or that there is only one God, and he fancies that at heart we do not believe what we preach, since the *bonzes* do not, preaching those things merely to bridle the people. Finally he wished the Father to show him our way from Europe to Japan on the globe, and, having considered, marvelling, he said that those who undertook such enterprises must be great-minded men, and, turning to the Father and the Brother, he said with a smile: 'As you expose yourselves to such dangers, either you are thieves who are compassing some fraud, or this Gospel of yours is really some fine thing.'"

In this year of 1580 the Jesuits were the recipients of an extraordinary and substantial mark of Nobunaga's favour. His new fortress of Azuchi, on the shore of Lake Biwa, had just been brought to a completion after more than three years' work, and a general invitation to all and sundry to come to see it was issued. The crowds that flocked to inspect it were immense. Among others, Father Gnecchi with some of his companions had proceeded thither, and Nobunaga, highly pleased that they should have come from Kyōto for the express purpose of admiring his handiwork, received them with great distinction Presuming upon this, Gnecchi begged him for a site for a house and a church in his new capital, and a site was not only granted forthwith, but a site which had been refused to all the importunities of Nobunaga's most favoured dependents. As chance would have it, the timber and furnishings of a fine house of thirty-four rooms had just been made ready at Kyōto, and Don Justo of Takatsuki now sent 1,500 men to convey these to Azuchi, where the promptness

with which the Jesuits availed themselves of Nobunaga's concession elicited a compliment from him.

"He exhorted us to erect a church also, which should be the
finest building in the whole city ; whether to ennoble that place,
or for some other secret intention he entertains with regard to the
law of God, or for some other end. . . . Such was the bruit of
these favours shown us by Nobunaga that it spread to Bungo and
Kyūshū. Some said that Nobunaga was a Christian ; others that
he was minded to become one ; others that the prince [his son
Nobutada] had been baptized, which would have been most pleasing
to God if it had been so ! We trust in the Lord that these will
be the preludes of what his Divine Majesty may be haply willed
to accomplish ; and if on account of their sins they shall not be found
worthy of such a great mercy, thanks to their favours, at least,
many people will be converted. Already many, and even chief
lords, begin to listen to discourses, but by reason of the wars not
much will be accomplished at once. However, from this the strife and
contentions we were exposed to in Kyōto will cease,—the Gentiles
endeavouring in every way to drive us thence, and continually
calumniating us to Nobunaga, and even offering him presents for
this purpose. But seeing the favours he has done us they have
retreated, and now all—*bonzes* as well as citizens—show themselves
more friendly to us."

In the spring of 1581 Valegnani, the Visitor-General,
accompanied by Froez and Mexia, came up to inspect matters
in the Kyōto district. Nobunaga was then in the capital for
the purpose of holding one of the fantastic and costly fêtes
which he frequently organised to "make display of his glory
and magnificence." When Valegnani paid his respects to him
there, the Visitor-General and his attendants met with the
kindest and most courteous of receptions. Nobunaga was
greatly surprised at the "Great Jesuit's" inches, and unbent
so far as to burst into hearty laughter at the odd appearance
of Valegnani's negro slave, and to determine by a practical
experiment whether the swarthiness of his complexion was due
to nature or to art.[8]   On Nobunaga's return to Azuchi the
Visitor-General followed him thither a few days afterwards,
and spent about two months in the new castle-town, during
which he saw much of Nobunaga. He was requested to take
all his *religieux* with him on his first visit to the fortress, so that
Nobunaga might make the acquaintance of them all, and after
a long interview the whole party was shown over the whole of
the fortress. As Nobunaga was exceedingly chary about allowing

---

8 This negro was presented to Nobunaga, and was with him when he was
murdered by Akechi in Kyōto on June 21st, 1582.

visitors to see the interior of his stronghold, this special at‑
tention to the foreigners was regarded by all as a very high
mark of favour indeed. The presents made to Valegnani also
furnished a fruitful subject of general conversation, people
crowding to see them; but the letters addressed to young Ōtomo
of Bungo and Shimadzu of Satsuma in favour of the Fathers,
and Nobunaga's assertion that he would greatly rejoice in the
universal spread of Christianity, perhaps afforded the Visitor‑
General greater satisfaction than anything else. Nobunaga's
consort was so much interested in Valegnani's conversation that
she " began to hear discourses," while her father, Asai, formerly
Lord of Ōmi, who had been stripped of his fief five years before
and was now living quietly in Azuchi, was actually baptized,
together with his spouse. Her three sons were frequent visitors
at the Jesuits' house; scarcely a week passed without seeing the
second one there, who assured the Fathers that he intended to
become a Christian as soon as he was certain that the step would
not be distasteful to his father. His elder brother, Nobutada,
Lord of Mino and Nobunaga's heir, was also minded to espouse
the foreign faith, and would have done so if there had been no
seventh commandment. Says the Annual Letter of 1582:—

"If sensuality did not pervert their intellect, most of these
lords would already be Christians. But the observance of this
precept seems so hard to them that it makes their conversion difficult,
so that many of them confidently allege that if the Fathers were
a little broader with them in this commandment, they would at once
become Christians. Among these lords the eldest son and successor of
Nobunaga has discussed this three or four times with a Brother,
wishing to persuade him that the Fathers should not proceed with
such rigour in this matter, maintaining that if they did relax their
rigour a great number of lords would forthwith be reduced to our
faith, and that so much was frequently said in the Court. Wherefore
the said prince asserted that it would be doing greater service to God
to dispense with this sixth [Protestant seventh] commandment, and
thus make so many converts than to ruin all hopes of their conversion
by our rigour in this precept, affirming that if it were [dispensed with]
he himself would be the first to receive holy baptism."

Altogether, even without having recourse to the elimination
of the seventh commandment from the Decalogue for the express
benefit of the territorial nobility, Valegnani was more than
satisfied with the prospects of Christianity in the Kyōto district.
It is true that there were not three hundred converts in the
capital itself, no more than one hundred in rich though far from
" godless " Sakai, and only 25,000 in the main island of Japan.

It was also true that as many as 18,000 of that number were to be found on one petty fief—that of Takayama Yushō at Takatsuki—while between 5,000 and 6,000 were on four still pettier holdings in Kawachi. But such Christians as these were wealthier, better educated, more intelligent, and, what was most important, more fervently devoted to the faith and much more submissive to the Fathers than were those of Kyūshū.[9] That their submission to the priests was really all that could be desired is clearly apparent from Froez's letter of April 14th, 1581, and from the Annual Letter of 1582, in the latter of which we are told among other things that "'Justo Ucondono' [Takayama Yūsho], a young man of twenty-eight, one of the bravest of Nobunaga's captains, is so humble and subject to the Fathers that in his intercourse with them he seems rather to be a servitor of the house than so great a lord." The capture of a few more territorial nobles of the stamp of Ucondono would rapidly swell the twenty-five thousand believers into hundreds of thousands, and Ucondono was sparing no effort to attract men of light and leading into the Christian fold. And beyond and beside all this the whole matter might one day be clinched by the conversion of Nobunaga himself. That the Jesuits, although not very sanguine, did not absolutely despair of this is plain from a remarkable passage in the letter from which we have just quoted. As soon as the Jesuits had erected their fine new

---

9 That the Jesuits had but small cause to complain of some of their Kyūshū converts even is apparent from Charlevoix's account of the landing of three new missionaries at Fukuda near Nagasaki in 1568. "Some prostrated themselves and even stretched themselves on the ground in the places where the missionaries were to pass, hoping to be trodden upon by the feet of those whose steps the Scripture says are full of charm; and what ought to pass for a miracle of humility in a people so proud, a missionary never appeared in a street without all the Christians he met, even to persons of the highest rank, assuming a respectful posture. The small people spoke only on their knees, and the others had always their eyes lowered and the body itself a little bent when they spoke. These *religieux* doubtless had great reasons for allowing such profound respect to be shown them, and it is good to observe that the *bonzes* having accustomed the people to this manner of acting, it was important to make them understand well that the God of the Christians deserved to be even more respected in the persons of his envoys than the false divinities of Japan in their ministers. The same memoirs add that the conversation of these fervent Christians had something celestial in it; and the examples of the virtues they were seen to practise filled every one with admiration. In 1577 eleven very rich Portuguese of good family were so struck with this that they asked to be received into the Company. Four were admitted; the others were sent to the Provincial of the Indies, and one named Amador de Castro, who was at Macao when the vessel that had carried them to Japan returned there, afterwards asserted that the crew spoke of the Japanese only with tears in their eyes, and said that to learn what it is to be a Christian it was necessary to go to Japan."

house in Azuchi, Gnecchi had got together some ten or twelve youths of the best families and had established a seminary in its upper storey. One of the things to which Valegnani had given much thought was the organisation of this new school on the same basis as the one just founded in Arima, for still greater things were expected from this institution in Azuchi than from its sister establishment in Kyūshū. Before the end of 1581 the number of pupils had advanced to twenty-five or twenty-six. One day, all unattended and unannounced, Nobunaga suddenly appeared in the Jesuits' house, rambled all through it, and went upstairs to see the priests and their pupils at work. The Jesuits paid much attention to the subject of instrumental music, and Nobunaga was delighted with the performances of the lads on the viola and various other European instruments.

"After conversing with the Fathers for some time, he withdrew, not wishing that the Fathers should descend to the basement, but that they should remain upstairs where they were. On reaching the castle he sent a present of things to eat to Father Organtino, at the same time giving him to understand that he was greatly pleased to have seen our house that day, and that it was as a token of the great pleasure he had received that he sent that present. With that and the other favours he frequently does us, the credit of the law of God increases apace, as well as the reputation of the Fathers among the Christians and Gentiles. May it please the Lord to enlighten him so that he may recognise the truth, to which he has frequently listened with attention in discourses. And although, if we consider his pride and his way of proceeding on the one hand, it may seem an impossibility that he should be subjected to the law of God, yet, on the other hand, seeing that the Lord has chosen him to destroy and undo the sects of the *bonzes*, always favouring us, and sometimes listening attentively to the things of another life, and of the immortality of the soul, it makes us believe and have hope that even for him *non sit abbreviata manus Domini*. With the great favours he has done the House of Azuchiyama this year, and with the intimate friendship and familiarity that arise from his proximity, it appears to us that for him a day has to come, as it came to the King of Bungo, of whom we always had less hope, and yet withal from his having favoured Christianity and the Fathers in his lands, our Lord deigned to convert him after thirty years, so that he might serve Him so devoutly as he now does."

These fair hopes, however, were to be ruthlessly dashed before many months were over. Nobunaga's eldest son, Nobutada, of whom the Fathers had so much good to say in previous letters, is referred to in bitter terms in Froez's Annual Letter of February 1583. He had done his share of the work in the final overthrow of Takeda of Kai early in 1583.

"Although naturally well disposed to our affairs, as has been said, yet, whether to pleasure his father, or through some wile of the

A WORD OF APOLOGY.

This book was announced to appear on or about the 1st of November, but its publication was delayed until this day. For this, I am alone responsible, neither Mr. Murdoch nor Mr. Young having anything to do with it. I undertook to prepare the index, and while working on it, some unavoidable obstacles occurred, which prevented me from continuing the work, with the result that the publication of the book was unduly delayed. I am exceedingly sorry for this, and sincerely crave the pardon of the subscribers.

ISOH YAMAGATA.

Tokyo, Dec. 12, 1903.

.Devil, he brought back a far-famed idol from these parts, and set it up in his kingdom of Owari. And passing to Kyōto, in token of gratitude for the victory he had achieved he went to visit another idol, Atanghu [Atago] by name, three leagues outside the city, and made it an offering of 2,500 *scudi*, with many other sacrifices and superstitions, among which was that he stripped himself naked, washing himself all over in those colds with snow. For these sacrifices and devotions he very soon had his guerdon, as we shall presently see."

The conduct of his father, Nobunaga, had been still more outrageous from Froez's point of view. After telling us about all the favours Nobunaga had done the Fathers, Froez proceeds :—

"He furthermore listened to sermons on various occasions, and although he showed that he was convinced by the reasonings, yet his arrogance rendered him incapable of receiving the influence and the light of the Divine grace. Finally, with much prosperity he advanced to such a height of presumption and extravagance that, not content with entitling himself the absolute Lord of all Japan and with being reverenced as such with such exacting and profound veneration as old men recollect never either to have seen or read of, he began, like another Nebuchadnezzar, to aim at being adored by all not as mere mortal man of this earth, but as God and Immortal Lord. To accomplish this most execrable and abominable design he built a temple on a hill hard by the fortress of Azuchi, with an inscription which, translated into our tongue, says thus : ' In the great kingdoms of Japan, in the fortress of Azuchi, on this mount which even from afar holds forth joy and content to him who looks upon it, Nobunaga, the Lord of all Japan, regard this temple of Sochenji. The rewards reaped by all such as shall worship it are as follows : In the first place, such as are already rich shall become richer ; the poor, the low, and the wretched shall become wealthy. Those who have no sons or successors to propagate their generation shall at once have descendants, and shall enjoy long life in great peace and repose. They shall reach a hundred years. They will be cured of sickness in a twinkling, and shall have the fulfilment of their desires in safety and tranquillity. Every month a solemn festival shall be held in memory of the day on which I was born, which shall be celebrated by a visit to this temple. All who put faith in what has been said will undoubtedly obtain all that is hereby promised. But the perverse and the unbelieving, whether in this life or in that to come, will be sent to perdition. Wherefore I repeat that it is very necessary that all should have the highest veneration and respect for this place.' With such an inscription the more easily to establish his own cult in that temple he caused the most celebrated and venerated idols of the different kingdoms to be conveyed thither. And since in the temples of these Gentiles it is customary to place a stone called ' Xintai ' (which means the heart or the essence of the idol invoked), for his own account he caused a stone to be placed higher than all the other idols, covered in the manner of a tabernacle or a chapel, and caused proclamation to be made throughout his kingdoms that from all the cities, castles, and villages every quality of men and women, noble as well as of base condition, should come on his birthday, the fifth moon of the year '82, to visit that temple and to pray to the stone placed by him there. And the concourse of people from remote and diverse parts was so great that it appeared something incredible. But from this spectacle, and from the reverence which is due to the Creator and Redeemer of the world alone, the Divine justice did not permit Nobunaga to draw delight for long, as we shall presently set forth, and as certain dread signs seemed to portend. For on the 8th of March, towards four o'clock of a very clear and calm evening, over the loftiest tower of the fortress of Azuchi the sky seemed as if on fire and so red that our people in the Residency were greatly perturbed. This appearance lasted till morning, so low and so close to the tower that it seemed that it could not be visible at a greater distance than twenty leagues, but afterwards we knew that it was seen in Bungo. On the 14th of May, about the same hour, a comet with a very long train appeared [and it continued] visible for many days to the great fear of every one. And a few days thereafter in Azuchi about mid-day a star fell from the sky, which seemed very portentous to our people."

The Annual Letter of 1583 is of more than ordinary historical value, for Froez devotes about thirty of its seventy odd pages to a circumstantial account of the murder of Nobunaga by Akechi Mitsuhide and of the stirring events of the subsequent fortnight. He was in a position to write on this subject with a good deal of authority, inasmuch as the Kyōto Jesuits saw most of the fighting on the fateful morning of June 21st, 1582. The church in Kyōto was only a single block distant from Nobunaga's quarters in the Honnōji, and a Jesuit Father (Carrion, apparently), while putting on his vestments to say Mass before dawn, "was advised to wait, as a tumult had arisen which ought to be of importance, as it was in front of the palace. At once arquebus-shots were heard and fire was seen, and very soon another came saying that it was no ordinary tumult, but that Akechi had turned traitor and the enemy of Nobunaga." It has been already remarked that the assassination of Nobunaga is one of the commonplaces in ordinary Japanese histories, and it has also been hinted that the researches of living Japanese historians have served to indicate that the popular and commonly accepted account of the incident stands in need of revision in more than one particular. On the other hand, these researches go far to confirm the general correctness of Froez's narrative. According to it, Hideyoshi (Faxiba), who had only some 20,000 or 25,000 troops with him, had written to his chief for reinforcements, saying that there was no need for him to come in person, for if he had 30,000 more men he would effectually settle matters with Mōri in a few days.

"But Nobunaga purposed to go to Kyōto and thence to Sakai and then to complete the subjugation of Mōri and the other princes, and thus, being lord of the whole of Japan, to pass to the conquest of China with a great Armada, leaving the kingdoms of Japan divided between his sons. . . . Before his departure from Azuchi he had dispatched his third son [Nobutaka], with 14,000 men, to reduce Shikoku. Then he went to Kyōto with his son, the Prince [Nobutada], and with the King of Mikawa [Iyeyasu] his relative, and other lords. This King of Mikawa [Iyeyasu] was to be quartered in our house, but he afterwards bethought him to lodge in another near-by, and a little later he made an excursion to see the city of Sakai—a thing which was no small providence of the Lord, as we shall see presently. . . . In Nobunaga's Court was a man named Akechi, of low birth, but so adroit in conversation, so brave in arms, and so skilled in architecture that from being the mean servitor of a certain gentleman, he so ingratiated himself with Nobunaga that he received from him the lordship of Tamba and Tango, beside the revenues of the *bonzes* of the University of Hiyei-san, which were almost equivalent to those of another province. But puffed up with these great favours, and scorning the obligations of fidelity and gratitude, he began to extend his impious hopes to the monarchy of Japan and the destruction of his lord. Nor did he fail to try to realise them, and to realise them in part on this occasion. Nobunaga having arranged that he should proceed from Azuchi with 30,000 men to join Hideyoshi by another route, when he heard that Nobunaga and the Prince his son [Nobutada] were in Kyōto with only a slender train, he collected all his troops in a fortress of Tamba, fifteen miles from Kyōto. There on a Tuesday, which was the eighth of Corpus Christi, he secretly summoned four of his trusted Colonels and disclosed his mind to them, and, as these Barbarians are very fickle, he easily suborned them, partly by means of intimidation, partly of promises. Perhaps he had already suborned some of the others,—although the particulars of this are not as yet known. After this he put his fortresses in order with good guards and sentinels, on the pretext of preventing disorder in his absence. On Wednesday, the 20th of June, at midnight, he gave the signal to march, and ordered the soldiers to have their arms in readiness and the matches alight on their serpentines, because entering straightway into Kyōto he was minded to give Nobunaga a view of the fine and well-drilled force he led. And thus marching briskly, the dawn began to whiten, some suspecting that perchance all this preparation had been ordered by Nobunaga to kill his relative the King of Mikawa [Iyeyasu]. But once in the city they were at once conducted by the Colonels and General Akechi (whom all obeyed without hesitation) to the palace of Nobunaga, which had formerly been a monastery, and surrounded it on every side."

Nobunaga had just got up and washed his face and hands, and was wiping them when he received an arrow in the ribs. He drew it out, seized a halbert, and laid about him lustily till his arm was shattered by an arquebus-shot. " Then he retreated into the rooms and shut the door with great difficulty. Some say that he cut his belly, and killed himself, according to the usage of the Japanese lords; others will have it that he was burned alive in the blazing palace, which the assailants speedily

N

fired. But be that as it may, it suffices that he who before made
every one tremble not merely with a word, but with his very
name, is now turned into dust and ashes." Meanwhile Nobutada,
who was lodged some six blocks off, had fled for refuge to the
palace of a son of the Emperor's. Akechi's men here ordered the
inmates to withdraw on foot, not in litters, and then fired the
building and made an end of the refugee, although he made a
gallant defence. The citizens were in great apprehension lest
the town should be fired and sacked, but Akechi kept a tight
hold upon his troops, and neither the city nor the Jesuits suffered
in any way. That same day, "towards the eighteenth hour,"
Akechi marched upon Azuchi. The great bridge over the Yodo
had been destroyed, but it was repaired with incredible diligence,
and Azuchi, stripped of its defenders, was soon in the hands of
the rebel. Here Gnecchi, his companions and their pupils were
at their wits' end. They did indeed manage to save the church
plate, but their house was ruthlessly pillaged and dismantled by
the rabble of the town. Gnecchi was persuaded to take refuge in
Okinashima; but on arriving there he found that they had fallen
into a robber's den, and that the boatmen who had so kindly
rescued them were simply fresh-water pirates. A good Christian,
however, whose nephew was a favourite of Akechi's, wrote "recommending the Fathers with such efficacy that he sent a boat to
succour them, and they were rescued with all their baggage and
taken to Sakamoto, where they met Akechi and were not badly
received by him." He had his own ends to serve in this. He
was exceedingly anxious to attach Takayama Yūsho (Don Justo
Ucondono) to his fortunes, and he now requested Gnecchi to use
his great influence with him in his (Akechi's) favour. "The
Father replied with good words, suitable to the circumstances;
but he afterwards secretly urged Justo not to identify himself
with such a tyrant in any way; otherwise, for this he would see
us all crucified." The Jesuits were provided with a safe-conduct,
and dispatched to Kyōto accompanied by one of Akechi's
pages.

When Azuchi fell into Akechi's hands it was not destroyed
by him, as is sometimes alleged; it was Nobunaga's own son, who
fired the fortress in a fit of insanity a little later on, who
was responsible for the ruin of the far-famed "paradise" of
his father. All that Akechi did was to rifle Nobunaga's strong

boxes, and to make a lavish distribution of their contents among his followers.

"As he divined that he was to enjoy his felicity for but a little time, he set himself to distribute the treasures without parsimony. Among other things there was a great quantity of gold piastres marked and distinguished by their weights; of these he gave as much as seven thousand *scudi* to some, three or four thousand to others, and to others two or three hundred according to their rank. He sent a sum to the Dairi, and to the five chief monasteries of Kyōto seven thousand each to celebrate the obsequies of Nobunaga, although he had been most cruelly assassinated by him. Thus all that had been amassed by the wars and the efforts of fifteen or twenty years was dissipated in the space of two or three days."

The Jesuits seem to have regarded Akechi's chances of maintaining himself for some considerable time as being by no means desperate. What chiefly contributed to his speedy overthrow was his strange inaction. The fortresses in the province of Settsu had been mostly dismantled by Nobunaga, and such as had been left intact were then practically defenceless, for their garrisons had all been dispatched to join Hideyoshi. If Akechi had sent out a few thousand men he could have at once seized every stronghold between Hiōgo and the capital. As it was, the commandant of Ōsaka castle, whose father had been one of Nobunaga's numerous victims, was supposed to have been a participant in the conspiracy. At all events, when Nobutaka, Nobunaga's third son, presented himself there he was refused admission into the citadel. As has been mentioned, Nobutaka had been dispatched with 14,000 men to reduce Shikoku, and he was just preparing to embark at Sakai when news of his father's assassination was brought. Thereupon the greater portion of Nobutaka's troops promptly deserted him, and so he hurried off to Ōsaka with those still faithful in order to be able to concert his measures in a strong and safe position. He only got possession of Ōsaka citadel through a *ruse* of one of the commandant's officers, who was no friend of Akechi's. After Ōsaka, Takatsuki was perhaps the strongest and most important fortress in the province, but Akechi, who took it as a matter of course that he would have Takayama's (Don Justo Ucondono's) support, so far from seizing it, sent the most reassuring messages to Takayama's wife.

Meanwhile the peasants on the various fiefs of Settsu had risen and rifled the castles there of all that could be carried

N 2

away; a fact that indicates how very easy it would have
been for Akechi to seize the whole province with a few
thousand troops if he had acted at once. All that Akechi
did was to occupy Toba with 10,000 men, and to seize and
garrison Shōryū, nine miles from Kyōto, and there he "kept
treating in order that the heads of the kingdom should
gradually pass over to him; and at the same time waited
to see what Faxiba Hideyoshi would do." The latter,
escaping the attempts of Akechi's assassins sent to lie in wait
for him, was very soon at hand. He sent forward three small
detachments—one through the hills, one along the Yodo, and
another under Takayama, while he himself, with Nobutaka
and the main force of 20,000 men, advanced some eight miles
behind these. Takayama, with less than 1,000 troops, was
the first to come into touch with the rebels. "They were so
fired with the ardour of battle, and so confident in the help
of God, that on seeing the enemy, Justo did not hesitate to
lead them into battle. And they so bore themselves that in
a twinkling they gained more than two hundred heads of
the nobles of Akechi." Presently the other two advanced
bodies came in upon Akechi's flanks, and a little later the
head of Hideyoshi's columns appeared in the defile less than
three miles distant. Thereupon the rebels broke and fled;
many of them took refuge in the castle of Shōryū, which was
forced on the following day, while others, prevented from
entering Kyōto by the citizens, held on towards Sakamoto.
These fugitives were slaughtered in scores by the peasants,
who were animated by no hatred of their treason, but merely
with a desire to get possession of their arms and horses. So
much appears in the case of Akechi himself. He had first
thrown himself into Shōryū, but he had left it in disguise,
"and, according to reports, somewhat wounded. Recommending himself to some countrymen with the promise of a great
sum of gold if they would escort him to the entrance to
Sakamoto, they wishing to get his scimitar and the little
he had about him, smote him with a lance, and cut off his
head. And the villains not being very eager to present it to
Nobutaka, another discharged this office." The head was
first "offered to the ashes of Nobunaga," and then sewn on
to the trunk, which was put on a cross and left to rot there

just outside the city. The slaughter of those who had taken
any part with Akechi was ruthless and unsparing. There had
been serious disorders in Nobutada's own fiefs; the castle of
Gifu was seized and sacked, while Ōgaki was the only place
in Mino where things had been quiet. Here, too, punishment
was swift. Akechi had indeed kept his own men well in
hand during his brief sway of twelve days; but elsewhere
the anarchy that ran riot was serious. If there had been no
Hideyoshi, it is extremely likely that all that Nobunaga had
achieved towards the re-establishment of a strong and efficient
central administration would have been totally undone and the
subsequent current of Japanese history changed entirely. Akechi
was an able architect, we are told, but it is more than
questionable whether his ability was of the order which is
demanded of the architects of empires.

From what has already been said, it ought to be tolerably
clear that the Jesuits had ample opportunities of arriving at
a definite estimate of the character of Nobunaga. From many
separate passages in their letters, the subsequent historians of the
Church, Crasset and Charlevoix, have essayed the task of painting a full and life-like portrait of this great figure in Japanese
history. Both efforts are certainly interesting. Says Crasset :—

"Nobunaga was a prince of a weak constitution and of a large
frame, although it did not seem sufficiently robust to bear the fatigues
of war. However, he had a heart and a mind that made good the
weakness of his constitution. Never was there a man on the earth
more ambitious than he. He was brave, generous, intrepid, and
he was not lacking even in moral virtues, being naturally inclined
to justice and the enemy of treason. As regards his intellect, it
was excellent—quick and penetrating,—and there was never any
business he could not unravel without trouble. Above all, he was
admirable in the science of war. He was the most able of captains
to command an army, to attack places, to trace works of all kinds,
and to select advantageous camps. He had only one head in his
Council, and that was his own, and if he asked the advice of his
people, it was to know their hearts rather than their minds. He
excelled in the practice of the counsel of those hypocrites who urge
that it is necessary to look at others without letting them perceive
it; for he was impenetrable to the most subtle politicians, and looked
at everybody without seeming to do so, so close and secret was he
and such a master of dissimulation. For the cult of the Gods he
mocked at it, being very well persuaded that the bonzes were impostors,
and for the most part great criminals who abused the simplicity
of the people and hid their enormous debauchery under a specious
veil of Religion."

Although Charlevoix's estimate is in the main equally

favourable, he yet gives us some dark shades which are absent from the foregoing sketch.

"He was reproached with having carried his mistrust to the point of killing his own brother with his own hand; but the short-coming with which he was universally charged was his pride. He treated the great with a haughtiness which was almost barbarous; the kings even whom he had subdued did not dare to look him in the face. A single look from him made everything possible for his officers when it was a question of obeying him, and made them accomplish things that were incredible. He never went abroad unless accompanied by a guard of two thousand cavalry; but as for his person, he was always very simply clad. A tiger-skin usually served him as a cuirass, and he often stretched it on the ground to sit upon it. He was temperate (in wine), but dissolute to excess, and this vice was for long regarded as the sole obstacle which hindered him from becoming a Christian. Apparently this view was a mistaken one; and it finally became very clear that Nobunaga's only god was his own ambition."

Most of the passages referring to Nobunaga in the letters written by the Jesuits were penned when he was showering benefits upon them, and when they might very well have been influenced by that expectant gratitude which consists in a very lively sense of favours to come. Such a peculiar position no doubt biassed their estimate of their patron considerably. It is therefore with considerable interest that one turns to what Froez has to say about his old acquaintance, if not friend, of fourteen years' standing, when he came to write his obituary. It must be kept in mind that although Nobunaga never withdrew his favour from the foreign priests, he had outraged them terribly by his assumption of divine honours six months before his death. Says Froez at the end of the Annual Letter of 1583 :—

"In truth the judgements of God as concerns Nobunaga are evident; since all his sumptuous edifices have been so unhappily consumed with the loss of inestimable riches and treasures, he being by nature not merely stingy but even rapacious, so that if he knew that anybody possessed any rare thing, he ordered that it should be handed over, and he could not be denied. Thus many, making a virtue of necessity, offered him such things spontaneously. Brother Vincent, a Japanese, who was well informed about such matters, assured me that two alone of his jewels (they were very different from those of Europe) were worth more than 85,000 *scudi*. Now of these none remain, for when Nobunaga went the last time to Kyōto he took them all with him to show to different kings and lords, and there they were burned together with him. In such a wretched and unhappy fashion has ended the man who fancied that there was no greater lord than he, not merely in the world but in Heaven itself. . . . And yet withal, as has been said, it cannot be denied that Nobunaga had good qualities. But finally his arrogance ruined him. *Et periit memoria ejus cum sonitu, et in puncto ad inferna descendit.*"

As regards the latter proposition in the final sentence of the extract it may be left to itself as a mild example of priestly assurance and ecclesiastical cocksuredness. With respect to the former, all that can be said is that subsequent facts have proved sadly destitute of consideration, for even at the present day many Japanese (mistakenly we venture to think) cherish the memory of Nobunaga as one of the three greatest statesmen the Empire ever produced. This is mainly to be attributed to the extremely lucky circumstance that at the death of Nobunaga the great master-builder was at hand ready to rear on the foundation laid by Nobunaga the political fabric which Nobunaga could never have achieved. Nobunaga certainly did a great day's work in his time, but Froez is not altogether blind to its limitations. "But what was of most import was that this people being so bellicose, and the land consequently subject to continual wars, he with his ability and prudence gradually reduced all to peace and tranquillity." The pacification and the establishment of a central control over some thirty odd of the sixty-six provinces of Japan was certainly no mean achievement. But how much did Nobunaga's narrow intensity, his domineering egotism and ruthlessness, his callous and brutal contempt for his vassals, with the faculty of terrorising them and making the utmost out of them for his own purpose, accomplish in the sphere of constructive statesmanship? What Froez here imputes unto him for righteousness is that he reared the far-famed hold of Azuchi, that he ensured his conquests by making the conquered live there as hostages, that he drove a fine road with magnificent bridges from there to Kyōto, and that he made roads in other provinces. "And where, before his rule, on all the ways at almost every league taxes were extorted and passports had to be obtained, he had abolished all that to the very great content of the people." Besides this, there was the erection of a palace for the Emperor and another for the Crown Prince, and the appropriation of a handsome revenue for the support of the Imperial Court. But that is the end of the record. When we come to deal with the Jesuit letters written during the sixteen years (1582–1598) Hideyoshi swayed the destinies

of the Empire, we find that there is scarcely one of them
without some reference to some real constructive measure or
project of wide compass and generally of public utility. Much
as the missionaries have to say in praise of their patron—before
he apotheosed himself—it is not difficult to perceive from
their accounts that Nobunaga in everything save soldiership
and ruthless force of will was a very small man when compared
with Hideyoshi, whom, after 1587 at least, they praise only as
Balaam blessed Israel, involuntarily and in spite of themselves.
Nobunaga, callous, forceful, masterful, the veritable *Übermensch*
of his time, was of the breed of Attila,—only an Attila
whose conduct and career were conditioned by a settled instead
of a nomadic environment. His dominant passion was power ;
the chief means he employed to attain it was destruction ;
his usual device for rendering an opponent harmless, the banal
device of extermination. Hideyoshi had a brain of a stamp
very different from this.

If there had been no Hideyoshi it is tolerably safe to
assume that Nobunaga would not now be regarded as one of
the three great national heroes of the great century of Japanese
history. How much Nobunaga actually owed to the genius
of his great retainer while alive may be open to discussion,
but there can be no question that Hideyoshi had much to
do with the making of the fortunes of his master while he
was alive, while it is he that has chiefly to be saddled with
the blame of belying Froez's prophecy, or rather assertion
of fact. As soon as it was known that Nobunaga had perished,
anarchy began to run riot in Central Japan, and but for
the prompt appearance of Hideyoshi on the scene to save
the situation the dominion Nobunaga had, if not consolidated,
at all events reduced and pacified, would have been shivered
into warring fragments. Not one of his two remaining sons
had anything of their father's ferocity or intensity of character ;
as soldiers they were in no wise remarkable in an age when
military ability was unusually common. Neither of them could
ever have held Nobunaga's conquests together, much less carried
them further afield. The House of Oda would have fallen
from its high estate no less rapidly than it had. attained to
it, and Nobunaga in all likelihood would have bulked no
more largely in the imagination of future generations than

the Hosokawas, the Ōuchis, and the Hōjōs, and less largely
perhaps than Takeda Shingen and Uyesugi Kenshin have
done. Happily, however, for his fame, and no less happily
for the best interests of the Empire, Nobunaga's handiwork,
such as it was, was not merely rescued from imminent and
almost certain destruction, but carried on to a full and thorough
and elaborate completion. He laid the foundation,—or rather
he dug the trenches for the foundation,—and on the ground
so prepared by him two men of very diverse and .vastly
greater genius than he raised the fabric of a stable, well-ordered,
and abiding national polity. And for a huge constructive
effort of this description, something better than the destructive
energy of a Japanese Attila was demanded.

It is extremely interesting to arrive at an analysis of
the motives which may have prompted the fierce and haughty
and inaccessible Nobunaga to take the poor and ill-clad
missionaries under his protection. In common with most
other Japanese rulers of the time he appears to have been
interested in the foreigners and their conversation from his
very first interview with Froez on the drawbridge of his new
castle in Kyōto. Apart from their religion, they could tell
him much of the great world to the west and of its science,
for they were men of a fine culture who had travelled far
and with alertly observant eyes. Furthermore, they were men
of an exquisite tact—a quality that was then, as it is now,
appreciated nowhere more highly than in Japan. Nobunaga
was quick to discern that he could afford to unbend in their
presence without the slightest risk of compromising his dignity,
or of meeting with any ill-bred presumption on their part.
There was no need for him to be under any constraint when
conversing with them, as there was when dealing with
his subordinates, his own people, and the subject lords whom
he ruled by inspiring them with an abject terror of his name.
This he doubtless felt as a relief, and when he had really,
although not confessedly, once convinced himself of their
sincerity, which, as we can see from the letters of the Fathers,
he was not slow to test on various occasions and in various
ways, it is not difficult to understand why they were admitted
to his presence when great lords were denied an audience. In
addition to all this, however, was the fact that he and they

were knit together by the sympathetic bond of a common hate. The Buddhist priests were Anathema Maranatha to him quite as much as they were to the foreigners, and his ostentatious favours to the priests from over-sea constituted a studied slight to the *bonzes*, who, in spite of their mutual hostility, were yet eager to enter into his good graces.

There is yet one question that may perhaps be profitably discussed. What was the precise value of Nobunaga's favour to the missionaries in the actual propaganda? How many new converts did it actually serve to bring into the Christian fold? It must not be forgotten that before the murder of the Shōgun Yoshiteru in 1565, Vilela and Froez had enjoyed his protection and countenance, that Miyoshi had been very well disposed towards them, and that Takayama, one of the most zealous and valuable proselytes the missionaries ever made, had been converted. All this was three years before Froez met Nobunaga on the drawbridge. It was Nobunaga, influenced by Vatadono, whom the Jesuits had to thank for their restoration to Kyōto. If Nobunaga had shown himself hostile to them, the fate of Christianity in Central Japan would have been sealed, till the year 1852 certainly, and for ever, probably. As it was, his good-will assured the missionaries ready admission into all the thirty-odd provinces he eventually reduced. But what was the net result of all that in converts? The number of these for the year 1582 has already been given. Of the 24,500 in the whole of Central Japan there were more than 18,000 on Takayama's fief of Takatsuki, and the bulk of the remainder on the estates of four petty lords in Kawachi. In all these five places the feudal chief was himself a convert. On him much, if not indeed all, depended. So much was evident in the case of Naitō, who held a fief in Tamba. He had been baptized by Vilela about 1565, and in 1573, when he cast in his lot with the Shōgun Yoshiaki against Nobunaga, he came down to Kyōto with 2,000 picked men, "whose banners all bore beautiful crosses, while on his own helmet was a great 'JESUS' in gold." At this date there were a good many converts on Naitō's lands. For the crime of espousing the losing side on this occasion he was deprived of his fief, which was then given to a non-Christian lord. From this date onwards for many years we find no reference to any

Christians on Naitō's former estates in the missionary letters.
The removal of Takayama from Takatsuki to Akashi about
1585 at once greatly reduced the number of converts on his
old domains. If he had made common cause with his over-
lord Araki in 1579 it would have been all over with Christianity
in the Home Provinces. The Takayamas—father and son—and
Naitō of Tamba were among the best, the most sincere, and
the most honourable converts the Jesuits ever made. By
accepting the foreign religion these three men had nothing
to gain from a temporal point of view, while they risked a
good deal. No such suspicions as not unnaturally arise about
the purity of Ōmura Sumitada's motives can be entertained
about theirs.

In quarters where there were no feudal lords or where the
feudal lords did not accept baptism themselves, Nobunaga's
favours did not do much to help to swell the Church rolls.
In Kyōto down to 1582 there were not three hundred Christians,
in Sakai one hundred, in Azuchi not so many, while the missions
made to Nobunaga's domains in Mino and Ōwari had been
attained with scanty success, except in one little corner, where
a sub-feudatory, on receiving baptism, proceeded to convert
his dependents by rather drastic methods. In 1581 Froes
made a visit to Echizen, where he was hospitably entertained
by the great Shibata in his castle of Kita-no-shō (Fukui);
but here, too, the harvest could scarcely be counted by hundreds.
Where Nobunaga helped most to augment the number of
proselytes was, strange as it may sound, in Kyūshū, where
he exercised no authority. His frequent receptions of the
Fathers did much to make their religion respectable, and
this was a consideration that weighed much with the young
Prince of Arima when he abandoned the *bonzes* in 1580,
and proceeded to impose his new faith upon his reluctant
subjects.

From all this it ought to be evident that there are considerable errors in the statements that "by 1582 the holy
name of Jesus had been carried into the furthest provinces
of the north, that the total number of Japanese Christians
at this time was estimated at 600,000, and that the apostolate
was exercised by one hundred and thirty-eight European missionaries." Froez had once got as far as Fukui in Echizen,

and missionaries had made flying visits to points in the neighbourhood of Nagoya on the Pacific coast of the island, but beyond these limits they had not reached.   The total number of converts in the whole of Japan is put in the Annual Letter of 1582 at "150,000 more or less," while at that date there were no more than seventy-five missionaries in the Empire, about thirty of whom were Japanese, none of whom had been admitted to the priesthood, however. Some Church historians are evidently of opinion that it shows a lack of due respect and reverence to the multiplication table to let it rest unused.

CHAPTER VIII.

HIDEYOSHI (1582-1585).

EVEN after the suppression of Akechi and his confederates, the fortunes of the House of Oda stood in no ordinary peril. A disputed succession to the headship of the clan had time and again been fraught with disaster to the greatest feudal families of Japan, and the death of Nobunaga's eldest son and heir together with himself now bade fair to give occasion to a bitter domestic quarrel. Although both the offspring of concubines, and both adopted into other Houses, Nobunaga's two surviving sons, Nobuo and Nobutada, were each inclined to urge their claims to be regarded as the family chief,—the former on the ground of age, the latter of the part he had taken in avenging the death of his father. Both were minded to set aside their one-year-old nephew, Sambōshi, the son of Nobutada, their elder brother. As the adult claimants were alike destitute of any real force of character, it became clear that the real struggle would be one among the chief captains of Nobunaga, who would merely avail themselves of the names of their *protégés* to advance their own interests. Among these captains there were four at this time who bulked more largely in the popular imagination than their fellows, and who really exercised a greater measure of influence than they.

The average Japanese, partly perhaps to escape from the perplexity of the bewildering kaleidoscope of proper names and titles which import so much confusion into the national records, has at all times shown great readiness and considerable happiness in devising nicknames for men prominently before the public, and the four captains of Nobunaga had all earned their patent in this peerage of popular creation, and were known as "Cotton," "Rice," "Attack," and "Retreat" respectively. The first was so fertile in resources that he could be employed for a multitude of purposes; the second was as indispensable as the common staple of food; the third was at his best at the head of a charge; the fourth in

conducting a retreat when things were desperate. Such was the
common and current view of the relative abilities of Hideyoshi,
Niwa, Shibata, and Ikeda. By 1582 it was tolerably clear that
the first of these had become at least *primus inter pares.*
Neither Niwa nor Ikeda seems to have had any heart-burnings
over this; but with Shibata it was very different. This Shibata,
now fifty-nine years of age, was Hideyoshi's senior by thirteen
years, had been much longer in the service of the House of
Oda,—had been, in fact, chief councillor of the clan even at the
date when Hideyoshi found menial employment with Nobunaga.
The rapid rise of the base-born monkey-faced adventurer had
been regarded with bitter feelings by the blue-blooded councillor,
and the almost superhuman astuteness and adroitness with which
Hideyoshi had foiled all the long series of efforts to ruin him
had served to intensify Shibata's hate by imparting to it a
strain of fear. It was now generally recognised that the
decently cloaked hostility that had prevailed between the twain
during the previous fourteen or fifteen years would soon be as
open as it had long been bitter. Neither of them would ever
submit to the other, and what Hideyoshi at least had long
perceived to be the crying need of the time was that the whole
Empire of Japan should have but one sole and single master.

A few weeks after the death of Nobunaga all his great
vassals assembled at the Castle of Kiyosu in Ōwari to decide
upon his successor. Nobuo, the eldest surviving son, was
supported by Ikeda and Gamō, a young and brilliant captain
of Ōmi, while Nobutaka's claims were strongly and hotly
urged by Shibata and a certain Takikawa, who had gained
considerable reputation and influence during the campaign
against Takeda of Kai at the beginning of the year, when he
had been made Daimyō of Kōdzuke. This Takikawa had an
intense hatred for Hideyoshi, and this community of sentiment
doubtless had much to do with the support he lent to Shibata's
view of how the feudal law of the Empire should be construed
in the case they had to decide. As might have been foreseen,
Hideyoshi came forward as the champion of Nobunaga's baby
grandson, Sambōshi. After a long and acrimonious wrangle
it was finally decided that Sambōshi should be acknowledged
as head of the House of Oda, that Nobuo should act as his
guardian, and that the administration of public affairs should-

be entrusted to a board of four—Shibata, Niwa, Ikeda, and Hideyoshi, who were all to rank as equals. "After this," says Froez, "Faxiba (Hideyoshi), with Shibata, Ikeda, and Niwa, divided the kingdoms (provinces) and revenues *ad libitum.*" To preserve the peace on this occasion Hideyoshi found it advisable to make great concessions; he patiently submitted to studied insults from Shibata, and even agreed to hand over his castle of Nagahama in Ōmi to him, thus facilitating Shibata's access to Kyōto.

On returning to the capital, however, Hideyoshi soon began to show that the advice of his colleagues on the Board of Administration was by no means indispensable to him. He took several important steps on his own sole initiative, among which was the erection of two first-class fortresses at Yawata and Yamasaki to secure the southern approaches to the capital. As it was Ikeda who held most of the neighbouring province of Settsu, it was from him that remonstrances might have been expected. Ikeda, however, was wise enough to say nothing, but objections came from another quarter. "Thereupon Shibata and Nobutaka in great wrath sent to Faxiba to say that in terms of the original conventions they were all equal, but from the signs he gave it appeared that he was aiming at the absolute dominion of the Tenza (Home Provinces). Let him dismantle the new fortresses, otherwise they would come to do it for him after the winter was over." To make clear the import of this, it ought to be stated that most of Shibata's great fief of Echizen was usually feet-deep in snow from mid-December till March, and that the difficult passes between his capital of Kita-no-shō, or Fukui, were practically impassable by any large force during that season of the year. As for Nobutaka, who had been installed at Gifu in Mino, it was very imprudent indeed for him to declare open war against Hideyoshi before the rains of spring had cleared the Echizen defiles. Hideyoshi's reply to the threat of the confederates was terse and to the point:—"He was waiting for them; the strong arm would decide who was to be master." And if he was laconic in the matter of words, there was no Spartan tardiness in his movements. "In the month of December (1582)," writes Froez, "marching with a great army towards Mino, he encamped around the city of Gifu, which he could

very easily have taken and fired if he had been so minded;
but Nobutaka, seeing the straits he was in, humbled himself
and begged for mercy, placing himself entirely in the hands
of Faxiba (Hideyoshi), who, exercising clemency, pardoned
him for the past, taking, however, as hostages his mother and
daughter and the most important persons in his household."

Hideyoshi had scarcely got back to Kyōto at the beginning
of 1583, when he was once more summoned to the field.
Takikawa, who held some very strong places in Northern Ise,
had mustered formidable powers, while Shibata had arranged
to support him with the levies of the southern corner of his
fief, counting upon being able to hold the common enemy
in play till the whole body of the Echizen vassals could get
over the mountains. Hideyoshi, however, like Philip of old,
fought with gold as well as with steel; and shortly after
his appearance before Nagahama, which he had ceded to Shibata
in the previous year, the commandant, Shibata's adopted son
Katsutoyo, Iga-no-Kami, not only surrendered the fortress to
him, but also joined him with the whole of the garrison.
With his rear thus protected against Shibata, Hideyoshi
wheeled round and broke into Ise, burning and ravaging Takikawa's
estates. An attack upon the castle of Kameyama was foiled
with a good many casualties, however, but in a few days it
was again invested by a force of 40,000 men. This siege
is interesting from the circumstance that it was then we first
hear of mines being employed in Japanese warfare. The
garrison was so surprised at seeing a bastion wrecked by this
new device that the besiegers had little trouble in making a
speedy end of the business.

Before the fall of Kameyama, Takikawa had sent a
messenger to Shibata urging him to move at once; and the
latter had dispatched his nephew Sakuma with an advance force
of 7,000 or 8,000 men. Hideyoshi now sent 20,000 troops
north to Nagahama, beyond which they threw up a cordon of
thirteen forts to block the progress of the army of Echizen,
while 15,000 more sat down before the stronghold of Miné in
Ise, which was also mined and carried. Just at this point
Hideyoshi found himself with another foe on his hands.
Nobutaka, recking little of the hostages he had given, now
ordered a levy of his vassals with the object of forming a

junction with Shibata. Not many of them responded, however, and Hideyoshi had entered Mino and seized Ōgaki before Nobutaka had been able to leave Gifu. Just as Hideyoshi was ready to give battle there he was surprised by what most regarded as very bad news from the Ōmi-Echizen frontier. There Hidenaga, Hideyoshi's half-brother, Katsutoyo the deserter, Takayama Ukon (Don Justo), and a certain Nakagawa had been left in command, the latter two holding Shizugatake and another fort which were the weakest in the cordon. Froez, who no doubt got his information from Takayama, differs somewhat from popular Japanese histories in his account of what followed. Shibata had already come up, when, on May 19th, 1583, 15,000 Echizen troops moved against Takayama and Nakagawa's (Xeiseo in Froez) positions. The latter wished to give battle, but as the two of them had no more than 2,000 men altogether, Takayama was for standing on the defensive merely. However, he unfortunately allowed himself to be over-ruled. The result was a terrific slaughter of their men, the death of Nakagawa, and the capture of Shizugatake, while Takayama had the greatest difficulty in retreating to the fort occupied by Hidenaga. The report that Don Justo had fallen spread all through the Home Provinces, and was carried to Bungo, "occasioning the greatest grief and fear to all the faithful of these parts, as he was the pillar of Christianity." The Japanese accounts, which have doubtless been somewhat embellished in order to make more interesting reading, will have it that Shibata sent Sakuma to the assault of Shizugatake with strict orders to return to headquarters at once, even if successful; that the attack on the fort was a secret one; that although Nakagawa fell, the garrison still held out; and that Sakuma, in defiance of reiterated messages from Shibata, sat down before the position and remained there. When news of this seeming disaster was brought to Hideyoshi, he was then at dinner. He merely asked whether Sakuma had retreated, and on being informed that there was no sign of his doing so, he threw down his chopsticks, drew his sword, and danced about the room, exclaiming, " I have won! I have won a great victory!" Froez merely says that "he heard of the ill-success of his two captains with such strength of mind that no change appeared in his countenance." Leaving 15,000

o

men to hold Nobutaka in check, he hurried off with the rest
of his troops, and by a wonderful forced march of two days
and nights, he joined his brother Hidenaga in front of Sakuma
before the latter fancied he could have quitted Mino.   On
getting intelligence of this, the Echizen men withdrew to
the heights they had formerly occupied, and next morning
Hideyoshi sent forward 6,000 men to assail them there.   The
fight raged bitterly till noon, when the whole southern force
was flung forward, and then the Northerners wavered, broke,
and fled in pell-mell rout and ruin, casting away spears,
arquebuses, swords, and even their clothes, as they scrambled
through the dense underwood.

"And in a trice there appeared on the top of the hill more
than 2,500 half-nude men.   Shibata was not in this battle, having
been posted with more than 1,000 men around the fortress of
Chiutarodono to block its garrison from taking part in the fight.
Wherefore Faxiba, advised that his chief adversary still remained
a-foot, sounded the recall, and turned the army against him.   And
he, fleeing by narrow and difficult paths, with only a few attendants,
came to the principal city of Echizen, called Kita-no-shō (Fukui), in
which was a most beautiful castle, roofed with tiles of stone so
smooth and so well made that they seemed as if made on a lathe.
But before entering the castle he fired the city, to prevent its
provisions or riches being of any avail to the enemy.   Faxiba,
following up his victory, entered Echizen with all his forces, and
laid siege to the castle where Shibata was.   He being now sixty
years of age, but a very valorous captain, exercised all his life in
arms, passed into a great room, and made a short address to the
gentlemen with him, saying thus:—'My retreat into this castle
has been, as you know, rather by the fortune of war than from my
cowardice.   And now being doomed to have my head taken by the
enemy, and to have my wife and yours, together with our sons and
relatives, outraged, to the eternal infamy of the name of the House of
Shibata,—according to the usage of the Japanese nobility I am resolved
before that comes to pass to cut my belly, and to have my body reduced
to ashes to prevent its being seen or found by the enemy.   As for you,
if there remains any hope of mercy, I will be pleased if ye save your
persons.'   Not only all they (the gentlemen), but their wives and
sons also, without a single exception, made answer that they would
follow him to the other world.   Shibata then added: 'I greatly
esteem the readiness of your minds, and the conformity of your
wills to mine.   My only regret is that I have no means of rewarding
the great fidelity and love I see in all.'   And with this he caused
many viands and instruments of music to be brought, and they
all began to eat, and to drink, and to play, and to sing with great
bursts of laughter and merriment, as if they had been at some triumph
or actual dance.   Already much dry straw had been placed in all the
rooms, while the doors and windows of the castle were kept well shut,
without a single arquebus or arrow being discharged therefrom at the
enemy, who were amazed at the quiet of arms and the loud sounds of
music and feasting.   Upon this, powder was strewn over the straw,

and it was fired, and the buildings began to burn. Then Shibata, first of all springing furiously upon his wife, the sister of Nobunaga (whom he had married a few months before), slew her with strokes of his dagger, and after her his other ladies, sons, and daughters in succession; and immediately after that, cutting his belly in cross fashion with the same dagger, the miserable and unhappy man perished. All the others did likewise, first killing their dear consorts, sons, and daughters. Whence, in place of the past songs, there suddenly rose cries and wailings so high and horrible that they drowned the roar of the flames. Some of them there were who, in lieu of cutting their own paunches, accorded to match themselves one against the other, and slew themselves with mutual wounds. And that not one vestige of such desperate ferocity should remain, the fire immediately coming on them devoured with every thing else these bloody and ghastly corpses."

On reading this very circumstantial account of this hideous hecatomb, one naturally asks how Froez came to be in a position to serve up all its gruesome details. He has his answer to that query quite ready:—"One old woman only, respected and skilled in discoursing, was left alive for the express purpose that she should afterwards pass out of the fortress, as she did, and relate to the enemy at full length the event that she had witnessed. And in this fashion ended the most valorous Captain there had been in Japan in the time of Nobunaga." This tribute to Shibata is a high one indeed, when we remember that those were the heroic days of Japan. It is doubtless true that Shibata's reputation for derring-do stood exceedingly high among his compeers, but we must not overlook the fact that Froez had been warmly befriended by him on more than one occasion, and hospitably welcomed by him at Kita-no-shō in May, 1581, when he "had made a splendid and regal banquet" for the missionary and his companions and asked him "about many things of Europe."[1] One odd thing is that Sakuma, Shibata's Captain-General, was specially mentioned by the missionaries for his extreme courtesy, the last thing which one would expect in a man known to his contemporaries as "Yasha Gemba"—"Demon Gemba."

Sakuma, now thirty years of age, was also involved in the

---

[1] See Froez's short letter of May 29th, 1581. From that of May 19th of the same year it is plain that Shibata, like most of his compatriots, was a staunch supporter of the grand principle of toleration for all beliefs not prejudicial to social order:—"After that we went to visit Shibatadono, who welcomed me courteously and told me that he would be pleased that the Law of God should be spread abroad; but that, notwithstanding, he was minded to do no violence to any one in that, adding in his own tongue, 'Tegoraxidori,' that is, that what proves of most worth will conquer."

ruin of his lord and uncle, Shibata. After the rout on the
frontier he had hidden in an Echizen peasant's hut, and was
betrayed by the honest-hearted, horny-handed son of toil " from
the hope of a reward." "A son of Shibata's, sixteen or
seventeen years of age, a youth of rare parts, whom Nobunaga
had chosen as the husband for one of his daughters, was
also captured. Both of them were conducted to Kyōto and
promenaded through the principal streets on a kind of cart (which
is the greatest infamy there can be, answering, approximately,
to being dragged at a horse's tail with us) to the appointed
place outside the city, where they were both beheaded by the
order of Faxiba." Though Froez says nothing of the matter,
it would seem that Hideyoshi was by no means anxious that
Sakuma should be sent to kneel at the blood-pit. " Thinking
it a great pity to lose so brave a man," says one Japanese
record, "Hideyoshi instructed a certain person to go to
Sakuma and urge him to take service with him, promising
to give him a large fief. Sakuma, however, defiantly repulsed
the overture, and was executed at Rokujōgahawa in Kyōto. He
died at the age of thirty, in a manner worthy of the nickname
of ' Demon Gemba.' "

It soon became apparent that the brilliant forced march
from Ōgaki to the Echizen frontier at Shizugatake had
served to decide the fate not only of Shibata, but of his two
confederates in the South as well. Nobutaka, put to sore
straits in Mino, made a desperate effort to join Takikawa in
Ise ; but his own vassals turned against him and put him to
death. As for Takikawa, he had been driven back into
Nagashima, and Hideyoshi now sent him a message to shave
his head in token of submission, to abandon his fortress, and to
come with his son to serve in his Court. The son was offered an
estate of 10,000 koku in Harima, and Takikawa himself a pension
of 4,000 koku if he obeyed. " If he did not obey, he (Hideyoshi)
would command the peasants of Nagashima to take his head
and bring it to him. Now (such are human vicissitudes)
Takikawa being originally one whom Faxiba might have
served with great honour to himself, constrained by cruel
necessity, accepted the conditions, surrendered his fortress,
shaved his head and beard, and with 1,500 persons of his
household came humbly to render obedience to Faxiba."

On returning to Kyōto from his Echizen expedition, Hideyoshi
at once began to show that he intended to carry matters with
a high hand.   First of all he celebrated Nobunaga's obsequies
with great circumstance and splendour.   His next step was
to remove Sambōshi from Azuchi, and to place him in the
Castle of Sakamoto "with a gentleman who should have care
of him without any pomp or grandeur."   His ostensible tutor,
Nobuo, the second and now the sole surviving son of Nobunaga,
who had previously held the greater part of Ise, had his fief
augmented by the addition of Iga and Owari, and was dismissed
to see to its administration with a stern hint to be contented
with what he had received, and to be very careful to keep
aloof from Kyōto and the Home Provinces.   Of the original
members of the Board of Administration, one, Shibata, had
just been made away with, and Hideyoshi now found means
to rid himself of all interference from the two others.   Niwa,
who had formerly held Wakasa, was now well content to be
removed from there to the much larger and wealthier fief of
Echizen, which placed him some forty miles further from
the capital.   Ikeda was a more delicate subject to handle.
Most of the province of Settsu was in his possession; the great
trunk road from the West lay through his domains, while
his proximity to Kyōto made it difficult to disregard him.
However, he had to consent to exchange Settsu for Mino,
Nobutaka's former province, although he "did so very much
against his will."   At the same time Hideyoshi removed
all the other petty princelets—Takayama of Takatsuki among
the number—from Settsu, and dismantled most of the fortresses
there, while he also appropriated Kawachi and Idzumi, and
thus effectually provided against any possible attack from the
south.   On the north-west, his brother Hidenaga, now invested
with the lordship of Tamba, Tango, and Inaba, kept ward over
the approaches to Kyōto from that direction.   Mōri, still lord
of some ten provinces in the extreme west of the main island,
was indeed formidable, but Hideyoshi managed to settle things
with him without drawing the sword again.   It will be
remembered that in June, 1582, Hideyoshi, on hearing of the
death of Nobunaga, "had concluded a very advantageous
truce with Mōri before divulging it."   From what Froez
says it is apparent that while Mōri had not actually

violated this pact of 1582, he had been on the outlook for
a chance of doing so.   Writes Froez (September 3rd, 1584) :—

"The King of Amanguci (*i.e.* Mōri), by the beginning of
1583 had sent to Hideyoshi an ambassador concerning the matters
in dispute between them, and Hideyoshi kept him always close to
himself on purpose that he might afterwards recount to his king
(*i.e.* Mōri) the events he had witnessed. And thereupon he gave
him a letter, which he first read aloud before many cavaliers, and
it was of the following tenor :—' Last year, not being yet much in
harness, I sent to say that you must let me have five of the nine
kingdoms (provinces) that remained to you, because you had so
promised to Nobunaga. You pretended not to understand, imagining
that my affairs would not go well. Now I will leave it to your
ambassador to tell how they have turned out.   I am not very
hungry for your kingdoms (provinces), but I wish you to keep
your word, and if you satisfy me in this matter we shall remain in
peace ; but if not, then we will see it with arms in our hands.
Success will be for him who has the better luck. And if you
resolve upon that alternative, I will take care to come and look
for you.' The King of Amanguci (Mōri), frightened by this letter,
and by the report of the ambassador, has found it best to accept
the bargain, giving him kingdoms and hostages. And so peace
has been preserved."

The provinces surrendered were very soon returned, however ;
and from then down to his death Hideyoshi was always on
very good terms with the House of Mōri.

Thus within two years from the death of Nobunaga,
Hideyoshi's power was greater than that of his former chief
had ever been. Not merely had the dominion acquired by
Nobunaga been prevented from falling asunder, but it had
been considerably consolidated and extended. However, even
within forty miles of the capital there was still some stiff
and stubborn fighting to be done. The monks of Negoro
had never been reduced, and now they were as powerful and
truculent as ever. Hideyoshi, apprised that they were about
to assume the offensive, ordered the muster of a large force
at Kyōto without specifying its objective. Just as he was on
the march to Negoro, news came that Nobuo in Ise had
killed three of his principal vassals who had given hostages
to Hideyoshi, and had entered into a secret alliance with his
uncle, Iyeyasu. In the latter Hideyoshi recognised an antagonist
of a very different stamp from Shibata. He had seen much
of Iyeyasu at various times between 1565 and 1576, and his
intercourse with him had served to convince him that the
Tokugawa chieftain was a leader of men with very few weak

spots in his armour. Brilliant he possibly was not; but in
combined soundness of judgement, breadth of view, tenacity
of purpose, dogged staying power in the face of ill-luck, and
circumspection in the midst of prosperity, Iyeyasu was unique
among all Hideyoshi's possible adversaries.[2] As for Nobuo,
it was a different matter entirely. With 60,000 men Hideyoshi
advanced swiftly into Ise, and reduced all the strongholds there
in a wonderfully short time. Iga was over-run with scarcely
any resistance, and the invaders moved so promptly that they
were able to seize the fords of the Kisogawa and press forward
into Owari and occupy the fortress of Inuyama. In this third
province, however, their difficulties began, for eight miles
from Inuyama Iyeyasu held Komaki with 20,000 men; and
Nobuo's force was now also under his orders. Hideyoshi offered
large bribes to certain of Iyeyasu's officers; they reported
the matter to their chief, and he promptly ordered them to
accept the overture. The result was that the Kyōto troops
were lured into an ambuscade, and lost heavily in the furious
action that followed. Although victorious on this occasion,
Iyeyasu's men had also suffered severely; so severely that it
was possibly for that reason that their commander judged it
inexpedient to assume the offensive. Most Japanese accounts
assert that Iyeyasu promptly retreated, that Hideyoshi followed
him up, intending to bring him to a general action, and that
just as he was coming into touch with the easterners Iyeyasu
again fell back so rapidly that his opponent was overcome
with astonishment. From Froez it appears that a force of
30,000 men, which had appeared to reinforce Hideyoshi, had
been sent back, as he had no need for so many troops, and
that his original army was occupied for several months in
a warfare of sieges and blockades. It was neither by sheer
military ability nor by mere superior diplomacy that Hideyoshi
was wont to worst his opponents, but by a unique combination
of the two; and Iyeyasu, well aware of the fact, took his

---

[2] In the person of Iyeyasu Japan supplied yet another instance of the
truth of the old Scotch saw to the effect that "gude gear is made up in
little buik." In the *Yeiya Meima* we are informed that "Iyeyasu was a
miserly man, writing a bad hand. He was small in stature, rotund and fat.
A man of few words, he had an ugly mien. When he gave commands on
the battle-field or when hawking he looked like a veritable war-god, and
his voice was then heard to a distance of seventeen or eighteen *chō*" (a
mile and a quarter). In all this there is nothing inconsistent with what
the missionaries tell us of him.

measures accordingly. He knew perfectly well that he could
never carry the war into Hideyoshi's own territory with any
permanent success, but he was no less well assured that he
could hold his own against even the genius of his antagonist
if allowed to fight on his own ground and under conditions
of his own choosing. Of so much Hideyoshi was also doubtless
convinced. At all events, he at last began to negotiate
seriously and in good faith. With Nobuo it was not difficult
to arrange terms; but Iyeyasu's caution made a speedy
settlement with him no easy matter. Early in 1585, however,
Hideyoshi adopted Iyeyasu's second son, Hideyasu, then eleven
years of age, and at the same time divorced his own younger
half-sister from her husband and bestowed her on Iyeyasu in
marriage. Still the latter showed no eagerness to proceed to
Kyōto; and it was only when Hideyoshi sent his own mother
to Iyeyasu's fief as a hostage that the latter went up to the
capital and made his submission to Hideyoshi.[3] Thus assured

---

3 Inasmuch as Hideyoshi's relatives play no inconsiderable part in the
history of the time, it may be well to deal with them compendiously here.
Hideyoshi's father was a peasant who did not enjoy the luxury of a family
name. Yasuke, as he was called, married a woman by whom he had two
children,—Hideyoshi, and a daughter older than he. When Yasuke died, his
widow married one Chikuami, by whom she had a son and a daughter.
Hideyoshi thus had an elder sister, and a younger half-brother (Hidenaga)
and half-sister. His family tree stands thus:—

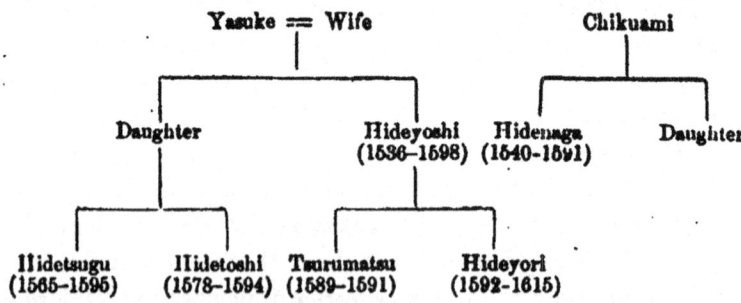

Hidenaga, the half-brother (known at first as Koichirō), rendered good
service during Hideyoshi's campaign in Harima in 1578, while in 1579 he
reduced the western half of Tamba. In 1583 we have found him serving
against Shibata, and appointed Lord of Tamba, Tango, and Inaba. For his
services against the monks of Negoro in 1585 he received Yamato, Kishiu,
and Idzumi with a revenue of 1,000,000 koku. With Hidetsugu he led the
expedition against Shikoku in the same year, and in 1587 he commanded
against Shimadzu of Satsuma. In 1590 he was in charge of Osaka during
the expedition against Hōjō, and in the following year he died at the age
of fifty-one. As he had no son of his own, he adopted his half-sister's second
son, Hidetoshi, who seems to have been almost as much of a monster as
his elder brother Hidetsugu. In 1594 he went to the hot-springs of
Totsukawa in Yamato, to be cured of a loathsome disease. While there

of the fidelity and good-will of perhaps the only man in Japan who could have held him at arm's length for a term of years, Hideyoshi now found himself free to deal with their reverences of Negoro. They had meanwhile been the recipients of a rough lesson from two of his officers. As soon as he had marched against Nobuo in Ise in 1584, 15,000 of these *bonzes* had come pouring down into Idzumi, burning and ravaging everything on their route to capture the new city of Ōsaka. As yet the city was unfurnished with ramparts, and most of its garrison had been sent to Ise. Consequently, on the approach of the 15,000 monks the confusion and panic that prevailed in it were intense. According to Froez, if the priests had once seized Ōsaka, it would have been very easy for them to march on the capital, for Hideyoshi had dismantled nearly all the fortresses of Settsu and Kawachi just a few months before. However, one of Hideyoshi's officers, Saiga Magoichi by name, had, in accordance with orders, assembled with the utmost secrecy some 6,000 or 7,000 men in Kishiwada Castle, half-way between Negoro and Ōsaka, and of this the monks were blissfully unaware. Saiga allowed their van to pass, and then fell upon the others with such effect that his men, not having time to take and count heads "according to the custom of Japan," had a busy half-hour of it lopping off ears. Four thousand *bonzes* were cut down here; and the peasants, seeing the others staggered when they received the news of the unexpected fate of their fellows, attacked them with bludgeons and clubbed them to death as they fled. Most of the fugitives tried to regain their monastery by the road along the sea-front. This was unfortunate for them, for Konishi (the Don Augustine of the Jesuits, who now makes his first appearance in the missionary letters) manned seventy vessels "with a great number of muskets and some pieces of artillery formerly given to Nobunaga by the King of Bungo, and, keeping along the Idzumi

---

he went to Yoshino, where he ordered some of his attendants to jump into the abyss of one of the great waterfalls there. They obeyed, but they were careful to take the young fiend with them.

Of Hideyoshi's elder brother, Hidetsugu, who was adopted by Hideyoshi in 1592, we shall have much to say in the text. Hideyoshi's younger half-sister had been happily married to a certain Saji, who was so broken-hearted when his wife was taken from him to be given to Iyeyasu that he committed suicide. This half-sister died in Kyōto in 1590 at the age of forty-eight.

Besides Hideyasu (Iyeyasu's son), Hideyoshi adopted several other sons, the most notable of whom was the young man afterwards known as Kobayakawa Hideaki, who is to appear in the *rôle* of the traitor at Sekigahara in 1600.

shore, put them to great straits." Accordingly, Hideyoshi had not
so much difficulty with the men of Negoro when he proceeded to
assail and burn their ecclesiastical eyrie. When it fell into his
hands, there was no Hiyei-san holocaust. He merely crucified
a few of the leaders, and allowed the others to withdraw. Many
of them found service with Iyeyasu; and a certain picked body
of their best marksmen formed the original of that "Guard of
a Hundred Men" which continued to hold a privileged position
in Yedo Castle down to the date of the fall of feudalism little
more than a generation ago. This conquest had the effect of
throwing the whole rich province of Kii into Hideyoshi's hands.
Hidenaga, his half-brother who had rendered good service in the
brief campaign, was forthwith invested with the lordship of the
new domain as well as of the adjoining provinces of Yamato
and Idzumi. Henceforth the only base from which the capital
could be assailed from the south was Shikoku, and with Shikoku
Hideyoshi was now in a position to deal effectually.

In the introductory chapter it was stated that something like
a first-class feudal power had arisen in Shikoku. While
Nobunaga had been prosecuting his conquests in Central Japan,
Chōsokabe of Tosa had reduced practically the whole of the
7,000 square miles of the island to obedience; and it was not till
1582 that Nobunaga found himself in a position to challenge
his pretensions. Then, just at the very time he was murdered,
a strong expedition against Chōsokabe was embarking at Sakai
under Nobutaka, while Niwa was soon to follow with an
additional force. The death of Nobunaga occasioned the
abandonment of the projected attack, and Chōsokabe was left
free to consolidate his conquests. By 1584 he was so strong that
he threatened Ōsaka during Hideyoshi's struggle with Iyeyasu,
and for doing so he was now called upon to pay the price. No
sooner had the monks of Negoro been brought to reason than
the troops employed against them were launched in two divisions, under Hidenaga and Hidetsugu, against Shikoku; while,
acting in concert with these, Kobayakawa, uncle of Mōri
Terumoto, fell upon the north-western end of the island with a
strong force from Mōri's provinces. A campaign of three months
served to convince Chōsokabe that he was hopelessly overmatched;
and when extremely generous terms were unexpectedly tendered
him at the eleventh hour, he was not slack in accepting them.

He was left with the single province of Tosa (220,000 *koku*), while Awa was assigned to Hachisuka, Sanuki to other captains of Hideyoshi, and Iyo to Kobayakawa as the reward of his co-operation.

Before this year of 1585 was out, the indefatigable Hideyoshi had won triumphs elsewhere. As a consequence of the Echizen campaign of 1583, Kaga, Noto, and Etchiu had all submitted. But when Niwa was transferred to Echizen, some of the barons in Etchiu had become restless, and while Hideyoshi was occupied with Iyeyasu and Nobuo, a certain Sassa Narimasa had openly revolted and had seized nearly the whole of Etchiu. Hideyoshi now moved a force against him and soon captured his stronghold of Toyama and brought him to order, and Etchiu was then given to Mayeda Toshinaga, the son of Hideyoshi's friend, Mayeda Toshiiye, who held Noto and Kaga. Niwa, the former member of the Board of Administration, would thus find plenty of occupation on his rear if he made any hostile movement against Kyōto. To make any such project on his part still hopeless, Hideyoshi now stripped him of the south-western half of his extensive fief of Echizen, and placed one of his own captains, Hori, there to guard the mountain passes.

To quote one Japanese authority: "Thus the whole of the Hokurikudō was brought under Hideyoshi's sway, except the province of Echigo, where Uyesugi Kagekatsu ruled supreme. Followed by no more than ten or twelve attendants, Hideyoshi crossed the Etchiu border into Echigo. To the astonished guardsmen of the frontier he said, 'I am Hideyoshi. Your master has already sent me messages of peace. I have therefore come to see him to settle matters with him personally.' This intelligence was immediately conveyed to Uyesugi, who at once hurried to meet Hideyoshi and came to a satisfactory and definite understanding with him." This account is probably correct; at all events it is in no conflict with Froez's statement (1583) that "the King of Gecigo in the region of Bando has sent hostages to Faxiba and concluded friendship with him."

There are other accounts of the affair which are much more circumstantial and dramatic. The great and impenetrable mountain-rampart which belts Etchiu off from Shinano and Echigo terminates in a lofty spur just where the Etchiu meets the Echigo strand. Here the only avenue from the one province to the other runs under beetling cliffs along a very narrow strip of beach often impassable when the strong gales of winter drive the Sea of Japan hard and high upon the coast. This spot is known as the Parent-forgetting Child-forgetting (*Oya-shiradzu Ko-shiradzu*) Pass, from the notion that the danger of the passage is such that it becomes a sheer case of each for himself. Just beyond this point stood Uyesugi's frontier castle of Otsurumi, then held by one Suga, a trusty captain of his. Hideyoshi, with a few followers, made his way to the vicinity of this fortress, and sent Kimura, one of his attendants, to request admission for "Hideyoshi's ambassador." When Suga refused the request, he was urged to meet the "ambassador" in his camp; and on proceeding thither, he was surprised to find that he had to deal, not with an ambassador, but with Hideyoshi himself. Hideyoshi now asked him to escort him to Uyesugi; but Suga replied that he was in a position neither to grant nor to deny the request; all he could do was to inform his master and to offer Hideyoshi the hospitality of the castle in the meantime. On receiving Suga's message, Uyesugi at once summoned his leading vassals to advise as to the best course of action in the extraordinary circumstances. The majority of the councillors urged the assassination of Hideyoshi, arguing that such was by far the simplest way of ridding themselves of the most formidable foe they could have, who had thus providentially delivered himself into their hands. However, young Naoye, who had been made one of Uyesugi's chief counsellors three years before, in 1582, at the early age of twenty-three, scouted the proposal in scathing language. "Hideyoshi's coming amongst us all unprotected," said he, "is evidence of his profound regard for our lord. With meaner men he would never take such a risk. It is because he has a just estimation of our master's real disposition that he trusts himself among us. Were we to abuse his confidence and slay him, the tale of our dastardly treachery would be told to generations yet unborn to our eternal shame. No! Let our lord meet magnanimity with magnanimity; let him meet Hideyoshi, and let them see whether they cannot come to an understanding. If they cannot agree, we will fight, but not till Hideyoshi has been sent back to his own people."

The result of the council was that Uyesugi set out with Naoye and no more than fifteen other followers, and met

Hideyoshi at Otsurumi. "Hideyoshi's manner was genial and free from all constraint; no one would have supposed that he was in the country of an enemy, utterly without defence. Uyesugi was so impressed with this that he began to perceive he was dealing with a greater man than himself." In a private interview an understanding was easily reached, and the solemn Uyesugi[4] was so charmed with his audacious visitor that he saw him safely past *Oya-shiradzu* and some twelve miles on his return journey to Kyōto.

Thus within the short space of three years from the death of Nobunaga in 1582, Hideyoshi had been able not merely to impose himself as over-lord upon all who had acknowledged his former chief as suzerain, but even to extend his authority over some 23,000 or 24,000 square miles of territory, where Nobunaga had never exercised the slightest influence. At this date he was lord of about exactly one-half of Japan, and that too by far the most populous and the richest half. The 40,000 square miles of the Kwantō and of the extreme north of the main island had yet to be reduced, while the Barons of Kyūshū (16,000 square miles) had hitherto treated his envoys with but scant respect. But Kyūshū and the Kwantō lay far apart, and could lend each other no support, even if they had been minded to do so, while the 56,000 or 57,000 square miles of Shikoku and the main island under Hideyoshi's sway lay all compactly together. Their levies could be readily combined and hurled in a single mass whether against the isolated and distracted southern island or against the unsupported and the disunited north. However, the time for any such enterprise was not yet ripe, although its fulness of days was maturing apace.

At this point it may be well to pause and consider how Hideyoshi so far compares with his predecessor. One Church historian would have us believe that the new man of destiny was merely a servile copier of Nobunaga, and that his great and abiding aim was to outdo his former chief in sheer crass purposeless megalomania. Let us look somewhat closely into this charge. As has been shown, the chief devices employed by

---

4 He is said to have been seen to smile but once in his lifetime, and that was when a pet monkey stole his nightcap, and, running up a tree, clapped it on his pate, and then glowered at Uyesugi with all his own solemnity.

Nobunaga to advance his empire and to consolidate his power were destruction and extermination. Between 1582 and 1585 how much had Hideyoshi destroyed,—how many foes had he exterminated? The monastery of Negoro is about the sum total of his achievement in the former direction, for Kita-no-shō had been fired by Shibata himself. As regards the victims who had been ruthlessly sacrificed to Hideyoshi's ambition, Shibata's son, Gonroku, and Sakuma about complete the list. Doubtless Shibata, if captured, would not have been spared, for his previous treatment of Hideyoshi and the deadly antipathy of the two men to each other rendered mercy impossible there; but as it was, Shibata was not sent to the blood-pit. As for Nobutaka, when he and his were in the hollow of Hideyoshi's hand, after dire offence had been given, not a hair of their heads was harmed, and it was after he had again taken up arms that Nobutaka was done to death by his own followers. When Takikawa stood at Hideyoshi's mercy, he was treated with contemptuous indulgence. With Iyeyasu, with Nobuo, with Uyesugi, Hideyoshi was utterly averse to pushing things to extremities; it is tolerably safe to assume that even if he had had them safe under ward in Kyōto he would have been in no hurry to send them to the execution ground. In his visit to Uyesugi—a very much saner proceeding than the visit of Louis XI. to Peronne, by the way—it is hard to discern what incident in the career of Nobunaga he was "copying." Then with respect to Chōsokabe, at the very moment he could have exterminated him, very honourable and handsome terms were proffered to the beaten chief. Besides Shibata's son and Sakuma, the latter of whom Hideyoshi actually endeavoured to save, there are the leaders among the Negoro monks to be considered. Several of these are indeed said to have been crucified; but there was no slight ground for regarding these mongrel men of God and of war as being really of the breed of bandits and brigands.[5] As it was, all but a few of them were allowed to retire to find service with Iyeyasu or elsewhere. How many of the inmates of Hiyei-san did Nobunaga allow to retire on September 29th, 1571? The monks of Kōya-san had given Hideyoshi infinite trouble while he was dealing with

---

[5] See Vilela's letter of 1563.

Iyeyasu in 1584, and he had threatened that he would burn their nest when his hands were free. As soon as his hands were free, Ōki, the chief priest, begged for mercy, and had no difficulty in obtaining it. If it had been Nobunaga, there would have been a big blaze on the Kōya-san about that time.[6] So far as regards destruction and extermination.

Nobunaga's constructive record has already been examined and found to be the reverse of important. Now, during the three years between 1582 and 1585, the peasant-ruler had so much warlike and so much diplomatic work on his hands that it would have been no wonder if neither time nor energy had been left for constructive effort either in statesmanship or in anything else. Yet here we find a thoroughly efficient system of central administration organised, with all its machinery supplied, and set to vigorous work. Justice was now administered as it had not been since the days of the Hōjōs in Kamakura. The coinage was reformed to suit modern tradal requirements. A comprehensive national land survey seems to have been already begun, although most modern Japanese authorities assign its inception to 1588 or 1589.[7] Brigandage and piracy, which had been exceedingly rife, were being vigorously suppressed,[8] wherever the power of the strong and efficient central administration extended.

[6] Ishida Mitsunari (of whom we shall have so much to say presently), afterwards the soul of the great coalition against Iyeyasu, was concerned in this matter. It was through him that Ōki the chief priest approached Hideyoshi. Ōki afterwards showed his gratitude to Ishida by working zealously for him just before Sekigahara. Among other services he then persuaded the Lord of Anotsu in Ise and the Lord of Ōtsu in Ōmi to surrender their castles to Ishida's partisans.

[7] In the spring of 1585, Aydono, Hideyoshi's Christian secretary, told Froes that "all the lands round Kyōto had already been surveyed, and that Hideyoshi was receiving from them a revenue of 900,000 *koku*, which is in silver 900,000 *tarris*—that is more than a million of gold."

[8] Even in 1586 the Inland Sea was far from safe. "The Vice-Provincial, proceeding to an island belonging to the greatest corsair of all Japan, Noximandono by name, who resides in a great fortress, had a great fleet of vessels which are constantly cruising, and is so powerful that along the sea-board of several provinces many cities pay him an annual tribute to be exempted from his attentions,—the Vice-Provincial, I say, endeavoured to obtain from the same a safe-conduct in order that our people, who traverse that sea, should be safe from his corsairs. Wherefore at this good opportunity he sent him a present, begging that favour. He received the brother who carried the present with much courtesy, and invited him to his fortress, finally giving him a banner of silk with his arms upon it, saying that when his people wished to injure us, we should show them that ensign." Other worthies of that kidney elsewhere were then meeting with short shrift, and after Hideyoshi's conquest of Kyūshū in 1587 the Inland Sea at once became as safe as a Ball-room or Scotland Yard itself.

Nobunaga's constructive efforts were almost entirely confined to fortress and palace-building. The erection of a palace for the Emperor, another for the Crown Prince, and a keep for himself was all that he had done either to extend or embellish Kyōto, which so late as 1577, at all events, was a miserable place enough in spite of its 900,000 or 1,000,000 inhabitants. Then there were the fortress of Gifu and the new city of Azuchi. The latter, apart from Nobunaga's own famous citadel and the *yashiki* of his chief retainers, never became of much consequence. In 1582 the town itself contained only some 6,000 or 7,000 houses,—smaller than Funai with 8,000 or Hakata with 10,000. Before the end of 1585 Kyōto had been greatly improved and enlarged; a grand new palace for the Emperor had been reared "which appears to be in no way inferior to those the Emperors of Japan had in the olden times." At the same time, 60,000 men were at work on an immense fortress-palace for Hideyoshi himself there. At first, indeed, it seems to have been his intention to remove the capital from Kyōto, for in 1583 Froez tells us he had requested the "Dairi (Emperor) and the principal monasteries of the *bonzes* to pass to Ōsaka." There, in that year, what was to be the greatest and strongest fortress ever seen in Japan had been commenced, and an army of 30,000 labourers had been set to work on it, toiling night and day. It took more than three years to complete it, although as time went on the host of workers was doubled. Froez was in the Home Provinces during the May, June, and July of 1586, and during all that time 60,000 men were employed in constructing the moats, and had been at the work for a long time previously.

"The walls are of great amplitude and height,—all of stone. In order that the multitude of workers should not cause confusion, it was ordained that each master should have his determined place, where he should work, a great number of people being employed during the night in emptying the water which continually kept rising in the fosses. What is the cause of much marvel in this matter is to see whence such a great number of stones of all kinds of sizes have been taken; there being a great lack of them there. For this reason he commanded the neighbouring lords for twenty or thirty leagues around to send boats loaded with them. In this way the city of Sakai alone has been charged to dispatch 200 vessels every day. So that from our house we sometimes saw as many as 1,000 entering under full sail and in good order together. On discharging, the stones are placed with such care and heed that none (without leaving his head there) might take a single one of them to place it elsewhere. And in order that the work might go forward with greater heat, it happening that a lord who supervised fell short either in men or industry, he was at once sent into exile, and stripped of his States and revenues. Besides the towers and the bulwarks around the fortresses, which are visible from afar by reason of their height, and the splendour of the tiles, which are all gilded, he is rearing many other remarkable edifices there."

Meanwhile, as has been said, another 60,000 men were at work in Kyōto, under the superintendence of Hideyoshi's nephew, Hidetsugu. "Nevertheless the said Quambacundono (Hideyoshi) being a prince of great industry takes it as a recreation to pass ten or fifteen days assisting at the works, now in Kyōto, now in Ōsaka." As for the city of Ōsaka as distinct from the castle, there were already four miles of continuous streets between the Yodo and Tennōji, while an equally extensive quarter was rapidly rising in another direction.

And how with all this was the peasant-ruler regarded by his subjects? Writes Froez in January, 1584:—"But in brief these manners of his do not please. The many lords oppressed by him and driven from their houses are watching for a good opportunity to avenge themselves." In October, 1586, he tells us that Hideyoshi "had far outstripped his predecessor Nobunaga in grandeur of State, in power, in honour, and in riches. . . . Into his hands come nearly all the gold and silver of Japan, together with the other rich and precious things; and he is so feared and obeyed that with no less ease than a father of a family disposes of the persons of his household he rules the principal kings and lords of Japan; changing them at every moment, and stripping them of their original fiefs, he sends them into different parts, so as to allow none of them to strike root deep." A little after this the missionaries discovered that if Hideyoshi was not loved, he was at least esteemed.

In 1585 the peasant ruler was appointed Kwanbaku, and from this year down to 1591, when he was named Taikō, we shall speak of him as Hideyoshi, or the Regent, indifferently.

P

CHAPTER IX.

HIDEYOSHI'S REDUCTION OF KYŪSHŪ AND CHRISTIANITY.

ANXIOUS as they were at the time, the Jesuits found no set-back to their immediate prospects in the death of Nobunaga. Their fine house in Azuchi which had been sacked and pillaged by the rabble of the town was indeed abandoned; but inasmuch as Azuchi had even already ceased to be of any importance, politically or otherwise, this was, after all, a matter of comparatively small moment.

"Our seminary was transferred to our church in Kyōto, but as the house was too small for thirty pupils, nearly all of illustrious birth, it was necessary for them to pass to the fortress of Takatsuki, where, besides the commodiousness and size of the dwellings, they are, as has already been said, under the discipline of our people, and under the protection of Justo and his father Darius, who treat them as their own sons. These youths progress greatly in virtue and in letters, and are of such good parts that what is learned in three years in the schools of Europe, they easily master in three or four months. Already some of them begin to show themselves adapted for preaching and for confuting the falsity of the *bonzes*, with great hope of notable service to the Lord."

However, the seminary was not destined to remain very long at Takatsuki. As has been said, Hideyoshi, after crushing Shibata, removed Ikeda and all the smaller barons from Settsu and Kawachi, and took possession of these provinces himself; and among the others, Takayama of Takatsuki was then called upon to surrender his estates, and to content himself with the fief of Akashi in Harima. Thanks to Takayama's prevision, however, this did not inconvenience the Jesuits so seriously as might have been expected. In the new city of Ōsaka Takayama had already built a fine *yashiki* for himself, and he strongly urged Father Organtino Gnecchi to ask for an interview with Hideyoshi and beg him for a site for a church and a house beside the great fortress. Although Hideyoshi "was wont to receive even persons of great quality *con severo ciglio e senza parole*, he welcomed Father Organtino with such cordiality—perhaps to acquire fame among foreigners and even to be celebrated in

Europe itself—that every one was amazed. He did not receive him in the common saloon, but introduced him into the interior rooms and kept discoursing with him for a good space in the presence of the treasurer and a secretary, who were both Christians; and not content with this, he went in person to assign to the said Father one of the most pleasant sites to be seen in the neighbourhood." Takayama at once set to work to build a magnificent church here; and the first mass was celebrated in it on the Christmas Day of 1583. Shortly after, the Seminarists were all removed from Takatsuki to Ōsaka. In 1584 we are told that "Hideyoshi was not only not opposed to the things of God, but he even showed that he made much account of them, and preferred them to all the sects of the *bonzes*. He puts much trust in the Christians, admires their customs, and particularly those of Justo, such continence and chastity as his in such a green age seeming to him to be beyond the strength of man.. . . . In brief, he is entrusting to Christians his treasures, his secrets, and his fortresses of most importance, and shows himself well pleased that the sons of the great lords about him should adopt our customs and our law." Three or four of the ladies of his Court were converts; Magdalene, the secretary of his legitimate consort, being a zealous propagandist. In the December of 1584 the baptism of Manase Dōsan, one of Hideyoshi's Court physicians, caused no small commotion, for this Manase passed for one of the most distinguished sages and scholars of his time. According to the Jesuits, he had studied in all the great schools of China as well as of Japan, where he had extended his attention to matters far beyond the limited scope of medicine and surgery. Be this as it may, we learn from Japanese sources that he had been born in 1507, that he was regarded as the reviver of medical learning in Japan, and that he had held important posts under Ashikaga Yoshiteru as well as under Hideyoshi. As he lived long enough to hold office under Iyeyasu after Hideyoshi's death, it becomes plain that he evidently knew very well how to look after his own constitution.[1] Over the

---

[1] See Whitney's "Notes on the History of Medical Progress in Japan," *Transactions of the Asiatic Society of Japan*, vol. xii. p. 305. The Japanese accounts of the introduction of Christianity into Japan given in the following pages of these Notes are interesting, or, to speak more correctly, amusing; for it is difficult to see how they could be more wildly inaccurate than they are. .

conversion of this old *savant* of seventy-seven years of age
the missionaries were jubilant, and not without reason either,
for his whole school of eight hundred pupils immediately
followed his example and became proselytes. The *bonzes* were
so concerned about this that they appealed to the Emperor
Ōkimachi, whom Dōsan had previously successfully treated
for a most serious disorder, to interfere; but his interference
was fruitless.

With all this, however, the Jesuits would have fared poorly
if there had been no Don Justo Ucondono (Takayama Yūsho).
What he was in his personal intercourse with the Fathers
has already been stated—practically their submissive tool. At
last he had yielded to them in the matter of making Christianity
compulsory on his estates. When he was removed from
Takatsuki, he stipulated that his former vassals should not
be called in question for their faith. Such a stipulation was
a highly proper one. But what detracted greatly from its
value was that it was not made on behalf of the great and
sacred principle of toleration of belief, for as soon as Takayama
was seated at Akashi in Harima (70,000 *koku*) he proceeded
to give his new subjects the choice between Christianity and
eviction from their offices or holdings. In Hideyoshi's Court
Takayama kept on preaching Christianity in season and out of
season; and his pertinacity and his undoubted sincerity of
belief did not fail to attract several notable converts to the
Christian fold. His reputation for courage and for military
ability stood very high undoubtedly, while, if we are to believe
the priests, his charm of manner was remarkable among a people
where manners were, and are, emphatically regarded as making
the man. Consequently his personal character had great weight
with his friends and intimates. Among these were two men of
brilliant parts who had risen high in Hideyoshi's service by the
exercise of what constituted the only passport to his favour—
ability, to wit. Kuroda Yoshitaka, if we are to trust certain
Japanese accounts, had started life as a horse-dealer; but at the
time we first meet with mention of him in authentic records, in
1578, he had attained a great local reputation in the employment of a petty baron of Harima, Odera by name. In that year
Hideyoshi was to enter upon the war with Mōri for the possession
of the Chūgoku, and Odera having made up his mind to side

with Nobunaga's commander, had then sent Kuroda to Azuchi
to offer his services as guide to the expedition. Kuroda was not
long in earning Hideyoshi's favourable regard, and in 1581 or
1582 he was appointed Chief of his Staff. It was just before
this appointment was made that the other "new man" we have
referred to came on the scene. This was Konishi Yukinaga, the
son of a druggist of Sakai according to the common story.
This story may be true, and it may not: at all events, when we
first hear of Riusa, Konishi's father, he was acting as Governor
of Murotsu in Harima, while in 1584 he was transferred to Sakai
in the same capacity. At the beginning of the Chūgoku war in
1578 Ukida Naoiye held the two provinces of Bizen and Mimasaka, as something like a sub-feudatory of Mōri. At first Ukida
had endeavoured to safeguard himself by a masterly policy of
inactivity, but his chief retainers were not long in perceiving
that Hideyoshi, whose success had been as substantial as it was
unexpected, would not be satisfied with this. Then determined
to make a merit of a timely submission, Ukida sent one of his
vassals to arrange terms with Nobunaga's lieutenant. The
emissary on this occasion was Konishi Yukinaga. In 1582
this Ukida Naoiye fell seriously ill, and just before his
death entrusted his son to Hideyoshi, by whom he was adopted.
This young man is the Ukida Hideiye of whom we shall
have a good deal to say presently. At first he was known as
Ukida Hachirō, and it is as Fachirandono that he makes his
earlier appearances in the Jesuit letters. Konishi's influence
with young Ukida was exceedingly strong, even after he
(Konishi) had taken service directly with Hideyoshi. Through
the exertions of Takayama, Kuroda, Takayama's fellow-officer in
the household troops, and Konishi, whom the Jesuits term
Captain-General of the Sea, were baptized in 1583, and shortly
afterwards Konishi's younger brother and his father also became
Christians.

During 1584 Hideyoshi was tolerably busy in the field; but on
the conclusion of the peace with Iyeyasu in 1585 he spent a good
deal of his time in Ōsaka, and it appears that he saw something
of the missionaries during this time. We hear of him suddenly
appearing at the seminary accompanied by a son and a brother
of Nobunaga and several other lords, and of holding a long and
familiar conversation with Cespedes, the Superior. "You

know," said he to the priest, " that everything in your law
contents me, and I find no other difficulty in it, except its
prohibition of having more than one wife. Were it not for that
I would become a Christian at once." He had previously said
something similar to his rival in ugliness, the one-eyed Japanese
Jesuit, Laurenco with " the comical face," in whose conversation
he took pleasure ; and the Brother had thereupon presumed to
administer to him a half-jesting, half-serious lecture, which
Hideyoshi deigned to take in good part enough.

All this not unnaturally led the Vice-Provincial Coelho to
believe that he would meet with a favourable reception from the
Regent when he went up from Nagasaki to visit the Kyōto
district in the spring of 1586. But the reception he did
meet with exceeded his most sanguine expectations.[2] Not
forgetting the important matter of presents for the Regent
and his consort, Coelho, accompanied by Froez, seven other
Jesuits, fifteen Catechists, and six alumni of the Seminary,
appeared in Ōsaka Castle on May 4th, 1586, and was ushered
into a great saloon by Aydono, the Christian secretary, and
one of the eight Court physicians—not Manase Dōsan, but
one Jacuin Toquun (Seyakuin Hōin), of whom the missionaries
will have much to say by-and-by. Hideyoshi, on learning of
their arrival, told Mayeda of Kaga, the Daimyō of Tango,
and the ambassadors of Mōri to attend him, as he wished to
show them with what respect he would receive the foreigners.
He took his place upon a sort of throne, and when they
appeared they saluted him in the Japanese fashion at so great
a distance that they could scarcely discern the features of
his face. This part of the business was as stiff and formal
as well could be. But the priests had scarcely withdrawn to
the entrance, when they were recalled and ordered to
approach the throne, while all the lords except Don Justo
(Takayama) were requested to retire. After ordering in some
refreshments, Hideyoshi left his throne and went and sat

---

[2] A long account of this audience appears both in Crasset and in
Charlevoix. The latter has evidently trusted to Froez's long letter of October
7th, 1586, almost entirely, and has paraphrased some passages in it in a rather
ingenious, if not very ingenuous, fashion, while Crasset gives a few additional
details, doubtless taken from some other letter which we have not been able
to obtain. There are slight inaccuracies in both accounts. Strangely enough,
both refer this audience to the year 1585. Froez, who acted as interpreter,
says the first interview took place on May 4th, 1586.

down beside Coelho, and began to speak freely with him of
many things he had in his mind to do. Presently he commenced to talk over old times with Froez, the interpreter,
whom he had known since 1568. Then he turned to Coelho
and said some rather extraordinary things to him, to which
reference will be made in the chapter on the Korean war.
One thing was that he was even then thinking of reducing
one half of Japan to Christianity, and that after conquering
China, as he purposed to do, churches would be built everywhere,
and all ordered to become Christians. Shortly afterwards he
got up, and insisted upon personally conducting the whole
party over the castle. They were shown into all the rooms,
some of which contained priceless treasures of all sorts, and
one of them some splendid European furnishings—four beds
being specially mentioned—and then warning them to pick
their way carefully at some risky passages, he led them up to
the eighth story of the donjon, and stood there talking
familiarly with them for some time, in full view and much
to the wonder of the 60,000 men working in the fosses below.
On descending, he again sat down with them, ordered tea to
be brought, and with his own hand "reached the cups first
to the Vice-Provincial, and then to the other Fathers and to
the Brothers." This time the conversation lasted between two
and three hours, and again some remarkable things were said.

"He told us how he was resolved to divide the southern kingdoms,
minishing something of the state of all the lords there, and how
he would destroy and ruin with a great army every one of them
who refused to obey him. This lord evinced such liveliness in his
countenance and such frankness as he uttered these words, that we
could perceive without the least doubt that he had not a shadow of
suspicion of us. He also added that in the division of Japan he
wished to give Justo Ucondono and Riusa, the father of Augustin
(Konishi), who were present, the kingdom of Hizen, leaving the
port of Nagasaki to the Church, and for that letters patent would
be issued,—but this, it was to be understood, was to be after he had
thoroughly settled the affairs of Japan, and taken hostages, because
he wished to do everything in such a way that the Fathers should
not be hated by the lords of Hizen. And he wished them further
to understand that he made that donation to them on his own
initiative, and not at the instance of others."

"On the following day Toquun, the senior physician, came to
our house congratulating us on the success of our visit. And seeing
the seminary where there were so many youths of noble birth, he
said to the Father that when he considered the distance of the
kingdoms whence we came to Japan, a country so strange to us,

and where we suffered so many travails as he had several times heard, and that in addition to that we made such expenditures in Ōsaka in educating so many youths and maintaining other people merely from zeal to extend our law, there was no man animated by similar motives but must favour us greatly, and that for himself, from such reasons on his part, he offered to do so always as far as he could."

Doubtless the Jesuits did not take much more than a passing notice of this honeyed speech at the time. Later on, however, they had ample reason to recall it and to remember it well, for in less than fourteen months its subtle and bitter irony had become only too apparent. Perhaps no one in Japan did so much to check the progress of the Christian propaganda in the Empire as this very smooth and soft-spoken and courteous senior physician of Hideyoshi.[3] Coelho had been saying many masses and prayers in order that he might obtain three things from the Regent. In the first place he wished to have license to preach the Gospel in all his States; in the second he desired to have the Jesuit houses and churches exempted from having soldiers billeted in them as they were in Buddhist temples, which were selected as their quarters by passing troops, this being *un obligo universale che è imposto a bonzi sopra i loro Monasteri.* Thirdly he was anxious to have his *religieux* exempted from the burdens the Daimyō and the smaller lords imposed upon their own vassals. The last two items were, to say the least of it, rather peculiar, for in these respects Coelho was clearly endeavouring to establish for himself and

---

[3] The whole of this letter of Froez's (October 7th, 1586) is worthy of attention, inasmuch as it is replete with details of the greatest interest. Hideyoshi in Ōsaka was served by female attendants solely. In 1584 there had been 120 of them; their number had now increased to 300. They were strictly forbidden to leave the Palace. On the night after the interview with Coelho the Regent spent all the evening talking to his consort, in the presence of her attendants, of the Jesuits and their religion, and said that he was sorry that he had not made her see the Fathers. "She replied that she did not think this strange, and that she did not believe such a thought had occurred to him, as she was not wont to see any man in his palace. But the King said that there would have been nothing improper (in her doing so), because we were foreigners, good people, and different in our customs from the Japanese. And because he was much pleased with a *dobuou*,—that is, a kind of garment which the Father had presented to him, he made the Queen put it on, and willed that she should pass once or twice through the room with it. Which being done, she remained thus clothed while the conversation lasted. We have also learned how the Queen said these words to the King: 'I was much afraid lest your Majesty should not receive these Fathers with the amiability I desired, because they were foreigners and because the honour of their law so demanded; but after I have learned with what courtesy you have received them, I am exceedingly glad, and I thank your Majesty for it.' This favour of the Queen, with the others she afterwards did us, was a singular mercy of God; because till then she had shown herself averse to the law of God and very little inclined to our affairs."

his people a privileged position in the empire whose hospitality
they were enjoying. It would have been interesting if Buddhist
missionaries had preferred analogous requests to Philip II. of
Spain and Portugal, or to any of the Catholic rulers of Europe.
The Vice-Provincial, after much consultation, determined to
approach Hideyoshi through his consort, his consort having
previously been won over by her Christian secretary, Magdalene,
and a fellow-convert among the maids of honour. " The Queen,
moved by God, took the matter so much to heart that she kept
watching for an occasion of finding the King in the vein when
he might grant her this." She sent word to Coelho to draw up
the patent himself, and the Fathers drafted it with the utmost
care. When it was presented to Hideyoshi (at the right
moment), however, it was not found altogether satisfactory. As
regards the first clause, he remarked that as he was Kwambaku
(Regent), there was no need for mention of "his kingdoms";
and " throughout all Japan " was substituted for this. With
respect to the third paragraph, he said it was unnecessary, " as
there was no man in Japan who wished to give trouble or
annoyance to the Fathers. Nevertheless, when the causes were
adduced why it should remain in the patent, as he is of rare
intellect he at once approved of the reasons and gave his
consent." He ordered two copies of it to be engrossed—one to be
kept in Japan, and the other to be sent to Europe "in order
that it might be known by the Christian lords how greatly he ·
favoured Christianity. Both copies were not merely sealed, but
actually signed by Hideyoshi. After they had been received at
the Jesuit house, the Vice-Provincial, accompanied by Father
Organtino Gnecchi and some others, went to thank the Regent,
and on this occasion they were received with even greater
frankness and cordiality than before. As it became late,
Hideyoshi detained them to sup with him, and proved himself a
most exemplary and most entertaining host. Konishi shortly
afterwards pointed out to Ukida (Fachirandono), Daimyō of
Bizen, that it would be well for him to imitate his father the
Regent in this matter ; and Ukida at once provided Coelho with
a similar patent for his own fief. About the same time Kuroda
proved no less helpful. It was he who had carried through the
negotiations with Mōri in 1583, and he was now starting on
another mission to that chief. Coelho was exceedingly anxious

to obtain admission for his *religieux* into Yamaguchi, whence
Torres had been hunted thirty years before; and Kuroda, who
was greatly appreciated by Mōri, now promised to arrange
this matter in a satisfactory manner. Says Crasset:—" He
obtained from Morindono, King of Amanguchi, his friend,
not only that the Fathers should preach in his States, but
that they should also have three residences there—one in the
city of Amanguchi, the other in the port of Shimonoseki, and
the third in the kingdom of Iyo. Admirable effect of the
providence of God, who was preparing an asylum for the Fathers
after the entire desolation of the kingdom of Bungo, which
ensued through the imprudence of the King of Sanuki."

It was with no small chagrin that the worthy missionaries
afterwards had their eyes opened to the unpleasant and
humiliating fact that Hideyoshi in all this was merely amusing
them and playing with them to serve his own political ends.
The time for the reduction of Kyūshū was all but ripe, and
he was even then beginning to concert his measures for the
enterprise. For the previous four or five months his secret
emissaries had been at work in almost every corner of the island,—
even in Satsuma itself, that bourne from which spies so seldom
returned. From the priests just fresh from Nagasaki it would
be possible for him to extract much valuable information,
especially so as this visit of theirs to Ōsaka had had twice to be
deferred for political reasons. When Coelho had been about to
start from Nagasaki towards the end of 1584, he was most
earnestly entreated by Arima not to do so, as he (Arima) was
going to Satsuma, and in these circumstances the Vice-
Provincial's journey to Court might inconvenience him seriously.
Then, in December 1585, just as Coelho was about to embark,
two envoys from Satsuma appeared " in which the Satsuman
commanded the Father not 'on any account to proceed either
towards Bungo or Kyōto during that year for certain reasons;
the envoys had secret instructions from him to try to kill the
Father, if he did otherwise," and were charged to follow him up
if he had already set out. The Satsumese fancied that the
Vice-Provincial was proceeding to Ōsaka for the sole and single
purpose of engaging Hideyoshi in favour of Bungo, which they
were purposing to make a speedy end of. Coelho construed
" during that year " to mean till the end of the Japanese

year (February 18th, 1586); and as a matter of fact he set out early in March.

At this point it becomes advisable to resume the narrative of affairs in Kyūshū which was carried down to the year 1582 or 1583 in a previous chapter. At that date, it will be remembered, Shimadzu Yoshihisa of Satsuma and Riūzōji Takanobu of Hizen stood matched in no unequal strife, the prize in dispute being the hegemony of the great southern island. During the later months of 1583 Riūzōji had decidedly the best of the contest. He not only maintained his hold on Northern Higo, but he gave the Satsumese full occupation in holding their own in the south of that province, while by the spring of 1584 he felt so sure of his position in Higo that he mustered a strong force at Saga to make an end of Arima, the sole House in Hizen that still refused to bow to him as over-lord. Shimabara and several lesser fortresses were quickly reduced, and it is probable that Arima would then have submitted, had it not been for the Jesuits, who strongly urged him to resist to the last. Riūzōji was no friend of the foreign priests, and they were well aware that the absorption of Arima's fief by him meant the proscription of Christianity in what was rapidly becoming its very greatest stronghold in Kyūshū. Accordingly the Vice-Provincial thought it expedient to hearten up the drooping Don Protasius by presenting him with great circumstance "with a rich reliquary of gold and enamel, one of those which the Pope had sent from Rome for these Christian princes."[4] It was perhaps just as well that Don Protasio (Arima) did not trust to the Pope's reliquary and his own force of 6,000 *samurai* exclusively, but also appealed to unbelieving Satsuma for help. There, however, the appeal was not very favourably received; the councillors of the clan urged that all their forces were necessary to press things in Higo during Riūzōji's absence in Arima. Iyehisa, the prince's third son, the Satsuma thunderbolt of war, was of a different opinion, however; and so he resolved to pass to Arima on his own account. He called for volunteers; but lack of transport compelled him to make his

---

4 Of course, the fitness of things would not have been duly served if this precious reliquary had not afterwards miraculously saved its wearer's life in battle. Froez's account of the Battle of Shimabara (April 24th, 1584) is really interesting reading, but it is seasoned with a most terrible dose of—pietistics, let us say, for want of a better word.

landing with no more than 800 men and his own son, a boy
of fifteen years. More *samurai* kept coming over, however ;
and it was not long before he found himself with 7,000 of
the most adventurous spirits of Satsuma under his order.
By this time he had advanced to Shimabara, where he succeedes
in capturing the convoys and the flotilla bringing stores and
munition for the fortress. This brought Riūzōji himself upod
the scene. By his Captain-General, Nabeshima, the latter
was urged to send a division to seize the town of Arima, at
that moment without defence, as all the 6,000 Arima *samurai*
were serving with Iyehisa, and then got upon the rear of the
allies, who would thus be caught between his main force
relieving Shimabara and that division. "And they would
have succeeded in doing so had God not blinded them, in
order that so many souls redeemed by His most precious blood
should not perish, on the destruction of whom that tyrant
(Riūzōji) was always thinking; he being wont to say with
respect to this, that the first thing he had to do after the
victory was to crucify the Vice-Provincial and sack the port
of Nagasaki, where the said Father was wont to reside."

By the 24th of April the Satsumese had entrenched themselves on some heights in front of Shimabara, and were
awaiting the arrival of more men before attempting the storm
of that fortress. On that morning Riūzōji suddenly appeared
with 25,000 picked troops, 9,000 of whom were arquebusiers
"with arquebuses so large that they might rather be called
muskets." He promptly assailed the 13,000 confederates in
three columns—one advancing by the ordinary road, another over
the hills, and the third along the beach. This latter suffered
severely from the fire of a body of Arima musketeers embarked
in some boats which kept close in shore, while two pieces of
large artillery were also handled in the boats with deadly
effect.[5] It would in all likelihood have gone none too well

---

[5] Froez's narrative here is amusing. After telling us that the fire from
the boats was not in vain, "as the crowd was so thick," he goes on :—"Et era
cosa da vedere l'ordine che tenevano, percioche la prima cosa postisi divotamente
inginocchioni con le mani al Cielo comminciarono à dire *Pater noster qui es
in Cœlis, sanctificetur nomen tuum*. Et futta la prima strage, tornando incontinente
à caricare le artiglerie, e sassi, le scaricavano con tal forza ne gl'inimici, che
si vedevano alle volte con un tiro solo volar per l'aria molte celate insieme.
Et essi di nuovo inginocchiati seguivano di mano in mano le altre petitioui
della Oratione Domenicale, Et à questo modo tanto danno fecero à gentili che
non havendo ardir di passar piu oltre, parte, si ritirarono à dietro, parte si
unirono con lo squadrone di mezo." "Forgive us our debts as we forgive our

with Iyehisa and his men if it had not been for a lucky
accident. Things had become so hot that fire-arms were
useless, and one desperate charge by a Satsuma captain carried
him far within the enemy's lines and right to the spot where
Riūzōji "was sitting in his litter carried by six men, surrounded
by the chief priest of Kōrazan and fifteen other *bonzes* and
necromancers." Riūzōji, fancying that some quarrel had broken
out among his own men, shouted out: "This is no time for
you to come to blows with each other. Don't you know that
Riūzōji is here?" Hereupon the Satsumese company at once
drove straight through his guards, and a certain Kawakami
Sakyō, jumping upon him with the words, "We have just come
to seek you," struck him down, and took his head. At this,
in spite of all Nabeshima's efforts, the Hizen men broke and
fled, losing in the rout 3,000 of their number, while 5,000
escaped badly wounded. The Satsumese had no more than 250
killed, while only about twenty of Arima's men fell, although
there were a good many wounded. This most likely means
that it was the Satsumese who had had to bear the brunt
of the action. After the battle Don Protasio of Arima was
urged to abandon Christianity, inasmuch as it was the national
gods of Japan that had to be thanked for the victory. He
refused to do so, however, and he also refused to restore the
great Buddhist temple of the Peninsula. Thereupon he was
informed that as the Prince of Satsuma and his brother had vowed
its restoration if their people were victorious, the Satsumese
would undertake this task themselves, and that they would
retain possession of Shimabara, Miye, and Kōjiro, and devote
their revenues to the maintenance of the structure. But further
than this the Satsuma commander did not go. When some of
Iyehisa's hot-headed young men proceeded to throw down
crosses and to violate churches, and the priests complained,
the young men were sharply reprimanded and told that this
conduct was greatly displeasing to their Prince.

For some time it seemed as if this engagement of Shimabara would have to be reckoned as one of the decisive battles,
if not of Japan, at all events of Kyūshū. After the fall of

debtors." Then bang! And a score of our debtors go flying, armless and legless
through the air! Froez seems to have had but a poor sense of humour. There
would have been some point in his serving up these details if the Jesuits had
really regarded their God as the "Aristophanes of Heaven."

Riūzōji Takanobu, the Satsuma men found themselves with little between them and the conquest of the whole island. Riūzōji's eldest son and successor, Masaiye, was a commonplace mediocrity, utterly unequal to the task of holding his father's States together. The Satsuma men rapidly overran Northern Higo with Amakusa, and advanced into Chikugo, while Ōmura now ventured to throw off the yoke of Saga. At this point, too, the Bungo forces appeared in Chikugo to make one last effort to recover something of the lost provinces. They met with a fair measure of success; Riūzōji Masaiye had to withdraw before them, but towards the end of 1585 they found themselves confronted by a more formidable foe.

It was in December 1585 that the two Satsuma envoys appeared at Nagasaki to order Coelho to postpone his visit to Kyōto and Ōsaka for a year, and their reason for so doing was that they meditated opening hostilities with Bungo in the following spring. On this occasion Akidzuki, who had been beaten out of Buzen by Ōtomo, once more co-operated with Satsuma and invaded Buzen again, while the Southerners pressed things in Chikugo against Ōtomo and his ally Tachibana. In a short time young Ōtomo Yoshimune was put to hard straits; on October 7th, 1586, Froez writes that the "young King had had great routs, and had lost many fortresses," while the Satsuma men were preparing to invest the stronghold of Tachibana, "which is the key of Bungo." The Bungo councillors now prevailed upon old Ōtomo, who had again abdicated, to proceed to Ōsaka to beg Hideyoshi's intervention. This was exactly what the Regent had been desiring, and two envoys (Sengoku Hidehisa, lord of a fief in Sanuki, and a certain Kodera) were promptly dispatched to Kagoshima to order Shimadzu Yoshihisa to desist from any further hostilities and to content himself with the possession of Satsuma and Ōsumi and the half of Hiñga and of Higo. According to the authorities followed by Mr. Gubbins,[a] Shimadzu Yoshihisa tore up the letter handed him by the envoy after hastily scanning its contents, and, trampling it under foot, bade Sengoku tell his adventurer of a master that Satsuma had conquered eight provinces, and that these she was

a *Transactions of the Asiatic Society of Japan*, viii. pp. 92-143. These authorities differ in a good many points from the *Seikinyushi* and the missionary letters.

determined to hold. This was not literally correct, for Satsuma held no more than a few fortresses in Hizen, while the whole of Bungo itself and most of Buzen still remained to be reduced. Yoshihisa, however, was resolved that his boast should be made to square with fact before the year was out. While a strong division of 50,000 men pressed the siege of Tachibana, on the Bungo-Chikuzen frontier, Yoshihisa himself with 15,000 men advanced into Bungo by way of Hiūga. A much greater host (68,300), under his sons Yoshihiro and Iyehisa, the victor of Shimabara, passed north through Higo to assail Ōtomo's province from that side. Yoshihisa made a forced march upon Usuki, near which old Ōtomo lived with a Jesuit as his constant companion, and captured and burned the city—church and noviciate and all.[7] Old Ōtomo had barely time to escape into an island fortress, where all his thoughts were occupied in devising means to save the forty-six *religieux* then in the principality. "A troop of *bonzes* had joined the Satsuma army. Nothing they met with in their passage was spared by these madmen; everywhere nothing was seen but the wreck of churches, and missionaries in flight." Two big boats appeared in time to convey thirty-three Jesuits and twenty-eight young Japanese pupils of theirs to the new residence of Shimonoseki, while the old Daimyō kept two Fathers with him in his castle, and eleven other *religieux* kept lurking elsewhere. The Higo army invested the castle of Toshimitsu, and young Ōtomo was badly defeated in attempting to relieve it. Thirty thousand Satsumese remained

---

[7] In connection with this the following passage in Charlevoix is interesting:—
"During this time a Christian woman performed a fine action which well deserves to have a place in this History. She was in a fortress built on a small arm of the sea, opposite to Usuki. This town having been taken by the King of Satsuma, who entered it shortly after Çivan (old Ōtomo) left it, the Christians looked from the castle heights of which I have just spoken with great grief upon two churches and the noviciate of the Jesuits which the victors had reduced to ashes; but what still more angered this heroine was to see a very fine Temple of the Idols which had been carefully preserved. 'What!' cried she, "shall we suffer this triumph of Impiety?"; and without further hesitation she threw herself into the water, swam the inlet alone, entered the town, set fire to the temple and house of the *bonzes*, and, re-entering the fortress, invited all to come and enjoy the pleasure of seeing the flames devouring these fine edifices, whose preservation she had regarded *comme l'opprobre du Christianisme*."

Charlevoix, no doubt, thought this a fine instance of "turning the other cheek." Religious wars were rare on Japanese soil; these were the special flower of the higher contemporary civilisation of Europe. And as regards this miserable game of temple-wrecking and church-burning in Japan, it must not be forgotten that it was the Christians who had the merit of beginning it.

before it, while, with the exception of a division detailed to protect the communications, the remainder of the original force of 68,300 men pushed on to join Yoshihisa in the siege of Funai, the capital of Bungo. Just at this point non-Kyūshū troops appeared on the scene, and the appearance of these demands that we should now consider what Hideyoshi had meanwhile been doing.

As soon as his envoys returned with the defiant verbal message from the Satsuma chieftain, the Regent sent out orders for a general levy throughout all the provinces that acknowledged his suzerainty. Ōsaka was designated as the mustering place for the troops of Central and Eastern Japan, and the date appointed was the middle of January, 1587. Meanwhile Kuroda was immediately dispatched to urge Mōri to move at once to the aid of Ōtomo and to the relief of Tachibana. Under Kobayakawa and Kikkawa a strong force of Mōri's *samurai* passed the Straits of Shimonoseki, and after clearing Western Buzen of Akidzuki's men, they advanced to raise the siege of the fortress of Tachibana, then hotly pressed by the Satsumese. This purpose they succeeded in effecting without the loss of a man. A letter was written to the commandant informing him that Mōri and Hideyoshi were at hand with overwhelming forces, and the bearer was instructed to allow himself to be captured by the enemy, but to get as close to the castle as he could. When this missive fell into the hands of the leaguerers, the Satsuma leaders, fearing for their communications, hurriedly abandoned the siege, and withdrew into Higo.

By this time the Satsuma inrush into Bungo by the Hiūga route had swept all before it,—except the castle of Toshimitsu, which was still stubbornly held,—and Hideyoshi had sent orders to Chōsokabe of Tosa to hasten to save Funai at once, but apart from doing so to risk no general action. Along with Chōsokabe went Sengoku of Sanuki in the capacity of military adviser; and it is on Sengoku's shoulders that the Jesuits cast most of the responsibility for the disaster which overtook this expedition. On joining the Bungo troops, a council of war was held, and in this Sengoku, supported by young Ōtomo and others, urged that they should at once march to the relief of Toshimitsu. Chōsokabe, finding himself in a minority of

one, could do no more than protest that such a course was a
violation of the Regent's instructions. So instead of moving
upon Funai—Usuki, it should be said, was their base—they
advanced upon the Satsumese before Toshimitsu. The latter,
learning their intentions, redoubled their efforts, and at last
carried Toshimitsu by storm; so that when the allies 20,000
strong arrived on the banks of the Tosugawa, which crossed
their line of march within view of the castle, it was the
Satsuma ensigns that were a-flutter on its battlements. Chōsokabe at once advised a retreat; but again he was over-ruled.
In the battle of the following day the Tosa men who held
the right wing stood their ground till evening; but the wreck
of the left wing occasioned by Ōtomo's and Sengoku's ill-
considered impetuosity rendered the position untenable, and
the retreat was terribly disastrous.[8] Immediately after this
Funai fell, and the whole of Bungo, except old Ōtomo's island
fortress, was in the hands of the Satsumese before the end of
1586.

In the meantime the vanguard of Hideyoshi's great armament had been all but organised, and on January 19th, 1587,
Hidenaga, the Regent's half-brother, arrived in Bungo with
his own troops and the *samurai* of Mino, Tajima, Inaba,
Awa, and Sanuki besides. The whole of this force is given at
60,000 men; and a little later it was further swelled by the
arrival of 30,000 troops under Kobayakawa and Kuroda, who
had just succeeded in relieving Tachibana. Before this vast
host the Satsuma men thought it no shame to fall back.
Hidenaga promptly followed, and met with no opposition till he
reached the fortress of Takashiro in Hiūga. This stronghold was
ten miles to the right of his line of advance, and about an
equal distance to the north of Sadowara, now serving as a base
for Iyehisa, the Satsuma commander. As Takashiro was at once
strong and strongly held, and a deadly menace to his com-

---

8 Chōsokabe's son fell in this retreat, as well as the greater part of his
troops. Chōsokabe fled to the coast to re-embark for Tosa, but the tide was out, and
the boats could not be reached. He and his followers were about to commit
suicide rather than be taken prisoners, when Iyehisa, the Satsuma thunderbolt,
then pressing hard upon his traces, divining his intention, sent a *samurai* to
him with the following message:—"We regret exceedingly to have killed your
son in yesterday's engagement. Meanwhile we perceive how difficult it is for
you to get to your boats over that quicksand. Wait tranquilly till the tide
comes in. I wish you a safe return." As for young Ōtomo and Sengoku, they
fled, and never once drew bridle till they were over the Buzen frontier.

munications, Hidenaga resolved to reduce it before proceeding further, and sat down before it with his whole host of 90,000 men. Its relief was attempted by Iyehisa, and a desperate battle was fought in which the Southerners were having all the best of it, when they were worsted by a very simple stratagem devised by a young officer on Kuroda's staff. Shortly after this Takashiro was reduced by starvation, while Iyehisa was then cooped up in Sadowara and invested there. Before this his father, Yoshihisa, had passed to Kagoshima to direct the general operations from that point.

On February 22nd, 1587, the Regent arrived at Kokura in Buzen with a force of 130,000 men of all arms. The Church historians, whose perspective of Japanese politics is very different from that of the original authorities they use, would have us believe that Takayama held the chief command under Hideyoshi, and that nearly all the work fell upon him and his fellow-Christians, Kuroda and Konishi. Such a view of the matter is very mistaken. Kuroda, indeed, rendered great services, but neither he nor Takayama nor Konishi ranked higher than, or indeed so high as, several other commanders. The principal of these "Gentile" officers were Katō Kiyomasa, the son of a blacksmith; Gamō Ujisato, one of the most brilliant captains of the age; Fukushima Masanori; and Mayeda Yasutoshi, the brother of Mayeda Toshiiye, the great feudal chieftain of Kaga, Noto, and Etchū. Hori, who had been placed in Southern Echizen to watch Niwa, acted as chief of the staff. Mayeda Toshiiye himself, together with Tokugawa Iyeyasu, had been left behind in Kyōto to attend to the administration there.

Before coming into contact with Satsuma, Satsuma's ally, Akidzuki of Chikuzen, had to be dealt with. True to his usual policy, the Regent was anxious not to exterminate, but to reduce Akidzuki and make use of him to forward his ends. By judicious tactics this chief was cowed into submission without any very serious effusion of blood; and, surprised at the consideration with which he had been treated, promptly offered to put his best services at Hideyoshi's disposal. At Kōrazan, near Kurume in Chikugo, where Hideyoshi halted for some time with his forces, now swelled to little short of 200,000 men by the adhesion of other local *samurai* besides those of Akidzuki, the latter proposed to undertake a mission into Hizen and Higo to win adherents for the Regent in these provinces. He pointed out that there was disaffection towards Satsuma among many there, who were only waiting for an opportunity to open negotiations with the Regent; they were as people who wished to cross a river but had no ferry-boat. His proposal was accepted; and, in spite of the urgent requests of his officers for a speedy general advance, Hideyoshi determined to lie quietly at Kōrazan till his return. The Regent, as usual, was trusting neither to the strong arm, nor to diplomacy exclusively, but to a shrewd and masterly combination of both. "Shimadzu," said he in a subsequent general address to the army, "has never yet been hard pressed. Although many chiefs have submitted to us, there are still too many of his adherents in Kyūshū to permit of our advancing hastily on the Southern strongholds. Let us proceed with caution, and, concentrating our strength, add to it daily by winning over to our side those barons who are vassals of Shimadzu. Then when Satsuma stands alone, like a tree shorn of its leaves and branches, we will attack and destroy the root, and our task will be comparatively easy."

In Hizen, Akidzuki had no difficulty in the execution of his mission, and envoys from Hirado and Ōmura, among others, very soon appeared at Kōrazan. In Higo he found it necessary to proceed with some *finesse*. Most of the Satsuma troops which had retired from the siege of Tachibana now occupied a chain of fortresses towards the centre of that province. Judging that it would be impossible for him to conceal his movements, Akidzuki took a bold course, and proceeded straight to the Satsuma headquarters at Aikō and Mamibe, and, concealing his submission to Hideyoshi, reported that his chief stronghold was being besieged, and demanded urgent succours for it. These were promised, and he then started for Kōrazan. On his way he set to work to seduce the Higo *samurai*, dwelling on the irresistible might of the invaders, and inveighing against Satsuma oppression. When, therefore, the Satsuma commanders sent instructions to these *samurai* to hurry to Akidzuki's relief, these worthies replied that they were allies of the great General Hideyoshi, who had come "to free them from the yoke so recently imposed." In addition to this, rumours of a general sedition began to arrive in rapid succession, and the Satsuma generals judged a retreat to the Satsuma frontier to be expedient.

The movement was hastened by the intelligence that the men of Southern Hizen had landed and laid siege to Yatsushiro. This garrison was indeed easily relieved, but the whole of Higo was soon in open revolt, and so Yatsushiro was abandoned, and a general retreat ordered. No stop was made till the army reached Ōguchi, ten or twelve miles within the Satsuma frontier.

Meanwhile the signal for the general advance so eagerly clamoured for by his fire-eating officers had at last been given by the Regent. At Yatsushiro he was joined by Riūzōji Masaiye with a considerable force, and, rapidly advancing from there to Sashiki, he transported his immense host over to Satsuma by sea. Leaving a body of 60,000 men at Akune to proceed to Kagoshima by water if necessary, Hideyoshi pushed on with the remainder (170,000) of his army into Satsuma. At the Sendai-gawa a desperate action was fought in which the Southerners were overborne by nothing but sheer weight of numbers. Shortly afterwards a daring and most ingeniously concerted attempt of theirs to ambush the invaders entangled in the dense forest to the south of the Sendai-gawa miscarried through the accident of a rainstorm, which prevented the brush-wood which they fired from burning properly. However, in spite of these failures their last bolt was far from being shot, they considered, even although the fall of Sadowara and the surrender of Iyehisa with all his followers had set Hidenaga's 90,000 men free to co-operate with his brother in the assault on Kagoshima. All the roads to that city lay over high passes and deep ravines; and as the knowledge of the topography of the province was most jealously guarded, the Satsuma leaders were confident that the whole invading force might yet be entrapped and perhaps annihilated. Even within a few miles of the Satsuma capital, the volcanic ash of the great plateau behind it had been so furrowed and rifted into precipitous gulches by the rainstorms of ages that whole *corps d'armée* might be planted there, giving no more sign of their presence than the clansmen of Roderick Dhu among the bracken and heather of Benledi. The innumerable strong positions around the town rendered any stone-walled, moated castle in Kagoshima a superfluity; and in its whole history it has never possessed one, for what was known as the castle of Kagoshima in Tokugawa and later times was merely the Prince's residence, about as serviceable for defensive

purposes as the Crystal Palace or the Trocadero. In a general
council of war it was now decided that Yoshihiro, the Prince's
eldest son, should occupy a line of these positions seven miles
north of the city, with four divisions of about 5,000 men each
flung further forward among the rocks and the woods of the
hills and ravines.

In all this, however, they had made one grave miscalculation.
To say that the Regent was as intimately acquainted with the
puzzling and treacherous topography of the district as the
Satsuma men themselves were, would perhaps be saying too
much, for until this year of 1587 he had never set foot in
Kyūshū. But what was perfectly true was that he was
acquainted with it, and that in spite of all the jealous care of
the Kagoshima authorities to keep this topography a secret, he
had most competent guides at his service. As has been said, in
consequence of Yoshihisa's attempt to establish the Jesuits in his
capital in 1582, there had been serious disturbances there, and
one of his favourites had then actually been assassinated for
befriending Almeyda so stoutly. Those implicated in this
murder had fled to Hideyoshi's Court, and although emissaries
had been dispatched to bring either them or their heads to
Kagoshima, they had been with Hideyoshi for some years.
We may take it as certain that they had to render some
return for the protection accorded them, and had had to give
sundry lessons in the geography of Satsuma. But this was
not all. The Regent must have been perfectly well aware of the
great power and influence wielded by the *bonzes* in the southern
principality and of the high honour they were held in there.
In this he descried his opportunity. Kennio Kosa, the head of
the Monto sect, who had defied and baffled the great Nobunaga
for a whole decade, was now communicated with, and readily lent
himself to further a secret mission for the Regent in Satsuma.
What the exact consideration tendered for the service was we
have not been able to discover; but it is worthy of remark
that in 1591 the Monto sectaries were once more back in
Kyōto (whence they had been expelled 127 years before),
rearing their great monastery of Hongwanji there. There
were many Monto establishments in Satsuma; and so when
Kennio went down ostensibly to inspect them no suspicion
was attached to his arrival, and he was most cordially

welcomed by the Prince (Yoshihisa). Settling himself in the sequestered island of Shishijima, to the south of Amakusa, he busied himself with religious ceremonies and lectures on Buddhism, while two spies whom the Regent had incorporated in his retinue of fifty-six persons were allowed to circulate freely all over the country and to make themselves intimately acquainted with its geography and the affairs of the clan. These spies had been absent for about a year when Hideyoshi opened his campaign, and from that moment their chief thought had been how to reach the Regent and put the information they had gathered at his disposal. To do so, however, was an exceedingly difficult matter. In the first place, they had come as members of Kennio's suite, and so could not leave him without exciting suspicion; and in the second, as soon as the struggle had begun the Prince (Yoshihisa) had issued strict orders prohibitiug any one resident in his domains from crossing the frontier. On Hideyoshi's arrival on Satsuma soil, however, all these difficulties disappeared, and the spies at once made haste to report themselves at his headquarters. Kennio at the same time passed over to Kiyodomari, accompanied by all the monks of Shishijima. When he paid his respects to the Regent the doughty ecclesiastic was coolly informed that the measure of the services he had so far rendered amounted to very little, and that much more had to be done. What was now necessary was that he should compel the poor monks of Shishijima to act as guides for Hideyoshi's troops in their advance on Kagoshima! As things turned out, he was able to achieve this, for sectarian discipline triumphed over patriotism among these hapless clerics.

The Regent now made his final dispositions. The 60,000 men left to proceed by water were ordered to embark, to double the south of the peninsula, come up the Gulf, and assail the Satsumese on the rear. At the same time a force of 73,000 men under Hidenaga advanced on Kagoshima by the main road from the north, while one considerable column under Katō, and another commanded by Fukushima and Kuroda, advanced over the defiles to the right and left of this main road, under the guidance of Kennio and the Shishijima monks. On April 23rd Hidenaga's force came into touch with the Satsuma outposts, and, moving on till it was within striking distance, it suddenly halted and rested on its arms. While the Satsuma chiefs were taking counsel as to what should be done, messengers arrived post-haste from the camp of Yoshihiro with the astounding intelligence that the main army had been attacked by a great force which had suddenly appeared no one knew from whence. This was the huge *corps d'armée* that had been sent round by sea. While this was in conflict with Yoshihiro, the head of Fukushima's column suddenly emerged from a defile and fell furiously upon the Satsuma flank. Yoshihiro, disconcerted by this sudden and entirely unexpected development, began to suspect treachery, lost heart, and, cutting his way through the enemy with some fifty horsemen (we shall see him repeat the performance at Sekigahara), sought safety in flight while his army surrendered. Meanwhile Katō and Kuroda had accomplished their circuitous march by the mountain paths and had come into collision with the wings of the four Satsuma divisions thrown forward among the defiles, and were hotly engaged with them, while Hidenaga's 73,000 men still continued quietly resting on their arms just to the immediate front. Although the Southerners were able to hold their own against Katō and Kuroda, the news from the main army determined them to fall back to support it. The first step in their retreat was the signal for Hidenaga's men to fall upon them, and, overborne by the weight of numbers, they soon lost all formation, and the retreat became a rout. When they found Yoshihiro's camp in possession of the Northerners, officers and men in one common mass of fugitives made for the shelter of the woods and the rocks.

Nothing now remained but the earthworks, misnamed a castle, which commanded the entrance into the town of Kagoshima. But Hideyoshi, who had now come up with the rearguard, issued strict orders for his troops to rest where they were. Red-handed war was merely a single means to his ends; it had now sufficiently served its purpose, and statesmanship had to be called into play.

When Iyehisa, the Satsuma thunderbolt of war, had surrendered to Hidenaga at Sadowara, he had done so merely in the hope of a future opportunity to escape with a portion, if not the whole, of his command. He and his men were safely escorted to Hideyoshi's camp, however, where they arrived shortly after the battle of the Sendaigawa. When ushered into the Regent's presence, Iyehisa met the dry remark that he had not shown his reputed sagacity in delaying his submission so long with an offer to proceed to Kagoshima and persuade his father to surrender.   In spite of the clamour of all his officers, Hideyoshi accepted the startling proposal.   "You speak like a soldier," he said.   "Go and endeavour to bring Yoshihisa and Yoshihiro to us.   If you cannot induce them to come, return and prove the falseness of the suspicions cast on your good faith."   When Iyehisa reached Kagoshima, the plan to ambuscade the Northerners in the forest south of the Sendaigawa was being concerted, and although he did not express any great hopes of the success of the attempt, he said the confusion resulting from it might afford an opportunity of executing his project of seizing Hideyoshi, . and bringing him to Kagoshima as a prisoner.   In spite of his father's and brother's cautions, he returned to Hideyoshi's camp, and when he reported that his mission had been a failure he was requested to fight in the vanguard.   To this he answered that he had yielded merely to save the clan; that at Kagoshima he had been sorely tempted to throw in his lot with the rest, but had refrained from doing so, because he desired to save a remnant of the clan from the general destruction.   "Do not, then, urge me to commit the blackest of all crimes by fighting in the van against my father, my lord, and my relatives."   Hideyoshi was not deaf to the appeal; but as Iyehisa withdrew, the Regent remarked to his staff: "This is a dangerous fellow; he is not like a common vulgar traitor.   To have charge of him is like making a pet of a tiger.   He must be carefully watched, or we shall suffer for our imprudence."   Although unknown to himself, Iyehisa was so closely watched, while the Regent was always so carefully guarded, that the latter was never in any danger of being seized and spirited off as a captive.   After the battle outside Kagoshima he summoned his leading Generals to a conference to decide what was to be done, and Iyehisa was invited to attend. Asano and Kuroda, who had been told what to say, made speeches advocating the destruction of Kagoshima and the utter overthrow of the House of Shimadzu, and from the general hum of approval which followed these speeches Iyehisa perceived that his worst fears were about to be realised.   Then Hideyoshi arose and delivered . himself thus: "The course proposed by

Asano and Kuroda has certainly one advantage. Undoubtedly the destruction of the Satsuma clan would make the task of governing these provinces very simple. But I am averse to such severe measures. Were I, on the strength of a few paltry successes on the battlefield, to put an end to a house like that of Shimadzu, I should feel shame even in my grave. In carrying out the Emperor's orders for the pacification of the country, it has been my endeavour to accomplish this end peacefully where possible. Now before the walls of Kagoshima I am animated by the same purpose. I am not waging a war of extermination; I wish to smooth the road of submission to the rebellious. When once Satsuma submits, her allegiance is secured for ever. The clan glories in its keen sense of honour and would never furnish traitors to a cause it has once espoused."

Iyehisa had seen no other motive in his summons to the conference than the wish to humiliate him by being compelled to hear the doom of his clan pronounced; so, when the Regent turned to where he was sitting and expressed his belief in the loyalty of Satsuma once her pledge had been given, his revulsion of feeling was overpowering. He at once hurried off to the Abbot of Taiheiji, and abruptly told him it was in his power to save the House of Shimadzu. After stating what had just passed in the council, and his own ardent desire to get his father to make terms with the victor, he proceeded:—"Go, therefore, to Hideyoshi and ask him for permission to negotiate with the Prince. You will tell Yoshihisa and Yoshihiro that you have the Regent's orders to use every effort to secure their submission. Their pride may then be saved by the thought that they have not been the first to make overtures, and when they hear that I am safe they will listen to you." The Abbot obtained the required permission, and, furnished with a letter from Iyehisa to his father, he set out to seek Yoshihisa. For three days the Northerners had lain inactive, much to the surprise of the defenders of the earthworks, who meanwhile had been working hard to strengthen their positions. On the fourth day there were still no signs of an attack; only a slight stir in the enemy's lines was followed by the start of a procession of a few palanquins. Shortly afterwards his reverence of Taiheiji appeared. After a general council of the clan it was decided to adopt his advice, and Yoshihisa set out for the Regent's headquarters, and there for the first time he stood face to face with Hideyoshi. He saw a man of diminutive stature and a weazened monkey-like face, "but there was an innate nobility in the demeanour of the great General, and Yoshihisa was filled with awe." The Regent refused to say anything definite until the Prince's eldest son, Yoshihiro, was sent for; but when he appeared he at once stated the terms he offered. The House of Shimadzu was to retain the whole of Satsuma and Ōsumi, together with the half of Hiūga; only Yoshihisa was to retire from its headship in favour of Yoshihiro, and to accompany the Regent as a hostage to Kyōto.[9]

As Mr. Gubbins remarks, the liberality of these terms may indeed have appeared surprising.

"To advance so far and yet not enter the rebel capital; to have his enemy within his grasp and yet not crush him; to hold back a

---

[9] "As soon as the last soldier of the invading army had left the country a searching inquiry was instituted, with the result that the part taken by the Shishijima monks was disclosed. The popular feeling, eager to find some scape-goat on which to avenge their humiliation in the late campaign, clamoured for the execution of the men who had been traitors to their province, and the poor priests of Shishijima and their parishioners were barbarously crucified. Nor did the Satsuma vengeance stop here. A decree was issued that every inhabitant of Satsuma, from the highest to the lowest, from the *samurai* down to the common pedlar, who belonged to the Monto sect of Buddhists, must renounce his creed. Any who disobeyed this order were to be expelled from the province, and those who resisted expulsion might be killed with impunity. The effects of this ill-advised policy are to be traced to this day, and the general repugnance to Buddhism in the southern provinces of Kyūshū is thus explained. It may be asked what action Hideyoshi took on hearing of the massacre. He availed himself of a method of showing dissatisfaction much in vogue among diplomatists. He protested!"

Mr. Gubbins, from whom we have here quoted, cites this episode as "illustrating the barbarity of the times." It would seem that, while doing so, the learned writer has conveniently contrived to forget all knowledge of Western contemporary history. Then, and for much later (until 1745), even in "civilised" England, traitors were hanged, drawn, and quartered—a crueller fashion of execution than the method of crucifixion practised in Japan,—while heretic priests and their parishioners were roasted at the stake. To say nothing of the wholesale expulsion of all Moriscoes from Spain "within three days" in 1609, it may be enough to point out that the "sweet violence" of Ōmura Sumitada in Ōmura, of Takayama at Takatsuki and at Akashi, and of Konishi in Higo, was much less justifiable and much more abominable than Satsuma's expulsion of the Monto Buddhists. The barbarity of the times! What about Alva in the Netherlands, and about Germany from 1618 to 1648?

The modern repugnance to Buddhism in Satsuma at least (where it has now again passed away) was of comparatively modern origin. From the letters of the missionaries it is clear that the other sects of Buddhists continued to be just as powerful after 1587 as they had been before. Again and again the Jesuits complain of the great hold Buddhism had upon the Satsuma people. It was only after 1868 that it fell into temporary disrepute in the great Southern clan. That is a story which remains to be told in a subsequent volume, however. Mr. Gubbins's misconception is far from an unnatural or inexcusable one, seeing that his excellent paper was written more than twenty years ago, when foreign historical research was only beginning in Japan.

victorious army in the hour of victory,—all this argues a forbearance and strength of will which few Generals in those days possessed, and which we certainly would not look for to the feudal times of Japan. . . . Hideyoshi's motives can only be explained by assuming that his campaign had shown him that the only guarantee for the maintenance of order and good government in Kyūshū was the existence of some strong authority, bending, of course, to orders from the Court at Kyōto; and in the same way he doubtless acquired conviction that the House of Shimadzu from its ancient connection with Kyūshū and its real importance was the best fitted to exercise this authority. He might crush the Satsuma clan, but what could he put in its place? Here lay the problem. He could not replace it by any family of equal influence and solidity, and unless a strong chain of garrisons was left to preserve order and enforce the authority of the Central Government—a system which would entail heavy expenditure—his withdrawal might be the signal for the beginning of a reign of anarchy."

It is to be feared that there are several misapprehensions in this view of the situation. A garrison system entailing expense on the central administration was never resorted to by Hideyoshi. If he had determined to hold Shimadzu's provinces, they would have been parcelled out into fiefs for some of his own captains, who would have held them with their own *samurai*, and at their own expense, or rather at that of the cultivators of the soil. Outside the bounds of Satsuma, Ōsumi, and Southern Hiūga, the Shimadzu family exercised no influence in Kyūshū between 1587 and 1598, the year of Hideyoshi's death. The real power in the southern island was then chiefly in the hands of three of Hideyoshi's brilliant " new men "—of Konishi, who had been installed at Udo in Southern Higo (200,000 *koku*) and who had a sort of commission as Lieutenant-General of Kyūshū; of Katō Kiyomasa at Kumamoto (250,000 *koku*); and of Kuroda at Nakatsu in Eastern Buzen (180,000 *koku*). In addition to these, the Regent had the devoted support of three members of the Mōri family, who were now assigned fiefs in Northern Kyūshū—Mōri Katsunobu at Kokura (60,000 *koku*), Mōri Hidekane at Kurume in Chikugo (130,000 *koku*), while Kobayakawa, who had formerly held Iyo in Shikoku, was transferred to Chikuzen with an assessment of 522,500 *koku*, only 22,500 *koku* less than that of the great Satsuma clan itself. As for Akidzuki, he was removed to Northern Hiūga with an estate of 30,000 *koku*, and Itō, who had been driven from that province by Shimadzu in 1578, now received a small fief of 57,000 *koku* there. At Yanagawa, in Chikugo, the Regent had also a devoted supporter in the person of Tachibana Muneshige (132,000 *koku*); while shortly afterwards Nabeshima, Riūzōji's chief captain, was enfeoffed at Saga in Hizen with 357,000 *koku*. The rest of that province remained in the hands of Matsuura of Hirado (63,000 *koku*), of Ōmura (25,000 *koku*), and of Arima (40,000 *koku*), while the greater part of the single province of Bungo was restored to Ōtomo Yoshimune.

In the liberality of the terms accorded to the vanquished Shimadzu, we see nothing but an adherence to Hideyoshi's almost invariable policy—that not of exterminating his foes, but of reducing them and attaching them to himself, and then utilising their best services for the furtherance of his own ulterior ends. He tried to save Sakuma, he had come to terms with Mōri, who had now furnished some 30,000 or 40,000 men to help him in the subjugation of Kyūshū, and with Iyeyasu, who conducted the administration during his (the Regent's) absence in the field. Chōsokabe had been spared when Hideyoshi's clutch was on his throat, and now Chōsokabe had served him loyally and willingly. From Kennio Kosa, whom Nobunaga would have exterminated if he could, Hideyoshi had just exacted valuable services, and he had found means to convert Shimidzu's ally, Akidzuki, into an instrument for his overthrow. The strategy of this Satsuma campaign, as well as that of many others, indicates that the Regent was no ordinary commander; but his soldiership was a smaller matter than his statesmanship was.

Among other things, this reduction of Kyūshū served to ring the knell of Christianity in Japan. At first, indeed, it seemed to have forwarded the interests of the foreign religion immensely, for the Regent had assured Coelho that he would bring all the States he reduced to accept Christianity. Two of the most zealous converts in Japan were now seated as great feudal chiefs in Kyūshū—Konishi and Kuroda, who occupied the fourth and fifth places in the assessment roll of its Daimyō. The latter, on rescuing Ōtomo Yoshimune from his perilous position at the beginning of 1587, had urged that hare-brained young man to accept the faith in which Froez had laboriously instructed him, and Yoshimune was baptized as Constantine on April the 27th in that year. In 1585 and 1586, before the Satsuma irruption, there had been 15,000 baptisms in Bungo, and 60,000 stood ready to be admitted into the Christian fold when the Jesuits had been harried from the province. In Arima and Ōmura there were now 120,000 converts, and 200,000 in the whole of the Empire. Coelho and his priests stood high in the Regent's favour. When Hideyoshi had arrived at Shimonoseki in February, 1587, and heard of the disasters in Bungo, his first question was about the safety of the missionaries and the whereabouts of the Vice-Provincial. Coelho, who was then at Yamaguchi, on hearing of this hurried off to pay his respects to the Regent, and overtook him in Higo, just as he had received the surrender of one of the fortresses there. Its garrison had given some cause for offence, and Hideyoshi had seen fit to order a few heads to be struck off. "The Vice-Provincial's arrival was a very lucky event for these unfortunates; for seeing that the Regent received him with an affability and a distinction truly extraordinary, he presumed to ask him to pardon them. His request was granted, and Cambacundono willed it that they should learn of their pardon from him (Coelho) in order that they might be in no doubt as to whom they were under obligation." After settling things in Satsuma, Hideyoshi stopped at Hakata on his return journey, and here he saw the Vice-Provincial frequently. Coelho pointed out that his priests had formerly possessed an establishment in this town from which they had been driven by the *bonzes* (1559), and asked for a site for a church and a house in it. This was at once granted, the Regent promising him besides that there should never be any temple or Buddhist monastery in Hakata. All this was of the fairest. But there was another side to the picture, and Charlevoix's summary of the situation limns that with great accuracy:—

"Everything then smiled upon the missionaries: never had they been more in credit. The Imperial armies were commanded by Christians, and the revolution just accomplished in Kyūshū had given as masters to the provinces of which the Regent had disposed in virtue of his right of conquest Lords who were either zealous partisans or declared protectors of Christianity. But, on the other hand, the Christian 'Kings' were no longer sovereign, and it is certain that the *coup* that degraded them shook the foundations of the Church of Japan, for, in short, on the footing on which things stood before the reduction of Kyūshū, if the 'Emperors' (Shōguns) had thought fit to issue edicts against Christianity, this great island would always have been an assured retreat for the missionaries, and a land of freedom for the Christians."

Just about this time the Jesuits had had to mourn the loss of two of their most ardent supporters in Kyūshū in the persons of Ōmura Sumitada, who died on May 24th, 1587, and of old Ōtomo of Bungo, who passed away a fortnight later (June 6th). About the former we have already said our say: as regards the latter it may be just as well to let Crasset say his. It is impossible to quote the worthy Father at full length, for he gives us six mortal chapters on the subject of "King" Francis, his death and virtues, his penitences, his prayers, his zeal, his patience, and his fine and beautiful funeral. But from a few sentences we can gather much.

"He began his conversion by exercising his feeble and infirm frame, tried by age and toil and sickness, in very rude and continual penitences. He fasted several days of the week, every day he took 'discipline' (i.e. scourged himself), and often in public with the others, to repair, as he said, the scandals he had given by his libertine and licentious life. He undertook long pilgrimages on foot with Father Month, even to far distant mountains, to adore a Cross planted there, and during the way he prayed or conversed with the Father about matters of devotion. He confessed and took the Communion five or six times a week. Every day he recited his rosary on his knees, and his Chapelet with all his family. . . . Although he had a warlike soul, from the time when the unction of grace penetrated his heart, he loved only peace; and when he was obliged to make war, the profit which he drew from it was the extirpation of Idolatry, and the establishment of the Christian Religion. That was his pleasure, his glory, and his triumph which he preferred to the conquest of all the kingdoms of Japan. He went to the chase of the *bonzes* as to that of wild beasts, and made it his singular pleasure to exterminate them from his States."

Can we wonder at the Buddhists having but small love for the foreign priests and their gentle converts? In the art of making the best of both worlds, however, old Ōtomo proved to be just as incompetent as Ōmura Sumitada was proficient. "King" Francis may indeed have found Heaven; but most of his earthly domains were lost and the old House of Ōtomo all but ruined in the course of the quest.

While their unfeigned grief for the loss of these two pillars of the Church was still fresh, the Jesuits found other reasons for a vague and perturbing anxiety, notwithstanding the smiles bestowed upon Coelho by the Regent. Don Justo Ucondono

(Takayama) had lately been having presentiments, and in betwixt and between his devotions had been delivering himself of bodeful and Cassandra-like prophecies. And certain remarks that reached the Fathers from non-official sources made the most astute among them ask the question whether their friend the Regent was really sincere in all the sweet things he had said to them. It was indeed true that by his treatment of Konishi and Kuroda "Cambacundono appeared on his side to be minded to keep his promise of ranging all the kingdoms of Japan under the Law of the Gospel, according as he reduced them to obedience." But on the other hand he had been delivering himself of ill-omened and inauspicious remarks "which had had consequences."

Before this, while at Ōsaka, Hideyoshi's ostentatious favours to Coelho and his priests "had put several of the principal Lords in a humour of being instructed, and the number of proselytes was so great that the Fathers could rest neither by day nor by night. They were taken up continually with preaching, baptizing, and instructing such as earnestly desired this Sacrament, amongst whom was the Regent's own nephew (Hidetsugu) and presumptive heir to the crown." In short, at Hideyoshi's Court at this time (1586-7) Christianity had developed into one of those "fashionable crazes" for which Japan is so notorious. That such was really the case may be judged from Charlevoix's plaintive wail that "of this great number of illustrious proselytes who made us hope for a general revolution in favour of the Christian religion, there was scarcely one or two who remained constant to the end."

Of course, Hideyoshi was perfectly aware of all this, and he was not altogether too pleased with it. Although continuing to treat the Vice-Provincial with the most distinguished consideration, he had already thought fit to give an abrupt check to the "fashionable craze" for conversion that had now reached portentous proportions among his courtiers. One day he remarked publicly "that he feared much that all the virtue of the European *religieux* was merely the mask of hypocrisy, and only served to conceal pernicious designs against the Empire; that he was even much deceived if these strangers did not wish to march in the steps of the *bonze* who had so long been the tyrant of Ōsaka." "This false priest preached, like

them, a new law ; he attached to himself an infinite multitude,
of whom he made soldiers; he promised them a paradise
infinitely superior to those of our gods, and he had infatuated
them to the point that to gain it there were no perils they
would not face ; by that means the impostor had made himself a prince, and he even thought of making himself Shōgun.
Nobunaga had been scarcely able to reduce him, and had found
more trouble from him than from all his other enemies put
together."

To any of his listeners really conversant with the actual
state of affairs, this deliverance of the Regent's must have
seemed at once humorous and sublime in the audacity of its
impudence.   At the very moment of its utterance, Hideyoshi
was hand-in-glove with this " false priest," the doughty and
ineffable Kennio, who was doing him rare service in
Satsuma by the perpetration of a piece of treachery as cunning,
if not as dastardly, as any ever devised and put in train by
the wit of man !

However, as it was not Hideyoshi's fashion to make premature
and imprudent disclosures of his underground workings, it is
not likely that the humour of the speech was apparent to any
but himself.   As it was, it answered his purpose, and the
overworked Christian priests at last were able to snatch a little
repose.   The open rupture was yet to come, however, and the
Regent's manner of effecting it was eminently characteristic
of himself.

An unusually large and fine Portuguese merchantman had
put in at Hirado, and Hideyoshi, then at Hakata, requested
Coelho to ask the captain to bring her round to that port
for his inspection.   The captain at once went to Hakata in a
smaller vessel, and, proceeding with Coelho to Hideyoshi, said
the only thing that prevented him from complying with his
request was the fact that he was asked to perform the impossible, as his ship had too large a draught for approaching
Hakata.   The Regent expressed himself as perfectly satisfied
with the explanation, and behaved most courteously to both
the captain and Coelho, who early in the evening returned
to their vessel together.   On the following afternoon Hideyoshi
went to see Coelho and the captain in their vessel, and spent
three hours with them there.   At midnight, a few hours

afterwards, the Vice-Provincial was roused from his slumbers in his cabin, and told that a messenger from the Regent insisted on having instant speech with him. On going on deck he was greeted by a man on shore with an order to land at once, the order being couched in the most insulting language. Poor Coelho dumfoundedly obeyed, and then the man who had summoned him told him that his Highness wished to know from him :—

1.—Why, and by what authority, he (the Vice-Provincial) and his *religieux* constrained his (Hideyoshi's) subjects to become Christians ?

2.—Why they induced their disciples and their sectaries to overthrow temples ?

3.—Why they persecuted the *bonzes* ?

4.—Why they and the other Portuguese ate animals useful to man, such as oxen and cows ?

5.—Why he allowed the merchants of his nation to buy Japanese to make slaves of them in the Indies ?

Before Coelho had time to collect himself, a second messenger appeared, read out a sentence of exile just passed against Don Justo Ucondono (Takayama), and, without saying a word more, at once returned ! " The Father was extremely surprised by a change so unexpected, and could not divine any reason for it; for on the preceding day Cambacundono (Hideyoshi) had done him the honour to come to see him in this same vessel, and to pass several hours with him, with promises of favouring the Christians and the Fathers of the Company in all things. As he remained in astonishment at such a strange resolution, the officer pressed him to make answer as soon as possible to the questions addressed to him." It was easy for Coelho to reply to the first query; all he had to do was to cite the Regent's patent of May, 1586. To the second and third questions (if we follow Charlevoix) he answered that the missionaries had never used violence; " that if the new Christians, knowing the falsity of the sects of Japan, and persuaded that the *Kami* and the *Hotoke* were anything but. Gods, had fancied it to be their duty to ruin their cult and wreck their temples, the Fathers must not be blamed for this, seeing that they had never contributed to it, except so far as the sovereigns approved; that they had never maltreated the *bonzes*, and that all the persecution they had raised against them was confined to convicting them of error in public

R

debates." Among a whole mass of evidence it is only necessary
to turn to Gnecchi's letter of 1577 and Froez's of 13th February,
1583, to perceive that the Fathers systematically instigated
temple-wrecking and idol-breaking; while there are many
passages in the missionary letters that prove that the persecution
of the *bonzes* was not confined to convicting them of error
in public debates. As regards the fourth count, Coelho urged
" that they never ate either ox or cow except at the tables
of the Portuguese, where they seldom appeared; that neither they
nor the merchants of their nation had fancied there was
anything to displease the Japanese in that, it being customary
in their country to make use of this meat; but that if his
Majesty did not approve of their doing so, they would desist
from eating it in future." The reply to the fifth charge is
exceedingly instructive. " The Fathers had left nothing undone
to prevent the Portuguese from purchasing Japanese to sell
them for slaves in the Indies; but his Majesty could easily
remedy this disorder, forbidding this trade to his subjects, and
by giving good orders about it in his ports."[10]

This admission alone is enough to establish the fact that
the Portuguese were carrying on an abominable slave-trade
at the expense of the Japanese. But how abominable a traffic
this was does not appear either from the Regent's query or
Coelho's reply. To realise that we must read the remarkable
document extracted from the archives of the Academy of
History at Madrid by M. Léon Pagés and published in the
Annexe to his *History of Christianity in Japan.*[11]

---

10 It may be well to give the gist of Crasset's version of the answers to the
last four questions: "That Christianity recognising only one God, the Creator
of Heaven and Earth, when his Majesty permitted his subjects to become
Christians, he permitted them to renounce the idols and to destroy their temples
as offensive to the true God; that the Emperor had often approved of their
acting in that fashion, and that Nobunaga, his predecessor, had pursued this
course towards the *bonzes*; that Christianity being as contrary to the cult of
the *bonzes* as light is to darkness and truth to error, it was impossible that they
should agree; that this same law forbade the use of violence, and that no one
could be forced to become a Christian; that it was true that the Fathers ate
oxen in Japan as they did in Europe, but that if his Majesty did not approve
of it, they would never eat any more of them; that as regards the Portuguese
the Fathers were in no wise responsible for their conduct, that they had no
knowledge of the evil they were doing (!) nor the power to prevent them;
that they had often reproved them for buying Japanese whom the people of
the country sold to them, but that they had been unable to exercise any
influence over them; that his Majesty could easily apply a remedy by prohibiting
under heavy penalties all the Governors of the towns and ports where the
Portuguese entered to sell any or to permit any to be bought."

11 *Consultation tenue par l'Évêque Cerqueira au sujet des esclaves achetés ou
engagés et transportés hors du Japan,* September 4th, 1598. One paragraph

These answers were given in writing, and when Hideyoshi ran his eye over them he made no reply beyond sending word to the Vice-Provincial to retire to Hirado, to collect all his *religieux* there, and to quit the country within six months. On the following day, July 25th, 1587, the following Edict, of which a copy duly sealed was sent to Coelho, was published and posted up in Hakata :—

"Having learned from our faithful councillors that foreign *religieux* have come into our estates, where they preach a law contrary to that of Japan, and that they had even had the audacity to destroy temples dedicated to our *Kami* and *Hotoke*: although this outrage merits the most extreme punishment, wishing nevertheless to show them mercy, we order them under pain of death to quit Japan within twenty days. During that space no harm or hurt will be done them. But at the expiration of that term, we order that if any of them be found in our States, they shall be seized and punished as the greatest criminals. As for the Portuguese merchants, we permit them to enter our ports there to continue their accustomed trade, and to remain in our estates provided our affairs need this. But we forbid them to bring any foreign *religieux* into the country, under the penalty of the confiscation of their ships and goods."

The Vice-Provincial pointed out that it was impossible for him to obey this Edict, for the reason that there was only one Portuguese vessel then in Japan, and that it would be six months before she sailed. The Regent admitted the force of the objection, and Coelho was then told to depart by the very first vessel, while orders were given that all Japanese members of the Company should leave the country together with the foreign priests.

When we turn to the Church historians for some adequate and intelligent explanation of this extraordinary *volte face* on

runs :—" Even the very lascars and scullions of the Portuguese purchase and carry slaves away. Hence it happens that many of them die on the voyage, because they are heaped up upon each other, and if their masters fall sick (these masters are sometimes Kaffirs and negroes of the Portuguese), the slaves are not cared for; it even often happens that the Kaffirs cannot procure the necessary food for them. These scullions give a scandalous example by living in debauchery with the girls they have bought, and whom some of them introduce into their cabins on the passage to Macao. I here omit the excesses committed on the lands of the pagans, where the Portuguese spread themselves to recruit youths and girls, and where they live in such a fashion that the pagans themselves are stupefied at it." It was Hideyoshi and his successors, not the Jesuits, who put down this accursed trade. One feature in it was contracts for years of servitude, and down to 1596 the Jesuits made no difficulty in giving their approval for these. Then on the representations of the (Christian) Otonas of Nagasaki, who cited Hideyoshi's severe law against the slave-trade and the execution of several Japanese for infringing it, Bishop Martines at last issued an excommunication against all buyers of slaves, at the same time imposing a fine of ten *crusados* for every slave bought. In 1598 this measure was reaffirmed by his successor Cerqueyra.

the part of the Regent, we meet with but scant satisfaction.
Crasset even pretends to be so simple as to believe that the
refusal of the Portuguese captain to bring his vessel round from
Hirado to Hakata had most to do with it; "and it was remembered that he had asked for two Portuguese ships for his war
with China." Besides this, Hideyoshi "wished to erect himself
into a God, and seeing that none but the Christians would oppose
him in this and refuse him divine honour, he took the resolution
of exterminating them as soon as possible so as not to give
them time to form a party in the State." Still further there
was the matter of his flagrant sexual immorality. He had left
his three hundred concubines behind at Ōsaka, and Jacuin
Toquun, an ex-monk who had become one of his physicians and
the minister of his pleasures, had been busy pimping for him in
Kyūshū. Toquun's "duties" had taken him into the Arima
country, where the women were very pretty, and here he had
met with such a bad reception that he returned to Hakata full
of wrath and vowing vengeance against the Christians and the
priests who had thwarted him. He arrived on the evening of
July 24th, shortly after the Regent's return from his three hours'
visit to Coelho on board his vessel, and when the port wine
he had brought back as a present had got into Hideyoshi's head,
Toquun's tale roused him to wrath, and the procurer adroitly
contrived to turn that against the Christians in general, and
Don Justo Ucondono and the Jesuits in particular. Charlevoix
also writes at great length of this trumpery Toquun episode.[12]
In all this the two historians are not very ingenuous, for both
of them had undoubtedly read Froez's document of 1597, in
which the whole general situation at this time is lucidly set

---

[12] To identify this Jacuin Toquun took some little time. At first we suspected
that Nagata Tokuhon (1512–1630), the most famous physician of the age, might
be meant. But this Nagata Tokuhon, who attained the patriarchal age of 118,
was in the service of Takeda of Kai, and later on in that of the Tokugawa
(see WHITNEY's Medical Progress in Japan, p. 806), and never in that of Hideyoshi.
The doctors at Hideyoshi's Court were Sakagami Chiun, Sakamori Jōkei. Takeda
Teika, Aki Teishun, Nanjō Sōko, Soya Jusen, Manase Dōsan (a Christian
convert), and Seyakuin Jensō. It was the last that was the Jacuin Tocun of
the missionaries. "Seyakuin Jensō was a native of Ōmi, and was at first a
priest of Hiyei-san, but he studied medicine, entered the service of Hideyoshi,
and, being much favoured by him, was constantly near his person. In the
Tenshō period (1573–1592) he was made head of the Seyakuin with the honorary
title of Hōin. This Seyakuin was a kind of free dispensary and charity hospital
founded by the Empress Kōken (740–758), but it had long ceased to exist
before Hideyoshi re-established it with the Emperor's sanction. Being made
head of this institution, Jensō adopted its name as his family name." Professional
jealousy of his fellow-leech Dōsan the Christian may have had something to
do with Jacuin's hatred of the foreign priests.

forth. From that paper we learn that Toquun (whom we have seen ironically complimenting the missionaries on May 5th, 1586) had noticed that the Fathers were devoting most of their efforts towards converting men of noble birth; and, believing that their pretext of saving souls was merely a device for the conquest of Japan, he had done his best to rouse the Regent's suspicions. Takayama (Don Justo Ucondono) he regarded as a very dangerous man—a fanatic entirely at the beck and call of the foreign priests. Hideyoshi had at first laughed at his suspicions; but "when he arrived in Kyūshū against the King of Satsuma, and noted that many lords with their vassals had become Christians, and that the same were bound to each other in great concord and exceedingly devoted to the Fathers, he began to recall what Toquun had already filled his ears with, and to understand (although in this he was auguring falsely) that the propagation of the faith would be prejudicial to the safety of the Empire. *And this is the true cause of the aversion he now declares.*"

Charlevoix would also have us believe that one great cause of the calamity that now overwhelmed the Fathers was the scandalous life the Portuguese traders were now beginning to lead. "It was remarked that they were eager to anchor only in the ports of infidel princes, and it was not doubted but that it was fear of having the missionaries as witnesses of their libertinage that had produced this change." The last clause in Hideyoshi's Expulsion Edict effectually disposes of this contention. A few pages later on Charlevoix labours hard to show that it was the ex-priest and procurer Toquun, who had just come in from Arima with tales of threats of murder and what-not, who was almost solely responsible for rousing his master to sudden and inconsiderate wrath against the foreign priests. The two statements are far from complementing each other, and in fact there seems to be as much, or rather as little, importance in one of them as in the other. In the matter of sexual morality the Regent was notoriously loose, and would never have found a cause for the banishment of the missionaries in such, to him, trifling considerations as either the debauches of the Portuguese seamen or his own pimp's broken head. The coarseness and the abruptness of his breach with the Vice-Provincial were the result neither of pique nor of caprice;

time and again he made use of similar outbursts of simulated
fury to mask the persistent continuity of designs long previously
conceived and put in train. And as regards Christianity,
Hideyoshi seems to have for some time been minded to treat it
exactly as the Buddhists, as Mōri, as Satsuma had been treated—
not to extirpate it, but to reduce it to the position of a serviceable
political tool. For the ideal prince, Hideyoshi would have
served Machiavelli as an infinitely better model than the latter
found in Cesare Borgia; for with far greater intellectual power
than the Borgia possessed, the Regent clearly grasped the fact
that neither ethics nor religion could be eliminated from politics.
At the same time, religion had to be put in its proper place and
kept there, and its proper place was that of a political tool.[13]

This consideration may help us to understand much. At
this time the only one among his own Christian officers
interfered with was Takayama, Don Justo Ucondono, cavalry
commander. Hideyoshi saw clearly that with all his great
military and other abilities, Takayama stood hopelessly at the
beck and call of the foreign priests. On two separate occasions
his course of action in important crises had been decided by a
letter from Father Gnecchi. And when some Japanese afterwards declared the banishment of the missionaries to be an
infringement of the freedom of belief and worship the nation
had hitherto enjoyed, the wrinkles of Hideyoshi's monkey-
face must have puckered into deeper creases as he recalled
Takayama's action in his own fiefs of Takatsuki and of
Akashi. So Takayama, being the hopeless tool of those the
Regent wished to use as his own tools, and being one of
the finest soldiers in the Empire, was a dangerous man, and
as such he was stripped of his command and of his fief and
banished. As for Konishi (Don Austin) and Kuroda (Simon
Condera), although Christians, Hideyoshi felt he might yet
trust them, and he had need of their services. Accordingly
Kuroda was, as we have seen, installed in Buzen, no doubt

---

13 "Cambacundono, to justify a conduct so *bizarre*, explained to the people
of his Court that he had acted so because the Law of the Christians was
entirely contrary to the religion which had hitherto been practised in Japan;
and that for long he had intended to abolish it, but that he deferred doing
so till he had become master of Kyūshū, where the Christians were most
numerous, and where they might have been able to form a party against him."
Crasset indeed cites this explanation; but he only does so to reject it by
implication as unreal.

charged to keep watch over the pagan Mōri in Yamaguchi, on the other side of the straits. Konishi in Southern Higo, and made Lieutenant-General of Kyūshū, could attend to the Christian-hating Satsumese, while he himself was to be kept under keen observation by his northern neighbour in Kumamoto, Katō Kiyomasa, one of the most bigoted Buddhist sectaries of the time.

Meanwhile the Vice-Provincial had hastily withdrawn all his *religieux*, with the exception of Gnecchi in Kyōto and one priest in Bungo, and assembled them in Hirado. All told, they amounted to one hundred and twenty. At the same time orders came from Hideyoshi that they were all to embark on the large Portuguese ship then on the point of sailing from Hirado, and to be gone at once. In a general council, however, it was resolved not to obey these instructions, and only a few priests needed for service in China departed. What made it possible for the *religieux* to act in this fashion was the practical sympathy of the Christian princes of Kyūshū,—especially that of Konishi, of Arima, and of Ōmura. Into the territories of the two latter Hideyoshi had sent troops with orders to dismantle the principal fortresses, to raze the churches, to obliterate all signs of Christianity, and to seize the port of Nagasaki. Arima and Ōmura appealed in person to Hideyoshi at Hakata, and met with a very bad reception; but on returning to their domains they found that the Regent's commissioners were by no means adamant when approached in a judicious manner. Under the genial influence of substantial bribes they developed a wonderful amount of "sweet reasonableness"; only one fortress and a few churches in Ōmura were demolished, while those in Arima and in Nagasaki were not touched. Nagasaki was not then appropriated even. Besides Nagasaki and Mogi, from which the priests drew an annual revenue of 300 cruzados, they now also held Urakami, worth 500 cruzados per annum, which had been bestowed upon them by Arima shortly after his victory at Shimabara in 1584. However, when the commissioners proceeded to seize these estates, they were met by representations from Arima and Ōmura to the effect that the missionaries had merely held the usufruct of them; and that as the missionaries had been banished, Nagasaki, together with Mogi and Urakami, naturally reverted to the feudal lord. The argument, supported as it was by a few trifling presents, was admitted to be unanswerable, and Nagasaki was left in the hands of Ōmura—that is to say, of the Jesuits.[14] Ōmura and Arima now wrote to the missionaries in Hirado, offering them an asylum in their domains, and Arima even went so far as to undertake to convert all his subjects who were still "idolaters," "above all the inhabitants of Shima-bara, Kojiro, and Miye, which had for long been under the rule of the King of Satsuma." Accordingly, as many as seventy *religieux* passed into the Arima fief, where the Daimyō "erected two very commodious houses, one for them and one for the seminarists they have brought from Ōsaka." Of the others twelve went to Ōmura, nine to Amakusa, two to Kurume in Chikugo, while four remained in Hirado and five were sent into Bungo.

In this last province, once the chief base of the missionary propaganda in Japan, Christianity had now indeed fallen upon evil days. In the war with Satsuma in 1586, the college and the novitiate had been burned to the ground, as well as most of the churches. Then the old Christian Daimyō, Çivan (Yoshishige), had died in May, 1587, and as his death had been shortly preceded by that of his second son, the Christian Sebastian, the foreign religion had lost most of its hold on the princely House of Bungo. It is true that the young Daimyō, Yoshimune "the Stammerer," had accepted baptism under stress of adversity and at the instance of Kuroda in 1587; but he was no enthusiastic Christian, and, being a prince of infirm purpose, he was entirely under the influence of his mother—the Jezebel of the Jesuits—and of her brother "Cicata" (Tawara Tsugitada), who was, in fact, the real ruler of the fief, and who hated Christianity with a most intense hatred. The chief friend the missionaries now had in Bungo was a certain "Paul Shiga Conixus," who had distinguished himself in the Satsuma war, and who is described as the most powerful vassal in the principality. Shortly after the arrival of the refugee priests, Yoshimune, or rather "Cicata,"

---

14 Either in the following year, or early in 1589, however, it was bestowed upon a son of Riūzōji's; and before 1591 it was at last really appropriated by Hideyoshi.

endeavoured to compel the Christians to take an oath of fidelity to Hideyoshi on a heathen altar; and when Shiga's opposition proved too powerful, the missionaries, with many honeyed apologies, were requested to withdraw from the fief. However, although some of them did so, eight remained in hiding on the lands of Shiga and of the prince's youngest brother. About this time Yoshimune had made two visits to Hideyoshi at Ōsaka. On the first of these he was severely snubbed, and among other things "was called a fool for not having known how to treat Shiga properly, who had rendered him such distinguished service in the war with Satsuma." On the second occasion he had gone up with Cicata and Shiga, and on the presentation of the latter to Hideyoshi, the Regent called him "the greatest man of war in Bungo," and invited him to dinner with him, entirely ignoring Cicata, much to the latter's mortification. In revenge for this, on his return to Bungo, Shiga was ordered to render obedience to the Imperial Edict, which forbade the profession of Christianity in the Empire, and to dismiss all his Christian dependents. Shiga at once made answer that he knew perfectly well how to account to the Regent for his conduct; that as for Yoshimune, he had no reason to complain of any shortcoming of his in the service he owed him; that at all times in Japan there had been complete freedom to embrace whatever religion one pleased; that he had made choice of Christianity, and, though it were to cost him his life, he would not renounce it; and that henceforth Yoshimune might dispense with sending him any more such instructions." It may be well to remark in passing that in no State in contemporary Europe could such an answer to a similar order have been returned with impunity.

Some time before this Yoshimune had apostatized, and he now began to persecute, and two of his Christian vassals (one with his wife, two children, and a servant) were beheaded for refusing to renounce their faith.[15] However, Yoshimune did not go very far in this direction; the councillors of the fief became apprehensive of a general rising of the Christian population, and persuaded him to let things rest.

---

[15] "Thus," says Charlevoix, "the first martyrs given to the Church by persecution in Japan perished by the order of a Christian king." In this connection it is interesting to examine the *Catalogus Occisorum in odium Fidei* given at the end of Cardim's *Fasciculus e Japponicis Floribus.* There it appears

That he could afford to leave his Christian subjects alone without any great risk of rousing Hideyoshi's wrath became pretty clear from a variety of circumstances. Arima and Ōmura, openly and unreservedly committed to the support of Christianity, had been twice to Hideyoshi's Court, and had there met with receptions whose courtesy was in marked contrast to the scant ceremony Yoshimune himself had been welcomed with, in spite of all his servile compliance with the letter of the anti-Christian Edict. Furthermore, his own Christian vassal, Shiga, continued to enjoy a high place in the good graces of the Regent. So Yoshimune came to the conclusion that he had after all trimmed his sails but badly; and by the middle of 1590 we find him piteously and abjectly whining for readmission into the Christian fold, and inviting Jesuits to resume their work in his fief.

Before this date Hideyoshi had seen fit to modify the stringency of his Edict somewhat, for a reason not given by Charlevoix, but plainly enough stated in the Annual Letters. The first hint of this is given in Froez's letter of February 24th, 1589. In 1587 Montero, captain of the vessel ordered to take away all the missionaries in 1587, had sent one Lopez with presents to Hideyoshi, and to ask him to leave those "few" priests he had been unable to find room for temporarily exempt from the scope of his Edict. Hideyoshi was enraged at the request,—said that he was determined to have no Christianity preached in his dominions, that it would cost any one doing so his head, and ordered all the churches in Kyōto, Ōsaka, and Sakai to be demolished at once. (The houses and the college were spared, however.) From this Froez began to believe that his expulsion of the missionaries was to be attributed to no drunken whim, but to deliberate and deeply-pondered policy. In October, 1588, this same Lopez was once more

---

there were five martyrs at Hirado in 1557, one in the island of Kamishima (Amakusa) in 1568, and two at Isahaya in Hizen in 1574. All these eight preceded these six Bungo martyrs of 1589. These cases were followed by that of a woman in 1591, and there were no others until the crucifixion of the six Philippine *religieux*, three Japanese Jesuits, and seventeen converts on the Martyrs' Mount at Nagasaki on February 5th, 1597. And for the death of these twenty-six only was Hideyoshi responsible. Besides these, Cardim counts four Jesuit Fathers, said to have been poisoned at Hirado—a Spaniard in 1590, a Fleming (died at Malacca 1592) in 1590, and a Venetian and a Fleming in 1593. Meanwhile, between 1549 and 1597 how many had suffered death for their religion in Europe?

sent up to Hideyoshi, on this occasion by Pereyra, the captain of the "great ship from Macao."

This time Lopez was received with the greatest affability and courtesy. On his saying, in reply to Hideyoshi's question, that the missionaries had gone, the Regent evinced much satisfaction, and added that he would have been glad to have been always friendly towards them, "but inasmuch as they preached a Law so hostile to the *Kamis* and *Hotokes* of Japan, he had been constrained to banish them. . . . The *Kamis* and the *Hotokes*, our gods, are none other than the Lords of Japan, who by their victories and their exploits have merited to be worshipped as deities by the people. Any Lord of Japan may aspire to this, provided he ends his life with some illustrious deed that may fire the minds of his subjects to render him this tribute of honour and reverence. Now this Law preached by the Fathers is entirely opposed to the *Kamis* and the *Hotokes*, and for the same reason it is directly opposed to the Lords and Monarchs of Japan; although it may be good for other parts, it is not good for Japan. Therefore I have ordered the Fathers away, as they were tending to the ruin and destruction of the *Kamis* and *Hotokes*,—thus tending to the abasement of my memory and glory after death; hence I cannot be the friend of those who are so opposed and hostile to myself." Lopez thought it well to say nothing in reply to this; but after answering a few questions, he ventured to remark that although the Portuguese had no right to question the dispositions made by Hideyoshi in his own realm, yet this departure of the Fathers was going to inconvenience them seriously, inasmuch as the King of Portugal did not wish them to sail to Japan or to continue their traffic there, unless they brought some priests with them from time to time. Thereupon Hideyoshi asked why the Portuguese who were merchants wished to have priests in their company, and on Lopez answering that the traders often had quarrels and dissensions, and that the priests were for reconciling them and re-establishing peace among them, the Regent said that if priests were necessary for the peace of the Portuguese, he was content they brought them, provided they returned in the vessel they came in.

As Froez was sure that Hideyoshi, "che è diligentissimo

investigatore di tutto quello che passa," was quite aware of
the presence of some one hundred old *religieux* in Japan, he
began to believe that the Regent had some purpose in talking
in such a strain. The purpose in question was the conserva-
tion of the Portuguese trade, but it is not till 1593 that the
missionaries say so plainly and distinctly. However, be the
reason what it might, the missionaries in Arima, Ōmura,
Nagasaki, and Amakusa now found themselves but little
interfered with, and profited by their enforced concentration
within these circumscribed limits to consolidate their position
there thoroughly. In 1589 there were as many as 23,000
baptisms in Kyūshū. Konishi, now Lord of Southern Higo
(200,000 *koku*), held a commission as Lieutenant-General, which
gave him great authority over all the small maritime fiefs of
Western Kyūshū; and, thanks to him, the priests remained
unmolested in Hirado, while he also found admission for them
into the Gotōs. Nor was this all he did for Christianity at
this time. In 1587 the Lord of Isahaya, a cousin of Arima's,
had been dispossessed of his fief, which was given to a son of
Riūzōji. As soon as Hideyoshi had returned to Kyōto, Arima's
cousin appealed to him for aid to recover his estates, and Arima
promised to help him with troops on condition that he accepted
baptism together with all his subjects. Before moving in
the matter Arima had consulted Konishi, and on the expulsion
of young Riūzōji from Isahaya, Konishi succeeded in making
Hideyoshi believe that Riūzōji had deserved to be expelled.
Two years later he contrived to extricate the Christianity
of Amakusa from a serious danger. In 1590 the bigoted
princelet, on being summoned to Court by Hideyoshi, refused
to go, and Katō Kiyomasa was at once sent to chastise him.
Konishi got himself associated in the commission, however,
and on Katō's losing many of his best troops in the siege
of Hiondo,[16] and therefore withdrawing, he found himself
sole commander, and soon induced the princelet to yield,
promising to make his peace for him with Hideyoshi. "What
is certain is that this storm passed, and that the island of
Amakusa, thanks to the good care of the Grand Admiral

---

16 This siege was a desperate affair. "In it three hundred women made
themselves especially admired, and for long rendered the victory doubtful. At
last they were all killed except two, and these were dangerously wounded."

(Konishi), was one of the parts of Kyūshū where religion for long was most flourishing."

All this was indeed most fortunate for the missionaries, but it was perhaps still more fortunate for them that Hideyoshi's attention was meanwhile wholly absorbed elsewhere and in a weightier matter.

CHAPTER X.

REDUCTION OF THE KWANTŌ AND FOREIGN RELATIONS (1590-1593).

WITH Kyūshū reduced and his power firmly established at
Kyōto, Hideyoshi now deemed the time ripe for extending
his supremacy to all the lands within the seas of Dai Nihon.
Of the sixty-six provinces of the Empire, eleven still remained
to be dealt with. These were Idzu, the eight provinces of
the Kwantō, and the vast stretches of Mutsu and Dewa in the
extreme north. In the latter districts there were some fifteen
or sixteen feudatories, none of them of any very preponderant
power, unless, perhaps, young Daté Masamune (22), who was
rapidly extending his boundaries at the expense of his neighbours. To deal with any or all of these in a summary fashion
would be no very difficult task. But the Kwantō was a very
different matter. In it were some half-score of independent
chiefs, but one of these occupied such a preponderant position
that the other nine existed more or less by his sufferance. In
the introductory chapter brief allusion was made to the sudden
rise of the House of the later Hōjō of Odawara. Now, under
Hōjō Ujimasa, its fourth head, it held Idzu, Sagami, Musashi,
Kōdzuke, and the greater part of Shimōsa, while it bade fair
to swallow up Kadzusa and Awa. Its strategic position was
an exceedingly strong one, for from the west of Idzu and the
Hakoné hills its western frontiers were ringed round with a
mountain rampart which made an invasion a really formidable
affair to those who should undertake it. The main approaches
were then, as now, by the Nakasendō and the Tōkaidō,—only
the Tōkaidō at that date ran round the north of the Hakoné
Lake instead of to the south of it as at present,—and the
provisioning of any large assailing force, unless supported by
a fleet, would have been a matter of great difficulty. The
Tōkaidō, on the western Hakoné slope, was dominated by the
keep of Yamanaka; the debouchure of the Nakasendo was
also protected by a chain of strongly-built fortified posts;

while the peninsula of Idzu was exceedingly well provided with places of arms. Due regard being had to the compactness and the extent of the Hōjō possessions, their geographical position and their difficulty of access, and the absence of any such local co-operation as Hideyoshi had received from Ōtomo, Riūzōji, and others in his conquest of Kyūshū, any campaign against Odawara would be likely to prove fully as serious an undertaking as that against Shimadzu in 1587 had been.

Perhaps it was this consideration that induced the Regent to endeavour to attain his end by peaceable means at first. At all events, when, in 1589, Hōjō Ujimasa vouchsafed no answer to Hideyoshi's first invitation to repair to Kyōto to pay homage to the Emperor, Hideyoshi at first contentéd himself with merely repeating the summons. Ujimasa now replied that he would appear at Kyōto if Numata, of which he had been stripped by Sanada Masayuki, were restored to him, and Hideyoshi at once ordered Sanada to restore that fortress. However, on the Regent now again urging Hōjō to repair to Kyōto, the other made answer that Hideyoshi "was merely trying to master the Kwantō by diplomacy, but that it would be more to the purpose for him to try bows and arrows." Of course this was a declaration of war. With the Emperor's sanction Hideyoshi called upon the levies of forty-five provinces, and, ordering Sanada to break in by the Nakasendō and Iyeyasu to advance at once by the Tōkaidō, he himself left Kyōto at the head of 170,000 men on April 5th, 1590. The whole punitive force is said to have amounted to 250,000 men. On May 1st the Regent arrived at Numadzu, and two days later his brother Hidenaga assaulted and carried Yamada after severe fighting and heavy loss, while about the same time Oda Nobuo succeeded in seizing the outer *enceinte* of Nirayama in Idzu, held by Ujinori (Hōjō Ujimasa's brother), but was beaten out of it a few days later on. After the fall of Yamanaka, Iyeyasu swept round Lake Hakoné, and, storming three castles on his way, advanced to Sakawa, three miles to the east of Odawara. Meanwhile, in a council of war Hōjō Ujimasa had proposed to stake everything on a decisive battle in the open, but in this he was opposed by Matsuda, his lieutenant (in whom he placed the utmost trust), who advocated a repetition of the tactics of Ujiyasu, who had foiled Uyesugi

Kenshin before Odawara in 1560 merely by sitting still. Now this Matsuda, bribed by the offer of Idzu and Sagami, had sold himself to Hideyoshi some time before. Early in May Hideyoshi arrived before Odawara, and, having been secretly informed by Matsuda that the Ishigaki hill to the north-west of the castle commanded a full view of it, he seized upon it, and, setting tens of thousands of men to work, he reared a castle there in a single night. The outside was pasted over with white paper, but from Odawara hold it looked just like the ordinary white plastered walls of a fortress. A few days after this Hideyoshi took Iyeyasu to the summit of the keep on Ishigaki hill and remarked to him, " I shall soon reduce all these provinces, and then I will give them to you," Iyeyasu thanked him, saying, " That were great luck indeed ! " Hideyoshi then whispered in Iyeyasu's ear, " Wilt thou live in Odawara, as the men of Hōjō have done ? " To this Iyeyasu answered, " Yes, my lord." " That will not do," said Hideyoshi ; " I have seen a map, and know that there is a place called Yedo about 21 ri distant from here to the east. It is girdled by rivers and the sea, and it is a fine position ; and that is the place where I would that thou shouldst live." Iyeyasu replied that he would respectfully obey his lordship's instructions. Such is the common tale of how it was that Yedo became the Tokugawa metropolis.

Odawara Castle was now closely invested on all sides, but the besieged sustained the siege with resolution and endurance. Finding it impossible to storm the stronghold, Hideyoshi ordered the siege to be converted into a blockade. " In consequence the leaguers now attempted no assault, but passed the time in giving feasts. Dancing-girls, musicians, and actors were brought into the various camps, and merry-making was the order of the day. It was indeed more like a gigantic picnic party than a great host intent upon slaughter. More than a hundred days passed in this fashion without a single encounter."

In the meantime, however, Hideyoshi had not been idle. On Hōjō's eastern flank, the Daimyō Yuki, in Shimosa, smarting under the supremacy of his too-powerful neighbour, had sent a messenger to the Kwanbaku (Hideyoshi), asking for one of his relations in adoption, and Hideyoshi at once went to visit him. He was accompanied by Iyeyasu's second son, whom he himself had adopted in 1585; and Hideyasu was now in turn adopted by Yuki. In September, 1590, Yuki retired from the headship of his clan, and Hideyasu then found himself chief of a fief of 101,000 *koku*. Hideyoshi had also meanwhile summoned the barons of Mutsu and Dewa to repair to his camp to do him homage, Daté Masamune especially being addressed in no over-courteous tone. After a council with his lieutenants Daté thought it best to yield, and on his appearance in the camp before Odawara, he was soundly rated and ordered to surrender all his late conquests to the Kwanbaku. These, however, were immediately restored to him, and Daté was received into grace.

Although there was little blood being spilt before Odawara itself, the campaign was being vigorously prosecuted elsewhere. The Nakasendō army corps under Sanada Masayuki, co-operating with Uyesugi of Echigo and Mayeda of Kaga, had stormed various castles in Kōdzuke and Musashi, while Asano and Kimura had been sent to deal with Awa, Kadzusa, and Shimōsa. Within a month sixty castles had fallen, and besides Odawara, only Nirayama in Idzu, held by Hōjō's brother, Ujinori, still continued to defy the assailants.

Yet after three months Odawara showed no signs of distress, and Hideyoshi was beginning to feel anxious—so much so that he offered to confirm Ujimasa in possession of the provinces of Idzu and Sagami if he would surrender. To this offer Ujimasa vouchsafed no reply. It will be remembered that these were the very provinces promised to Matsuda the traitor, and it thus becomes questionable whether Hideyoshi really made the offer in good faith. As for Matsuda, he had meanwhile concerted with Hori, one of Hideyoshi's captains, to admit his troops into the castle, and the treachery only miscarried through Matsuda's endeavour to make his own sons parties to it. One of these, Matsuda Fusaharu, was Ujimasa's favourite page, and on his trying to dissuade his father from proceeding any further in the dirty business, he was put in ward to keep him quiet. However, he contrived to get conveyed out of the house in a case of armour, and, first stipulating for his father's life, apprised Ujimasa of what was toward. Matsuda, however, met with the fate he deserved. On the miscarriage of the plot, Hideyoshi again renewed his offer, and repeated it several times. Ujifusa, Ujimasa's second son, whose wife and children had been captured and held prisoners at Iwatsuki, now urged his father to yield, while it was known that some of Ujimasa's captains were inclined to desert. Suspicion and mistrust had become rife among the besieged, and so at last in August Ujimasa sent his eldest son Ujinao to deliver the castle to Iyeyasu, while at the same time Ujinori evacuated Nirayama and joined his brother in captivity at Odawara. Ujimasa and his party were taken to a physician's house, and here they were waited upon by messengers from Hideyoshi with an order to—commit suicide!

The messengers were too ashamed to state the purport of their visit, but Ujimasa, inferring it from their demeanour, asked for a few minutes' leave, and he and his brother Ujiteru first took a bath and then calmly disembowelled themselves. Ujinori was on the point of following their example, but was arrested in the attempt by the officials. As for the sons, Ujinao, Ujifusa, and the others, Hideyoshi allowed them to withdraw to the monastery of Kōya-san with a revenue of 10,000 koku for their support, and here Ujinao died in the following year at the age of twenty-one. The gallant Ujinori had won Hideyoshi's respect, and a few years later he was made lord of Sayama in Kawachi with an assessment of 10,000 koku.

The contrast between the measure meted out to Hōjō of Odawara in 1590 and the treatment accorded to Shimadzu of Satsuma in 1587 is certainly remarkable. But then Shimadzu was a necessity in his position; and his provinces in the extreme south of the Empire, so far from being wanted, could not be kept in order by anyone else. Hōjō, so far from being a necessity, would continue to be a serious disturbing element; and, besides, Hideyoshi had very great need for his fief. In Mikawa and the adjoining provinces Iyeyasu was too powerful and too near for the Regent's mental comfort; and it was only by some such advantageous exchange as that of the Kwantō just proffered him that Iyeyasu could be induced to remove. And Hideyoshi doubtless fancied that, though beaten for the time being, Hōjō Ujimasa, while the breath of life was in him, would never rest till he had done his best to upset the contemplated re-arrangement and settlement of the feudal map of Eastern Japan. At all events, be the reasons what they may, this is one of the very few instances in which Hideyoshi had recourse to the very banal device of extermination so much affected by Nobunaga. Mikawa and the other provinces evacuated by Iyeyasu, after being offered to and refused by Oda Nobuo (who was sent into temporary exile at Akita for his refusal), were portioned out among eight of Hideyoshi's followers, while in Kai, Owari, and Northern Isé there were also great changes made at this time. At this date also, Gamō Ujisato, with 800,000 *koku*, was planted in Aidzu, marching with the domains of Daté, of Uyesugi, and of Iyeyasu.[1] The overthrow of Hōjō had brought with it the surrender of the whole of Northern Japan to Hideyoshi. Before Odawara had fallen, Nambu, Akita, Sōma, Tsugaru, and other Daimyō of Mutsu and Dewa had given in their allegiance to the Kwanbaku, and the others now hastened to make their peace with him. Furthermore, about the middle of the Ashikaga period, Matsumaye Nobuhiro had settled at the place which now bears his name; and he and his descendants had brought the Ainu of that locality into subjection. The Regent now recognised that conquest, and confirmed Yoshihiro, the great-grandson of Nobuhiro, in the lordship of Yezō.

Hideyoshi was now undisputed master of the empire from Tanegashima in the south on to snowy Yezo in the north; the

---

[1] This Gamō Ujisato was one of the finest soldiers of the time. His father had left Sasaki to join Nobunaga, and in the struggle between Shibata and Hideyoshi young Gamō had taken part with the latter, and had then done him brilliant service, as he afterwards did in the Satsuma campaign and on other occasions. "He was a military genius. After a certain battle in which he played a leading part, Ishida Mitsunari, who witnessed his operations, brought Hideyoshi the following report:—'From what I saw of the way he conducted the campaign, I judge him to be an extraordinary man. For seven days continuously I saw his troops marching before my eyes, and in that vast host there was not one single breach of discipline. If he remains steadfast to your Highness's cause, he will be the best general in your service. He is indeed a man to be closely watched.' At this time, when he was made lord of Aidzu, he retired from the presence of Hideyoshi to an adjoining room, and as he there sat against a pillar his eyes were seen to fill with tears. Seeing this, a near attendant of the Kwanbaku approached him and said, 'You are quite right to feel so grateful for the favour you have received.' In reply, Gamō whispered, 'No! it is not so!' Were I placed near the capital even in a small fief I might some day do something of worth. But now that I am sent away to remote Aidzu, my hopes are dashed, and so my tears arise in spite of myself.' Some time after Hideyoshi began to fear Gamō, and it is said that in the spring of 1593, while in the camp at Nagoya in Hizen, poison was administered to him by Ishida Mitsunari at the instigation of the Taikō. Gamō died at Kyōto on March 17th, 1595." He was an intimate friend of Justo Ucondono, and through him he was baptized by Father Gnecchi, as was also his chief councillor later on, in 1595. He was very friendly towards the Jesuits, in whose letters he appears as "Findadono" (Hida-no-kami), and they lamented his death greatly.

s 2

work of mere territorial centralisation was complete. It had been generally expected that he would fail in his attempt to reduce Hōjō;[2] hence Hideyoshi's return to the West was all the more of a triumphal progress. Accordingly, when he took up his quarters in Ōsaka he was not unnaturally in a very good humour,—"il étoit d'une affabilité donc ceux qui connoissoient son humeur atrabilaire, etoient extrêmement supris."

This frame of mind was promising for the prospects of a favourable reception of the embassy from the Viceroy of the Indies which had just then arrived in Japan. During the travels of the Japanese ambassadors to, in, and from Europe, Valegnani had remained in Goa; and here, in 1587, he had received a letter from the Vice-Provincial Coelho, informing him of the favours Hideyoshi was then heaping upon the missionaries, and suggesting the dispatch of an envoy by the Viceroy of the Indies to thank the Regent for all these favours, and to request a continuance of them. De Menesez, the Viceroy, heartily approved of this project, and nominated Valegnani himself for the office. Meanwhile, in May, 1587, the four Japanese ambassadors on their way back from Europe arrived at Goa; and some months later came intelligence of Hideyoshi's sudden and startling change of front towards Christianity. It was then deemed expedient to associate the four Japanese youths in the projected mission. On arriving at Macao, in the summer of 1588, Valegnani proceeded cautiously, and at first wrote to the Christian princes of Kyūshū for their advice. Their counsel was that the matter should be entrusted to a certain pagan lord, who was at once an intimate friend of Konishi and very influential at Hideyoshi's Court.

---

2 Writing on July 25th, 1590, to the Jesuit General, Father della Matta says:—" Saranno cinque mesi, che il Tiranno si parti con grand' essercito per suggettarsi un Signore orientale, che non voleva venire a presentarsi a lui in capo dell' anno col solito tributo, ne riconoscerlo per superiore. Costui dicono che hà aperte le porte di alcune fortrezze al nemico e lasciatolo entrare, riserandosi egli in una, che è di circuito dodici miglia, dove haveva fatta provisione in particolare per l'habitatione della gente, che era in molto numero di due mila case, con vettuaglie per due anni; e dicono che il pensier suo è di straccar questo Tiranno, al quale cominciano già a mancar le provisioni, e cosi consumargli le forze con mira di succedergli nell' Imperio del Giapone. E opinione poi, che questo Signore non possa esser superato, e che cosi Quabacundono [i.e. Hideyoshi] ò muoia li, ò se ne torni (che è piu possibile) assai humiliato il che fara buona congiuntura per l'Ambascieria del P. Visitatore." In explanation of the last remark, it ought to be observed that the Visitor-General, Valegnani, had come into Nagasaki four days before as ambassador from the Viceroy of the Indies to Hideyoshi.

This was Asano, the Minister of Justice, who was then in
Kyūshū in connection with the new land-survey of the empire
and with the settlement of the affairs of some of the fiefs.
Asano willingly enough undertook the commission; and on
his showing Valegnani's letter to Hideyoshi, the latter at
once said that the envoy of the Viceroy of the Indies would
be welcome. Valegnani, on learning this, set sail with his
companions, and on reaching Nagasaki on July 21st, 1590,
he immediately wrote to the Regent notifying him of his arrival.
Hideyoshi, on receiving the letter, charged Asano and Kuroda
with the conduct of the embassy to Kyōto, and ordered them
to see that it should want for nothing on the route. However,
just at this time Valegnani was taken ill and was unable to
leave Nagasaki for some months, and the delay thus occasioned
gave some of his courtiers an opportunity of suggesting to
Hideyoshi that the mission was not genuine, but merely a
trick of the foreign priests. Asano had sent a courier to say
that a vessel would be sent to fetch the envoys; but no vessel
appeared, and Asano himself was dismissed to his fief in Kai,
while Hideyoshi began to speak contemptuously of the embassy.
It was Kuroda and Konishi who sent this news to Valegnani,
and they at the same time urged him to start at once, taking
as few *religieux* and as many Portuguese with him as possible,
and to make a strong effort to eclipse the Korean ambassadors,
then in Japan with a suite of three hundred persons. Accordingly, at the end of November Valegnani set out with
Gnecchi and Mesquita and two other priests, some young
Japanese Jesuits, the four returned Japanese ambassadors with
their attendants, and twenty-six or twenty-seven Portuguese
from Nagasaki and the neighbouring ports, "who might have
been taken for great lords." At Murotsu in Harima it was
learned that Hideyoshi had just lost his infant son and his
half-brother, Hidenaga; and in consequence of this news the
envoys remained there for some two months, Gnecchi being
sent on to act as intelligence agent in Kyōto. As might
have been expected, the four [8] young Japanese just returned

___

[8] As has been said, all were admitted into the "Company of Jesus" in
1592. Chiji-iwa soon left it, however. Itō died in 1612 at the age of 45,
and Nakaura suffered martyrdom at Nagasaki on October 18th, 1633. When
Hara died is not known. He was noted as a translator of Portuguese works
into Japanese.

from Europe after eight years' wandering found themselves
a centre of universal attraction. They had brought maps
and globes and scientific and musical instruments with them,
and they had much to say about "the majesty of the Sovereign
Pontiff of the Christians, about the power of the monarchs of
Europe, and about the august manner in which divine service
was celebrated at Rome and in all the great churches." Mōri
of Nagato, we are told, could not leave them, while young
Kuroda was, if possible, still more attached to their company.
Among the great crowd of notabilities that thronged to greet
them from all sides "conversions" again became numerous. Itō,
one of the ambassadors, had been the representative of Ōtomo
Yoshishige of Bungo; and it was now that Yoshishige's son,
Yoshimune of Bungo and Itō's cousin, cut such a sorry figure.
He had sent Shiga to make his peace for him, first with
Gomez, and then with Valegnani, and now on his way to
Kyōto he appeared at Murotsu "more in the character of a
penitent than of a prince." After copious tears and piteous
prayers, he at last succeeded in engaging Itō in his behalf;
and after Valegnani had made him pledge his princely word
that he would make full reparation for all the evil he had
done, he was once more admitted to the fold. "The ceremony
of reconciliation was conducted in a manner which gave the
infidels a great idea of the Christian religion." With all
this, however, Valegnani's mind was by no means free from
anxiety. News had come from Kyōto that Hideyoshi had
again been expressing himself in terms not very complimentary
to the mission. Kuroda had ventured to speak to him about
it, and had met with a rude rebuff. Nothing dismayed by
this, however, Kuroda engaged the good offices of Masuda, the
Minister of Works, to smooth the way; and although Masuda
also met with a repulse at first, he ultimately succeeded in
getting Hideyoshi to consent to receive the envoy. "If Father
Valegnani wishes to do me reverence," at last said the Regent,
"I will receive him; but if he comes as ambassador to ask
me on behalf of the Viceroy of the Indies to revoke the Edict
of banishment I have issued against his *confrères*, I wish
neither to see him nor to speak to him; above all, let him
bethink himself well not to say anything to me in favour
of his diabolical religion." Masuda and Kuroda were then

commissioned to make all due arrangements for the reception of the mission, and towards the end of February, 1591, it left Murotsu for Kyōto.

In Froez's "Annual Letter" (Froez, though, was not with Valegnani, Lopez and Mesquita being his attendants) we have a full account of the magnificence of the embassy, of its presents (among which was an Arab jennet) and of its reception by Hideyoshi in Kyōto on March 3rd, 1591. After the formal audience was over, and Valegnani and his companions were at dinner with Hideyoshi's nephew and eight great lords, the Regent strolled in *en déshabillé* and talked and acted in the most frank and free and simple and unconstrained manner—a usual practice of his, by the way, as Japanese authorities show. A great deal of his best work was done in this very unconventional guise, and that evening he effected a noteworthy stroke by the device. Among the presents offered by the embassy was a clock, and Hideyoshi sent for Rodriguez, a young Jesuit (priest in 1596) whom Valegnani sometimes used as interpreter,[4] and asked him to show him how to mount it. The Regent kept him with him far on into the night, talking with him about all manner of things, and in the course of his remarks he said he was going to start for the province of Owari next morning, and that meanwhile, till the letter to the Viceroy of the Indies was ready, Valegnani was free to go anywhere in Japan, "but caution him to act so that the *religieux* who accompany him comport themselves with much discretion, and not compel me, by an ill-considered zeal, to make a bold stroke which would have consequences." The hint was not lost upon the Visitor-General. Although no objection was raised against his open celebration of the Mass (a thing unknown in Japan, except in out-of-the-way places in Kyūshū, since 1587), yet when he returned to Kyūshū he thought it well to put a restraint upon the very injudicious zeal of the converts there. He had delayed handing over the presents from the Pope to the Christian princes who had sent the envoys to his Holiness, and now he insisted on their delivery being made without any elaborate celebration, while the college and novitiate in Arima were removed to lonely

4 Fathers Mesquita and Lopez had acted in this capacity at the formal reception of the embassy.

seats in Amakusa at the same time that the seminary was transferred to a site in an impenetrable forest near Hachirō. So prudent were the measures taken by Valegnani that at his departure with Hideyoshi's reply to the Viceroy of the Indies, in spite of the proscription of the priests by the newly-established central government, there were no fewer than one hundred and forty Jesuits in twenty-three houses left behind in Japan. And from the judicious manner in which the latter comported themselves, they were able to carry on a propaganda—albeit now an underground one—attended with most remarkable results. The protection of the Christian Daimyōs stood the priests in good stead, and even the number of these kept on increasing; Sō Yoshitoshi, Daimyō of Tsushima and Konishi's son-in-law, had been secretly baptized by the Visitor-General at Kyōto in 1591, and one of the last things Valegnani had done before his departure was to administer baptism to the Prince of Hiūga. In Kyōto itself even Christianity was making substantial progress. There old Kuroda, himself a favourite of Hideyoshi's, had engaged the sympathies of the Governor of Kyōto in favour of the proscribed priests. This Governor, called " Guenifoin " by the Jesuits, seems to have been Hōin Mayeda Geni, who stood high in his master's good graces. In 1594 these two induced Hideyoshi to consent to Gnecchi's remaining in the capital, while at the same time we are told the Governor winked at the presence of many other missionaries in the city. Yet, withal, we cannot but be at least mildly surprised to be assured that in 1596, when Martinez, Bishop of Japan (arrived August 8th, 1596), in his quality of ambassador from the Viceroy of the Indies, had an audience with Hideyoshi (now become Taikō), the Christianity of Kyōto was the most flourishing in all Japan.

Before Valegnani's departure in October, 1592, there had been a good deal of plotting and counter-plotting on the part of the Jesuits and of their enemies. After his arrival in 1590 the Visitor-General had not availed himself of the good offices of the two Governors of Nagasaki to introduce his mission at Court, and they had taken great umbrage in consequence. Accordingly, on their visit to Kyōto at the next Japanese New Year (February, 1592) they informed Hideyoshi that Kyūshū was full of missionaries who continued to discharge their functions in defiance of his edicts, and endeavoured to make him believe that the late embassy was entirely fictitious and a mere device of the priests to regain his favour. It would seem that Masuda, the Minister of Works, had meanwhile quarrelled with Kuroda, for Masuda, as well as "Jacuin Tocun," now lent himself to serve the purposes of the slighted Governors. Kuroda, however, had recourse to Mayeda Geni, Minister of Worship and Governor of one of the two sections of Kyōto, who seems to have been on no very good terms with Masuda, and Mayeda (Guenifoin) proved sufficiently astute not only to effect the miscarriage of the intrigue, but even to obtain permission for a certain number of priests to remain openly in Japan! He got Rodriguez, whom Hideyoshi had just taken into his service as interpreter, to suggest to the Regent that if he had any doubts about the genuineness of the mission, he might detain Valegnani's suite as hostages at Nagasaki until he thoroughly sifted the matter; and on Hideyoshi asking Mayeda's opinion of the proposal, the latter at once replied that the more he detained of the *religieux* who had come with the ambassador the better, and Hideyoshi acted upon his advice. Now Valegnani had brought with him a strong reinforcement of missionaries for work in Japan; and so all these could now appear in Nagasaki without any disguise whatsoever! At the same time Mayeda induced the Regent to modify the terms of his dispatch to the Viceroy of the Indies, and to excise from it an invective against the missionaries similar to that which had accompanied his Edict of 1587.

Shortly after this the Korean war began, and Hideyoshi went down to Nagoya in Hizen and established his headquarters there in September, 1592. "The presence of the Taikō (Hideyoshi) occasioned the missionaries great alarm; all the more so, since almost all the Christian princes were in Korea or in the fleet, and since this monarch, surrounded by idolaters, and at the head of nearly the whole of Japan in arms, could in a moment exterminate Christianity in this part of the empire, where it had always been most flourishing." Valegnani accordingly now withdrew all the priests from Hirado and Ōmura to Nagasaki, where in the terms of Mayeda's arrangement

he could claim immunity for them as members of his suite.
At the same time, acting on the advice of the Christian lords
at Nagoya, he sent De Melo, captain of· the vessel he was to
leave in, together with Rodriguez, to visit Hideyoshi to explain
why he had not gone, the Portuguese having been unable to
effect their sales promptly on account of the war. The
messengers were well received; and when Rodriguez assured
Hideyoshi that Valegnani was charmed with his presents for
the Viceroy, the Taikō said: "I am delighted to hear that
the presents are to his liking. Tell him to make his arrangements at his leisure; and as for yourself, I allow you to make
Kyōto your ordinary place of residence." And yet within a
month of this the magnificent church in Nagasaki had been
razed to the ground !

As for Nagasaki, its history at this time is somewhat
difficult to elucidate. We know, however, that before this
date it had been appropriated by Hideyoshi. In 1587 we
have seen that a bribe induced the commissioners charged
with its appropriation and the demolition of the churches in
it to leave the town in the hands of the Prince of Ōmura.
When it was actually made an Imperial town does not appear
very clearly. We know, however, that the twenty-six or twenty-
seven Portuguese merchants in Valegnani's suite took the
opportunity, when Hideyoshi strolled in among them after
dinner on March 3rd, 1591, of asking him "for justice against
the Receiver of his Majesty's dues in the port of Nagasaki
who had been guilty of malpractices; that he promised it
readily, and that the Receiver was cashiered." As the embassy
had left Nagasaki in November, 1590, we may conclude that
Nagasaki must have been appropriated by the central
authorities in 1589 or early in 1590. In 1592 its two Governors
interfered with a Portuguese merchantman that entered, and
tried to possess themselves of all the gold on board of her;
and on the matter being reported to Hideyoshi they were
removed. For a year after this Nagasaki was without a
Governor; and when one was appointed, he was appointed for
the special purpose of dealing drastically with the Christians
there. And this visitation was brought upon the Christians
by nothing but jealousy and intrigue among themselves,
European Christians, too, being mainly to blame.

In the following chapter a somewhat detailed account of the Philippine imbroglio will be found. Here it will suffice to say that two envoys from Manila waited upon Hideyoshi at Nagoya shortly after his arrival there, and that they and their Japanese friends filled his mind with suspicions of the Jesuits and of the Portuguese. They said they believed it to be their duty to inform him that the Portuguese were the masters of Nagasaki, that they alone profited by the foreign trade, that they acted in the most arbitrary manner there, and that in defiance of his Edicts they protected the Jesuits, who had all remained in Japan. They added that it was the Jesuits who persuaded the Portuguese to refuse the Spaniards liberty to trade with the Japanese, a thing which deprived his Majesty of very great advantages. As trade was what Hideyoshi was extremely anxious for, this last revelation or accusation at once roused his wrath. "What!" he burst out in a tone which made all present tremble, "these strangers whom I have put to the ban wish to act as masters in my States! I will soon stop them from that!" He immediately appointed Terasawa, a favourite of his own and a protégé of Jacuin Tocun, to the Governorship of Nagasaki, with orders to demolish the great church and the splendid houses of the Jesuits and to reduce the contumacious foreigners to order. So demolished the church and the houses were, and their timbers transported to Nagoya, to be used in some of the buildings there.[5] However, in the new Governor the missionaries were destined to find not a harsh enemy, but a valuable friend. Terasawa, whom Charlevoix describes as an open-minded young man of twenty-five or twenty-six, and, after Guenifoin, the best favourite of the Taikō, soon convinced himself that the charge against the foreigners was a trumped-up one, and thereupon he was not slow to display a sympathy for them at once sincere and practical. By next year the demolished church had not only been restored, but the Governor had even obtained from the Taikō leave for twelve Jesuits to reside in Nagasaki for the service of the Portuguese merchants, while in 1595 he himself was baptized, albeit secretly.

---

5 The Fathers note that on the very day Hideyoshi at Nagoya issued the Edict for the destruction of their church, his mother died in Kyōto, in fulfilment of a Christian prophecy which had much to do with the conversion of the Prince of Hiūga.

This, it may be remarked, is Charlevoix's account of the matter; but a perusal of the Annual Letter of 1593-4 (Gomez's) serves to disclose the fact that the worthy Father has here been somewhat economical of the truth, and has passed over some very interesting and informing passages in that epistle. That he had it before him when he wrote is presumable from the circumstance that he all but reproduces its very language when recounting certain episodes of the year. In the letter referred to, Gomez complains bitterly of Terasawa's hostility to the Christians, citing his removal of the crucifixes from the cemetery, of his forbidding Christian funerals and Christian marriages, of his attempt to upset Mayeda Geni's arrangement with respect to Valegnani's suite, of his threat to destroy the eleemosynary institutions of the Jesuits. His underlings even levied petty blackmail upon the priests, accusing them of stealing some of the timbers of the razed church, and "finally it became necessary to close their mouths with five piastres of silver, which are twenty-and-odd *scudi* in gold."[6] The Fathers made strong efforts to conciliate the goodwill of Terasawa's beadledom by all the means they could think of, but for some months with very little effect; and the underlings, gloating in the opportunity of "making themselves important," harried and harassed the Fathers in innumerable petty ways. At the same time, the position of the priests in Arima and Ōmura was even worse than it was in Nagasaki. These districts, in common with all the maritime fiefs of Kyūshū, were now filled with Hideyoshi's emissaries, searching for timber and provisions, requisitioning boats, impressing boatmen, and making lists of able-bodied men. The priests lurking there had consequently to keep flitting from one retreat to another in all manner of disguises and under the darkness of night, and to one scamp who succeeded in compiling a list of their names and their whereabouts they had to pay a considerable sum of hush-money. Their great house in Ōmura they saved by getting the Dowager Princess to occupy a few of its rooms and to assert that it was her property; and they prepared to save their great college in Amakusa by a similar device. Then some kind friend informed Hideyoshi that the Christians of Nagasaki were exceedingly and suspiciously well-provided with

---

6 Several other instances of blackmailing are given; one of them amusing and another most ingenious in its rascality.

arms, and he promptly issued instructions for all peasants, mechanics, and merchants to be stripped of their weapons, and sent out a commission to enforce it with the utmost strictness. This investigation took the officers into almost every house, very much to the inconvenience of the concealed priests. However, when things seemed to be going from bad to worse, they suddenly mended. Writes Gomez:—

"While this was passing, and the time for the arrival of the (annual) ship was approaching, we had another cause for fear. This was that after the destruction of the church and the houses at Nagasaki it was the general opinion among the Gentiles that the Portuguese, disgusted by the destruction of their church, would not return with their ship to Japan, and that thus that important and profitable commerce would be lost; on account of which they feared greatly; and universally all the lords and grandees of Japan said that it was very foolish to have destroyed that church, and greatly blamed Quambacundono, saying that if the ship did not come to Japan, that kingdom would be ruined and undone, and that it was not reasonable to endanger the Portuguese commerce for such a trifle; and, above all, they greatly blamed Terasawa, as it was he who had put that into the head of Quambacundono, and had been the principal cause of the destruction of the church and the houses, doing a notable injury to the Portuguese. But we, who knew well that the Portuguese ship would not cease to come for that, were in great fear, on the contrary, that with the coming of the ship Quambacundono might learn that although he killed the Fathers and made an end of Christianity, the Portuguese were not to cease coming to Japan; and the church and the houses having been already destroyed in their presence, if they returned this year to Japan he would lose all apprehension—(until now he has taken great care not to scandalise the Portuguese)—and henceforth treat Christianity and us as seemed good to him. . . . But Quambacundono returning from Kyōto to Nagoya, hearing that the destruction of the church and houses at Nagasaki was taken so ill by the lords of Japan, and that there was risk that the Portuguese ship would return no more, became greatly frightened and anxious to repent of what he had done; and Terasawa still more so, because he knew that if the ship did not come and this trade were lost on his account, he would not only lose the favour of Quambacundono, but might very readily be ordered to cut his belly. . . . Thus Quambacundono began to discuss with Terasawa and Terasawa with him how the mistake might be remedied. And Quambacundono remarked that if the Fathers were already gone, it was easy to send a letter to Macao to invite them back."

As Father Gomez is somewhat long-winded, it may be just as well to give a *précis* of the rest of the passage. Juan Ruiz, Valegnani's interpreter, having gone to Nagoya, was received exceedingly well by Hideyoshi, and on his saying that the Portuguese would return, Hideyoshi's good-humour increased still more. He asserted that he wished to bestow great favours on the Portuguese, that he wished them to have much liberty, and that none of his officials should have any jurisdiction over them.   Terasawa was even more polite to Ruiz, while his underlings in Nagasaki now began to be very civil to the priests.   The Vice-Provincial was not slow to meet their advances, and Ruiz and Antonio Murayama (Tōan), a dependent and fellow-provincial of Terasawa's, " were sent to disabuse him of any false imaginations or opinions he entertained of us," and to offer him a present.   " And God gave them (the envoys) so much grace in this that they changed Terasawa in such a way that from being a persecutor and an enemy he resolved to become our patron and friend."   He at once began to give advice as to how the priests should conduct themselves, saying that as Hideyoshi was still opposed to Christianity, it was necessary for them to do all their work quietly and secretly, and promising that if they followed his counsels he would forward their interests with the Taikō, and on the arrival of the ship would obtain permission for them to rebuild their church at Nagasaki.   He also told them that on the arrival of the ship a Father ought to go with the captain to see Hideyoshi, pretending that he had come in the vessel, and that he then would be received in audience.   Gomez was fully convinced that all this had been prompted by Hideyoshi himself.   At all events, on the arrival of the ship the comedy thus outlined by Terasawa had all its details filled in.   Da Rova, the captain, took Father Paez with him, and the ecclesiastic was received by Hideyoshi with the utmost consideration.   He asked Paez whether this was the first time he had been in Japan; and on Paez (who was one of the best linguists among the missionaries) pretending not to understand him, he kept a perfectly serious face.   Then he invited the captain and the priests into his *cha-no-yu* house, " which is a chamber all made of plates of gold, and where all the vessels are likewise of gold; which thing he has caused to be done these last few years to show his grandeur.   Where entering Quambacundono caused the Father, the captain, and the interpreter to enter with him, and there he gave them *cha* (tea) to drink, which is a beverage made of hot water with a certain herb which is very medicinal and useful for the stomach.   And there he talked for a long time of various things with the Father and the captain, but he said not a single word about the priests." A little later Terasawa, who had meanwhile joined them, suddenly and abruptly told Hideyoshi that the Portuguese were anxious to rebuild the church in Nagasaki and to keep some ten priests in it, and Hideyoshi said he was quite agreeable, provided the priests confined their services to the Portuguese and refrained from converting the Japanese, and told Terasawa to go to Nagasaki at once to select a site for the church. In spite of Terasawa's advice not to make the restored building too sumptuous, the priests shortly had a new church built, but little if at all inferior to the old one in size and magnificence. "And," insists Gomez again, "from this it was easy to perceive that Hideyoshi changed from dread of losing the commerce of the ship; because with all this it appears that he could not have believed that he would see the ship return to Japan in the same year as he had destroyed the church in, and that to make sure that it would not fail to continue to come he gave permission to rebuild the church and the houses, and that they should maintain ten priests in it." While in Nagoya Paez had been completely occupied in hearing confessions and in other professional duties, and Hideyoshi must have been perfectly well aware of this. Justo Ucondono (Takayama), who had entered the service of Mayeda of Kaga, was now in camp, and at his instance a Father and a Brother had spent the Lent of 1593 only a few furlongs from Hideyoshi's head-quarters saying mass and celebrating the other offices of the Church. Furthermore, the Court interpreter, the young Jesuit Rodriguez, now passed most of his time at Nagoya; and as Hideyoshi had no objection to his seeing his foreign friends, his quarters were generally shared by *religieux* from Nagasaki, who dispensed ghostly comfort to the converted and worked zealously to multiply their numbers. Rodriguez at this time made the acquaintance of Iyeyasu and won his esteem. It is interesting to hear of Iyeyasu denouncing the ignorance and immorality of the *bonzes*, remarking that he knew how little reason Hide-yoshi had for his hostility to the foreign priests, and actually offering the latter a secret retreat in his own domains.

Some of the remarks in Gomez's letter about the eagerness of the Japanese for the continuance of the Portuguese trade

may strike one as being ridiculously extravagant. However,
their general truth is abundantly confirmed from other sources.
The vessel of 1594 was so late in coming that hopes of her
arrival were abandoned ; and Gnecchi, writing from Kyōto,
speaks of the great dissatisfaction of the lords and the
merchants at being deprived of their annual supply of silk
and the Chinese, Indian, and European commodities brought
by the "great ship from Macao." "In Kyōto, where we live,
we suffer from such a dearth of these commodities that it is
a subject for commiseration to hear the daily complaints of
the people about the failure of this year's ship." Since the
appearance of Valegnani's embassy in 1591 there had been
a veritable Portuguese craze among the Japanese. When he
had heard of that mission Hideyoshi had more than once
asserted that these strangers came to Japan for bread (or rather
for rice), because they had none in their own country; but he
changed his tone on hearing of the magnificence of the envoy's
cortège; and when Valegnani and his twenty-six merchants
arrived in Kyōto, "Japonii omnes tantopere eorum comitate,
humanitate, morumque suavitate obstupefacti fuerunt ut ab
illo tempore semper declararint se non mediocriter erga illos
affectos esse."[7]   It soon was fashionable to be Portuguese in
everything.   European dress became so common that on
casually meeting a crowd of courtiers it was difficult to say
at once whether they were Portuguese or Japanese.   To imitate
the Portuguese some of the more ardent votaries of fashion even
went so far as to commit the Paternoster and the Ave Maria
to memory.   Reliquaries and rosaries were eagerly bought—as
much as ten or twelve scudi being paid for a rosary,—while
all the lords, Hideyoshi and his nephew the Regent included,
went about with crucifixes and reliquaries hanging from their
necks—a tribute not to piety but to fashion. All this being
taken into account, then, Gomez's explanation of Hideyoshi's
leniency towards the Jesuits in 1593 must probably be admitted

---

7 The Italian copy of this letter here reads:—"Et realmente quando il P.
Visitatore venne qua come Ambasciadore, à visitare questo Rè, con 26 Portughesi,
restorno tutti questi Giaponesi attoniti per li loro buoni portamenti et costumi
et già da quel tempo in quà li sono restati sempre molto affettionati. Et
veramente pare che N.S. Iddio volesse cosi, che il P. Visitatore venisse lui
à fare questa imbasciata da parte del Vice Rè dell' India, perche tenendoci
prima per huomini sospetti, et gente vile, et bassa à fatto, si levorno poi da
questi pensieri, et rimasero loro molto affettionati et conseguentemente alle
nostre cose" [i.e. to Christianity].

to be correct. Besides, from Froez's Annual Letter of 1595 we know that Hideyoshi himself was a keen trader. In the Philippines, jars called "Boioni" were manufactured cheaply; but in Japan they were in great esteem, "because in them a most noble liquor called *cha* [tea] may be excellently kept. Jars which in the Philippines cost two *soudi* are reputed among the greatest treasures of the Japanese, and are valued like precious stones. Accordingly, Taicosama sent two men to the Philippines to buy as many of these jars as could be had, thinking that he would make a great profit from the transaction. But learning that many Japanese Christians trade at Manila and bring many of these jars from there, he used every effort to have them all confiscated, and besides, he punished their purchasers very severely. In this matter Taicosama (for where the desire of gain holds sway there is no escape) proceeded so severely against those of whom he had notice that he collected a great treasure." [8] It must not be forgotten that this was a time of luxury and profusion in Japan; it was part and parcel of Hideyoshi's policy to involve his courtiers, the feudatories, and their vassals in a lavish expenditure of their resources; and thus the Portuguese commerce might very well have then been considered of vastly greater importance than it really was. This consideration tends to render Gomez's exposition of the situation all the more credible.

How mild Hideyoshi's so-called persecution of Christianity had been may be gathered from a review of the position of the Jesuits in Japan in the years 1595–96. At that time the Society had altogether 187 members in the Far East, fifty of whom were in China and the rest in Japan. Of these latter

---

[8] The remainder of this paragraph is somewhat amusing:—" Hæc nimia severitas redundavit etiam in quosdam viros primarios Nagasachanos, qui Meacum captivi sunt abducti. Sed antequam se in viam darent, veriti, ne Taicosama hac occasione ipsos tolleret 'è medio, confiteri et communicare voluerunt. Alii vero qui erant culpabiles (si modo in hac re aliqua culpa est) quia tamen tales non habebantur, remanserunt, et quoniam verebantur ne detegerentur, aliud perfugium non habuerunt, in hac vita, pro innocentiæ suæ patrocinio, quam ut ab auxilio divino penderent, eoque orationes suas omnes referrent. Itaque conspirarunt, ut præter pœnitentias, quas ordinarie domi fiebant, oratio, quæ dicitur quadraginta horarum, prolongaretur ad centum sexaginta, eoque ampleus dies, idque sine intermissione ulla, tam nocturnis quam diurnis horis, sic ut unusquisque, præsto esset quando vocabatur. Ac viri quidem conveniebant in Ecclesia Misericordiæ, feminæ vero in primaria domo, in qua instituta erat oratio quadraginta horarum. Denique constantia eorum in tam sancto exercitio a Domino nostro impetratum est, quod erat in votis. Taicosama enim omnes e vinculis dimisit, sanosque et incolumes ad suos remisit."

T

137 no fewer than 125 were in the empire without licence ;
for Hideyoshi had only sanctioned the presence of ten priests
in Nagasaki for the service of the Portuguese solely, and of
Father Gnecchi in Kyōto on condition that he had no church
and that he should not baptize, while Rodriguex had official
employment. These *religieux* were distributed in five principal
houses and fifteen residences, attached to which there were
more than 660 seminarists, catechists, and other agents.
There were at that date 300,000 Christians, 65,000 of whom
were adults, baptized since Hideyoshi had launched his anti-
Christian Edict of July 25th, 1587, at the head of dumfounded
Coelho. And the quality of the proselytes was no less
remarkable than were their numbers. In 1587 the only
Christian Daimyō in Japan had been Ōtomo of Bungo, Arima,
Ōmura, Amakusa, and Takayama of Akashi. In that year
old Ōtomo had died (May 24th), and his son Yoshimune had
apostatized shortly after, while Takayama had been stripped
of his fief. But, on the other hand, Konishi had been made
Daimyō of Southern Higo (200,000 *koku*), and Kuroda of
Buzen (180,000 *koku*), while Itō, re-established at Ōbi in Hiūga
(57,000 *koku*), had been converted in 1591, and Mōri Hidekane,
who was then installed at Kurume in Chikugo (130,000 *koku*),
was baptized shortly after his marriage with a Christian
daughter of old Ōtomo of Bungo. Since that date at least
half-a-dozen territorial chiefs had been captured. Sō of
Tsushima had been (secretly) baptized by Valegnani in 1591 ;
Nobunaga's grandson, Sambōshi, Lord of Gifu, in Mino (135,000
koku), together with his younger brother, in 1595 ; Kyōgoku
of Ina in Shinano (100,000 *koku*) in the same year ; while
in 1596 Froez records the circumstances of the conversion
of the lords of three different provinces whose names he
withholds for prudential reasons. But the most illustrious
proselyte the Jesuits had made in these years was Gamō Ujisato,
who had been seated in Aidzu (1590) with an assessed revenue
of 800,000 *koku*. It is true that Gamō died about this time ;
but his chief retainer, to whom the guardianship of his son
and successor was entrusted, was a most zealous believer and
had promised the missionaries that young Gamō should be
made a Christian. As for the sons and relatives of Daimyō
then brought into the fold, they are too numerous for detailed

mention. Tsugaru, the son of the Daimyō of Hirosaki in Mutsu, in the extreme North, was bitterly disappointed because no missionary could be spared for service in his father's fief,[9] while from a neighbouring fief in Dewa, Ise-no-kami, a great man of war, came to Kyōto to be baptized with all his attendants. Three of the five most powerful feudal chiefs in Japan at this time—Mōri of Aki, Mayeda of Kaga, and Ukida of Bizen—all had Christians among their *karō* or Chief Councillors, while all three of them had cousins or other relatives who were most ardent believers. The two sons and the nephews of Mayeda Gen-i, who now resigned the governorship of Upper Kyōto to become Minister of Worship and of the Household of the Dairi, were among the missionaries' most devoted followers. The wife of Hosokawa of Tango, Akcchi Mitsuhide's daughter, had been baptized as Grace in 1587, and now Hosokawa's brother, " Joannis Gemba," became a convert. Although not converts, Hachisuka of Awa and Fukushima of Ōwari are mentioned as doing everything in their power to forward the cause of Christianity in their domains.[10]

Most of all this had been the result of the work of Father Gnecchi and of the two priests and five brothers he had under him in the Kyōto and Ōsaka circuit. The old man was deliberately devoting the best of his efforts to the conversion of the nobles, of their chief vassals, and of people of rank and influence, reasoning that if they were once firmly secured, their example would at once be followed by the nation at large as soon as Hideyoshi should either die or withdraw the ban against the foreign religion. In the Court of Hideyoshi's designated successor, his nephew the Kwambaku (Regent) Hidetsugu, Gnecchi had many friends, and was so well thought of by the Kwambaku himself that on two separate occasions Hidetsugu sent him 200 bags of rice when supplies from Europe ran short. From any anxiety of such a contingency in future, the mind of the priest must have been relieved when, through his wife, he drew Sō, the richest

---

[9] In this connection we again hear of Yezo and its inhabitants in the missionary letters. Froes calls the Ainus Tartars, "admodum barbaros, colore fusco, capillis barbaque promissis uti Moscovitæ."

[10] Fukushima, we are told, at one time had the reputation of being the most cruel and the most savage man in Japan; and it was a sermon by the Japanese Jesuit, Vincent, which constrained him to abandon his ferocity.

merchant in Kyōto, into the Christian fold. This Sō had been a most devoted member of the *Nichiren-shiu*, the most bigoted and almost the only aggressive Buddhist sect in Japan, and had had the reputation of being its main financial prop in the metropolis. Sō not only became a Christian himself, but he brought his brother and eight more of his fellow-sectaries with him, one of these being nearly as wealthy as himself.[11] In 1594 a Buddhist priest moving in the very best society had been sentenced to death for debt; Mayeda Gen-i's son paid the money on condition of his becoming a Christian. The baths of Arima behind Kobe had become famous since Hideyoshi had visited them, and at this time there were always three or four thousand real or imaginary invalids there, most of them fashionable people. After some instruction, the *bonze* was sent off there to talk Christianity; at the end of a year Gnecchi went there also, in the first place for his health, in the second "that he might institute some spiritual fishing among leisured folk. There he baptized several nobles converted by the *bonze*, who was thoroughly versed in all Buddhistic lore. Returning to Kyōto, he took the *bonze* with him in order that he might hear a few sermons; then, more firmly instructed by these, he began at Fushimi with happy effect to cast the net of the Christian doctrine among the crowd of noble lords there, many of whom he knew; and in a few days he brought four or five of the chief of them to the shore of the Church of Christ, among whom was a very noble lord, by name Caminokawa, from the Kwantō, whose revenue is 120,000 sacks of rice." At this time the blind were organised in a corporation which extended all over Japan; the upper ranks and offices in it were eagerly sought for, huge bribes being paid to obtain them, for the power and privileges attaching to them were immense. These blind men of higher rank were often employed by the Daimyō in very important and very delicate matters; one section of them, fifty in number,

---

11 "Special mention," writes Froez, "ought here to be made of these Hokkes; because theirs is the most pestilent and the most pertinacious among the sects of Japan, and exceedingly few of them have hitherto passed over to ours. Although it has been found that, once they have done so, they are much firmer and more constant in our faith than the others." Curiously enough, in the same letter he says something similar of the people of Owari:—"Est enim gens illa admodum elata a natura et ferox, et licet initio ægre se dedat alicui rei, tamen si semel vel bono vel malo se applicaverit ei tenaciter adhærescit."

could freely appear before the greatest potentates in Japan
to rehearse the ancient story of their houses and of the empire.
Six of these men were now captured by Gnecchi. " Thus as
soon as these Quenguii (*Kengyō*) have obtained some knowledge
of the mysteries of our faith, and begun to be taken with
the sense of heavenly things, they act as preachers among
the nobles, many of whom they have already brought over
to their views." One of the things that then marked a
gentleman was a mastery of all the elaborate details of the
cha-no-yu, or tea-drinking ceremony. The *chajin,* or masters
of this ceremony, exercised great social influence, for they were
the arbiters of contemporary taste and propriety.[12] Hideyoshi's
own *chajin* now fell a prey to Gnecchi, and " brought many
nobles into the Christian fold. And since he himself is of
noble birth, and once governed a great State, he is known to
many at Court, of whom, whenever an opportunity presents
itself, he does not neglect to lure some into the Christian fold."
Among the ladies of Hideyoshi's Court the old priest was no
less indirectly active. Magdalene, whom the Church historians
mistakenly call Konishi's mother, was the secretary of Kita-
mandokoro, Hideyoshi's legitimate consort, and her fishing
was no less successful among the women than the *chajin's*
was among the men. Yodogimi, the secondary spouse of the
Taikō and the mother of Hideyori, the Taikō's heir, was not
a Christian ; but her younger sister Maria, the mother of
Kyōgoku, the lately converted Daimyō of Ina in Shinano, was
a most zealous one ; we find her writing to Gnecchi for some
pious books, " because she had none except one entitled
' Contemptus Mundi or Gerson.' "[13] Nor was this all. Many

---

12 For an account of *cha-no-yu* (to which there is frequent reference in the
missionary letters of those years), see Professor CHAMBERLAIN'S *Things Japanese,*
4th ed., pp. 450-454.

13 Gnecchi sent her the Catechism, the Ratio Confitendi, and a book of
Meditations. " In a separate part of the College of Amakusa a press has been
set up for the Latin and Japanese languages. This year (1596) has been given
forth the Catechism of the Council of Trent in Latin, which is read in the
seminary. The tract called 'Contemptus Mundi' in Latin and Japanese has
also been issued. Likewise the Exercises of Father Ignatius in Latin." In
the Letter of 1595 Froez says :—" Ut autem doctrina Christiana majores haberet
progressus, opusculum quoddam editum est 10 capitibus comprehensum, in quo
succincte et perspicue declaratur, quod cuique Christiano credendum pariter et
agendum sit. Quod opusculum tam huic genti gratum est, ut hactenus nulla
ex re ampliorem videatur cœpisse voluptatem: unde et fructus ex illo consecutus
est plane singularis et notabilis. [Gnecchi made a very liberal distribution of it
among the noble lords at the baths of Arima.] Quanquam et ex aliis libellis
eadem lingua excusis, nempe de modo confitendi, rosarium recitandi, aliaque

of the highest officials were, if not Christians, at all events very favourably disposed towards the priests. To say nothing of the fact that the important post of Governor of Sakai was held by Konishi's Christian brother, and that Terasawa, the Governor of Nagasaki, and their former foe, was now a special patron of theirs—he is said to have been secretly baptized by Gomez in 1595—three of Hideyoshi's five *Bugyō* or Ministers were, as events showed, prepared to take no small trouble and to incur no small risks in order to protect them and to serve their interests. As has been said, Mayeda Gen-i's two sons, his nephews, and many of his retainers were zealous Christians; and he himself had already on more than one occasion given the priests substantial help, as had also a second Minister, Asano; while Ishida, the ablest of the five, was soon to save them from what at first looked like certain and irretrievable ruin.

All this considered, it is not strange to find that the Jesuits laid the flattering unction to their souls that nothing stood between them and the spiritual conquest of the empire but the life of Hideyoshi. While pretending to have yielded a meek and willing obedience to his drastic Edict of 1587, they had for nine years been carrying on a burrowing and a mining propaganda which had sapped all the power and the prestige of Buddhism and of Shintō in the highest and most influential quarters. Of this Hideyoshi was perfectly cognisant, and the missionaries were perfectly aware that he was cognisant of it. And yet he held his hand. This Froez piously attributes mainly to the special providence of God; but he gives as secondary causes the care the Jesuits had taken to avoid all open flouting of his authority and his anxiety to ensure the continuance of the Portuguese trade. As regards the grounds of Hideyoshi's hostility to Christianity, Froez's letters are a curious study. At first in 1587 it was because of Hideyoshi's own immoral life and his determination to extirpate a cult the general dissemination of which would effectually mar all prospects of

---

pietatis Christianæ officia exercendi, non multo minor fructus constitit inter Christianos." The succeeding paragraph of this letter is also of interest:— " Verum illud præcipuum quoddam adjumentum ad hujus vineæ Dominicæ culturam attulit, quod multis in locis, iisque primariis instituta sit conceptionis serenissimæ Angelorum Reginæ Sodalitas; quæ sic Japoniorum animos commovit, tantoque sensu et affectu illam complexi sunt, ut nobilissimi quique et omnium principes honorificum reputent, si nomen illi dare possint."

that apotheosis at which he aimed. In succeeding letters less
and less is said about the first cause, and more and more
stress is laid upon the second. Over and over again Froez
quotes Hideyoshi's own very words that he had expelled the
missionaries "not because they were wicked men or that the
law they taught was bad in itself—[although on other occasions
he reports Hideyoshi as calling it "diabolical"]—but because
they and their doctrine, so hostile to the *Kami* and the *Hotoke*,
were utterly subverting our sects and all the ancient and
hallowed ceremonies of our Empire, to the mock and ignominy
of our *Kami*." Even in his letter of December 13th, 1596,
Froez writes that "whenever the conversation turns upon us
in the presence of many lords, Hideyoshi pronounces us to be
upright and sincere in our faith, and says that he himself
would readily become a Christian if he did not dread that the
bonzes would die of hunger, since they would get no more
alms; and that so many temples which are the ornaments of
Japan would be left destitute." Now, while Froez neither
lies nor invents, he knew as well as anyone that Hideyoshi
could speak in jest, and was wont to give anything but the
true reasons for the measures he adopted and the policy he
pursued. And all this while Froez had perfectly grasped the
true reasons for Hideyoshi's sudden change of front towards
Christianity in 1587. But until 1597 he deemed it advisable
to keep his discovery to himself. Then at last in that year,
in the anxious hour of peril and tribulation, when Hideyoshi
really stretched forth his hand and laid it heavily upon the
foreign priests, and when the responsibility for the outbreak
of the real persecution then instituted had to be apportioned,
Froez delivers himself of his knowledge fully and without
reserve. Of the many able pieces penned by him, his
"Narrative of the Death of the Twenty-six Crucified" is
perhaps the most remarkable. In the next chapter more will
be said about it, but one paragraph of it must be cited here.
Says the writer :—

"In order more rightly to understand this determination of the
King [Hideyoshi], it must be known that the Jesuits, especially in
Kyōto and its vicinity, have devoted all their chief efforts to convert
men of noble birth; for they once converted to God, the others will
readily follow. Jacuin [*i.e.* Seyakuin Hōin], noting this, believed
that we were adopting this stratagem rather as a means of seizing
upon Japan than of procuring the salvation of souls; and that for

that purpose we had come from Europe. For, as we have insinuated, Jacuin regards the immortality of the soul, among other false dogmas, as a mere dream, and impiously and absurdly believes that the souls of men, as of brutes, are extinguished with (the bodily) life. Resting on this same suspicion, which already before we were ordered to be banished (1587) had been increased by the great zeal of Justo Ucondono in exciting the nobility to the faith, he had dinned the same into the ears of the King, who, however, then declared that he thought nothing of that accusation. However, when he arrived in Kyūshū against the King of Satsuma, and noted that many lords with their vassals had become Christians, and that the same were bound to each other in great concord and exceedingly devoted to the Fathers, he began to recall to memory what Jacuin had already filled his ears with, and to understand (although in that he was auguring falsely) that the propagation of the faith would be prejudicial to the safety of the empire. *And this is the true cause of the aversion which he now declares,*—not hatred of Christianity or any zeal for the idols, for it is generally known how slightly he esteems the *Kami* and the *Hotoke,* as they are called in the Japanese idiom ; for he has no doubt that a future life is a mere fiction, and therefore laws looking to that are merely the decrees of men devised for the ruling of kingdoms, in order that by the dread of the punishments of another life people may be bridled, so to speak, and restrained from crime."[14]

This remarkable admission, for such it really is, was, as we have said, penned when the responsibility for the institution of a real and death-dealing persecution had to be apportioned. For at last, after ten years of forbearance, Hideyoshi had raised his hand to strike, and had smitten heavily indeed.

---

14 " The fear o' Hell's the hangman's whup tae haud the wretch in order."

CHAPTER XI.

THE BEGINNING OF SPANISH AND PORTUGUESE RIVALRY IN JAPAN.

IN a previous chapter the general position of the Spaniards in Manila and of the Portuguese at Macao and in the Far East has been sufficiently indicated. It is only necessary to recall the fact that in 1580 the crowns of Spain and Portugal had been united in the person of Philip II., who in the Cortes of Thomar (1581) pledged himself to recognise the individuality of Portugal, and promised that "he would maintain the rights and liberties of the people, that the Cortes should be assembled frequently, that all the offices in the realm should be entrusted to Portuguese alone, that no land or jurisdiction in Portugal should be given to foreigners, and that there should be a Portuguese Council which should accompany the King everywhere and have entire charge of all Portuguese affairs." And a special Article in the Concordat then drawn up confined the trade with Japan to the Portuguese exclusively, while four years later Philip II., exercising his prerogative of the Protectorate of the Church in the Portuguese Orient, gave his assent to a Bull of Gregory XIII. that equally confined the teaching and preaching of Christianity in Japan to the "Company of Jesus," which, in its Oriental missions, from the very first had been under Portuguese patronage. Now, naturally enough, the merchants in Manila chafed at being excluded from the lucrative Japanese trade, and the Governor and his subordinate officials, to whom it would have undoubtedly meant perquisites and pickings, were in full sympathy with them in the matter. At the same time the Franciscans and the Dominicans settled in the Philippines resented the Jesuit monopoly of religious teaching in Japan, and when after 1587 tales of the miserable plight to which Christianity was reduced in the Island Empire began to reach them, over-credulity inflamed them with an ardent desire to proceed to the forbidden land and achieve a brilliant success where the "Society of Jesus" had failed so

wretchedly.[1] The Bull threatening them with the pains and
penalties of excommunication if they ventured to infringe
that monopoly was a fatal bar to their aspirations, however,
and they were fretting their souls with vain and unsatisfied
longings, when a train of circumstances put it in their power
to evade it.

Among the converts made by the Jesuits was a certain
Harada, who later on had found his way to the Philippines
as a trader, and had taken full note of the weakness of the
Spaniards in their new possessions. In that weakness he saw
his own account, and he made haste to return to Japan,
where he struck up an acquaintance with one Hasegawa, a
courtier of Hideyoshi. Through Hasegawa, Harada represented
to the Regent how easy it would be for him to take possession of
the Philippines. Hideyoshi, who by his conquest of the Kwantō
in 1590 had just brought the task of the territorial centralisation
of Japan to a completion, and who wished for nothing better
than some enterprise over-sea to keep the unemployed blades
of his restless subjects busy, listened to Hasegawa's exposition
of Harada's notions readily enough, and in 1591 he penned
a very haughty letter to the Governor of the Philippines calling
upon his Excellency, Don Gomez Peres de Marinas, to recognise
him (Hideyoshi) as his suzerain. Harada was entrusted with
the missive, and, wishing to pose as an ambassador, he went to
Valegnani at Nagasaki and tried to get him to write to the
Governor of the Philippines and the Jesuits there in his favour.
Valegnani, taking the measure of the man,[2] refused his request
on one specious ground or another, and straightway wrote to the
Jesuits of Manila a statement of what he conceived to be in train,
and advised them to inform the Governor of what was toward.
Harada after this had not the assurance to present himself in
the guise of an ambassador, but he got a nephew of his to act

---

[1] The report was that only six Christians had been left in Japan, and that
these six had lately been reduced to two.

[2] Charlevoix's characterisation of Harada is so vigorous, and so applicable
to a modern type, by no means confined to the somewhat slender ranks of
Japanese Christians, as to be worthy of citation. "Faranda," writes he, "of
obscure birth, a bad Christian, and one of those men who wish to intrigue at
any price to make themselves a name, and whom it costs nothing to sacrifice
their honour, their conscience, the safety and the tranquillity of the State to
their itch to make themselves important, having gone to the Philippines to
trade there, took it into his head to oblige the Governor of these islands to
recognise the 'Emperor' of Japan as his Sovereign."

as such, and to present Hideyoshi's dispatch to de Marinas. To follow all the tortuosities of this complicated intrigue is impossible. It must suffice here to say that the Governor sent over as representative a certain Llano, accompanied by a Dominican named Cobos, in 1592; that these kept aloof from the Jesuits; that they were joined by two rascally Spaniards[3] then stranded in Japan; that from that circumstance, and from their being utterly in the hands of their interpreters, Hasegawa and Harada, they were led to do both Portuguese and Jesuits much damage by their envious and disparaging remarks during their stay; and that on their being drowned on their return voyage, Harada, who had gone by another vessel, was able to pose at Manila as Hideyoshi's ambassador, on the plea that his credentials had been lost in the ship that carried Llano. De Marinas, now doubtless apprised of the purport of Valegnani's letters to the Manila Jesuits, had become suspicious, and wished to gain time before moving any further in the matter. This did not suit Harada at all; and so he determined to avail himself of the Franciscan jealousy of the Jesuit monopoly of religious teaching in Japan, and drew up a memoir of the reasons, for which he pretended Hideyoshi had sent him. In this document the chief articles were that Hideyoshi desired to be on friendly terms with the Spaniards in the Philippines, that he wished to establish a commerce between them and his subjects, and that he asked for Franciscan Fathers, of whose sanctity and contempt for the things of the world he had heard the best report. This memoir Harada first communicated to the monks, and then, seeing that they took the bait, to the Governor. The Franciscans did much to allay the latter's suspicions about the letter, and the result was that Don Gomez dispatched an embassy with a dispatch to Hideyoshi on May 20th, 1593. The embassy consisted of Caravajal, Father Baptiste,

---

[3] These Spaniards—one a waif from Peru, the other from the Philippines—seem to have been the first non-Portuguese traders to reach Japan. They both arrived utterly destitute about 1590, one being befriended by the Jesuits and the other by the Portuguese merchants. However, a money dispute with the latter, in which the priests, on being invoked, refused to interfere, drove the Spaniards into an appeal to the Japanese law—possibly the first case of its kind in the country (1591)—in which they had the worst of it. Katō Kiyomasa was one of the two judges appointed to deal with this suit. Hence they were eager to ruin both Jesuits and Portuguese, and when the Manila mission appeared in Satsuma, where one of them (Solis) then was building a ship to go to Peru or to New Spain in, they saw a fine opportunity to accomplish their desire. This, be it remarked, however, is the Jesuit, not the Dominican, account of the matter.

and three other Franciscans, who thus succeeded in evading the letter of the Bull of 1585 by entering Japan not as missionaries but in the quality of ambassadors ! The Governor's dispatch was non-committal; his Excellency could not comply with Hideyoshi's demand without first communicating with his master the King of Spain, but meanwhile he was anxious to see a trade between Japan and the Philippines instituted.

A perusal of this letter occasioned one of the Taikō's simulated volcanic outbursts of passion, and on Baptiste's offering to stay with his priests as hostages, Hideyoshi angrily refused his consent until they swore beforehand that the Philippines would be submissive and faithful to him. Permission was then accorded the four priests to visit the palaces at Ōsaka, Fushimi, and Kyōto, but only on the express condition that they should refrain from preaching. They were put under the care of Hasegawa and Harada, who fondly fancied that they had their charges helplessly at their mercy by reason of their ignorance of Japanese. That precious pair of rascals, it ought to be remarked, had already served their own account by misinterpreting to Hideyoshi in the most scandalous manner. Meanwhile, the Jesuits had furnished the newcomers with a Japanese grammar,[4] and they had furthermore been joined by Garcia, who from having been a merchant in Japan before he had become a priest, knew the language passably well, and who, in the course of a late interview with Hideyoshi, had staggered the intriguers somewhat seriously. This unexpected development did not suit Hasegawa and Harada at all, and accordingly they resolved to ruin their Franciscan *protégés* at the earliest opportunity.

In their eager and inconsiderate zeal the unwary priests soon played straight into Harada's hands.[5] On reaching Kyōto they had been assigned a lodging there. However, as they kept on vaunting the magnificence of Hideyoshi everywhere and on every occasion, and as they paid their court to him very adroitly when they went to see him at Fushimi, they got

---

4 This was probably a copy of Alvarez's *De Institutione Grammatica, libri* iii., printed at Amakusa in 1593. Valegnani had brought back a printing-press with him in 1590. For information regarding its publications, see Sir ERNEST SATOW's paper in the *Transactions of the Asiatic Society of Japan.*

5 Harada meanwhile had received a handsome revenue from Hideyoshi for his services. In modern times Harada would be styled a *Sōshi,*

permission to build a house of their own. But they built a fine church as well as a house, opened it with as much circumstance as if they had been in the middle of Spain, and from that time continued to sing in the choir, to preach publicly, and to discharge all their functions "with an incomprehensible confidence." The Christian commonalty was consequently much edified, and began to institute comparisons at the expense of the Jesuits, and dissensions in the Christian fold were imminent. At the end of 1594 they had been joined by three more friars from Manila, with presents from the Governor for the Taikō, which were accepted, and with a letter which was pronounced to be unsatisfactory. Thus reinforced, the Franciscans established the convent of Bethlehem in Ōsaka, and at the same time sent two of their number to Nagasaki. The latter seized upon a church of the Jesuits, now used only secretly and clandestinely by its owners, and began to celebrate the holy offices in it with the utmost publicity. The Governor of Nagasaki, however, promptly checked this ill-advised zeal on their part and compelled their return to Kyōto. The Franciscans were not slow to accuse the Jesuits of having been the real prompters of this rebuff, nor to publish the accusation among the Christians of Kyōto, and to endeavour to enlist their sympathy against the Company of Jesus. "This caused the appearance of a schism among the faithful of which the consequences were very baneful. On this subject we have a very beautiful letter of Father Gnecchi to Father Acquaviva, his General, in which that venerable old man, whom all Japan so very justly regarded as the greatest worker there had been for long in the empire, deplores his misfortune at being obliged to witness every day, without being able to remedy them, things which filled his heart with bitterness,—to see the best-founded hopes of soon seeing Christianity dominant in the Empire vanishing by reason of this fatal disunion." Matters became so bad that the Jesuits at last called the attention of the Franciscans to the Bull of 1585. "But they made answer that it did not apply to them; that they had come to Japan as the envoys of the Governor of the Philippines on a purely political mission, not in the quality of missionaries; that as they were staying with the permission of the Emperor, no one had any right to restrain them from

discharging the functions of their ministry with the fullest
freedom, and that such had never been the intention of the
Sovereign Pontiff.   What was more surprising was that they even
refused to defer to the authority of the Bishop of Japan, who
at this crisis arrived at Nagasaki invested with all the authority
of the Apostolic See."   It was perhaps not so very surprising
when we consider that this first Bishop of Japan to arrive
in the country was a Jesuit, who had no *vis coactiva* in his
diocese.[6]   Thus in spite of the Jesuits the Franciscans went
boldly on with their own propaganda ; in spite, too, of the
very friendly cautions of Mayeda Gen-i and others of Hideyoshi's
ministers to the effect that such a breach of promise and such
a wanton flouting of the Taikō's edicts would be sure to
eventuate in dire disaster to themselves and to the whole
Christianity of Japan.   In the interview with Hideyoshi at
Nagoya in Hizen, in 1593, when he agreed to their going to
Central Japan, the misguided Franciscans *"being resolved not to
obey him, gave no promise, but made a low reverence."*   The Taikō
knew all about Gnecchi's puerile trick towards Akechi in 1582,
and also about Coelho's towards the Satsuma envoys in 1584,
and neither trick can have done much to raise Hideyoshi's
opinion of the foreign priests, either as honest men or as very
proficient liars.   Liar on a colossal scale as he was himself on
necessary occasions, he yet had the highest respect for honesty,
as many incidents indicate, but for small trickery and for the
men that practised it he had nothing but scorn and contempt.
Accordingly the poor friars were sadly astray if they fancied
that one of the greatest masters of the arts of simulation and
dissimulation that has ever lived could be circumvented by any
such infantile device as that of Father Baptiste at Nagoya in
Hizen in 1593.   In mere erudition Hideyoshi was inferior to the
average bucolic in the ruck of the novices in the Franciscan or
in any other Order; in practical statesmanship and politics, and
in all their arts and devices, Dominic or Loyola or Machiavelli
would have come badly off in any encounter with him.   The
deluded Franciscans had to learn by dour experience that it was
but ill work for pigmies to set their powers against those of a

---

6 A Bishop of Japan had been nominated in 1566, another shortly
afterwards, and yet another in 1587, but none of them had reached their
diocese.

giant in the art of deception,—as well as of statecraft generally. But, in common with most Caucasians, they no doubt believed, rashly enough, that great men were (and are) only to be found in Caucasian, if not Christian, lands. Meanwhile, in 1594, in 1595, and till the autumn of 1596, the Taikō was too much occupied with other affairs of the weightiest moment to be able to devote his attention either to the over-zealous Franciscans, or, indeed, to Christianity at all, which even Charlevoix in stray passages perceives—albeit perceives but dimly—to have been merely an insignificant pawn in the gigantic political chess-game Hideyoshi was then playing.

Towards the end of 1596, however, an incident occurred that had the effect of bringing the conduct of the Philippine priests directly to the Taikō's notice. A great and richly-laden galleon, commanded by a certain Captain Landecho, on her way from Manila to Acapulco got caught in a typhoon, and at the end of it she found herself crippled and becalmed off the coast of Tosa. Although the captain protested he was in a condition to proceed, the Prince of Tosa (i.e. Chōsokabe) insisted upon his entering the port of Urado to refit; and on Landecho's showing no great willingness to accept the hospitality so pressingly proffered, his Highness sent two hundred armed boats to tow him into the harbour. As she entered, the *San Felipe* (that was the vessel's name) was purposely run upon a sand-bank and broke her back, and there-upon the Prince appropriated her remaining cargo, worth 600,000 crowns,—about 400,000 or 500,000 crown's worth of the original freight had already been jettisoned,—coolly telling Landecho that this procedure was in accordance with the law of Japan, which declared all stranded vessels and wrecks the property of the authorities! In reply to the captain's vehement protests, it was suggested to him that he should appeal to Hideyoshi himself, the Prince offering to exercise his own good offices (?) with the Taikō on behalf of the Spaniards through his own intimate friend, Masuda (Maxita of the Jesuits), then Minister of Works! Acting upon the hint, Landecho dispatched two of his officers to the capital, instructing them to avail themselves of the services of the Franciscans there, but to keep severely aloof from all intercourse with the Jesuits. The officers were thus brought into contact with Hasegawa, and he and Masuda represented to the Taikō that 600,000 crowns would do something to fill a sadly depleted treasury. Hideyoshi quickly fell in with Masuda's views; and as Hasegawa then thought fit to inform him of how the Franciscans had defied his authority in spite of all his (Hasegawa's) warnings, and that Landecho was working through them, the Taikō promptly dispatched Masuda and Hasegawa to Tosa to confiscate all the *San Felipe's* cargo. At the same time he ordered the arrest of the contumacious Franciscans, three of whom were seized in Kyōto and as many in Ōsaka, while in the latter city three Japanese Jesuits were also made prisoners. The Bishop of Japan, Martinez, a Jesuit, then in the capital in his capacity of Ambassador from the Viceroy of Goa, on two occasions had proffered his services to Father Baptiste, the Franciscan commissary, in the affair of the *San Felipe*, but on both occasions he had been coldly thanked, and when Mayeda Gen-i (Guenifoin), Governor of Kyōto, was through him at last approached in the matter, Mayeda at first refused to move, since he was offended because Masuda's good offices had been invoked in preference to his. When he did take up the case, Mayeda found all his efforts useless, inasmuch as his colleague, the Minister of Works, had already obtained the Taikō's consent to the course he had suggested.

Landecho meanwhile had come up to Ōsaka, while his officers in Tosa were trying every device to get their cargo out of the clutches of the Japanese. After exhausting the resources of soft speaking and cajolery, the pilot was so ill-advised as to attempt to intimidate Masuda and the Prince of Tosa by dwelling on the power and greatness of the Spanish King. He produced a map of the world, and on it pointed out the vast extent of the dominions of Philip II. Thereupon Masuda asked him how it was so many countries had been brought to acknowledge the sway of a single man. And then, to quote Charlevoix, "this unfortunate inflicted a wound on Religion which is bleeding still after the lapse of a century and a half." "Our Kings," said this outspoken seaman, "begin by sending into the countries they wish to conquer *religieux* who induce the people to embrace our religion, and when they have made considerable progress, troops are sent who combine with the new Christians, and then our Kings have not much trouble in accomplishing the rest."

This speech was carefully reported to Hideyoshi, and nothing, we are told, was equal to the impression it made upon his mind. "What!" he cried in fury, "my States are filled with traitors, and their numbers increase every day. I have proscribed the foreign doctors; but out of compassion for the age and infirmity of some among them I have allowed them to remain in Japan; I shut my eyes to the presence of several others, because I fancied them to be quiet and incapable of forming any bad design, and they are serpents I have been cherishing in my bosom. The traitors are entirely employed in making me enemies among my own subjects, and perhaps even in my own family; but they will learn what it is to play with me!" He then swore that he would not leave a single missionary alive; but shortly after, taking a more moderate tone, he went on: "I am not anxious for myself; so long as the breath of life remains, I defy all the powers of the earth to attack me; but I am perhaps to leave the empire to a child, and how can he maintain himself against so many foes, domestic and foreign, if I do not provide for everything incessantly?"

So far Charlevoix, who asserts that he has followed the *procès verbal* sent to Madrid, signed in Japan by all the officers of the *San Felipe*, by the Franciscans and Augustins on board of her, and by several other trustworthy persons. In several passages he lays the greatest stress upon the indiscreet speech of the pilot of the *San Felipe*. And in a letter of the Bishop of Japan, written sixteen years later on (November 15th, 1612), we meet with the following reference to it:—

"It (*i.e.* the Spanish survey of the Japanese coast) confirms the opinion which many pagan and even some Christian Japanese have conceived in consequence of the speech of the pilot of the galleon *San Felipe*, which came to the province of Tosa in 1596. This pilot, interrogated by one of the principal Governors of Taicosama, after a survey of the map of the world, how the King of Spain, such a far-distant country, had made himself master of so many kingdoms and provinces, replied imprudently that the Catholic King first sent ministers of the Gospel to convert the natives, who afterwards, uniting with the captains of his Majesty, made their work of conquest easy."[7]

---

[7] In a much earlier letter (October 22nd, 1602) of the same Bishop of Japan to the Vice-Provincial of the Jesuits at Manila, requesting him to move the authorities to prevent the influx of Philippine *religieux* into Japan (sixteen of these had just arrived there), we meet with another reference to this affair of the Spanish pilot:—"Iyeyasu and all the pagan Japanese lords—(and several Christian lords have difficulty in persuading themselves to the contrary)—have the same opinions and the same suspicions as Taicosama entertained; that is

U

On the other hand, in Father Santa Maria's *Relaçion del martirio que VI. Padres desoalços Franciscos etc. padecieron en Japan*, published at Madrid in 1599, nothing is said about the culpable frankness of the pilot, although two whole chapters of that monograph are devoted to the affair of the *San Felipe*. It is to be noted, however, that the author was Provincial de San Joseph de los descalços, that he would not be likely to advert to a fatuity of which the Spaniards were ashamed, and that, besides, in many points his work is untrustworthy, the very title containing an inaccuracy. The omission of all allusion to this episode in Froez's very able *Historica Relatio de Gloriosa Morte XXVI. Crucifixorum* is a more serious matter, although his mere silence is no proof that the speech was not made. That narrative is of special value, for Froez, then thirty-three years in the country, had a grasp of the inner history of the times which no contemporary of his evinces.

In a previous chapter reference was made to the account Froez gives of Jacuin's (Seyakuin Hōin's) anti-Christian efforts in and before 1587. This Jacuin was now again active.

---

to say, that the Spaniards are a conquering race always going with arms in their hands, and that their chief design in these countries—(witness the facts of Manila itself and of New Spain)—is to possess themselves of foreign States, and that the preaching of the Gospel is a mere artifice for conquest; and (in consequence of the imprudent discourse of the pilot of the *San Felipe*, the galleon lost on the coast of Tosa, held with one of the Governors of Taicosama and which the Japanese lords remember perfectly) they are persuaded that the manner in which the Spaniards have proceeded in their conquest of so many kingdoms in the New World has been to send *religieux* in advance to Christianise the natives; so that later on these join the Spaniards and rise against their own rulers and put the Spaniards in possession of the kingdoms; and although such is the opinion of their own warlike resources and of their valour that they appear convinced that no neighbours could ever conquer their empire, and that they are rather in a position to conquer others, yet the suspicion which they continue to cherish about the Spaniards and the *religieux* of Luzon rouses the apprehensions of the rulers, and this suspicion cannot fail to produce a very great impression and a very profound irritation, as happened in the time of Taicosama. This prince, as a matter of fact, had written to Manila some four or five years ago that his reason for crucifying the Franciscans was that these *religieux* had come as spies, and that the Gospel and the teaching of the Franciscans had merely been devices for the conquest of kingdoms, adding that no more of these same *religieux* must be sent to Japan; whence it may be inferred—although Taicosama was in error—what the opinion of the Japanese lords is. And although these lords are well-informed about the affairs of China, and are not ignorant that the Portuguese, with whom they have maintained commercial relations for so many years on a thoroughly friendly footing, are a peaceful race with no ideas of conquest, yet as these lords know that we are at present under the authority of the same sovereign and that we profess the same religion, the members of the Company who come to Japan *viâ* the East Indies and Macao, and whose pacific character the Japanese appreciate, experience in part the effect of their suspicions. It is thus that all this Church is exposed to calamities having their origin in the arrival of these *religieux* of Luzon."

Froez here tells us that he had amassed enormous wealth, thanks to his opportunities at Hideyoshi's Court; that he was spending that wealth lavishly in the re-erection of the Hiyei-san temples, demolished by Nobunaga, and that he was greatly concerned at the conversion of so many of the upper classes to Christianity. Accordingly he availed himself of the open and recklessly defiant propaganda of the Franciscans to denounce the foreign priests to Hideyoshi. Just at this time, too, Martinez, the first Bishop of Japan, charged by Albuquerque, the Viceroy of the Indies, with presents for Hideyoshi, and a letter certifying the genuineness of Valegnani's embassy of 1590–91, and acknowledging the due receipt of Hideyoshi's dispatch and presents, appeared in Japan. Arrived at Fushimi, Martinez was received in audience by Hideyoshi, "who first asked him why the Viceroy had been so long in writing to him. He answered this question to the satisfaction of that prince, who, after showing great consideration for his person and for the character with which he was invested, caused him to be served with tea, and dismissed him, very well satisfied with his manners, but very poorly with respect to the disposition he seemed to be in with respect to Christianity." After this the Bishop passed some time at Fushimi and Ōsaka confirming the converts. "Such," says Froez, "was the zeal of the Christians in taking the said Sacrament; in such numbers did they flock from various and far-distant parts, that the good prelate could take no rest either by night or by day; and much effort had to be made to repress the universal ardour so that not the faintest rumour should reach the ears of the King or of his intimates. And for this reason the Bishop was compelled to withdraw from Court as soon as possible. But the said ardour could not be repressed without the physician (Jacuin) getting hint of it, and he did not remain silent before Taicosama." Then at this moment "Masuda, another minister of iniquity, loaded the Christians with fresh suspicions and false reports on account of the passengers of that ship, specially mentioning that among them were some *religieux*[8] who had come as spies of the Christian princes to promulgate their law. Thus

---

[8] There were four Augustins, one Dominican, and two Franciscans on board the *San Felipe*. The Augustins and the Dominican were sent back to Manila, but the two Franciscans remained in Japan, and one of them was to be numbered among the twenty-six martyrs of February 5th, 1597.

the King, already spontaneously roused, now poured forth all
his wrath upon the faithful."

As for the unfortunate Landecho, who was vigorously
insisting upon the restoration of his freight in accordance with
international law, he was told that the Taikō had every reason
to regard and treat him as a pirate; but that he would be
granted his life. Only he had to return to Manila with all
his equipage [9] and passengers at the first opportunity. If we
are to believe Charlevoix, if it had not been for the Jesuits
the whole of the Spaniards would have starved. However,
they at last got back to the Philippines, where their appearance
and the story they had to tell excited the most intense indignation. A pamphlet was issued and scattered all over the Spanish-
speaking world charging the Jesuits with being entirely
responsible for Landecho's misadventure and the ruin of the
Franciscans, and accusing them of many enormities, among
others of the wealth they were accumulating by engaging in
trade. [10]

"Those who made the most noise about this were some Spaniards
in the Philippines, who, jealous of the commerce of the Portuguese
in Japan (baneful source, as has been already remarked, of so many
scandals which shook the Church of Japan to its foundations), sought
every way to drive them hence in order to establish themselves on
their ruins, in which they believed they could not succeed unless
they also procured the expulsion of the Jesuits, who were of the
same nation, or who depended upon it; and as these Spaniards
perceived that the Jesuits could neither subsist nor maintain their
Catechists in Japan without the succours they drew from commerce,
they left nothing undone to render them odious on this ground in
order to strip them of this resource; and they had the address to
get the calumnies they devised on this head published by some
missionaries coming from the Philippines, whom they found means
to seduce to their designs by the false reports of apostates."

Meanwhile at Ōsaka, in order to conserve at least some
vestige of their credit with Hideyoshi, Hasegawa and his son
Ushiōye, supported by Jacuin (Seiyakuin Hōin), were actively
bestirring themselves to involve the Jesuits in the irremediable

---

9 Santa Maria says Hideyoshi detained the negroes on board the *San Felipe*
for his own service.

10 In his defence of the Jesuits, Charlevoix enters into an account of the
sources of their revenues in Japan, which is obviously misleading. In connection
with this pamphlet a statement by Charlevoix is interesting as showing the
enterprise of the Japanese as traders in those times:—"An Augustin, Emmanuel,
who happily found himself at Acapulco at the time these calumnies began to
spread in this part of America, made a very fine reply to them, which was
signed by *a number of Japanese who traded to Mexico*, and by several Castilians and
Portuguese who had been in Japan."

ruin that had so suddenly fallen upon their *protégés*, the over-
zealous Franciscans. But the members of the Company now
reaped the reward of their persistent efforts to associate with,
and to make friends of, the upper classes. Mayeda, the Daimyō
of Kaga, who was no Christian,[11] and Ukida Hideiye's cousin
and chief retainer, who was a very earnest one, exerted themselves very vigorously on behalf of Gnecchi and his companions,
while two of the Ministers, Mayeda Gen-i and Ishida Mitsunari,
now Governor of Lower Kyōto, did not hesitate to lie stoutly
and lustily in order to save them. Ishida was all the more
zealous on their account, because, luckily for the priests, young
Hasegawa, in searching for them and compiling a list of their
converts, had mortally offended him by trespassing upon his
jurisdiction as Governor of the capital. The result was that,
with the exception of the Brother and two servitors already
in ward in Ōsaka, no Jesuit was arrested.[12] Gnecchi appealed
to Ishida on behalf of the Brother and the two servitors;
but he was told nothing could be done, since, if Hideyoshi
heard of their having been in Ōsaka, there might be an
ebullition of wrath that would prove disastrous to all the
hundred and forty Jesuits in Japan. Some Christians offered
lordly bribes to the Governor of Ōsaka to let the prisoners
escape; "but the said Minister, contrary to the custom of
similar officials, who readily become mild at the sight of

---

11 His cousin was a Christian, however, and Justo Ucondono, who was in
Mayeda's service, was very intimate with him (Mayeda).

12 The account given to Gnecchi by Ishida of his interview with Hideyoshi
when he called upon him for instructions is not devoid of interest. Ishida
asked him if he wished the priests who had come with the Portuguese to be
arrested. "The King replied, 'Do you not know that Mexico and the Philippines have been subjugated by those men who came in the ship to Tosa?
Now, in order to reduce Japan in the same way and by the same method they
have sent those *religieux* of theirs to spy out the land, and to attach the people
to themselves by preaching, intending to follow with a great and powerful
armament to assail all these realms in open war with the support of the
Christians already suborned. [From this it may be inferred that, although
Froez says nothing about it, the rash speech of the pilot was actually made.]
Ten years have gone since I prohibited that Law, and those of the Company
obey my edict; whence, therefore, do these new men appear, daring to preach
what I forbid, and to sap and subvert the Empire of Japan? Shall I suffer
that?' Ishida replied that His Highness's reasons were just, and that what
he had said of the Fathers of the Company was true, purposely adding other
things to mitigate the mind of the King towards the Company. Thus Taicosama
then openly showed that he was in no wise offended with the Company, and
he presently added, 'Because our interpreter [Rodriguez] may be much disturbed
by this news, dispatch a swift ship to assure him that he may be free from all
anxiety, and tell the old man who lives in Kyōto [Gnecchi] to be of tranquil
and easy mind.' He also pardoned the Fathers of Nagasaki, the Bishop, and
all those who had come into his sight."

gifts, always declared himself inexorable and harder than flint." Thus "Dominus Deus quod decreverat hoc beneficium præstare iis quos præ sua occulta sapientia elegerat, non passus est eorum diligentiam suum consequi effectum," and the three Jesuits were to have the privilege of attaining the martyr's crown in the company of their rivals from Manila.[13]

Besides those already seized, Ishida was commissioned to arrest all the Japanese who had frequented the Franciscan churches in Kyōto. The list proved so formidable, however, that he had a new one prepared, in which were entered only fifteen names—mostly those of the priests' own domestics. This list being laid before the Taikō, who was then leaving for Ōsaka, he said he would send the Ōsaka prisoners to the capital, and then went on :—

"I wish to have them promenaded in carts through the streets of Kyōto, their noses and ears cut off; then sent to Ōsaka, and there promenaded through the streets also ; that the same thing be repeated at Sakai, and that this sentence of death be carried before them on the carts.

"TAICO SAMA.

"I have ordered these foreigners to be treated thus, because they have come from the Philippines to Japan, calling themselves ambassadors, although they were not so ; because they have remained here for long without my permission ; because, in defiance of my prohibition, they have built churches, preached their religion, and caused disorders. My will is that after being thus exposed to public derision, they be crucified at Nagasaki."

---

13 Froes also counts among the secondary causes of Hideyoshi's leniency towards the Jesuits, "the arrival of the Bishop to visit him, bringing the answer of the Viceroy of the Indies, by which, as far as we understand, his hands were completely tied, as he himself also confessed to Ishida when he expressed his opinion to him about the royal Edict." His statement of what he regards as the chief and primary reason is noteworthy. "Some one may inquire of me the reason why the King was unwilling to arrest us, when we preach the Gospel, and with so many colleges and residences cherish and foster 300,000 souls in the faith and true piety of Christ. In order that the solution of this question (although it may be gathered from the interview with Ishida) may be understood, I add as the principal cause the Providence of God, who distributes his treasures according to the profound and impenetrable judgement of his own wisdom, and knowing what is fitting for the salvation of His elect, with paternal benignity directs all things to His greater glory. Hence His Divine Majesty, aware that the sower of tares had by recent events disturbed the faithful somewhat, willed with an all-powerful hand to draw this good from it,—in other that the good-will and the works of the Franciscan Fathers being rewarded—(to wit, in order that to the six living at Kyōto he might give access to the palm of martyrdom, and that thus this new vine of Christ might be watered by their blood and by that of some others; but that He might allow the five others to be driven from the Empire)—*in order, I say, that in this way the little seed of discord, which might cause great harm to this Church, might be destroyed.*" When the interests of his own Society are intimately concerned, even fine old Froes can assume the unctuous professional smirk.

This sentence was duly carried out,—only Ishida ventured to restrict the mutilation to the lobe of one ear. From Sakai they had to make a terrible overland journey to Nagasaki in the dead of winter, and here all the twenty-six of them (two had been added to their number on the way down) were crucified in the Japanese fashion on February 5th, 1597. It is to be noted that they had had to make the circuit of all the Imperial towns of the time, and also that at Nagasaki it was not the secretly baptized Terasawa, who was then busied with preparations for the second Korean Expedition, but his brother Hasaburo,[14] acting as his deputy, who had to superintend the execution.[15] The excitement produced by this event in

[14] One of the most pitiful things in connection with this tragedy was that Paul Miki (*ætat.* 33), one of the three Japanese Jesuits that suffered, had been Terasawa Hasaburo's bosom-friend in their school-boy days. For years the twain had lost sight of each other, and when they *did* meet at Nagoya in Hizen, whither Hasaburo had gone to meet the cavalcade of *condamnés*, the meeting was a most moving one. And poor Hasaburo, who seems to have been a thorough gentleman in the real sense of the word—honest, upright, devoted to duty, and tender towards the feelings of others—was the more to be pitied of the twain.

[15] The literature on this episode is most voluminous, and some of it, to tell the truth, far from trustworthy. For example, when we get a treatise "de la muerta de 12 religiosos *dominicos*, tres P.P. de la Compañia de Jesú i 17 Japones martyres," we may well begin to ask ourselves whether such a thing as accuracy can ever be attained in history. Not a single Dominican then suffered death. De Santa Maria, Provincial de San Joseph de los Descalços, gives a "Relaçion del martirio que VI. *Padres* Descalços Franciscos y XX Japones Christianos padecieron en Japon," whereas only three of the Spaniards were Fathers. There were really, it seems, according to Froes's letter to Acquaviva, six Franciscans, three Japanese Jesuits, and seventeen Japanese Christians, mostly domestics of the Franciscans, crucified on this occasion. Of this very voluminous literature we have plodded through a fair amount with interest and edification, and here and there with disgust. It is somewhat upsetting to find the good old Charlevoix, after telling us how the bones of the Jesuit martyrs had been safely conveyed to Macao, simperingly insinuating that the Franciscans of Manila had not been so lucky! On this occasion Jesuit and Franciscan in common had died like brave men, loyally and fearlessly and ungrudgingly, for what they believed to be duty. If the spirit of their work, of their sacrifice, and of their accomplishment survived, there was surely no need for a contemptible rivalry over the respective number of Jesuit big-toe joints and Franciscan big-toe joints that might have been carried off to play the part of properties in the miserable tomfoolery of miracles worked by the relics of holy Saints.

In 1587, the very year when Hideyoshi thought fit to drop the mask *vis-à-vis* the missionaries, Sixtus V. instituted the Congregation of Sacred Rites, whose most serious work consists in processes for the beatification and canonisation of the servants of God, the honours paid to Saints, and the recognition of martyrdoms suffered for the Catholic faith. In this last special matter, its first case was that of the twenty-six victims crucified on the Martyrs' Mount at Nagasaki. The two instruments (one for the Franciscans and another for the Jesuits) attesting its findings were issued by Urban VIII. on September 14th, 1627,—nearly thirty years after the tragedy.

The following from Léon Pagés is interesting:—"The news of the canonisation of the twenty-six martyrs of 1597 reaching Manila towards the end of 1629, was the occasion of solemn rejoicings there. St. Pierre Baptiste and his companions had resided at Manila, and had set out from there on the mission to Japan. The Franciscans began their fête on January 2nd; one of the Crosses of the Blessed was borne in the procession, and the banner was deployed by Captain Diego de Mercado, who had been present at the martyrdom. Then

Nagasaki' and Kyūshū generally was intense; among others
the Princes of Arima and Ōmura, on their way to the Korean
War, came in solemn pilgrimage to the scene of the execution.

Meanwhile Hideyoshi, although allowing Gnecchi to remain
in Kyōto, took means to arrest his further efforts among the
upper classes, and issued a special order forbidding any Daimyō
to embrace Christianity, while measures were adopted to render
the Edict of 1587 something better than the virtual dead letter
it had been before. The Lieutenant-Governor of Nagasaki
strictly ordered that no Japanese should enter a church, that
there should be no Christian assemblies or meetings there,
deported the three or four Franciscans then in the city, and
made vigorous search for the one (Jérome de Jesus) who had
eluded him. Then, later on, he caused the Bishop of Japan,
Martinez, to return to Macao, while a few days after he
received instructions to send away all the Jesuits, with the
exception of two or three for the service of the Portuguese
in Nagasaki. How this order was really executed may be
judged from the fact that in October, 1597, a small junk
carried away eleven of the one hundred and twenty-five Jesuits
then in the country. Such is Bishop Çerqueyra's account of
the matter (January 12th, 1603); but Charlevoix's narrative
is more detailed :—

"There were one hundred and twenty-five Jesuits then in Japan,
of whom forty-six were priests. Twelve of these remained in Arima
and Ōmura, eight in Amakusa, four in Bungo, as many in Hirado
and the Gōtōs, while two passed to Korea. Father Gnecchi remained
in Kyōto with two priests, and with four or five religieux who were
not so. The others showed themselves at Nagasaki, making pretence
of preparing to depart for Macao. In effect, in the October following
(1597), a Portuguese vessel being on the point of sailing, all the
bridge seemed to be filled with Jesuits, although there were only a
few students with their professors, two sick priests, and some catechists;
the others were Portuguese disguised as Jesuits, and by this innocent
stratagem, which had doubtless been concerted with Terasawa, Father
Gomez saved his mission. But inasmuch as in spite of the wise
precautions he had taken to prevent the religieux from being discovered, it might happen that such a misfortune might overtake
some of them, he caused the report to be spread that all of them
had not had time to reach the port before the departure of the ship,
and that he would profit by the first opportunity to make them
embark."

there was also to be seen the original sentence of the tyrant Taicosama, who
condemned the martyrs as propagators of the faith of Jesus Christ. The Jesuits
(who celebrated the fête later) possessed a bone of the right fore-arm of each
of the martyrs sent with authenticated certificates by P. Morejon, Rector of
Macao, and P. Palmeiro, Visitor of the Province of Japan and China."

· · However, as there were persistent rumours that Hideyoshi was again coming down to Kyūshū, the Lieutenant-Governor of Nagasaki deemed it time to act in earnest; the priests were still continuing to discharge all their functions, and if the Taikō heard of that, it would be serious. So early in 1598 Hasaburo sent out a force to destroy the churches; and in Arima, Ōmura, and Hirado one hundred and thirty-seven of them were demolished, while the college in Amakusa, the seminary in Arima, and the houses and residences of the priests, also went to the ground. At the same time Ishida in Kyōto sent word to Gnecchi that the Jesuits could not doubt he was their friend, but that if they desired to retain his friendship they must at once repair to Nagasaki to embark there at the first opportunity. "So Gnecchi remained there with four or five Japanese Jesuits who were not priests, and who could more easily disguise themselves."

We are told by Çerqueyra, the new Bishop of Japan— (Martinez had just died at Malacca)— who, accompanied by Valegnani and four priests, arrived at Nagasaki in August, 1598, that he found Terasawa had assembled all the Fathers and Brothers of the Company who had not been able to remain in hiding, and that he kept them at Nagasaki to be deported to Macao by the ship of the year; "however, a great many Fathers and Brothers remained concealed by the Christians themselves in the lands of Arima, Ōmura, and Amakusa, cultivating these Christianities as well as they could in a time so unfavourable."

From the foregoing statement of the facts of the case, it becomes clear that if due regard be had to the provocation received, the attitude of the Taikō's officers towards the Christians cannot fairly be characterised as either cruel or ferocious. And yet, with perhaps the exception of Katō Kiyomasa, "*vir ter execrandus*,"[16] no Japanese statesman has been

---

[16] It is to be noted that this much-quoted epithet was no coinage of the missionaries, however. After many difficulties Konishi (Katō's great rival) had at last got a Chinese embassy to appear in Japan in 1596, and on proceeding to Fushimi he was there warmly commended by the Taikō for his efforts. "Subjungebat deinde (Taicus) minime se ignorare rem hanc etiam ante biennium, trienniumve confici potuisse, si non Toranusque (Katō) *homo ter execrandus*, et capitalis ipsius hostis obstitisset; quem dicebat se simulatque e Corai reverteret de medio sublaturum, hancque poenam meritis ejus longe fore inferiorem: tamen expenso accuratius facto in gratiam ipsius Ecuno-cami (Konishi) se vitam condonaturum, atque ita tracturum ut omni auctoritate exueretur." See Froez's letter of December 28th, 1596,

so much assailed by the missionaries and their sympathisers as Hideyoshi.[17] Yet Charlevoix himself is sufficiently open-minded to point out that this is exceedingly unjust,—that it is true that Hideyoshi began the persecution, but that it is equally to be remembered that of some two hundred *religieux* and 1,800,000[18] believers, who had lived under his sixteen years' rule, no more than twenty-six were killed, and these without any refinement of cruelty. And the execution of some of the said twenty-six amounted to something very like a political necessity. So much appears from an incident of this same or of the following year. Tello, who had succeeded Marinas as Governor of the Philippines, had then sent Navarette as his representative to Japan with presents and a letter for the Taikō. In the dispatch the Governor had ventured on a mild expostulation about the fate of the Franciscans. Hideyoshi's reply (inserted in the histories of Guzman and Bartoli) was very moderate. It pointed out that the *religieux* had broken their promise and had been guilty of causing grave disorders in the State, asked the Governor how *he* would have acted towards Japanese priests preaching an aggressive Shintoism in the Philippines, and, inviting him to imagine himself in Hideyoshi's place if he wished to understand the reasons for the execution of the Franciscans, assured him that if any of the numerous Japanese subjects then in the Philippines infringed the laws of Spain, His Excellency had the amplest liberty to deal with them without any risk of interference on the part of the Japanese Government. It is to be specially marked that Hideyoshi never attempted to interfere with the religion of the foreign merchants in Japan; we have seen that he more than once admitted that it was only reasonable that priests for their service should be allowed to reside in Nagasaki. And this, it must be remembered, was also the position of the Tokugawa Government in its early days; we shall presently see that it was only because the Portuguese captains would persist in smuggling

17 Don Vivero y Velasco, Governor of the Philippines, was Iyeyasu's guest from 1609 to 1611. In his Memoirs this Governor mentions Taicosama, " whose soul is in hell for all eternity."

18 Where Charlevoix got these figures from we are at a loss to discover. In two passages, in separate letters, Froez distinctly says that in 1596–97 there were three hundred thousand Christians in Japan. And in January, 1603, Çerqueyra, Bishop of Japan, writes:—" As to the number of the Christians before the war of the year 1600, . . . this might nearly amount to three hundred thousand."

religieux into the country, in defiance of the prohibition to do so, that they ultimately drove the Shōgunate to shut its ports against them. But this is to anticipate matters somewhat.

Charlevoix's summary of the general attitude towards Europeans in Japan is well worthy of remark.

"However little attention," writes he, "one may have paid to what passed as regards Christianity in Japan since the first Edict of Taicosama (1587), one will scarcely hesitate to recognise that the danger of entire destruction to which this flourishing Church found itself exposed came chiefly from the eagerness of the Spaniards in the Philippines to share with the Portuguese in the commerce of these isles and the little concord among the evangelical workers which had been the consequence of this. Indeed, there is every reason to believe that if the missionaries had always comported themselves as they had during the first years of the persecution, the Emperor (Hideyoshi), who witnessed with tolerable equanimity the progress of a religion he could not help esteeming, would not have been forced to any *coup d'état* to arrest it; and after his death the numbers and the rank of the Christians would have constrained the Government to treat them with respect. It is still more certain that at the time of which I speak the good under-standing which had existed from the beginning between the Japanese and the Portuguese had not yet been impaired in any way, and that the Court was in no wise on its guard against the latter even as regards the missionaries, as sensibly appeared from the arrival of the new Bishop, Dom Louis Çerqueyra, whom 'the ship from Macao'[19] brought at this conjuncture to Japan, together with Father Valegnani[20] and several other Jesuits, without any one finding any reason to object. It is true that the news which suddenly spread, that the Emperor (Hideyoshi) was at the last extremity, prevented either the missionaries or the Christians from being any longer thought of."

Accurate in the main as this *exposé* may be, its penultimate sentence yet calls for qualification. When the Bishop arrived he found that the Christians of Nagasaki were being sorely and shrewdly harried and harassed by the orders of Terasawa, the Governor. "Everybody," writes Çerqueyra, "apprehended lest Terasawa, then in Korea, should be informed of our arrival, and that becoming still more wroth, should have us conducted to Kyōto; but Our Lord permitted that at the time of our arrival Taicosama should fall mortally sick, and that he should die in the course of the same year,—a circumstance which procured for ourselves and the Japanese Church more calm and security."

---

[19] This is a mistake. Çerqueyra says he came in the "junk" of Nuño de Mendoza.

[20] Absent since October, 1592.

It was perhaps little wonder, though, that Terasawa was enraged at the Christians. The escaped Franciscan, Jêrome de Jésus, had at last been detected, and after some time deported to Manila. No sooner had he reached that port than he, in company with another Franciscan, took passage in a Chinese junk for Nagasaki, where the two duly arrived. News of their departure from Manila had got abroad and reached Terasawa in Korea; and the first intimation of the arrival of the proscribed missionary the Lieutenant-Governor got was in a fiery letter from his superior. Aided by the Jesuits, who were in the most profound anxiety lest Hideyoshi should hear of the affair, the Japanese succeeded in arresting one of the monks; but de Jésus made good his escape into the interior and was put to the ban, the Jesuits earnestly praying for his speedy capture and quiet removal from the country. The death of Hideyoshi, however, relieved them from their worst apprehensions.

In the letter of Paez (October 13th, 1598), from which these details are taken, there is an interesting account of the last days of the illustrious Taikō. At Fushimi towards the end of June, 1598, he was attacked by dysentery, " accompanied as ordinarily is wont to be the case by a distemper of the stomach." At first the attack seemed slight, but on the 5th of August Hideyoshi seemed to be at the point of death. " But not losing a spark of his courage by reason of that, he began with an intrepid heart, and with the extraordinary circumspection which has characterised every action of his, to set things in order just as if he had been in the most perfect health. And all his aim was that his son, who is six years of age, should succeed him in the Empire." After recounting the measures he took, about which something will be said in a subsequent chapter, Paez goes on :—

"At this time (in September) Father Juan Rodriguez, with some Portuguese from the captain of the ship, arrived at Fushimi with the presents which the ship is accustomed to make when she arrives in Japan. Taicosama, hearing of their coming, sent an officer to congratulate them on their happy arrival and to request Father Rodriguez to see him; but he did not wish to receive the visits of the others. The Father went as he was notified, and, before entering where the Taikō was, he passed through so many saloons, corridors, galleries, and chambers, that on his departure, if he had not had guidance, he could not have found his exit. Finally arrived at the place where Taicosama was, the Father found him lying on a couch among velvet cushions, so wasted that he had lost nearly all human semblance. And making the Father draw near, he said to him that he was not a little rejoiced at his presence, as he had been so near death that he had not expected to see him again; and that he thanked him for the trouble he had taken to visit him not merely then, but also for years past. He caused him to be presented with two hundred bags of rice, a Japanese garment, and a vessel for coming and going. He also presented certain garments to the Portuguese who had come to Fushimi with the Father; to each of the two *fragate* of the captain two hundred bags of rice, and another two hundred to the ship. He also wished that the Father should visit the Prince (his son, Hideyori), having first instructed him to receive the Father and his Portuguese companions kindly, because they were foreigners. His son did so, and presented each of them with a silken garment as his father had done. On the day following, which was that on which the marriages between the sons and the daughters of the five Regents were celebrated, he summoned Father Rodriguez and willed that he should be present at the feast which was held on the occasion of the said marriages. And finally, the Portuguese recommending themselves earnestly to him in order that he should procure their favourable dispatch, he dismissed them with many words and tokens of kindness.

"Thus the Father took his leave with great grief at seeing a man so wise and prudent in all other things, except in that which was of the greatest importance,—his own salvation to wit; and in that he was so blinded by obstinacy not to listen to the words the Father so much wished to address to him on this occasion. But it was not possible, he not wishing to give place to such discourses."

On the 4th of September, after a temporary rally, there was a terrible relapse, and the Taikō lingered on in agony until the 15th, "when he fell into a frenzy, saying a thousand absurd things in all other matters, except what touched the providing for his son being monarch of Japan, because in that he spoke much to the point even till the very last date, which was the early morning of the following day."

Thus, on September 16th, 1598, passed away the greatest man Japan has ever seen, and the greatest statesman of his century, whether in Japan or in Europe. Three days before him died Philip II. of Spain, the most powerful contemporary ruler in Christendom. How much religious freedom did Philip II. allow his non-Catholic subjects? Let those who presume to speak of the barbarity of those days in Japan, ponder that question well before proceeding with their parable.

CHAPTER XII.

THE KOREAN WAR.

EVEN a superficial study of the life and work of Hideyoshi serves to impress one with the strength of his grasp upon the actualities of the situation, his unerring sense of political perspective, his prescience of the future and the problems it would present, and the grand unity, continuity, and comprehensiveness of his statecraft. The unification of the *disjecta membra* of the Empire under his own administration was undoubtedly the primary object he kept before him. That accomplished, however, he knew that his task was by no means finished. How to give lasting and abiding permanence to his handiwork was a problem that insistently called for the strenuous exercise of all his faculties. By 1590 the most pressing aspect of the problem had been solved, and a brief glance at the contemporary map of feudal Japan is sufficient to disclose how astute the solution devised was. As in that year, Nobuo, Nobunaga's second and only surviving son, who had at first held Owari, Ise, and Iga, and latterly Owari only, was stripped of his remaining fief and banished to Dewa, Hideyoshi's grasp on all his master's dominions was fully and firmly rivetted.[1] All the strongholds for leagues round Kyōto

---

[1] Nobuo is said to have been banished for declining the proffer of Iyeyasu's original provinces after the conquest of the Kwantō in 1590. "Hideyoshi was very angry, and exclaimed, 'You are not fit to govern; but remembering that you are a son of my former lord, I wished to befriend you particularly. Do you presume to think my gift too small?'"

In Froez's account of the death of the Kwanbaku (Hidetsugu, Hideyoshi's nephew) there is a curious passage about Nobuo. Just before breaking openly with his nephew, Hideyoshi invited him to Fushimi, to take part in the play (probably a *Nō* dance) enacted in the palace there. It seems that Hideyoshi also took a part in it; for we are told that he was consumed with envy of the superior acting and dancing of his nephew, and was greatly concerned that the palm should be awarded to the young man and not to himself:—"Nam nonnunquam et ipse se ingerebat in tripudia et saltatum, sed motu corporis' tam incomposito et incondito, ut decrepitum et delirum senem exprimeret." Nobuo had a great reputation as an actor and a dancer; and Hideyoshi, to minish his nephew's laurels, called upon Nobuo to perform. But the crafty Nobuo purposely made many mistakes, as a courtier should, and Hideyoshi was so pleased that he at once gave him 6,000 bags of rice, and, "speaking with him, all witnesses being removed, made no end of enumerating the benefits he had received from Nobunaga; alleging that he was very sorry for having acted with too much severity towards him in banishing him to the extreme

were held by his own garrisons, while the possession of Sakai
and Ōsaka made him master of all the over-sea routes to the
capital. His reduction of Negoro in 1585 had thrown the
rich province of Kii into his hands, and about the same date
the whole island of Shikoku had been reduced and, for the
most part, parcelled out among his officers. In the previous year
Mōri of Nagato had been stripped of three of his ten provinces,
and Ukita Hideiye, one of Hideyoshi's trusted men, kept a
watch upon him from Bizen and Mimasaka. The campaign
of 1587 had resulted in limiting the sway of Shimadzu to Satsuma,
Ōsumi, and part of Hiūga, while Konishi, stripped of his
lands in Harima, had been made Lord of Southern Higo in
order to keep his great southern neighbour in check, and at
the same time old Kuroda had been established in Buzen to
watch Mōri across the Straits. At Kanazawa in Kaga, Mayeda
had been placed to block Uyesugi Kagekatsu, with whom
Hideyoshi had come to an understanding; from 1590 Uyesugi
was further placed under observation from the south-east by
the establishment of another of Hideyoshi's lieutenants, Gamō
Ujisato, in the fief of Aidzu, charged also with the duty of
paying attention to his sea-board neighbour, Daté of Sendai,
who had tendered his submission to the Regent during the
siege of Hōjō's stronghold of Odawara. That campaign of
1589–90 against Hōjō had put Hideyoshi in possession of his
provinces, and these were given to Iyeyasu, who had at the
same time to surrender his fief of Mikawa and its adjacent
provinces to Hideyoshi. Iyeyasu, the Regent felt, he could
trust; and of the old great Houses only five were now left,
and all these were in isolated parts of the Empire, and under
the jealous surveillance of Hideyoshi's " new men "—Satsuma
in the extreme south, checked by Konishi in Higo; Mōri at
the western extremity of the main island, observed by Kuroda
in Buzen, and by Ukida Hideiye on the east; Uyesugi in
Echigo, with Mayeda on one flank and Gamō on the other,

confines of Japan; although that had not been done in order that he might be
for ever stripped of his fiefs, but in order that better ones might be bestowed
upon him—an assertion which the copious tears flowing from his eyes made
credible. But this time he was not dealing with an inept and foolish man,
for Nobuo well knew the old man's crafty tricks, and was aware that his tears
were crocodile's tears. . . . For it was then five years since he had been stripped
of his States and banished; and when Hideyoshi had recalled him, he had
not indicated by even a word that he wished to restore them to him, much less
to give him better ones."

who, together with Iyeyasu at Yedo, might safely be counted upon to keep Daté in Sendai and Satake in Mito out of all mischief. However, it was not so much the five old Houses and Iyeyasu that needed to be kept employed, as Hideyoshi's own immediate followers. So much has been clearly set forth by Rai Sanyō in his *Nihon Gwaishi*. Writes the Japanese historian :—

"Although Hideyoshi subdued the great barons of his day, he was well aware that they would not, without some good reason for doing so, remain subject to him long. So he thought to himself, 'As I have risen from obscurity and obtained power over others by the sword, so soon as ever my position in the State seems to the great barons to be only used for my personal benefit and advancement and ceases to confer anything on them, they will no longer allow me to rule over them. I must make it worth their while to keep me in power.' So he gave away land and money right and left without stint, thus making men anxious to fight for him. He bestowed the wealth he had acquired as freely as though he were giving away dust. And the persons who received it valued it at no higher rate. They did not look upon it as a special favour bestowed on them by the Taikō, but rather as the due reward of the services they had rendered him. Their thirst for gain was never satisfied. For every new effort they put forth in his cause they expected some additional rewards. But though their desire to receive was unbounded, Hideyoshi's power to give was limited by the size of the country over which he ruled, and consequently it came about that rewards for his generals had to be sought in other lands. Accordingly, before the wounds received in the battles they had fought here in their own country were healed, his generals were dispatched to Korea—a country entirely unknown to them— where during a series of years they spent their strength in a fruitless war." [2]

However, there is the best of reason to believe that this Korean expedition was no sudden freak on the part of Hideyoshi, whose prescience of the future, as has already been said, was remarkable. So far back as 1578, when starting on his expedition against Mōri, then master of the Chūgoku,

[2] It is to be noted, however, that Rai Sanyō, whose wonderful popularity among his countrymen is to be attributed rather to the lucidity and picturesqueness of his style than to any great command over original authorities, very often rests content with presenting one side of a question merely. Hideyoshi gave lavishly, it is true; but the giving was by no manner of means all on his side. The missionaries make frequent reference to his enormous exactions from the Daimyō. At the New Year all the Daimyō without exception had to appear at his Court; whoever failed to do so would have been regarded as a contumacious and manifest rebel. In 1589 Arima "carried with him three thousand cruzados to present to Quabacundono on his first arrival, besides many other precious things, since Quabacundono did not wish such visits to be made with empty hands. And with these, and with the changes of States and kingdoms in Japan, and with other diverse tyrannies, it may be said that he has accumulated an immense quantity of gold and silver and of other rich and precious things."

he is represented to have used the following language to
Nobunaga :—" When I have conquered the Chūgoku, I will
go on to Kyūshū and take the whole of it. When Kyūshū
is ours, if you will grant me the revenue of that island for
one year, I will prepare ships of war and supplies and go
over and take Korea. Korea I shall ask you to bestow on
me as a reward for my services, and to enable me to make
still further conquests ; for with Korean troops, aided by your
illustrious influence, I intend to bring the whole of China
under my sway. When that is effected the three countries
(China, Korea, and Japan) will be one. I shall do it all as
easily as a man rolls up a piece of matting and carries it
under his arm." [3]

That some such speech may have been made is rendered
probable by the tenor of certain remarks made to Froez on
the occasion of his and Coelho's visit to Hideyoshi at Ōsaka
in 1586 :—

" He also said that he had reached the point of subjugating
all Japan ; whence his mind was not set upon the future acquisition
of more kingdoms or more wealth in it, since he had enough, but
solely upon immortalising himself with the name and fame of his
power ; in order to do which he was resolved to reduce the affairs of
Japan to order, and to place them on a stable basis ; and, this
done, to entrust them to his brother Minodono (Hidenaga), while he
himself should pass to the conquest of Korea and China, for which
enterprise he was issuing orders for the sawing of planks to make
two thousand vessels in which to transport his army. And for
himself, he wished nothing from the Fathers, except that through
them he should get two great and well-equipped ships from the
Portuguese, whom he would pay liberally for everything, giving the
very best wages to their officers ; and if he met his death in that
undertaking he did not mind, inasmuch as it would be said that he was
the first Lord of Japan who had ventured on such an enterprise ;
and if he succeeded, and the Chinese rendered obedience to him, he
would not deprive them of their country, or remain in it himself ;
and because he only wished them to recognise him for their Lord,
and that then he would build churches in all parts, commanding
all to become Christians, and to embrace our Holy Law (!) "

Again, five years later, when on the expedition against
Hōjō in 1590, he visited the Shrine of Yoritomo at Tsurugaoka,
near Kamakura, and there, patting the back of the image of
the great Shōgun, he is said to have addressed it thus :—

" You are my friend ! You took all the power under Heaven
(in Japan). You and I only have been able to do this ; but you

---

[3] Dening's translation.

V

were of high and illustrious descent, and not like me, sprung from peasants. But as for me, after conquering all the empire, I intend to conquer China. What do you think of that ?"

The subjection of the Kwantō in that year of 1590, as has been said, made Hideyoshi undisputed master of Japan from one end of the archipelago to the other. The problem then was how to maintain his rapidly acquired supremacy. Without employment of some sort, the mettlesome feudatories would never remain quiet, and so much Hideyoshi had foreseen from the first. To engage them to spend their resources and energies in an over-sea war was the best and easiest solution of the problem ; and as early as 1587, immediately after the reduction of Kyūshū and the subjugation of Shimadzu of Satsuma, the Regent had taken the preliminary steps to provoke the necessary quarrel. In that year an envoy was sent to the Korean Court to complain of its discourtesy in having latterly failed to send the embassies to Japan that had previously been wont to come. To make this and subsequent developments clear, however, it becomes advisable to say something about the general relations that had subsisted between Korea and Japan.

Since their commencement in the first century B.C. these relations had undergone many vicissitudes. At an early date Korea figures as the instructor of Japan in Chinese learning, in Buddhism, and in the arts of civilisation. Koreans swelled the numbers of the host of Kublai Khan which had attempted the conquest of Japan in 1281 A.D. At other times we read of Korea being over-run by Japanese invaders, of its being governed in part by Japanese officials, or paying Japan a heavy tribute in token of submission. Then, in 1392, the whole 80,000 square miles of the peninsula got unified under the sway of a single strong and stable government; for such at first the government of the first royal ancestors of the present helpless and hopeless Korean monarch undoubtedly was. Even then Korea stood under the protection of China, but that did not prevent her from meeting Japan on equal and friendly terms. Embassies bearing letters and presents were periodically exchanged between the two countries. Somewhere between 1418 and 1450 Japanese traders from Tsushima had been granted settlements of sixty houses at each of the ports of Ché-pho, Fusan, and Yŏm-pho ; but they came over in greater numbers than provided for, and in 1510 they rose against the Korean authorities, who were exacting from them what the islanders held to be an undue amount of forced labour. At first the Japanese had the best of it; but being defeated with a loss of two hundred and ninety-five heads, the survivors were compelled to withdraw. For some time after this there was but little intercourse between the two nations, although a few Japanese returned and established themselves on sufferance. In 1572, however, the Japanese sent a friendly message, requesting a resumption of the old relations, and as the Prefect of Fusan supported the request, they were permitted to resume operations at Fusan alone, three *li* below the prefecture, which means about half-way down the bay from the present village of Fusan. From that time the former relations were renewed,—only no envoys were sent from Korea to Japan. It was decreed by the Korean Government that a Japanese landing anywhere except at Fusan should be treated as a pirate. This perhaps is not to be wondered at, as from various passages in the missionary letters we learn that at this time the islanders were exceedingly addicted to piracy, and that their operations were by no means confined to Japanese waters.

In 1587, then, Hideyoshi, as has been said, saw fit to send a messenger to Seoul to complain of the non-appearance of Korean embassies in Japan, and to demand that they should be sent in future. The envoy was one Yuya Yasuhiro, a vassal of Sō Yoshitoshi, Daimyō of Tsushima, who, as a response to Hideyoshi's harshly worded and insulting letter, carried back a polite note, in which the Korean King stated that as the journey by sea was a long one and the Koreans were not good sailors, he would have to be excused from complying with the demand. Yuya's failure cost him his head.[4]

Next spring another mission was sent, consisting of Sō, the Daimyō of Tsushima himself, Yanagawa his retainer, and a monk, Genso. At first no notice of these envoys was taken

---

4 According to the Japanese accounts, Yuya with all his family was put to death by his lord the Daimyō of Tsushima (Sō), not for his failure in his mission, but because he and his brother had accepted official titles from the Korean King some time before, and because he had acted too favourably to the Koreans in this mission. These accounts attribute the rudeness of which the Koreans accuse Yanagawa (Taira-no-Shigenobu) to him.

by the Korean Court, and Sō and his companions as the months
dragged on became apprehensive of sharing Yuya's fate. At
last the King privately sent word that an envoy would be sent
to Japan on one condition, viz., that the Japanese should seize
and send to Korea some dozen or so of Korean renegades,
who, under the leadership of one Sa Wha-dong, had fled to
Japan, and since then had acted as guides to Japanese pirates
in their descents on the Korean coasts. As Hideyoshi was
eager to stamp out piracy, the envoys were overjoyed at this,
and Yanagawa was at once dispatched to Japan to seize the
renegades. In August, 1589, three Japanese pirates, with Sa
Wha-dong and his companions, were delivered up to the Koreans
at Seoul, where they were at once beheaded. Then Sō was
called to the Palace for the first time, where he was presented
by the King with a handsome steed, while he in turn gave
the King a peacock and some match-locks, *the first ever seen in
Korea.*

In April, 1590, the King redeemed his promise by dispatching
three envoys to Japan, in company with Sō and his companions.
After a voyage of three months they arrived at Kyōto, where
they were housed in the temple of Daitokuji. This was the
very Korean embassy with its suite of three hundred whose
splendours Valegnani laid himself out to surpass with the
assistance of twenty-six or twenty-seven Portuguese merchants
of Nagasaki and the neighbouring ports, all of whom " might
have passed for Lords." About the object of and the success
that attended this Korean mission Charlevoix professes to be
ignorant, but Mr. Aston and Mr. Hulbert, availing themselves
of Korean sources, here come to our assistance. At the arrival
of the ambassadors Hideyoshi was in the Kwantō reducing
Hōjō, and when he returned in the autumn he postponed
granting them an audience on the pretext that he must first
repair the Hall of Audience in order to receive them with
due ceremony. How much Hideyoshi really cared about the
ceremonial part of the business may be inferred from Mr.
Aston's translation of the Korean account of the manner of
their reception :—

"The ambassadors were allowed to enter the palace-gate borne
in their palanquins. They were preceded the whole way by a band
of music. They ascended into the Hall, where they performed their
obeisances. Hideyoshi is a mean and ignoble-looking man, his

complexion is dark, and his features are wanting in distinction. But his eyeballs send out fire in flashes—enough to pierce one through. He sat upon a threefold cushion with his face to the south.[5] He wore a gauze hat and a dark-coloured robe of state. His officers were ranged round him, each in his proper place. When the ambassadors were introduced and had taken their seats, the refreshments offered them were of the most frugal description. A tray was set before each, on which was one dish containing steamed *mochi*,[6] and *saké* of an inferior quality was handed round a few times in earthenware cups and in a very unceremonious way. The civility of drinking to one another was not observed. After a short interval, Hideyoshi retired behind a curtain, but all his officers remained in their places. Soon after a man came out dressed in ordinary clothes, with a baby in his arms, and strolled about the Hall. This was no other than Hideyoshi himself, and every one present bowed down his head to the ground. Looking out between the pillars of the Hall, Hideyoshi espied the Korean musicians. He commanded them to strike up all together as loud as they could, and was listening to their music, when he was suddenly reminded that babies could despise ceremony as much as princes, and laughingly called for one of his attendants to take the child and to bring him a change of clothing. He seemed to do exactly as he pleased, and was as unconcerned as if nobody else were present. The ambassadors, having made their obeisance, retired, and this audience was the only occasion on which they were admitted to Hideyoshi's presence."

For a long time Hideyoshi did not deign to reply to the letter of the Korean King delivered by the ambassadors,[7] and suggested that they should return without an answer. They refused to do so, naturally enough, and after being made to wait at Sakai for a long time, they at length received the Regent's reply. Here we give Mr. Aston's translation, which is nearly but not quite identical with what we find in the missionaries' letters:—

"This Empire has of late years been brought to ruin by internal dissensions which allowed no opportunity for laying aside armour. This state of things roused me to indignation, and in a few years I restored peace to the country. I am the only remaining scion of a humble stock, but my mother once had a dream in which she saw the sun enter her bosom, after which she gave birth to me. There was then a soothsayer, who said 'wherever the sun shines, there will be no place which shall not be subject to him. It may not be doubted that one day his power will overspread the empire.' It has therefore been my boast to lose no favourable opportunity, and, taking wings like a dragon, I have subdued the East, chastised the West, punished the South, and smitten the North. Speedy and

---

[5] An assumption of royal style.

[6] A sort of cake made of rice.

[7] His procedure *vis-à-vis* Valegnani and the missive from the Viceroy of the Indies was similar.

great success has attended my career, which has been like the rising
sun illuminating the whole earth.

"When I reflect that the life of man is less than one hundred years,
why should I spend my days in sorrow for one thing only? [8] I will
assemble a mighty host, and, invading the country of the great Ming,
I will fill with the hoar-frost from my sword the whole sky over
the four hundred provinces. Should I carry out this purpose, I
hope that Korea will be my vanguard. Let her not fail to do so,
for my friendship with your honourable country depends solely on
your conduct when I lead my army against China."

The envoys at last returned to Korea after a year's absence,
accompanied by Yanagawa and the monk Genso, who, according
to some authorities, were instructed to endeavour to persuade
the Korean Government to assist Hideyoshi in renewing the
long-interrupted relations with China. However, from the
tone of Hideyoshi's letters, as well as from the observations
they had made during their stay in Kyōto and Sakai, the
ambassadors were satisfied that war with Japan was inevitable,
and on reaching Fusan the senior envoy at once sent a dispatch
post haste to Seoul intimating as much. On their way up to
the capital Yanagawa's conduct could scarcely be described as
tactful. At Tai-kou (Tai-Kyu) he insulted the aged Governor,
remarking to him: "For ten years I have followed war, and
thus my beard is grey; why should you grow old?" Again,
calling for a Korean spear, he said: "Your spears are too long,"
insinuating that the Koreans were cowards. Even the gentler
sex did not escape his scathing criticisms. He threw a basket
of oranges to some dancing girls, and when they scrambled
for them he told the bystanders, "Your nation is doomed.
You have no manners." At a banquet in Seoul, the monk
Genso whispered to the senior envoy:—"The reason why
Hideyoshi wants to attack China is because the Emperor
refuses to receive a Japanese envoy. If Korea leaves us but
a clear road to China, we will ask nothing else. No troops
need be given." The Korean replied that China was the
mother country, and that Korea could not so desert her as
to give a road to an invading army. Then the monk insisted
that inasmuch as Korea had given a way to the Mongol hordes
for their attack upon Japan three hundred years before, she
should now do as much for a Japanese army when Japan
was seeking her revenge. This, however, was considered too

---

8 He had recently lost his infant son, Tsurumatsu.

preposterous to be even discussed, and it became plain to Hideyoshi's emissaries that for the Japanese there was no road through Korea, unless they cut one for themselves with the sword. From the Korean King's dispatch to Hideyoshi Mr. Hulbert gives the following extract:—

"Two letters have already passed between us, and the matter has been sufficiently discussed. What talk is this of our joining you against China? From the earliest times we have followed law and right. From within and from without, all lands are subject to China. If you have desired to send your envoys to China, how much more should we? When we have been unfortunate she has helped us. The relations which subsist between us are those of parent and child. This you well know. Can we desert both Emperor and parent and join with you? You doubtless will be angry at this, and it is because you have not been admitted to the Court of China. Why is it that you are not willing to admit the suzerainty of the Emperor instead of harbouring such hostile intents against him? This truly passes our comprehension."

Hideyoshi was enraged at the indifference to his overtures shown by the Koreans, and was especially indignant because the Korean King said to the envoys that his project of conquering China was like "measuring the ocean in a cockle-shell," or "a bee trying to sting a tortoise through its armour."

Meanwhile a messenger from the Chinese Government had arrived in Seoul to inquire into what was going on, for ominous rumours of the intentions of the Japanese had reached the Court of Peking from another source. Shortly before, in this same year, Hideyoshi had sent the King of Lūchū a peremptory message through the Daimyō of Satsuma commanding him to pay tribute to Japan. Now, Lūchū had neither army nor navy, the traditional foreign policy of the little kingdom being comprised in the words "good faith and courtesy"; while the King was young, and more anxious to devote himself to the domestic affairs of the islands than to become embroiled in foreign quarrels. "For the sake of peace, therefore, he sent to Hideyoshi an envoy with a shipload of presents, which the latter was pleased to receive very graciously. The envoy, a priest, was treated with the greatest civility, and Hideyoshi condescended personally to impress on him the advantages Lūchū would derive from placing herself under Japanese protection, and ceasing to send tribute to China. He made no secrets of his projects against that country, and the King of Lūchū, on the return of his envoy, requited Hideyoshi's candour by at once dispatching a warning message to the Chinese Government." Soon after this, and before the landing of the Japanese in Korea, a messenger had been sent from Seoul to Peking to state that an invasion was almost certain ; but the Chinese did nothing to meet the rapidly gathering storm of war now about to burst with dire and fell results upon Korea.

Here it is well to pause in order to consider what condition Korea was in to withstand it. As has been said, the 80,000 square miles to the south of the Yalu and the Tuman had been unified under a strong and stable central government in 1392 A.D. Since that date the prosperity of the country and its progress in the peaceful arts had been more than considerable. Printing with metal types had originated in Korea in 1324, one hundred and twenty-six years before the invention of the art in Europe, and during the early years of the fifteenth century the presses working under royal patronage and at the royal expense had been exceedingly busy and productive. At the time when a knowledge of letters was a rare accomplishment in Japan, the higher learning was widely diffused among the upper class in the peninsula. In metal work the Korean artists or artisans were skilful, while the Korean potters of those days enjoyed a high reputation, their wares being eagerly sought for in Japan, where fabulous sums were paid for the products of their best kilns. However, in spite of a tolerable diffusion of the arts, the country was mainly an agricultural one, rice being the chief crop, although the fisheries, then prosecuted with much energy and success, also proved a fruitful source of wealth. In all these respects, Korea in 1592 had reached a much higher degree of culture or cultivation than had Japan. Yet notwithstanding all this, and surprising even to the verge of paradox as the statement may seem, it is unquestionable that from the point of sociological development Korea lagged seriously behind Japan. With the spread of the feudal system and the complete transference of the government from the hands of incompetent and effeminate Court nobles to those of the sturdy and vigorous military class, it is indeed true that in course of time the island empire had become one wild welter of seething intestine strife from end to end. But this was far from proving all pure loss. The old system of predial serfdom was meanwhile thoroughly broken up and abolished; and even the Japanese peasant and artisan became almost as expert in the use of arms as in that of his tools. That this proposition is true will abundantly appear from the authorities cited in connection with Hideyoshi's devices to strip the non-*samurai* classes of their weapons. Now, just as in contemporary England the possession of arms did much to foster that sense of self-reliant, self-respecting individuality among the commons which made them so superior to the peasants of France, still in a state of helpless serfdom, so this consequence of the unending feudal strife in Japan made the Japanese labourer and artisan much more than a mere thing with a body and two hands. The full advantage of this was reaped when the empire was at last unified under the capable rule of a statesman of the very highest order of administrative genius.[9] In the practical sphere of war and of administration it is questionable whether any contemporary State was so rich in talent as was the Japan of Hideyoshi. Such aristocracy as then ruled her was a real aristocracy of brains. The Daimyō of Satsuma, with his lineage of four hundred years, was indeed no creature or creation of Hideyoshi, nor was Mōri, who was rising to greatness when Hideyoshi was a groom. But these princes were emphatically men of ability, and as for the other feudatories they were nearly all Hideyoshi's own men. Of the present Japanese peerage, one Prince and a full dozen Marquises are the representatives of Houses whose founders had risen from comparative, indeed in most cases from absolute, obscurity to greatness in the service of the illustrious peasant ruler. In Japan then (except perhaps Takayama, Don Justo Ucondono) there was no man of ability, whether *samurai*, merchant, farmer, or artisan, who was not allowed full scope for the free and full development of all his best faculties.

---

9 Charlevoix, writing of Hideyoshi's administration in 1591, says very truthfully:—"Nothing was better administered than Japan, and it became perfectly clear that in order to be submissive and peaceful, the Japanese have no greater need than the generality of other nations of anything beyond being under the sway of a prince who knows how to rule. Crime was punished, virtue rewarded, *merit placed, turbulent spirits occupied*, or put in a condition not to give trouble, and apart from the Christian persecution, in which Hideyoshi always showed a moderation which could scarcely have been expected from his character, no one had any grounds to complain of the government. In truth this monarch was not loved, but he was feared and esteemed, and that sufficed to maintain all in their duty."

In Korea things were vastly different. There were only
two classes—a class of nobles, leisured and learned indeed,
but effeminate and generally destitute of practical ability in
everything except venal intrigue, in which they were extremely
proficient; and a horde of slaves who were bought and sold
and passed from hand to hand like so much landed property.
"At that time there was no lower middle class at all. Society
was composed of the upper class and their retainers. Almost
every man in the lower stratum of society was nominally the
slave of some nobleman (or of the Government), though in
many places it was nominal serfdom only. At the same
time the master had the right to sell them at will, and they
were in duty bound to assume mourning at his death."
Another weakness in the social organisation was the disastrous
lack of cohesion and the extreme mutual jealousy that was
prevalent among the ruling class. Factional strife had
originated in 1575, and since that date every man had been
fighting for his own hand, and plotting and intriguing dirtily
for his own wretched self, and even with the enemy sweeping
the country with fire and sword the filthy cabals still went on.
"No sooner did a capable man arise than he became the
target for the hatred and jealousy of a hundred rivals, and no
trickery or subterfuge was left untried whereby to have him
disgraced and degraded." Jealousies there also were in
Japan in plenty; but then, so far from allowing them to
work any scathe on the body politic at large, Hideyoshi knew
how to profit from them richly. Again, for two centuries
the Koreans, apart from repelling an occasional inroad of the
wild tribes beyond the Yalu and the Tuman, and repulsing
the not infrequent descents of Japanese pirates, had had no
experience in practical warfare whatsoever. Thus it came to
pass that the Government found it advantageous to permit
the militia to commute the military service due by a monetary
payment. The result was that only the very poorest of the
poor served with the colours, and that the army was more of a
mob than anything else. Once more, although there were
small cannons, matchlocks had never been seen in Korea
previous to 1590 or 1591.

Against all this, warfare had never been prosecuted so
seriously and so scientifically in Japan as in the days of

Hideyoshi, when, according to the missionaries, the art was actually revolutionised.[10] In Korea, too, forts and fortifications had been neglected, and had fallen into a miserable state of dilapidation ; and the hurried task of repairing these in the extreme south at this time made the people complain loudly.

Against all this there were two great factors in favour of the Peninsulars in the approaching struggle with Japan on Korean soil. The surface of the country is so hilly and undulating that it has been compared by a French missionary to the sea under a strong gale. This means that it is an ideal ground for a wearing and wasting guerilla warfare. In the next place, for ultimate success in this contest it was absolutely necessary that the way between Korea and Tsushima should lie perfectly open to the Japanese, and that they should maintain undisputed command of the sea. Now, strange indeed as it may sound to us nowadays, the Koreans were undoubtedly better seamen than the Japanese were then. Says Charlevoix :—
" Taicosama had no absolute need of Korea in order to make war on China, but the Koreans, powerful and expert on the sea, might have molested his troops; besides, Korea once conquered, Japan could maintain the war for long, without drawing at all seriously upon her own resources." Elsewhere he says :—" The Koreans cannot stand before the Japanese on land, but they are their superiors on the sea because they have the better ships."[11]

---

10 "Accordingly, we confidently believe that shortly, in diverse parts of Japan, a very great number of conversions will follow as soon as this universal erection of new castles and the demolition of very many old ones are at an end, *which is occasioned by nothing else* than that under Taicosama a new method of warfare was devised which calls for new and much more strongly fortified castles."—VALEG- NANI, October 10th, 1599. The introduction of fire-arms into Japan had doubtless no small influence upon the military tactics of the time. That they were employed pretty extensively we know from the missionaries. Two heavy pieces of artillery had been used by Arima at the battle of Shimabara on April 24th, 1584; Otomo of Bungo had presented several such pieces to Nobunaga, and these were employed by Konishi against the monks of Negoro in their retreat from Kishiwada in Idzumi in 1585; while in the battle of Shizugatake, fought in the preceding year, we hear of a hot artillery fire being kept up by Hideyoshi's troops. As regards matchlocks, we know that Otomo's troops used them against Mōri's men with great effect, that the monks of Negoro were formidable chiefly by reason of their fire-arms, and that of the 25,000 men Riūzōji had had under him at Shimabara in 1584 as many as 9,000 had been equipped with the arquebus. In his war with Takikawa in 1583 Hideyoshi had captured the castle of Kameyama and Miné by springing mines under them, the first instance of the thing in Japan.

11 He quotes from the Dutchmen wrecked there in 1653, to the effect that "their ships have ordinarily two masts with from 30 to 35 oars each, with five or six rowers; so that on each of these galleys, what with soldiers and

Clearly to follow the vicissitudes of the Japanese invasion
of Korea it will be found advisable to pay some little attention
to the accompanying map of the peninsula.[12] The kingdom
was then, as now, divided into eight *dō* or provinces, the largest
of which, covering some two-fifths of the whole peninsula,
were P'yen-an and Ham-gyung in the extreme north. Of
the remaining six provinces four fronted the Yellow Sea,
and from north to south were Whang-ha, Kyung-geui (the
metropolitan province), Ch'ung-ch'ung and Chul-la, the last
also facing towards Kyūshū. Of the two on the Sea of Japan,
Kang-wun and Kyung-san, the topography of Kyung-san calls
for special study, inasmuch as it was on Kyung-san that the
first fury of the storm of invasion broke, and some of the
hardest fighting took place within its limits. In the centre
and north of the whole peninsula flow four rivers whose position
must be carefully noted. These are the Han, on which Seoul,
the capital, stands; the Imjin (Rinshin), which joins the
estuary of the Han; the Ta-dong, with the important town
of P'yeng-yang, the capital of P'yen-an province, on its northern
bank; and the Yalu, which separates the kingdom from the
Chinese province of Liao-tung. So much it is indispensably
and absolutely necessary to grasp before proceeding any further
with the text.

Having thus glanced at the state of affairs in the country
that was to have the ill-fortune of being the seat of operations,
we will now return to Japan. The missionaries assure us
that all the wisest in the empire detested the proposed expedition, and that remonstrances against it were not heard merely
because the haughty Hideyoshi had made it known that the
first man who dared to remonstrate would be shortened by
the length of his head. He had sent his Admiral, Kuki, to
superintend the construction of several hundred vessels in the
Bay of Isé, while the maritime Daimyō of the Chūgoku,
Shikoku, and Kyūshū were ordered to equip two large ships

---

sailors, there are nearly 300 men, with some pieces of artillery, *et quantité de
Feux d'artifice.* Each village is obliged to maintain a vessel completely equipped
and manned."

12 Any map of Korea in which Roman characters are used will be found
no easy study, for although the place names are expressed by the same characters,
yet they appear differently according as the characters are read in the Korean,
or the Japanese, or the Chinese fashion. In this map the Japanese renderings
of the characters are given within brackets below the Korean.

for each 100,000 *koku* of their assessed revenue, and to man
them every fishing village was compelled to furnish ten sailors
for every hundred houses it contained. In addition to the
complement of seamen thus raised a fighting force of 9,200
men was distributed among the vessels; the commanders, besides
Kuki, being Tōdō Wakizaka, Katō Yoshiaki, Kurushima, Suga,
and some others. Nagoya in Hizen had been designated as the
seat of the general headquarters, and here something like
a city quickly sprang up. Hideyoshi went down there in
September, 1592, and remained until the beginning of 1594,
making one visit to Ōsaka and Kyōto in the interval, however.
He had frequently given out that it was his purpose to proceed
to Korea, and there assume the supreme command in person;
but that he never did. So far as there was any supreme
command in the first Korean campaign it was held by Ukida
Hideiye, Daimyō of Bizen, Bitchū and Mimasaka, whom
Hideyoshi had once adopted as a son. But as a matter of
fact, the chief of each division was left with a comparatively
free hand, and acted to a large extent on his own initiative.

Of these divisions (in addition to the naval force) there
were ten in all—those of Konishi, Katō Kiyomasa, Kuroda the
younger, Shimadzu, Fukushima, Kobayakawa, Mōri, Ukida,
Asano, and Hashiba, footing up altogether to some 190,000 or
195,000. All these actually crossed to Korea, while besides
Hideyoshi's own household troops, amounting to over 28,000
men, 74,000 troops belonging to the Eastern and Northern
Daimyō remained behind at Nagoya, as a provision against
any possible attack from China."[13]

---

13 "The following table is translated from Mr. Kinoshita's *Hōtaikō Seigai
Shinshi* ("A New History of the Foreign Conquest of Toyotomi Taiko," written
in Chinese—5 vols., 1893), not yet completed. The author bases his statements
on the best authorities, and his book is considered the best that has ever appeared
on the Korean war.

FIRST CONTINGENT (KYŪSHŪ).		
Konishi	7,000	
Sō	5,000	
Matsuura	3,000	
Arima	2,000	
Omura	1,000	
Gotō	700	
		18,700
SECOND CONTINGENT (KYŪSHŪ).		
Katō Kiyomasa	8,000	
Nabeshima	12,000	
Sagara	800	
		20,800

In most foreign histories of this war, Konishi and Katō Kiyomasa are represented as sharing the chief command

THIRD CONTINGENT.

Kuroda Nagamasa	6,000
Ōtomo Yoshimune	6,000
	——— 12,000

FOURTH CONTINGENT (KYŪSHŪ).

Shimadzu Yoshihiro	10,000
Mōri Yoshinari	2,000
Takahashi	2,000
Akizuki	1,000
Itō	1,000
Shimazu Tadatoyo	1,000
	——— 17,000

FIFTH CONTINGENT (SHIKOKU).

Fukushima	5,000
Toda	4,000
Hachisuka	7,200
Chōsokabe	3,000
Ikoma	5,500
	——— 24,700

SIXTH CONTINGENT (KYŪSHŪ).

Kobayakawa	10,000
Mōri Hidekane	1,500
Tachibana	2,500
Takahashi Mototsugu	800
Tsukushi	900
	——— 15,700

SEVENTH CONTINGENT.

Mōri Terumoto } Kikkawa } Mōri Motoyasu }	30,000

138,900

The above seven contingents were to start first and open the roads to China.

EIGHTH CONTINGENT.

Ukida Hideiye	10,000
Masuda (Bugyō)	3,000
Ishida (Bugyō)	2,000
Ōtani	1,200
Mayeno	2,000
Katō Mitsuyasu	1,000
	——— 19,200

NINTH CONTINGENT.

Asano (Bugyō)	3,000
Miyabe	1,000
Nanjō	1,500
Kinoshita	850
Nakagawa	3,000
Inaba	1,400
	——— 10,750

And troops of Tokimura, Akashi, Bessho, Hattori, Hitotsuyanagi, Takenaka, Tani, &c.

TENTH CONTINGENT.

Hashiba Hidekatsu	8,000
Hashiba Tadaoki	3,500
Hasegawa	5,000
Kimura	3,500
Onogi	1,000
Kamei	1,000
	——— 22,000

between them. This mistake arises partly from the fact that their divisions constituted the extreme van of the invading host, and that consequently the brunt of the fighting fell on them. But besides this there was an exceedingly strong rivalry between these commanders, which was greatly inflamed by religious animosity. Katō was a staunch adherent of the Nichiren-shiu, the only really aggressive Buddhist sect in Japan, while Konishi was the main prop of the new foreign religion introduced by the Jesuits. His division of 18,700 men was composed almost entirely of Christians, for Matsuura of Hirado was the only one of his superior officers that was not a convert,

---

And troops of Makimura, Okamoto, Kasuya, Katagiri, Fujikake, Furuta, Shinjō, Hayakawa, &c.

The above three contingents were to enter Korea after the preceding seven contingents.

NAVAL FORCES.

Kuki	1,500
Tōdō	2,000
Wakizaka	1,500
Katō Yoshiaki	1,000
Kurushima	700
Suga	250

And troops of Kuwayama, Horiuchi, &c.

These distributions of troops are based on the *Tenshō-ki, Chōsen-Seibatsu-ki, Buke Bunshō-shū,* and *Taikō-ki.* The *Taikō-ki* puts the troops of Takahashi Mototane and Akizuki at 1,000, and those of Itō and Shimazu Todatoyo at 1,000. The *Chōsen-Seibatsu-ki* gives the following numbers:—

Kuroda Nagamasa, 5,000; Fukushima, 4,800; Toda, 8,900; Chōsokabe, 3,600; Ikoma, 5,000; Masuda, 2,000; Ōtani, 2,000; Mayeno, 1,000; Katō Yoshiaki, 750.

The *Buke Bunshō-shū* gives the following numbers:—

Sō, 1,000; Katō Kiyomasa, 10,000; Nakagawa, 1,500; Tōdō, 2,800; Wakizaka, 1,200; Katō Yoshiaki, 2,400.

About the rest all the authorities are agreed.

The troops who remained at Nagoya were as follows:—

Upwards of 5,000, constituting the front-guard of Hideyoshi.
Upwards of 5,000, constituting the rear-guard of Hideyoshi.
Upwards of 1,000 archers and musketeers led by Ōshima, Miyagi, &c.
Upwards of 1,000 under Kinoshita Yoshitaka.
500 retainers and guards of Ashikaga Yoshiaki, the former Shōgun.
6 bands of inspecting horsemen.
6 bands of immediate attendants of Hideyoshi.
Upwards of 12,000 messengers, foot-soldiers, and others.

All the above belonged directly to Hideyoshi. Besides them, there were:—

Upwards of 74,000 troops under Hashiba Hideyasu, Tokugawa Iyeyasu, Mayeda of Kaga, Oda Nobuo, Oda Nobukane, Uyesugi Kagekatsu, Gamō Ujisato, Yūki Hideyasu (Iyeyasu's second son), Sataké, Daté, Mogami, Mori (of Shinano), Niwa Nagashige, Kyōgoku. Satomi, Hashiba Hideyori, Hashiba Katsutoshi, Hori Murakami, Mizoguchi, Mizuno, Nambu Sanada, Sengoku, &c.

The grand total was upwards of 305,000.

The *Taikō-ki* gives the total of troops who crossed over to Korea as 205,570, and of those who remained at Nagoya as 102,450, making a grand total of 307,985.

The *Tenshō-ki* gives the number of troops who crossed over to Korea as 201,000 and of those who remained at Nagoya as 102,800, a grand total of 303,500.

The *Seibatsu-ki* says 208,650 crossed over to Korea, while 97,460 remained at Nagoya.

and many of Matsuura's three thousand men had received baptism. As Konishi was hand-in-glove with the priests (to whom he was extremely subservient), and kept constantly writing to them, as did also Arima and Ōmura, the Jesuits were uncommonly well informed about the work of Konishi's division, and about his differences with Katō Kiyomasa. So much interest did the priests take in these two special divisions that they neglected the others almost entirely, and as foreign accounts of this war are based chiefly upon passages in the missionary letters of the time, it comes to pass that attention has been almost exclusively directed to the work of these two generals of divisions, whose united commands amounted to no more than 38,700 men in a total land force of 190,000 or 200,000 troops. From the very first it was a hot and eager race between Konishi's persecuting Christians and the persecuting Katō with his pagans. However, Konishi had the best of the start from Tsushima, and actually succeeded in effecting a landing on Korean soil while Katō was still invoking his *Hotoke* for a favouring wind to swell his limp and empty sails, or rather anathematising his rival for having appropriated most of the transports.[14] The early morning of the 24th of May, 1592, was misty, and Konishi, seizing the opportunity to elude the formidable Korean cruisers, got his division on board and worked safely and unopposed across the stretch of some fifty miles of salt water that lay between him and Fusan. Curiously enough, the Commandant of Fusan happened that day to be hunting on Deer Island, at the entrance to the harbour, and he it was who first descried the approach of the invading host. He at once hurried back to his post, determined to meet the foe resolutely. What followed will best be told in the words of Charlevoix :—

"Konishi summoned the Governor to surrender, promising him his life. The summons was received with contempt, the Governor replying laughingly that he was going to send to ask the King his master for permission to yield to it. Konishi made no answer, but he employed all the next night in preparing the assault. He began it at four in the morning; the Koreans fought like brave men;

---

14 Some Japanese accounts say that it was Katō who got away first. But on this matter the missionaries, hand-in-glove with Konishi as they were, may be regarded as the better authorities. Recent research has served to disclose that on many points they are perfectly right, where popular Japanese histories are sadly astray.

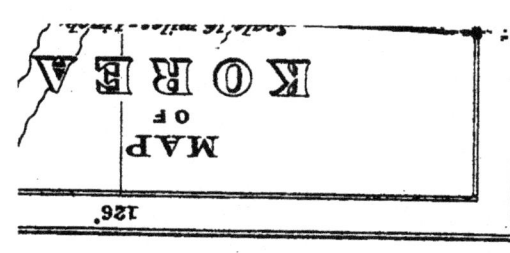

MAP
OF
KOREA

but the Governor having fallen, the Japanese broke in on all sides, and put every one who showed a sign of resistance to the edge of the sword. That day and the following they rested in Fusan; on the next they laid siege to Tong-nai (Tō-rai), a still stronger fortress, less than three leagues distant. The walls were better built and higher, and as it was the principal defence of the district it had been occupied by 20,000 of the best troops of the country. Konishi approached it about noon, having with him only the half of his army, and about 20,000 sailors and camp-coolies. The commandant was a young lord of twenty-two, a very brave man. Konishi at once planted ladders against the walls, and was the first to mount them himself. He was so well supported that after a very stiff fight of three or four hours (the Koreans say eight), in which, however, he had only one hundred killed and four hundred wounded, he filled the fosse with five thousand dead (among whom was the commandant) and found himself master of a place, which its position and its magazine full of a prodigious quantity of arms and of provisions made pass as the chief of all that frontier. Thus after this conquest, although there were still five strongholds to reduce before reaching the capital, the consternation throughout the country was so general that none of them ventured to expose themselves to the lot of the first two, and all opened their gates to the conqueror."

It may be as well to supplement the summary statement in the last sentence by a few details from Japanese and Korean sources. Three great roads lead up to Seoul from Fusan, and it was the central one of these that Konishi followed immediately after the storming of Tong-nai (Tō-rai). Passing through Yong-san (Ryo-san), which he found deserted, he crossed the Chak-won Pass on May 29th, routing the force holding it with a loss of three hundred men; and then pushing on through Mir-yang (Mitsuyō) and In-tong (Jindō), he forded the Naktong and entered Syen-san (Zenzan) on June 3rd. On the following day he drove the Korean General, Yi Gak, from Sang-ju (Shoshiu), and on June 5th he arrived at Mun-gyung (Bunkei), where he was joined by Katō Kiyomasa with the second (Kyūshū) division of 20,800 men. The latter had landed at Fusan on May 28th, four days after Konishi, and, following the Eastern route, stormed Kōng-ju (Keishiu) on the last of the month, putting three thousand Koreans to the sword. Thence advancing by, and quickly reducing, Yeng-tchyen (Yei-sen), Shin-ryeng (Shinnei), Eui-heung (Giko), Kun-wi (Gun-i), and Pi-on (Hian), he left the great Eastern road and joined Konishi at Mun-gyung (Bunkei) on June 5th, as has just been said. In front of the united commands of some 39,000 men lay the Cho-ryung (Chōrei) Pass, a strong defensive position where a handful of resolute men might have given serious trouble to a host.

Contrary to their expectation, and not a little to their satisfaction, the Japanese commanders found this position unheld, and their troops swarmed over the Cho-ryung "singing and dancing." A day's march beyond this lay Chung-ju (Chūshiu), perhaps the strongest fortress in the peninsula, but the fate of this stronghold was decided by a pitched battle in the open before it was reached.

When news of the fall of Fusan reached the Korean capital, Yi Il, practically the Commander-in-Chief, was ordered off to block the further advance of the Japanese. But when the military rolls were looked up it was found that the army was mostly on paper, and that a large majority of the men were either "sick" or "in mourning." So the whole force General Yi Il could muster amounted to just three hundred men. Even these could not be mustered at an hour's notice, and so, in order to obey the King's command, the unfortunate General had to start off alone, trusting that this pitiful handful of men would follow him. Of course the intention was to gather soldiers as he went, and he did succeed in getting at least the semblance of an army together. However, the course of events quickly disclosed that Yi Il was just as useful without as with an army, for as soon as he heard of the approach of the Japanese he bolted up the Cho-ryung Pass, making not the slightest attempt to block it, while the provincial levies that had meanwhile gathered dispersed, as they not unnaturally refused to be commanded by a coward. In the meantime Sil Yip, the Vice-Minister of War, had been sent to Chung-ju (Chūshiu), and had there collected a considerable force. It was his intention to hold the Cho-ryung Pass, the key to the whole situation, but when Yi Il appeared as a fugitive, Sil Yip determined to remain at Chung-ju. One of his lieutenants strongly urged him to seize the Cho-ryung at any price, but he made answer: "No, they are infantry, and we are cavalry. If we can once get them into the plain we can use our battle-flails on them with deadly effect." To carry out this project, "Sil Yip selected a spot that seemed to him most suitable. It was a great amphitheatre made by high mountains, while on the other side, like the chord of an arc, flowed the river T'an-geun-da. The only approaches to this plain were two narrow passages at either end where the mountains came down to the river bank. In this death-trap, then, General Sil drew up his entire command and awaited the coming of the invaders. It is easy to imagine the glee with which the Japanese saw this arrangement, for it meant the extermination of the only army that lay between them and Seoul. Strong detachments were sent to block the passages at the ends of the plain, while the main body scaled the mountains and came down upon the doomed army as if from the sky. The spears and swords of the descending legions flashed like fire, while the roar of the musketry made the very earth to tremble. The result was an almost instantaneous stampede. The Koreans made for the two narrow exits, but found them heavily guarded by the Japanese. They were now literally between 'the devil and the deep sea,' for they had the appalling spectacle of the hideously masked Japanese on the one hand and the deep waters of the river on the other. The whole army was driven into the river or mercilessly cut down by the swords of the Japanese. General Sil Yip himself made a brave stand, and killed with his own hand seventeen of the enemy before he fell. Out of the whole army only a handful escaped, and among them was the coward Yi Il, who managed to get across the river."

Mr. Hulbert's authorities allege that Katō's division, as well as Konishi's, was engaged in this affair. The missionaries, who doubtless get their information from Konishi, tell another story, however. Katō had come into the main central road just ahead of Konishi's advance, and had insisted on pushing forward in the van. Konishi objected to this, and Katō had had un-willingly to make way for him. When Konishi's division came upon Sil Yip's army of cavalry, Katō had quietly halted and did nothing, expecting that Konishi would be overborne, and that he (Katō) could then have the glory of extricating his rival's com-mand from destruction.[15] When Konishi achieved a brilliant victory, Katō was apprehensive lest his conduct might be reported to Hideyoshi, with inconvenient results to himself. Accordingly he asked to be allowed to join Konishi in his advance and contem-plated siege of Seoul, whereupon Konishi made answer that Katō

[15] According to the Jesuits, Sil Yip's force amounted to nearly 70,000 men, of whom 8,000 were killed and many made prisoners. The Japanese put the Korean losses at 3,000 dead and several hundred prisoners. See Charlevoix, vol. iv. p. 171 seq.; Crasset, vol. i. p. 617.

might follow him, but that it was the Taikō's intent that each division should remain under the orders of its own original commander. "Upon this answer Toranosque (Katō) decamped secretly, and advanced by side roads in the hope of reaching Seoul first; but the Great Admiral (Konishi) suspected his design, and, as he had the better guides, he preceded him by several hours." This account of the matter, as has been hinted, was doubtless obtained from Konishi himself, and is probably fairly correct. At all events, what is certain is that the two divisions separated at Chung-ju (Chūshiu), and that while Konishi pressed on hot-foot by his original route, the main central road, Katō swung off to the *West* (not the East, as Mr. Hulbert says), and, hurrying rapidly through Chuk-san (Chikusan) and Yong-in (Ryojin), reached the southern bank of the river Han, opposite the western suburbs of the Korean capital. No boats were to be found, but seeing some waterfowl peacefully swimming about on the further side of the stream, Katō judged that it was held by no hostile force. One of his retainers swam the river and brought back a boat, and thus the second division managed to cross the Han, and to enter Seoul by its southern gate on the forenoon of June 12th, 1592. It was with considerable mortification that Katō found the city already in the occupation of Konishi, who had passed through its eastern gate some hours earlier that same morning, while both must have been disappointed to learn that if they had been four days earlier they would have captured the Korean King and all his family. Both Konishi and Katō had certainly made good time on their way up to Seoul, the former arriving there in nineteen, and the latter in fourteen days from the landing in Fusan.

Four days after the occupation of the capital by the first and second (Kyūshū) divisions, the third made its appearance there. Young Kuroda, with his 12,000 men, had landed at Fusan almost immediately after Katō, and had at once turned off along the coast to the West. On May 31st he assaulted and captured Kim-hai (Kinkai), inflicting terrific damage on the enemy, and then pushed on to Syeng-ju (Seishiū). Here he was joined by 3,000 men of the fourth division (Shimadzu's), who had stormed Tchyang-wun (Shōgen) under the leadership of Mōri and Itō. Their way from Syeng-ju (Seishiū) lay through Chiré (Chirei), Kim-san (Kinzan), over the Chiu-p'ung-ryung

(Shū-fū-rei) Pass and by Yong-dong (Yei-dō). After killing some thousands of the enemy at the storming of Ch'ung-ju (Seishiu) Castle, they reached Seoul on the 16th of June. On that same day Ukida Hideiye, who, besides bringing his own (eighth) contingent of 19,200 troops, acted as the Japanese Commander-in-Chief, arrived in the capital, while the fourth (Shimadzu), sixth (Kobayakawa), seventh (Mōri), and fifth (Shikoku) *corps d'armée* had all effected a landing, and the Japanese fleet of several hundred vessels had been anchored near Fusan since June 7th. An order was soon issued by Hideyoshi detailing the commanders to the charge of the various provinces of Korea. Katō was to operate in Ham-gyung, and Konishi in P'yen-an, while Kuroda was to reduce Whang-ha, and Mōri Yoshinari Kang-wun. Mōri, with his thirty thousand troops, was to occupy Kyung-san; Kobayakawa, Chul-la; the men of Shikoku (Fukushima, Chōsokabe, Hachisuka, and so forth), Ch'ung-ch'ung; and Kyung-geui, the metropolitan province, was to be kept in order by Ukida, the Commander-in-Chief, from his headquarters in Seoul.

Having accompanied the Japanese thus far in their triumphant march, or rather rush, let us now pass to the side of the Koreans for a little. One morning, shortly after the wreck of Sil Yip's cavalry force to the south of Chung-ju, a naked soldier came panting through the south gate of Seoul with intelligence of the disaster from which he had escaped. "I have escaped with my life and I am come to tell you that flight is your only hope," was the conclusion of his tale. In the Korean authorities followed by Mr. Hulbert there is a vivid and graphic account of the panic that at once ensued, of the distracted councils in the Palace, and of the general hopelessness of the situation. The Minister of War received orders to detail troops to man the city walls. But in these walls were thirty thousand battlements, each with three embrasures; and in lieu of the ninety thousand men for whom provision had thus been made, no more than seven thousand could be drummed together. Flight was really the only resource left open, and while one Royal Prince was sent into Ham-gyung and the other into Kang-wun, the King, his concubines, and his courtiers passed out of the city for the North, with the view of ultimately taking refuge on Chinese soil if such a necessity should be forced upon him. With "the moving account" of the Royal flight given by Korean authorities we will here dispense; doubtless the drenching rain and the short commons of the retreat to Song-do (Shōto) did trouble his Korean Majesty, his eunuchs, and his courtiers somewhat, but they would have mattered but little to any real ruler of men—an Alexander, a Cæsar, a Peter of Russia, a Napoleon, a Hideyoshi, or an Iyeyasu. What perhaps is worthy of citation from "the moving account" is the circumstance that as the King and his escort passed through the "Peking Pass" his Majesty could see that the city behind him was in flames, and that it had been fired not by invaders, but by his own dutiful subjects. Even before his midnight flight his own palace had been looted by the city rabble, and now it, together with three other Royal residences, the treasury, and the granary, was burning furiously. In one store-house all the deeds of the Government slaves, and in another all those of privately owned thralls, were kept; and both these buildings, together with their contents, became ashes. On June 12th, the day of Konishi and Katō's entry into Seoul, the Royal fugitive reached Song-do (Shōto); and when Kim Myung-wun, who had been entrusted with the defence of the river Han, fled to the Imjin (Rinshin) river, and thence sent a letter telling the King of the occupation of his capital by the Japanese, his Majesty again set his Royal face towards the North, and did not pause until he was comparatively safe in P'yeng-yang beyond the Ta-dong (Dai-dō)

Now that Seoul and the line of the Han were lost, the only thing that remained for the Koreans to do was to block the Japanese advance at the Imjin (Rinshin) stream. Orders were issued for the muster of a huge force at its ferries; and in a few weeks an army, formidable as far as mere numbers went, was massed there. But before dealing with this episode in the campaign, let us see what was meanwhile passing to the south of the Imjin and in the East. In these quarters the Peninsulars had even by this time begun to pluck up heart, and to endeavour to make some real head against the invaders. The fourth Japanese division (Shimadzu's) had been sent into the province of Kang-wun; and although it rapidly over-ran this great tract of territory, the reduction of Yung-wun, held by no more than five thousand Koreans, cost the Satsuma *samurai* a heavy bill in casualties. Before this had happened, however, the Japanese had had another considerable success elsewhere. The Governor of Chul-la had raised eight thousand men and had set out to join the King in the North; but his heart had failed him, and he had retreated to Kong-ju (Kōshiu). Here he was joined by the levies of Ch'ung-ch'ung and Kyung-sang, and the whole force, put by the Koreans at one hundred thousand and by the Japanese at fifty thousand men, then set out for the Imjin (Rinshin) river. Not far from Seoul, however, they came across a Japanese force entrenched on Puk-du-mun (Hokutomon) Mountain, and they resolved to attack it. While the action was raging, Japanese reinforcements arrived from the capital, and the Southern Korean army of fifty thousand was scattered with the loss of over one thousand killed and several hundred prisoners. Some of its battalions made for the Imjin, and participated in the subsequent engagement there. Before this, however, the Koreans had actually for the first time scored a real victory. Sin Gak had been associated with Kim Myung-wun in the defence of the Han, but after Kim had thrown all his engines of defence into the stream, and fled, Sin had likewise to retire. He at once began to gather troops in Kyung-geui, the metropolitan province, and he was soon joined by a contingent from Ham-gyung. The huge granary at Ryong-san (Ryuzan), near Seoul, from which the invaders were drawing all their supplies, had been fired by the Koreans, and this had made foraging necessary. A considerable body of Ukida's own special division had got as far as Yang-ju (Yōshiu) on this duty, when they found themselves confronted by Sin Gak's levies. A desperate contest followed, in which the Japanese were thoroughly beaten, and were forced to retreat with serious loss. Naturally, the moral effect of this was immense. But just at this point the incurably weak spot of Korea disclosed itself. While all Kyung-geui was ringing with the exploit of the successful commander, and people were beginning to see that all was not lost, a swift messenger was on his way from the King bearing a sword and a letter ordering the instant execution of Sin Gak. Kim, to cover his own cowardice at the Han, had accused Sin Gak of desertion, and another General, Yu Hong, recognising a powerful rival in Sin, had urged that the coward should be slain. Not long after the death-messenger was dispatched, news of the exploit at Yang-ju (Yōshiu) came in. A messenger was at once hurried off by the King to countermand his former order; but when this emissary arrived at Yang-ju the gallant Sin Gak had been shortened by the length of his head an hour before.

At this time Konishi and Katō's columns were on the route northwards. No opposition was met with till the Imjin was reached, but here progress seemed to be barred most effectually. The northern bank of the stream was a long flat stretch of sand,—an ideal place for deploying the huge Korean host that had meanwhile assembled here. Contrariwise, the southern bank was a long steep bluff, pierced by only one narrow gulch, through which the great northern road ran down to the ferry. This was the only point whence a crossing could be effected; and in any passage of the stream only a few boats could cross together, and these would be exposed to the concentrated arrow-fire of a great portion of the force deployed on the flat where the landing had to be made. Besides all this, there were no boats, the stream was wide, and the current strong. It was no wonder, then, that here the quick step of the Japanese advance was abruptly stopped for the time. For ten long days the islanders sat upon the bluff, gazing down upon the exultant Koreans beyond, and impotently chafing to bring matters to the shock of battle. It is probable that if the Korean commanders had been content to hold their position, meanwhile imparting discipline and cohesion to their levies, the subsequent course of the campaign would have been confined to the southern half of the peninsula, and possible that, in view of the results of the contemporaneous naval operations, the islanders might ultimately have been either annihilated or starved into surrender. What, however, the Koreans lacked at this time were commanders; or, to speak more precisely, what they lacked at the Imjin stream was a commander, for of officers that presumed to act as commanders they had more than enough. The nominal chief of the army here was that Kim who had abandoned the line of the Han in such precipitation. But "a number of other generals were there, and each held his own troops in hand, and each wished to distinguish himself and so step over the heads of the rest into the good graces of the King. This would mean preferment and wealth. There was absolutely no supreme command, there was no common plan, there was nothing but jealousy and suspicion."

Accordingly things were by no means so desperate for the Japanese as they seemed. When the eleventh morning broke, the Koreans noticed a great stir among the enemy on the opposite bluff—they were running to and fro carrying bundles from place to place. Soon smoke and flame showed the islanders had fired their camp; and presently the whole force was seen defiling off towards the south. A shout of exultation rose from the sandy flat on the north of the stream as the Koreans perceived that the advance had been abandoned. A young commander, Sin Gil by name, who knew nothing of war, impetuously and clamorously called for an immediate and energetic pursuit. Some of his men urged that some preliminary scouting should at least be done, and Sin answered their representations by ordering their heads to be struck off at once. An old general then expostulated with this Korean fire-eater, but Bobadil drew upon him, and called him a coward. This nettled the old man so keenly that, throwing all thoughts of sound tactics to the wind, he at once declared that he would lead the advance and be the first to fall. Thereupon Sin had perforce to follow; and the two commands at once passed the ferry. Of course they found themselves ambushed by the Japanese; and the wreck of their commands found that most of the boats had re-crossed the stream, and so got annihilated at the water's edge. This was bad, indeed; but yet in itself it did not necessarily spell disaster. The Japanese had secured only a few boats—too few to be of much service in face of the main Korean army, which still remained intact on the sandy flats beyond. However, the Korean commanders came most gallantly to the assistance of the invaders. As soon as they witnessed the terrific slaughter of the pursuing force on the other bank, they mounted their horses and fled. "The moment the soldiers saw the flight of their generals they raised a decisive shout, 'The generals are running away'; and forthwith followed their example."

Konishi, who had left Seoul on June 27th (1592), had been

the first to reach the Imjin. Here he was joined by Katō a few days after his arrival, and on passing the stream the two divisions (first and second) passed on together to Song-do (Shōto). At this point they separated—Katō swinging off to the east towards the province of Ham-gyung, while Konishi held straight on the northern road, which the Japanese fondly believed was to lead them to Peking. This was on July 9th. The common story is that it was the mutual jealousy of the two leaders (and feudal neighbours) which made this separation necessary, and that their respective routes were decided by the time-honoured method of casting lots. The latter proposition may be doubted; by Hideyoshi's instructions sent to Seoul, Ham-gyung had already been assigned as Katō's sphere of action, while P'yen-an had been marked out for Konishi, who had the best of the luck in this matter, for it was he who had to follow the direct line of advance. But Katō's work, although not so full of interest perhaps, was at once necessary and meritorious. The men of Ham-gyung were the best soldiers in the kingdom, and if that province had been left to itself, the main Japanese communications would infallibly have been cut by determined flank attacks from the north-east. The resistance Katō here met with was really a stubborn one. Several detachments of his were very roughly handled, while his main force on one occasion found itself in a very precarious situation. Even when nominally reduced, the province remained far from quiet, and the winter of 1592-3 was a tolerably lively one for the men of Kumamoto and Saga among the snow-drifts of frozen North Korea. One important incident in this special campaign was the capture of two Royal princes, which proved a strong piece for the Japanese when it came to the game of diplomacy.

Let us now follow Konishi on the direct great western road to the north. On July 15th, six days after his separation from Katō, he arrived at the Ta-dong (Dai-dō), just in front of P'yeng-yang, where the Korean King still lingered. At this time he had no more than his own single division of seventeen or eighteen thousand men; but he was almost immediately joined by young Kuroda (third division) with some twelve thousand more. The force that now lay before P'yeng-yang was mainly a Christian one. All its superior officers—Konishi, Kuroda, Ōtomo, Arima, Ōmura, and Sō— were converts, with the single exception of Matsuura of Hirado. Of course this circumstance had no influence upon the military operations, but it is an interesting one to note. The islanders were here again confronted with the problem they had solved at the Imjin—a broad swift stream to pass, and no boats to cross in. Besides this, beyond it lay the best fortress in Northern Korea, well provisioned, and held by a formidable garrison.

On the night of his arrival, Konishi sent a Korean prisoner across the river with a letter for the King asking for an interview in mid-stream, with a certain Yi Dok-hyung (Ri Toku-kei) as his representative. Next morning Yi was sculled to the middle of the river, where Konishi, Sō of Tsushima, and the monk Genso met him. Konishi at once came to the point. "The cause of all this trouble," said he, "is that Korea would not give a safe conduct to our envoys to Nanking, but if you will give us an open road into China, all the trouble for you will be at an end." Yi's answer was: "If you will send this army back to Japan we can confer about the matter, but we will listen to nothing so long as you are on Korean soil." Konishi continued: "We have no wish to harm you. We have wished such a conference as this before, but have not had such an opportunity until to-day." "Turn about and take your troops back to Japan," repeated the Korean. Konishi lost his temper at this, and cried out: "Our soldiers always go forward, and know nothing about going backwards." Thus the conference proved abortive.[16]

Strangely enough, as at the Imjin, it was by the Koreans assuming the offensive that the Japanese were freed from their unpleasant position before P'yeng-yang. Kim and his fellow-

---

[16] Two attempts had been made to negotiate on the way up from Fusan to Seoul. The Governor of Yölsan (Ursan), captured by Katō, had been released and sent with a letter to the King. But his Excellency, not wishing to appear as a released prisoner, said he had escaped and destroyed the letter. At Shang-chin, in Kyung-san, Konishi captured a Korean, Oshiun, who knew Japanese, and this man was sent to Seoul with a letter from Hideyoshi, and a communication to the Korean Foreign Minister asking why no reply had been given to the dispatch forwarded by the Governor of Yölsan, and saying: "If the Koreans wish for peace, let them send Ri Tokukei (Yi Dok-hyung) to Chung-ju (Chūshiu)." This Ri (or Yi) had been the official entertainer of the early Japanese embassy. He now undertook this mission and set out with a letter from the Foreign Minister, and accompanied by Oshiun as interpreter. On his way he heard of the fall of Chung-ju (Chūshiu), and sent Oshiun forward to find if the report was correct. The interpreter fell into the hands of Katō's troops and was executed as a spy, and Ri (Yi) thereupon abandoned the mission and returned.

commander, Yun Du-su, thought to make short work of the
business by a sudden night attack upon the camp of "the
dwarfs." With a picked body of troops they set out to ford
the stream at Neung-no-do, a little above the city. But the
fording of the river, always a difficult operation at night, took
longer than had been allowed for; and the summer dawn was
already trembling in the sky when the expedition came in
touch with the Japanese outposts. The only thing now open
for the Koreans was to retrace their steps; and this was fatal,
for it revealed the position of the fords. After a hearty break-
fast the islanders got into order, and made for the passage
in the highest of spirits. They swarmed across in such numbers
that the defenders of the bank were almost at once hopelessly
overborne; and the Japanese, following hard upon their traces,
entered the city along with them. The Korean commanders
now could do no better than to order the Ta-dong gate to be
opened and to tell the people to escape for their lives, while
the soldiers threw all their heavier arms into a pond as they
poured out of the town in headlong confusion. They had no
time to fire the granaries, however, and these, filled to repletion,
fell into the hands of the Japanese, who now quickly settled
down in P'yeng-yang, and waited till the necessary developments
of the grand strategy of the campaign had been completed
elsewhere. As for the Korean King, he had fled from P'yeng-
yang, whence, after one or two halts on the road, he made
his way to Eui-ju (Gishiu), a few miles south of the Yalu, the
north-western limit of his realms. From here urgent messengers
were again sent to Nanking to implore assistance.

But before dealing with this part of the story it is necessary
to obtain a clear idea of the general strategy of the campaign,
the reason for Konishi's and Kuroda's inaction in P'yeng-yang,
and why it was that the Japanese never set foot on Chinese
soil. To clear the way, the following remarks of Mr. Hulbert
are helpful :—

"We notice that the military prowess of the Japanese, their
thorough equipment, and their martial spirit took Korea by surprise.
It caused a universal panic, and for the first few weeks it was
impossible to get the soldiers to stand up and fight the enemy, to say
nothing of the generals. The troops and the generals were mutually
suspicious of each other, and neither seemed to have any faith in
the courage or loyalty of the other. But now the time had come
when the impetuous sweep of the Japanese was stopped for the time

being by their occupation of Seoul. The fall of the capital was
looked upon by the King and the people as a great calamity, but
in reality it was the very thing that saved the King from the necessity
of crossing the border, and perhaps it saved Nanking itself. If the
Japanese had kept up that impetuous, overwhelming rush with which
they came up from Fusan to Seoul; and, instead of stopping at the
capital, had pushed straight for the Yalu river, they would have
been knocking at the gates of Nanking before the sleepy Celestials
knew that Hideyoshi dreamed of paying back in kind the haughty
summons of Kublai Khan four hundred years before. The stop at
Seoul gave the Korean forces a breathing space and an opportunity
to get into shape to do better work than they had done. The people
came to see that, instead of painted devils, as they had at first
appeared, the Japanese were flesh and blood like themselves, and
the terror which their fierce aspect at first inspired gradually wore
off and in so far lessened the discrepancy between the two combatants.
On the side of the Japanese there was only one favourable factor,
their tremendous fighting power in battle. There they had it all
their own way. But, on the other hand, they were in a thickly
populated and hostile country, practically cut off from their base
of supplies, and dependent entirely upon forage for their sustenance.
Under these circumstances their position was sure to become worse
rather than better, and the real strength of the Koreans was sure to
show itself. If a Korean regiment was swept off in battle there were
millions from which to recruit, while every Japanese who fell caused
just so much irreparable injury to the invading army. We shall
see that it was the abandonment of the 'double quick' that eventually
drove the Japanese back across the straits."

And in connection with Konishi's halt at P'yeng-yang
Mr. Hulbert writes:—

"Here again the Japanese made a grand mistake. Their only
hope lay in pushing on at full speed into China, for even now the
force that was to crush them was being collected, and every day
of delay was lessening their chances of success."

This may indeed be true; but it seems to show a misconception of the strategy projected by Hideyoshi. How long did
the Japanese really dally in the Korean capital? Konishi had
been nineteen days on the march between Fusan and the
capital, and during this space he had stormed two strong
fortresses and fought one great battle. He may well have
fancied that a short breathing space would be no bad thing
for his troops. Yet he allowed them no more than fifteen
days, for he entered Seoul on June 12th, and his division
defiled through its gates for the North on the 27th of the
same month. Katō, who arrived in the capital on the same
day as his rival after a march of fifteen days, stayed a
day or two longer in it than Konishi, but he was still able
to effect a junction with him at the Imjin. As for Kuroda,

who had reached Seoul on June 16th, he marched sufficiently
well to join Konishi on the southern bank of the Ta-dong in
front of P'yeng-yang on July 15th.   Now all these three
advance divisions amounted to no more than fifty thousand men.
Were these enough for a race on Nanking?   It must be
remembered that even in Korea their communications would
have been infallibly cut by the men of Ham-gyung province,
while in China they would simply have been engulphed and
swallowed up.   And events soon showed that every man of the
other divisions (fourth, fifth, sixth, seventh, and eighth) that
had landed was necessary to hold the South and centre of
the peninsula.   All this Hideyoshi had made allowance for.
His purpose was that the reinforcements he held at Nagoya
should be dispatched by sea to join Konishi at P'yeng-yang, and
the latter, with his two divisions swelled by four or five fresh
ones from Japan, should then be thrown forward, while no
effort was meanwhile to be spared either to reduce or conciliate
the Koreans, and, if possible, actually to secure their co-operation.
If the six divisions employed in holding them down could be
set free for service beyond the Yalu, the Chinese would then find
that a unified and united Japan was really a redoubtable
antagonist.   But, unfortunately for the Japanese, their strategy
was utterly dislocated at this point.   To ensure the success of
their gigantic project, it was absolutely necessary that they
should hold complete command of the sea, and on the blue
water they very soon found themselves as thoroughly overmatched and out-classed as the raw Korean levies had been
on land at the beginning of the campaign.   Hideyoshi had
shown himself very eager (May 4th, 1586) to secure the services
of two first-class Portuguese vessels with their fine artillery for
this campaign, and his failure to secure these was to prove costly.

It has been mentioned that several hundred vessels of the
Japanese fleet had arrived at Fusan on June 7th.   Whether
it was at the sight of these, or of another fresh squadron,
that the Admiral of Kyung-sang province lost heart and
thought of scuttling his ships, does not clearly appear.   The
point is not material; but what is material is that this Admiral
was induced to send and ask for help from Yi Sun-sin, the
Admiral of the neighbouring province of Chul-la.   The appeal
was promptly answered, and Yi soon joined his colleague of

Kyung-sang with a squadron of eighty vessels at the island of Ok-po, where a Japanese squadron rode at anchor. With the wind behind them the Koreans swooped down on the islanders, and soon had twenty-six of their craft in flames from their fire-arrows. So sturdy was the Korean onset, so determined their efforts at grappling and boarding, that the enemy were constrained to give way, and crowd on all sail to escape. Admiral Yi succeeded in cutting off a good many of the fugitives, while the others hurried back to seek safety in Fusan. Shortly afterwards he captured or sunk another dozen Japanese war-ships in a stiff fight at No-ryang; and this made him really respected by the enemy. To quote Mr. Hulbert:—

"The main reason for his unparalleled successes on the sea was the possession of a peculiar war-vessel of his own invention and construction. It was called the *Kwi-sun*, or 'tortoise-boat,' from its resemblance to that animal. There is no doubt that the tortoise furnished the model for the boat. Its greatest peculiarity was a curved deck of iron plates like the back of a tortoise which completely sheltered the fighters and rowers beneath. In front was a hideous dragon's head, erect, with wide open mouth, through which arrows and other missiles could be discharged. There was another opening in the rear, and six on either side for the same purpose. On top of the curved deck there was a narrow walk from stem to stern, and another across the middle from side to side, but every other part of the back bristled with iron spikes so that an enemy who should endeavour to board her would find himself immediately impaled upon a score of spear-heads. This deck, being of iron, rendered the ship impervious to fire arrows, and so the occupants could go into action with as much security as one of our modern battle-ships could go into engagement with the wooden war-vessels of a century ago. In addition to this, she was built for speed, and could easily overtake anything afloat. This made her doubly formidable, for even flight could not avail the enemy. She usually did more execution after the fight commenced than before, for she could overtake and ram them one by one probably better than she could handle them when drawn up in line of battle. It is said that the hulk of this remarkable ship (though others say it is only a *facsimile*) lies in the sand to-day in the village of Ko-sung, on the coast of Kyung-sang province. It was seen there by Lieutenant Geo. C. Foulk, U.S.N., in 1884. The people of the town have an annual festival in his honour, when they launch a fleet of boats and sail about the harbour in honour of the great Yi Sun-sin and his 'tortoise-boat.'"

In the engagement last described, the Japanese in their flight were so terrified by this strange craft, which pursued them and sank them one by one, that they stamped their feet and cried out that it was more than of human workmanship. And indeed it was almost more than human for that century, for it anticipated by nearly three hundred years the ironclad war-ship. In this battle Admiral Yi was wounded in the shoulder, but made no sign. He urged on his men to the very last, and finally, when they drew off, weary of slaughter, he bared his shoulder and ordered the bullet to be cut out.[17]

Shortly after this he fell in with Kurushima's squadron (seven hundred fighting men besides the crews), and destroyed the whole of it. "Kurushima fought desperately, and when all his men had fallen and his ship had been burned he effected a landing on an island and committed *hara-kiri.*" A few days later a Japanese convoy, with supplies, escorted by twenty-six war-vessels, was captured, while this remarkable naval campaign was closed by the destruction of a few Japanese vessels near Yong-deung Harbour.

This was a brilliant beginning indeed; but it was merely the earnest of greater achievements. No doubt divining what the strategy devised at Hideyoshi's headquarters was, Admiral Yi retired to the south-western end of Chul-la province and had all the coast eastwards from this point patrolled by swift cruisers. One day in the eighth month (July 9th—August 7th)—just about the time that Konishi had seized P'yeng-yang—one of his scouting vessels appeared driven at full speed with the intelligence that the head of a vast Japanese Armada, with nearly one hundred thousand men on board, would soon appear on the horizon. This number, taken from Korean sources, is doubtless exaggerated; but it is probable that possibly two divisions or so had embarked at Tsushima, or perhaps Fusan, to make

17 About Yi Sun-sin's "tortoise-boat," Mr. Hayashi, in his *Chōsen Kinsei-shi* ("History of Modern Korea"), writes as follows:—"The 'tortoise-boat' was invented by Yi Sun-sin. The Korean history of the war (*Kokuchō Hōkan*) says that the boat was covered with boards like a tortoise-shell. On all the other parts sharp iron spikes were closely planted. In front was a dragon's head, the mouth of which served as a port for bullets to pass through. At the stern was the tortoise's tail, under which there was another opening for bullets. On each side there were six openings. In this way guns could be fired from the four sides. Besides, the boat could be propelled in every direction, and was so fast that it seemed to fly. In the *Ching-pi-nok* and some other books descriptions of this boat are given. A book called *Richūbu Zensho* (which describes the career of Yi Sun-sin) gives the most particular description, and also contains two illustrations of the boat. But no book says that iron plates were used in its construction. As a matter of fact, Japanese war-ships of the time were covered with iron plates at some points. But a Chicago newspaper gives a report, on the authority of a British Naval Report of 1883 from Korea, to the effect that the Korean war-ships of the sixteenth century were covered with iron plates like a tortoise-shell, that the wooden ships of the Japanese were therefore no match for the Korean ships, that a relic of a tortoise-boat was found at Yong-yong (?), and that the Koreans were the first to build an ironclad. This report appears to me to be erroneous."

their way round and up to Konishi by water. The Korean
Admiral promptly weighed anchor and went out to meet the
hostile fleet. Before it came within striking distance, Yi turned
and fled, and the Japanese vessels, pressing on in headlong
and impetuous pursuit, broke their line and fell into disorder.
When opposite Han-san Island, however, Yi ordered *not his
ship, but his rowers about*; and with what had been his stern,
but now his prow, promptly rammed the leading vessel among
his astounded pursuers. Leaving her to go to the bottom at
her leisure, he rapidly passed on to deal with the others in
a similar fashion; and presently his whole fleet, which had
meanwhile put about, came down upon the confused Japanese
in splendid order and with terrific impetus. "Seventy-one
of the Japanese vessels were sunk that day, and it is said
the very sea was red." But this was merely one instalment
of the day's work. Before the evening fell a reinforcing squadron
came up from An-gol Harbour near Han-san.

"The attack straightway began, and soon the Japanese were put
in the same plight as their fellows had been. Many, seeing how
impossible it was to make headway against the iron ship, beached
their vessels and fled by land; so on that same day forty-eight ships
more were burned. The few that escaped during the fight sped
eastward towards home. So ended, we may well believe, one of
the great naval battles of the world. It may well be called the
Salamis of Korea. It signed the death-warrant of the invasion.
It frustrated the great motive of the expedition—the humbling of
China; and thenceforth, although the war dragged through many
a long year, it was carried on solely with a view to mitigating
the disappointment of Hideyoshi."

In all this, except as regards the motive for the war and
its prolongation, Mr. Hulbert is probably perfectly correct. The
humbling of China and the mitigation of his disappointment
no doubt did weigh much with Hideyoshi, but, as we shall
presently endeavour to show, there were other important considerations involved. Leaving that point for future discussion,
however, what we have to note here is that it was a naval
battle that really decided the campaign and saved Korea, even
when a hostile force of close on two hundred thousand of the
finest soldiers of the age were encamped upon her soil. This
may well raise the question whether an enemy double or triple
as strong could hold Great Britain, providing the islanders
contrived either to retain or to regain complete command of
the blue water. The discussion of the practicability and the

possible utility of a modern "tortoise-boat" ramming with bow or stern indifferently may be left to naval architects,— and his Majesty the German Emperor.

Meanwhile, before proceeding to deal with the troubles of Konishi at the farthest point of the Japanese advance, let us see how it was faring with the army of occupation in the various provinces of Korea, to the south of this, for of the fortunes of Katō in Ham-gyung we have already treated—not exhaustively. but sufficiently for our purpose. Nearly all the districts held by the Japanese had been stripped of what should have been their natural defenders, for all the regular provincial levies had been drafted to the north beyond the Ta-dong River, to protect the King and to block the advance of the invaders. But this proved to be the reverse of an evil either for the occupied provinces or for Korea at large. The ordinary levies were mostly commanded by incompetent cowards, who had obtained their commissions not by merit, or on the ground of any suitability for their posts, but by the adroit flattery and wholesale bribery that become such potent arts when the destinies of a kingdom are at the mercy of the eunuchs and the flunkeys of a corrupt and effeminate Court. Many of these officers had thought it no shame to bolt precipitately even when their commands evinced a disposition to stand firm, and some of them had actually been dragged from their lurking-places and forced to resume their posts by their own men! It is not hard to understand that the absence of commanders of such a type was much preferable to their presence. The result was that the peasantry, enraged by the devastation of their crops and their homesteads by the Japanese foragers, had to find their own natural leaders when they came to the conclusion that it was just as well to die fighting as to perish from starvation. It soon appeared that there was no lack of bold and resolute captains for the innumerable guerilla bands which now formed in every one of the occupied districts. The list of these leaders given by Mr. Hulbert is far from complete; yet it gives the names of two formidable chiefs in Chul-la, eight in Kyung-sang, seven in Ch'ung-ch'ung, as many as eleven in the metropolitan province of Kyung-geui, and two each in Ham-gyung and P'yen-an. Besides the actual damage they did in cutting off stragglers, they wore down the enemy, both men and horses, by keeping them perpetually on the alert and in motion, and by subjecting them to the strain of a haunting sense of continual insecurity.

One of these leaders, known as "the General of the Red Robe," seemed to pervade nearly the whole of Chul-la, so rapid were his changes of base. His intelligence department was efficiency itself, "and whenever the Japanese encamped the Koreans gathered on the surrounding hills at night, each carrying a framework that supported five torches, and so the islanders fancied they were surrounded by great numbers of Koreans, and anxiety kept them always awake. The best of the Korean soldiers were detailed to watch mountain passes and defiles and look for opportunities to cut off small bodies of the enemy's forces. Traps of various kinds were set into which they occasionally fell, and they were so harassed and worried that at last they were compelled to withdraw entirely from three whole districts of the province."

Before many months were over a union of some of these bands in Chul-la contrived to inflict punishment upon the enemy which led to the evacuation of nearly the whole of the province. On entering the town of I-ch'-i (Riji) a large body of Japanese had been so roughly handled that they had to beat a retreat, and after some desultory fighting in the vicinity, in which they at last got the best of it, they again advanced upon I-ch'-i. The Koreans, however, blocked a mountain pass they had to negotiate; and as the Japanese had to come creeping up it on their hands and knees, the peninsulars easily held their ground. All day this fierce fight raged, and when the long summer's day ended, the bodies of the assailants were piled in heaps where they had fallen, and the records say that "the ground was covered with one crimson matting of leaves." A few weeks later a body of seven hundred volunteers, commanded by one Cho, and a monk, held their ground against terrible odds, and after their weapons were gone they all fell fighting with stones and naked fists. The Japanese loss was so serious that it "took the survivors four days to burn the dead, and when it was done they broke camp and went southward. They never regained the ground lost by this retreat, and it was a sample of what must occur throughout the peninsula, since Admiral Yi had rendered reinforcements from Japan impossible."

Shortly after this the Governor of this province of Chul-la was able to muster a force of close on twenty thousand men, with which he harassed the islanders in the adjoining provinces severely. He refused to be drawn into any general action, and by clever tactics was able to establish communication with the North so that messages soon passed freely from the southern districts to the King. He as well as other independent leaders also rendered a valuable service in making an end of those of their countrymen who had been base enough to act as spies for the enemy. About the same time a plot for the seizure of Seoul itself was discovered at the Japanese headquarters, and the townsmen who had been parties to it were roasted to death at slow fires.

In the matter of walled towns and sieges the invaders were much more fortunate than they were in the open country. But even in this respect they had not been having all the fortune of war on their side latterly. In an attempt on the fortress of Yu-nan (Yen-an), in Whangha province, Kuroda with three thousand men had been badly foiled, while Hosokawa (the Jecundono of the Jesuits) and Mōri Hidemoto had sustained a positive disaster at Chin-ju (Shin-shiu) in the south of Kyung-san. The King before his flight had ordered some of the Royal treasures to be sent thither, as the place was one of the strongest in the South. Ukita, the Commander-in-Chief, ordered an attack upon it by a column of ten thousand men. At that time its garrison numbered no more than three thousand; but luckily the commandant was no average officer, for he knew a good deal about the art of war in general, and of siege-warfare in particular, and was a stout-hearted, gallant man to boot. To make a summary end of the story, the assailants were beaten off with the loss of nearly half their numbers. This repulse was a great mortification to the Japanese, and, as we shall presently see, it rankled even in the mind of Hideyoshi himself when he heard of it. Failure before a fortress was bad, but failure to hold one against the Korean levies was worse. This affair is so interesting that we here reproduce Mr. Hulbert's account at length:—

"In the ninth month (October 6th—November 3rd) General Pak Jin of Kyung-sang advanced to the attack of the walled town of Kyöng-ju (Keishiu). It is said that he made use of a species of missile called 'The Flying Thunderbolt.' It was projected from a kind of mortar made of bell metal, and having a bore of some twelve or fourteen inches. The mortar was about eight feet long. The records say that this thing could project *itself* through the air for a distance of forty paces. It doubtless means that a projectile of some kind could be cast that distance from the mortar. The records go on to say that the 'Flying Thunderbolt' was thrown over the wall of the town, and when the Japanese flocked around it to see what it might be, it exploded with a terrific noise, killing twenty men or more instantly. This struck the Japanese dumb with terror, and so worked upon their superstitious natures that they decamped in haste and evacuated the city. The inventor of this weapon was Yi Jang-son, and it is said the secret of its construction died with him. It appears that we have here the inventor of the mortar and the bomb. The length of the gun compared with its calibre, the distance the projectile was carried with the poor powder then in use, and the explosion of the shell all point to this as being the first veritable mortar in use in the East, if not in the world."

Having thus given a rough general sketch of events south of the Ta-dong, we will now return to Konishi sitting quietly on its northern bank in P'yeng-yang awaiting the reinforcing divisions expected by sea, and to the Korean King eagerly looking to China for help. Two messengers had already been sent to the Chinese capital without result, and a third dispatched in August had had no more success. A fourth at last did produce some effect, possibly partly because the Chinese Prefect of Liao-tung had sent word that the King of Korea was on the point of being driven to take refuge on Chinese soil, for down to this point the Chinese Government had suspected the Koreans of being actually in collusion with the Japanese! Orders were issued for a force to be mobilised in the Liao-tung, and five thousand men at once set out to drive the Japanese from P'yeng-yang. They arrived there on or about October 3rd, and, finding the gates open, marched into one of the simplest but deadliest traps possible. The Japanese lying in every house first decimated them with their arquebus-fire, and then sprang upon them with the sword. The second-in-command and about three-fifths of the Chinese fell, while their chief made a ride to the Yalu in record-breaking time.

On hearing of this rout the Chinese Government immediately set to work to set a really formidable army on foot; but to gain time they meanwhile sent an envoy to Konishi to amuse him with proposals of peace. This envoy, Shin Ikei by name (the Juquequi of the Jesuits), is characterised by Mr. Aston as a dissipated worthless fellow, but Froez speaks of him in very different terms, while his conduct indicates that he was a man of rare nerve and resolution. From Su-nan

(Jun-an) he sent a communication to Konishi telling him that he had been sent by the Emperor of China to inquire why the Japanese were trampling Korea under foot; and on Konishi requesting an interview with him at a point some three miles to the north of P'yeng-yang, he promptly repaired to the rendezvous entirely alone and unescorted. His courage in thus venturing among the Japanese astonished the Koreans, and drew a high compliment from Konishi. "Not even a Japanese," he said, "could have borne himself more courageously in the midst of armed enemies." An armistice of fifty days was agreed upon, during which the Japanese were not to pass 10 *li* beyond P'yeng-yang, while Shin Ikei was to proceed to Peking to arrange a satisfactory peace.

If we are to believe the missionaries, the truce was a very fortunate thing for Konishi. He and Kuroda had now less than thirty thousand men under them, and large detachments of these were necessary to hold the series of forts that maintained their communications with Seoul, while the Koreans, elated with the news of Admiral Yi's great naval victory and of the successes in the South, and besides having been hardened by a few months' real warfare, were now becoming antagonists that had to be seriously reckoned with. Mr. Hulbert seems to be perfectly right in his contention that before China raised a hand to help Korea the invasion had virtually collapsed. "The Koreans without the aid of China could probably have starved the Japanese out of P'yeng-yang and driven them southward, cutting them off on the left and right till they would have been glad to take ship for home." Soon supplies were no longer to be obtained in the open country, while to all the insistent demands for supplies from Japan Hideyoshi practically turned a deaf ear. He did indeed dispatch small convoys on two occasions, but one fell into the hands of Admiral Yi's men, and the other into those of the Korean guerillas on the way up from Fusan. At all events so the Jesuits say. Thus, in a way, the Chinese counter-invasion was really a calamity for Korea, for just at the time the dormant energies of the people were being thoroughly roused, everything was thrown into the hands of the Chinese, and " the Koreans leaned back upon China and relapsed into their old self-complacent fool's paradise."

The Jesuits and the Koreans are at one in asserting that the Chinese army of counter-invasion was a thoroughly efficient force, and they are also in accord as regards its equipment. It had no matchlocks, but it had a large artillery train of small field-pieces, while it was very strong in cavalry, all the horse-men being in iron mail " on which the best swords of Japan could made no impression." On the other hand, the short blunt Chinese sword was a poor match for the long heavy Japanese blade, with its edge of razor keenness. As regards the numbers of this force there is great discrepancy among the authorities. The Jesuits and Japanese speak of 200,000 troops; the Korean historian says it amounted to 51,000 men all told. It crossed the Yalu in the dead of winter (January 27th, 1593), and early in February it was before P'yeng-yang. Konishi made a gallant stand with his 18,000 or 25,000 troops; but the odds were too great, and after losing 2,300 men in the desperate street-fighting that followed the Chinese escalade, he had to make shift to slip out through the Ta-dong gate and cross the river on the ice under cover of night. Although there was no immediate pursuit the retreat was a trying one. To safeguard his communications Konishi had garrisoned a chain of forts a day's march apart from each other on the road from Seoul; and he now found the feather-headed young Ōtomo of Bungo, who had held the two nearest to P'yeng-yang, had abandoned them in a panic, carrying all the provisions with him. For this Ōtomo was stripped of his fief, and the once proud princely family of Bungo had to be partly supported by the alms of the Christians of Nagasaki.

This disaster at P'yeng-yang entailed the evacuation of Ham-gyung by Katō, who had to fight his way stoutly before he was able to join Konishi at Han-shiung. At the same time orders were issued by the headquarters in Seoul for all the troops beyond the Han to concentrate in that city. This order was promptly obeyed by all the commanders except one, and this brings us to the subject of Kobayakawa's worth and achievements.

This grizzled old warrior of sixty-one was the son of the famous Mōri Motonari, and had done his full share of the work in raising the House of Chōshū to the proud position it occupied. We have seen him installed as Daimyō of Chikuzen in 1587. In this Korean campaign he held the position of Chief of the Staff in addition to the command of his own division (the sixth). On the way up from Fusan he had been careful to keep his men fresh, marching no more than seven or eight miles a day, and his fellow-commanders began to make uncomplimentary remarks. But these did not ruffle the old man's serenity much. In July, 1592, Ishida, whom we have seen befriending the Jesuits to such good purpose, together with his friend Ōtani, and his colleague, Masuda, Minister of Works and "of iniquity," who appeared in the *San Felipe* incident, proceeded to Seoul as *Kangun* (military overseers) to administer rewards and act as general commissioners. (Latterly we shall find them taking part in Konishi's peace negotiations.) Ukida and others sketched a plan for the prosecution of operations, and Ishida submitted it to Kobayakawa, and asked his opinion on it in a very confident tone. The veteran looked at it and said nothing ; and Ishida, disconcerted at this, pressed him to speak. "Your plan is a fine one," said Kobayakawa very coolly at last, "but it foresees nothing but victories. In case of a reverse, where is your salvation?" Ishida at once sketched in several chains of castles and fortified posts, and Kobayakawa then nodded approval. Later on, when a council of war was anxiously discussing how the Japanese could get back to Fusan without the Koreans and Chinese falling upon their rear as soon as they moved, Kobayakawa sat quietly with his back against a pillar apparently soundly asleep. Ishida shook him and reproved him sharply, telling him that that was no time for slumber. " Oh ! " said Kobayakawa, "why all this bother? Fire all the camps, and let us get away under cover of the smoke. The thing is simple enough." But before this retreat the cool-headed old man, who could be impetuous enough in season, had already saved his countrymen from disaster.

When the order for withdrawal reached Kobayakawa, then in Kaishung (Kaijō), he stoutly refused to budge. Ōtani, one of the three commissioners, was thereupon dispatched to persuade him to fall back, pointing out that it was advisable for him to join the other divisions in order to fight a general action. He then consented to retire if he were assigned the place of danger and of honour in the contemplated battle. On his retreat to the Imjin (Rinshin) his rear was assailed by the Chinese, but he wheeled round and beat them off, and then resumed his leisurely march to Seoul. On arriving there he refused to enter the city, saying to Ishida and others who urged him to do so, "You have always been under the great Taikō (Hideyoshi), who has been ever victorious. You know nothing of defeat, and consequently nothing of how to turn defeat into victory. But that's an old experience with me; so leave this matter in my hands. There is a vast difference between our numbers and the enemy's. Suppose we do win one or two battles; they will yet keep pestering us like so many swarms of flies. Unless it is a life-and-death fight, these fellows won't be cowed. We've gone back far enough; now is the time to seek life in the midst of death." The Japanese authorities give long accounts of the brilliant tactics and the dashing impetuosity of the phlegmatic old warrior and his men when they met nearly the whole of the Chinese army (with Korean auxiliaries) in the great battle of Pyŏk-jé-yek (Hekiteiyeki), a few miles out of Seoul. It appears to have been really a stiff action, during which it was hot hand-to-hand work from ten o'clock till noon. At mid-day the Chinese gave way, and in the hot pursuit that followed they lost close on 10,000 men. "Li-joshō, their commander," say the Japanese records, "was thoroughly disheartened and wept all through the night." Mr. Aston tells us that he at once withdrew to Tong-pa (Tōha), and thence to Kaishung, beyond the Imjin. As for old Kobayakawa, he was quite modest over his brilliant exploit. "When the Empress Jingo of yore subjugated Korea," said he, "she was helped by the gods. In the present case, who knows but the gods helped us again?"

However, in spite of the victory of Pyŏk-jé-yek (Hekiteiyeki), the Japanese position in Seoul was desperate; and the islanders sent a letter to the Korean Prime Minister making proposals of peace. This missive was handed to the Chinese commander, and he sent Shin Ikei to meet Konishi and Katō in mid-stream off the village of Yong-san near Seoul. The interview was short and business-like. The Japanese were told: "You must give up the two princes; you must leave the capital and move south to the coast of Kyung-sang province. Then, and not till then, will we conclude peace and the Emperor recognise your king as his vassal." The terms were promptly accepted; and so in the name of the thirty-seven Japanese commanders Konishi and Katō agreed to evacuate Seoul on May 9th, 1593—that is, 360 days after Konishi's landing at Fusan, and 341 days after his entry into the Korean capital. The Japanese faithfully kept their pact, and by the day appointed their columns were all heading for the South. On May 20th the Chinese generalissimo entered the city.

"The condition in which he found things there is almost indescribable. The country all about was lying fallow, and a great famine stared the Koreans in the face. A thousand bags of rice were hastily brought out and made up into soup or gruel, mixed with pine leaves, and a few of the starving thousands were fed. As General Sa Dasu was passing along the street he saw a young child trying to suck milk from the breast of its dead mother. The sight aroused his compassion, and he carried the child to his quarters and ordered it to be cared for. Rice was so scarce that a whole piece of cotton cloth could be purchased with about three quarts of it. A horse cost but three pecks of rice. Famishing men fought and killed each other, the victors eating the vanquished, sucking the marrow from the bones, and then dying themselves of surfeit. It is even said that, when a drunken Chinese soldier vomited, half-starved men would crawl towards the place and fight over the possession of this horrible substitute for food. This state of things naturally brought on an epidemic of the native fever, a species of typhus, and the dead bodies of its victims lay all along the road, the head of one being pillowed on the breast of another. The dead bodies in and immediately around Seoul were gathered and piled in a heap outside the Water Mouth Gate, and it is affirmed that the pile was ten feet higher than the wall."

Li-joshō was in no haste to follow up the islanders in their retreat. He presently allowed one of his subordinates, whom the Koreans call General Yi Yo-bak, to do so with ten thousand men, however. A day or two after his departure this doughty warrior returned with the alarming intelligence that he had a pain in the leg. In July a dispatch from the Chinese Military Censor still in P'yeng-yang arrived ordering a general pursuit. Then at last Li-joshō bestirred himself, and actually got as far as the Cho-ryung Pass, of course without seeing any sign of the Japanese except the ravages they had committed; and then turned back to his cosy quarters in Seoul. The Koreans had clamoured loudly for vigorous measures, but the Chinese had actually burned all the boats on the Han so that the national levies from the North could not get across. They explain all this by the fact that before leaving the capital the Japanese had dispatched large sums of money to the quarters of the Chinese Commander-in-Chief and the Military Censor. At all events, the Chinese, although reinforced by five thousand men, came into no further collision with the Japanese. Early in October Li-joshō and the censor collected all their forces, with the exception of ten thousand men left to serve as a body-guard for the Korean King, and departed for Nanking. "In spite of their suspicions of the corruptibility of General Yi Yo-song, the Koreans speak in high terms of him. They describe him as a young man of thirty, of handsome person, broad mind, and possessed of great skill in the art of war. When he was on the eve of returning to China he bared his head and showed the Koreans that his hair was already turning to gray. He told them it was because he had worked so hard for them, which piece of pathos seems to have impressed them deeply."

Meanwhile, although the evacuation of Seoul had decided the campaign, what the Koreans call its greatest engagement yet remained to be fought. Even after the negotiations for peace, of which we shall speak presently, had advanced to a satisfactory initial stage at Hideyoshi's headquarters at Nagoya, he "ordered all the other troops in Korea to recross the sea, but first to render him an account of a Korean lord, a near relative of the King, who held one of the strongest places in the country, and who had greatly harassed the Japanese during the whole course of the war by the bands he had sent against him. All this was executed; the Korean was besieged, his fortress taken, his garrison passed to the edge of the sword, and he himself being found among the dead, his head was carried to the Emperor (Hideyoshi)." This passage from Charlevoix evidently refers to the bloody affair of Chin-ju (Shinshiu). It will be remembered that a column of ten thousand men under Hosokawa, Mōri Hidemoto, and other commanders had failed disastrously before this walled town in the previous year, and that their miscarriage had rankled in the mind of Hideyoshi himself. The concentration of the Japanese in the South now enabled them to assail the position with an unusually large force, while the Koreans were now massed here in as great numbers as they had been anywhere else, perhaps, in the course of the war. In the actions before the town and in the

capture of the town itself the Koreans admit a loss of between
sixty thousand and seventy thousand men, which is probably
correct.[18] Their statement that the assailants' lost an equal
number, however, cannot be taken quite so seriously, though we
must not forget that the fighting was hot, heavy, and prolonged.
Close on a hundred assaults were directed against the fortress
before it finally fell on the ninth day, thanks in a great measure
to Katō Kiyomasa, who devised a tetsudo of ox hides stretched on
a framework, which was pushed forward on wheels to the base of
the wall, whose corner stones were dislodged with crow-bars.

After this most sanguinary affair all the troops who had
served through the campaign were withdrawn, with the exception of Konishi's division, mostly composed of Christians,
among whom Father Cespedez and a young Japanese Jesuit
were soon busy. The missionaries say that previous to the
storm of Chin-ju fifty thousand fresh men had been dispatched from Nagoya to help to hold the cordon of twelve
fortified camps Konishi had established along the southern
coast of the peninsula. About the precise number of these
camps, all of the same general kind, overlooking the sea from
a bluff and protected landwards by a moat and earthworks,
there is a want of agreement among the various authorities.
Mr. Hulbert says there were between twenty and thirty of them,
some ten miles apart from each other, beginning with the
harbour of So-sang in the Ul-san district of Kyung-sang and
extending to Sun-ch'un in Chul-la, a distance of over two
hundred and seventy miles. The Japanese limit their number
to eighteen, and their extent from Ul-san to Tongna (Tōrai)
and Koje-do (Kyosai-tō), a very much shorter distance.

Meanwhile, as has been said, the initial peace negotiations
had considerably advanced. There were numerous difficulties
in the way; among other things, Katō Kiyomasa was unwilling
to give up the captive princes, and so he had to be peremptorily
recalled to Nagoya and sent into temporary banishment from
Hideyoshi's presence. The Koreans, still burning to revenge
their wrongs, were insistent that there should be no peace with
the Japanese brigands. Shin Ikei and two colleagues passed

18 In several passages Froez puts the Japanese losses in the first campaign
at more than fifty thousand men and more than five hundred vessels. He tells
us that Ōmura had not lost one single vessel, and that out of his contingent
of one thousand men only two had perished!

the sea to Nagoya, however, where they arrived on June 22nd, 1593; and after being fêted and regally entertained by Hideyoshi, they exchanged the most friendly assurances with him, both parties agreeing to throw the blame of all that had happened on the unlucky Koreans, who were now kept in the dark about all that passed. The latter were bitterly dissatisfied with this Chinese embassy—especially so with Shin Ikei, whom they accused of systematically amusing his Government with the fiction that the Japanese were suppliants suing for pardon. He was said by them to have always substituted in his dispatches to Nanking the word "submission" for "peace," the word actually used by the Japanese; and a document brought over by a Japanese envoy, Naitō, Hida-no-Kami, who accompanied him on his return to Seoul, was described to the Koreans as "Hideyoshi's letter of submission."[19] Naitō proceeded with this dispatch as far as Liao-tung, where he was detained by the Chinese Government, which had heard of the affair at Chin-ju (Shinshiu), and could not reconcile it with Hideyoshi's pacific assurances, and suspected that the missive entrusted to Naitō was a forgery of some of the Japanese generals tired of the war. Shin Ikei succeeded in smoothing over matters, however; and at last, in 1594, a Chinese official induced the Koreans to give a reluctant consent to a peace. Naitō was then allowed to proceed to the Chinese Court, where he gave his adhesion to the three articles of peace thus briefly recorded by the Korean historian:—(1) To grant investiture—not tribute; (2) all Japanese to leave Korea; (3) never again to invade Korea. The envoy's Christianity did not prevent him from fibbing in true diplomatic

---

[19] Mr. Aston calls the envoy Konishi, Hida-no-Kami. But the Jesuits say that it was Naitō, the Christian ex-Prince of Tamba, who acted in that capacity on the occasion. He was also called Hida-no-Kami. Like Xenophon with Proxenus, he had accompanied his friend Konishi, Settsu-no-Kami, Commander of the 1st Division, as a "simple volunteer." Writes Charlevoix under the year 1596: "Konishi had long ago fathomed his master's passionate desire that the Chinese Emperor should send a formal embassy to ask for peace; he had undertaken to induce the Chinese monarch to do so, and it was chiefly for this purpose that he had sent his old friend John Naytadono, formerly King of Tamba, to the Court of Peking. This lord had negotiated very happily in favour of Christianity, which he was on the point of introducing into China, when he was recalled to Japan; he had even tolerably well persuaded the Chinese Emperor to do what the Grand Admiral (Konishi) wished; but it was Juquequi (Shin Ikei), who, intimidated by Konishi, finally determined his master to a step which surprised all the Orient and which would have covered Taicosama with glory, if he had known how to moderate himself sufficiently and to extract from it all the advantage it ought naturally to have procured him."

fashion on this occasion. Among other startling assertions he is said to have assured the Chinese that the *Ten-nō* (Emperor) and *Koku-ō* of Japan were one and the same person! [20]

As for a real peace, however, it was still far from being assured. When the Chinese ambassadors, on their way to Japan to invest Hideyoshi as King, arrived in Korea, they found the Japanese still cantonned in a number of their fortified camps. They protested against this, and said they were forbidden to proceed to Japan so long as a single Japanese soldier remained on Korean soil. The Japanese thereupon withdrew from some of their positions, but insisted on retaining Fusan and one or two less important places as a guarantee of Chinese good faith. They ultimately agreed to evacuate Fusan if the Chinese envoys would come into their camp. As soon as the ambassadors did so, fresh difficulties arose. Some of the war-party among the Japanese generals refused to give up Fusan without renewed instructions from Hideyoshi, and Konishi, the strenuous advocate of peace, had to pass the sea to consult him. Even when Konishi returned to Fusan in February, 1596, he brought no instructions with him, and shortly afterwards he again left for Japan, taking with him Terasawa, Governor of Nagasaki, and Shin Ikei, who went for the ostensible purpose of arranging the ceremonies for the reception of the two ambassadors. Shin Ikei was left at Nagoya in Hizen, while Konishi and Terasawa hurried on to Kyōto, where they were greatly commended by Hideyoshi for their exertions on behalf of peace.

Anxious as Hideyoshi was for its conclusion, he still kept the Chinese envoys waiting in the camp at Fusan. Froez says the reason for this, *non alia fuit, quam quod Taico incredibili cupiditate flagrans, amplificandi nominis sui gloriam et perpetuam apud posteros potentiæ et magnificentiæ suae relinquendi, prorsus*

---

[20] To do Naitō justice in this matter, however, it may be well to direct attention to the following passage from Froez's *Historica Relatio de Legatione Regis Chinensium, &c.*:—"The Chinese King, after many discussions (for the King of the Chinese with the utmost arrogance deems that he is the Lord of the whole world, and that there is no one like himself), ordered it to be indicated to the Taikō (Hideyoshi) that it was neither becoming nor fit that he (the Taikō) should allow the Dairi (the Emperor), a private individual subject to the King of Japan, to retain his pristine place of dignity, when he, by his exertions and his bravery, had subjected the sixty-six kingdoms of Japan to his sway. If he stripped the man (the Dairi) of these, he promised that he would send a Royal crown and patent, and that by the same ambassadors he would reply to the articles sent by the Taikō, together with terms and conditions about the entire evacuation of Korea by the Japanese and their return to Japan."

constituerit dictos Legatos splendidissimo et omnibus numeris absolutissimo apparatu et pompa excipere. The preparations for the reception of the Chinese embassy were on an unprecedented scale of magnificence, and immense sums were spent upon them. But this cost Hideyoshi but little, if anything; it was the feudatories that were loaded and crippled with debt to defray them.[21] Shin Ikei was at last brought up to Fushimi, where there were several keen bouts of fencing in conventional propriety between him and the Taikō in which the astute and daring Chinaman had by no means the worst of it.

Before this, Konishi and Terasawa had started to bring over the envoys and to withdraw all the Japanese troops from Korea. Midway, seven leagues from the island of Iki, they were met by a dispatch-boat with the intelligence that the senior ambassador had fled from the Japanese camp towards China. Some of Konishi's pagan enemies had frightened this poltroon by telling him that the Japanese did not want investiture, that he and his companion were detained there merely because the Taikō saw fit thus to avenge himself on the Chinese, and that presently he would find his life in danger. When he reached Peking he was severely punished for his cowardice, while his colleague who had remained was promoted to his post and Shin Ikei associated with him as junior ambassador. Konishi, who was not blamed for the *contretemps*, received orders to leave his troops still in Fusan and to escort the remodelled embassy to Kyōto.

Meanwhile there had been a succession of perhaps the greatest and most disastrous earthquakes ever known in Japan, and all the stately edifices reared in the capital and Fushimi had either been levelled with the ground or so seriously shaken that they were untenable. One corner of Ōsaka castle had been proof against the shocks, and here it was determined that the embassy should be formally received. This reception, which is fully described in all its extravagant magnificence by Froez, took place on October 21st, 1596, Hideyoshi, however, refusing to see the Koreans who had come with the Chinese mission. Froez is at one with the Japanese authorities in stating that the ceremony of investing Hideyoshi as King of

---

[21] For a full account of them, see Froez's *Relatio.*

Japan was performed with great state in the presence of all the Court, and that he was then presented with a patent of investiture, with a golden seal, a crown, and robe of state. As to what immediately followed the Jesuit is far from being in accord with the native accounts. According to Froez, everything continued to be on a most satisfactory footing until the return of the envoys to Sakai on October 24th. Hideyoshi then sent four *bonzes* to call on them there, and these priests brought back a dispatch requesting that all the Japanese forts in Korea should be dismantled and their garrisons withdrawn, that Hideyoshi should pardon the Koreans as the Chinese Emperor had already done: they had, indeed, merited destruction, but would derive no benefit from visiting them with that penalty. "When the Taikō in reading the letter came to the request for the demolition of the fortresses, he became inflamed with as great anger and fury as if a legion of devils had taken possession of him. So loudly did he vociferate and perspire that vapour exhaled from his head. His rage was increased by the fact that he had understood the Japanese were intensely feared by the Chinese, and much more by the Koreans, *neo primœ suœ cogitationis ut pro conficienda pace mediam tantum Coraini regni partem retineret, oblitus esset.*" Mr. Aston, who summarises Japanese authorities, says that this outburst came earlier, and that it was occasioned by something very different. After a banquet to the envoys on the 22nd, Hideyoshi retired to a summer-house and commanded his reverence Shōda and a fellow-priest to translate the patent of investiture for him. Konishi had already besought them to modify any expressions in the document which might be likely to wound Hideyoshi's pride, but the *bonzes* (looking upon the Christian Konishi as their foe, doubtless) interpreted faithfully enough. Mr. Aston's translation of this important piece is as follows:—

"The influence of the holy and divine one (Confucius) is wide-spread; he is honoured and loved wherever the heavens overhang and the earth upbears. The Imperial command is universal; even as far as the bounds of ocean where the sun rises, there are none who do not obey it.

"In ancient times our Imperial ancestors bestowed their favours on many lands; the Tortoise knots and the Dragon writing were sent to the limits of far Fusang (Japan), the pure alabaster and the great seal character were granted to the mountains of the submissive country. Thereafter came billowy times when communication was interrupted, but an auspicious opportunity has now arrived, when it has pleased us again to address you.

"You, Toyotomi Taira Hideyoshi, having established an Island Kingdom, and knowing the reverence due to the Central Land, sent to the West an envoy, and with gladness and affection offered your allegiance. On the North you knocked at the barrier of ten thousand *li*, and earnestly requested to be admitted within our dominions. Your mind is already confirmed in reverent submissiveness. How can we grudge our favour to so great meekness?

"We do therefore specially invest you with the dignity of King of Japan, and to that intent issue this our commission. Treasure it up carefully. Over the sea we send you a crown and robe, so that you may follow our ancient custom as respects dress. Faithfully defend the frontier of the Empire; let it be your study to act worthily of your position as our minister; practice moderation and self-restraint; cherish gratitude for the Imperial favour so bountifully bestowed upon you; change not your fidelity; be humbly guided by our admonitions; continue always to follow our instructions.

"Respect this!"

This language was arrogant, but it was less so than that of the letter of instructions which accompanied the patent. Hideyoshi was roused to the intensest fury. "I don't need his help to become King of Japan!" he burst out. "What Konishi led me to believe was that the chief of the Mings was to acknowledge me as Ming Emperor!" He tore off the crown and robes and flung them on the ground, together with the commission,[22] and sent for Konishi that he might cut off his head on the spot for deception. He was somewhat pacified, however, when Shōda and the other priest pointed out to him that it was an ancient custom for the countries neighbouring to China to receive investiture from her, as she surpassed them all in civilisation, and that it was really an honour to Hideyoshi that his fame and deserts had compelled so signal a recognition. Konishi, too, had no difficulty in showing that the three commissioners, Ishida, Ōtani, and Masuda, were equally responsible with himself for all that had happened; and so, although he was driven from Court, he was soon received back into favour. From this point onward there is nothing in Froez at all

---

[22] Japanese schoolboys are religiously taught that the Taikō tore this document to pieces. As a matter of fact, it is still in perfect preservation in the Imperial University of Tokyo. I am informed that the opening sentence of the translation should run: "The Emperor, who respects and obeys Heaven, and is favoured by Providence, commands that he be honoured," etc. Also, "As a mark of our special favour towards you, over the sea we send you a robe and crown contained in a costly case," is suggested instead of Mr. Aston's "Over the sea we send you," etc.

at variance with Mr. Aston's terse summary of the Japanese
authorities :—

"Hideyoshi ordered the ambassadors to leave Japan at once
without any answer or even the compliments to themselves and their
sovereign demanded by Eastern diplomatic usage. On reflection,
however, he judged it politic not to carry his quarrel with China any
farther just then, and allowed himself to be persuaded to give suitable
presents to the Chinese ambassadors. All his anger was turned
against Korea, which as usual was made the scapegoat. He vowed
that he would never make peace with that unhappy country, and at
once gave orders to prepare a fresh expedition. Even the heads of
the two Korean officers were for a moment in danger. The embassy
left Kyōto on the following day. At Nagoya, where they were
detained by contrary winds, they were overtaken by a messenger
bearing a letter from Hideyoshi, which they hoped might be an
apology, but which turned out to be nothing but an enumeration of
the wrongs which that meek and inoffensive personage had suffered
at the hands of the Koreans, viz., when the Korean ambassadors
came to Japan some years before, they had concealed the state of
things in China—offence No. 1. At the request of Shin Ikei, the
Korean princes had been released, but they had not come to render
thanks in person: they had sent instead two officers of mean position—
offence No. 2. The Koreans had for several years impeded the
negotiations of peace between China and Japan—offence No. 3. On
the return of the ambassadors to Korea in the twelfth month of 1596,
this document was communicated to King Riyen, who in great alarm
appealed again to China for assistance to repel the new invasion
which now threatened him."

Shin Ikei and his colleague had gone back to the Chinese
Court with no dispatch from Hideyoshi, but with a plausible
account of his respectful acceptance of investiture. But some
articles bought in Japan, which they tried to palm off as
presents from Hideyoshi to the Emperor of China, had already
betrayed them before the Korean King's urgent appeal for help
arrived.

Meanwhile the Taikō had shown that he was really in
earnest. On March 19th, 1597, orders were issued for the
mobilisation of five divisions from Kyūshū (56,700 men), two
from Shikoku, one of 30,000 from Mōri's and another of
10,000 men from Ukida's fiefs; and when these were thrown
into Korea, together with the Japanese garrisons there, there was
a total of 141,500 invaders in the peninsula. Some Japanese
authorities indicate that it was Hideyoshi's purpose to coerce
the Koreans into peace by a mere display of force, and in
support of this contention they adduce the inaction of the
army for some time after the landing was effected. Katō
Kiyomasa, who led the first division on this occasion, sought

an interview with Shōkei-jin, a Korean official, and is said to have informed him that the Japanese would withdraw if a Korean prince of the blood were sent to Japan on a mission of apology. Shin Ikei also exerted himself on behalf of peace, but in July, while on his way to Katō, he was arrested as a traitor by some Chinese troops, who had meanwhile arrived in the South of Korea. This put a stop to all peace negotiations, and hostilities were forthwith resumed. It is to be noted, however, that the Korean authorities explain the delay in the Japanese advance by commissariat difficulties. Their commanders had asked for supplies from Japan, and had pointed out that if these were not forwarded they would have to wait till the grain ripened in Korea; but Hideyoshi, in consistent adherence to the maxim of subsisting the war in the enemy's country, had ordered his generals to wait till harvest-tide.

At first, indeed, he might well have been anxious about the probable fate of convoys from Japan in view of the naval superiority developed by the peninsulars in the great campaign of 1592–93. It was true that the Japanese had already profited by the lessons they had then received, and had meanwhile devoted much attention to bringing their fleet to a high state of efficiency. And although the Japanese, perhaps, were not aware of the fact, the Korean navy was now far from being the exceedingly formidable force it had been five years before. Then it had been handled by a stout-hearted seaman of the type of Nelson; now it was commanded by a drunken poltroon, who had obtained his post by the adroit exercise of dirty Court intrigue at the expense of the gallant Yi Sun-sin. This worthy, Wŏn-kiun by name, was utterly incompetent and extremely unpopular with his men, and under his command the Korean navy had rapidly drifted into disorganisation and demoralisation. A strong Japanese fleet under Katō Yoshiaki, Tōdō, and Wakizaka lay not far from Fusan, and Wŏn-kiun received orders to disperse it. Although fully aware of the folly of attacking, he could not well refuse to do so, as he had been the loudest in inveighing against the alleged supineness of his predecessor. This time the Japanese had but little difficulty in beating off the peninsular vessels; and on the Koreans making the island of Ka-tök, the men immediately rushed ashore to quench their thirst, and four hundred of them were cut down by the Japanese garrison. Wŏn-kiun then retired to Köje-do; and to hearten him up somewhat, the Commander-in-Chief ordered him to be flogged! But this drastic measure only served to bring on one of his periodical fits of drunkenness, and a little later nearly the whole of his fleet was either captured or destroyed by Konishi, who in this campaign acted chiefly as an Admiral.

This victory threw the sea open to the islanders, and they now prepared for a general advance. By this time there was a large and formidable Chinese force in the South of Korea, and it was against a section of this, entrenched in Nam-wŏn (Nan-gen), in Chul-la, that Katō directed his operations by land, while Konishi co-operated with him with the fleet. In the assault upon this place, according to one account, 3,726 heads were taken, those of the officers and the noses of the private soldiers being pickled in salt and lime and forwarded to Hideyoshi. The Japanese advance presently occasioned the evacuation of many fortresses, and in a few weeks the islanders were again masters of nearly the whole of Kyung-sang, Chul-la, and Ch'ung-ch'ung. At last, near Chik-san, in the extreme north of the last province, the allies made a stand; and an obstinately contested battle was fought, in which both sides claimed the advantage. To the islanders, however, anything short of a decisive victory which would have enabled them to establish themselves in the Korean capital, was almost equivalent to a defeat. The winter was at hand, and the pinch of hunger was again beginning to be felt. The Korean fleet, too, had been reorganised and again taken in hand by Admiral Yi Sun-sin, and was once more formidable. The island of Chin-do (Chintō), at the south-western extremity of Chul-la, was its station, and it had already beaten and killed the Japanese Admiral Suga' in a stiffly-fought action near that place. It had also been reinforced by a Chinese squadron, with whose commander Admiral Yi contrived to maintain cordial relations, rather to the surprise of his Government, which had expected that the overbearing arrogance of the Chinese would render anything like friendly co-operation impossible. In view of all these circumstances the Japanese judged it advisable to retire to their long chain of entrenched camps fringing the southern seaboard to pass the winter.

Not long after this—on January 4th, 1598—a fresh Chinese army of 40,000 men arrived in Seoul, and its commander dispatched it to operate in the South shortly afterwards. Reinforced by a large proportion of the Chinese already in the peninsula, and a great body of Koreans, it advanced upon Yŏl-san (Urusan), the most westerly of the Japanese positions, then held by Katō Kiyomasa with the first division. Yŏl-san was naturally strong, with convenient communication with Fusan both by land and sea; "but the Chinese quickly cut the land communication, and invested the place, which, apart from its natural strength, was in other respects ill-prepared to stand a siege. The Japanese were soon driven from an outer line of hastily constructed palisades into the castle itself, which the Chinese made repeated but fruitless attempts to take by assault. The losses were so considerable that it was decided to convert the siege into a blockade, a plan which the scarcity of provisions among the Japanese almost rendered successful. Their supplies of rice were soon exhausted, the cattle and horses in the castle followed next, and officers and men alike were in a short time reduced to the greatest extremities. They chewed earth and paper, and, stealing out by night, thought themselves fortunate if they could find among the corpses lying outside the walls some dead Chinaman whose haversack was not entirely empty." However, before February was out, Yŏl-san (Urusan) was relieved. Fifty thousand men under Hachisuka, Kuroda, and others hurried to its relief by land, while Konishi appeared with his fleet, and a simultaneous attack by these forces, supported by a determined sally on the part of the beleaguered garrison, was pressed home so vigorously that the besiegers had to retire, leaving everything behind them.

A little later, in the spring of 1598, the Chinese received still further reinforcements and once more took the field. On hearing of their advance, Konishi advised the evacuation of the outlying fortresses of the sea-board chain, and a concentration of all the troops in Fusan; but Hideyoshi, to whom the proposition was referred, indignantly refused to entertain it. He recalled the greater part of the army, however, leaving only the Kyūshū divisions and a few other bands, sixty thousand men in all, to hold the fortified camps.

Most of the summer was spent by the Chinese in fruitless

attempts against Sun-chŏn and Yŏl-san. They were at first
more successful at two intermediate points, at Kong-yang
(Kon-yō) and at Sŏ-chŏn (Shisen), the latter of which was
held by the men of Satsuma under Shimadzu Yoshihiro and
his son. At first this Satsuma camp was in serious danger, but
the Kagoshima *samurai* rose to the demands of the occasion,
and repulsed the allies with terrific slaughter, pursuing them
hotly for miles and taking as many as 38,700 heads. These
were buried under a tumulus; but the ears and noses had
previously been cut off, packed in barrels, and sent to Japan,
where they were subsequently deposited near the Temple of
Dai-butsu in the capital, and that *Mimi-dzuka*, or " Ear-mound,"
raised over them which is still shown to travellers as one of
the sights of Kyōto by Japanese *ciceroni.*

This great battle, fought on October 30th, 1598, was speedily
followed by a brilliant victory of Konishi's at Syoun-tyen (Jun-
ten), and these unexpected and crushing reverses drove the
Chinese commanders to make overtures for peace. Konishi and
several of his colleagues welcomed their advances heartily; and
as just about this time two messengers arrived with intelligence
of the death of Hideyoshi, an armistice was arranged. Before
his decease, Hideyoshi had shown himself anxious to bring the
hostilities to a close, and had requested Iyeyasu and Mayeda
Toshi-iye to arrange for their termination. From an old
Satsuma record we learn that these latter dispatched two agents
to Korea with secret instructions to inform the Koreans that
peace would be made if a Korean prince were sent to Japan,
and that the Japanese troops would be withdrawn if some
tiger-skins and ginseng were sent to Kyōto as presents.

A general withdrawal was at once begun; but it soon
proved to be anything but a simple operation. In spite of the
armistice, the Korean and Chinese squadrons fell upon Konishi
and Shimadzu's transports, and, if we are to trust the Korean
accounts, forced the Japanese to abandon their vessels and take
refuge on the island of Nam-hai (Nankai), whence they were
subsequently rescued by one of the other commanders. The
Japanese will have it that they were severely handled indeed,
but that they beat off the assailants, killing the gallant Admiral
Yi Sun-sin as well as his Chinese colleague, and then made
Tsushima safely.

About the exact date of the resumption of diplomatic relations between Japan and Korea there is some discrepancy among the authorities. Some assign 1601 as the year, which Mr. Aston gives as 1607, while in the Annual Letter of 1605–6 we meet with mention of a Korean ambassador in Kyōto about that time.

Such was the lame and impotent conclusion of the great Korean struggle,—a war which the Jesuits in their famous slave-trade memorial very frankly condemn as "unjust." That it really was so there can be but little doubt. As regards that not unimportant matter, it is to be feared that we must be content to follow the missionaries. But when we come to deal with Hideyoshi's motives for this wanton aggression we may well question whether the Church historians have grasped them fully and firmly. That he was actuated by lust of conquest and a burning desire to immortalise his name is no doubt perfectly correct. But when both Crasset and Charlevoix assure us over and over again that a prime object with him was to extirpate Christianity in Japan by finding fiefs for all the Christian *daimyō* in Korea, and removing them with all their converted *samurai* thither, we cannot but believe that their notions of the importance of Christianity in Japan at this time were wildly exaggerated. At one time there were 200,000 Japanese serving over-sea, the greatest force that ever was sent on such service down to the date when Great Britain was called upon to preserve her supremacy in South Africa. Of all this vast host not more than twenty thousand were Christians. The single pagan division levied in Mōri's fiefs alone amounted to thirty thousand men. Hideyoshi may indeed have been minded to transfer Konishi, Arima, and Ōmura to the peninsula when conquered; but after all, they, as well as Christianity, were merely so many insignificant pawns in the gigantic game the Taikō was playing.

CHAPTER XIII.

HIDEYOSHI'S DOMESTIC POLICY.

THUS far we have occupied ourselves with tracing the course of two currents of events, and as regards what is perhaps the more important of the two our treatment of the theme has hitherto been but cursory. From what has been advanced the reader may perhaps glean a fair notion of the introduction of Christianity into Japan and of its progress there, and also of the general attitude of the islanders towards foreigners and foreign Powers. But even these matters cannot be adequately understood unless we carry along with us tolerably clear ideas of the great work of re-establishing a strong central power in the country then in full progress. Upon one feature of that task we have indeed touched at some length; yet the mere subjection of the feudal chiefs to his sway accomplished by Hideyoshi is by no means synonymous with that task as a whole. The organisation of a strong and efficient administrative machine at the central seat of authority was of equal moment with the reduction of Shimadzu, of Mōri, of Hōjō, of Daté, and of most unclerical mail-clad clerics like Kennio Kora and the monks of Negoro, to obedience. To a consideration of Hideyoshi's Government, and especially of its relations to the Imperial Court on the one hand and to the feudatories on the other, it is now advisable to devote some little attention.

Although the Jesuits at an early date seem to have penetrated the fact that it was the Dairi, as they call him, who was the real Emperor, they very rarely speak of him as such in their letters. We have seen the profound astonishment with which the missionaries were struck when "this Prince" endeavoured to assert himself towards Nobunaga in connection with the recall of the Christian priests to Kyōto in 1568. However, we meet with several other instances of the Dairi's essaying to make his voice heard in the administration of affairs. After the murder of Ōuchi by Suye Harukata in

Yamaguchi in 1552, the Emperor ordered the Shōgun to punish the rebel. The Shōgun failed to comply with the Imperial command, and thereupon the Emperor entrusted the commission to Mōri Motonari, who carried it out effectually. In 1569–70 Mōri of Nagato and Ōtomo of Bungo were fighting for the possession of Buzen, and the Emperor intervened and succeeded in making them cease hostilities and compose their differences. Again, in 1580 it was the Emperor's fiat that caused the evacuation of Ōsaka by Kennio Kosa, a thing Nobunaga had utterly failed to effect by force of arms. Yet, in spite of these sporadic instances, the Emperor's intervention in State affairs was exceedingly infrequent, while his real power was exceedingly small,—under Hideyoshi, indeed, almost nothing.

The deference evinced for the Imperial Court by Nobunaga would appear to have been much greater than that shown by any of his predecessors. Nobunaga, indeed, seems to have been anxious to act in what might be called a constitutional fashion. At the outset of his career he asked for the Shōgun's sanction to his wars with his neighbours; when he ousted Miyoshi from Kyōto, and restored the last of the Ashikaga Shōguns there, he himself was appointed the Shōgun's deputy; and after he had been driven to depose—or had found an excuse for deposing—his superior in 1573, he pursued his career of conquest in virtue of a commission from the Emperor to pacify the country. The title of Shōgun he never assumed (not being of Minamoto stock); but he took the style of Naidaijin, or Inner Great Minister of the Imperial Cabinet, a body which at the time exercised no real power whatever.

On the death of Nobunaga in 1582, the guardianship of his heir, his grandson Sambōshi, was assumed by Hideyoshi, and within three years the guardian felt himself strong enough to compel Sambōshi and all the stock of Nobunaga to acknowledge him as their suzerain. Hideyoshi now bethought himself of the advisability of assuming the style of Shōgun, and approached the deposed but still titular Shōgun, Ashikaga Yoshiaki, with a proposal to adopt him and confer his titles upon him. Yoshiaki refused to do so, and thereupon one of Hideyoshi's advisers suggested that he should assume the office of *Kwanbaku* or Regent. The commonly accepted, but not very probable, story is that Hideyoshi was entirely ignorant of the nature of the office, but when informed that the *Kwanbaku* was second to none but the Emperor, he eagerly adopted the suggestion, and prevailed upon the Emperor to remove the existing occupant and to install himself in the position. At the same time, by the assumption of the family name of Toyotomi, he put forth pretensions to kinship with the Fujiwaras, of the oldest and most illustrious stock in Japan.

It was at this time that he nominated the five *Bugyō*, or Ministers, who formed the most essential part of the administrative machinery devised for the maintenance and consolidation of the centralised authority he was now engaged in establishing at the expense of the great feudatories. These Ministers, like their master, were all " new men "; and, like him, they owed their position to nothing but their own proved capacity. With some of them we have met already while dealing with the subject of Christianity. Masuda Nagamori, Minister of Works, as we have seen, had no small share in the intrigue of Hasegawa and Harada in connection with the *San Felipe* incident of 1596 which precipitated the Taikō's wrath upon the heads of the overzealous and imprudent Franciscans, while it was in his capacity of Chief of Police and Minister of Criminal Affairs, as well as of Governor of Lower Kyōto, that Ishida Mitsunari (Xibonojo of the Jesuits) was entrusted with the unwelcome duty of arresting and mutilating his own Christian *protégés*, and of dispatching them to Nagasaki for execution. Mayeda Gen-i (an ex-priest), seemingly from his acquaintance with neglected Court ceremony, had attracted the favourable notice of Hideyoshi, and was now appointed Governor of Kyōto and Minister of Worship. Even then he continued to bear the title of *Hōin*,[1] and by appending this to his personal name of Gen-i the Jesuits introduce him to us as " Guenifoin." Strangely enough, although the missionaries always speak of him as one of their most powerful protectors, we meet with the following in a Japanese account of him :—

" When Hideyoshi prohibited Christianity, Mayeda Gen-i proposed, as a means of testing Christian converts, the following measure: Christ's image was engraved on a copper plate, and anybody who

---

[1] A title of reverence among Buddhist priests,

was suspected of being a Christian was ordered to trample on it. Those who hesitated to do so were judged to be Christians. This method was afterwards adopted by the Tokugawa Government."

Asano Nagamasa was Minister of Justice; and Nagatsuka Masaiye, as Minister of Finance, was the first to begin the minting of gold and silver on an extensive scale in Japan, and as Minister of Agriculture instituted the grand survey of the Empire carried out between 1586 and 1596. Although the Emperor's Cabinet, with its eight subordinate boards, was still theoretically in existence, the suspended functions of its inanimate frame served only to bestow high-prized but empty titles on Hideyoshi's officers and favourites. All real power in domestic matters was in the hands of the *Bugyō*; as regards the external relations of the Empire, the Taikō was his own Foreign Minister.

Besides acting as Ministers in Kyōto, all these *Bugyō* were at the same time territorial magnates of no small importance. Ishida held a fief in Ōmi of some 194,000 *koku*, and Nagatsuka another adjacent one of 50,000; to the south Masuda had large domains (200,000 *koku*) in Yamato; Asano after 1590 held nearly the whole province of Kai (218,000 *koku*); while his reverence Mayeda Gen-i was in possession of an estate of 50,000 *koku* in Tamba.

With the internal administration of his feudatories in their own fiefs neither the Regent nor his Ministers seem to have interfered—at least at first. The following incident at all events would suggest as much. Hideyoshi, as has been said, made Takayama (Don Justo Ucondono) exchange Takatsuki for Akashi :—

"As soon as Justo had taken possession of it, his first thoughts were to reduce it under the obedience of Christ. The *bonzes*, having scent of his design, with their idols went to cast themselves at the Queen's feet. The Queen, touched with ardent zeal for her religion, spoke to the King in their behalf. But Hideyoshi, who was no bigot, answered her briskly that he had absolutely given Justo that place in change for Takatsuki; *and for the rest, every one was free to dispose of his own.* Let the *bonzes*, if the idols be troublesome, drown them in the sea, or dry them for fuel. Don Justo, much pleased with Hideyoshi's answer, took then a resolution to oblige all his subjects to become Christian."

Yet withal, in spite of this large measure of authority left vested in the territorial nobles, their power to cause trouble to the central administration was by no means great. By means of his Korean expeditions and similar enterprises the Taikō

involved those that might otherwise have occasioned him
grave apprehensions in a lavish expenditure of the men and
resources that might have rendered them formidable.   It
is needless to say that this expenditure must have driven
them to levy taxation and contributions within their domains
to an extent that made those on whom the burden fell eagerly
anxious for less exacting rulers.   And as regards those princes
that remained at home the Taikō was at no loss to devise a
means of crippling and curbing them in a very effectual
manner.   It was his practice to request the attendance at his
Court of those potentates he had even the slightest grounds
to suspect of disaffection.   There they would be kept for
months and even for years—Hideyoshi associating with them
at *cha-no-yu* (tea-ceremony) parties and other similar functions,
penetrating their designs, and reading their minds and characters
with far greater facility than he could read one of his own
Edicts.   Meanwhile the extravagance and the profusion a sojourn
with Hideyoshi meant entailed the heaviest demands upon the
already tax-burdened peasantry in their fiefs.[2]

Apart from presents to the Taikō, and to his Ministers
with their underlings—no inconsiderable item, by the way—
mansions had to be maintained in Kyōto and Ōsaka, and,
after 1594, in Fushimi, where the Taikō expected the assistance
of his dutiful dependents to help him to develop these cities
into something that might add lustre to the glories of the
newly-reared, or rather lately resurrected, centralised empire
of which he was the architect.   Then the Taikō's *fêtes* were
both magnificent and costly, and yet in several instances they
cost the Taikō but little.   At the reception of Valegnani's
embassy the expenses were not inconsiderable; but it was
Kuroda of Buzen and Minister Masuda of the Works Department that had most to do with meeting them.   Again, at
Nagoya in Hizen in 1593 the *fêtes* in honour of the envoys
from Korea were still more sumptuous; but to furnish them

---

2 Writes Froes (1569):—"A quo tempore Taicus regnum iniit, is Principes et
Dominos Japoniæ semper miserabiliter afflixit, tam in bello Coraino, quam in
ædificiis suis et structuris infinitis excitandis, quibus continenter operam suam
locare debuerant.   Consequenter verò afflixit et eorum famulos.   Accedit quod
rarò vel ad breve tempus eis potestatem fecerit, ut Regna sua et status invisere
possent, imò vult eos cum uxoribus et liberis sedem in aula sua figere: idque
facit quod vereatur, ne uspiam conjuratio aliqua, vel seditio contra suam
personam excitetur."

forth it was neither the citizens in the Imperial towns nor the peasants in the Taikō's own home estates that were burdened with exactions. Three years later on, preparations were being made to receive the Chinese embassy (Shin Ikei and his senior colleague) at Fushimi, and of these preparations Froez writes that "this expenditure accomplished the ruin of the princes and the lords, and that such was the purpose of the monarch,"—Hideyoshi to wit. As many as 100,000 workmen had been employed on these preparations for the best part of a year, and most of these had been furnished by "the princes and lords," as also most of the 100,000 troops, mostly cavalry, mustered to do honour to the embassy. And then when all had been brought well-nigh to completion the earthquakes of September, 1596, levelled the whole of magnificent Fushimi with the dust, wrecked Kyōto and all the Taikō's new structures therein—the Daibutsu included,— and left only a few wretched corners intact within the *enceinte* of the great stronghold of Ōsaka![3] And thereupon orders were given to have Ōsaka Castle restored and put in order forthwith, and it was restored and put in order and furnished with the most costly furnishings that had been left intact in Japan,—and all this, too, before the next 21st of October, that is, within six weeks. For the whole of this immense expense Hideyoshi had by no means to answer. Then the procession of gold-bedizened barges that escorted the Chinamen back to Sakai, as has been said, was gorgeous enough to have

---

[3] Charlevoix's account of this calamitous season (a revamp of Froez) has been translated into Japanese, thence retranslated into English, and then religiously quoted in what purport to be histories of Japan. The good Father's paragraphs may be condensed thus: On the 20th July for half-a-day there was a rain of ashes at Kyōto and Fushimi and of red sand at Ōsaka, and then later a rain of grey hairs covered all the Northern provinces. Three weeks later a haired comet shrouded in black vapours appeared and hung over Kyōto for fifteen days.—August 30th, a general earthquake over all Japan. Renewed on September 4th, when in half-an-hour the Taikō's palaces in Ōsaka were overthrown. On the 5th another shock destroyed Fushimi and many other towns utterly, the Taikō's losses amounting to some 3,000,000 "of gold." In his palace only the kitchen remained standing, and in that the Taikō, carrying his son in his arms, took refuge. Seven hundred (?) of his concubines (Froez's words here are: "Ipsumque Taici domicilium amplissimum corruit, et, ut fama est, *Septuaginta* ejus feminas ac quasdam nobilitate illustres oppressit ") were crushed under the ruins. Not a single Christian is said to have perished. At the same time there was a huge tidal wave, so extraordinary that the country was flooded to Kyōto on one side, and on the other to the extremity of Bungo and to Hakata. Shortly afterwards Lake Biwa rose like a storm-tossed ocean and inundated all the neighbouring country. The Taikō at first looked upon this calamity as a punishment for his having undertaken tasks too great for mortal man, but soon, like Pharaoh of old, he hardened his heart and gave orders for the re-erection of all his overturned edifices.

made not merely good contemporary Queen Bess in her somewhat niggardly magnificence, but even Solomon in all his
glory, or the Queen of Sheba herself, uncharitably envious.   In
this procession the Taikō was represented by one comparatively
poorly-equipped vessel; it was the submissive *daimyō* that
furnished forth all the items in the splendours of this Japanese
floating Field of the Cloth of Gold, and the finest and most
magnificent item in the whole inventory was that supplied by
the recently subjected Daté Masamune, of Sendai, in the
far and frosty North.   And all this grand and sumptuous
display at Ōsaka would go but a very little way towards
endearing Daté to those subordinate *samurai* of his he had
left at home to make themselves unpopular in their districts
by having to squeeze extra taxes out of their retainers in
order to defray the expenses of this precious contribution to
the pomp with which the erstwhile peasant Hideyoshi contrived,
or at least endeavoured, to impress a sense of the greatness of
himself (and incidentally of Japan) upon the ambassadors of
the most haughty and the most punctilious Court there has
ever been, not merely in the East, but in the world.

That the Taikō's government by no means pressed heavily
upon the *bourgeoisie* of the Imperial towns or upon the peasants
in his own domains becomes abundantly clear from the
assertions of the Jesuits—assertions which are all the more
credible from the circumstance that after they and Coelho
had been thrown over by Hidéyoshi in 1587 their comments
upon his personality and his administration become not merely
caustic, but rancorous in the extreme.   And yet we find
Charlevoix synthetising their remarks on the attitude of the
commonalty towards the Taikō in a very remarkable and
very suggestive fashion.   In the festivities that had marked
Hideyoshi's ostensible demission of the office of *Kwanbaku*
(Regent) in favour of his nephew Hidetsugu, and his own
assumption of the style of Taikō in 1592, there had been a
most fantastic hunting-party near Kyōto, in which the knightly
hunters had been rewarded with a bag of 15,000 brace of
birds.   " After the chase," writes Charlevoix, " Hideyoshi thus
entered the capital, amidst the acclamations of the people,
by whom he was more loved than by the grandees, because,
in spite of his great expenditures, *he in no way crushed them*

with imposts, and because the multitude fed itself gladly on those vast projects and on those great shows *which cost it nothing,* and which it fancies give great lustre to the nation."

In spite of this most express testimony in favour of the mildness of the Taikō's administration from his bitterest foes, an English author has charged Hideyoshi with the oppression of the commonalty, and adduces three specific instances of arbitrary and tyrannical exactions from the lower orders. In the first case, the unit of land-taxation for nine hundred years had been the *tan* of some 1,440 square yards; and this *tan* the Taikō reduced to its present dimensions of 1,210 square yards, and levied the same amount of taxation on the reduced unit as had been previously paid on the original and larger one. This regulation, of course, brought into the treasury an extra 20 per cent. of revenue from taxation throughout all the Imperial domains. But, on the other hand, it must not be forgotten that, all things considered, an increase of taxation was neither unreasonable nor unjust. Hideyoshi's government had given the farmers of his own fiefs that peace and security so essential for their industrial prosperity; and for that peace and security they and their ancestors had sighed in vain for generations. For that inestimable boon the addition of a fifth to the old rate of taxation was surely no extravagant ransom to be called upon to pay. Furthermore, the improvements effected by Hideyoshi's *Bugyō* of Works and Agriculture in such matters as irrigation works and better transport facilities had greatly raised the annual value of the average holding in the home provinces at least. And some of the Daimyō were not slow to profit by the object-lesson; the fine system of aqueducts and canals in Kaga, for example, dating from shortly after this epoch.

Another instance is found in the circumstance that in 1589 Hideyoshi distributed as much as 365,000 *ryō* in gold, and as much in silver, among the territorial nobles. It is said that large sums were obtained from the lower orders. Such a proposition may well be doubted, however. It was only after the establishment of his own mint in Kyōto that gold and silver began to be coined on anything but the smallest scale in Japan, and the 730,000 *ryō* had all most probably been struck by Hideyoshi's own Minister of Finance. The bullion would come partly from the mines in Hideyoshi's own domains, and possibly in still greater part from the presents offered by the large feudatories recently subjected. To a certain extent, then, the Daimyō would merely be receiving back in an altered form the material of their own gifts. What stands seriously against the hypothesis that the 730,000 *ryō* distributed in 1589 were exacted from the lower orders is that down to the issues of Hideyoshi's own mint the gold and silver coinage in the hands of the commonalty was extremely small—in short, about *nil*. Down to this date the currency of Japan had been almost entirely a copper currency, and for an adequate supply of coins the islanders had been largely dependent on China. Now, in the matter of foreign trade Hideyoshi had always shown himself keenly interested; while he was anxious to debar the Portuguese and Spanish priests from his dominions, he always accorded the Iberian traders the warmest welcome. The question of the most advantageous medium of exchange must surely have occupied his attention, as well as that of his Minister of Finance, and just as the Japanese financiers of Meiji have deemed it advisable to adopt a gold standard in order to bring the country in line with the great trading nations of the West, so Hideyoshi would seem to have come to the conclusion that if full advantage was to be reaped from the prosecution of the trade with the gold-and-silver hunting merchants from Macao and Manila, her copper standard would have to be abandoned by Japan, and copper coins used as token money merely. One of the most considerable problems that Count Matsukata had to face on the adoption of the gold standard by Japan in 1897 was the disposal of the bulk of the silver coinage then in circulation. A similar problem in the matter of the old copper coinage appears to have confronted Hideyoshi about 1587 or 1588, and one device he adopted in its solution, curiously enough, is fixed upon by his English biographer as his third example of the Regent's high-handed treatment of his meaner subjects. Writes Mr. Dening:—

"As an instance of an exploit which involved an enormous amount of suffering and hardship among the poorer classes, and yet which had no object beyond the gratification of his love of notoriety, we may mention the erection of the great Buddhist idol at Nara (*sic*). Hideyoshi was no believer in Buddhism; and hence his large expenditure for this object had no religious motive to palliate it. The erection of the idol was undertaken as a mere pastime. It was the project of a mind to which the conception and the carrying out of giant schemes was a second nature: its chief object was to create astonishment. It was true that, as he boasted, Hideyoshi did in five years what it took another twenty years to accomplish; but the question is, what did this increased speed involve? It involved the ruin, the reduction to the most abject poverty, of hundreds and thousands of those who were engaged on the work. One would think that the Taikō had had abundant opportunity for displaying his Herculean powers in the number of lawful undertakings in which he had been engaged without resorting to such childish methods as this. But the greatest geniuses have their weak points, and this love of being the author of prodigies was one of Hideyoshi's most prominent defects."[4]

Now, apart from the fact that the huge idol then cast, much larger than the one still to be seen at Kamakura, served a

---

[4] The following from a letter of Froez's is interesting,—all the more so as Froez could often see what things really meant. "Hideyoshi's third device was to rebuild the Daibutsu, a most stately temple of an idol, together with a great monastery which the *bonzes* had adjoining. This structure had been reared with great magnificence and at immense cost in the city of Nara by the Emperors when they exercised universal dominion. And apart from the fact that this temple was dedicated to such an abominable cult, it was truly a marvellous and kingly structure; having among other things an idol of Shaka of such size that it exceeded the largest statue and colossus now found in the world. It was of metal, all gilt, and the Japanese of all parts crowded to worship it with marvellous devotion and veneration. But some few years ago [1567] it was destroyed by a Christian, who could not endure that the Devil should be so zealously worshipped in that place, and so set fire to it; hence both the temple of the idol and the monastery went to the ground. Now the Tyrant has determined to re-erect not merely the said monastery and temple, but also the same idol—not, however, in the city of Nara, but in his new city of Kyōto [Hideyoshi added a section to Kyōto], in order that the work may be more celebrated and greater than has ever before been seen during all these centuries in Japan, as will be really the case. And all this not from the devotion he has for the idol, but out of mere ostentation and for the greatness of his name in order the better to gain the minds of the populace, who, devoted to this idol, greatly praise this undertaking; and still much more by this and other devices to mask his tyranny and the sordidness of his mind; giving to understand that of the great hoard of gold and silver he is accumulating he does not wish to make use for his own advantage or his own gratification, but for the content and general weal of the people, and for the honour and glory of the gods. And he is astutely planning to possess himself of all the iron in Japan, *having ordered that all the mechanics and common people should leave off wearing swords and carrying any other sort of weapons (with which such people are here always well provided)*, and bring them to a place indicated for the purpose to be converted into the iron work necessary in the temple. Thus the populace is disarmed, and he the more secure in his arbitrary dominion. And this device is a thing never yet heard of or seen in Japan; it could have proceeded only from the brain of Quambacundono [Hideyoshi], cunning and crafty beyond human belief. Now he is depriving the people of their arms under the pretext of devotion to Religion, and he does it with the greatest advantage to himself, alleging the excessive expenses he would otherwise have to be at. And thus he contrives in such an artful way to colour his principal design of rearing this temple, in which is to be erected an idol representing—himself! whereby he may become one of the gods and be worshipped by all the people of these kingdoms. But the Lord our God, who knows how to make mock of all wisdom of the flesh, and to humble all the wickedness of this world, will, we trust, soon bring him low, and render all his astuteness and all his iniquity vain and naught!"

A A

useful purpose in absorbing a great amount of the bad copper coins Hideyoshi wished to remove from circulation, the erection of the image and its shrine was not undertaken as a mere pastime. Such a project would do much to conciliate the good-will of the devout Buddhists in the empire, who were at once numerous and powerful. Among them were to be reckoned some of the Regent's own best captains—notably Katō Kiyomasa, while among his most trusted councillors there were others of the faith besides his Minister of Worship, his reverence Mayeda Gen-i ("Guenifoin"), Governor of Kyōto. Having once tamed the warrior priests of Negoro, Hideyoshi, true to his wonted policy, aimed at attaching them and their followers, and such as they and their followers, to himself, and of making use of them when possible. Only a few months previously Nobunaga's direst and invincible foe, Kennio Kosa, had rendered Hideyoshi the most substantial services in the course of his campaign against Satsuma. And these services had been possible only from the Regent's having been able to conciliate the High-priest, and from the High-priest's consenting to exercise his influence over the monks of Satsuma. As by Henry IV. Paris had been considered to be fully worth a Mass, so Hideyoshi deemed a new Daibutsu no very extravagant price to pay for the material (if not the very moral) assistance of such potent factors in the empire as Kennio Kosa and his brethren. Besides, on the Buddhist priests would fall all the odium (if any) of collecting the material necessary for the image, and also of finding the workmen. And the story of the rebuilding of the Eastern Hongwanji in Kyōto in modern times indicates how easy it is for the Buddhist priesthood to raise almost fabulous sums by appealing to the piety or the superstition of even this comparatively enlightened and very materialistic age. The sum expended (Yen 7,000,000) on this modern structure must have been as great as that devoted to the erection of Hideyoshi's Daibutsu, and yet we hear no complaints of the rebuilding of the Eastern Hongwanji " having involved the ruin, the reduction to the most abject poverty, of hundreds and thousands of those who were engaged on the work."

That vainglory as well as policy entered into the motives that prompted the erection of the colossal image is no doubt perfectly true. The Jesuits are emphatic in their assertion of Hideyoshi's somewhat astonishing megalomania, although they are altogether astray as to the precise model on which the Regent endeavoured to form himself. Says Charlevoix:—

"It was his craze to copy Nobunaga in everything, and to endeavour to surpass him in the same things wherein this great prince had made himself admired; but if his ideas were as vast, they were far from being as just; he always lacked a certain taste in everything he carried out, and was satisfied provided the multitude, who judge by the eye, or rather by the fathom, was charmed. However, as he sometimes employed excellent workmen, he did not entirely fail to accomplish very fine things."

Now, strangely enough, this assertion is followed by an elaborate comparison between Nobunaga's and Hideyoshi's methods of administration, and in most details the comparison actually amounts to a contrast. From this fact the extent to which Hideyoshi's mania for "copying" his former chief— a great man indeed, but in almost every respect, except perhaps taste, his successor's inferior—was carried may be inferred. Sir Ernest Satow comes much nearer the truth when, in connection with this Kyōto Daibutsu of Hideyoshi's, he remarks that it was undertaken in imitation of Yoritomo, who had originated the project of erecting a Daibutsu at Kamakura. A careful analysis of the Taikō's work shows that it was not Nobunaga, but Yoritomo, he had set before himself as a pattern, if indeed he had such a thing as a pattern at all.

To speak in homely language sadly inconsistent with that revered figment, the dignity of history, a wonted practice of the peasant-ruler's seems to have been not so much to endeavour to kill two birds with one stone, as to disable many fowls with a single missile, and, after catching them, to utilise them in the inglorious but beneficial function of providing eggs for his own table. In the light of this truth—for truth it was, as anyone with average patience and intelligence can easily discern—even the vainglorious project of the Daibutsu, set afoot by the impious and irreligious Taikō Sama, "whose soul is in Hell to all eternity," stands forth as no mean item in Hideyoshi's plethoric bag of statecraft tricks. There is nothing in contemporary—or indeed in subsequent—records to indicate that this erection of the Daibutsu by the Taikō was regarded either by the commonalty, by the Buddhist priesthood, or by the Japanese nation at large as an act either of reprehensible vainglory, of oppression, or of extortion. As regards the origin, the value, and the sociological importance of religious beliefs and cults, Hideyoshi would seem to have thought out all the vital questions connected with them.

The two cardinal points that have mainly determined Japanese historians in their estimates of the various Regents or Shōguns that swayed the real authority in the Empire from the twelfth century down to 1867 have been the attitude of these statesmen towards the Imperial House, and the measure of success with which they have sustained the prestige of Dai Nippon *vis-à-vis* foreign Powers. The Hōjō Regents of Kamakura (1201–1333), in spite of their undoubtedly able and, on the whole, beneficent administration of the country, have been covered with the blackest obloquy—stigmatised as "fiends, serpents, beasts"—on account of their very cavalier treatment of the divine line of the Sun-goddess. Yet in connection with the famous episode of 1281—the Japanese analogue of the Spanish Armada—Rai Sanyō asserts that "the repulse of the Tartar barbarians by Hōjō Tokimune, and his preserving the dominions of our Son of Heaven, were sufficient to atone for the crimes of his ancestors." The conduct of the Ashikaga Shōguns (1338–1573) towards the Emperors has also brought the invectives of Japanese annalists upon them, but the special act in the whole course of their two hundred and fifteen years' administration that has evoked the bitterest reprobation was Yoshimitsu's acceptance of investiture as King of Japan from the Emperor of China.[5] In view of these considerations it may be well to consider Hideyoshi's attitude towards the rightful sovereign of Japan somewhat minutely.

As we have already seen, the Emperor Okimachi (born 1571, died 1593) occasionally endeavoured to assert himself and to make his influence felt in the administration of the affairs of the State. About the time of the Satsuma campaign of 1587 he was induced to abdicate in favour of his grandson Go Yōzei, and in 1588 or 1589 the Regent contrived to turn the formal investiture of the youthful Emperor with the Imperial

---

[5] In the Chinese Emperor's letter of instructions accompanying Hideyoshi's patent of investiture this event is alluded to. "The investiture was first granted to your country by an ancestor, Emperor Ching-tsu (1403–1425), so that this is now the second time of doing so. Our favour to Japan may well be said to be of old standing."

dignity to his own advantage. To enable the reader to grasp the real meaning and intent of Hideyoshi in organising the elaborate pageants that marked this event it may be well to cite both a foreign and a Japanese account of the circumstances. Says Charlevoix (summarising the missionary letters of the year):—

"The dedication of Daibutsu accomplished, Cambacundono (*i.e.* the Lord Regent) bethought himself to have it published abroad that he was going to reinstall the Hereditary Emperors in the possession of all their authority. He began by the erection of a superb palace; and as the Dairi had just abdicated the crown in favour of his son,[6] he took occasion of the ceremony of the coronation of the new monarch to give a splendid *fête* to this Court. The young Dairi appeared there as Emperor, but after the comedy had lasted some days, matters were put in the same condition as they had been in before, and all the gain the new Emperor made, therefore, was the magnificent palace that had been built for him."

So far the able and judicious Charlevoix, condensing the material supplied by the astute and keenly-observant members of his Society at work in Japan a century and a half before he wrote. Now let us listen to Mr. Dening, who speaks after a collation of Japanese authorities:—

"The following year Hideyoshi determined to celebrate his triumph in the south by entertaining the Emperor at his own palace. During the preceding tumultuous times little attention had been paid to royalty, and few were acquainted with the proper ceremonies to be observed on the occasion of an Imperial visit. Mayeda Gen-i being one of these few, after conference with the various nobles he decided on the ceremonies that would most befit the occasion. In the main they resembled those which had been observed by Ashikaga Yoshimitsu. The preparations for the pageant occupied three months. When all was complete, Hideyoshi and all the great officers of State accompanied the Emperor from his own palace to the Jūraku, Hideyoshi's own recently erected palace. The sensation caused by the royal reception was very great. No such thing had happened for over a hundred years, and many were those to whom the Emperor was as mysterious a personage as one of the gods. The Emperor remained five days in the Jūraku as Hideyoshi's guest. On the second day of his visit, Hideyoshi assembled all the chief barons of the land and made them swear allegiance to the Emperor *and to his chief Minister, the Kwampaku. They agreed that anyone who broke his oath should be punished by his fellow-barons, and, after the manner of the time, pronounced curses on such an one in the name of all the gods of the sixty-six provinces of the empire.* The number and magnificence of the gifts presented to the Emperor on this occasion were the wonder of the age."

---

[6] His grandson, as a matter of fact.

If it be remembered that Hideyoshi was then (in 1588–89) still engaged in the task of extending and consolidating his power, and when we recall the fashion in which he had utilised Nobunaga's puppet heir in that undertaking, the italicised portion of the foregoing citation will become pregnant with significance.

When Nobunaga had restored the Ashikaga Shōgun and occupied Kyōto in 1568, it was Hideyoshi who had urged upon his chief the advisability of rebuilding the Mikado's palace and of supplying the Imperial household with a substantial maintenance. But when Hideyoshi became the real chief of the State himself, there appears to be evidence to establish the fact that, so far from his being true to the policy he urged on Nobunaga, the Civil List he doled out for the support of the Court was niggardly. And in no matter of any real moment does the Emperor seem to have been consulted by him. The Jesuits were indeed aware that the Dairi was the legitimate Emperor of Japan, and that he had once been the real ruler of the Empire, but it was not Hideyoshi they had to thank for the information; while persistent efforts to hoodwink the Koreans and the Chinese in this matter were actually made. At the opening of his negotiations with the Koreans, they had taken great offence at Hideyoshi's presumption in making use of the word *Chin* (We), which appeared to them an assumption of equality with the Emperor of China. When the Korean ambassadors did reach Japan in 1590, they were still further outraged to discover that in Japan Hideyoshi was merely a subject, and that the homage due to the sovereign was reserved for the Tennō. Furthermore, in the dispatch addressed to the Korean Monarch through this embassy by Hideyoshi, it will be observed that no allusion whatsoever is made to the Mikado, the real sovereign of Japan. And in connection with the negotiations at Peking in 1594 that led to the dispatch of the Chinese embassy of 1596, the following remarks of Mr. Aston are instructive:—"Konishi's [7] language on this occasion has been fully reported, and is eminently suggestive of the well-known witty definition of a

---

[7] Mr. Aston represents Konishi as having gone to Peking on this mission. The missionary writers assert that it was Konishi's friend, Naitō, the ex-Prince of Tamba, that conducted the negotiations in question.

HIDEYOSHI'S DOMESTIC POLICY.   375

diplomatist. One of his most astounding assertions was that
the Tennō (Mikado) and Koku-ō (Shōgun) of Japan were one
and the same person."

Yet again, in the language of his communications to the
Viceroy of the Indies (1591) and to the Governor of the
Philippines (1597) there is nothing to indicate that Hideyoshi
was merely the deputy of a higher power. These two documents
are so remarkable for this as well as for various other reasons
that the reproduction of at least one of them will be profitable.
There is such a wonderful consistency in the tone and spirit
of these two missives, separated as they are by an interval of
six years, that they cannot be dismissed as the mere chance
productions of an upstart intoxicated with a temporary fit of
crazy and capricious vainglory. To the Viceroy of the Indies
the Regent wrote as follows:—

"Most Illustrious Lord,—I have received the letter you have
addressed to me with pleasure, and from reading it I fancy I can
appreciate the prodigious distance which separates us, as Your
Excellency has very well remarked. Japan comprises more than
sixty 'kingdoms' or principalities, which for long have been
agitated by troubles and civil wars, from the refusal of those who
have seized upon them to render to their Sovereign Lord the obedience
which they owed him. The sight of such calamities affected me very
keenly from my tenderest youth, and from then I thought of the
means to remedy them. With that view I have strenuously applied
myself to acquire three virtues, the most necessary for success in
the achievement of such a great project. In the first place I have
studied to make myself affable to everybody in order to win all
hearts. Secondly, I have endeavoured to accustom myself to judge
sanely of all things, and to comport myself with much prudence
and discretion. In the third place, I have omitted nothing to give
a great idea of my worth. By this I have succeeded in subjecting the
whole of Japan to my laws; and I govern it with a mildness which in
no way yields to the valour I displayed in conquering it. Above all,
I have made my tenderness felt among the workers who cultivate
the soil and maintain abundance in my Empire; all my severity is for
those who remove themselves from the paths of virtue. To-day
there is nothing more tranquil than Japan, and this tranquillity
constitutes her strength. This vast monarchy is like an immovable
rock, and all the efforts of its enemies are vain to move it.
Thus not only am I at peace in my States, but men come here
from the most distant countries to render me the obedience which is
my due. At present I am purposing to subject China to myself, and
as I entertain no doubts of my success in this design, I trust that soon
we shall be much nearer each other, and that communication between
us will be easier. With respect to what regards religion, Japan is
the realm of the *Kami*, that is to say of *Shin*, which is the origin of
all things; the good order of the government which has been
established here from the beginning depends on the exact observance
of the laws on which it is founded, and whose authors are the *Kami*

themselves. They cannot be deviated from without involving the disappearance of the difference which ought to subsist between sovereign and subject, and of the subordination of wives to husbands, children to fathers, of vassals to lords, of servants to their masters. In a word, these laws are necessary for the maintenance of good order at home and of tranquillity abroad. The 'Fathers of the Company,' as they are called, have come to these islands to teach another religion here; but as that of the *Kami* is too surely founded to be abolished, this new 'law' can only serve to introduce into Japan a diversity of cults prejudicial to the welfare of the State. It is for this reason that by Imperial Edict I have forbidden these foreign Doctors to continue to preach their doctrine. I have even ordered them to quit Japan, and I am resolved no longer to allow any one to come here to spread new opinions. I nevertheless desire that trade between You and Us should always be on the same footing (as before). I shall have care that the ways are free by sea and by land; I have freed them from all pirates and brigands. The Portuguese will be able to traffic with my subjects in all security; and I will in no wise suffer any one to do them the least wrong. . . ."

As in the case of those addressed to the King of Korea and to the Governor-General of the Philippines, there is nothing in the language of this dispatch that would have led its recipient to believe that its writer was not the real sovereign of Japan, or that the pacification of the country and the subjection of its sixty odd provinces to his sway, on which Toyotomi dilates at such length, had been prosecuted and accomplished in virtue of a commission from a superior power. In this respect the tone of Hideyoshi's dispatches is in marked contrast with the phraseology employed by modern Japanese statesmen, whose invariable wont it is to ascribe everything to the virtue of the Emperor. And as a matter of fact, in the actual disposal of the fiefs Hideyoshi acted as if he and not the Emperor had been the lord-paramount of Japan. In this disposal of the soil of his empire, the Mikado now ceased to be consulted, even formally. In Yoritomo's time everything in this regard had been done with the Imperial sanction; under the Ashikaga Shōguns the great provincial offices had often been made hereditary in the families of their own nominees. Now, under Hideyoshi, the third stage in the development of Japanese feudalism is reached; and from this date down to the end of the Tokugawa supremacy, the Emperor of Japan is removed from all contact with, and from all control over, the feudatories.

As we have said, this missive to the Viceroy of the Indies

is remarkable on other grounds as well as on that to which
we have just adverted. The exposition of the writer's position
towards Christianity and religion generally—and the gist of
the statement is repeated in but slightly varying language in
the communication to Tello, Governor of the Philippines in
1597—is exceedingly clear and exceedingly striking.

It will be observed that nothing is said of Buddhism, and
that no allusion is made to the cult of Confucius or to
Chinese philosophy. According to the Taikō (*Kwanbaku*, when
he replied to Valegnani's embassy), the religion of Japan was
Shintō, the indigenous cult of the autochthonous *Kami* that
had been worshipped by the nation for centuries before the
introduction of exotic Buddhism in the sixth century. In his
attitude towards this Buddhism, as well as towards Chinese
philosophy, Hideyoshi presents a great divergence from his
Tokugawa successors. While in the interests of statecraft and
internal quiet Buddhism was not merely to be tolerated, but
even placated by such devices as the Daibutsu and the
re-erection of the sumptuous temples so remorselessly razed by
Nobunaga, yet the Taikō was far from being inclined to make
it practically the State religion of Japan, or to vest its priests
with the important censorial and semi-administrative functions
afterwards imparted to them by Iyeyasu.

Under the latter ruler and his successors the study of the
Chinese classics received such exceptional encouragement that
they soon became widely diffused all through the land. On
Chinese literature Hideyoshi set such little store that he once
declared that when he had accomplished the conquest of China
and Korea he would compel those countries to adopt the Japanese
syllabic system of writing. In the dispatch we have cited a
careless reader might fancy that the phrases referring to the
subjection of vassal to lord and so forth contain an implicit
reference to the *go-rin*, or five relations, of Confucianism.
However, it will be observed that of two of these relations—that
of younger brother to elder brother, and of friend to friend—Hideyoshi says nothing whatsoever. What he pronounces in favour
of is autochthonous Japanese Shintō, pure and uncontaminated
by the leaven of any exotic cult or any foreign philosophy.
Not that he purposed to force this Shintō upon a people
reluctant to re-adopt it; his later attitude towards Buddhism

supplies ample evidence that in the matter of religious
toleration he was far in advance of any contemporary ruler
in Christendom. Only in this toleration the professors of a
religious cult were to find no pretext for aggression on their
fellow-subjects who happened to be of a different faith. There
can be but little doubt that this consideration had great
weight in the Taikō's proscription of the Christian priests,
who preached a creed at once aggressive, intolerant, and
persecuting. So much had appeared from the conduct of
Takayama in Takatsuki and Akashi, of Ōmura Sumitada in
Ōmura, of the Lord of Amakusa in his island, while, when
the foreign priests had been supreme in the new city of
Nagasaki, they had strictly prevented any non-Christian from
living within its limits. With the worship of the ancestral
gods in the Shintō pantheon these fanatic foreigners would
be sure to come (as they had done in Ōmura, Hirado, Bungo,
Chikuzen, Yamaguchi, and elsewhere) into dire collision, and so
give rise to commotions that would be nothing short of disastrous
to the internal peace it had cost him so much effort to establish.

The Jesuit writers tell us that one chief motive that
constrained Hideyoshi to banish them was "a design of ranking
himself among the gods, by which he hoped to make himself
adored by all his subjects as one of the chief conquerors of
Japan. Now, knowing that none but Christians would dare
to oppose him, he took a resolution of exterminating them
forthwith before they could have time to make a party against
him." That the Taikō did look forward to an apotheosis is
indeed indisputable. For the last few years of his life he
fostered and favoured the ancestral worship of the *Kami* (the
Shintō gods) and the indigenous cult of Dai Nippon in a very
pronounced manner. In the new quarter he had recently added
to the capital city of Kyōto, he had prepared a site for a
temple whose chaste splendours were to eclipse those of any
of the fanes of the land. And the deity to whom this nascent
sanctuary was to be dedicated was—himself.

Before all things a warlike people, to none of their eight
million ancestral divinities did the Japanese more frequently
or more fervently appeal than to their War-god. And, strangely
enough, the form under which the War-god was invoked seems
to have been the outcome of Buddhist priestly ingenuity. The

fable has it that the Empress Jingō, on starting to accomplish the conquest of Korea in 201 A.D., discovered that she was pregnant, but by the favour of the gods she found a stone (at Hirashiku, near Nagasaki) which, being placed in her girdle, delayed her accouchement until her triumphant return from the peninsula. After the reduction of Korea, Jingō, on her arrival in Japan, was delivered of her thirty-six-months child, destined to hold in the popular estimation even a higher place of honour than his Amazonian mother, who was credited with having effected her conquests through the power of her yet unborn son. After leaving her couch Jingō erected at Toyoura in Nagato a shrine dedicated to the Spirit of War that had guided her army. Her new-born son thus honoured was called Ōjin, of whose name Hachiman is the Chinese form; and in mediæval times it was Hachiman Dai-bosatsu that the Japanese *samurai* invariably invoked as his tutelary deity. Now of Ōjin, or Hachiman, no warlike exploits are recorded in the national annals, his reign seeming to have been one of almost unbroken tranquillity, while he himself is represented to have done much to foster rural industry and to promote navigation and the introduction of new arts, of *savants*, and of Chinese books from Korea. When in later ages the Buddhist monks contrived to establish him in the position of a War-god, they probably were not altogether unconscious of the irony of foisting upon this most warlike nation a divinity whose claim to be invoked as the God of Battles was strictly of the *lucus a non lucendo* order.

Of the absurdity inherent in this cult of Hachiman, Hideyoshi no doubt was sensible; and in the correction of the absurdity it is more than possible he fancied he detected his best chance of being able to obtain sure and exalted position in the national pantheon himself. At all events, in the magnificent structure rising to completion on Amida-ga-mine in Kyōto, with all the iron-work in it made from sword-blades, he was after his death to be worshipped as Shin Hachiman, or the New Hachiman. In various other quarters of Japan similar but naturally less splendid shrines were also being reared, to be dedicated in due time to this new and very real incarnation of the War-god.

A modern reader may well fancy that such a project on the

Taiko's part was nothing short of vainglorious insanity. Hide-yoshi, however, knew perfectly well that men who had deserved far less than he at the hands of his fellow-countrymen had been made the recipients of divine honours shortly after their decease. Even Taira Masakado, the only rebel that ever attempted to aspire to the Imperial dignity, had been honoured with a splendid temple in the Kwantō a few years after his defeat and death. At the present day, indeed, there is no Shin Hachiman in the Japanese pantheon. But an explanation of this fact is not difficult to find. Shortly after Hideyoshi's death the Regents to whose charge he had committed the Empire con-ducted the apotheosis of the dead hero with the greatest pomp and magnificence, and for several years the shrine was thronged with devotees. Then in 1619, four years after the struggle between Iyeyasu and Hideyori (1615), in which the death of the latter brought the House of the Taikō to an end, the temple of Shin Hachiman was demolished by Itakura, the Governor of Kyōto, who no doubt took his cue from Iyeyasu's sarcastic remark to the effect that the new God of War had proved of but very little service to the cause of his own son.

The miscarriage of the Taikō's endeavour to establish himself as a divinity after death was occasioned simply by the ill-success that attended his attempt to found a family. His efforts in this latter direction are interesting to follow. Just before the Korean expedition he had for a second time lost an only son, and the loss appears to have touched him very keenly, as he then (ætat. 57) seems to have abandoned all hopes of further posterity. The only thing left for him to do was to arrange for the ultimate transmission of his power to one of his relatives. For this purpose his nephew, Hidetsugu (the Dainangandono of the missionaries), a young man of twenty-seven, was selected, and in 1592 he was associated with Hideyoshi in the govern-ment and invested as *Kwanbaku* (Regent) by the Mikado, Hideyoshi ostensibly demitting that office and assuming the style of Taikō. All Hideyoshi's palaces and much good advice were conveyed to the new Regent, but very little real power. Then, after tracing the plan for the new citadel and city of Fushimi and laying the foundation stone of the former, the Taikō proceeded westward to direct the Korean expedition from Nagoya in Hizen, arriving there in September 1592. His sojourn in Kyūshū lasted until the autumn of 1593, and by the time of his return to Kyōto relations between him and his nephew had become so unsatisfactory that the latter thought it advisable to evade his uncle's request to come to welcome him (most probably in Ōsaka).

The explanation of this is that meanwhile, in 1592, one of the Taikō's secondary wives, Yodogimi, daughter of Asai, dispossessed Lord of Ōmi, had given birth to a son; and although many believed the child to be no son of Hideyoshi's, yet the Taikō not only acknowledged the paternity, but evinced the greatest joy over the propitious event. Seemingly, in the course of 1593, the *Kwanbaku* (Hidetsugu) began to receive a succession of letters from his uncle, urging him to take command of an augmented armament against China, and to proceed to the conquest of the empire, which he was promised as his own special appanage. However, Hidetsugu showed himself in no way inclined to engage in the pursuit of a chimerical empire that might involve the ruin of his substantial prospects in Japan, and so he remained quiet at Kyōto. He was not slow to perceive that the Taikō merely wished to remove him from the way of his own late-born son, and he was in no mood to efface himself on behalf of Yodogimi's progeny.

On the return of the Taikō to Ōsaka in 1593 the apprehensions of the Regent were further roused by the request to adopt the Taikō's infant son as his own—a measure, of course, that would have had the effect of preventing him from transmitting his power to any of his own children, of whom he already had several. The ill-feeling thus already aroused between uncle and nephew was sedulously fanned by the dependents of the two different Courts, for the future prospects of the courtiers depended upon the answer to the question as to who was really to be the ruler of Japan. In the evil work of intensifying the mutual jealousy and distrust of the Taikō and of the *Kwanbaku* to a degree that made the co-existence of the relatives an impossibility, Ishida Mitsunari, Minister of Criminal Law and Administration, is charged by Japanese historians with having taken the chief share. Many of these authorities will have it that Ishida looked forward to grasping the supreme direction of affairs on the death of Hideyoshi, and that he exerted all his immense powers of intrigue to effect the speedy ruin of the Taikō's nephew, who stood so seriously in his way. That this view is correct is not unlikely; in this connection, although they speak in general terms of the intrigues of the courtiers in the rival Courts, the Jesuits make no explicit mention of Xibunojo's (Ishida's) name. However, it must not be forgotten that although no convert himself, Ishida was regarded by the missionaries as one of their most influential patrons. Whatever be the measure of truth in this charge, it is at all events clear that things soon came to such a pass that the uncle's distrust of his nephew was complete, and that he adopted every device to drive the *Kwanbaku* to compromise himself irretrievably.

At Kyōto, early in 1595, the Taikō celebrated an extraordinarily sumptuous *fête* to mark the ostensible formal completion of his surrender of power to his nephew. Thereupon the latter furnished a return *fête*, where some 26,000 tables were set forth, but the Taikō at the last moment professed himself unable to attend, and all the preparations went for nothing. And the same thing happened a few weeks later. This was very significant, for two similar incidents had counted as no small items in the provocation that led Akechi Mitsuhide to murder Nobunaga thirteen years before. The Regent fell into the trap, and through one of his retainers began to intrigue with the great feudatories. The first one of these he approached was Mōri, and Mōri at once informed the Taikō, who ordered him to pretend to enter into the cabal. A few weeks later on, one morning the Regent found himself confronted with a demand for plain answers to four of the very plain questions it was Hideyoshi's wont to address to those on whom he wished to fix a quarrel or whom he purposed to crush. Briefly they were:—(1) Why, while the Regent was so unwell that he could not go to see his uncle, he yet was able to take horse-exercise and to engage in archery every day? (2) Why he disgraced himself by executing criminals with his own hand?[8] (3) Why he had lately so greatly

8 For this see DICKSON's *Japan*, pp. 188–189, where, however, there are several errors of detail. Froez, after telling us that while the Regent "was handsome, well-formed, of a quick and penetrating wit, of an admirable discernment, of a noble presence, of engaging manners, wise, prudent, sober, modest, far removed from gross pleasures, a lover of the fine arts, taking much

increased his escort when he went abroad? and (4) Why he had lately endeavoured to impose a new form of oath upon Japanese subjects?

The fourth query sufficed to disclose to the Regent that Mōri had betrayed him, for he had asked Mōri to take a special oath of fidelity to himself. In his reply Hidetsugu confined his attention to the last two questions, and his uncle professed to find the answers so satisfactory that he openly declared that whosoever henceforth spoke ill of the Regent would meet with short shrift as a pestilent slanderer and backbiter. Meanwhile, in the utmost secresy, troops were being massed from all the neighbouring provinces in Ōsaka and Fushimi, and at last, when he felt himself secure and all the exits from Kyōto were effectually blockaded, the Taikō in Fushimi abruptly raised the mask. He wrote to the Regent informing him that all his intrigues were known, and that he had to retire to Kiyosu in Ōwari at once; otherwise he would be dealt with summarily. When the Regent went to Fushimi in abject submission his uncle refused to give him audience, and ordered him at once to make his way to Kōya-san, the monastery reserved for the reception of great political exiles. The whole course of the subsequent tragedy is traced at great length in Froez's monograph;[9] suffice it here to say that after a short interval the Regent, together with the few pages that had not been previously withdrawn from his retinue, was ordered to commit suicide. A young page of nineteen years of age performed the last friendly offices of a Japanese warrior in such circumstances for the Regent and his companions, and then received the fatal stroke himself from

pleasure in the society of men of letters, and himself cultivating with care all the sciences becoming a Prince destined to govern a nation such as the Japanese," he had yet one terrible weakness. "All these excellent qualities were quite obscured by a strange and most inhuman vice. He took a strange kind of pleasure and diversion in killing men, insomuch that when any one was condemned to die he chose to be the executioner himself. He walled in a place near his palace, and set in the middle a sort of table for the criminal to lie on till he hewed him to pieces. Sometimes, also, he took them standing and split them in two. But his greatest satisfaction was to cut them off limb by limb, which he did as exactly as one can take off the leg or wing of a fowl. Sometimes, also, he set them up for a mark, and shot at them with pistols and arrows." "On ajoûte," says Charlevoix, "qu'il prenait des femmes enceintes, et qu'il les dissequait toutes vivantes pour examiner la situation de leur fruit. La religion Chretienne aurait sans doute adouci des mœurs si monstreuses, s'il est vrai, comme quelques-uns l'ont assuré, que Cambacundono (the *Kwanbaku*) songeait sérieusement à l'embrasser; mais Dieu ne l'en jugea pas digne."

9 *De Morte Quabacundoni*, October 1595.

the Taikō's emissary.[10] Shortly after, all the ladies of the Regent's household, to the number of thirty-one, arrayed in their most sumptuous apparel, were sent to the common execution-ground in Kyōto and there beheaded, Hidetsugu's three children having first been executed before the eyes of their doomed mothers; and all the bodies were thrown into a hole in Sanjō-machi, over which a stone was placed with the inscription, "The Mound of Beasts." And then every structure that had been erected by the Regent Hidetsugu was razed to the ground, and every measure taken to erase his memory from the minds of his contemporaries and from the history of Japan.

On this occasion Hideyoshi did indeed have recourse to the banal and commonplace device of extermination—extermination thorough, utter, ruthless, and relentless. That he considered he had imperative reasons for divergence from his almost invariable policy of clemency towards those with whom he had had a clash of wills we cannot for a moment doubt. Hidetsugu's investiture with the Regency had been effected only when his uncle seems to have abandoned all hope of future offspring. The subsequent birth of Yodogimi's son, Hideyori, had introduced a new and wholly unexpected factor into the situation. For the problem with which he found himself thus suddenly confronted the Taikō at first endeavoured to find a solution in dispatching his nephew to conquer an empire for himself over-seas in China. When this device proved ineffectual, Hideyoshi had recourse to the common Japanese expedient of adoption, and attempted to get his own son acknowledged as his (the Regent's) heir by the Regent. When this attempt also proved abortive, the Taikō thought that he had very strong reasons for believing that on his own death Yodogimi and her son would almost surely be put out of the way by Hidetsugu. And as regards the latter, Hideyoshi may well have begun to question whether this cultured vivisector of criminals and of pregnant women was the man either to rule Japan or to transmit the power of the Toyotomi family to future generations. Furthermore, the Regent's conduct towards himself afforded grounds for suspicion, and the suspicions thus raised seem to have been sedulously intensified by Ishida and

10 DICKSON's account of this (*Japan*, p. 190) is more sensational, but—incorrect.

others of the Taikō's own immediate *entourage*. When proof
was at last supplied by Mōri that the Regent was actually
tampering with the fidelity of the great feudatories,[11] the
Taikō felt that the situation had become so desperate that it
and the future could be saved only by recourse to the most
desperate expedients.

In the June of the following year (1596), in the very midst
of the elaborate and sumptuous preparations for the reception
of the Chinese embassy, the infant Hideyori (*œtat.* 3) was
solemnly invested with the title of *Kwanbaku* (Regent), and
from that date onward the chief object of solicitude to the
Taikō was the safeguarding of the prospects of his heir and
successor. When, in June, 1598, his exceedingly robust constitution gave sudden but unmistakable signs of breaking
down, all his thoughts were occupied with the future of
Yodogimi's son. Yodogimi herself was a woman of no high
mental ability and no great force of character, but in her
the Taikō's trust was considerable, and the trust he reposed in
his legitimate consort (*née* Sugawara, the Kita Mandocoro-sama
of the Jesuits) was still greater. But without further loyal
support from the greatest of the barons, the infant Regent's
mother and Hideyoshi's chief spouse could not be expected to
maintain the power and prestige of the House of Toyotomi
during a long minority of fourteen years. Among these barons,
Tokugawa Iyeyasu was at once the most powerful if not the
most trustworthy. So Iyeyasu was summoned to the Taikō's
sick-room, and there the dying ruler told him that after his
(the Taikō's) death there would be great wars, and that
only he (Iyeyasu) could keep the empire tranquil. "I
therefore," Hideyoshi proceeded, "bequeath the whole country
to you, and trust that you will expend all your strength
in governing it. My son Hideyori is still young. I beg
that you will look after him. When he is grown up, I

---

11 Among others, Daté of Sendai was, if not indeed actually involved, at
all events suspected. At this date (August, 1595) he suddenly found himself
called upon for answers to two of those very plain questions it was Hideyoshi's
wont to address to such as he meant to deal with drastically. And Daté's
leading retainers were compelled to take an oath of allegiance to Hideyoshi,
swearing to report the slightest trace of treachery they might observe in
Daté's conduct, and binding themselves to serve the Taikō and his heirs for
ever. If they failed in any of these pledges they invoked upon themselves
the plague of foul leprosy, the anger of heaven during seven generations, and
everlasting suffering.

leave it to you to decide whether he shall be my successor or not."

Iyeyasu, however, declined the task the Taikō wished to impose upon him, and on being once again pressed to undertake it, persisted in his refusal to do so. However, he was afterwards installed as the chief of the Board of Five Regents the Taikō appointed immediately before his decease (September 16th, 1598). The other members of this Board were the great feudatories,—Mōri of Aki and nine other provinces, Ukida Hideiye of Bizen, Mayeda Toshi-iye of Kaga, and Uyesugi Kagekatsu, lately removed from Echigo to Aidzu. Of these, Mayeda was specially entrusted with the guardianship of Hideyori, who, with his mother, was to reside in the stronghold of Ōsaka, while Iyeyasu, installed in Fushimi, was to supervise the general administration of the empire. The five Ministers or *Bugyō* appointed by Hideyoshi in 1585 still remained in office, and were to discharge their functions under the direction of the Regents, who collectively *vis-à-vis* the *Bugyō* occupied the position of the Taikō. However, between the Regency and the Ministry a new Board of *Chū-rō* (Middle Councillors) was introduced, composed of three Daimyō of secondary rank, whose duty it was to be to effect the compromise of all difficulties that might arise between the five Regents and the five Ministers.

. Scarcely had these arrangements been completed when the Taikō, who had meanwhile rallied somewhat, again began to sink rapidly, and on the morning of September 16th, 1598, the greatest man Japan has ever seen passed peacefully away.

. For some time the death of the Taikō was kept secret, and such as ventured to speak of it were summarily and sharply dealt with. However, before the end of the year Iyeyasu and his co-regents felt themselves strong enough openly to cope with the situation. The Taikō's corpse was interred in Fushimi in the greatest state, and shortly afterwards, as has been mentioned already, the sumptuous shrine on Amida-ga-mine, behind Kyōto, was with the utmost pomp solemnly and formally dedicated to the New War-God of Japan.

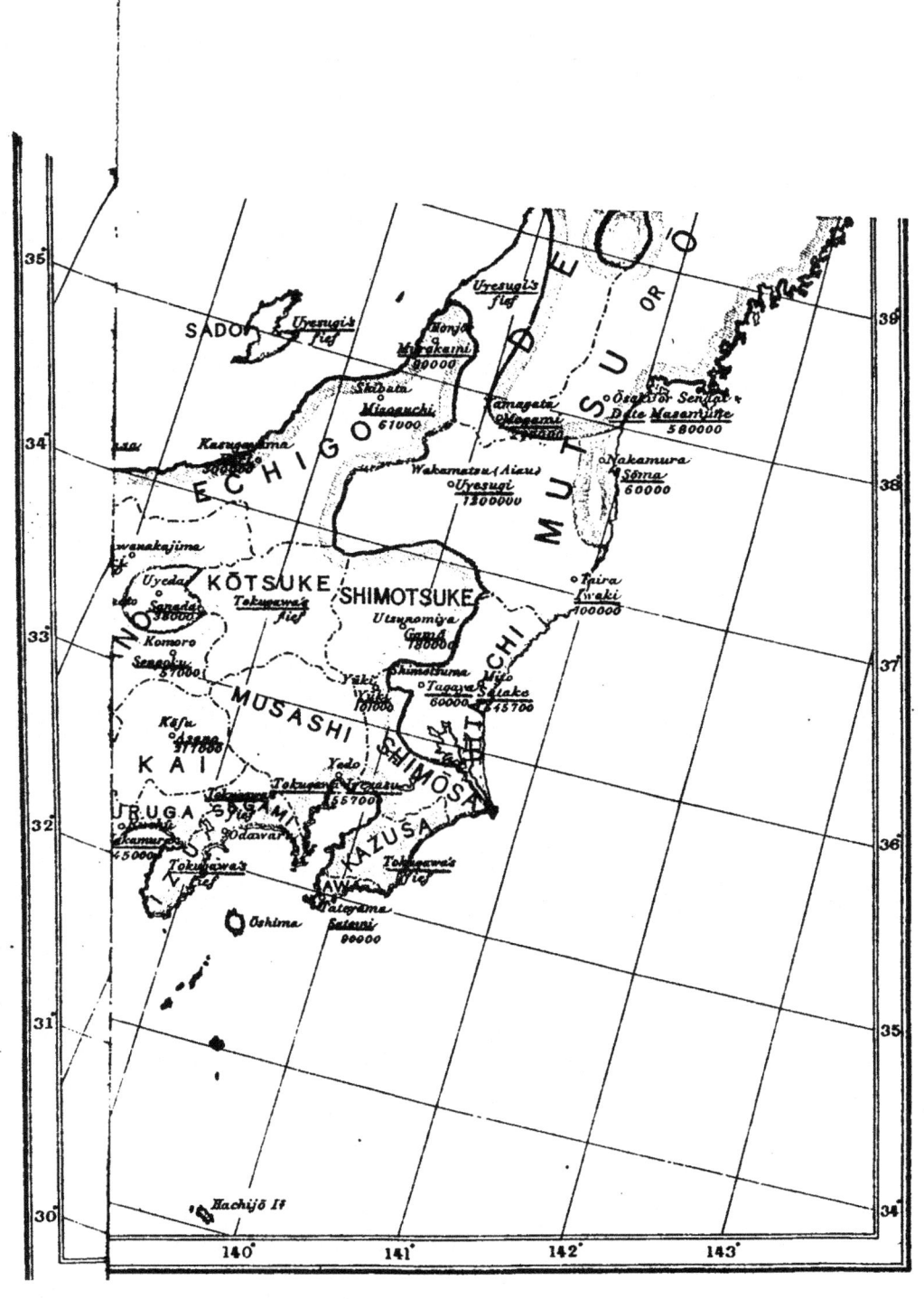

CHAPTER XIV.

SEKIGAHARA.

TO have a correct apprehension of the immediate course of events that followed the death of the Taikō, it is necessary to devote some little attention to the contemporary map of feudal Japan.

Leaving out of consideration the territories still held by the Buddhist priests and a numerous assemblage of smaller landholders, we find the soil of the Empire partitioned out among two hundred and fourteen Daimyō, each with an *assessed* revenue of 10,000 *koku* of rice, or over. The sum total of the assessment of these two hundred and fourteen fiefs amounted to 18,723,200 *koku*, and to this total the domains of the five members of the Board of Regency contributed more than a third (6,341,000 *koku*). Of these five, Tokugawa Iyeyasu, ruling the greater part of the Kwantō from his rapidly growing new fortress-town of Yedo, with a revenue of 2,557,000 *koku*, was by far the most powerful. The second place on the list was disputed by Mōri and Uyesugi, the former being set down at 1,205,000, and the latter at the same figure less the odd 5,000—at 1,200,000 *koku*. Equal as they were in the matter of assessed revenue, the geographical position of Mōri Terumoto's estates tended to make him a much more influential figure in Japanese politics than Uyesugi could hope to be. Mōri ruled the nine provinces of the main island to the immediate east of the Straits of Shimonoseki, and thus access to the capital, whether by land or by sea, was comparatively easy. Furthermore, across the Straits one cadet of the House, with a revenue of 60,000 *koku*, was settled at Kokura in Buzen; another held a fief of 130,000 *koku* further south in Chikugo; while in between these two, Kobayakawa, of the stock of Mōri, occupied Chikuzen, with an income of 522,500 *koku*, a revenue that gave him the ninth place among the Japanese Daimyō of the time. As for Uyesugi, although his new immense possessions in Aidzu (to which he had been removed in 1598) stretched from the northern

confines of the Tokugawa domains right on to the beat of the
surf of the Sea of Japan, his way to Kyōto was hopelessly
blocked, whether by the northern, central, or southern route.
The fourth member of the Board of Regency, who also occupied
the fourth place in the roll of the great feudatories, in this
respect was much more fortunate than Uyesugi. From his
domains in Kaga and Etchū, which were assessed at 835,000
koku, Mayeda Toshi-iye could march his *samurai* to the centre
of affairs with but very little to impede his progress. The
fifth Regent had the smallest revenue, but the most favoured
geographical situation of all the members of the Board. Ukida
Hideiye's resources were assessed at no more than 574,000 *koku*;
but then his stronghold of Okayama in Bizen was little more
than one hundred miles from Ōsaka, and just one hundred and
thirty miles from Fushimi or Kyōto. In point of revenue
Ukida was only sixth among the great barons, for the assessment
of Daté of Sendai stood at 580,000 *koku*. But inasmuch as
Daté's conduct in connection with the Hidetsugu tragedy in
1595 had placed him under grave suspicions, and inasmuch as
Sendai was far removed from the centre of authority, Daté, fifth
as he was in the assessment list, found no place on the Board
of Regents.

Hideyoshi's five *Bugyō*, or Ministers, have been already
alluded to as territorial magnates. Three of them might
be counted of second, and the other two of third rank
among the Daimyō. Of the five, Asano Nagamasa (Minister
of Justice), with a fief of 218,000 *koku* in Kai, occupied the
fifteenth place in the list of the Taikō's feudatories, and
Masuda Nagamori (Minister of Works, the Maxita Yemondono
of the Jesuits), with one of 200,000 *koku* in Yamato, the
seventeenth.[1] The Minister of Criminal Affairs, the notorious
Ishida Mitsunari (Xibunojo of the Jesuits), was twenty-first
in the roll with a fief of 194,000 *koku* in Ōmi; while Nagatsuka, the Finance Minister (sixty-fifth in the list), had
another of 50,000 *koku* at Minakuchi in the same province; and
Mayeda Gen-i, Minister of Worship and Governor of Kyōto (the
" Guenifoin " of the Jesuits), another (with Akechi Mitsuhide's
old castle-town of Kameyama) of the same value in Tamba.

---

[1] Equal with Fukushima in Owari and Konishi in Southern Higo and a
certain Miyabe in Inaba, whose domains were confiscated after Sekigahara.

As regards the three *Chū-rō*, or Intermediate Board, Ikōma (twenty-eighth in the list) had domains assessed at 150,000 *koku* in Shikoku (at Takamatsu in Sanuki); Nakamura (twenty-ninth in the list) a fief of 145,000 *koku* in Suruga; and Horio (thirty-fourth in the list) another of 120,000 *koku* in Tōtōmi. From this it will appear that the five *Bugyō*, even reinforced by the three *Chū-rō*, weighed but little against the *Go-Tairō*, or Regents, as regards resources, since the combined revenue of the eight members of the lower Boards amounted to no more than 1,127,000 *koku*, only one-seventeenth of the resources of the Empire, while, as has been said before, the five Regents together represented more than one-third of the same.

Of the remaining 11,000,000 *koku*, nearly one-third was in the hands of nine great barons. We have already referred to Daté in Sendai (580,000 *koku*) and to Kobayakawa in Chikuzen (522,500 *koku*). Both these feudatories will be found either openly or covertly friendly to Iyeyasu at the crisis of Sekigahara, when they found something of a counterpoise in Shimadzu and Satake. The former's domains in Satsuma and the extreme south of Kyūshū were rated at 555,000 *koku*; and Satake, in Hitachi, on Iyeyasu's eastern flank, with 545,700 *koku*, was no mere *quantité negligéable*. In Hizen, Nabeshima's fief was the most considerable—357,000 *koku*. Hori, who marched with Uyesugi to the west, held lands to the value of 300,000 *koku* in Uyesugi's former domains in Echigo. The next two Daimyō on the list, occupying the twelfth and thirteenth places, were staunch adherents of Iyeyasu, but the fourteenth was to be found in the ranks of his foes. Katō Kiyomasa (twelfth), Konishi's great rival and the bitter foe of the Christians, ruled a domain of 250,000 *koku* from his castle of Kumamoto—even then the second best in Japan—in Northern Higo; while at the other extremity of the empire Mogami (thirteenth) held a fief of 240,000 *koku* at Yamagata in Dewa. The most powerful chief in the island of Shikoku was Chōsokabe in Tosa (fourteenth), with 223,000 *koku*.

To enter into any minute account of the remaining one hundred and ninety-two fiefs and their possessors would serve no useful purpose. Only a careful scrutiny of the roll serves to disclose one or two points of interest, and enables us to correct some of the impressions conveyed by the historians of the Church. At this date in Japan there were no more than six openly-professed Christian Daimyō.[2] In Southern Higo, Konishi at Udo, as has been said, was rated at 200,000 *koku*; at Nakatsu in Buzen old Kuroda had estates of the value of 180,000 *koku*; and Mōri Hidekane held a fief of 130,000 *koku* at Kurume in Chikugo. The famous "King" of Arima, of whom we hear so much from the Jesuits, was only a petty princelet of 40,000 *koku*, while his relative in Ōmura had no more than 25,000 *koku*. Thus the united assessment of all the Christian princes in Kyūshū (575,000 *koku*) scarcely exceeded either that of Shimadzu or of Kobayakawa. The sixth Christian Daimyō stood thirtieth in the list of contemporary feudatories. This was none other than that grandson of Nobunaga of whom Hideyoshi had constituted himself the guardian in 1582. Sixteen years later the guardian died master of the Empire, while the ward, Ota Hidenobu, was Lord of a paltry fief of 135,000 *koku* at Gifu in Mino! Thus, all told, the revenues of the Christian Daimyō amounted to no more than 710,000 *koku*, less than one twenty-sixth of the total assessment of the empire. Such is the simple fact; yet from a cursory perusal of Crasset or of Charlevoix a reader might easily infer that Arima and Ōmura stood nearly in the very first rank of the territorial potentates. The foregoing analysis may also serve to indicate that the missionaries had no very just perspective of the general situation when they wrote that the Taikō's Korean venture was mainly prompted by the desire to remove the Christian Daimyō from Kyūshū. Arima and Ōmura were too insignificant to call for any very close attention from Hideyoshi, while both Konishi and Kuroda were "new men" of his own—brilliant captains, thoroughly devoted to his cause. What the Taikō more likely had set his mind upon was the appropriation of the broad lands of Mōri, of Kobayakawa, and possibly of Satsuma. It may suffice also to disclose the precise

---

[2] Charlevoix writes that Valegnani baptized the "King" of Iga in 1592. Iga is here a mistake for Hiūga, Itō of Oba being referred to. Hachisuka of Awa in Shikoku is also said to have been baptized secretly, while the two brothers Kyōgoku—one Daimyō of Ina in Shinano (100,000 *koku*), the other Lord of Otsu in Ōmi (70,400 *koku*)—were also claimed as Christians. About their Christianity, in 1600 A.D. at least, there seems to be room for doubt. As regards that of their mother, Maria Kyōgoku, one of Hideyoshi's Court ladies, and a zealous propagandist, there is no doubt at all.

amount of wisdom or practicability in the scheme of regency
the Church historian maintains Hideyoshi should have adopted
to safeguard the real interests of his infant son. According
to him, the Board should have been composed of Ishida
Mitsunari (Xibunojo), Mayeda Gen-i ("Guenifoin"), Konishi,
and Kuroda! The recommendation, of course, of these four
comparatively uninfluential men [3] to the position was the circumstance that they were either Christians or friendly towards
Christianity.

Two other "princes" may also be noted, since we meet
with their names not merely in the missionary letters, but
also in the records of the Dutch and English factories of
Hirado. This island, the domains of our erstwhile friend
"Taqua Nombo" (Takanobu) and of the Matsu-ura family,
was assessed at 63,000 koku, while Terasawa, the Governor of
Nagasaki, said to have been secretly baptized in 1595,[4] was
also Lord of Karatsu in Hizen with 80,000 koku, to be increased to 120,000 koku by reason of his having been on the
right side on the field of Sekigahara, in October, 1600.

The first measure that occupied the attention of the
new administration was the withdrawal of the troops from
Korea in accordance with the last solemn injunctions of the
Taikō. To superintend this undertaking, Asano, Minister of
Civil Law, and Ishida, Minister of Criminal Affairs, were at
once dispatched to Kyūshū, and by the beginning of December,
1598, the evacuation of the peninsula had begun. About
a month previously the Japanese had won a great victory
at Sō-Chŏn, in the south-west corner of Kyŏng-sang-do,
when, according to one writer, they took 38,700 heads of the
enemy, the ears and noses of which, as has been mentioned,
were cut off, packed and pickled in tubs, and sent to Kyōto,
where they were interred in the well-known "Mimi-dzuka," or
Ear Mound. Coming immediately after this success, as they
did, the orders for evacuation were by no means pleasing to
some of the commanders, and among them there was a sharp
division of opinion as to the precise manner in which the

---

[3] Total revenue, 624,000 koku. Revenue of members of the actual Board,
6,341,000 koku.

[4] If actually baptized, he remained for no very long time constant in the
faith, as we soon find him persecuting his former fellow-believers.

instructions were to be construed. One party insisted that the acquisitions already made should be safeguarded by a treaty; the other regarded the orders of the Regents as absolute, and this faction at once began the retreat, and the other had to follow. The two parties carried their differences back with them to Japan, to find that there the two Commissioners, Ishida and Asano, were likewise themselves strongly at variance on the subject. The former, in favour of unconditional withdrawal, was supported by Satsuma, Konishi, Arima, Ōmura, Terasawa, and the various Princes of Chikuzen and Chikugo, while Asano found partizans in Katō Kiyomasa of Kumamoto, young Kuroda of Nakatsu, Mōri Katsunobu (Iki-no-Kami of the Jesuits) of Kokura, and Nabeshima of Hizen. It may be noted that of the five Christian Daimyō of Kyūshū three were in one camp and one in the other. About the latter's Christianity, however, there seems to have been now some manner of doubt. The missionaries complain that on his return from Korea the old Kuroda showed but a lukewarm devotion to the cause of his creed, while the younger, his son, Kai-no-Kami, seems to have fallen away from the faith entirely.[5] This acrimonious quarrel—for such it really was—was ostensibly composed by the Regents early in 1599; but it had scarcely been disposed of when another of a much more serious nature broke out, and the three *Chū-rō,* or Board of Mediators, found ample opportunity for the exercise of their functions.

The chief among the Regents had given his colleagues and the *Bugyō* serious grounds to question, if not his fidelity to the House of Toyotomi, at all events his conformity to the dying injunctions of the Taikō. The latter had, among other things, directed that there should be no giving or receiving of hostages or sureties among the Daimyō, and that there should be no marriages (*i.e.* political marriages) arranged without consultation. To quote from Mr. Dening :—

"This injunction was not followed by Iyeyasu. In order to strengthen his position, he sanctioned, if indeed he did not instigate, the celebration of three important marriages. The daughter of Daté Masamune became the wife of Kazusanosuke Tadateru; Fukushima Masanori married the daughter of Matsudaira Yasumoto; and the daughter of Ogasawara Hidemasa was given to Hachisuka Munéshige.

5 Charlevoix assigns 1604 as the exact date of his apostasy, but complaints in the letters of the missionaries indicate that it took place some time before.

These marriages were all political, and their contraction being in direct violation of Hideyoshi's commands, the *Tai-rō* and the *Bugyō* no sooner heard of them than they went to Iyeyasu in a body and proposed that he should retire from the Government, since he had proved himself disloyal to the House of Toyotomi. Iyeyasu retired, and this was the signal for a general commotion."

Although there is a measure of truth in this passage, yet errors of detail and omissions tend to divest it of a good deal of its real serious significance. It ought to be stated that Kazusanosuke Tadateru was Iyeyasu's own son—his sixth; that Matsudaira's daughter had been adopted by Iyeyasu before she was married, not to Fukushima himself, but to Fukushima's son, and that Hachisuka's son's bride was actually Iyeyasu's great-granddaughter. Another instance of the same tactics is supplied by the betrothal of yet another of Iyeyasu's multitudinous and very convenient granddaughters to the twelve-year-old son of Konishi, whom the old statesman was very eager to attach to his cause. Again, the Regents and the Ministers did not go to Iyeyasu in a body; neither did Iyeyasu retire from his position. The *Tai-rō* and *Bugyō*, then in Ōsaka, merely sent a letter to Iyeyasu in Fushimi, censuring him and threatening him with dismissal from the Board if he failed to tender reasonable explanations for the contraction of these alliances. Iyeyasu refused to do so; and things became so serious that both in Ōsaka and Fushimi the rivals hurriedly brought up troops from their fiefs to be ready for the last emergency. In a short space fully 200,000 armed men were mustered in the two citadels or cantonned in the neighbourhood. However, during the several weeks in which matters stood at such a critical pass, discipline of the strictest was maintained, and not a sword left its sheath. Ultimately the three *Chū-rō*, or Mediators, succeeded in patching up a hollow peace, as the price of which the *Bugyō* (Ministers) had to express their regrets for the steps they had taken. This they did merely to gain time to enable them to weaken their opponent by intrigue.

In plotting and in all the arts of cabal the master-mind in the opposition to Iyeyasu was singularly proficient. This was Ishida Mitsunari, who, with no military prowess or prestige whatsoever, had yet, by dint of surpassing ability as a civil-administrator, raised himself from the utmost insignificance to the position of the most powerful man at the Court and in the councils of the Taikō. Although he had been a Minister for a decade and a half, he was still no more than forty years of age, and so felt utterly averse either to retiring from the political stage, or to remaining in the position of comparative eclipse he had been temporarily thrown into by the death of the Taikō. Although easily the first man among the *Bugyō* (Ministers), he found himself overshadowed by two members of the Board of Regency, and the problem that presented itself to him was how to remove these two men from the way. Between Mayeda Toshi-iye, in charge of Hideyori in Ōsaka, and Iyeyasu in charge of the administration of the empire in Fushimi, strife sooner or later was almost certain; and if the mutual distrust and jealousy of these, now the two most powerful leaders in Japan, could once be excited, Ishida counted upon being able to fan jealousy into a flame that would ultimately consume one or other, or perhaps both, of the only men that stood between him and greatness. Hence in the quarrel between Iyeyasu and his co-regents and the *Bugyō* Ishida made an endeavour to rouse Mayeda Toshi-iye to implacable resentment against the President of the Board. Doubtless, too, had it not been for two unexpected developments, success would have attended his efforts. Mayeda and Iyeyasu had each his own coterie of adherents among their fellow-feudatories; and these would have been only too eager to see the decision as to which of the two chiefs was really to be master of Japan put to the sharp arbitrament of the sword. Behind Iyeyasu stood Daté, Kuroda, Gamō, Ikeda, and other more or less powerful chiefs, while, down to the end of 1598 at least, Mayeda had staunch partisans in Asano, Katō, Hachisuka, and Fukushima, the latter two of whom we have just seen Iyeyasu endeavouring to attach to the fortunes of the Tokugawa by the forbidden device of political marriages. Luckily for the interests of both parties, however, Iyeyasu and Mayeda Toshi-iye had a staunch friend in common in the person of Hosokawa Tadaoki, Daimyō of Tango (230,000 *koku*).[6] In the course of the dispute just

---

[6] In passing it may be well to say that this Hosokawa was the husband of Akechi Mitsuhide's daughter, the Christian Princess Grace of Tango, of whom we hear so much from the Jesuits. Hosokawa (transferred to Buzen with a revenue of 369,000 *koku* in 1601) appears as Jecundono in the missionaries' letters,

referred to, Hosokawa, who seems to have penetrated Ishida's designs, exerted himself to bring Mayeda and Iyeyasu together; and, in spite of his own serious illness, Mayeda went to call on Iyeyasu at Fushimi in March, Iyeyasu returning the visit at Ōsaka twelve days later on. Then in the following May, Mayeda died in Ōsaka, and thereupon, through Hosokawa's efforts, all the Mayeda adherents promptly attached themselves to Iyeyasu.

Naturally this development came as a serious blow to the projects and the prospects of Ishida, who, instead of being able to play off one faction against another as he had purposed to do, now found himself called upon to confront both factions fused into one. At the same time his own party, although far from a match for the united followings of Iyeyasu and of Mayeda, was by no means a contemptible one. With the exception of Asano, he was on the best of terms with all his fellow *Bugyō*, while he was hand-in-glove with Konishi, one of the greatest captains of the age, and with Sataké, who could muster as many as 70,000 or 80,000 *samurai* in his sea-board province of Hitachi on Iyeyasu's eastern flank. Besides, three of the Regents (Ukida, Mōri, Uyesugi) and Shimadzu of Satsuma were neutrals; and to win these great feudatories to his support Ishida worked with signal success.

Meanwhile, however, his own immediate fortunes seemed at the very lowest of ebbs. Thanks to Hosokawa's interference, he not only found himself helpless on the death of Mayeda, but even in deadly peril of his life in consequence of the exposure of his intrigues. While attending Mayeda's death-bed in Ōsaka (April, 1599) he learned that the so-called " seven Generals "[7] had sworn to have his life. They were enraged

His title was Etchū-no-Kami, and Etchū becomes Jecun in Charlevoix ! In the interests whether of accuracy or of pedantry—call it what you will—it ought to be said that Hosokawa's fief at Miyadzu in Tango was rated at only 170,000 *koku*. Iyeyasu had recently given him an additional estate of 60,000 *koku* in Bungo. This is interesting as being one of the very rare cases in Japan we have met with of one man holding two distinct and widely-separated fiefs. William the Conqueror's special device to enfeeble his feudatories seems never to have been adopted in Japan.

[7] These were Katō Kiyomasa (*ætat.* 39); Katō Toshiaki (37), Daimyō of Matsuyama in Iyo (100,000 *koku*); Ikeda (36), Daimyō of Yoshida in Mikawa (152,000 *koku*); Hosokawa (36), the Jecundono of the Jesuits; the younger Kuroda (32); Fukushima Masanori (39); and the son of Asano Nagamasa, Ishida's fellow *Bugyō*, Asano Yukinaga, then 20 years of age. It is to be clearly grasped and carefully kept in mind that these " seven Generals " were *not* Iyeyasu's retainers, as Ii Naomasa, or Honda, or Sakai were; but independent feudatories of equal rank with himself—of course with much smaller fiefs.

against him not merely on account of his late intrigues, but also from the fact that these doughty warriors, in an age when military prowess was everything, had a most proper contempt for the mere civilian, who by inglorious but very safe and very profitable stay-at-home pettifoggery had reaped a richer harvest of honours and rewards than they had been able to do themselves in spite of all the stricken fields most of them had witnessed in Korea as well as in Japan. And besides that consideration, a further stimulus to the enmity of certain of the seven was not wanting. In his later years the Taikō had treated his legitimate consort, *née* Sugihara, somewhat coldly, and had lavished attention, if not affection, upon his "secondary" wife Yodogimi, *née* Asai, the mother of Hideyori. Ishida was not slow to perceive the quarter where it would be most profitable to pay court for his future advancement, and soon succeeded in attaining a high place in the regard of Yododono, as the Jesuits term the mother of the Taikō's heir. Now this gave great umbrage to Katō, to Fukushima, and to the other relatives of Hideyoshi's lawful spouse; and when to this cause for resentment against the dexterous and adroit Minister of Criminal Affairs was added the disclosure of his abortive attempts at mischief-making between Iyeyasu and Mayeda, their respective chiefs, the hatred of the Captains for the intriguing pettifogging civilian, as they considered him, became simply implacable. Apprised by some of the horde of spies he maintained in his service that the "seven Captains" had arranged to make an end of him when he withdrew from Ōsaka Castle after the death of Mayeda Toshi-iye, Ishida, putting himself under the escort of Sataké, hurried to Fushimi and there abjectly threw himself upon the mercy of Iyeyasu. The old statesman, who, besides being a soldier with a record of eighty-seven battles in the course of his eight-and-fifty years, was even more proficient in intrigue on the grand scale than was the very adroit Minister of Criminal Affairs, "having some plan" refused to listen to the seven hot-headed Generals and contented himself with advising the suppliant Ishida to resign his official position and quietly to retire to his fief of Sawayama in Ōmi. After deeply considering the situation for several days,—during which, by the way, he seems to have had a secret interview either with Naoye, Uyesugi's very able lieutenant, or with Uyesugi himself, and arranged to co-operate with him against Iyeyasu on some future day,—Ishida adopted Iyeyasu's advice, and under the escort of Hideyasu, Iyeyasu's second (but now eldest surviving) son, withdrew to Sawayama. Here, as we learn from the missionaries, he was soon joined, if not accompanied, by Konishi, who was induced to append his name to the secret list of confederates—Mori, Uyesugi, Ukida, and "the flower of the Japanese nobility"—that the intriguing pettifogger had already knit together in an underground alliance against the seemingly so magnanimous Iyeyasu,—who, by the way, "had a plan."

Charlevoix, it may be parenthetically remarked, goes out of his way to explain that the priests expressed to Don Augustin (Konishi) their extreme dissatisfaction with the step he had taken in thus joining the confederates, and labours hard to prove that the Christians were not hostile to Iyeyasu's—that is, to the winning—cause. The good Father assures us that Arima and Ōmura (puissant potentates, indeed!) zealously supported Iyeyasu. This is simply untrue; these two very wary and prudent men just sat quietly on the fence and remained strictly non-committal during all the course of the subsequent struggle. The two Kurodas were indeed zealous partisans of the Tokugawa cause; but the younger one had already dropped his Christianity for good and all, while at this date the missionaries plaintively complain of Simon Kondera's (old Kuroda's) lukewarmness for the faith. As for another Christian Daimyō, Oda Hidenobu (Nobunaga's grandson) of Gifu, on the representations and promises of Ishida, with whom Konishi then was, we shall see him join the confederates at the very moment when the Tokugawa vanguard was only a few miles distant from his fortress. Iyeyasu, in afterwards good-humouredly accusing the Christians of "having been of the counsel of his enemies," was really perfectly correct; if Ishida had proved triumphant it is not at all unlikely that the Jesuit writers would have had a great deal to say about the high worth of Konishi's procedure on this occasion. "Nothing succeeds like success,"—even the very best of the sons of men may prove cowards and sneaks and trimmers and time-servers upon occasion, and almost utterly unconsciously to themselves.

As for the seemingly very magnanimous Iyeyasu who "had a plan," he ordered the seven puzzle-headed and impetuous Captains to disband their musters; and shortly afterwards through Masuda, Minister of Works (our old acquaintance of the *San Felipe* episode), and Nagatsuka, Minister of Finance, he communicated to Ukida, to Mōri, and to the other Generals who had taken part in the Korean war his "desire" that they should return to their respective estates for "well-earned rest," and then reappear in Ōsaka by the autumn or winter of the following year (1600 A.D.). In compliance with this "desire" Ukida retired to Bizen, Mōri to Aki, old Kuroda to Buzen, Katō Kiyomasa to Northern Higo, and Hosokawa to Tango. At the same time Uyesugi (Canzugedono of the Jesuits) hied him to Aidzu, pleading that he had to see to the administration of his new fief, as "not many days had passed since his removal to it" from his ancestral domains of Echigo (April, 1598). At the same time, with a somewhat similar excuse, Mayeda Toshi-iye's heir, Toshinaga,[8] withdrew to Kanazawa in Kaga; while Iyeyasu was graciously pleased to allow the three hard-worked and most meritorious *Chū-rō*, or Middle Councillors—they all had their revenues handsomely raised after Sekigahara—to retire to their own estates to snatch a little of the repose they doubtless found themselves so much in need of. As the Japanese Army General-Staff's most meritorious compilation puts it, "this permission of Iyeyasu's to the Generals to with-draw is considered to have been the result of his well-conceived plan to strengthen his position. In the first place, Toyotomi's (Hideyori's) men would censure him for his arbitrary acts; secondly, they would intrigue against him, thus furnishing him with a pretext for removing them; and thirdly, alarming rumours would arise everywhere. The subsequent course of events abundantly justified Iyeyasu's forecast."

On the 7th of the ninth month (October 25th), 1599, Iyeyasu proceeded to Ōsaka to pay a complimentary visit to Hideyori, and while there he was secretly informed by Masuda, Minister of Works, that Mayeda Toshinaga had woven a plot against him, and had given instructions to Asano (Minister of Law

---

8 The Jesuits tell us he was sufficient of a freethinker to shoot foxes with his arquebus—a crime of almost as deep a dye in the Japan of those days as it would be in modern Leicestershire.

and Ishida's opponent), to Ōno Harunaga (now, or soon to become, Yodogimi's paramour), and another to kill him. One result of this was that Asano was dismissed from office and ordered to return to his fief (Kai), while Iyeyasu, a little later on, convoked his allies and informed them of his intention to move an army against Mayeda in Kaga. However, there is the strongest reason to believe that Iyeyasu was fully aware that this plot was a mere fabrication of Masuda's, or rather of Ishida's, for Masuda was often Ishida's mouthpiece merely. Rumours of treachery on the part of Hosokawa were also originated and sedulously disseminated by Ishida. Early next (Japanese) month (November 28th), however, Hosokawa came to Ōsaka to proffer Iyeyasu a written declaration of fidelity and to offer to send his son to Yedo as a hostage for his good faith, and shortly afterwards Mayeda sent his own mother to Fushimi in a similar quality. When Iyeyasu spoke of transferring this lady to Yedo, Masuda, Nagatsuka, and others protested against this glaring infraction of the Taikō's direction that there should be no giving or receiving of hostages among the Daimyō. The protest went unheeded, however, and Hosokawa's son and Mayeda Toshinaga's mother became the first of the innumerable political hostages that were taken to and kept in Yedo between the years 1600 and 1863. Meanwhile, Iyeyasu was perfectly aware of the fact that Ishida was busily strengthening his castle of Sawayama and turning it into a Cave of Adullam. Konishi had either accompanied Ishida thither or had joined him there since, and other captains of note had also become Ishida's guests. Iyeyasu mentioned the matter to Ishida, but when Ishida explained, he professed to be satisfied with the latter's explanations. And so the plotting and counter-plotting went on apace all through the winter of 1599–1600.

It was on May 12th (old style) of this latter year (1600) that Will Adams had his first meeting with Iyeyasu. This interview, as well as his second on the 15th, and the third forty-one days later on, took place at Ōsaka, where "the King" (*i.e.* Iyeyasu) then lay. This raises the question of how it came to pass that Iyeyasu had his headquarters in Hideyoshi's stronghold and not in Fushimi, which had been designated as such by the Taikō. When Iyeyasu had paid his complimentary visit to Hideyori early in the ninth Japanese month of 1599, Masuda and Nagatsuka had pressed him to remain there on the plea that his separation from Hideyori would lead to suspicion and discord. Iyeyasu accordingly then established himself in the western citadel of Ōsaka Castle and remained there down to the 16th of the sixth month, 1600—that is, till within a few days after his third interview with Adams, and the dispatch of the pilot and his companions in the *Liefde* to Uraga[9] in the Kwantō, whither "our passage was long, by reason of contrarie windes, so that the 'Emperor' was there long before we."

What had led to this rapid movement of Iyeyasu's was the outbreak in the North-east, which Ishida had arranged either with Uyesugi himself, or with Uyesugi's most trusted captain, Naoye, at the very time he (Ishida) had sought protection from Iyeyasu in Fushimi against the infuriated seven Generals in the spring of 1599. On returning to Aidzu, early in the autumn of the same year, Uyesugi at once began to prepare for war. Of this Iyeyasu was informed by his friends and retainers near the Aidzu frontiers, but he paid no overt attention to the matter till the May of 1600. Then, acting on the advice of Ukida and of Mōri and of Matsuda and Nagatsuka (all parties to the plot), he sent an envoy to Uyesugi to order him to come to Ōsaka to explain his actions. As Iyeyasu expected, his emissary returned bearing a defiant reply (June 13th, 1600); and accordingly he rapidly pushed on the mobilisation of troops he had meanwhile secretly begun, and, appointing Fukushima and Hosokawa to the command of the advance guard, sent word to his friends on Uyesugi's rear and flanks to be ready for emergencies. Then, just at this point, the *Bugyō* and the three *Chū-rō* (who seem not to have been really hostile, however) protested against the expedition on the ground that his departure from Ōsaka amounted to the abandonment of Hideyori! Iyeyasu, who, there is good reason to believe, was either fully informed of, or at least divined, the extent of the intrigue against him, gave no heed to the protest, but dispatched all his allied Daimyō in Ōsaka to their fiefs to levy

---

9 Her eighteen guns and her great store of ammunition had been taken out of the *Liefde*, and guns and ammunition alike no doubt proved very serviceable in the subsequent campaign.

troops; and then sent instructions to his northern allies regarding the strategy to be adopted against Uyesugi.

While Iyeyasu himself was to head the main invading force advancing by the Shirakawa road from the south, Uyesugi's principality was to be simultaneously assailed from four other different quarters. From the extreme north-east Mōgami (240,000 *koku*) was to move from Yamagata by the Yonezawa route. Daté of Sendai (580,000 *koku*) was to break in also from the north-east, but at a point much further south (along the Shinobu route). From Hitachi, Sataké (545,700 *koku*) was to push Uyesugi on the south-east, while on the west Mayeda of Kaga (835,000 *koku*), and Hori, who had just (1597) obtained a fief of 300,000 *koku* in Uyesugi's former province of Echigo, were to press on towards Wakamatsu from the coast of the Sea of Japan. As a matter of fact, only two of these four forces ever came into action with the Aidzu *samurai*. Hori found enough to occupy his attention in a sudden revolt of Uyesugi's former vassals who had been transferred to him only three years before, and Mayeda was so hotly assailed on his rear by a confederacy of the Daimyō of Daishōji, of Komatsu, and of Fukui and the rest of Echizen that Sekigahara had actually been fought before he had been able to begin his march. As for Sataké, in him Uyesugi had not a foe but an ally, for Sataké was one of Ishida's own immediate friends. Sataké, indeed, did take the field with 70,000 men; but he held them in readiness to fall upon the flank of the main invading (Tokugawa) army from the South after it should have passed the Kinugawa.

Thus in the Aidzu campaign of 1600 A.D. it was Mōgami and Daté that had to bear the brunt of the fighting. The former, acting on Iyeyasu's instructions, at first merely stood on the defensive, and a sudden swoop of Uyesugi's men under the capable Naoye stripped him of some of his border forts and even put his capital of Yamagata in danger. However, a seasonable reinforcement from Daté soon enabled Mōgami to retrieve the situation and to hurl the invading force back upon its base. Daté meanwhile had maintained a vigorous offensive from the very inception of hostilities, and his efforts had been so embarrassing to Uyesugi that the latter had been constrained to a strictly defensive attitude on the south, where

cc

he soon found himself threatened by a Tokugawa force of
69,300 men.

In this latter army, besides the levies from the Tokugawa
domains proper, marched all the troops from the western
provinces that had espoused Iyeyasu's cause. He himself and
his third son, Hidetada, headed its respective divisions, and
under them Fukushima, Kuroda the younger, Hosokawa, Katō
(Yoshiaki), Ikeda, and young Asano (the dismissed *Bugyō's* son)
held commands. Iyeyasu, at the head of the rear-division
(31,800 men), arrived at Koyama on September 1st, and at
midnight of the same date he was roused from his sleep to
receive the messenger who brought definite intelligence of
Ishida's revolt in the West. Next day he called a council of
war at Koyama, to which Hidetada and his officers from
Utsunomiya—the first division, 37,500 men, then lay there—
were summoned. At this council the position of affairs in the
West was set before the commanders, and they were informed
that they were at liberty, if they wished, to retire and join
Ishida, who, having seized their wives and families in Ōsaka,
had thus contrived to put them into a very difficult position.
As the result of a conference, the officers refused to avail
themselves of Iyeyasu's magnanimous offer—as he knew very
well they would, no doubt—and handed him a document under
their joint seals pledging their unfaltering devotion to his cause.
They then went on to consider whether Ishida or Uyesugi
should first be dealt with in full force, and since they proved
unanimous about the advisability of wheeling round upon the
Western enemy, Fukushima and Ikeda were immediately
dispatched as an advance guard, while Kuroda, Hosokawa,
young Asano, Katō Yoshiaki, and other captains (*not* retainers
of Iyeyasu) quickly followed with their commands.

Meanwhile Iyeyasu stayed behind to arrange for an army
of observation to hold Uyesugi in check for the time being.
A force of 20,000 men drawn mostly from the small local fiefs
was left under Hideyasu (Iyeyasu's second son) at Utsunomiya,
while provision was also made for holding Saalso in play
if he should assume the offensive. But neither Satake nor
Uyesugi gave Hideyasu any immediate trouble; the latter
was altogether preoccupied with Daté and Mōgami, who,
carrying out Iyeyasu's orders, continued to threaten Uyesugi's

rear so cleverly and so seriously that a forward movement against the Tokugawa division in Utsunomiya was too dangerous to be attempted. As a matter of fact, the news of the battle of Sekigahara surprised Uyesugi while still in the midst of an evenly-balanced contest with his two northern neighbours, Mōgami and Daté.

Iyeyasu in person returned from Koyama to Yedo on September 11th, and saw to the dispatch of the division of his auxiliaries that was to advance against the Westerners along the Tōkaidō, or sea-board route. At the same time he ordered Hidetada (his third son) to make ready to push along the Nakasendō, or great central highway, with his force of 38,000 men, reducing the enemies in his path, and to join himself in the province of Mino, where, according to his forecast, the decisive battle of the campaign would be fought. The two great highways, it may be remarked, run into each other at Kusatsu, sixteen miles from Kyōto, after a course of three hundred and eight (Tōkaidō) and three hundred and sixteen (Nakasendō) miles respectively, but at Miya (two hundred and thirty miles from Tōkyō) in Owari the Tōkaidō is, if anything, little more than twenty miles distant from the nearest post-station on the Nakasendō in Mino. The success of the strategy of the Easterners accordingly depended a great deal upon the answer to the question whether they could anticipate Ishida's confederates in seizing upon all the strong positions in Owari and in Southern Mino. Once allow the Westerners to possess themselves in force of the front of twenty odd miles between the sea at Miya and Unuma on the Nakasendō, and it would bid fair to spell disaster to the Tokugawas, with the possibility of Uyesugi and Sataké freeing themselves from Daté and Hideyasu's army of observation at Utsunomiya and falling tempestuously upon the rear or flank of Hidetada, isolated from the Tōkaidō division. Accordingly the work of Fukushima, Ikeda, and their fellows with the Tōkaidō advance-guard became of supreme importance for the moment; and when, on September 21st, they occupied Nobunaga's old fortress of Kiyosu, well-advanced in the centre of the twenty-mile stretch between the Tōkaidō and Nakasendō just alluded to, the junction of the two army corps was practically assured so far as mere frontal opposition was concerned. Here Fukushima and his men remained quiet for some time, and while they are waiting here it may be well for us to pass to the side of Ishida and his allies and to follow the course of events in the West since Iyeyasu passed out of Ōsaka on July 26th, 1600.

On his way to the prosecution of the Aidzu campaign Iyeyasu had passed the night of July 27th in the keep of Fushimi; and there he sat talking with Torii Mototada, the commandant of the fortress, far into the morning. This Torii was a grizzled, war-beaten veteran of sixty-two, four years Iyeyasu's senior, and as the twain had been together since boyhood, the old companions revived many a pleasing and many a sad reminiscence of their past united fortunes. Among other things Iyeyasu now told his trusty henchman that they were on the threshold of great events; charged him to use the gold in the castle vaults freely; and enjoined him to keep him fully apprised of everything that transpired in the West. When they parted they did so with tears in their eyes, for they felt that the present might prove their last meeting on earth. Two days later on, in Ise, Matsudaira Yasushige informed Iyeyasu that there were indications of a revolt on the part of Ishida, and Iyeyasu replied that he was perfectly aware of the fact. Thus there are good grounds for believing that the subsequent events in the West came as no great surprise to the far-seeing old statesman.

That very same day (July 30th) Ishida dispatched a messenger to inform Uyesugi of Iyeyasu's departure, and then he redoubled his exertions to extend the sweep of the confederacy he had already secretly formed. That Ishida had the power of making and permanently attaching friends to himself is attested by the strange episode of the next month. On August 10th Ōtani Yoshitsugu (38), Daimyō of Tsuruga (50,000 koku), passed Sawayama with his troops on his way to join Iyeyasu. Ishida sent for him, and, disclosing his projects, invited him to abandon Iyeyasu and to join his own faction. Ōtani strongly endeavoured to dissuade Ishida from his purpose, assuring him that he was playing a losing game; and on Ishida's refusing to listen to his advice, Ōtani sorrowfully said good-bye to him on the 15th and proceeded on his way to the East. However, his anxiety for his friend of twenty years' standing was so deep that at Tarui he halted three days and dispatched one of his captains back to make one more attempt to save Ishida from what Ōtani believed to be inevitable destruction. When the messenger returned with the news that Ishida was firm in his determination, Ōtani thought there was nothing more for it but to return and share his old friend's fate; and so that evening he wheeled round and rejoined Ishida at Sawayama on the following day. Here, meanwhile, Ishida had been joined by the *Bugyō* Masuda and Nagatsuka—that Konishi also was with him we know from the Jesuits—and, as a result of their councils, on August 25th a letter was dispatched to Iyeyasu under the joint seals of the three *Bugyō*, Masuda, Nagatsuka, and Mayeda Gen-i,[10] charging him with the breach of the instructions of the Taikō in thirteen specific instances. This, of course, amounted to an open declaration of war. At the same time they sent off urgent messengers with letters to the various Daimyō calling upon them to join them on Hideyori's behalf, and holding out promises of the richest rewards if they did so. Before this, as has been said, Ishida had come to a secret understanding with Mōri Terumoto; and Mōri, now leaving Hiroshima by sea on August 23rd, arrived in Ōsaka on the night of the following day. Here he was received by Masuda, Nagatsuka, and Ankokuji,[11] who made him the leader of their own particular faction.

Just at this moment Matsuda had been instructed by Ishida to seize the wives and children of the Daimyō who had gone with Iyeyasu against Uyesugi and to intern them in Ōsaka castle as hostages. The execution of this order at once led to a tragedy which is differently related by the Japanese, by the

---

10 Both Ishida and Asano had been forced to retire from office in 1599, it will be remembered.

11 Of this Ankokuji Yekei, who then held a fief of 60,000 *koku* in Iyo, we learn that he had been Superior of the Buddhist Temple of Ankokuji in Aki, and had been a great friend of Mōri Terumoto, whom (along with Kuroda) he had assisted to come to an understanding with Hideyoshi. Afterwards he become a favourite of Hideyoshi's by reason of his discourses on military and religious affairs at leisure moments. Various Daimyō, who wished to get audience of Hideyoshi, bribed him to obtain it for them. Likely enough he was one of those Buddhist priests employed by the Taikō to conduct his negotiations with the Chinese, who were pitted against Rodriguez at Nagoya in Hizen in 1593 in Iyeyasu's presence, when, according to Charlevoix, the Buddhists came off so badly as to excite Iyeyasu's laughter at their expense. Ankokuji Yekei, at all events, gave up Buddhism and became a Daimyō, and distinguished himself at Sekigahara by showing a very nimble pair of heels. Iyeyasu, we are told, hated him exceedingly because he (Ankokuji) had abandoned his original profession and had taken part in the conspiracy against him.

missionaries, and by the Dutch. Among others, Hosokawa's wife and family were then in Ōsaka; and it was they that Masuda first attempted to arrest. What followed is told tersely and pithily enough by the Japanese historian :—

"She (Hosokawa's wife), however, was a heroic woman, and committed suicide after killing her children with her own hand, while her retainers set fire to the mansion and followed their mistress on the dark path. The wives and children of Kuroda, of Katō Kiyomasa, and of Ikeda contrived to make good their flight; and Masuda, cautioned not to proceed too energetically by the example of Hosokawa's wife, contented himself with fencing in and setting guards over the residences of the others."

Unfortunately there is reason to question the accuracy of this very direct and very compendious account of the incident. This wife of Hosokawa was no other than that Grace, Princess of Tango, who appears so often in the pages of Charlevoix, and over whose virtues and trials the worthy old Father now and then waxes a trifle nasal. He devotes several pages to the circumstances of her death, and from these it appears that she killed neither her children nor herself; but that after hours of prayer she meekly extended her neck to receive the fatal stroke from the sword of the steward, whom Hosokawa before his departure had secretly charged with the performance of the office in the case of need. M. Léon Pagés' account, which is much shorter than Charlevoix's, is yet in substantial accord with his. Naturally, being a devout believer in that Christian religion where the canon is set against self-slaughter, Hosokawa's wife would not have been likely to die by her own hand.[12]

---

12 As is well known, she was a daughter of Akechi Mitsuhide. Her husband, while averse to her seeing the foreign priests, allowed her to bring up their children (a son and two daughters) as Christians. "She appreciated to such a degree the happiness of being able to communicate her thoughts to the missionaries, that with this sole aim she learned to read and write Portuguese, having as the only means of doing so an A B C and the writings her brother sent her, without ever seeing Father or Brother; and already she read and wrote tolerably well, and perhaps better than her teacher." She had a most sumptuous Christian funeral; and afterwards, down to 1611-1612, her husband showed great favour to the Christians, welcoming the missionaries in his new fief of Buzen. In 1604 we read that "an annual service was always celebrated for D. Gracia. This year Jecundono (Hosokawa) on this occasion delivered to the Father seven men condemned to death, whom he pardoned; and finding it was not enough, he delivered twenty others on the day after: these unfortunates, grateful towards the Church, asked to be instructed, and received baptism. Jecundono seemed to be inclined to become a Christian. But political interest and the difficulty of observing the sixth (Protestant seventh) commandment were always the principal obstacle to the conversion of the Princes." The Dutch account of the Ōsaka episode of 1600 is worthless; it is therein attributed to the year 1614 or 1615.

Meanwhile Ōsaka was rapidly filling with the levies of the league, and before the end of the month there were as many as thirty-five or forty "Generals" in the city. The most noted of these were Mōri Terumoto (1,205,000 *koku*), with his two subordinate officers, his cousin Mōri Hidemoto, and his relative Kikkawa[13]; Ukida of Bizen (574,000 *koku*), his fellow-regent; Shimadzu of Satsuma (555,000 *koku*); Kobayakawa of Chikuzen (522,500 *koku*); Nabeshima of Hizen (357,000 *koku*); Chōsokabe of Tosa (222,000 *koku*), with the *Bugyō*, besides one of the *Chu-rō*, Ikoma, whose son was with Iyeyasu, however. Altogether their combined commands footed up to 93,700 men, and more were still coming in—a formidable host, indeed. But among these, unfortunately, were some who had, if not Iyeyasu's, at all events their own interest more at heart than that of the confederacy. Kikkawa, Kobayakawa, and the small Daimyō Wakizaka[14] of Sumoto in Awaji (33,000 *koku*), and three others afterwards played a double game in the supreme crisis of Sekigahara. Three undoubtedly able captains there were, all in dead earnest in their opposition to the Tokugawa cause—Ukida, Shimadzu, and Konishi—but their ability was minimised by the fact that none of them exercised the real powers of a Commander-in-Chief, as Iyeyasu did undoubtedly.

Still, at the general council of war held in Ōsaka it seems to have been Ukida, the generalissimo in the Korean war of 1597-98, that was mainly responsible for the strategy of the confederates. While Mōri (Terumoto) and Masuda were to remain in Ōsaka professedly to protect Hideyori, the army as a whole was to assume the offensive. A small corps was to be dispatched north into Tango, where Hosokawa's father was making head for Iyeyasu; but it was against Iyeyasu himself that the main host was to be thrown. It was to march along the Tōkaidō to Seta, at the southern extremity of Lake Biwa in Ōmi, and thence, while the main division under Ishida, with whom went Satsuma and Konishi, was to

---

13 Mōri Terumoto (47) was the son of Takamoto, eldest son of Mōri Motonari, first Daimyō of Yamaguchi; Hidemoto (24) was the son of Motokiyo, sixth son of Motonari. Consequently Mōri Terumoto (48) and Mōri Hidemoto (21) were cousins. Kikkawa Hiroiye was thirty-nine years of age at the time of Sekigahara.

14 One of the seven spearmen of Shizugatake (1584).

skirt the Lake and then press forward along the Nakasendō
into Mino and Northern Owari, Mōri Hidemoto, Ohōsokabe,
and Nagatsuka, with 30,000 men, were to make a rapid dash
into Ise, there reduce the four out of the seven local princelets
that adhered to the Tokugawa, and then to advance rapidly
into Northern Owari, there to rejoin Ishida's *corps d'armée*.
From this it will be seen the primary objective of the Westerners
was to seize upon the strategic positions between Miya on
the Tōkaidō and the Nakasendō to which we have already
alluded.

But before reaching Lake Biwa the stronghold of Fushimi,
held for Iyeyasu by old Torii Mototada (62), had to be dealt
with, and an immediate assault upon it was ordered. It was
at this point that young Kobayakawa (22) of Chikuzen (522,500
koku) gave the first indication of his real sympathies. Almost
at the very moment that Torii received the letter from the
Bugyō summoning him to deliver up the citadel, a captain
of Kobayakawa's had secretly appeared and told him that
Kobayakawa was ready to join him in defence of the fortress !
But Torii, suspecting a *ruse*, promptly rejected the overture,
and on August 27th he found himself and his garrison of 1,800
invested by an army of full 40,000 men, led by Ukida,
Kobayakawa, Mōri Hidemoto, and Shimadzu.

Although this siege of Fushimi is only a minor operation
in the great struggle of 1600 A.D., it may yet be not unprofitable
to dwell upon it at some length, as certain incidents in it
serve to throw a flood of clear and illuminating light upon
the spirit then animating the military class in Japan and
upon the *ethos* of the times. Torii, after indignantly rejecting
the summons to surrender his charge, assembled the garrison
and addressed them in a soul-stirring harangue. " I have
already," he said, "sent a messenger to our liege-lord informing
him of our steadfast determination to hold this citadel to the
last gasp. If there be any among you who loathe to die, the
way is still open for such to withdraw. We are now going
to hold this castle with no prospect of outside succour whatsoever, and with little more than a thousand men against a
host. Let us leave our corpses in the breach for the sake of
our liege, and so make ourselves exemplars of what faithful
vassals and high-spirited *samurai* should be," He then held a

farewell banquet with his subordinates, and after enjoying it to their heart's content each soldier returned to his post.

On the evening of August 27th forty thousand men began the assault with a furious bombardment of the castle. For the following eight days the attack was maintained; but all assaults were baffled and beaten back by the garrison, whose commandant, the grizzled Torii, meanwhile passed a good deal of his time in playing *go* (checkers)! After the siege had thus gone on for ten days, on September 6th Ishida, on his way from Sawayama to Ōsaka, appeared, and vehemently urged the assailants to press matters more energetically and to make a speedy end of the business. Accordingly, on the following day four terrific but ineffectual assaults were delivered. Meanwhile gold had been found to open a way into the fortress where steel had failed; on the morning of the 8th September forty men of the garrison, seduced by the enemy, set fire to the castle, broke down part of the rampart, and made good their escape. The wind was then blowing a gale, and it drove the flames rapidly before it this way and that; and in the resulting confusion the besiegers poured in "like a tidal wave," and seized on two of the outer forts. In one of these Matsudaira had his command of eight hundred men virtually annihilated before he himself committed suicide. In the other, Naitō fought with the greatest gallantry, but seeing that all was hopeless, he told his subordinate officer, Andō, "to fight on, while I retire and dispatch myself." He then withdrew to a bell-tower, and after collecting a heap of fuel he said to his immediate follower, Harada: "You must make good your escape and inform my lord and my son Samanosuke how the castle of Fushimi fell." He thereupon calmly disembowelled himself; and Harada, setting fire to the fuel, saw his master's corpse reduced to ashes, and then escaped. Naitō's son, a lad of sixteen years, who had fought like a seasoned veteran, also disembowelled and threw himself into the flames of his father's funeral pyre. By 10 A.M. the main tower of the castle was ablaze; and seeing this, Torii's retainers, deeming everything lost, counselled the commandant to kill himself like a brave *samurai*. Torii, however, pointed out that he was not fighting for his own personal honour,—what was precious above all things to his liege-lord Iyeyasu at this crisis was *time*—and that to gain even one single hour for his master he would not think it shame to meet his fate at the hands of even the very humblest foe. Therefore, no *hara-kiri*; the word was—fight to the bitterest end. He further called upon the little band of two hundred still left not to heed the fall of comrades, not to select their antagonists, but to cut down every foe indiscriminately. Then he sallied out upon the swarming enemy, sweeping them back with terrific slaughter. At the end of the third sortie Torii found himself covered with wounds and with no more than one hundred followers left. Two more desperate onsets reduced these to ten, and then the commandant retired to the inner citadel, and was sitting on a stone step resting when a certain Saiga ran upon him about to smite him with a spear. Thereupon Torii got up, saying, "I am Torii Mototada, commandant of this castle." Saiga fell upon his knee, and respectfully said: "Fire has already got possession of the main citadel. All is now lost. I beg you will now commit suicide and give me your head. 1 shall thereby reap eternal honour!" Torii thereupon calmly removed his armour, committed the "happy dispatch," and Saiga took possession of his head. "In such a way," says the Japanese historian, "was the castle of Fushimi taken. The besieged were killed almost to a man; but the siege was a very costly operation to the Western army, its casualties having been about 3,000."

On the fall of Fushimi (September 8th) Ukida seems to have returned to Ōsaka to meet Ishida there. Four days later the latter returned to Sawayama to lead the advance along the Nakasendō. Meanwhile Mōri Hidemoto, Chōsokabe, Nagatsuka and Nabeshima, with 30,000 men, had pushed into Ise, where they met with an unexpectedly stubborn resistance from the local princelets that there held for the Tokugawa. Only one castle (Anotsu, with a garrison of 1,700 men) was carried after a fierce assault, in which the Westerners lost heavily; and then the exigencies of the campaign forced the main body to hurry on into Mino, leaving Nabeshima to complete the reduction of Ise.[15]

15 In this he had made no very great headway when, on the 14th of the ninth month, he was summoned by Ishida to join him at Ōgaki. But on the evening of the 21st news of Sekigahara reached him, and he hurriedly withdrew to Ōsaka by the Iga route.

In the meantime Ishida, with 6,000 troops leading the advance along the Nakasendō, had reached Tarui on September 16th, and two days later he moved on to Ōgaki, where the castle was surrendered to him. Here he remained for some days awaiting the arrival of various contingents, till on the evening of the 21st he learned that the strategy of the Westerners had miscarried. On that day, as has been said, the Tokugawa advance-guard under Fukushima, Ikeda, and Kuroda had seized upon Kiyosu, and, owing to the dilatory movements of the allied contingents, the intended offensive of the confederate commanders had to be converted into the defensive—at all events for the time being. All that Ishida could do for the moment was to exert himself to win over the holders of the three or four fortresses that lay between Ōgaki and Kiyosu. Of these the castle of Gifu, held by Oda Hidenobu, Nobunaga's Christian grandson, Hideyoshi's former ward, was the most important. Although Iyeyasu was the young man's (20) grand-maternal uncle, yet Oda allowed himself to be seduced by the specious promises of Ishida, and, mustering 6,500 troops, undertook, together with the Lords of Inuyama and of Takega-hana, to bear the brunt of the Tokugawa attack while the main columns of the confederates were coming up.

Having thus detailed the respective preliminary movements of the contending forces, and brought their advance guards within striking distance of each other, we will now pass to the side of the Easterners. After seizing Kiyosu on September 21st, Fukushima and his fellow-commanders remained quiescent; for the date of Iyeyasu's departure from Yedo was not yet fixed, and no orders to assume the offensive had so far been received. On the 26th, however, a messenger arrived from Yedo urging them to make an immediate forward movement, and intimating to them Iyeyasu's intention to start *as soon as he was convinced of their fidelity.*[16] Hearing this, they were much ashamed at having been idle so long, and at a council of war held on the following day it was resolved to march at once on Gifu and reduce it. In order to do so the Kisogawa had to be crossed. The river was fordable at two places—at Ōkoshi above, and at Kōda below the town. It

[16] It must be strongly borne in mind that the Eastern van did not consist of Iyeyasu's vassals, but of his allies.

was arranged that Fukushima and Kuroda, with 16,000 troops, should advance from Ōkoshi, while Ikeda and Asano, with 18,000, should make a simultaneous movement from Kōda. Leaving a detachment at Haguro to mask the castle of Inuyama, both divisions left Kiyosu on September 28th. Ōda's troops sallied out of Gifu to check their approach, but both at Ōkoshi and Kōda the Easterners made good their passage of the stream and hurled Oda's men back upon Gifu with great slaughter; and on the following morning Fukushima seized Takegahana by a *coup de main*. Flushed with this initial success, the Easterners at once pressed on to the storm of Gifu, and in spite of an obstinate resistance they were in possession of the citadel and of the person of Oda Hidenobu early in the afternoon, while at the same time Inuyama surrendered unconditionally. On September 30th they pushed on some five miles further to the river Gotō, whither Ishida in Ōgaki, twelve miles distant, had thrown forward about 1,000 men to guard the stream. The Easterners made very short work of this meagre band, and on October 1st they occupied Akasaka; and, selecting the high land of Okayama (present Katsuyama) at the south end of the town for Iyeyasu's future headquarters, they there remained quiet for about twenty days awaiting the arrival of their Commander-in-Chief.

At the date of the fall of Gifu, Ishida, sixteen miles distant at Ōgaki, had with him only the troops of Shimadzu and of Konishi there. However, just at this juncture Ukida arrived with 10,000 men. He had left Ōsaka on September 22nd, intending to march on Ise; but an urgent message from Ishida caused him to hurry on to Ōgaki, where he appeared on September 30th, the day of the skirmish at the Gotō stream. Nine days later (9th October) Ōtani came in from Tango with his troops that had been reducing Hosokawa's castles there, and encamped at the village of Yamanaka, south-west of Sekigahara, some ten or twelve miles to the rear of Ōgaki. On the 13th Mōri Hidemoto, Chōsokabe, and Nagatsuka arrived with 30,000 troops from Ise, and took up their quarters on the Nangu hill, to the west of Akasaka, where the Tokugawa van then lay. Lastly, a week later, on the 20th October (eve of the battle of Sekigahara), Kobayakawa came in with 8,000 troops and occupied the heights of Matsuo, above Ōtani's right flank, and so also about twelve miles to the rear of Ōgaki.

However, this latest accession to the strength of the mustering Western host was of more than questionable value. Before the assault on Fushimi, Kobayakawa, as has been said, had sent one of his captains with friendly overtures to Torii, the Tokugawa commandant, and since then the young man's conduct had been such as to make him an object of suspicion to his confederates. After the fall of Fushimi (September 8th) he had returned to Ōsaka, and only left it in response to Ishida's urgent summons on the 24th. Even then he showed no great haste to join the main army; on the pretence that he was in bad health he loitered here and there by the way for the best part of a month. When he did reach the neighbourhood of Ōgaki on October 20th he sent word to Ishida that as he knew he was under suspicion he would refrain from entering the castle until he had regained the confidence of his fellow-commanders by delivering battle to the Easterners. The inference was obvious. However, at this very moment Ishida's attention was fully occupied by the general commotion that had suddenly arisen in the ranks of his army. Spies had just come in with the intelligence that on the noon of that very day the generalissimo of the opposition host had arrived in the headquarters of Akasaka with a reinforcement of more than 30,000 men and had assumed supreme command of the Eastern army.

This report was perfectly correct. Iyeyasu, who had returned to Yedo from Koyama on September 13th, had quietly remained there contemplating the whole situation. However, when the capture of Gifu fully assured him of the fidelity of his allied captains—Fukushima, Ikeda, Kuroda, Asano, and the others—he at last made up his mind to proceed to the front. So, leaving his younger brother Matsudaira Yasumoto with a garrison in Yedo, he left his capital on October 7th at the head of a force of 32,700 troops. On the 17th he reached Kiyosu, and after resting there an entire day he left on the 19th for the extreme front, and by noon on the 20th October he was receiving his generals on the " high ground of Okayama, at the southern end of the town of Akasaka."

Three hours after his arrival there was a sharp affair of
outposts, in which the Westerners had the best of it, and this
did something to restore the waning confidence of the rank and
file in their leaders. However, in spite of this, by the evening
the Westerners were rapidly falling back. Iyeyasu had issued a
general order to the effect that while a division should be left at
Akasaka to confront the confederates in Ōgaki, his main army
should next morning begin their march on Ōsaka, capturing
Sawayama on the way. As he had intended, this order was
promptly communicated to the confederate commanders by their
spies; and in consequence they at once resolved to fall back upon
Sekigahara, where with Ibukiyama on the north and Matsuo hill
to the south it would be impossible for Iyeyasu to march on
Ōsaka merely by turning their flank. He then would have to
fight a general action to clear his way, and a general action was
just what Iyeyasu wanted to force. In addition to having been
apprised of the lukewarmness of Kobayakawa (on Matsuo-san) in
the confederate cause, that very afternoon he had received
overtures from Kikkawa, virtually in command of Mōri
Hidemoto's division on Nangu hill, and also from a subordinate
commander, Wakisaka of Awaji.

Early in the evening four divisions of the Westerners made
ready for their march of ten miles to Sekigahara. It was a
cheerless night to be abroad in. Rain had begun to fall, and
the drizzle had developed into a terrific downpour, while at the
same time a westerly October gale beginning to scream and
whistle through the defile from Lake Biwa drove it fast and
hard in the faces of the retreating troops, who had to march in
Cimmerian murk and mud up to the calves of their legs. It
was not till one o'clock in the morning of the 15th day of the
ninth month—October 21st, now also the anniversary of
Trafalgar—that Ishida's own troops arrived at Sekigahara and
there took up their comfortless position in the village of Koseki.
Three hours later on Shimadzu's troops came in and occupied
Koike, immediately to the right of Koseki. Yet later on
arrived Konishi's command, which came into position to the right
of the Satsuma men, its rear resting on Tenmanyama to the
north. Last of all, Ukida's big division came straggling in all
bedraggled and mud-bespattered shortly after daylight—if there
can be such a thing in a cross between a London November fog

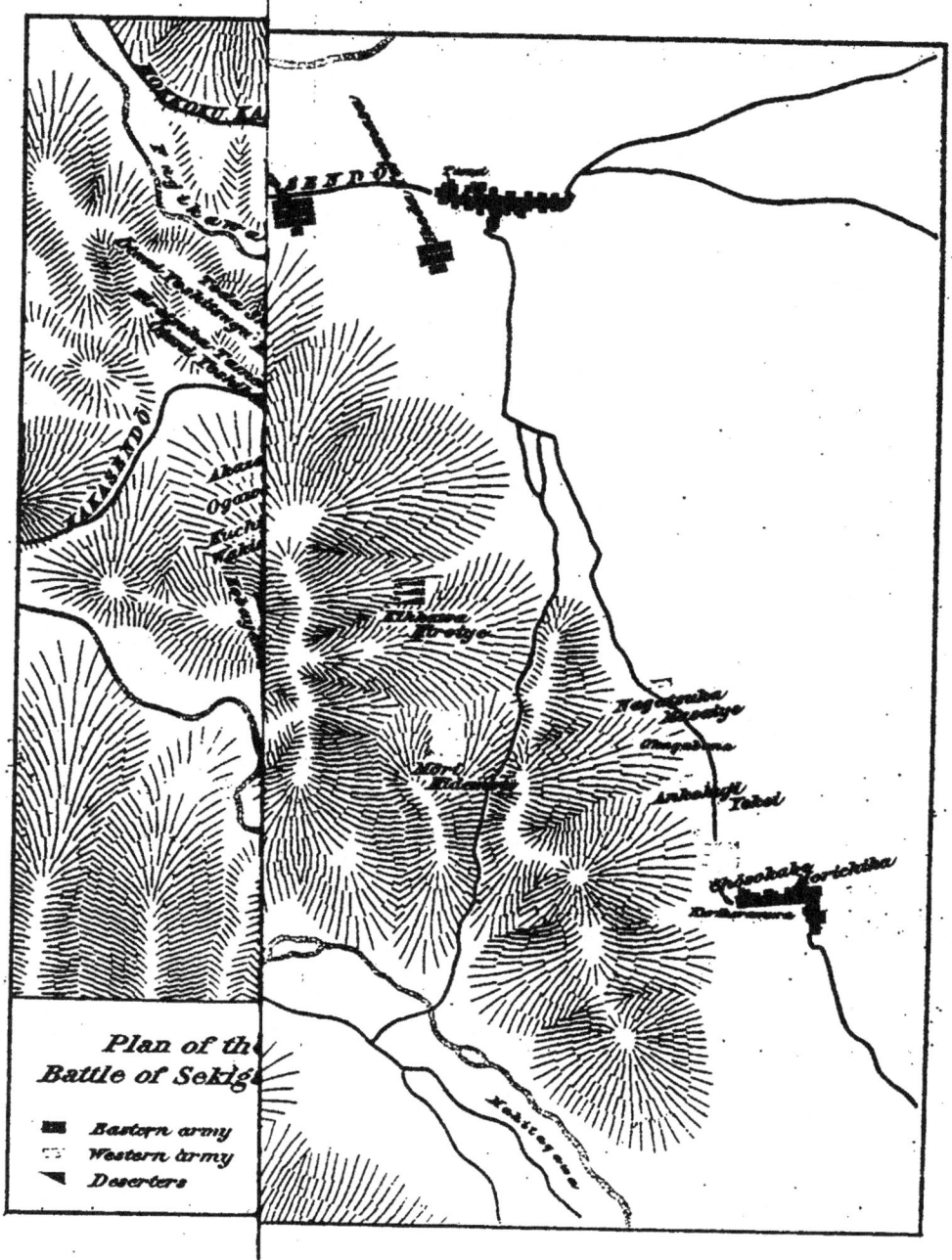

Plan of the
Battle of Sekig...

- Eastern army
- Western army
- Deserters

and an intensified Scotch mist—and somehow or other managed to get into order on Konishi's right flank. Meanwhile Ōtani had moved up from Yamanaka, and, posting himself on Ukida's right, completed the allied front which occupied the gap through which the Tokugawa must force his way in order to march on Ōsaka. A glance at the map will thus show that the road diverging from the Nakasendō and running round the base of Ibukiyama north into Echizen was beset by Ishida's troops and the men of Satsuma, while Konishi, Ukida, and Ōtani blocked the Nakasendō more or less effectually. Some distance to their extreme right, and slightly to their front, the heights of Matsuo-san, a position of prime importance, were held by 8,000 men under—Kobayakawa ! Between Ukida's division and Ōtani's troops ran a rivulet crossed by the Nakasendō a few hundred yards below Ōtani's left front; and on the other side of the Nakasendō along the banks of this stream, on the ground below the slopes of Matsuo hill, were placed the battalions of the small Daimyō Wakisaka, Ōgawa, and two others. This disposition calls for disproportionate notice from the circumstances that all these officers were, like Kobayakawa, tarred with the traitor's brush. As for the other generals of the Western army, Mōri Hidemoto, with Kikkawa, was on the Nangu hill; Chōsokabe on Kuriharayama; and Nagatsuka and Ankōkuji at Okagahama—all on the right, or southern, flank of the Tokugawa advance along the Nakasendō, and about eleven or twelve miles in advance of the main western front now at Sekigahara.

If there had been no such thing as treachery in the Western army, these dispositions would have blocked the Tokugawa advance almost infallibly. But Kikkawa on Nangu hill, on the flank of Iyeyasu's march, had already come to an understanding with the Tokugawa, while Kobayakawa with his 8,000 men on Matsuo-san, on the extreme right of the confederate line of battle, had already pledged himself to desert his allies when the strife should be at its hottest. At this supreme crisis Kobayakawa and Kikkawa virtually held the future of Japan in their hands. The fortunes of the opposing hosts now depended almost entirely on the practical answer to be returned by these trimmers to the question, "To which party have you really lied honestly?" For the disparity between the

armies in point of courage and ability was little, and in mere
numbers it was not great. In fact, the relative figures were
almost the same as at Waterloo.—79,000 in the Western host;
under Iyeyasu, "about" 70,000 men.

The dispositions of the Westerners were not yet completed
when the Tokugawa van arrived (not appeared) and began
to deploy to the right (Tokugawa) of the Nakasendō opposite
the left front of the confederates, and only a few bow-shots
distant therefrom. In fact, before Ukida's column had left
the Nakasendō, Fukushima's men had tumbled into and become
mingled with its rear ranks, much to the mutual surprise of the
confederate rear and Tokugawa advance guards, for the fog at
7 A.M. lay still so thick that one could scarcely descry anything
two paces off.

In the Tokugawa camp the *reveille* had sounded at 3 A.M.,
and the vanguard was soon under way to accomplish the
thirteen or fourteen miles that lay between it and Sekigahara.
The storm had somewhat abated its violence, but a drizzle still
dripped from the impenetrable fog. Fukushima, on stumbling
into Ukida's rear, called a halt; and as the rest of the
van came up it wheeled off the road to the right and took
up its position between the great highway and a spur of
Ibukiyama. Kuroda's right rested on this high ground; and
from his left, in order, the troops of Hosokawa, of Katō
Yoshiaki, and of Tanaka fell into line. As the centre under
Iyeyasu's fifth son (Tadayoshi) and Ii Naomasa came up, it
also broke off to the right of the road and occupied the positions
between that road and Tanaka's left. At this juncture
Iyeyasu, with the rear, was still advancing a mile or two behind,
while at various intervals on the Nakasendō, several more miles
to the rear, Yamanouchi, Asano, and Ikeda had been left to
deal with the Western troops of Mōri, of Chōsokabe, and of
Nagatsuka on Nangu and the neighbouring heights in case
they should show any disposition to descend on the main road
and close in on the Tokugawa rear. If they should do so,
the Tokugawa host would be likely to find its fortunes in truly
evil case.

Such was the posture of affairs at 7 A.M., but the dense fog
still swathed and enveloped everything in its folds, and it was
merely by the hum of voices and other sounds that the opposing

hosts could judge of each other's presence. At last about eight
o'clock it began to lift and roll away up the slopes of Ibuki and
of Matsuo. Then from the Tokugawa centre Ii Naomasa, with
thirty spearmen, dashed forward upon some Western skirmishers
and drove them in, while at the same time Fukushima, leaving
his position on the Nakasendō, swung forward over the open
ground to its left, and then, facing somewhat to the right,
opened a vigorous fire on Ukida's division. Fukushima's
advance was at once followed up by the troops of Kyōgoku,
Tōdō, Terasawa (Governor of Nagasaki), and Honda; and they,
passing on beyond him, took up their positions on the extreme
Tokugawa left and at once came into action with Ōtani. In the
course of half an hour the battle had become general, and
raged furiously all along the line. The determined Tokugawa
onset was met by quite as determined a Western resistance, and
after a series of charges and counter-charges, repulses and counter-
repulses, at noon the fell hurly-burly, swaying this way and that,
still raged with equal fortunes. By this time the Tokugawa
reserves had come up, but the narrowness of the ground prevented
them from coming into action with full effect. Possibly no more
than half the Western host (40,000 men) had yet been engaged,
and by noon 60,000 Tokugawa troops were pressing on their
opposing front.

During all these four hours Kobayakawa, with his 8,000
men, from his perch on Matsuo hill had remained quietly
looking on, passively and seemingly unconcerned. It seems
that it had been arranged between him and Ishida[17] that at
a given signal from the latter, Kobayakawa should, when the

---

[17] It may seem odd that, despite his purely civilian record, Ishida should
have held such high command in the confederate army. It ought to be remarked,
however, that Ishida had been a keen student of military strategy under Shima,
noted as one of its most competent exponents. About 1590 Hideyoshi had put
Ishida in possession of the fief of Minakuchi in Ōmi, with a revenue of 40,000
koku. Shortly afterwards, when Ishida returned to Kyōto, Hideyoshi asked him
how many new *samurai* he had engaged since his revenue had been increased.
Ishida replied that he had engaged only one, a man called Shima. Hideyoshi
remarked that Shima's name was familiar to him, and that he was a man who
would not serve a master of Ishida's type unless his allowance was a very
handsome one. "How much do you give him?" he asked. "You give me
40,000 *koku*," answered Ishida, "and of that I give Shima 15,000 *koku*." "It is
rare indeed to find such little difference between the income of master and man,"
laughed Hideyoshi. Shima was together with Ishida on the allies' extreme left
at Sekigahara, and doubtless had his share in formulating the strategy and the
tactics of the confederates. Ishida used to remark that a public servant should
spend all the income he gets from his employer, that if he failed to do so he
committed theft, and that if he spent too much and ran into debt he was a
fool.

D D

strife was at the hottest, swoop down the slope, get upon the left rear of the Tokugawa, and then fall furiously upon the left wing, which would thus suddenly find itself between the hammer and the anvil. However, when at noon the signal was raised by Ishida, Kobayakawa gave no response. As has been said, he had already come to a secret understanding with the enemy; yet as regards the enemy he now remained equally quiescent and non-committal. Informed of this, just at the moment the tide of war seemed to be setting in strongly against him, Iyeyasu bit his finger in anger and exclaimed, "What! Is the wretch to spoil my cause?" He at once gave orders to put the trimmer to the test by opening a hot fire upon him; and thus unavoidably constrained to declare himself at last, Kobayakawa put a battalion of six hundred men in motion to descend the slope and to take Ōtani's command in flank. As for Ōtani, he was not very much disconcerted by this development, for he had already conceived suspicions of Kobayakawa's good faith, and consequently had been keeping a keen eye on his camp all through the strife. Accordingly he now at once called in his advance guards, and, wheeling round, presented a solid front to the attack of the Chikuzen men. Twice he broke them and drove them back with great loss; and then, to his real surprise, the troops now on his left flank—Wakisaka's and Ōgawa's and two other battalions—turned round and fell furiously upon him! Hereupon Kobayakawa again pressed his attack; and thus taken really unexpectedly, Ōtani, seeing that all was now hopeless, disembowelled himself, while his troops almost to a man fell in their traces where they stood.

In the meantime, under pressure of superior numbers Konishi's troops had been borne back from the line of battle, and, seeing this, Kobayakawa's main body swept down and round the rear of Ukida's division and completed the rout of Konishi's men. A cry of "Treachery" now arose in the Western ranks; and in the confusion this caused Kobayakawa fell upon Ukida's rear and broke the big division utterly. In the débâcle Ishida's troops, who had fought manfully, were the next to go, and then only Shimadzu remained; and in a few moments he found himself like an islet in a raging sea of enemies, assailed front, right flank, left flank, and rear alike. Seeing that all was lost, the Satsuma chieftain at the head of seventy horsemen cut his way through the swarming foe,. sped through the pass and on to Ōsaka, where he forcibly seized the best ships in the harbour and in them made his way to Kagoshima.. As for the *débris* of the Western force, it was swept through the defile of Sekigahara and down the Ōmi slope in hopeless and headlong rout.

As regards the casualties, though heavy, they were by no means extraordinarily so. Those of the Tokugawa are not exactly known, but it is generally admitted that they were fewer than those of the Westerners. These latter lost just 8,000 of their 40,000 men that came into action—that is, about 20 per cent. If we allow 7,000 out of the 60,000 Tokugawa troops engaged, we reach a total of 15,000 out of 100,000 men—15 per cent., almost exactly the percentage of that of Mars-la-Tour and Gravelotte, and less than half that of Salamanca or Borodino or Eylau (33 per cent.).

A little study of the general situation will serve to disclose that in forcing a general action at Sekigahara Iyeyasu was taking no inconsiderable risks. Even at noon, after four hours' fighting and just before Kobayakawa's defection ruined the allied cause, the tide of war was seemingly running in favour of the Westerners; and had the deserters thrown themselves in force upon the Tokugawa left rear at this critical juncture instead of assailing their own right flank, the result would infallibly have proved very different.

Nor was this all. As has been pointed out, away back on Nangu hill and the adjoining heights, ten miles or so to the east (or in advance) of Sekigahara, and a few miles south of the Nakasendō along which the Tokugawa had to march to the battle, was posted nearly the whole of the grand division of more than 30,000 troops of the Western army that had marched into Mino *viâ* Ise, while the remainder, Nabeshima's command, was supposed to be hurriedly advancing to their support. To deal with this body of nearly 30,000 men, only a slender force of observation—at most 8,000 men—had been stationed at various points of the Nakasendō under Ikeda, Asano, Yamanouchi, and Arima.[18] And for this Westerner

---

[18] Arima Noriyori of Arima in Settsu, the watering-place behind Kobe (10,000 *koku*, doubled after Sekigahara). Arima Toyouji of Yokosuka in Totomi

division of well-nigh 30,000 men to descend and drive in
these 8,000 men upon the rear of the Tokugawa army, then
hotly engaged at Sekigahara, and to press the attack home
with disastrous results to Iyeyasu and his fortunes, would have
been a very easy thing.

But of all these 30,000 troops not a man moved. To
understand the reason of this it is necessary to glance at
the map. There it will be observed that on the low ground
the extreme rear was occupied by the Tosa troops under
Chōsokabe, while in front of him were Ankokuji's battalions,
and still further in front those of Nagatsuka (*Bugyō* of Finance).
As has been said more than once, the strong division of Mōri
Hidemoto was on the summit of Nangu hill, while a little
in front of him, and in the extreme van of the Ise division,
was his chief of staff, Kikkawa, with his own levies from the
provinces of Hōki, Idzumo, and Oki, which he held as a
feudatory of the House of Mōri. *Now, this Kikkawa, all unknown even to Mōri Hidemoto, and still more so to Nagatsuka,
Ankokuji, and Chōsokabe, had come to a secret understanding with
the Tokugawa headquarters early on the 20th of October. And it
was in consequence of this understanding, as well as of that with
Kobayakawa and Wakisaka, that Iyeyasu had issued the general
order for an immediate march on Osaka which had led to the
precipitate retreat of Ishida, Konishi, Satsuma, and Ukida upon
Sekigahara.* To quote the Japanese Army General Staff's
publication :—

"The troops of Nagatsuka, Ankokuji and Chōsokabe, stationed
near Nangu-san, did not take part in the fighting. They were
detained by the inactivity of Mōri's troops. Kikkawa Hiroiye, the
chief lieutenant of Mōri, had promised Iyeyasu to pass to his side,
and, faithful to this promise, he did not stir, although he had been
urged by Nagatsuka and the others to move together with them
and attack the Tokugawa rear. Nagatsuka and his companions
thus lost the opportunity of helping Ishida, and soon after learning
the result of the battle they precipitately retired to Ise."

From this it will be seen that neither the Ise division
(30,000 men) of the Western army, nor the Nakasendō division
(38,000) of the Tokugawa army, under Hidetada, ever came

(30,000 *koku*) was transferred to Fukuchiyama in Tamba with 60,000 *koku* after
this war. Arima Harunobu of Arima in Hizen, the "great" Arima of the
Jesuits (he and Omura, 25,000 *koku*, were called the "two pillars of the
Church"!), with 40,000 *koku*, prudent man, just sat quietly on the fence till he
found time to make up his mind as to which was the proper (*i.e.* the winning) side.

into action. Also it will appear that apart from unforeseen treachery and defection—against which it was almost impossible to provide—the strategic dispositions of the Western commanders were excellent. If all the allies had been staunch to the cause, the Tokugawa must infallibly have been bucketed to pieces in the *cul-de-sac* into which they had so venturously thrown themselves. On the other hand, knowing what he knew, Iyeyasu's resolution and procedure clearly vindicate that his head was set upon the shoulders of a genius. It must not be forgotten that Iyeyasu was no mere medley of isolated capacities, but a definite, a distinct, a far-reaching and a versatile idiosyncrasy. The art of war is only one among the arts that contribute to empire, and while in that he was proficient, he was by no means so unintelligent as to fancy that that alone was the only factor of importance in the struggle for place and power. Ishida's capacity for intrigue he never undervalued for a moment; and although conscious of superiority to Ishida in statecraft, and of equality to Konishi, Shimadzu, and Ukida in the mere ordering of a campaign, he yet recognised that Ishida's ability as an intriguer had by no manner of means to be discounted. At this supreme crisis of his life Tokugawa Iyeyasu did indeed venture on a bold risk; but the result amply testified to his ability not merely as a soldier but as a master of men—master because he could read character and utilise the lore conveyed in the print in fashion long before Valegnani brought his new-fangled press and types to Japan in 1590.

Apart from any secret understanding with Kikkawa and Kobayakawa, Iyeyasu would most likely have remained quiet at Akasaka until the Nakasendō division, whose arrival might be expected at any hour, had come in. Its 35,000 troops (for some had been left to reduce Sanada in Uyeda Castle) would have swelled the Tokugawa forces to a total of 105,000 men, thus giving Iyeyasu a numerical equality to the forces the allies could hope to mass against them within the next week. Then, of course, the chances would have been fairly equal.

These considerations raise the question of the whereabouts of Hidetada's Nakasendō division at the time of the great battle. This division had left Utsunomiya on October 1st, and had arrived at Komuro in Shinano on October 9th. Here, instead of pushing resolutely forward, Hidetada allowed himself to be drawn into an ineffectual attempt to reduce the castle of Uyeda (held by Sanada), twelve miles to the north off his direct line of advance. Sanada (38,000 *koku*) had been ordered by Iyeyasu to join him in the Aidzu campaign, and accordingly, with his two sons Nobuyuki and Yukimura, he set out to meet Hidetada at Utsunomiya. While on his way he got (August 29th) an invitation from Ishida to join *his* party. The father then informed his sons that they were free to choose which of the sides they would espouse. Nobuyuki declared for Iyeyasu; but Yukimura, the future hero of the great siege of Ōsaka (1615), pronounced for Ishida, as did also his father. The two latter returned to Uyeda, and here they received a summons to surrender from Hidetada when he arrived at Komuro on October 9th. To this Sanada made answer that he would give a definite reply after he had persuaded his retainers to yield. Hidetada waited two days, during which Sanada contrived to make his fortress impregnable. When another messenger from Hidetada appeared he was sent back with an insolent challenge, and on the 12th Hidetada left Komuro to reduce the refractory Daimyō of Uyeda. On the 16th, after an unsuccessful assault on the castle, Hidetada was back in Komuro, and here a courier from his father appeared, instructing him to meet Iyeyasu in Mino, as he intended to leave Yedo on October 7th. The messenger had started on October 6th, but had been retarded by floods. Hidetada now left a detachment to mask Uyeda, and on October 6th set forward by cross roads to save his rear from the risk of attack. On October 23rd he was at Tsumagome, seventy-nine miles from Sekigahara, and here he received news of the great battle of October 21st. He now hurried on by forced marches of thirty-eight and forty miles a day, and on the 26th he formed a junction with the main army, which had meanwhile advanced to Kusatsu, forty miles beyond the battle-field of Sekigahara. Iyeyasu in person was nine miles ahead at Ōtsu, and Hidetada at once pushed on to meet him. But the old statesman was so wroth with Hidetada for the tardiness that might have dislocated and wrecked the whole campaign—wrecked even the fortunes of the House of

Tokugawa—that he refused, and very justly refused, to see him; and it was only after earnest pleading on the part of Sakakibara, Honda, and other old and devoted retainers that the son was admitted into his father's presence on October 29th.

However, to return from this digression to Sekigahara, we are told that on the afternoon of October 21st Iyeyasu shifted his headquarters from Okayama to a height by the Fujikawa, where Ōtani had previously been encamped. Here he received the congratulations of his allied generals; and when one of them proposed to raise the pæan of triumph, he made reply that he had been confident of victory from the first, and that the right time to raise the pæan would be when the hostages in Ōsaka had been recovered. That night he passed in his new camp, while his troops bivouacked in and around Sekigahara.

However, for the traitors there was no such repose. Immediately after the battle the victorious commander ordered Kobayakawa, Wakisaka, and the other deserters to march upon Ishida's keep of Sawayama and reduce it. That very night they started, fifteen thousand strong, with Ii Naomasu to watch their operations. Sawayama was gallantly held by Ishida's brother with 2,800 men; but here the treachery of Fushimi was repeated, and after killing Ishida's wife and children, his brother disembowelled himself and was buried in the wreck of the blazing fortress.

Iyeyasu soon started on his march to Ōsaka, and from Ōtsu on October 26th he sent a messenger to Ōno Harunaga (Yodogimi's paramour) to tell him that although Ishida and his fellow-conspirators had made use of Hideyori's name to forward their designs, he (Iyeyasu) did not hold either Hideyori or his mother, Yodogimi, in any way responsible for this, for he was quite convinced that they had been no parties to the conspiracy. To Yodogimi this was more than welcome news, and Ōno was at once dispatched to Ōtsu, there to thank Iyeyasu for his message in the warmest possible terms.

In Ōsaka, since the morning of October 22nd, when news of Sekigahara arrived, all had been terror and confusion. After Nagatsuka had departed for the front on September 12th, Mōri Terumoto had been left with Masuda and Mayeda Gen-i ("Guenifoin" of the Jesuits) as counsellors. The latter, really averse to Ishida's projects from their inception, under the plea

of ill-health retired to his estates and to private life about the
beginning of October; and from that time Mōri had to rely
for counsel upon Masuda (Maxita Yemondono) alone. On
October 22nd the survivors of the Sekigahara *débâcle* began
to pour in through the gates with the wildest and most
exaggerated tales of disaster, and shortly afterwards the
unbeaten commands of Nabeshima, of Chōsokabe, and of Mōri
Hidemoto came tumbling in one after the other. The more
courageous among these—notably Mōri Hidemoto and Tachibana
—were strongly for proceeding with the struggle. Ōsaka, they
pointed out, with its triple *enceinte* and its huge store of
provisions and the 70,000 or 80,000 troops now in it to man
its ramparts and bastions, was virtually impregnable to all the
forces—at the utmost 120,000 men—that Iyeyasu could bring
against it; and meanwhile new levies could be brought up
from Bizen, from Mōri's domains, and from Kyūshū. Besides,
Uyesugi and Satake must still be making head strongly in the
North, and there also in Ōsaka were the wives and children of
several of the superior officers in the Tokugawa army.

However, in spite of all this Mōri Terumoto was by no
means eager to prolong the contest with Iyeyasu. If he could
come off with no territorial loss he would be more than
content to surrender Ōsaka and all that it contained and
quietly withdraw to his capital of Hiroshima, which he was
now doubtless sorry that he had ever left on behalf of the
cause of Ishida, whom he half suspected of the endeavour to
make tools of himself; of Shimadzu, of Ukida, and of the
" flower of the Japanese nobility." Terumoto (49) was also,
unlike his cousin Hidemoto (22), aware that Kikkawa had
been exerting himself to come to an arrangement with Iyeyasu
and to agree with the adversary speedily on his behalf; and
of Kikkawa's action or inaction at Sekigahara, which had
so disgusted young Mōri Hidemoto that he at once parted
company with his diplomatic lieutenant, Mōri Terumoto
expressed his approval. His approval was all the greater
when he received a letter, evidently written by Iyeyasu's
orders and·signed by Fukushima and Kuroda, assuring him
that, in recognition of the service done by Kikkawa, the
Mōri domains would be left intact. On October 28th, just a
week after Sekigahara, and while Iyeyasu was at Ōtsu, Mōri

sent an assurance of his fidelity to the latter, and on being in turn assured by Ii, Honda, Fukushima, and Kuroda that Iyeyasu would strictly keep his promise not to punish him in any way, he evacuated Ōsaka and retired to his private residence at Kizu, while at the same time Masuda withdrew to his own domains of Koriyama in Yamato. Three days later, on November 1st, Iyeyasu entered Ōsaka Castle, and this peaceful entrance of his into the impregnable stronghold that had been the base of the confederacy indicated in unmistakable terms that the battle of Sekigahara had been decisive of the immediate fortunes of Japan.

CHAPTER XV.

AFTER SEKIGAHARA.

ALTHOUGH the great fight on the Moor of the Barrier had sufficed to stamp out the main and central blaze of civil war, yet the flames of the strife continued to crackle and sputter in more than one outlying section of the empire. In Ise and Shima the reduction of some of the castles that had held for Ishida gave a certain amount of trouble, while in Tango and the bordering provinces work still remained to be done. There Hosokawa's castle of Tanabe (now Maizuru, the naval port), held by his father Nagaoka Yusai, had been assailed by a force of 15,000 men under Ōnogi of Fukuchiyama (31,000 *koku*); but it had held out staunchly until October 9th. On that day an envoy from the Emperor arrived at the place in order to arbitrate. Nagaoka Yusai was perhaps the most eminent scholar and poet then living, and the Emperor would have regretted his death deeply. His Majesty therefore dispatched this envoy, with the result that Yusai was allowed to march out from the castle. After Sekigahara, Hosokawa got permission from Iyeyasu to assail Ōnogi in Fukuchiyama, and after receiving the surrender of Kameyama (Mayeda Gen-i or "Guenifoin's" castle) on the way, he was soon in possession of the person of Ōnogi, who on being sent to Ōsaka was there requested by Iyeyasu to commit *hara-kiri*.

Mōri had dispatched an expedition against Katō Yoshiaki's domains of Matsuyama in Shikoku, but the news of Sekigahara brought about its precipitate recall. The fighting in Kyūshū was of a much more serious nature. At the beginning of the great upheaval our old acquaintance Ōtomo Yoshimune had been living in retirement in the domains of Mōri, and when Mōri cast in his lot with Ishida, he at once furnished Yoshimune with means to pass into his ancestral province of Bungo, there to rouse his former vassals in support of the confederate cause. At first Yoshimune had no small measure of success in his mission; the old retainers of Ōtomo were not slow to muster to the standard of their former chief, and for the moment it bade fair to go ill with the upstart princelets among whom the Bungo domains had been partitioned in the Taikō's time. However, in a week or two these fair prospects were hopelessly blasted. On former occasions we have seen old Kuroda (Simon Condera of the Jesuits) laying a friendly but very firm restraining hand upon the vagaries of the scatter-brained Yoshimune, and old Kuroda happened now to be in a position to repeat the service once more. At this time he was at home in his neighbouring fief of Buzen, and from there, hastily collecting 8,000 men, he advanced into Bungo, beat Yoshimune to his knees on the Moor of Ishigaki two days before Sekigahara, and, pushing on, made short work of all the partisans of Ishida in the province. Then wheeling round, he hurried to assault Kokura (near the Straits of Shimonoseki), held by Mōri Katsunobu (60,000 koku), the Iki-no-Kami of the Jesuits, and it surrendered on November 19th. Meanwhile Kuroda had also fitted out a fleet of junks in the Bungo Nada, and between these and the retreating squadron of Shimadzu a desperate naval engagement was fought on the twelfth day after Sekigahara.

In the meantime in Higo no less signal services had been rendered to the cause of Iyeyasu. As has been said, the northern half of that province was held by Katō Kiyomasa, who had married one of Iyeyasu's numerous adopted daughters, and at the outbreak of the civil war Katō had been promised Southern Higo and Chikugo if he could effect their reduction. Southern Higo, with its castles of Udo, Yatsushiro, and Yabe, was the fief of Katō's great rival and enemy, Konishi, who was now with Ishida; and into Southern Higo Katō at once poured his troops. As regards this special campaign we are in a very fortunate position, for the Japanese accounts of it are substantially corroborated by the letters of the missionaries, five of whom were besieged in Udo.[1] This fortress was invested on October 26th, and sustained the siege to the 25th of the following month. When Katō got news of Sekigahara he

---

[1] Unfortunately for the other incidents of 1600 A.D. the Jesuits are not of much assistance. The "Annual Letter" for that year seems to be lost, and the details of the Sekigahara campaign and of the events that led up to it receive very inadequate treatment both from Charlevoix and Léon Pagés, the latter of whom has followed Guerreiro's somewhat scrappy narrative.

caused letters to be sent into the castle by attaching them
to arrows, in which (by the letters) he informed the besieged of
the defeat of their cause and invited them to surrender. But
the besieged would not respond.

"The fact was that there were five Christian missionaries who
attended to the burial of the killed and the nursing of the wounded.
They made the soldiers promise not to see such letters, and so they
burned them without ever opening them. On the 20th of the tenth
month (November 25th), however, some of Konishi's retainers who
had escaped from Sekigahara and returned were seized by Katō
and sent into the castle. From them Konishi Yukikage, the
commandant, learned the truth, and thereupon decided to yield. He
begged Katō to pardon his soldiers, as he would surrender the castles
under his command. Katō agreed, and so Yukikage surrendered
the castle of Udo and went to Kumamoto, where he subsequently
died by his own hand. The commandants of Yatsushiro and Yabe
fled to Satsuma, while the Satsuma troops who had entered Higo
to support Konishi's cause retired."

Thus far the Japanese historian. Now to quote the
missionaries as summarised by M. Léon Pagés, who, while
much more terse and direct, is yet in substantial accord with
Charlevoix.

"But the chief misfortunes were for the fortress of Outo (Udo),
the chief castle of Don Augustin (Konishi), and for the whole
province. In the estates of Don Augustin, including the islands
of Amakusa and Chiki, were 100,000 Christians, with seven
houses of the Company in them. Canzouyedono (Katō) came to
besiege Outo, which defended itself heroically. Among the besieged
were two Fathers, three Brothers, and some Catechists. Canzouye
(Katō) wished to use the missionaries as intermediaries, and through
them to obtain the surrender of the place: he addressed himself
to the Visitor and the Vice-Provincial, who were at Nagasaki.
These excused themselves as religieux and as foreigners, alleging that
they would give the Christians of Japan grounds for thinking ill
of them if they interfered in politics. Canzouye (Katō) waxed
angry and threatened the Fathers; but they did not flinch, and
the besieged continued to resist. Meanwhile there arrived at Outo
one of Don Augustin's officers, the bearer of the baneful news of
the lost battle and of the captivity of the Admiral (Konishi). It
was then resolved to treat, since they had no longer a Lord to
fight for. The place was surrendered; but Canzouye (Katō) caused
the chief commandant, the brother of Don Augustin, to be put
to death. Canzouye (Katō) detained the missionaries and their
domestics as prisoners. They suffered cruelly, and the Father
Rector, Alfonso Gonsalvez, died of exhaustion at Nagasaki in March
1601."

To the reply of the Visitor-General and the Vice-Provincial
that they could not intervene in Japanese politics, Katō
might very well have retorted that the five missionaries in the
besieged citadel were intervening therein with a vengeance,

and that on two separate and notorious occasions Father Gnecchi had actually intervened in Japanese politics in the most effectual manner. But then there were such things as "innocent stratagems," to say nothing of "sweet violence," in the missionary bag of tricks.

Immediately on the surrender of Southern Higo, Katō turned upon Chikugo, where Tachibana of Yanagawa (132,000 *koku*) and Mōri Hidekane of Kurume (130,000 *koku*)—the "virtuous" Simon Findenadono of the Jesuits—had declared for the confederacy. The former, Tachibana, had done some stiff fighting at Ōtsu on Lake Biwa on Ishida's behalf just two or three days before Sekigahara; and on the news of the great battle had hurried back to Ōsaka, and failing to induce Mōri Terumoto to make a stand there, had returned and reached Yanagawa on November 14th. Two days later his neighbour, Nabeshima Katsushige (son of the Daimyō of Saga), came down to Saga, bearing a commission from Iyeyasu to attack Yanagawa! Young Nabeshima (20) had originally set forth to join Iyeyasu on the Aidzu campaign; but on reaching Ōsaka, Ishida's men had compelled him to make common cause with them, and so instead of helping Iyeyasu he had fought stoutly against his cause at Fushimi and at Anotsu in Ise. However, after Sekigahara he contrived to make his peace with the Tokugawa chief through the good offices of Ii and Kuroda, and was dismissed to his father's estates, there to give practical evidence of sincerity in his original political faith by bringing the local partisans of Ishida to reason and subjection. In three days after his arrival, he and his father were at the head of 30,000 Hizen *samurai* ready to invade Tachibana and Mōri Hidekane's fiefs, while at the same time that indefatigable old son of Mars and of Christ, Simon Condera (Kuroda the elder), was advancing upon them hot-foot from Buzen. Mōri Hidekane, the "virtuous Simon Findenadono," yielded his capital of Kurume without striking a blow, but Tachibana proved a man of tougher and more robust fibre. It was not till November 30th, when his beleaguerers had been joined by Katō Kiyomasa from Higo, that he yielded; and even then it was more to persuasion than to force that he gave way. Katō and he were great friends, so "Katō invited him to surrender and to atone for his fault by leading the

van in the projected attack on Satsuma. Tachibana accepted
the invitation and surrendered his castle. Later on, however,
the attack on Shimadzu was abandoned, and Tachibana went
to Kumamoto, where he was very well treated by Katō, who
gave him a residence and supplied him abundantly."

With respect to this "projected" attack on Shimadzu, it
must be mentioned that while Hidetada (22) was to lead it,
Terasawa, Governor of Nagasaki, was to have had an important part in the conduct of it. The bulk of the forces
employed in it were to be supplied either by the former
confederates of Shimadzu—such as Tachibana and Nabeshima—
or by those local Daimyō who so far had sat quietly and in
non-committal fashion safely (as they thought) upon the
fence. Of such—Dante would have doubtless pronounced
them "hateful alike to God and to the enemies of God"—
were the most powerful and most puissant princes of Arima and
of Ōmura—"those two Pillars of the Church" (one of them
at least soon to apostatize when his religion no longer brought
him lucre) whom the Jesuits would have us believe had all
along made such head for the cause of Iyeyasu! Even
Siebold, by the way, refers to moving Christian troops under
an apostate captain against a pagan adversary as a striking
instance of Iyeyasu's craft and cunning. The Ōmura and
Arima levies would after all have constituted merely a fraction
of the punitive force. Down to the year 1612 Iyeyasu seems
to have regarded the Christian party—if, indeed, he believed
there was such a thing—in Japan as too utterly insignificant
to be a ground for any serious apprehension. The simple fact
of the matter appears to be that at the bottom of his heart
Iyeyasu had a most proper contempt for turncoats and trimmers, and invariably used them,—if not to do his dirty work
for him, at all events for dealing either with their former
associates still in arms, or with those antagonists of his with
whom the trimmers would have hastened to associate themselves
in the case of his own defeat. Immediately after Sekigahara,
Kobayakawa, Wakisaka, Ogawa, and their fellow-deserters
found themselves charged with the reduction of Sawayama,
the stronghold of Ishida, their former chief; Nabeshima had
had to advance upon Tachibana; while Tachibana, in turn,
would have had to lead the van in the attack upon Satsuma.

However, the projected attack upon Shimadzu with his great resources and his strong position at the extreme confines of the empire had to be considered very carefully and only ventured upon when all other means of bringing him to submission had failed. Negotiations were set on foot, and as the final result of them the young prince (Tadatsune, 25) appeared at Fushimi in the spring of 1602, and was there received by Iyeyasu. So far from suffering any territorial loss in consequence of Sekigahara it would appear that about this time Shimadzu even received an addition to his domains. At all events, whereas at the death of the Taikō in 1598 his fief was rated at 555,000 koku, under Iyeyasu we find it returned at 605,000 koku, exactly the same as Daté of Sendai, whose virtuous attachment to the Tokugawa cause sufficed to add no more than 25,000 koku to his revenue.

Before Shimadzu's submission early in 1602 Iyeyasu's Northern adversaries had already been constrained to give up the contest as bootless. Just when the whole might of the Tokugawa was to be thrown against Uyesugi in Aidzu in the spring of 1601, Uyesugi tendered his surrender to Hideyasu, Iyeyasu's son, at Utsunomiya, and on the seventh month of that year he repaired to Fushimi, there to be told that he was to be removed from Aidzu to Yonezawa, and that his resources were to be somewhat clipped and curtailed. Henceforth, instead of 1,200,000 koku he was to receive no more than 300,000 koku, and in the new list of Daimyō he was to content himself with the eighteenth instead of the third place he had held at the death of the Taikō. A little later on Sataké also thought fit to make his peace with the victor and to submit to being removed to Akita in Dewa, with a revenue of 205,800 koku in lieu of the 545,000 koku he had enjoyed at Mito in Hitachi.

Having thus briefly sketched the course of the civil war in the outlying portions of the empire, and outlined the fortunes of some of the limbs of the conspiracy or of the confederacy, it may now be well to return to a consideration of matters at the centre of affairs, and more especially to the measure meted out to the vanquished leaders there.

Of the chief confederate commanders actually engaged in the great battle of October 21st, only one, the chivalrous

Ōtani, died on the field, and Ōtani there fell by his own hand. Nor were any of the others then made prisoners. We have already alluded to the fashion in which the gallant Shimadzu extricated himself from the *débâcle* of the stricken field; and Shimadzu was either accómpanied, or at least soon joined, by Ukida in his flight. When at last, in 1602, the Satsuma chieftain made his peace with Iyeyasu, Ukida, who had been some eighteen months his guest, surrendered himself to the victor and was then exiled to the island of Hachijō, the most southerly of the seven islets in the Idzu chain.[2]

---

[2] It is odd that while Charlevoix is in error about the fate of Ukida, Kaempfer, or rather Caron, should have been misled with regard to Hachijō. The former tells us that Bigendono (Ukida) was killed by a sabre-stroke while fighting stoutly in the van at Sekigahara. In the latter (Kaempfer) we find the following:—"Fatsisio Gasima, which is as much as to say the Eighty Fathom Island, is the most remote island the Japanese have in possession southward. It lies under the same meridian with Jedo, and is reckoned to be about eighty Japanese water leagues distant from the continent of Japan, being the furthermost of a long row of small islands, almost contiguous to each other. *It is the chief island where the great men of the Emperor's Court, when out of favour, are usually confined, pursuant to a very ancient custom, and kept prisoners on a rocky coast,* from the extraordinary height of which the whole island hath borrowed its name. *As long as they continue on this island, they must work for their livelihood.* Their chief occupation is weaving, and some of the silk stuffs wrought by them, as they are generally men of ingenuity and good understanding, are so inimitably fine that the Emperor hath forbid, under severe penalties, to export or to sell them to foreigners. This island, besides being washed by a rough tempestuous sea, is so well guarded by nature itself, that when there is some provision of the common necessaries of life, or some new prisoners to be brought in, or the guard to be relieved, the whole boat, with all the lading, must be drawn up, and again let down by a crane, the coasts being so steep and rocky as to admit of no other access."

Now, strangely enough, the sole and single personage of Daimyō rank for whom Hachijō served as a place of banishment was Ukida Hideiye. Ukida seems to have proved a real and permanent benefactor to the islanders. At all events, until of late years one of the leading industries of the place has been the manufacture of Ukida relics, the supply of which appears to have been well-nigh as inexhaustible as that of the True Cross, or of the tobacco-pipes smoked by Cromwell's men who once garrisoned Dunnottar Castle.

On this passage of Kaempfer Sir E. Satow, who visited the island in 1878, writes:—"In this notice of Hachijō, which reads almost like a passage from the Arabian Nights, the only correct statement is that which relates to the situation of the island. No one was ever banished to it before 1603, scarcely a century earlier than Kaempfer's stay in Japan, and therefore it cannot well be said that confining any class of persons there was a very ancient practice in his day. Of great men belonging to the Court of the Mikado (*Kugé*) none was ever exiled to Hachijō, though Ukida Hideiye was sent there in 1603. There is no reason to suppose that he or his descendants were weavers. On the contrary, the manufacture of silken cloth in the island dates from the fifteenth century, and it was the means of furnishing the annual tribute of the farmers, which was paid in the products of the loom instead of in rice, money, or any of the other various kinds of payment in vogue on the mainland. The statement that the coast is so steep and rocky that the only way of gaining access is by being drawn up by a crane, boat and all, is an absurd exaggeration. It is true that there are no commodious, almost land-locked, harbours in the island, but there are several small coves and beaches where a landing can be easily effected in calm weather, and it is very doubtful whether landing is impossible at any time, except, perhaps, during the most violent storms."

A Japanese visitor to Hachijō in 1874, among other things, says:—"The islanders used to wreck all vessels cast on the island, seizing all money, food,

As for Konishi, he was not captured till four days after the battle, and if he had really been very anxious to do so he might have escaped.

"At Kusakabe-mura, on the eastern flank of Ibukiyama, on October 25th, he declared himself to the village headman of Sekigahara, and asked him to arrest him, as he would be rewarded for so doing. But at first the simple villager refused to touch him, saying that it was improper for humble folk like himself to arrest so great a man. Thereupon Konishi [3] said:—'It is easy for me to commit suicide, but as a Christian I may not do so.' The villager had to be urged repeatedly before he would consent to take Konishi with him to his house. The headman at last complied with the request, and sent word to the local Daimyō, by whom Konishi was handed over to Iyeyasu, then at Hachiman."

At this crisis Ishida evinced no such submissive and complaisant meekness. When he saw that the great battle was lost, he fled across Ibukiyama, and, foodless for several days, he was lurking in the disguise of a woodman in a cave near Furuhashimura, when, on October 27th, six days after Sekigahara, he was discovered by some soldiers of Tanaka, who had been specially charged with the task of seizing him. He was at once conveyed to Ōtsu, "where Iyeyasu gave him clothes and medicine, as he was suffering from a stomach disease. He

---

and implements that might have been on board of them. They have recently somewhat improved in this respect. They allow a vessel to remain in a dangerous place until it is about to break up, when they purchase the cargo, etc., for a low price, and, leaving the crew nothing but their lives, put them in a miserable hut and sell food to them at extortionate prices. There is another important point to be noticed. The banished persons, in order to gain a livelihood, pass themselves off as physicians, and frequently poison the people by giving them drugs of the nature of which they are ignorant. The islanders, too, are not ashamed to squeeze newly-born children to death, and the lives of both mother and child are often destroyed by attempts to procure abortion with mulberry leaves and another plant."

The writer of this latter sketch, it may be remarked, was a native of Tosa, and possibly a descendant of those ancient Japanese Cornishmen who showed themselves such proficients in the gentle art of wrecking at the expense of the *San Felipe* in 1596, and who essayed to practice it on Ulloa's ship six years later on. Two of a trade can never agree.

[3] It is exceedingly difficult to arrive at any very definite estimate of Konishi's character and real abilities. Even in the pages of Charlevoix, where he has paragraph upon paragraph devoted to him and his doings, his figure is a shadowy and illusive one—*ce grand homme,—ce grand homme,* such is the burthen of them. He strikes one as a sort of Christian Pius Æneas—a man of undoubtedly great ability in war, and no mean proficient in diplomacy (in the missionary letters we have met with three instances at least where he lied rather neatly),—but withal something of a prig. Unfortunately he was at bitter enmity with Katō Kiyomasa—now a Buddhist Saint—who has been fortunate or unfortunate enough to get idealised by subsequent perfervid patriotic historians. Konishi's services in Korea were incontestably great—as great, perhaps, as those of his rival Katō Kiyomasa. But as an administrator of his fief Katō seems to have been the better man, for the impulse he gave to the civilisation of Higo by the introduction of Korean arts and artists, and of Korean industries, and of Koreans to instruct his subjects in these industries, was considerable.

had been bent on escaping to Ōsaka, there to rally his defeated partisans and to make vigorous head against the victor." At Ōtsu, among others, Kobayakawa came to look at him. Ishida, on seeing him, at once burst out into a scathing invective, calling him the meanest coward and traitor on the face of the whole earth. Kobayakawa was young (22) and sensitive; and this biting, burning indictment hit him so hard that he "repented of his conduct and became a sorrowful man from then."[4] Some little time afterwards, as Ishida was sitting bound with a rope on a mat in front of Iyeyasu's quarters at Ōtsu, Fukushima, and, later on, Kuroda, came up on horseback. The former looked down upon the prisoner scornfully, and contemptuously remarked, "You have provoked a useless disturbance; and now see where you are!" Ishida hotly retorted, "It is only fate that I failed to capture and bind you even as I am bound now!" Fukushima pretended not to hear, and passed on. When Kuroda appeared, he at once got down from his horse, saluted Ishida respectfully, and said to him, "You have indeed had bad luck. Use this." And therewith he took off his own *haori* (cloak), put it on Ishida, and went on his way. "All who heard of the incident praised Kuroda and condemned Fukushima." When Iyeyasu proceeded to Ōsaka on November 1st he took Ishida, Konishi, and Ankokuji with him, and had them paraded through Ōsaka and Sakai on pack-horses, placarded as disturbers of the public peace of the empire. Asano and Hosokawa here mockingly remarked, "What a difference between the clever fellow he was lately, and the miserable captive he now is!" Ishida, on hearing the taunt, turned round and said, "They seem to laugh at me for not having died on the battle-field. But this is what any average puzzle-headed general could do. A really great commander would escape, and think how to rise again. I fled, not because

---

4 However, of all the Sekigahara double-dealers Kobayakawa was the only one to profit by his treachery. He was removed from Chikuzen (522,500 *koku*) to Ukida's former fief of Bizen (574,000 *koku*), with an increase of 51,500 *koku* in his assessed revenue. Yet Kobayakawa did not really profit either much or long from having played the part of a Judas. The Japanese annalists tell us that "he became extravagant and indulged in luxury." In fact he became insane, and, acting lawlessly, lost most of his old retainers. He returned to his fief on the ninth month of 1602 without having obtained permission to do so, and died there in the following month. Ikeda Tadatsugu, second son of Ikeda Terumasa, was invested with the fief of Okayama (Bizen) in the following year. Wakizaka was allowed to retain his fief of 33,000 *koku* in Awaji, but Ogawa (70,000 *koku*) was stripped of his in Iyo.

I was a coward, but because I purposed to return to Ōsaka and risk another battle. They do not understand the mind of a great leader."

From four, and from four only, of his vanquished antagonists was Iyeyasu's mind resolutely set upon exacting the last and extreme penalty, and of these four one had already passed beyond his reach. Nagatsuka, Hideyoshi's Minister of Finance, whose share in the work of weaving the conspiracy had been second only to Ishida's, had retired to his castle of Minakuchi, in Ōmi, and had there committed the happy dispatch. This, however, did not save his head from being severed from his lifeless trunk and exposed together with those of his accomplices—or confederates—on the public pillory in Sanjō in Kyōto. As for Ankokuji, if he did not actually spin much of the spider's web himself, he certainly did a great deal to lure many big flies, Mōri among the number, into its meshes. Ankokuji had been a Buddhist priest before he became a Daimyō of 60,000 *koku*; and his readiness with his pen, or rather with his ink-brush, chiefly proved his ruin, for it was he who was responsible for the composition of most of the dispatches and proclamations issued by the allies. On the 1st of the tenth month (November 6th)—sixteen days after Sekigahara—Ankokuji, together with Konishi and Ishida, was decapitated on the common execution-ground in the capital. And on this occasion Ishida gave one more taste of his quality —indomitable resolution, steadfast to the very last. On his way to the execution-ground he asked for a cup of hot water, as he felt thirsty. Hot water could not be obtained, so the guards offered him a persimmon, saying the fruit would serve to appease his thirst. Ishida declined to eat it, on the plea that "it was not good for the health"! The guards laughed, saying it was ridiculous for a man about to be beheaded to be so very careful of his health. Thereupon Ishida burst out, "It is natural that to men like you it should seem ridiculous. But a man who aims at a great thing is ever bent upon accomplishing his object even to the very moment when his head is to fall into the blood-pit. It is a case of the proverb, 'Sparrows cannot understand eagles.'" No! Ishida was no coward, and yet the Church historians contrast the courage of Konishi the Christian with the abject cowardice of "Xibunojo" the Pagan on this fateful occasion ! [5]

The leniency with which Iyeyasu treated Ishida when the latter's intrigues were fathomed and divulged by Hosokawa in 1599 has often been commented on by historians. It will be remembered that on that occasion the Tokugawa chief refused to allow the enraged "Seven Generals" to put Ishida out of the way, because "he himself had a plan." He was perfectly aware that the intricate system of administration, with its numerous internal mutual checks devised by the Taikō, could be no permanent one. It would sooner or later involve Japan in the whirlpool of civil strife from which it had just been rescued by Hideyoshi; and he himself was resolved to make the contest when it came as sharp and as decisive as might be. In order to accomplish that purpose it was necessary that matters should be brought to a head; and to force the situation, and to knit his (Iyeyasu's) opponents together in an open league when they could be all dealt with effectually, there was no one more capable than Ishida. Doubtless this consideration had much to do with Iyeyasu's attitude towards the ambitious Minister of Criminal Affairs in 1599. If such a forecast really influenced Iyeyasu's conduct on that occasion, the subsequent course of events bore ample testimony to the correctness of his prescience of the future and to his ability in reading the minds of men.

To dwell upon the "might have beens" of history is, as a rule, a bootless task. However, now and then the "might have beens" must be briefly considered; and the probable consequences of a triumph of the confederates in the great war of 1600 are worthy of some slight attention. The apparent result of the Tokugawa's cause kicking the beam on that occasion would have been to replunge Japan into that welter of civil strife from which she had just emerged. Among the allies there was no one great and undisputed head, as there was in the opposing party. Ishida had woven the conspiracy, and for the moment he was its political chief. But the great feudatories, his allies, as soon as the common foe was disposed of, would almost at once have challenged his pretensions; and as Ishida's ambition was more than equal to his ability, the

---

[5] The original authority here is Carvalho's letter of February, 1601.

victorious allies would soon have fallen into two or perhaps several hostile camps, and the clang of arms would have continued to resound all over the length and breadth of the empire. In short, although professedly acting in support of Hideyori, each chief was really fighting for his own hand. All central government would have been at an end, and as the foreigner was then in the land, foreign influence, by playing upon the mutual jealousies, the hopes, the fears, and the interests of the warring feudatories, would have grown apace in the empire. Japan then might very probably have become professedly Christian in cult; possibly might, in part at least, have for a space passed under the sway of the "Protector of Spain."

The crying need of the time was a strong central administration, and that could be furnished by one man alone—by Tokugawa Iyeyasu. In every way the results of the great strife of 1600 A.D. made for the substantial welfare of the nation.

On his entry into Ōsaka Castle Iyeyasu found himself practically master of the empire, with fully one-third of its extent, in the shape of confiscated fiefs, to dispose of. Of the 6,480,000 *koku* of revenue these confiscations represented, more than one-eighth—836,000 *koku*—had been taken from Mōri. Under the guarantee of Fukushima and Ikeda that Iyeyasu would not punish him in any way, Mōri Terumoto was congratulating himself upon his good fortune. But he was soon cruelly disillusioned. On November 7th Kikkawa received a letter from Kuroda, undoubtedly written by Iyeyasu's instructions, stating that the guilt of Mōri Terumoto in having joined the conspirators, in having signed his name to proclamations against Iyeyasu, and in having dispatched a hostile force to operate in Iyo, was too manifest to be passed over; and that in consequence he must inevitably be dispossessed of his estates, but that one or two provinces of his fief would be bestowed on Kikkawa. In reply to this Kikkawa urged that Mōri had joined the conspirators, not so much from approval of their motives, as from the wish to testify his fidelity to Hideyori; that henceforth he (Mōri) would be faithful to Iyeyasu, and that the provinces promised himself (Kikkawa) should be left to Terumoto, so that the line of Mōri might be preserved. On November 15th Mōri was stripped of the provinces of Aki, Bitchū, Bingo, Inaba, Hōki, Idzumo, Iwami, and Oki (836,000 *koku*), and confined to Suwō and Nagato alone with an assessment of no more than 369,000 *koku*.[6]

Fully and clearly to understand how Iyeyasu used his triumph to consolidate the power of his House, it is absolutely necessary to devote close attention to the fashion in which he re-arranged the map of feudal Japan. To begin with, it must be clearly apprehended that the victor had spoils to the extent of 6,480,000 *koku* to dispose of. Of this amount fully one-third came from four Daimyō whose fiefs were reduced. Mōri, as has been said, was lopped of 836,000 *koku*; Uyesugi, transferred from Aidzu to Yonezawa, of 900,000 *koku*; Sataké, removed from Hitachi to Akita, of 339,000 *koku*; and Akita, shifted from Akita to an estate of 50,000 *koku* in Hitachi, of 140,000 *koku*. Besides all this, ninety others of the two hundred and fourteen fiefs in Japan, representing a total of 4,464,000 *koku*, were entirely and unreservedly confiscated.

In the opening year of the seventeenth century the re-modelled feudal map of Kyūshū stood as follows:—In the extreme south Shimadzu continued to hold. Satsuma, Ōsumi, and the half of Hiūga with an assessment of 605,000 *koku*. The rest of Hiūga and the greater part of Bungo were portioned out among nine small Daimyō. On the west Shimadzu's northern neighbour was Katō Kiyomasa, whose original fief of Kumamoto (250,000 *koku*) had absorbed Konishi's (200,000 *koku*) and some other lands, and now stood rated at 520,000 *koku*, with the eighth place in the roll of the feudatories. On Katō's north flank a new fief had been formed out of the confiscated domains of Tachibana and Mōri Hidekane; and Tanaka (whose soldiers had captured Ishida) was transferred from Okazaki in Mikawa, where he had had a

---

. [6] Charlevoix (quoting from Carvalho) is very strong in his remarks upon a piece of very dirty work he attributes to Mōri—or rather to some of his officers—at this crisis. Pagés' summary (also based on Carvalho) is, as usual, more condensed, and therefore more convenient for citation:—"The eldest son of Don Augustin (Konishi), twelve years of age, having a safe conduct from Morindono, had taken refuge in the lands of this Lord, but apprehending that he would be put to death, he summoned the missionary from Hiroshima and confessed. In reality Morindono soon broke his word, and caused the boy, who knew how to die like a Christian, to be executed. Morindono sent the head of his victim to Daifou-sama; but the latter evinced the liveliest indignation at this barbarous act." Although the missionary statements are wonderfully clear and explicit on this point, it must be remembered that Mōri, from persecuting his Christian subjects, was no favourite with the foreign priests. It will be remembered that this son of Konishi's had either married or had been betrothed to one of Iyeyasu's countless swarm of grand-daughters,

revenue of 100,000 *koku*, to Kurume, with an assessment of more than thrice. as much (325,000 *koku*). To the west Nabeshima still remained in Saga with 357,000 *koku*; Arima in Arima with 40,000 *koku*; Ōmura in Ōmura with 25,000 *koku*; Matsuura in Hirado with 63,000; while Terasawa, the Daimyō of Karatsu and the Governor of Nagasaki, had his assessment raised from 80,000 to 120,000 *koku*, the extra 40,000 *koku* coming from the island of Amakusa, which was now added to his original domains. As has been said, Kobayakawa was removed from Chikuzen to Ukida's old fief of Bizen (574,000 *koku*), and Kuroda of Buzen (180,000 *koku*) had been installed in his place with a revenue of 523,000 *koku*, which gave him the seventh place in the new *Bukan*, or register of the feudatories. Kuroda's former estates in Buzen, augmented by Kokura and some appanages in Bungo, were bestowed on another of the "Seven Generals"—on Hosokawa of Tango, the "Jecundono" of the Jesuits, who entered upon them with an assessment of 369,000 *koku*, exactly the same as the reduced revenue of his neighbour Mōri in Nagato and Suwō across the Straits of Shimonoseki. It will thus be seen that of the "Seven Generals" three were very well provided for in Kyūshū; of these three, two (Kuroda and Hosokawa) were friendly towards the foreign priests, while the other, Katō Kiyomasa, was, not without reason, their bitter enemy.

As regards Shikoku, it was now portioned out between five feudatories of the second rank. Ikoma, the *Chū-rō*, while taking part with Ishida ostensibly, had taken the precaution of sending his son to assist Iyeyasu; and now as the result of his prudence (the Scotch prudence of the famous '45) the assessment of his fief of Takamatsu in Sanuki was raised from 150,000 to 173,000 *koku*. His immediate neighbour, Hachisuka of Awa, who had maintained a benevolent neutrality in the strife, at the same time had his revenue raised from 177,000 to 187,000 *koku*, while Katō Yoshiaki of Matsuyama in Iyo, one of the "Seven Generals," had his original assessment of 100,000 *koku* exactly doubled as a reward for his efforts at Sekigahara. At the same time his neighbour Tōdō of Imabaru reaped even a richer reward than he, for Tōdō's fief was increased from 83,000 to 203,000 *koku*. And Tōdō in turn might have found just cause to become uncharitably envious of the new Lord of Tosa. At the beginning of Ishida's revolt, Yamanouchi, the small Daimyō of Kakegawa (68,600) on the Tōkaidō, had proposed that all the princes on the route along which the Tokugawa forces were to march should place their castles in the hands of Iyeyasu as a guarantee of their good faith; and now Yamanouchi, who had never come into action at Sekigahara at all, was, as a reward for this proposal, put in possession of the greater portion of the confiscated fief of Chōsokabe of Tosa (202,600 koku).

In the main island, Fukushima, removed from Owari, was installed in Mōri's former capital of Hiroshima with 498,200 koku; and another of his fellow "Generals," Ikeda, was removed from Yoshida in Mikawa to Himeji in Harima (520,000 koku), with an increase of 368,000 koku. At the same time, the last and youngest of the "Seven Generals," Asano Yukinaga, was seated in Kishū (not Kyūshū) with 395,000 koku—178,000 koku more than his father the Bugyō had received in the province of Kai, which was now for the most part incorporated with the Tokugawa estates.

The two Chū-rō who had been established in Iyeyasu's old provinces—Horio, 170,000, at Hamamatsu in Tōtōmi, and Nakamura, 145,000, at Shidzuoka in Suruga—were transferred to Matsuye in Idzumo, and Yoneko in Hōki, with increases of 70,000 and 30,000 koku respectively.

Among other things these dispositions had the effect of throwing the provinces of Owari and of Kai, together with the former Tokugawa fiefs in Mikawa, Tōtōmi, and Suruga, into Iyeyasu's hands, and all this vast territory was now either directly incorporated with the Tokugawa domains or entrusted to devoted vassals of the Tokugawa House who, under the name of Fudai Daimyō, were destined to play an all-important part in the future administration of the country.[7] Besides all this, in Mino there had been twelve, and in Ōmi four confiscations, and in these positions Fudai were now also installed.

---

[7] In the so-called "Legacy of Iyeyasu" it is laid down that "all Daimyō and Hatamoto who adhered to me and my cause before the war at Ōsaka (1615) are to be Fudai. Those who since that date have given in their adhesion and remained steadfast are Tozama—outside Lords. . . . . Tozama Daimyō, however able they may be, cannot have seats in the Go-rōjū, or take any part in the administration." As has been said, at this time Fudai Daimyō were those hereditary vassals of the House of Tokugawa that had been invested with fiefs of more than 10,000 koku.

A single glance at the map will serve to indicate the significance of this. In the previous chapter we incidentally referred to the course of the Tōkaidō and of the Nakasendō, the two great routes connecting Kyōto and Yedo. As has been said, they run into each other at Kusatsu, sixteen miles from the ancient capital. Now at Zeze, only seven miles from Kyōto and nine miles in advance of the great junction, the castle made a western Tokugawa outpost, held by the Fudai Toda (30,000 koku); and from that point right on to Yedo both routes were entirely commanded either by Tokugawa fortresses or by the keeps of Iyeyasu's Fudai, or vassal lords. Of these, at this time fifty-eight in number, the most important were Ii, installed in Ishida's former fief of Sawayama with 180,000 koku; Honda at Kuwana in Ise (100,000 koku); Takeda in Mito (150,000 koku); one Okudaira at Kanō in Mino, and another Okudaira at Utsunomiya, each with 100,000 koku; the son of the gallant old Torii, the hero of Fushimi, at Iwakidaira in Mutsu, and Sakakibara at Tatebayashi in Kōdzuke, each with an equal assessment. All told, the revenues of these fifty-eight retainers of the House of Tokugawa amounted to 1,856,000 koku—about one-eleventh of the total of those of the empire.

Nor was this all. Two of Iyeyasu's sons had done sterling work in the previous campaign, and one of them (the fifth), Matsudaira Tadayoshi, was now vested with nearly the whole of the rich province of Owari (520,000 koku), with his seat at Kiyosu, Nobunaga's original castle-town, subsequently occupied by Fukushima, now removed to Aki. Even greater recognition than this was received by Iyeyasu's second son, Hideyasu, for his services with the army of observation left at Utsunomiya to hold Uyesugi in check while Iyeyasu himself was dealing with Ishida and his confederates in the West. In Echizen there had been wholesale confiscations—no fewer than nine princelets losing their lands there—and all this territory was bestowed on Hideyasu, who, with a revenue of 751,000 koku, found himself the second in the reorganised list of Daimyō. His assessment was exceeded only by that of his immediate neighbour, Mayeda of Kanazawa, which was at the same time advanced from 835,000 to 1,195,000 koku. Thus it will readily appear that apart from mere territorial gains, which were great, the strategic value of the positions now seized upon by the Tokugawas, and held either directly by them, or indirectly for them, by the vassal lords of their House, made Iyeyasu master of all Central Japan.

The settlement effected in the extreme north of the main island has yet to be glanced at. There, as has been remarked, Uyesugi was soon to be stripped of Aidzu and removed to Yonezawa, while Satake at the same time was transferred from Hitachi to Akita. The latter province of Hitachi was for the most part parcelled out among Fudai Daimyō, or Hatamoto. It will be remembered that Mogami and Daté had done yeoman service in keeping Uyesugi's captains employed in protecting his rear. The rewards they now reaped were singularly unequal. All Daté's exertions had sufficed to add no more than 25,000 *koku* to his former revenue of 580,000, and his dissatisfaction at this scant return for his exertions cannot have been diminished by seeing his neighbour and late ally, Mogami of Yamagata, advanced from 240,000 to 570,000 *koku*. Yet even so, with all this great accession to his resources, it was not Mogami who profited most by the removal of Uyesugi to Yonezawa. As has been incidentally mentioned more than once, Uyesugi's tenure of the Aidzu domains had dated only from the year 1597, when he was transferred to them from Echigo. For the seven years previous to that date Aidzu had been held by one of the most distinguished men of Hideyoshi's time, by Gamō Ujisato, of whom it was whispered the Taikō himself stood somewhat in dread. There is no need to believe the gossip that Gamō was poisoned at a *cha-no-yu* function by Ishida, acting on a hint from Hideyoshi, but what is incontestable is that on the death of Gamō, at the age of forty, his fifteen-year-old son, Hideyuki, was removed to Utsunomiya with a greatly reduced revenue (180,000 *koku*). This son Iyeyasu now restored to his father's former dominions, with an assessment of 600,000 *koku*, greater than that of Mogami, and all but equal to Daté's. Over on the western side of Aidzu, Hori was left in undisturbed possession of his fief of 300,000 *koku* at Kasuga-yama in Echigo.

Thus the extreme north of the main island was mainly in the hands of six great feudatories, whose united assessments, running as they did from 205,800 (Satake's) to 605,000

(Daté's), footed up to 2,589,800 *koku.* Here, no more than in Kyūshū or Shikoku, or to the west of Kyōto, were any Fudai established. The interspersing of these vassal lords of the dominant House among the great independent feudatories to observe and curb them was a device to be adopted only some little time later on. Meanwhile Iyeyasu relied upon the mutual jealousies and antipathies of the Daimyō in the outlying parts of the empire to bar any concerted movement among them that might possibly be directed against the Tokugawa supremacy.

It may now be not unprofitable to cast a glance at the fate of the *disjecta membra* of the cumbrous and complicated administrative machine devised by the dying Taikō to govern the empire in the interests of the House of Toyotomi. Of the five Regents, Mayeda Toshiiye had died in 1599; Ukida, now in hiding in Satsuma, was soon to be exiled to lonely wave-beaten Hachijō, there to originate a new, a permanent, and a not unremunerative local industry—the manufacture and sale of Ukida relics; while Mōri and Uyesugi had both been (or were soon to be) constrained to cry " peccavi " and withdraw to insignificance, with wings and talons sadly clipped. As regards the *Bugyō,* or Five Ministers, Asano, of the Civil Law Department, had retired in 1599; Ishida and Nagatsuka (of Finance) had just had their heads set upon the public pillory in Sanjō in Kyōto; Masuda (Works), stripped of his 200,000-*koku* fief, was now a prisoner at Iwatsuki, not far from Yedo, while his reverence Mayeda Gen-i ("Guenifoin") had retired to his estate in Tamba, there to enjoy *otium cum dignitate,* ruffled only by the obstinacy with which his two sons would persist in their perverse attachment to the Christian faith.[8]

As for the three very worthy *Chū-rō,* or Middle Councillors —well, they found themselves in the position of Othello after the detection of the supposed infidelity of Desdemona. The

---

[8] One, if not both, of the lads had played a manly part in the gruesome episode of 1595, when the Taikō and his nephew quarrelled so disastrously. In 1602, we are told, "this year died piously Sachondono, the eldest son of 'Guenifoin,' whom his father had banished for becoming a Christian. Solemn obsequies were celebrated at the church by the orders of Paul Chougendono, his brother, equally a Christian; but 'Guenifoin' caused the corpse to be delivered to the *bonzes,* who buried it with their idolatrous ceremonies. . . . Chougendono nobly confessed his faith on the occasion of the obsequies of his father, when, in presence of the whole nobility and of three or four thousand (!) *bonzes,* he repulsed with horror the *insignia* they tendered him. (1610) Chougendono, son of 'Guenifoin,' had in his youth given proofs of a sincere piety, and

President of the Board of Regency had, like Aaron's rod, swallowed up all his colleagues or rivals, and for the present there was no saying what his exact co-efficient of expansion might be. As for the *Bugyō*, they had either vanished into endless night or disappeared into honoured or unhonoured obscurity, as the case might be. Thus the worthy *Chū-rō*, most honourable mediocrities, finding the task of mediating between nothing and possible infinity altogether beyond their capacities, were very well contented to be respectfully bowed off the scene with increased revenues to remote parts of the country, like Aristophanes' Kleruch of the Chersonese, to live

> " retired upon an easy rent,
> Hating and avoiding party, noble-minded, indolent,
> Fearful of official snares, intrigues, and intricate affairs."

" Uneasy lies the head that wears a crown"; still more uneasy the head and eke the more adipose sections of the anatomy of the wight who essays to play the *rôle* of a buffer between infinity and nothing; for the chances are that infinity will smite him shrewdly and terribly as to his hinder parts.

Now what is to be said about this Iyeyasu, who has emerged so decisively victorious from all this imbroglio? In the first place, we must set down to his credit account that Tokugawa

---

under Taico-sama had even prepared himself for death. But with age, and in his new estate, after he had succeeded his father, he became cold, and, without apostatising, abandoned himself to the disorders of the senses. Divine providence arrested him in this descent by permitting him to be accused before the Coubo-sama (Iyeyasu) by one of his retainers of being a Christian. Chougendono, full of wrath [somewhat un-Christian, it may be remarked], had the informer killed; then, frightened at his deed, he gave signs of mental alienation. Then the Coubo, declaring him incapable as an administrator, confiscated all his property, but spared his life. Later Chougendono, recovering his reason, recognised the divine chastisement, and henceforth lived as a Christian."

In this connection it may be well to allude to the following passages in M. Pagés:—"(1601) Maria Kiogocou, whose husband had been Prince of Omi, and whose two sons had received from Daifou-sama the first Tango and the second Wakasa, contributed all her efforts to multiply the conversions. . . . (1602) Sachondono, Prince of Wakasa, likewise received baptism. Chourindono, his brother, Prince of Tango, was already a Christian, and great hopes for the estates of these two princes might be conceived." However, about the Christianity of these two princes there seems to be more than a little doubt. Kyōgoku Taketomo, Daimyō of Ina in Shinano (100,000 *koku*), had been rewarded for his services at Sekigahara with the greater portion of Hosokawa's former fief in Tango (123,000 *koku*), while his brother Takatsugu, who had made a most gallant defence of the Ōtsu on the 17th, 18th, and 19th October, 1600 (Sekigahara was fought on October 21st), was made Daimyō of Obama in Wakasa (92,000 *koku*), with an increase in his revenue of 21,600 *koku*. Says M. Pagés (1602): "A greater number did not become converted, in spite of their convictions, in order not to trangress the law of the Taikō, lately renewed by Iyeyasu, forbidding nobles to become Christians, and by reason of the idolatrous oath which the Lord of the Tenka caused his principal officers to take."

more than once refused the office of Regent, or of guardian to the heir of the Taikō. The position was forced upon him. In the second place, few Japanese really believed Hideyori to be of the seed of the aged loins of the Taikō. Hideyoshi, at the time of Hideyori's birth, was eight-and-fifty years of age; and although his constitution had originally been of the very hardest, it had been enfeebled not merely by the fatigues of war and of rule, but by sexual debauchery notorious even in an age notorious for its profligacy. Besides that, Hideyori's mother, Yodogimi, was no Cornelia, no mother of the Gracchi; her subsequent relations with Ōno Harunaga were patent to all. In the third place, in spite of the fact that the Taikō, by vaulting into the seat of his former Lord, Nobunaga, had undoubtedly rendered a great service to the best interests of Japan, yet it could not be denied that he had most flagrantly betrayed the interests of Nobunaga's heir—that three-year-old grandson Sambōshi, whose claims he professed to have espoused so chivalrously at Kiyosu in 1582. As has been said, the guardian in 1598 died master of the empire; at that date the ward stood thirtieth in the guardian's roll of Daimyō,—Lord of a petty fief of 135,000 *koku* at Gifu in Mino. Now, by the whirligig of Time, or Fate, or Providence, or of whatsoever you will—this ward of Hideyoshi's,—this grandson of Iyeyasu's former Lord and relative by marriage (Nobunaga to wit)—from having been foolish enough to lend himself as a catspaw to Ishida and the others who were using his (Sambōshi's) former guardian's (Hideyoshi's) supposed son (Hideyori) as a puppet for the advancement of their own interests, the grandson of Nobunaga, the rightful heir,—*not* to the Shōgunate, but to the Vice-Shōgunate—found himself at Kōya-san as a prisoner of war to Tokugawa Iyeyasu, who, being of undoubted Minamoto stock, had, apart from his actual achievements, an undoubted claim to the position of Shōgun, just left vacant by the death (1597) of that last of the Ashikaga family deposed by Nobunaga in 1573.

It is perfectly true that two wrongs—or three either, for the matter of that—do not make a right; but surely Iyeyasu might be forgiven for reasoning that the general interests of the empire were paramount to those of the Taikō's heir, or to those of the House of Toyotomi. For Hideyoshi's usurpation of the

supreme power the only justification that could be urged was
that at the time he (Hideyoshi), and he alone, could give peace
and stable government to the distracted country. Now that
that great ruler was no more, could his successors be expected
to continue his work? The infant Hideyori, of course, was
merely a puppet; the real head of the House of Toyotomi was
Yodogimi, an able woman in some respects perhaps, but a
woman swayed by favourites, among whom a paramour more
distinguished for his good looks than for his genius held a
high place of influence. Clearly from such a quarter an
administration strong and vigorous enough effectually to curb
the restless ambition of the feudatories and to keep them quiet
in their fiefs could not be looked for. In short, the House of
Toyotomi had no longer anything to justify it in its pretensions
to be the ruling House in Japan. Every argument that
Hideyoshi could have urged in support of the rectitude of
his conduct towards Nobunaga's heir in 1585 could be urged
with equal force by Iyeyasu *vis-à-vis* Hideyori.

It may be asked why Iyeyasu, instead of waiting for
fifteen years—until 1615—did not now in 1600 summarily
sweep Hideyori from his path. In reply. to this query many
considerations can be adduced in support of the proposition
that at that date such a procedure would not merely have
been highly impolitic, but even fraught with the gravest
danger, not merely to the best interests of the House of
Tokugawa itself, but to the permanent peace of the empire.
In the first place, in the autumn of 1600, if the 70,000 or
80,000 beaten and still unbeaten confederate troops in Ōsaka
had resolved to hold that fortress till reinforcements could be
brought up, Sekigahara would have by no manner of means
been likely to prove the decisive victory it did. To obtain
peaceable possession of Ōsaka was then an object of prime
importance to Iyeyasu; and hence the reassuring message
dispatched from Ōtsu to Yodogimi and Hideyori five days
after the battle. This message had a powerful effect; and
once in Ōsaka, a breach of his word, plighted so spontaneously
and so openly by Iyeyasu, could not be thought of.

But behind this was a far more vital consideration. Many
of the captains of Hideyoshi were honestly devoted to the
fortunes of his House, and it was in no small degree by

reason of the vigorous and effective co-operation of these independent chiefs that Iyeyasu had been able to crush Ishida and his confederates. Any harsh treatment of Hideyori would have roused the profound resentment of the allied chiefs that marched to Sekigahara in the Tokugawa van, or protected its rear on that occasion; and the probable outcome of this would have been the formation of a new hostile confederacy far more difficult to deal with than the one that had just been broken up. Shimadzu, Mōri, Ukida, Uyesugi, and Sataké were all alive,—the first with unimpaired, and the others with still formidable resources,—and if these were supported by Fukushima, the Katōs, the Kurodas, Asano, Tanaka, and Ikeda, the House of Tokugawa would find itself called upon to face more than its match. At best, a long and disastrous civil war, or rather series of civil wars, must ensue. In every way, then, not merely the immediate Tokugawa interest, but the general welfare of the empire was consulted by leaving the House of Toyotomi with moderate revenues and a plethora of empty honours and respect in quiet and undisputed occupation of Ōsaka—for the time being, at least. To keep Shimadzu and Mōri, and Kyūshū, Shikoku, and Western Japan generally quiet, the good-will of Katō Kiyomasa, of Kuroda, of Tanaka, of Fukushima, and of Ikeda was all-important. Besides, Hideyori had been betrothed to Hidetada's daughter (consequently another of Iyeyasu's grand-daughters), and in September, 1602, the marriage was solemnised with extraordinary pomp at Ōsaka. While Iyeyasu could as yet put forward no legitimate claim to be the official Father of the Japanese people, he could, on the other hand, claim with justice to be either the father or grandfather-in-law of a very large fraction of the most powerful Daimyō of the time. Among other things this enabled him to extend the ramifications of the unique Tokugawa secret service in a very effectual manner, and so to put himself in a position to take timely precautionary measures to avert any necessity for an open rupture with those it was to his interest to use and humour for the time. The establishment of the train of Hidetada's daughter in Ōsaka simply meant the introduction of so many Tokugawa spies into the great stronghold of the House of Toyotomi. From them Iyeyasu no doubt found corroboration of the fact that the heir of the Taikō was regarded with affection by the valorous captains who had earned promotion from Hideyoshi; and so we learn from the missionaries that to conciliate the good-will of these Daimyō, the Tokugawa chieftain "treated Hideyori and his mother with the greatest respect by reason of the recollection which the Lords preserved of the former Sovereign; and he often went in person to visit the young prince at Ōsaka. He did more, and to please the Lords, without abandoning anything of his own special authority, he undertook to exalt the memory of the Taikō by celebrating his elevation to the rank of the *Kami* as Shin Hachiman, or the New God of Battles. The temple built for the new god was the most magnificent of all Japan; it was inaugurated with splendid celebrations, and an annual *fête* was instituted for Shin Hachiman as for the other *Kami*.[9] On this occasion considerable alms were distributed among the poor, the Japanese nation being naturally *aumônière*, and solemnising its *fêtes*, and *especially its funerals*, by immense liberalities."[10]

Any endeavour to discover a European analogy to the condition of affairs in Japan at the opening of the seventeenth century is, it need scarcely be said, utterly hopeless. To dub Iyeyasu the Richelieu and his grandson Iyemitsu the Louis XIV. of Dai Nippon, as a brilliant but somewhat superficial French historian has done, is entirely beside the mark. In some few respects Hideyoshi had done for Japan what Louis XI., Henri IV., and Richelieu had done for France at

---

[9] Seeing that Japan has some 8,000,000 *Kami*, we must conclude that the New God of Battles came off much better than the great body of his *confrères* in the Pantheon.

[10] It is a most ungracious task to have to find fault with an author who has furnished us with so much valuable assistance as M. Pagés has done. Elsewhere we have had jokingly to accuse him of "being sometimes as confused as chaos." By that we mean that he is frequently inherently inconsistent. The passage we have just cited is in page 70 of his "History." Now on page 63, in dealing with the funeral of Sachondono, son of "Guenifoin," he writes as follows:—"A rich alms offered by Chougendono was distributed among the poor, *a thing that singularly edified the pagans*. Really the *bonzes* acted very differently, and enriched themselves without measure." Nor is this by any manner of means a very glaring case of inherent inconsistency on M. Pagés' part. The way he wobbles from year to year in his estimate of the character of Iyeyasu, of young Kuroda, of Hideyori, and of Yodogimi is remarkable—and exasperating somewhat. The fact of the matter seems to be that while M. Pagés has (for the period 1598-1651) raked over a greater amount of original material than Father Charlevoix has, he is vastly inferior to the old Churchman in the matter of judgement. To co-ordinate his abundant details, M. Pagés has failed most signally. At the same time, over such Japanese sources as there are he shows no earthly command whatsoever. Yet, in spite of all that, his work is, and will remain, a most valuable one.

various epochs. And in the days of Henry IV. there was for
the time in Japan a strong Hideyoshi legend—a legend quite
as strong as the Napoleonic legend was in France between
1815 and 1850. Of the strength of this Hideyoshi legend,
Iyeyasu was perfectly aware, and to grapple with it before
its inherent flaws and the impotency of the representatives of
the House of Toyotomi disclosed themselves, he was by no
means inclined.

At the same time, as only those of Minamoto lineage were
eligible for the office of Shōgun, Iyeyasu was fortunate enough
to be able to request and obtain from the Emperor his
investiture with the dignity that neither Hideyoshi nor
Nobunaga had been able to assume. As has been mentioned,
the last Ashikaga Shōgun, deposed by Nobunaga in 1573, had
died in 1597; and the title of Shōgun, after being in abeyance
for six years, was now formally bestowed upon Iyeyasu in
1603. Inasmuch as Hideyoshi from his birth could never
aspire to the Shōgunate, it was not exactly easy for his
supporters to maintain that Iyeyasu, in assuming the office,
was stripping the Taikō's heir of any of his just prerogatives.
At the same time, as the duties of Shōgun were "to preserve
the Emperor and his palace from danger, and to preserve peace
and tranquillity in the empire in every direction," Toyotomi's
men might have found in the commission substantial grounds
for apprehension. However, to any representations Hideyoshi's
former captains might have made on the matter, Iyeyasu could
have made answer with perfect correctness that during all the
years of Hideyoshi's ascendency there *had* been a Shōgun in
Japan, and that the existence of that Shōgun had in no wise
militated against or compromised the position of the Regent
or of the Taikō. In 1598 Iyeyasu had been nominated *Nai-
dai-jin*, or "Interior Great Minister," and this title was now
formally conferred upon Hideyori.

Withal, during the years immediately subsequent to Sekigahara, Iyeyasu proceeded with the utmost caution. In the
settlement of the country then effected, it is to be observed that
in Shikoku and in all the main island west of a straight line
drawn from Tsuruga in Echizen to Kyōto, and thence to Ōsaka,
the House of Tokugawa had absolutely no direct territorial
foothold whatsoever. In all that vast stretch of territory not

a single Fudai Daimyō had been as yet established. In Kyūshū, at the same time, the sole and single Tokugawa appanage was the Imperial town of Nagasaki; and even the government of Nagasaki was vested not in a Tokugawa retainer, but in Terasawa, the Daimyō of Karatsu (120,000 *koku*). On the other hand, the whole of Central Japan, from the Nikkō mountains and the embouchure of the Tonegawa, on to Fushimi, and from thence north to the Sea of Japan and along its coast to the confines of Kaga, had been firmly clutched by Iyeyasu; and on these broad domains he now set himself to rivet his grasp. At Ōsaka, shortly after Sekigahara, there had been a long and earnest consultation between him and Hidetada as to whether it was in the East or in the West that the future seat of their power should be established; and after an exhaustive casting up of *pros* and *cons*, the decision had been rendered in favour of maintaining Yedo as the Tokugawa capital.

There, since the occupation of five of the eight provinces of the Kwantō ten years before, very considerable work had been done. In 1590, what is now part of the site of the Imperial palace of Tōkyō was crowned by a small fortress, of which the original had been the stockade thrown up by Ōta Dōkwan, a captain of Uyesugi's, in 1456. All around on the landward side was a tangled wilderness of reeds and sedge on the low ground, where the Sumida and the rest of the network of streams struggled seaward through the marshes; on the heights, dense copses and a luxuriant growth of bamboo-grass. At the date Iyeyasu rode in to take possession of his new capital (1590), what is now the most valuable building-ground in Japan, the Nihonbashi district, was feet if not fathoms below salt water, while along the line of moat near which stands the Mitsui Bank and some of the finest modern structures in Tōkyō the wavelets of Yedo Bay rippled in upon the shingle or the shells, for then from Wadagura to Hibiya was "a sea-beaten beach, with only fishermen's huts thereon."

Of Iyeyasu's first entry into Yedo we have an interesting record in the archives of the Temple of Zōjōji, written by Genyo Sonō, the incumbent, who stood before the gate to see the procession go by. Mr. McClatchie translates as follows:—

"My Lord, riding on horseback, was just passing in front of the temple gate when, strange to say, his horse stood still of himself, and would not advance. My Lord looked to left and right and perceived a priest before the gate. He gave orders to his attendants, saying, 'Inquire what priest that is.' They therefore questioned me, when I replied, 'The temple is of the Jōdō sect, and my own name is Sonō.' But before the attendants had repeated to him my answer, my Lord caught the words as he sat on horseback, and said, 'Then you are Sonō, the pupil of Kanyo?' (Kanyo was the priest of the temple of Daijiuji, in Iyeyasu's own native province of Mikawa.) I could only utter in response an exclamation of surprise. 'Then I'll halt awhile at your temple,' said he, and he entered Zōjōji. My Lord next observed, ' I wish to take a meal by myself in this temple to-morrow morning, but it is quite unnecessary for you to make any extensive preparations '—and with these words he went on his way. True to his promise, he arrived early next day. I was in the greatest delight, and offered him a humble repast. Then said my Lord, 'My sole reason for stating my desire to take a meal here this morning was as follows: For a General to be without an ancestral temple of his own is as though he were forgetful of the fact that he must die. Daijiuji, in the province of Mikawa, has been, of course, the temple of my forefathers for generations back, but what I have now come to beg of you is to let me make this my own ancestral temple here, and to enter with me into a compact as priest and parishioner.' With tears of joy I assented. He with all reverence pronounced his acquiescence in the Ten Buddhist Precepts, and then went back to the castle. After this he was pleased to remove Zōjōji to Sakurada; but on the ground that it rendered the frontage of the castle too confined, it was shortly afterwards (in 1598) removed once more to its present site to the west of the sea-beach at Shiba." [11]

The so-called "castle" enclosure which Iyeyasu had just entered we are told was limited in extent and unsightly in appearance; the flights of steps were built of old ship's boards. Honda Masanobu remarked, "In such a place as this my Lord cannot receive guests! I pray that it may be put in repair." The Dainagon (Iyeyasu) laughed and replied, "Do you entertain such a womanish idea as this? The question of repairs is one that can be deferred awhile." Safety from attack was

[11] How does this square with the following passages from M. Pagès? In connection with Iyeyasu's dedication of the temple to the Taikō as Shin Hachiman in 1608, he writes:—" The Coubosama (Iyeyasu), by this illustrious example, proposed to prepare for himself the honours of an apotheosis. Such pride was the result of temporal prosperity, and made it plain that the thought divine did not dwell in the heart of the sovereign. This prince was besides but little favourable, and one might say opposed, to the Christian religion; but he 'humoured' it in the interests of politics and of trade. *At the same time he evinced for the bonzes a profound aversion.*" (1608) "From the point of view of Religion, with advancing years the Coubosama (Iyeyasu) became more superstitious towards the *Kami* and the *Hotoke*, and more hostile to the true faith; but he had no recourse to persecution [What would a most Christian King of Spain have done to *bonzes* in his country, M. Pagès?] and allowed *Religion* to gather strength among its converts, and to extend its dominion among the infidels. The princes, from the example of the sovereign, were for the most part tolerant, and some of them even entirely sympathetic appeared to wait for nothing but the permission of the Coubosama to become converted." (1612) "The Coubosama (Iyeyasu) remained plunged in the disorder of morals [he was then seventy years of age—and so, if we are to believe M. Pagès, not

the all-important consideration at the moment; and to ensure
this, a cordon of some thirty fortresses was established all round
Yedo at distances varying from ten to fifty or sixty miles.
Many, if not most, of these a little later on became the seats
of Fudai Daimyō. The work of converting the old-fashioned
keep, with dry ditches and earth embankments only for its
defences, into a modern moated and stone-bastioned castle was
then undertaken; and in 1600, when Iyeyasu's younger brother
was left behind with a garrison in Yedo, he was left to hold
one of the strongest fortresses in Japan. It was not till 1606,
however, that what was known as the Nishi-maru, or western,
was added to the Hommaru, or main enclosure. This was done
by the forced labour of 300,000 men drawn from the domains
of the vassal lords, who then found themselves called upon to
maintain this huge army of labourers for fully six months.

Later on, in 1610 or 1611, Iyeyasu's ninth son,
Yoshinao, established in Owari,[12] found Nobunaga's old keep
of Kiyosu altogether too confined for his requirements, and
in consequence the magnificent castle of Nagoya was constructed
for him, almost entirely by forced labour, which Fukushima
of Aki, Katō Kiyomasa of Kumamoto, and Kuroda of Chikuzen

merely a scallawag, but a most persevering and persistent one], and became
more and more subservient to pagan superstitions. This year he convoked the
bonzes of all sects in order, he alleged, to reassure his conscience. He listened
to them, and chose for his doctrine that of the Tendaishu, disciples of Dainichi.
After his conversion to this sect he exclaimed, 'Ah! poor me, if I had died
two days before this, where would my soul have been! I was in a bad way!
See in what I placed my trust!' It had been suggested to him to hear the
Nanban—that is to say the *religieux* of Europe; but Sahioye (then Governor of
Nagasaki) and other courtiers were opposed to this, and the criminal life of
the prince opposed a so-to-speak invincible obstacle to the divine mercy."
(1613) "The old Daifousama (Iyeyasu), whose idolatrous superstition and
hatred for *Religion* increased with his years, was restrained only by his love
of lucre and the desire of preserving the trade with Macao and the Philippines.
He still humoured the Portuguese and the Spaniards, and tolerated some
missionaries. This year again this prince and his son (Hidetada) received with
benevolence the envoys of the Bishop and of the Father, the Vice-Provincial
of the Company." (1614) "From the effect of years (then 72) Daifousama
(Iyeyasu) irresistibly submitted to the ascendency of the *bonzes*; they inspired
him with terrors, and threatened him with the vengeance of the national gods,
if he should delay to annihilate the Christian religion. Everything, said these
perverse ones, was to be feared from the votaries of Jesus Christ, a malefactor
put to death on a cross of shame between two thieves. The Christians, they
added, feared neither death nor the loss of their fortunes, and they rendered
worship to individuals condemned by the authority of the law. Lately they
had seen them worship Jirobioye, crucified for having bought 'lingots' of bad
alloy, and to steal from the funeral pyre the bones of eight other criminals,
burned alive by order of the prince."

12 Tadayoshi, the fifth son, who had obtained Owari with a revenue of
520,000 *koku*, had died in 1607 at the age of 27; and the ninth son, Yoshinao,
then a child of eight, was appointed Lord of the fief, with an increased
assessment of 619,500 *koku*.

had chiefly to furnish. Iyeyasu himself, leaving Hidetada in possession of Yedo, established his own Court at Shidzuoka in Suruga in 1607, and here also the castle was greatly extended and strengthened, while at Kōfu, in the recently acquired province of Kai, there was another great effort in the same direction. Although, unlike Shidzuoka and Nagoya, Kōfu commanded none of the great routes between east and west, yet at Kōfu a strong citadel was a necessity, for the population of this mountainous district was a bold, an energetic, and a turbulent one. For generations down to 1584 Kai had been ruled by the Takeda family; and the penultimate chief of this House, the great Takeda Shingen (1523–72), had in his time been famous not merely as one of the finest soldiers, but as the ablest feudal administrator in Japan. So excellent was his system of government that Iyeyasu is credited with having made a most exhaustive study of it, and to have adopted not a few of its features for his own estates. It is also alleged, seemingly on the best authority, that when Kai was incorporated with the Tokugawa domains the former retainers of Takeda showed themselves so resolute in the maintenance of the old regulations and customs that Iyeyasu and his successors never ventured to deviate from them in any respect. It was ever the policy of the old statesman to conciliate, where such a thing was possible; yet a stronghold in Kōfu was a desideratum in case the policy of conciliation should miscarry there.

Still, all this was far from occupying the whole of Iyeyasu's energies. The missionary writers dwell insistently upon his fondness for money, and there can be no doubt that he addressed himself to the task of filling his treasury vaults in good earnest. Yet in common fairness it must be conceded that he accomplished this without imposing any undue burdens upon his own immediate subjects, for taxation bore less heavily upon the peasants of the Tokugawa domains than upon those of the independent fiefs. One item in his extra-ordinary revenue did indeed fall upon the non-Tokugawa farmers and merchants in the last resort—the large presents the Daimyō had to furnish him with from time to time. When Vivero had his first audience with Iyeyasu at Shidzuoka in 1609, "he saw a Lord of high rank introduced, who, prostrating himself, remained for several minutes with his face to the earth, and then

withdrew, *leaving a present in gold, in silver, and in silk of the
value of 20,000 ducats.*"

But it is questionable whether these presents from the
Daimyō constituted more than a mere tributary to the great
stream of wealth that was flowing into the coffers of Shidzuoka
and of Yedo from sources other than those of the ordinary
taxation levied from land and domestic trade. It must not
be forgotten that Iyeyasu's great economical aim was not so
much to appropriate the then existing national wealth as to
obtain a revenue legitimately earned from the stimulation of
new industrial and commercial enterprises, and so form a
consequent positive addition to the material resources of the
empire. Under 1603 M. Pagès tells us: "Gold and silver
mines discovered in his reign in the province of Sado returned
him 1,500,000 cruzados annually. He had declared all the
mines already discovered, as well as all those to be discovered,
to be his property." In explanation of this passage it must be
stated that when Uyesugi had been removed to Yonezawa,
this part (Sado) of his former extensive domains had been
appropriated by Iyeyasu himself. With regard to *all* the mines
being declared Tokugawa property, it is to be surmised that at
this date the declaration extended only to the direct Tokugawa
estates and to those of the Fudai Daimyō. Later on, subsequent
to the capture of Ōsaka in 1615, the regulation was no doubt
extended to the domains of other feudatories. Kaempfer
(writing in 1691–92) tells us that " of the produce of all the
mines that are worked he (the Shōgun) claims two-thirds,
and one-third is left to the Lord of the province in which
the mine lies; the latter, however, as they reside upon the
spot, know how to improve their third parts so as to share
pretty equally with the 'emperor.'" Moreover, at this early
date of 1603 any Tokugawa claim to levy toll, much more to
appropriate all the produce of the mines of Satsuma or the
underground wealth of any of the other great fiefs, would
have been not merely ill-advised but utterly illusory. Yet
despite that, the revenue of Iyeyasu from the hitherto undisturbed metallic treasures of his own broad domains must have
been considerable. Sado was not by any means the only
locality where prospecting had been attended with more than
merely remunerative results. In 1605 Idzu had furnished

a great deal of gold and silver, and there Ōkubo Chōan and Watanabe were continually making fresh discoveries. In the following chapter we shall see how strenuous Iyeyasu was in his efforts to develop this new source of wealth, and what sacrifices he was prepared to make in order to attract Spanish miners to the country to instruct his subjects in metallurgy and in all the secrets of the miner's art.

His third source of extra-ordinary revenue was his perquisites from the foreign—chiefly the Portuguese—commerce. Japan at this time was practically a free-trade country; of regular Custom-dues the foreign merchants had to pay none whatever. All that was expected from each vessel that arrived was a present, or rather presents, to the prince of the territory into whose ports it had entered. As Nagasaki had been the chief port frequented by the merchantmen from Macao since 1568, and as Nagasaki had been declared an Imperial town about 1588 or 1589, for the last ten years of his life it had been the Taikō who had been the chief recipient of the free-will offerings of the Portuguese captains. Nagasaki, as we have said, had just been declared a Tokugawa appanage, and as a consequence it was Iyeyasu's favour the Lusitanians now had to conciliate. The presents they tendered, while perhaps no very heavy tax, must yet have been considerable, for the cargoes they brought were extremely valuable. For example, the *Madre de Dios*, which was attacked and destroyed by Arima's men in the harbour of Nagasaki in the early days of 1610, had a lading worth more than 1,000,000 crowns, while the unfortunate *San Felipe*—no Portuguese ship or Japanese trader, by the way, however—carried goods to about an equal value. However, from the opening of the seventeenth century there was a serious drop in the importance of the Portuguese commerce. The Dutch rovers had appeared in the East, and annually lay in wait to make prize of the "Great Ship" from Macao. In 1603 they accomplished their purpose, and again in 1604, while in 1608 fear of them kept the annual galleon fast in the roadstead of the Portuguese settlement in the Canton River. Nor was this all; the Japanese of the independent fiefs, notably of Satsuma and of Arima, had thrown themselves with great vigour into maritime enterprise, and their junks now carried on a large proportion of the

over-sea trade.   Raw silk and silk fabrics from China formed
the chief item in Portuguese cargoes; for then Chinese silk
was much more esteemed than the native product in Japan,
and all direct trade between Japan and China remained
impossible down to 1643; at least, the Portuguese as middlemen
at Macao had had for long a monopoly of the Chinese silk
trade with Japan.   Now, however, Japanese junks obtained
the commodity from Cochin-China and also from Manila, with
the result that of the 5,000 quintals imported into Japan in
1612, the Portuguese vessels brought no more than 1,300.
From all the foreign trade with non-Tokugawa portions of
Japan—and it seems to have been not inconsiderable—Iyeyasu,
down to the year 1609, received no special advantages.   Yet
until then, directly at least, he was by no means minded
to hamper this commerce—in fact, there is strong evidence
in favour of the belief that down to that year he did his best
to encourage it.   Still at the same time he showed the utmost
eagerness to attract the foreign ships to Uraga and to other
ports in his own family domains; and, in the interests both
of Japan and of foreigners, it is much to be regretted that
the exceedingly liberal inducements held out to Europeans
to frequent the harbours of Eastern Japan were so sparingly
responded to by Spaniards from Manila, Spaniards from New
Spain, Dutchmen, and Englishmen alike.

CHAPTER XVI.

CHRISTIANITY AND FOREIGN RELATIONS (1598-1614).

ALTHOUGH the often-repeated assertion that the Battle of Sekigahara was the greatest battle ever fought on Japanese soil is simply untrue, and although the cognate statement that the victory in question gave peace to the empire for more than two hundred and sixty years is equally erroneous, yet it is correct to say that that battle threw the central administrative power, such as it was at the time, into Iyeyasu's hands. It is also correct to allege that from shortly after that date down to within less than half-a-century ago the Government of Iyeyasu and his successors had supreme control of the relations of the empire with foreigners and foreign Powers.[1] As it was this Government that was responsible for suspending all intercourse between Japan and the outside world[2] from 1639 to 1853, it is of the utmost importance to attain clear and precise notions of its early attitude towards foreigners, the foreign religion, and foreign trade. This purpose will be best served by setting forth the facts available, and allowing these to speak for themselves.

It will be remembered that just at the time Terasawa, the Governor of Nagasaki, had received orders in the summer of 1598 to collect and deport all *religieux* from Japan, the arrival of two disguised Franciscans from Manila threw the Jesuits into the greatest consternation. One of the twain, from his ignorance of the country and of the language, was speedily detected, arrested, and sent back; but the other, the zealous and indefatigable Jérôme de Jésus, who had once already been summarily deported from Japan, and who knew Japanese passably well, eluded the search of the officials, and, making his way to the province of Kii, went into hiding there. On December 7th, 1598, he was discovered, and was ordered

---

[1] Daté's embassy to the Pope and to the King of Spain (1613-1618) was in all likelihood sanctioned by the Tokugawas.

[2] With the exception of a few Dutch and Chinese merchants in Nagasaki and an occasional embassy from Korea.

into the presence of Iyeyasu. What then happened will be best told in the priest's own words:—

"When the Prince saw me he asked me how I had managed to escape the preceding persecution. I answered him that at that date God had delivered me, in order that I might go to Manila and bring back new confrères from there—preachers of the law divine—and that I had returned from Manila to encourage the Christians, cherishing the desire to die on the Cross in order to go to enjoy eternal glory like my (former) confrères. On hearing these words, the 'Emperor' began to smile, whether in his quality of a pagan of the sect of Shaka, which teaches that there is no future life, or whether from the thought that I was frightened at having to be put to death. Then looking at me kindly, he said, 'Be no longer afraid, and from now no longer conceal yourself, and no longer change your habit, for I wish you well; and as for the Castilians who every year pass within sight of the Kwantō where my domains are, when they go to Mexico with their ships I have a keen desire for them to visit the harbours of that "island," to refresh themselves there, and to take what they wish, to trade with my vassals, and to teach them how to develop silver mines; and that my intentions may be accomplished before my death, I wish you to indicate to me the means to take to realise them.' I answered him that it was necessary that Spanish pilots should take the soundings of his harbours, so that ships should not be lost in future as the *San Felipe* had been, and that he should solicit this service from the Governor of the Philippines. The Prince approved of my advice, and accordingly he has sent a Japanese gentleman, a native of Sakai, the bearer of this message. . . . It is essential to oppose no obstacle to the complete liberty offered by the 'Emperor' to the Spaniards as well as to our Order, for the preaching of the Holy Gospel. . . . The same Prince (who is about to visit the Kwantō) invites me to accompany him to make choice of a house, and to visit the harbour which he promises to open to us; his desires in this respect are keener than I can express."

Iyeyasu's first envoy to the Philippines does not seem to have been very successful in his mission, for the Spaniards there, having lent all their spare vessels and men to aid the King of Cambodia in his struggle with the Siamese, were in no position to respond to his requests with anything but polite promises. Iyeyasu, suspecting that it was on account of the depredations of the Japanese pirates in the Philippines that the Governor had given such a lukewarm reception to his overtures, had two hundred of the sea-rovers arrested and executed, and sent a second envoy with another letter written by Jérôme de Jésus, who meanwhile had built the first church and celebrated the first Mass in Yedo. It was not until the arrival of the new Governor, d'Acuña (in May, 1602), however, that any answer was returned to Iyeyasu's proposal for reciprocal freedom of commerce, his offer to open the ports of the Kwantō, and his request for *competent naval architects*. And then having got an answer—favourable in all respects except with regard to the last-mentioned item— the envoy set homewards, only to perish by shipwreck off Formosa. Meanwhile Iyeyasu, impatient at the delay, had dispatched Jérôme de Jésus himself to Manila, and after another shipwreck the Franciscan returned to Japan with the Governor's reply before the end of the year. He was well received by Iyeyasu, who promised him a site for a house in Kyōto, and who, on the death of de Jésus soon after, allowed another Franciscan (de Burgillos) to proceed to the Philippines to seek for further missionary assistance.

Meanwhile there had been a succession of events that luckily furnished Iyeyasu with an opportunity of giving incontestable proofs of the earnestness and sincerity of his desire for a legitimate trade and friendly intercourse with Manila. In 1601 that harbour had been frequented by numerous Japanese merchantmen, several from Satsuma, and some with Christians among their crews. The captain of one of these was asked by the Dominicans if the priests might go to Japan and preach the Gospel there; and on Kizayemon, the captain, saying they might do so, and offering them a passage in his vessel, the Provincial of the Dominicans wrote to the Prince of Satsuma offering some of his *religieux* for service in the Prince's provinces. Towards the end of the same year, Captain Kizayemon brought back an answer from one of the councillors of Satsuma, inviting missionaries to the number of not more than twenty into the principality. To quote M. Léon Pagés:—

"On the other hand, the Spaniards, who saw themselves opening the gates of Japan, and who were eagerly seeking for commerce with that Empire, desired at the same time, with a marvellous zeal, the advancement of religion. The Governor convoked both the Councils, the ecclesiastic and the secular; and the whole assembly decided with one accord that missionaries of the various Orders should be sent with a view to the propagation of the Christian faith, and *for the service of the King of Spain* (Philip III.). Dominican, Franciscan, and Augustin *religieux* were designated by their respective provinces, and were assigned the districts where they were to preach the faith."

This, be it observed, was really trenching at once on the Portuguese monopoly of trade with Japan, and on the Jesuit monopoly of missionary work in that Empire. The concordat of 1580 had confined the Japanese trade to the Portuguese, and it was only in 1609 (July 25th) that a decree was issued by Philip III. (1598–1621) permitting the citizens of Manila to trade freely with Japan and China. Equally the Papal Bull of 1585 had confined the propagation of the Christian faith in Japan to the Jesuits. That of 1600 had allowed the Begging Order to participate in the work, provided they entered the empire *viâ* Goa and Macao, and under the Portuguese flag. It was only in 1608, after a great deal of agitation, that Pope Paul V. issued a Bull annulling the restrictions of the former two, and according free access into Japan to *religieux* from any quarter.

The Dominicans naturally proceeded to Satsuma—only to find, however, that, as of old, the Prince merely wished to use them as decoys for foreign trade, and that a miserable existence in the sequestered and surf-beaten islet of Koshiki was the limit of their prospects. In 1603 they obtained a precarious footing on the fronting mainland at Kiyodomari, but about 1607 they were constrained to quit Satsuma and to transfer their chief seat to Isahaya in Hizen.

As many as nine Franciscans set out for Japan, their chief being entrusted with a letter and presents from the Governor of the Philippines for Iyeyasu. The latter, however, expressed his dissatisfaction at seeing so many priests and so little trade, and then allowed four of the *religieux* to pass on to Yedo, where one of them soon contrived to make a fool of himself as the result of a dispute with the heretic English pilot, Will Adams, the Kentishman from Gillingham.[3] The others remained in

---

[3] Charlevoix sets forth the whole matter—Bishop's investigation and report to the Pope on the incident and all—with malicious wit and pleasantry. Cocks's account of the matter, written to Wilson, Cecil's Secretary, corroborates Charlevoix in all essential particulars. After setting forth how a young friar argued with Adams at Uraga that by the mere strength of faith one could make mountains disappear or trees move, or the sun stand still, he goes on: "Mr. Adams told him he did not believe he could do either the one or the other. Not that he was in doubt but that the power of God was able to do them, and greater matters too, but that he firmly believed that all miracles ceased long since, and that those of late times were but fiction, and nothing to be respected." The friar, however (to quote Dr. Riess's summary), insisted on demonstrating that he could walk on the sea, so that thousands of people came to behold and see the event. He appeared provided with a great piece of wood made in the form of a cross, reaching from above the girdle to his shoes, and boldly went into the water. But he would have been drowned if Melchior van Sanvoort (supercargo of the *Liefde*, of which Adams had been the pilot) had not saved him with his boat. The next day Adams went to

Kyōto, and their good offices there proved of great assistance to the Augustin Father, de Guevara, who appeared in Japan a little later on. Through the Franciscans, de Guevara obtained permission from Iyeyasu to settle in Bungo, and at Usuki in that province a church and a convent were soon erected. Before de Guevara had been many weeks in his new quarters he found himself called upon to intervene in favour of some of his secular friends from Manila.

Towards the end of 1602 one of the three ships from the Philippines for New Spain—the *San Espirito*—was driven out of her course by contrary winds, and had sought refuge in one of the harbours of Tosa. The men of that province seem to have been the Cornishmen of Japan, looking upon wrecking as not merely a profitable, but a very honourable industry. They had deliberately run the *San Felipe* aground at Urato in 1596 with no inconsiderable advantage to themselves, and now they quietly and unobtrusively prepared to get possession of the *San Espirito* in some such similar fashion. Guevara, however, hurried to the scene and put the Captain, Lope de Ulloa, upon his guard, and at the same time addressed a petition to Iyeyasu, while Ulloa sent his own brother and an Augustin monk he had on board to back up the petition with rich presents. Meanwhile the Tosa wreckers acted in a way that left no room to doubt what their gentle intentions really were. Thereupon Ulloa summarily threw all the Japanese placed as

see the friar and found him ill in bed. "Had you but believed," he said to his visitor, "I had accomplished it." For the very same thing the friar had to leave Japan and return to Manila, where the Bishop punished him with imprisonment for this rash attempt. This account is more accurate in some details, but not so witty as Charlevoix's:—"When the friar was reproached by his *confrères*, he coldly replied to them that he had brought forward such good arguments against the heretic that he had believed it impossible that God would refuse to confirm them by a miracle." We must remember that Charlevoix was a Jesuit, and that the Franciscans had begun their mission in Yedo "by declaiming with violence against the Fathers of the Company (of Jesus)." Charlevoix, however, recounts the fatuous tales of the miracles worked by the crosses discovered in persimmon trees and what not in Kyūshū in 1612, with all imaginable pious unction. M. Pagés' account of the attempt of the Jesuit from Nagasaki to deal with Adams is also entertaining reading:— "There still remained at Yedo (1605) the Englishman Adams, and several Hollanders, his companions. The missionary saw Adams himself, and on the part of the Bishop offered him a safe-conduct to proceed to Nagasaki and thence wherever they wished! Really, there was reason to fear lest these heretics should sow the false seed among the people. But the offer of the prelate was declined by Adams, who alleged as a pretext that the Cubosama (Iyeyasu) would not allow him to quit his dominions. The Father at the same time put everything at work to convert these unfortunates; but he found them rebels and hardened in their error." Charlevoix and Pagés have both drawn upon the Annual Letter of 1605-06 somewhat liberally.

guards on the ship overboard, dead or alive; hoisted sail; opened fire upon the guard-boats that endeavoured to intercept him and sunk most of them, with great carnage among their crews. When Iyeyasu heard of all this, he said the Tosa pirates had got nothing but their deserts. A safe conduct was granted to the few Spaniards who had been left behind on shore, and orders were given that they should be allowed to proceed to Manila by the first ship sailing thither. And, what was most important of all, in order to prevent a recurrence of such "accidents," Iyeyasu caused the delivery of eight identical patents providing for the security of all foreign vessels that might appear in the waters of Japan,[4] and according them perfect freedom to trade in any of the ports of the country. The documents also offered foreigners full liberty to reside in any quarter of the empire; only they were to abstain from all propagation of the Christian religion.

However, the Spaniards showed no very great eagerness to prosecute the trade with Eastern Japan. A splendid site had been offered for a settlement of Spanish merchants in Yedo, but none ever came to occupy it. A vessel with presents for Iyeyasu and some Franciscans on board put in to a harbour of Kii in 1604; and on the captain sending word that he had not proceeded to Yedo by reason of the dangerous navigation, Iyeyasu offered to send an English pilot (Will Adams) to bring the ship round safely, as he had just brought round another Spanish ship a little time before. When the captain declined this offer, Iyeyasu gave orders for all the Franciscans he had brought to be seized, put on board the ship and sent back again.[5] However, one or two Spanish ships do seem to have come to the Kwantō since 1602. So much

---

[4] "Laws enacted to be observed in Japan with respect to foreign merchants:—If any foreign vessel by stress of weather is obliged to touch at any principality or to put in to any harbour of Japan, we order that, whoever these foreigners may be, absolutely nothing whatsoever that belongs to them or that they may have brought in their ship shall be taken from them. Likewise we rigorously prohibit the use of any violence in the purchase or the sale of the commodities brought by their ship, and if it is not convenient for the merchants of the ship to remain in the port they have entered, *they may pass to any other port that may suit them, and therein buy and sell in full freedom. Likewise we order in a general manner that foreigners may freely reside in any part of Japan they choose,* but we rigorously forbid them to promulgate their faith. Given in the 9th moon of the 7th year of Keicho (1602) to Don Pedro de Acuñha." Translation into Portuguese verified by Costa, Notary of the Diocese, by order of Çerqueyra, Bishop of Japan.

[5] They appear, however, to have been able to elude the officers and to escape into hiding.

may be inferred from a remark in a dispatch an envoy of Iyeyasu carried to the Governor of the Philippines in 1605, for in it he complains that "the number of ships sent has been reduced instead of increased."[6] While this ambassador was in Manila, some Spaniards had arrived in the Kwantō, and had dropped some very ill-advised remarks there. On being asked how many ships had lately come to Manila from New Spain, and what cargoes they had brought, they boasted that a whole fleet had arrived with nothing but men and munitions of war—for the conquest of the Moluccas. This made Iyeyasu very suspicious. He at once had all the Christians in Yedo registered and the Franciscans put under the surveillance of some of his officers. And at the same time he judged it well to endeavour to open up commercial relations with other foreigners besides those of Manila, who seemed bent not so much upon the prosecution of trade as upon the propagation of their religion and possibly the conquest of new territories.

Luckily the means of doing so lay ready to hand. We have already on more than one occasion referred incidentally to the Kentishman, Will Adams, pilot of the Dutch ship *de Liefde*, whose eighteen or twenty pieces of artillery may have done good service in the great campaign of 1600. But to make clear the general course of the contemporary foreign relations of Japan, much more than a mere incidental reference to the *Charity* and to Will Adams is necessary. A recapitulation of some of the salient incidents of contemporary European history becomes indispensable.

It was about 1566 that the revolt of the Netherlands and the subsequent so-called Eighty Years' War with Spain began. Alva entered the provinces in 1567, and was only in any way checked when the "Water Beggars" seized upon Briel in 1572, and the insurgents began to trust to their little navy. In 1581 Holland and Zealand declared themselves a free country, severed alike from Spain and from the Empire. On

---

[6] A strange sentence in this dispatch recommends the Governor not to allow the Japanese established in Manila to return to Japan. Of these there appears to have been a numerous body. In this very year "the Japanese settled at Dilao in the Philippines, *who amounted to about* 15,000, had a difference with the Spaniards. A Japanese was killed; his compatriots flew to arms, constructed a camp and entrenched themselves. A *religieux* who spoke Japanese succeeded in appeasing the parties and in preventing great calamities." In 1608 the Japanese again rose at Manila, and had to be reduced by fighting.

the murder of William of Orange in 1584, his second son, Maurice of Nassau, then seventeen years old and a student at Leyden, was named Governor of the United Provinces; and by 1594 these seven provinces were entirely cleared of Spanish troops. Desultory fighting for the possession of what is now the kingdom of Belgium went on for fifteen years longer, until in 1609 a twelve years' truce on the *uti possidetis* basis was signed between Spain and Holland. This left the Hollanders in entire possession of the northern provinces, whose well-being ever since 1590 had been steadily increasing. Thousands of ingenious workers, turning in despair from the hopelessness of their condition in the Spanish Netherlands, brought their skill and industry into the North, which soon became as famous for its manufactures as for its energy in commerce. It was to this latter, however, that the Hollanders mainly owed their wealth. Ever since 1572 more and more attention had been devoted to the navy, which also played the part of a mercantile marine; and by 1609 the burghers of the Seven Provinces— especially of Holland and Zealand—had become lords of the sea and the chief traders of the world. In 1609 Dutch ships had utterly ruined the Spanish fleet in the sea-fight off Gibraltar, and the over-sea trade of the Peninsulars was for the time left unprotected.

But already, long before this, the Hollanders had set themselves to work to ruin the Spanish and Portuguese trade thoroughly. As has been repeatedly asserted, Philip II. of Spain became King of Portugal as well in 1580; and in his person, or in that of his son and his grandson, the two crowns remained united down to 1640. The "Sixty Years' Captivity," as this period is termed by the Lusitanians, proved disastrous to Portugal. In the conduct of their monopoly of the Eastern trade the Portuguese had merely brought the commodities to Lisbon, and instead of distributing them over Europe them- selves, had rested content with letting foreign nations come to fetch them. As a matter of fact, it was Dutch merchants who, from an early period, had played the chief part as distributors. Accordingly, Philip II., by way of dealing a deadly blow at the interests of his "rebel subjects," closed the port of Lisbon to them in 1594. The result might have been foreseen. Excluded from the terminal depôt of the lucrative Portuguese commerce in the West, the venturesome heretics resolved to tap its sources in the Orient; and when Houtman, who had escaped from a Portuguese prison, approached the "Company for Remote Countries" with a proposal to fit out an East Indian expedition, the Directors at once entrusted him with the command of three vessels for this purpose. After eight-and-twenty months' absence, Houtman returned with only one of his ships—but so richly laden as to rouse the enthusiasm of the Hollanders. Six different Companies were at once formed for trade with the Far East, and in 1598 as many as twenty-two Dutch ships left for the Indies, fully armed and with instructions to "attack and overpower all merchants of the dominions of the King of Spain, those residing within them as well as those trading there." With most of these squadrons we have little or nothing to do; but one of them, fitted out by the Rotterdam Company, was destined to open up relations between both Holland *and* England with Japan. The third of these Dutch ventures of 1598—that of Oliver van Noort of Utrecht—is remarkable chiefly because it brought home intelligence of the fate of one of the five vessels in this Rotterdam expedition which had been Van Noort's only Dutch predecessors in passing through the Straits of Magellan. In January, 1601, Van Noort, then in a harbour of Borneo, learned from one Manuel de Luis, a Portuguese, who traded between Japan and the Malay Archipelago, that one of the Rotterdam Company's five vessels in a state of the direst extremity had reached Japan in the Spring of 1600, and that the surviving score of her original ship's company of 110 men were detained there as prisoners. This was but cheerless news to bring home to an already bankrupt Company.

The vessel to which we refer was *de Liefde*, which carried the "pilot-major" or second-in-command of the squadron of five vessels of which the ill-fated Mahu had been admiral. This "pilot-major" was not a Dutchman, but, as was usual at the time, an Englishman—Will Adams, from Gillingham, in Kent. So far, Englishmen alone had been found venturesome enough to question the application of Pope Alexander VI.'s Bull of 1493 in the Pacific. Drake had been the only sailor since the return of Del Cano with his seventeen fellow scarecrows (the sole survivors of Magellan's intrepid crew) in 1522, who had circumnavigated the globe. His enterprise of 1577–1580 had been followed up and successfully repeated by Thomas Cavendish, "a gentleman of Suffolk" (1586–1588); and in 1593 Richard Hawkins had had to yield to ill-luck and the Dons at Atacames, fifty-seven miles north of the Equator, after his good ship the *Dainty* had passed into the Pacific by the Straits of Magellan. In 1591 James Lancaster (James was no "Sir" at this time) conducted a buccaneering squadron to Malacca, whence he returned in 1594—after rendering the name of "Englishman" in East Indian waters synonymous with that of "pirate." Many former members of the crews of these early English rovers and others besides were only too ready to take service with the enterprising Hollanders who were now so sturdily bent upon breaking the Peninsular monopoly of Eastern trade,[7] and the Dutchmen were keen to utilise their services.

This "pilot-major" of *de Liefde*, Will Adams the Kentishman, was destined to play an honourable, albeit a modest, part in the history of the early Tokugawa relations with foreign countries; and his own account of the matter, instinct with the charm of a virile simplicity, is at once of enthralling interest and of high historic value. In his letters we meet with a spelling delightfully phonetic, a syntax which is equally delightfully go-as-you-please, and a phraseology that is piquant in its crisp quaintness; but as we read on, we find it abundantly borne in upon us from far weightier considerations that we are veritably here face to face with one to whom the atmosphere of "the spacious times of great Queen Bess" was natal.

On April 19th, 1600 A.D., when *de Liefde* was towed into a harbour of Bungo by the local boatmen, out of her surviving crew of four-and-twenty men Adams says in one letter that "there were no more but five men of us able to go." A few days later three of the twenty-four spectres died, and a little later on still three more. It was a lucky thing for Adams and his heretic companions that the old Christian Daimyō, the patron of the Jesuits, was no more (died 1587),

---

[7] For example, John Davys, the famous explorer, before going as pilot to Michelbourne in 1604, had been pilot of the Dutch Indiaman *de Leeuw*; while the second pilot in Mahu's fleet was also an Englishman, Timothy Shotten.

and that Funai was no longer the centre of Jesuit influence in Kyūshū. As it was, the waifs had grounds for serious misgivings.

"After wee had been there fiue or sixe days came a Portugall Jesuite, with other Portugals, who reported of vs, that we were pirats, and were not in the way of merchandising. Which report caused the governours and common people to thinke euill of vs: In such manner that we looked alwayes when we should be set upon crosses; which is the exccution in this land for theeuery and some other crimes. Thus daily more and more the Portugalls incensed the justices and the people against us."[8]

"Nine days after our arrivall," Adams goes on, "the great King of the land sent for me to come to him." Starting with a single companion, the "pilot-major" reached Ōsaka on May 12th, 1600 (O.S.), and was at once conducted into Iyeyasu's presence. What then happened will be best told in Adams's own words:—

"Coming before the king, he viewed me well, and seemed to be wonderfull fauourable. He made many signes vnto me, some of which I vnderstood, and some I did not. In the end, there came one that could speake Portuges. By him, the king demanded of me of what land I was, and what mooued vs to come to his land, beeing so farre off. I shewed vnto him the name of our countrey, and that our land long sought out the East Indies, and desired friendship with all kings and potentates in way of marchandize, hauing in our land diuerse commodities, which these lands had not; and also to buy such marchandizes in this land, which our countrey had not. Then he asked whether our countrey had warres? I answered him yea, with the Spaniards and Portugals, being in peace with all other nations. Further, he asked me, in what I did beleeue? I said, in God, that made heauen and earth. He asked me diverse other questions of things of religions, and many other things: As what way we came to the country. Hauing a chart of the whole world, I shewed him, through the *Straight of Magellan*. At which

---

[8] This account is fully substantiated by the missionaries themselves. Writes Guerreiro (condensing their reports):—" A missionary having had speech with them, recognised that they were heretics; on their disembarkation they at first declared that they had come to trade with Japan; but the Prince at once comprehended that they had other intentions, and that it was only a tempest that had driven them towards his empire; for they brought no merchandise similar in quality or in quantity to that of the other ships, neither did they have the noble and opulent appearance of the other merchants, nor as much plate nor as many servants as they, and appeared really come as soldiers and sailors, all the more so as they had with them a great quantity of artillery and arms. All this made it perceived that they were not folk of good alloy, and Daifousama (Iyeyasu), on the advice of the Governor, at once sent an officer to Bungo to conduct the vessel to Kyōto (*sic !*) or Sakai; he confiscated this vessel as a wreck, according to the laws of Japan, and sent her to a port in the Kwantō, as well as the Hollanders of the crew and 18 or 20 pieces of artillery; at the same time he appropriated all the rest of the cargo, consisting chiefly of arms and a great quantity of powder." No doubt a fair amount of this Dutch powder was burnt in course of the Sekigahara campaign some five months later on.

he wondred, and thought me to lie. Thus, from one thing to another, I abode with him till mid-night. And hauing asked mee, what marchandize we had in our shippe, I shewed him all. In the end, he beeing ready to depart, I desired that we might haue trade of marchandize, as the Portugals and Spanyards had. To which he made me an answer; what it was, I did not vnderstand. So he commanded me to be carried to prison. But two dayes after, he sent for me againe, and enquired of the qualities and condition of our countreys, of warres and peace, of beasts and catell of all sorts; and of the heauens. It seemed that he was well content with all mine answers vnto his demands. Neuertheless, I was commanded to prison againe: but my lodging was bettered in another place. . . ."

Shortly afterwards the *Liefde*, which had meanwhile been brought up from Bungo to Sakai, was sent round with Adams and all his companions to the Bay of Yedo; and for the next few months Iyeyasu was too much occupied with the most serious affairs to have any time to spare for further interviews protracted to midnight and conducted mainly by the language of signs. However, after he had solved the problem of the disposal of the *débris* of Sekigahara and the general rearrangement of the Empire for the time being, he gave order that the Hollanders, ship and all, were to stay where they were. How it fared with the "pilot-major" we leave Adams himself to tell. Writes he:—

"So in processe of four or fiue yeeres the Emperour called me, as diuers times he had done before. So one time aboue the rest he would have me to make him a small ship. I answered that I was no carpenter, and had no knowledg thereof. Well, doe your endeavour, saith he: if it be not good, it is no matter. Wherefore at his commaund I buylt him a ship of the burthen of eightie tunnes, or there about: which ship being made in all respects as our manner is, he comming aboord to see it, liked it very well; by which meanes I came in more fauour with him, so that I came often in his presence, who from time to time gaue me presents, and at length a yearely stypend to liue vpon, much about seuentie ducats by the yeare, with two pounds of rice a day, daily. Now beeing in such grace and fauour, by reason I learned him some points of *jeometry*, and vnderstanding of the art of *mathematickes*, with other things: I pleased him so, that what I said he would not contrarie. At which my former enemies did wonder; and at this time must intreat me to do them a friendship, which to both Spaniards and Portingals have I doen: recompencing them good for euill. So, to passe my time to get my liuing, it hath cost mee great labour and trouble at the first: but God hath blessed my labour.

"In the ende of fiue yeeres, I made supplication to the king to goe out of this land, desiring to see my poore wife and children according to conscience and nature. With the which request, the emperour was not well pleased, and would not let me goe any more for my countrey; but to byde in his land. Yet in processe

of time, being in great fauour with the Emperour, I made supplication
agein, by reason we had newes that the Hollanders were in *Shian* and
Patania; which reioyced vs much, with hope that God should bring
us to our countrey againe, by one meanes or other. So I made
supplication agein, and boldly spake my selfe with him, at which
he gaue me no aunswer. I told him, if he would permit me to
depart, I would bee a meanes, that both the English and Hollanders
should come and traffick there, but by no means he would let mee
goe. I asked him leave for the capten, the which he presently
granted mee. So by that meanes my capten got leave; and in a
Iapon iunk sailed to *Pattan*; and in a yeares space cam no *Hollanders*.
In the end, he went from *Patane* to *Ior*, where he found a fleet
of nine saile: of which fleet *Matleef* was General, and in this fleet
he was made Master againe, which fleet sailed to *Malacca*, and
fought with an armado of Portingalls: in which battel he was shot,
and presently died: so that as yet, I think, no certain newes is
knownen, whether I be liuing or dead."

This brings us down to the year 1605, and to the point
where Iyeyasu was beginning to wax impatient over the large
promises but scant performances of the Spaniards of Manila
in the matter of sending merchantmen to the Kwantō. It
was just possible, he doubtless fancied, that he would be better
served by their Hollander rivals. Accordingly the "Capten,"
Quaeckernaeck, who by the way was accompanied by the Cape
merchant Santvoorts when he departed, took with him the
Shōgun's licence for the Dutch nation to trade in Japan. This
practically amounted to an invitation to the Dutch East India
Company to establish a factory in the Empire, for three
years before (1602) the States-General had ordered all the
rival companies (especially the Zealand and the Holland
associations) to amalgamate.

This new body, with its capital of 6,000,000 livres and its
patent for twenty-one years, was the second great chartered company established, and differed from its only predecessor, the
English East India Company, instituted in 1600, mainly in that
its (the Dutch) conquests were made in the name of the State, and
ranked as national colonies, not as private possessions. By this
time (1605) it already had numerous factories in the Far East;
and it was to the chief of its establishments at Patani, on the
eastern side of the Malay Peninsula, that Iyeyasu's letter was
delivered in order to be forwarded to the Stadtholder, Maurice
of Nassau, who, now thirty-seven years of age, had been at
the head of affairs in the United Provinces since 1584.
However, the constant naval wars of the Dutch with the

Portuguese in the Far East—presently we shall see how shrewdly the Jesuits in Japan suffered from them—prevented the speedy transmission of Iyeyasu's first letter to the Stadtholder; and in 1608 the Factor of Patani sent Santvoort with one letter to Iyeyasu and another to Adams explaining the long delay in the answer from Holland. In the meantime, in Holland the new Company had instructed the commander of the fleet that left the Texel on December 22nd, 1607, to send at least one of his vessels to Japan to deliver a letter to the "Emperor" from the Stadtholder and to establish a factory there. In accordance with these instructions two Dutch ships were dispatched from Patani, and they arrived at Hirado on July 6th, 1609. A site for a factory was selected there, and Jacob Spex—who gave his name to the straits between the island and the mainland—became its first chief.

To understand why it was that Hirado was selected as the site of the Dutch factory (in 1609), and of the English one four years later on (in 1613), a brief explanation may be necessary. It will be remembered that from the middle of the preceding century the princelet of the island had evinced the greatest eagerness to attract the Portuguese merchantmen to his harbours, and that that had been discovered to be the sole consideration that had induced him to pen his honeyed and flattering invitation to the Jesuit Superior-General, Barretto, then at Canton. It soon became palpable to Torres and his priests that Matsuura Takanobu, of Hirado (Taqua Nombo, as they call him), was using them merely as decoys to lure the freighted galleons to his ports. The sharp lesson that Torres administered to him in the early '60's provoked him exceedingly; and the opening of Yokoseura in Ōmura as a rival harbour enraged him still more. But the erection of the new town of Nagasaki, also in Ōmura, in 1568 had been the severest blow he had received. Exceedingly averse as he was to the foreign religion and its priests, his overmastering desire for foreign trade had driven him to extend a sullen toleration to their presence; and even after Hideyoshi's Edicts of 1587 and 1596 a few of them were permitted to lurk concealed in Hirado.

However, on the death of Takanobu (Taqua Nombo) in 1599, his son and his successor ordered all his vassals, without exception, to celebrate certain "pagan" rites and to sacrifice to the *manes* of the departed Daimyō. His Christian retainers, headed by his brother and his brother's wife, a daughter of Sumitada of Ōmura, stoutly refused to comply with the order; and when a persecution was instituted, six hundred of them withdrew from Hirado in a body, and these were followed by so many others that the Daimyō, seeing his estates being depopulated, was constrained to call a truce. This emigration was in defiance of the law of the Taikō which denounced severe pains and penalties against vassals who should withdraw themselves from allegiance to their Lord without his permission; and as Terasawa, the Governor of Nagasaki, had shortly before abjured his Christianity, and was not particularly friendly to the Jesuits at the time, the Fathers in Nagasaki, whither the exiles bent their course, found themselves saddled with a serious responsibility. Besides, just then they were in sore financial straits. However, some of the emigrants got settled in Higo, and later on, after 1601, in Hosokawa's (Jecundono's) new fief of Buzen. On hearing of the incident of the *Liefde* with her crew of heretics, the keen-witted Daimyō of Hirado was not slow in finding means to put himself in communication with the captive Hollanders; and he actually succeeded in engaging a number of the eighteen survivors to cast cannon and to teach the art of gunnery to his subjects. And when, thanks to Adams's intercession, his "Capten," Quaeckernaeck, and the Cape merchant, Santvoort, were allowed by Iyeyasu to quit Japan in 1605, it was the wide-awake Daimyō of Hirado who enabled the twain to avail themselves of the permission by granting them a passage in the trading junk he that year dispatched to Patani. The Daimyō's exceptional kindness to the Dutchmen, and afterwards to the Englishman Saris in 1613, was mainly prompted by the circumstance that he wished to be free from all foreign priestly influence in his own domains, and to be exposed to no such risks as his orders of 1599 had involved him in.

Having dealt with Iyeyasu's somewhat ineffectual attempts to open up trade between Manila and the Kwantō, and having traced the chain of circumstances that enabled him to entice the Hollanders to Japan to break the Portuguese monopoly of foreign trade there, we must now, in order to make the general situation perfectly clear, devote our attention to the fortunes of the Portuguese traders and of the Jesuit priests since the death of the Taikō in 1598. The interests of the priests and of the merchants were closely interknit; so much so that Hideyoshi, who was really desirous of the maintenance of the Portuguese trade, felt constrained to pretend to be ignorant of the fact that his Edict of 1587 was to a large extent a dead letter. The incidents of 1596–97 roused him to sharp and vigorous action, and the tragedy of the Martyrs' Mount at Nagasaki was the result. However, in spite of renewed mandates for the deportation of all missionaries from Japan, the officers entrusted with the commission do not seem to have shown any very great amount of zeal in its execution—possibly, perhaps, in consequence of secret instructions from Kyōto. On the demise of Hideyoshi in 1598, although there was no repeal of the Edicts of 1587 and of 1596, and although no infringement of the Taikō's law forbidding the Daimyō to become Christians was overlooked, yet Iyeyasu proved by no means hostile to the Jesuits. Although he accused them of being of the council of his enemies before Sekigahara, yet in 1601 he issued two official patents permitting the Fathers to reside in the Imperial towns of Kyōto, Ōsaka, and Nagasaki. This was a great improvement in their position, for "since 1587, the date of the Edict of Exile, no such favour had been conceded, the missionaries never having had more than a mere verbal permission to reside at Nagasaki." The reason of this liberality on the part of Iyeyasu becomes tolerably apparent from the following passage from M. Léon Pagés. After recounting the intrigues of Terasawa, the Governor of Nagasaki, against the Daimyō of Arima and of Ōmura, to which we have incidentally alluded in a previous chapter, M. Pagés proceeds:—

"Daifousama (Iyeyasu) was again irritated by the effect of a new artifice of Terasawa's, but this artifice turned against its author. One of Terasawa's servants, having gone to Nagasaki to make purchases for the Sovereign, had in no way consulted Father J. Rodriguez, *interpreter of the Tenka in the affairs of the Portuguese.* Iyeyasu having shown himself dissatisfied with his purchases, the servant cast the blame upon the Father and the Portuguese. But the Prince wished to elucidate the matter, and (after an investigation), recognising the innocence of the Fathers, *caused a patent to be delivered, in order that thenceforth all his purchases should be made through the medium of the missionaries,* and without Terasawa's assistance."

One result of this incident was that for two years Iyeyasu would not admit Terasawa into his presence. The latter had to conciliate the missionaries by giving them free admission into his Amakusa possessions; and even so, in 1604, he was stripped of the governorship of Nagasaki, when the administration of the town was entrusted to a commission of five citizens, all of whom were Christians. All this, however, was not to prove so much pure gain to the Jesuits. In that year of 1604 orders were issued by Iyeyasu's Government for the incorporation of the rapidly rising suburbs known as New Nagasaki with the Imperial town proper; and as this New Nagasaki had stood within the Ōmura domains, and had been a chief source of the Prince's revenue, the Prince was exceedingly wroth. He loudly blamed Rodriguez, then at Court, and the Vice-Provincial, Paez, for having failed to give him timely intelligence in advance that such a step was contemplated; and went so far as to evince the depth of his resentment by apostatising and summarily throwing his Christianity overboard. As old Kuroda died this year, Arima thus now found himself the sole Christian Daimyō in Japan; and the old law of the Taikō, zealously enforced by Iyeyasu, interposed a fatal obstacle to any new accessions to the number. Terasawa, too, although for the moment constrained to be conciliatory, bore the missionaries no real goodwill, and immediately on regaining favour with Iyeyasu gave evidence of his true feelings by instituting a mild persecution of his Christian subjects.

Meanwhile the Jesuits had been the recipients of other tokens of favour from the Shōgun. Rodriguez, who attracted Iyeyasu's favourable regard at Nagoya in Hizen as early as 1593, had been interpreter at the Taikō's Court; and Iyeyasu had appointed him to a similar position at his own—mainly for commercial matters, it would appear. About this time Iyeyasu showed marked attention to the interpreter at a great palace function; and, fond of money and slow to part with it as he was, presented him with a gift of 500 crowns. Nor was this the only similar solid evidence of regard that he bestowed upon the Jesuits about this date. In 1603, the Dutch "pirates" (Heemskirk was the captain) had for the first time successfully achieved what was to become a regular annual venture with them—the capture of the "great ship from Macao"; and as she carried the over-due supplies of several years for the Japan mission, the Fathers were reduced to the greatest extremity.[9] This came to the knowledge of Iyeyasu—most likely through Rodriguez. Then "God touched the heart of the Coubosama (Iyeyasu) himself, who sent 350 taels as a pure gift, and offered spontaneously 5,000 taels under the title of a loan until the date when the arrival of the new subsidy would enable the amount to be liquidated. This was truly a gift from heaven, for these alms and some presents from the Christians enabled the year to be passed. The alms of his Catholic Majesty the King of Spain and Portugal were not paid, and remained in arrears for many years."

Certainly so far the Jesuits had had but little cause to declaim against Iyeyasu—except, perhaps, with regard to the very ready welcome he tendered the Spaniards from Manila. When at last, in 1605, the Bull of Clement VIII., issued nearly five years before (December 12th, 1600), arrived in Japan—"Dutch 'pirates' now audaciously meddling with our 'great ship from Macao,' and shutting off our communications"—and the Fathers of the Company insisted that in terms of it all those interloping Franciscans and what-not from Manila must quit the country at once, Iyeyasu must have again "begun to smile," as we have seen him do at an outburst of that hot-headed cowled Boanerges, Jérôme de Jésus. It is more than possible that, like the Taikō, he maintained that religious rivalry was no good thing for the peace of the country; but it is perfectly clear that he certainly adhered to the doctrine that competition is the soul of trade and exceedingly advantageous to the interests of commerce—from a Japanese point of view. The favours he bestowed on the priests of the rival sects seem to have been graduated in accordance with their proved efficiency as decoys for foreign merchantmen to the harbours of the empire.

In 1605, where we have now arrived, we have seen that Iyeyasu was beginning to get into bad humour with the Manila combination of allies in the service of God and Mammon. In this the Jesuits and the Portuguese—most

---

[9] In this year there were 109 Jesuits—53 of them priests—in Japan.

probably thanks to their astute priest-interpreter—seem to have descried their opportunity. When Rodriguez went up to Kyōto in connection with the affairs of the annual Macao galleon, as had been his wont since the times of the Taikō, he carried with him some fine presents for Iyeyasu; among them a wonderful clock, something like the one Hideyoshi had shown himself so pleased to receive from Valegnani in 1591. Shortly afterwards an officer of the Court, sent to Nagasaki professedly on mercantile business, succeeded in arranging that Iyeyasu should formally receive the Bishop of Japan. The missionary writers are frank enough in their account of the matter; what they state virtually amounts to an admission that the Coubosama (Iyeyasu) wished to maintain the trade with the Portuguese, and as he perceived that Çerqueyra's position as Bishop of Japan gave him great credit with the merchants, he (Iyeyasu) thought it well to show the powerful Church dignitary some amount of attention. So in 1606 the Bishop in full canonicals was received by Iyeyasu—at Fushimi (where, by the way, the Jesuits meanwhile had been allowed to establish themselves) according to some accounts; at Kyōto according to others. On this occasion the Bishop took care to make himself especially agreeable to Canzoukedono, the principal favourite of the Prince, and to Itacouradono, the Governor of Miaco, by whom, of course, we understand Honda, Kōzuke-no-suke, Chief of Iyeyasu's Council of State—afterwards known as the Gorōjiu—and Itakura, Governor of Kyōto, who was afterwards to score a point with his master by wrecking the shrine of Shin-Hachiman, and at the same time the Taikō's prospects as a durable War God. This was sound policy on the part of the Bishop. During the next few years the flattered and powerful Canzoukedono was to do the priests—and through them, himself—more than one good turn. This same Canzoukedono, to do him justice, seems to have been enamoured not so much of the Bishop's gorgeous canonicals as of the colour of his face, for towards all Caucasian men the worthy Honda professed himself to be exceedingly well-disposed. Will Adams and equally heretic Dutchmen received a ready welcome from open-minded Honda at all times—worthy Honda, who, sometimes in the fearful and wonderful guise of "Codskin," appears no fewer than thirty-one times in the heretic Cocks's Diary, and always with kindly mention.[10] This special procedure of the Bishop's may well be believed to have been inspired by the astute and able Rodriguez, who held what is vulgarly called the "inside track" at the Court of Iyeyasu. So much might at least be inferred if we take this incident in close connection with pages 140 to 145 of M. Léon Pagés.

Of the said M. Léon Pagés, who on occasion can be almost as confused as chaos itself while still keeping highly service-able as a very superior ecclesiastical almanac, the following paragraphs, limning the broad outlines of the situation with lucid accuracy as they do, are invaluable:—

"The Coubosama had not become favourable to religion; he had allowed the Edicts of Taicôsama to remain, and the missionaries were always considered as exiles. However, since the last reign [i.e. the death of the Taikô in 1598] there had been no general persecution; some isolated victims only had perished by the orders of the Yacatas (Daimyôs), those Lords having in their domains an absolute authority, dependent on the Coubosama (Iyeyasu) only under the title of great vassals. But, as always happens in the life of the Church, this relative peace sufficed to confirm the faith of the old converts, and to multiply the conversions of the infidels."

Since the sentence of exile (in 1587, when Coelho's junketing with Hideyoshi was abruptly brought to an end in such a volcanic manner), no Superior of the Company had been received as such by the "Sovereign"; and Father Valegnani, the Visitor, had not been received as Visitor, but as the Ambassador of the Viceroy of the Indies (1591). The Vice-Provincial, Father Paez, who had never omitted to send his annual salutations to the Coubo (Iyeyasu), and to offer him European presents, encouraged by the reception accorded the Bishop in the preceding year (1606), "now undertook to go in person to visit this Prince. He was then at Foutchou [Shidzuoka] in Suruga, where he was building a fortress. Canzoukedono, consulted by the Father Provincial, sounded the will of the Coubo (Iyeyasu), and answered the Father that his visit would be welcomed."

On arriving with his suite of four *religieux* at Shidzuoka, where he was also joined by Rodriguez, the Vice-Provincial had a most courteous reception from Iyeyasu, who meanwhile had been purposely kept in ignorance of the death of his son,

---

10 We shall see this Honda play rather a questionable part in the great Osaka war of 1614-15.

Hideyasu, Daimyō of Echizen, which had happened a few days before. To prevent the interview being deferred in consequence of the receipt of this untoward intelligence, "Canzoukedono" (Honda) had even gone so far as to intercept and delay the delivery of all letters from Echizen. In 1605 silver mines had been discovered in Idzu, and the Vice-Provincial was requested to inspect them on his way to visit Hidetada in Yedo.[11] All this did much to restore the confidence of the Jesuits, "for it was said that the Fathers might consider themselves as re-established without any other sign of the Prince, since, in accordance with the Japanese law, if he who pronounced a sentence of exile afterwards admitted the exile into his presence, the exile finds himself effectually and irrevocably restored to favour." On reaching Yedo, where the castle had just been finished by the forced labour of 300,000 men in the previous year, the priests met with an equally encouraging welcome from the Shōgun Hidetada, who "requested that a Jesuit clockmaker should be left with him."

The Vice-Provincial thus had good grounds for considering that his mission had at last emerged from the long eclipse it had lain under (twenty years, since July 1587) in Japan; and in this belief he ventured on a step of questionable policy on his way back to Nagasaki. This was a formal visit to Hideyori in Ōsaka. We are told that this visit was especially advantageous in assuring the Christians of Ōsaka of the good graces of the young Prince, and *that Hideyori's mother herself testified her satisfaction at this mark of deference shown to the heir of Taikōsama.* In the course of two years a wonderful change seems to have taken place in the attitude of Yodogimi (Hideyori's mother) and her councillors towards the Christians. In consequence of the baptism of some of her own intimate relatives in 1606 she actually denounced the missionaries to Iyeyasu; and the latter, to satisfy her, issued an Edict couched in the vaguest terms—for strictly local consumption in Ōsaka.[12]

---

[11] Rodrigues instead of Paez went to Idzu on this occasion.

[12] "His Highness having learned that several persons have embraced the doctrine and the religion of the Fathers, is exceedingly displeased at this infraction of his Edicts. His Highness makes it known that he enjoins his servants, the nobles, and the ladies of the Household to observe the preceding Law, and declares that in future the said servants and vassals must take great pains not to embrace the religion of the Fathers, and those who have adopted it must adopt another instead."

Now from this time onwards we find the Ōsaka Court extremely favourable to Christianity—so much so that the subsequent persecution of 1612, 1613, and 1614 scarcely extended to Ōsaka, and that some of Hideyori's chief commanders in the great struggle of 1614–15 were either actually, or at all events had been, Christians.

In spite of all his efforts to open up commercial relations with others, it was upon the Portuguese that Iyeyasu had mainly to depend for his foreign purchases down to 1609. Hence, during this time the Jesuits were in the ascendant. One ship, indeed, had sailed from Manila for the Kwantō in 1606,[18] but stress of weather drove her to Hizen, where some of the monks she carried were allowed to settle in Nabeshima's fief of Saga. Later on we hear of stray Spanish ships frequenting Uraga at the entrance to Yedo Bay. However, towards the end of 1609 (the Hollanders had just settled in Hirado, by the way), an incident occurred which tended greatly to brighten Iyeyasu's prospects of trade, if not with Manila, at least with the Spanish possessions elsewhere. On the 25th July, after handing over his authority to Silva (who was to signalise his tenure of office by administering a terrible drubbing to the Dutchmen in the following year), Don Rodrigo Vivero y Velasco, who had been acting Governor-General of the Philippines for some ten months, embarked at Manila for Acapulco on the *San Francisco*, a ship of 1,000 tons with a crew of 350 men, which was accompanied by two smaller consorts, the *San Antonio* and the *Santa Anna*. A furious typhoon separated the vessels, and only the *San Antonio* could hold on her course. The *Santa Anna* was driven ashore in Bungo (where she was got off in the following year, however), while the *San Francisco* was completely wrecked on the Pacific side of Bōshū, " ten leagues from Ōtaki and forty from Yedo (September 30th, 1609)." Thirty of her crew or passengers were drowned, but the survivors were received most hospitably; the Prince of Satsuma (ever eager for trade), then in Yedo, visiting Vivero, and maintaining all his people for thirty-seven days. Conducted to Yedo, Vivero met with a most flattering welcome from the

---

[18] Sotelo, afterwards to become so notorious, was one of her passengers.

Shōgun Hidetada, and then passed on to greet Iyeyasu at Shidzuoka. Here the reception accorded him was equally courteous, and two of the three requests he urged upon Iyeyasu were granted the day after they were preferred.

These requests were for—

(1) The Imperial protection for the Christian priests of different Orders who might reside in the empire, as well as the free use of their houses and churches.
(2) The confirmation of the alliance between the "Emperor" and the King of Spain.
(3) In testimony of this alliance, the expulsion of the Hollanders, the sworn enemies of the Spaniards, and pirates of the worst description.

As regards the last demand, Iyeyasu cleverly eluded it, while thanking Vivero for "informing him of the true character of the Dutch foreigners." At the same time he offered to put one of the foreign-built ships constructed by Will Adams at Vivero's disposal to enable him to proceed to Mexico; and requested him to ask the King of Spain for fifty miners, since he had heard the miners of New Spain were very expert, while those of Japan as yet could get from the ore scarcely half the metal it contained. In reply Vivero said he would first go down to Bungo to see if the *Santa Anna* could be made seaworthy, and on coming back would give definite answers. On his return from Bungo—where the *Santa Anna* seems to have been still aground, or at least not repaired—Don Rodrigo thankfully accepted the offer of Adams's ship. Now, on the subject of the miners, he put forward some rather startling propositions. Half the produce of the mines was to go to these miners, while the other half was to be divided between the Spanish King and Iyeyasu. His Spanish Majesty furthermore might have factors and commissioners in Japan to attend to his mining interests there; and these commissioners might bring with them *religieux* of different Orders, who should be authorised to have public churches and to celebrate the divine offices in them. Then Don Rodrigo went on to repeat his representations on the matter of the Hollanders; and afterwards asked that "if for any reason vessels belonging to the King of Spain or his subjects should come to Japan, His Highness should be pleased to guarantee their safety,[14] to issue safe-conducts for

---

[14] The Dons still bore the *San Felipe* episode in mind, doubtless.

their crews and cargoes, and to order that they should be
treated like his own subjects." He asked that "in case the
King his master should wish to construct men-of-war or
merchantmen in the harbours of Japan to send to Manila,
and also to provide munitions of war or stores for the
fortresses in his dominions in this quarter of the world,
factors and commissioners might be established in Japan to
superintend these operations, with liberty to make their
purchases at the prices current of the country." Finally he
asked that "when the King of Spain should send an ambassador to the 'Emperor' of Japan, that ambassador should
be received with all the honours due to the representative of
so great a monarch."

Strangely enough, with the exception of the demand for
the expulsion of the Dutchmen, all these articles were at once
promptly conceded. But then Iyeyasu was keenly bent upon
three things, in which foreign assistance for the time being
at least was all-important. These three things were the
development of foreign commerce, the creation of a Tokugawa
mercantile marine, and the development of the newly-discovered
mines in Idzu, Sado, and elsewhere. To obtain this foreign
assistance in carrying out these important projects the early
Tokugawas were clearly willing to make great concessions
to the Peninsulars in the matter of that religion to which
they themselves were so indifferent.

The Treaty with Don Rodrigo was concluded on the 4th
of July, 1610, and to convince Vivero of the sincerity of
his intentions the "Emperor" resolved to send an embassy
to the Spanish monarch, with rich presents for his Majesty
and for the Viceroy of New Spain. So, entrusted with
dispatches and presents from Iyeyasu and also from Hidetada,
Vivero set sail in Adams's ship (rechristened the *Santa Buena-
ventura*) on August 1st, and arrived at Matanchel in California
on the subsequent October 27th, 1610.[15]

---

[15] Adams in one letter gives the tonnage of this vessel as one hundred
and twenty, and in another at one hundred and seventy tons. Iyeyasu furnished
4,000 ducats to equip her, and she was manned by a Japanese crew, who,
after having a magnificent reception in Mexico, again arrived in Japan with
Sotomayor (ambassador from the Viceroy of New Spain) on July 13th, 1611.

Don Rodrigo, who died at the ripe age of eighty-one in 1636, in spite of
an evident fondness for big figures, is certainly an entertaining and informing
writer. He tells us that Shidzuoka had then 600,000 inhabitants, Yedo 700,000,
Osaka nearly 1,000,000, while Kyōto with 1,500,000 (50,000 of whom were

Iyeyasu, having the Dutchmen in Hirado, and having just received the most encouraging assurances of a trade not only with Manila but also with New Spain, now thought it well to administer a strong hint to the Portuguese that they were no longer so indispensable to him as they fancied themselves to be. Neither in 1607 nor in 1608 had any "great ship" come from Macao, for the Dutch rovers were abroad. In the latter year a Japanese vessel from Arima was wintering in Macao, and the crew, supported by other Japanese sailors, got into a quarrel with the Portuguese, which occasioned deaths on both sides. Pessoa, then Commandant of the settlement, forced the Japanese to sign a declaration setting forth that they alone were to blame; but the islanders on returning to Japan sent a very different account of the matter to Iyeyasu, and he, giving credit to their accusations, resented the episode deeply. He said nothing, however, for some time; and when in June, 1609, the *Madre de Dios*, with Pessoa himself as captain, arrived in Nagasaki with a dozen Jesuits and a cargo worth more than 1,000,000 crowns, he pretended to accept the Portuguese explanations of the Macao affair of 1608. Meanwhile he sent secret instructions to the Daimyō of Arima (now the only Christian Daimyō in Japan) to seize the *Madre de Dios* and Captain Pessoa—alive or dead. The Daimyō, who had been greatly enraged by the Macao incident, at once surrounded the doomed ship with a flotilla of boats manned by more than twelve hundred fighting-men. After three days' terrible fighting, Pessoa in desperation exploded his powder magazine; and the *Madre de Dios*, crew, priests, and 1,000,000 ducats worth of cargo and all, went to the bottom of Nagasaki harbour, the Japanese massacring the few swimmers that survived the explosion.[16]   Among other things two years'

---

prostitutes) he pronounces the largest city in the world. When he was there, 100,000 men were engaged in re-erecting the Daibutsu of Taikōsama, "whose soul is in Hell to all eternity." He tells us, among other things, that the Japanese "are clever at *invention* (?) and imitation," that "the grandees were clothed in *Chinese* silk, which was better than their own," that "they ridiculed the extraordinary value Westerners attach to diamonds and rubies, considering the worth of the thing to lie in its utility," and finally that, "if he could have prevailed upon himself to renounce his God and his King, he would have preferred that country to his own." According to him, there were then 1,800,000 Christians in Japan,—a statement which is exceedingly wild, as it is questionable whether there were ever more than 300,000.

16 In his account of this affair, Pagés has simply followed and condensed the Annual Letter. Charlevoix, who devotes about twenty pages to it, has in this instance written with a good many more original documents before him. He shows that Kämpfer had been entirely misinformed about the incident.

II H

supplies for the Jesuit mission in Japan disappeared when
Pessoa set the match to his ammunition on January 14th,
1610; and the good Fathers had to break up their seminary
from sheer want of funds for the time being. And what
by no means helped to console them for the calamity was the
report that they were all to be deported from Japan, and
the Philippine *religieux* put in possession of their establishments! At this time, it must be remembered, Vivero was in
great favour with Iyeyasu, as was his agent, the Manila
Franciscan, Luis Sotelo, destined soon to become famous or
notorious. Another point, and an extremely noteworthy point,
in the history of Japanese Christianity is this: "Don John
of Arima and his son Michael went to render to the Shōgun
an account of the execution of his orders. This was a title
to the Imperial favour, and a few months later the Shōgun
wished Michael, already married, to espouse one of his grand-
daughters.[17] The unhappy (?) Prince had the misfortune to
consent, and did not fear to repudiate his legitimate wife,
Donna Martha, whom he had espoused in the face of the
Church. His new wife had by the violence of her character
occasioned the death of her first husband. This baneful union
inspired Michael with pride that caused his ruin, as we shall
soon see." As a matter of fact, it brought about his formal
apostacy and his succession to the Arima fief two years
later on, and then the last Christian Daimyō in Japan
disappeared.

Naturally enough this *Madre de Dios* incident created a
great commotion in Macao; and after recovering from their
horror and consternation, the Portuguese there spent much
time in debates over the course to be adopted in consequence
of the outrage. At last it was determined to send an embassy
to Iyeyasu at Shidzuoka, but the ambassadors were to enter
Japan *viâ* Satsuma. They were charged to ask for the re-
establishment of trade between Japan and Macao; and, on
the one hand, to make excuses for the slaughter of Arima's
men in Macao three years before, and, on the other, to demand
compensation for the loss of the *Madre de Dios* and her cargo.

---

[17] As already indicated, ready-made or adopted grand-daughters were kept
in stock by the early Tokugawas, and a remunerative item of political commerce
they seem to have proved.

In spite of their splendid suite and of the rich presents they offered, the envoys produced no very great impression upon Iyeyasu. He accepted their presents, but their requests he left unanswered. This is perhaps not so very much to be wondered at when it is stated that about that time there were no less than three other rival "embassies" from foreign Powers in Japan, and that Iyeyasu, seeing himself with good prospects of the establishment of that healthy rivalry among foreign traders at which he had long been aiming, felt the Portuguese were no longer so necessary to him as they had been, and that accordingly there was no further need to humour them over-much.

This feeling may have been all the stronger from the circumstance that one of these missions was composed of those "pestilent and piratical rebel Hollanders" against whom Portuguese and Spaniards were at one in inveighing so bitterly. To understand the exact significance of this mission of 1611 in the general political and commercial situation in the Far East at the time, a few words on non-Japanese relations may be necessary.

It has been already remarked that the Dutch East India Company was formed in 1602 and that a twelve-years' truce was signed between Spain and the United Provinces in 1609,—in which year, as has been also said more than once, Philip III. formally declared the Japan trade open to his Spanish subjects of Manila, as well as to the Portuguese, to whom it had hitherto been confined by the Concordat of 1580. Meanwhile, between 1602 and 1609 the new chartered company had been making serious inroads upon the Far Eastern territorial possessions of the King of Spain and Portugal. In 1605 or 1606 the Dutch had seized some of the Moluccas with their wealth of spices, and in the latter year they had made a determined assault upon Malacca, where the Japanese formed no inconsiderable portion of the garrison that beat them off.[18] On the conclusion of the truce of 1609 the States-General turned their best attention to fostering the Company, and Pieter Both was then sent out as the first Governor-General of the national possessions in Asia and the Malay Archipelago.

---

[18] In this affair Adams's old companion, Captain Quaeckerneck, was killed.

As might have been expected, little attention was paid to the twelve-years' truce in these far-off quarters; the Dutch continued to make their annual effort to capture the "Great Ship of Macao" and the Acapulco fleet to and from Manila just the same as before. It will be remembered that in 1609 the Dutchmen promised Iyeyasu to send ships every year. This promise had not been kept in 1610, and its failure was simply owing to the fact that Admiral Wittert's attempt on the Manila fleet that year had utterly miscarried. Silva, the Governor of the Philippines, had fallen upon him with a superior force; and Wittert, with three of his vessels, was captured, while one other was sunk, only two of his whole squadron of six ships making good their escape. As two of these vessels had been meant for Japan, it is easy to understand why the Dutchmen in Hirado looked in vain for their East Indiamen in the offing there during the year 1610.

In the next year, however, Governor-General Both, who had meanwhile established a factory at Jacatra (now the city of Batavia), had ordered the *Brach* to sail from Patani for Hirado, where she arrived with an inconsiderable cargo of pepper, cloth, ivory, silk, and lead on July 1st, 1611.

"The cargo of the *Brach* being of little importance in comparison with the Spanish and Portuguese cargoes, the merchants of those two nations did not fail to point out the disproportion to the Japanese authorities. Spex, considering that in the circumstances one ought to endure a present loss to assure considerable future advantages, declared that he had come merely to return thanks for the former favours accorded, and, taking with him the best things in the cargo, betook himself to Shidzuoka, where Iyeyasu held his Court. He had written to Adams in order to make sure of his assistance."

Spex and Segerszoon, the envoys, were entirely successful in their mission. After a visit to Hidetada in Yedo, and another to Hideyori in Ōsaka, they returned to Hirado with a patent which, while not so clear and precise in its phraseology as that issued in consequence of the *Ulloa* incident of 1602, was still very liberal and highly satisfactory. What tended to make it all the more satisfactory to the Dutchmen was that it had been accorded them in spite of most strenuous efforts on the part of Spaniards and Portuguese alike to have them summarily expelled from Japan.

One imposing Spanish embassy, headed by Captain Domingos Francisco, had just arrived from Manila specially charged with the task of "settling the matter regarding the Hollanders." But so little attention was paid to it that no answer was ever returned to the Governor-General's dispatch. Francisco, thus rebuffed, had got as far as Nagasaki on his return, when he was instructed again to repair to Shidzuoka "with a new message from the Governor of Manila, but with the recommendation to say nothing about the Flemings." On this occasion Francisco met the Macaoese envoy (Nerete) at Court, and conveyed to him the cheering information that "Conzoukedono [our old friend Honda Kōdsuke-no-suke, who practically was Iyeyasu's Prime Minister] had allowed neither the Japanese interpreter usually employed by the Portuguese and the Spaniards, nor a Franciscan (who accompanied him, and who was an excellent interpreter) to speak, but had called upon Adams (to whom he entrusted many matters) to fill this office, whence the results to be expected might be judged."

Before this, the other Spanish embassy—that from New Mexico—although faring better in some other respects, had met with an equally mortifying repulse in the matter of the Hollanders. This "embassy," besides rich presents, had brought a cargo of cloth for sale. The presents were accepted, but Sotomayor, the envoy, by his Castilian hauteur soon got into trouble. He preferred four demands in writing :—

(1) That the Spaniards should be allowed to build as many and such vessels in Japan as they pleased.
(2) That their pilots should be allowed to survey the coast and harbours of Japan.
(3) That the "Emperor" should forbid the Hollanders to trade in the countries subject to him; in which case the King of Spain would send men-of-war to Japan to burn the Dutch ships.
(4) That when Spanish vessels came to Japan, they should be free from all search, and have liberty to sell their merchandise to whomsoever they pleased.

The first and second points were granted, while nothing seems to have been said about the fourth. But as regards the third it was emphatically asserted that "the lands of His Majesty being open to all foreigners, none ought to be excluded from them; if the respective princes of foreign States were at war it was expected that they should be left to decide their differences in their own countries, and no exclusion (from Japan) could be made." In this position, it is to be observed, from first to last the early Tokugawa administration was consistent and undeviating; on subsequent occasions, to similar representations of the Dutch and English analogous answers were returned, while in 1600 Iyeyasu had told the Portuguese pressing him to make a summary end of Adams and his companions that "we [Adams is speaking] as yet had not doen to him nor to none of his lande any harme or dammage: therefore against Reason and Iustice to put vs to death. If our countreys had warres the one with the other, that was no cause that he should put vs to death." What Iyeyasu wanted was foreign trade and foreign instruction in certain matters for his subjects; and the greater the number of rival and competing nationalities that could be enticed to Japan, the better it was for the economic interests of the country. With foreign monopolists or foreign trádes-unionism Iyeyasu had not the slightest sympathy. Competition was the life of trade and the death of profits—Portuguese, Spanish, English, and (at one time) Dutch alike. Hence the firmness of his reply to Sotomayor, and eke to all others on this point. It has to be added, however, that Sotomayor had given great offence on the occasion. Although he had been requested to appear at the audience unarmed and with no train, he had presented himself before the palace with his armed escort, the standard of Castile flauntingly displayed, and trumpets defiantly blaring. At the meeting with Iyeyasu he was compelled to appear alone and unattended.[19]

---

[19] Apart from Charlevoix and Léon Pagés, we have made use of Carvailho, the Jesuit Provincial's "Report on the Introduction of the Dutch into Japan," which, while inaccurate in many details, is yet of importance. Among other things, he tells us that William Adams was a great engineer and mathematician. "After he had learned the language, he had access to Iyeyasu and entered the palace at any time. In his character of heretic, he constantly endeavoured to discredit our Church, as well as its ministers. . . . The Spaniards of New Spain established themselves at Uraga [at the entrance to Yedo Bay, since made famous by Commodore Perry in 1853], where the Hollanders resided; and the Franciscan religieux obtained a licence to build a church there. The English pilot was always on friendly terms with the Spaniards, willingly assisting them, and receiving them into his house when they were sick; but on the subject of the Catholic faith he was inaccessible. . . . Sotomayor spoke of the Hollanders, and insisted to the 'Governors' that they should no longer be allowed to stay in the ports, denouncing them as rebels against their King and people who could bring no other merchandise than what they had stolen from the Portuguese and the Chinese. But Sotomayor was not listened to, *the favour of Adams always protecting the Hollanders.*"

As showing the measure of success that had attended Iyeyasu's persistent and unwearying efforts to develop foreign trade and to create a Tokugawa mercantile marine, the following paragraphs from Carvailho's report (Macao, February 8th, 1615) are worthy of quotation in full:—"To all these incon-

Apart from the fact that communications had been re-opened, with Korea by 1607, and that the course of events that was to bring the English East India Company's ships to Japan in 1613 was already in train, the foregoing sketch succinctly depicts the aspect of Japan's foreign relations at the end of the year 1611. Down to this date, be it remarked, the Tokugawa Government, apart from enforcing the law that no Daimyō should receive baptism, had shown no hostility to Christianity. The following year, however, marks a new departure in its attitude towards the foreign religion. "In the year 1612," writes Adams to Spalding in Bantam, "is put downe all the sects of Franciscannes," while at the same time the Jesuits had no fewer than eighty-six churches or houses razed.[20] Before proceeding to investigate the why and the wherefore of this sudden change in the policy of the Tokugawa Government it may be well to cite the following passages from Léon Pagés:—

1612:—"As to the Church of Ōsaka, which was in the private domains of Hideyori, and which had been erected in virtue of the licence of Taikōsama, his father, it enjoyed a complete immunity." 1613:—"The 'Jesuit' house of Ōsaka was always favoured, and even assisted, by Hideyori and his mother." 1614:—"At Ōsaka the Governor, Ichi-no-Kami (Katagiri Katsumoto), had the Christians registered, and persecuted them *without the power of putting them to death.*"

Ichi-no-Kami, it may be observed, the priests allege had already secretly sold himself to Iyeyasu, and on his treason being discovered by Hideyori, soon fled from Ōsaka.

Naturally enough, for an explanation of Iyeyasu's abrupt

---

veniences it is to be added that a great volume of merchandise flows into Japan from all parts: a circumstance that makes the failure of our 'ship'—the 'Great Ship of Macao'—still more felt. For example, in 1600 and 1602 the Japanese scarcely sailed abroad at all; only some cargo-junks carried rice to Manila. In 1612 the Portuguese ship brought only 1,200 quintals of silk, but of silk 5,000 quintals were imported (without speaking of other merchandise) by *Japanese junks*, by Manila ships, and by the Chinese. This is the chief cause why the Portuguese are no longer considered as they were before. With Cochin-China a very damaging traffic has been opened, because the Chinese carry much silk thither, which the Japanese go to buy and take to Japan in their junks; and for the enticement of pay Portuguese pilots are not wanting to navigate those junks." N.B.—At this time no direct, trade between China and Japan was allowed by the Chinese Government. Hideyoshi's request for a market at Ningpo had been refused, and since the Korean War of 1598 there had been no communication between China and Japan.

20 The list of *religieux* in Japan at this time shows 122 Jesuits (66 priests, 56 brothers), 14 Franciscans, 9 Dominicans, 4 Augustins, 7 Secular Priests. Total, 156 *religieux.*

break with the foreign priests one turns to the pages of the historians of the Church.   None of them, it may be said, seems to cover the situation exhaustively, although Charlevoix, as usual, seems wonderfully dispassionate and judicial in his analysis of the causes.   He holds that the immediate incidents which prompted it were two in number.

In the first place, the Christian Prince of Arima, who had burned the *Madre de Dios* and had found his reward in a matrimonial alliance between his son and a grand-daughter or a grand-niece of Iyeyasu, set on foot an intrigue to recover certain territories he had lost some time before.   To accomplish this end he opened up communications with Okamoto Daihachi, the secretary of Honda, Kōdsuke-no-suke (Canzoukedono), who was often consulted by Iyeyasu in questions concerning the redistribution of fiefs, and bribed the secretary heavily.   Now Okamoto (the secretary) was a professed Christian, as were not a few others in analogous positions in Japan at the time, for the Jesuits seem to have made a point of capturing the subordinates, who really then, as now, pulled the strings to no small extent.   Okamoto proved no better than a pious trickster, however.   He forged a "privilege," which he professed to have obtained from Iyeyasu, transferring the disputed territory to Arima, and later on asserted that this privilege had been revoked in consequence of the efforts of certain calumniators, above all of Hasegawa Sahioye, now Governor of Nagasaki and the sworn enemy of the Christians and of the old Prince of Arima himself.   Arima then resolved to look after his interests in person, went up to Court with his son and his daughter-in-law; and there the hopeful pair disclosed the intrigue to Iyeyasu, who at once ordered his Council to investigate the matter.   As a result of their report Okamoto was sentenced to be burned alive; old Arima was stripped of his principality and exiled to Kai, where his head was cut off a little later; and his apostate son invested with his fief.   So enraged was Iyeyasu at the episode that he deprived all the other Christian officers in his service of their revenues, banished them with all their households, and forbade all the Daimyō to receive any of them into their domains.

In this first point Charlevoix is at one with the other Church historians.   As regards what constituted the second "immediate" cause he is also in accord with them, although he varies considerably from them in the details of the matter,—in which variance it seems that the good old Father must be held to be more or less inaccurate. For example, he represents the embassy from New Spain to have been headed by skipper Sebastian, and puts down the *contretemps* at Shidzuoka to the worthy seaman's ignorance of diplomatic usage. But skipper Sebastian was, it seems, only in the train of Sotomayor. Be this as it may, when Sebastian, taking Father Sotelo with him, proceeded to survey the coasts of Japan—especially of Central and Western Japan—in virtue of the permission accorded, whether by Hidetada or Iyeyasu (the point is disputed), there was at once a great outcry. And, according to the missionaries, this outcry was prompted by—Will Adams.[21] It will be remembered that so long before as 1604 a Spanish ship that had put in to Sakai or one of the neighbouring ports had been piloted to the Kwantō—to Uraga, most probably—by Adams. The Kentishman seems now (1612) to have been asked by Iyeyasu why the Spaniards were so eager to explore and chart the Japanese coasts, and the pilot at once replied (quite correctly in normal conditions, but then the Spaniards had got express permission) that in Europe such a proceeding would have been considered a hostile one, and then went on to recapitulate (also quite correctly) the course of the Spanish and Portuguese conquests in America, in the Philippines, and the East Indies. All this chimed in exactly with the tenor of the remarks of the pilot of the *San Felipe* (1596), which were still (1612) kept in mind in Japan. Then Adams, on being questioned closer about the priests, replied that the Romish *religieux* had been expelled from many parts of Germany, from Sweden, Norway, Denmark, Holland, and England, and that although his own country preserved the pure form of the Christian faith from which Spain and Portugal had deviated, yet neither English nor Dutch considered that that fact afforded them any reason to war with, or to annex, States that were non-Christian solely for the

---

[21] The Dutch authorities allege that it was only from Hidetada, not from Iyeyasu, that the Spaniards from New Spain obtained leave in 1611 to survey the coasts of Japan. The point is really immaterial in view of the concession to Vivero in 1609-10 and in view of the reply of Iyeyasu to Jérôme de Jésus' representations in 1598 or 1599.

reason that they *were* non-Christian. Such is the gist of the missionaries' very own accounts. According to Charlevoix, who, however, is honest enough to explain that he was not perfectly acquainted with all the details, Sebastian, on re-appearing at Court to take his leave, was somewhat brusquely informed that although Spaniards might trade with Japan as before, Christian priests were no longer to be brought into, or tolerated in, the country.[22]

Charlevoix, it is to be noted, has enough of the historical sense to be able to distinguish crisply enough between causes and occasions. He points out very clearly that the orthodox Spaniards and the orthodox Portuguese in their eagerness either to secure or to participate in the lucrative Japanese trade descended to a mutual calumniation that only needed the corroborative testimony of the heretic Dutch to convince the Japanese that Spaniard and Portuguese were, like Jew and Christian in Heine's *Disputation,* "both in stinking bad condition." But what the good Father omits to say explicitly—although he gives a thousand and one instances of it inciden-tally—is that the rivalry between the Jesuits from Macao and the *religieux* from the Philippines did far more to arouse Japanese distrust of the Peninsulars than all the squabbles of the traders. The simple truth of the matter is that, from 1594 down to 1614 at least, between Jesuits and Franciscans in Japan it was all but war to the knife, just as it was in Paraguay a few years later on. No amount of Church historianizing will suffice to conceal that truth from any one who takes the trouble to spend some little time over the letters sent by the rival Order and Society to their respective headquarters. Even in the very midst of the throes of the persecution of 1614, Franciscans and Jesuits—both supposed to have been evicted from Japan—fell into the most unseemly strife over the appointment of a Bishop (Cerqueyra died in

---

22 In his fascinating monograph on *Ein unentdecktes Goldland*, Dr. Nachod, who devotes forty-three of his one hundred and forty-two pages to this episode of Captain "Sebastian" (really Sebastian Viscaino), incidentally shows that Charlevoix (to whom he makes no reference) was not so very far wrong in his account of the embassy of 1611 from New Spain, after all. Vizcaino's real mission was to discover this supposed El Dorado—to speak correctly, yet like an Irishman, there were supposed to be two of them, one of gold and the other of silver—situated in the North Pacific off the Japanese coast. We must not forget that those were the days when the world was young.

1614) who had no longer any diocese left to him! Incidents of such a nature were quickly seized upon and pressed home by the Buddhist priests, who meanwhile under Iyeyasu's patronage had recovered no small amount of the prestige, if not of the wealth and power, that had been theirs before the rise of Nobunaga. It would appear that some of the *bonzes,* such as Yamato, one of the three renegade commissioners appointed in Arima in 1612 for the suppression of Christianity in that principality, had pretended to become Christians, and had received baptism merely for the purpose of being able to assail the enemy with more accurate knowledge, and consequently with greater effect. So early as 1605 we hear of an implacable war against the Church in Ōmura being *waged by a Japanese priest ordained at Rome, who had repudiated the faith immediately on his return to Japan.* In many places in the missionaries' accounts we meet with instances of the Buddhists denouncing the foreign priests to Iyeyasu's Government as violators of the laws of Japan. Now, although so much wedded to the grand principle of religious toleration that in 1610 he felt constrained to administer a sharp lesson to the persecuting fanaticism of the Nichiren sect,[23] yet it must be remembered that, unlike both Nobunaga and Hideyoshi, Iyeyasu was a professed Buddhist himself. At his Court priests like Tenkai and Takuan were frequently consulted on matters of policy. This being so, Buddhist opposition to Christianity was now a much more serious matter than it had been a dozen years previously. But behind all these considerations there were factors at work of which we get no hint in

---

[23] "One of the Nichirenshū went to preach his doctrine in Owari, and poured forth torrents of insults against the Christians and the Jōdō sect of Buddhists, and went on repeating the same invectives in a hundred places. Hence brawls and challenges to a public disputation. All this commotion came to the ears of Iyeyasu, who was himself of the Jōdō sect, and he summoned the adversaries into his presence. On the day appointed the Nichiren champion stammered and could not speak. Iyeyasu gave orders to strip this *bonze* and all his *confrères* of the marks of their dignity. He had them ignominiously promenaded in Yedo and in all the places where the *bonze* had spread his calumnies, and finally he had the ears and most of the nose of the chief *bonze* cut off. These unfortunates became the talk of the whole people, and were banished from Kyōto, leaving there twenty-one magnificent houses." What made the satisfaction of the Jesuits especially keen over this mishap to the Nichirenshū was that this sect, to which Katō Kiyomasu (died 1611) and his son belonged, had inspired and fanned the persecution in Higo that had (1601–1602) all but exterminated Christianity in Konishi's former domains. It is to be observed that this measure of Iyeyasu's—solely in the interests of social order—was of a much milder nature than was Nobunaga's procedure after the Azuchi-ron, in 1579.

the historians of the Church.   It seems that by a mere
accident about this time (1612–13) Iyeyasu came into
possession of documents clearly implicating some of his own
high officers in a treasonable intrigue with the representatives of his Catholic Majesty the King of Spain and
Portugal (Philip III.).

   In Dr. Dickson's " Gleanings from Japan " will be found
a Japanese account of the introduction of Christianity into
the country, and another of Hanai's—by whom he evidently
means Ōkubo's—conspiracy.   The two chapters, although both
interesting, are of singularly unequal worth.   In the first
we merely meet with a few grains of wheat in an infinite
deal of chaff; in the second there is a solid substratum of
truth underneath the layers of more or less imaginative varnish
liberally applied to give artistic finish to the incident.[24]

---

[24] Professor Naitō (Chiso), who seems to be entirely ignorant of the foreign
"sources" for this period, is certainly one of the leading authorities on early
Tokugawa history.   Mr. Yamagata has supplied the following summary of the
results of Professor Naitō's researches on this Christian conspiracy.   The
missionary writers, not unnaturally, make no reference to it; yet the details in
Professor Naitō's exposition are far from irreconcilable with what the Church
historians tell us:—
   "One of the chief reasons why Iyeyasu determined to exterminate
Christianity in Japan appears to have been his discovery of a conspiracy on
the part of Japanese Christians to conduct foreign troops into the country
and to overthrow his Government.   The central figure of this conspiracy was
a small Daimyō called Ōkubo Nagayasu.   This man was a son of a certain
actor of saru-gaku ('monkey-dance'), who had been in the service of Takeda
of Kai.   After the fall of the Takeda family he was introduced to Iyeyasu
by one of the latter's immediate vassals, and he served him for some time
as an actor of the 'monkey-dance.'   In 1590 Iyeyasu was appointed by Hideyoshi
ruler of six of the eight provinces of the Kwantō, with his headquarters at
the new town of Yedo.   About that time Iyeyasu said one night in the
course of conversation with his retainers that nobody in the whole country,
except Mōri, was governing as many provinces as he at that time; and as
the expenses of such an extensive administration were great, he wished to
get as much gold and silver as possible.   Without the precious metals, he
continued, he could not act as he wished; but to get them in large quantity
he had to levy heavy taxes from his subjects, to their great mortification.
Iyeyasu then asked his retainers whether they knew any means of obtaining
much gold and silver without mortifying his people.   None ventured to give a
reply to this difficult question.   Ōkubo, who was then called Ōkuratayū,
happened to sit behind them.   The next day he betook himself to Aoyama
Tadanari, and said to him that he had a plan to get for Iyeyasu as much gold
and silver as he wished; but as it was a great matter, he had hesitated to speak
in the presence of so many persons, and that he would be glad to speak
about it directly to Iyeyasu himself.   Aoyama was pleased with his proposal,
and forthwith told Iyeyasu about the matter.   Iyeyasu was not inclined to
believe that a mere actor had any grand scheme to offer, but just to be amused
he summoned Ōkubo into his presence.   Ōkubo then explained to him his plan,
which was to open gold and silver mines within his dominions, and said that
this was the only means of getting the precious metals without burdening the
people.   Iyeyasu began to be interested, and asked: ' Is this your own devising
or did you hear about it from professional men?' 'There are many miners
in the Western countries,' replied Ōkubo; 'I have heard from them all about this
matter.'   Iyeyasu then said: 'Have you no mind to give up your present

It would appear that besides Ōkubo himself, who before his death in 1613 was superintendent of the rich gold mines of Sado, several of the Daimyō were considered to have been

---

occupation and take this mining business into your hands?' Ōkubo gladly replied in the affirmative, and making one of his pupils his successor, he invited miners from various countries. With them he tried some mines in the province of Idzu, and was so successful in his first attempt that he was able to forward to Yedo a large quantity of gold and silver. Iyeyasu was highly satisfied with his work, and granted him the honour of becoming a *samurai*. Now he had been much patronized by Ōkubo Tadachika, one of the most powerful and trusted vassals of Iyeyasu, who was very fond of *saru-gaku*. This Ōkubo now permitted him to take his family name, and so the actor Ōkuratayū became Ōkubo Jubei Nagayasu, and was also granted the honorary title of Iwami-no-Kami. He opened mines in several places, and constantly supplied gold and silver to Iyeyasu, who was thus enabled to have little concern about monetary affairs in conducting the Sekigahara campaign. Ōkubo steadily rose in Iyeyasu's favour, and was given a fief of 30,000 *koku* at Hachiōji, twenty miles from Yedo. But he was a man of a greedy turn of mind, and during his superintendence of the mining works he secretly appropriated large quantities of gold and silver; but so adroitly did he manipulate the official accounts that his crime was never discovered during his lifetime. He was also entrusted with the collection of taxes in Ōmi, in Sado, and in some other places, and in discharging this duty he misappropriated no little amount of the public money. In this way he became very rich, and led a luxurious and extravagant life, keeping many concubines. In going to and coming back from the island of Sado he often passed through Yechigo, the province of Matsudaira Tadateru, the sixth son of Iyeyasu. Thus Ōkubo became intimate with Hanai Mondo, the chief retainer of Tadateru. Ōkubo's son, Ukyo, married Hanai's daughter, and, becoming one of Tadateru's chief vassals, he wielded his power in a fashion that was injurious to the happiness of the people of Echigo.

"On the 25th of the second month of the eighteenth year of Keichō (1613) Ōkubo died. According to his will, his sons asked permission to bury his remains in Kai, his native province, in a gold coffin. This was not granted. Ōkubo had promised his concubines large sums of gold in the event of his death. Accordingly, when he died his concubines requested his heir, Tōjurō by name, to hand over the gold they had been promised by his father. Tōjurō, however, delayed to pay them, excusing himself on the ground that he would see to their demands after he had settled all accounts with the Government which had been left unsettled by his father. The dissatisfied concubines then appealed to Iyeyasu, and the result was that the late Ōkubo's books were subjected to a close audit. It was then found that Ōkubo had been guilty of many irregularities in his monetary matters. At the same time a most astounding discovery was made. In a box which was the most prized treasure of Ōkubo in his lifetime were found several important documents. From these writings Iyeyasu learned, to his intense amazement, that Ōkubo, who had been a Christian, had had communication with foreign Christians, and had concocted a conspiracy to overthrow the Shōgun's Government with the aid of foreign troops. In that letter the name of Ōkubo Nagayasu was mentioned. Thus assured of the treason of the late Ōkubo, Iyeyasu ordered all his sons, seven in number, to be arrested and examined. On the 6th of the fifth month (June 18th, 1613) they were all condemned to death and the fief and the properties of their father were confiscated. Many persons were punished in connection with the affair. Among them was a brother of Takayama Ukon.

"Connected with this affair, Ōkubo Tadachika (of Odawara) was put into disgrace. As before said, he was one of the most powerful and trusted vassals of Iyeyasu. He had his castle at Odawara (70,000 *koku*). Honda Masanobu was his rival in power. They differed radically in their characters. While Ōkubo was a man of sincere and generous nature, Honda was a man of intrigue, cold-hearted and shrewd. They were not on good terms with each other. When the treason of the late Ōkubo Nagayasu was discovered, Ōkubo Tadachika, who had patronised him and given him his family name, was much ashamed, and shut himself up in his house for many days. A certain Baba, who hated Ōkubo for some grievance, went to Honda and accused Ōkubo of being a party to the treason. Honda was glad to have an opportunity of humiliating his rival, and

implicated, among others Ōkubo of Odawara and Iyeyasu's own son Tadateru being suspected. Tadateru, it will be remembered, had married the daughter of Date Masamune; and we shall soon find Date despatching an embassy of his own to the King of Spain and to the Pope. Iyeyasu is said to have kept the discovery a profound secret, and to have quietly set to work to clip the wings of the conspirators. Ōkubo's sons were ordered to commit suicide, Ōkubo of Odawara and several other Daimyō had their domains and their revenues curtailed, while shortly afterwards Tadateru was removed from his fief of 480,000 *koku* to one of 30,000 *koku*, and kept in banishment during all the rest of his long life of ninety years.

It is to be remarked, however, that it was not till 1615, after Iyeyasu had made a final settlement with Hideyori and his Christian generals—with " their flags inscribed with Jesus and Mary, even with the Great Protector of Spain "—that Tadateru was actually degraded, and Japanese records attribute his fall to incidents that happened in the course of the campaign. While in front of Osaka some of Tadateru's men had a fatal brawl with certain of Iyeyasu's own retainers; and it was this, and also Tadateru's own slackness in the operations that preceded the great assault, which had so enraged Iyeyasu that

---

brought the information to Iyeyasu. The latter was greatly perplexed; but in order to test Ōkubo he ordered him to go to Kyōto and to persecute the Christians of the city. Accordingly Ōkubo went up to Kyōto in the 1st month of the 19th year of Keichō (February 9th, 1614) and set himself to carry out his Lord's order. He destroyed the Christian churches in that city, burnt to death sixty native converts, and banished the foreign priests to Nagasaki. While in Kyōto he received a message from Iyeyasu, in which he was given to understand that for the offence of having privately contracted a marriage with Yamaguchi Shigemasa without obtaining the permission of the Shōgun his fief would be confiscated and he would be sent to Omi as an exile. He received the message calmly and went to live in Omi, where he was given 5,000 *koku*. His two sons were also exiled to the remote North of the Empire. He wrote to them expressing a wish that they would refrain from taking any rash step such as committing suicide, for that would only add to his disadvantage, and said that he trusted in the wisdom of his Lord to see his innocence, and that if they were summoned to service once more they should not refuse to accept even a humble position. He declined to receive the allowance of 5,000 *koku* allotted to him, saying that he could not honestly receive it when he was not doing his duty. He relied upon the support of Ii Naotaka, Lord of Omi, for his livelihood, and passed his days in seclusion, as if he were a real prisoner. Sympathising with him, Ii offered him his friendly service to try to establish his innocence before the Shōgun. Ōkubo begged him not to do anything of the kind, as he was unwilling to expose the mistake of his Lord. At such an expression of loyalty Ii was moved to tears. In the second year of Kanyei (1625), his grandson Sadachiyo, afterwards Tadato, was given a fief at Kisai with 20,000 *koku* revenue, and after-wards was removed to Akashi (near Kobe), where his revenue was raised to 70,000 *koku*. His son Tadatomo was re-established at Odawara with 113,000 *koku* revenue. As for old Ōkubo, he died in the fifth year of Kanyei (1628) in the place of his exile in his seventy-sixth year."

he forbad his sixth son to look upon his face again. Yet, as it was the old statesmen's invariable custom to bide his time, it is possible that he waited till Ōsaka was his before dealing drastically with the malcontents that Ōkubo had secretly banded together three years before.

However, making all due allowance for a very liberal amount of the apocryphal in the account of Ōkubo's conspiracy, we nevertheless find ourselves confronted with abundant evidence of the fact that the Tokugawas were beginning to become suspicious of the foreign priests. For instance, we are told that "in the Keichō period (1596-1614) Iyeyasu sent Nishi Soshin to Western countries with a commission to investigate Christianity. This man was an inhabitant of Sakai and a master of the tea-ceremony (cha-no-yu). He was known to Hideyoshi as well as to Iyeyasu. While abroad for three years he became a Christian and studied it (Christianity), and then, returning, gave Iyeyasu a minute report on what he had studied. Iyeyasu now clearly saw the harmful nature of Christianity, and resolved to prohibit it altogether."

So what with Japanese priests "ordained at Rome" turned renegade and waging an implacable war on the Church after their return to the country, and what with secret official emissaries like your Nishi Soshin, master of cha-no-yu (we shall presently meet with others of the kidney), the authorities suffered from no lack of information on the social and political effects of Christianity in its home-lands. No doubt the worthy tea-master made full report of how Catholics and Protestants alike were burning at the stake such as they were severally pleased to consider heretics, duly dilating upon the previous religious wars in France and in the Netherlands, upon the strife going on between Christians and Mahomedans (some of the tales embodied in Don Quixote disclose the spirit in which it was conducted admirably), upon the Christianising conquests of the Spaniards in America and of the Portuguese in the East, with a passing allusion to St. Bartholomew's Day, to the tender mercy and loving-kindness of the Holy Office, and to the Pope's pretensions to excommunicate heretic monarchs and to dispose of their dominions even as Iyeyasu would dispose of the fief of a revolted Fudai Daimyō. To the broad, tolerant mind of Iyeyasu, centuries in advance of European statesmen in his attitude towards freedom of religious belief and profession, the aggressive, intolerant, and persecuting spirit of contemporary European Christianity must have seemed at once loathsome and dangerous in the extreme to the best interests of any country whose ruler was eagerly bent (as he himself was) on the maintenance of domestic peace and order. The report of the secret commissioner sent abroad to investigate all the aspects of Christianity cannot have failed to resuscitate the recollection of the Spanish pilot's remarks in 1596, and of the Spaniard's indiscreet mention of the mustering of fleets and men and munitions at Manila in 1605 for the conquest of the Moluccas,[23] consonant, moreover, as it must have been, in all essential particulars with the repeated representations of the trusted Will Adams, it must have convinced the Tokugawa of the expediency of taking prompt and resolute action. On having been informed by Adams some time before that the Romish priests had already been expelled from Protestant countries, Iyeyasu is said to have exclaimed, "If the Sovereigns of Europe do not tolerate these priests, I do them no wrong if I refuse to tolerate them."

Now in justice to Iyeyasu the following facts must be noted. His resolve to bring the work of the foreign priests in his realms to an end was taken in 1612, and the Church historians date the persecution from that year. *Yet during the lifetime of this great ruler (died 1616) not one single European missionary was put to death!* The first execution of foreign missionaries did not take place until May 22nd, 1617, and that execution (by decapitation) was carried out without any torture or any indignity whatsoever. The two priests then killed were treated like *samurai*—Japanese gentlemen. The executioner was not of the *Eta*, or pariah class—the outcasts who were employed to dispose of ordinary criminals. According to the usage observed in Japan with respect to persons of distinction, the headsman on this occasion was one of the chief officers of the "Prince" of Ōmura. And a calm and dispassionate consideration of all the circumstances as detailed by themselves impels any impartial

---

23 The Dutch had beaten the Portuguese out of Tidore and Lantore in 1605-1606, and they in turn were evicted by this Spanish expedition from Manila. In 1610 the Dutch Admiral Verhoeven and most of his officers were killed in an ambuscade in Banda; but shortly after they made good the conquest of most of the group of the Spice Islands, and dominated them by seven well-manned forts.

mind to the conviction that the blood-guiltiness—if such there was—as well as the responsibility for the horrors of the subsequent persecution, was on the heads of the foreign *religieux* rather than on that of the Tokugawa Government. That Government, be it remarked in common fairness, claimed no more than what every European Government of the day did—to be really master in its own realms. Suppose the said Tokugawa Government had insisted on sending Buddhist missionaries to most Catholic Spain or Portugal—how would these missionaries have been received? They would not have been deported; they would have simply been burnt at the stake as infidels! Now the Tokugawas aimed at nothing more than the justifiable deportation of foreigners whose continued presence they had reason to believe was prejudicial to the peace of Japan; and it was only when the foreigners *would* persist in returning to a land where they were not wanted that the Japanese Government had recourse to very regrettable, but very necessary, methods of dealing with aliens that made a merit of flouting its decrees. In thus flouting the fiat of the rulers of Japan the *religieux* no doubt honestly believed they were perfectly in the right. But it surely must be conceded that the missionary—or even the Christian—standpoint is not the only one, and that people's rights in their own houses are even more valid than the arrogated "rights" of fanatical outside propagandists to disturb their domestic peace and quiet. It is surely only the essence of common-sense and of justice to maintain that people have not only a right, but a duty, to protect themselves against unjustifiable aggression of all sorts—that of zealot alien propagandists included.

Now for the facts as set forth by the missionaries themselves, apart from all Japanese presentations of the case. Since the death of Hideyoshi in 1598 there *had* been martyrs in some of the fiefs, notably in Higo and Yamaguchi (Mōri's domains); in the latter only a few. But for the internal administration of the great feudatories the Tokugawas at the time were not responsible. On the other hand, in many of the great fiefs, notably those of Aki (Fukushima's), Chikuzen (Kuroda's), Buzen (Hosokawa's), and the greatest of all, Kaga, the domain of the fox-shooting Mayeda—all in close relations with Iyeyasu, in fact his most zealous supporters—the

1 1

missionaries had been welcomed.   And in the immediate
Tokugawa domains themselves, down to 1612, subject only to
the qualification that no superior vassal was allowed to receive
baptism, the foreign priests really had liberty to propagate
their faith.   In these domains until that year of 1612 no
Japanese Christian had suffered merely on account of his
being a Christian.

In the Tokugawa possessions the first Christian put to
death was Okamoto, Honda's secretary, and he suffered not
because of his faith but on account of his venality in the
Arima intrigue.   In short, Okamoto's attempt to serve God
and Mammon at the same time miscarried; and he had to
pay a penalty whose exaction in similar cases would do
much towards teaching the sinful sons of men the value of
honesty and sincerity and the inherent vileness of an esurient
hypocrisy.   The attention bestowed on this criminal by the
Christians at his execution seems to have excited Iyeyasu's
disgust, and to have prompted some of the phraseology of
the Edict of 1614.   When Iyeyasu did, in consequence of
this and other things, set his face against Christianity, he at
first plainly said that merchants and farmers and those below
them in social status might do as they listed in the matter;
what he was resolved on was that the officers that served him
should not be Christians.   Even when the Franciscan Church
in Yedo was pulled down later on in the same year (1612)
Christian farmers, artisans, merchants, lepers, and outcasts
were in no wise interfered with.

It was only in the August of the following year (1613) that
any Japanese lost their lives for their religion in Yedo, and for
so doing they had mainly to thank the indefatigable, intriguing,
blue-blooded Father Sotelo, whose activity, whether in diplomacy, or in proselytising, or in fighting rival Orders, was well-
nigh limitless.   About Sotelo in the *rôle* of diplomatist more
will be said later on; here it must suffice to remark that it
was really he who had done the chief share of the work in
negotiating Vivero's Spanish Treaty of 1610, and that he had
in 1612 started on an alleged diplomatic mission from Hidetada
the Shōgun to the King of Spain.   He was shipwrecked shortly
after starting, and as Hidetada had recalled his commission,
Sotelo was not in particularly good odour when he returned to

Yedo. Notwithstanding this circumstance, and notwithstanding the prohibition against the preaching of Christianity, he erected an oratory in Asakusa in the leper quarter, and there publicly celebrated Mass. The members of his congregation were arrested, and those of them that refused to apostatise were beheaded at Tonka—"a place situated between Yedo and Asakusa,"—which, in contemporary England, would be equivalent to saying "between London and Westminster."[24] Among the victims was Sotelo's own Japanese catechist, while yet another catechist was kept in prison for four years. Sotelo himself was also at the same time put in ward, and the Shōgun seems to have been hard put to it to know how to get rid of him, for at this date the Tokugawas were utterly averse to imbruing their hands in the blood of the foreign priests. He was indeed condemned to death, but at the request of Daté Masamune of Sendai he was released, and Daté took him to his own capital in the North, and shortly after sent him as his ambassador to the King of Spain and to the Pope.

Having thus disposed of Sotelo, the Government now addressed itself to getting rid of *all* the foreign missionaries, as well as of those Japanese Christians who might be influential enough to excite disturbances in the country. On January 27th, 1614, Iyeyasu issued a proclamation ordering the suppression of Christianity in Japan, together with a set of fifteen Articles instructing Buddhist priests how they were to act in the matter.[25] At the same time all the Daimyō were ordered

---

[24] Eight executed August 16th; fourteen August 17th; five September 7th, 1613.

[25] In connection with Iyeyasu's expulsion of the missionaries the following documents are worthy of consideration.

In a letter from Çerqueyra, Bishop of Japan, to Philip III. of Spain (October 5th, 1613) we meet with the following passage:—

"Among the principal means of persevering, inspired in the Christians by the Holy Spirit, has been the formation of certain associations called *Kumi*, into which are only admitted Christians resolved to die for the faith, and to keep the Christian law, taking Our Lady the Holy Virgin for their special patroness. They meet frequently, now in one house and now in another, and confer on subjects of a nature to fortify their souls in the faith, and to maintain their devotion. For this purpose they have spiritual manuals, and they observe certain regulations. Independently of the faithful Christians, the most of those—a small number—who failed in the persecution of last year, have presented themselves to do penance and to enter those fraternities, and they have accomplished the legitimate satisfactions. These holy exercises have extended to all the district, and children of ten, eleven, and twelve years and upwards have formed similar *confréries* among themselves with regulations appropriate to their age. The fire of the Holy Spirit has, for the greater

to send all the *religieux* in their domains to Nagasaki, and thereafter to demolish all the churches and compel the converts

glory of God, been propagated far beyond Arima—that is to say in the islands of Chiki and Conzoura, bordering on Higo and opposite to Tacacou (*i.e.* Arima); so that what the missionaries have been unable to accomplish by their preaching and their councils during a great number of years has been accomplished in little more than a year by a miracle of the Holy Spirit. The *religieux* of the Company formerly in charge of Arima, although in exile at present, do not hesitate to return there to visit the faithful and to assist them spiritually."

It must be remembered that Christianity had been proscribed in Arima in the preceding year (1612); and these associations were regarded as seditious by the authorities.

Carvalho, the Jesuit Provincial, deported from Japan in November, 1614, writing from Macao to the Pope on December 28th of the same year, says:—

"The reasons which have moved the King to persecute us and the Christians are chiefly these two:—(1) Some Gentiles, enemies of the faith, have persuaded the King that our gospel teaches that those who disobey their Lords should be venerated, and that criminals and violators of the laws of the realm are worshipped by the Christians. What gave occasion to the first calumny was the happy end of those who refused to obey the orders of their Lord (in Arima) to abandon their faith, and who suffered death in consequence, and who are venerated by the Christians for preferring to obey·God rather than their Lords. The ground of the second calumny was that when a certain Christian who had exchanged a certain kind of silver for another against the Royal Edicts was crucified, the Christians on bended knees commended him to God as he was dying. This gave rise to the calumny that a criminal on the gallows was worshipped by the Christians. When these calumnies reached the ears of the King, and he believed them, he burst out in anger: 'A Law in which doctrine of that sort is taught is of the Devil!' And straightway he enjoined the Gentile Governor of Nagasaki, who was present, to root out all the *religieux* and clerics from Japan. He also ordered the dynasts not only to crucify and persecute the native Christians till they should return to their old superstition, but also to drive the preachers of the Gospel from their domains and to destroy and burn their houses and churches. And in sooth all have obeyed the royal mandate. It appears that these calumnies were the cause of this persecution, as well from general talk and report as from two letters addressed to us by two courtiers very high in the King's favour."

The next paragraph deals with the Japanese suspicion that "the *religieux* are sent to Japan, *ut prætextu prædicandi Evangelii regna invadant*," and with the ill service done by the Dutch and the English in connection with the Spanish survey of the coasts.

A reference to the Annual Letter of 1614 serves to elucidate several points in Carvalho's communication. Says de Mattos:—"The King (Iyeyasu) did not hesitate to let this blow (*i.e.* banishing the missionaries) fall at once, as much by reason of the hatred he cherished against our holy faith, as from the desire to preserve his kingdom. It was no fault of the *bonzes*, who, being sworn enemies of the Christian faith, said the worst they could of it on every occasion in the presence of the King. But the Dutch and English merchants who trade in this country have been those who have greatly inflamed the King. By false accusations these have rendered our preachers such objects of suspicion that he fears and readily believes that they are rather spies than sowers of the Holy Faith in his kingdom. Notwithstanding this, in our banishment the King has made no mention of the fear he entertains, nor of the hatred he bears us, although this may be the principal motive. But to make it believed that we are justly expelled, and that the Christians are not wrongly persecuted, he adduces two things, which are rather excuses for himself than matter of accusation against us. We have learned this chiefly from two letters, the one written from the Court to the Father Rector of Kyōto by Safioye, Governor of Nagasaki, and the other from a favourite of the King named Gotō Shōzaburō, also a Gentile, written to a Christian of Kyōto, his friend. The first, translated from the Japanese, is as follows:—' From this letter which I send to you by this courier express, you will understand what the King's opinion and judgement of you is, for a few days ago, having heard that certain Christians had gone out of their houses to worship a certain citizen of Nagasaki named Jirobioye (who was justly executed for having

to abjure Christianity. On February 11th, 1614, the fifteen Jesuits in Kyōto received orders to withdraw, and on the 21st

---

contravened the law which forbids the purchase of silver bullion), he said that without doubt that must be a diabolic faith which persuades people not only to worship criminals condemned to be executed for their crimes, but also to honour those who have been burned or cut in pieces by the order of their Lord. Likewise they are still more wicked who preach such a faith. The King has spoken to me in such a strain, not without causing me pain. Consequently I send you this messenger expressly to inform you in what condition your affairs are at Court.—11th of 11th month (1613). HASEGAWA SAHIOYE.' The second letter sent to the citizen of Kyōto ran thus: 'A few days ago in the presence of his Highness there was talk of the Law of the Christians, on the occasion of an individual of Nagasaki who had purchased silver bullion, not marked as coin of the realm (which is forbidden), which individual Igadono, Governor of Kyōto (i.e. Itakura, the Shōshidai), had sentenced to be crucified and whom the Christians had gone to worship. Likewise Arimadono, having ordered several men to be burned alive for refusing to renounce their Christianity, the sectaries of that same Law came equally, and eagerly cut off portions of their bodies and carried them away as relics. His Highness, informed of these facts, said that it was a very bad thing to worship such people, and he blamed the preachers of the Christian Law severely; and although it is probable that he will not cause the Christians to be chastised, it seems to me useless and dangerous to adhere to a Law which his Highness holds in horror. What I have written has been repeated in Yedo by merchants who have gone there from Kyōto, and the merchants of Yedo soon informed his Highness of it. The Prince, regarding the preaching of the Christian Law as strange and suspicious, will perhaps address some questions to the *religieux* on the matter.—11th of 11th month. GOTŌ SHŌZABURŌ.'"

(This Gotō Shōzaburō, it may be remarked, was a skilful engraver whom Iyeyasu had made Master of the Mint; and as he was intelligent in affairs of State, he had taken him into his confidence. Gotō appears in Cocks's Diary more than once.)

The writer of this Annual Letter of 1614 gives a clear account of this Jirobioye incident. "In the November of last year (1613) a certain Christian was crucified for having purchased some silver bullion—a thing strictly forbidden by law. On the same day and at the same place five Gentiles were beheaded for various crimes. Now, in order that by the example and the punishment of these, all should be taught to respect the laws, the criminals to be executed were conducted through all the principal streets to the place of punishment, so that a huge crowd of people assembled to see justice done upon them. The Gentiles were beheaded and the Christian was crucified. Now it is the custom in Japan that as soon as the victim is elevated on the cross, he is pierced to the heart with a lance. When this was done to the Christian, and the poor man rendered his last sigh, the Christians who were present, moved with compassion, and holding their rosaries in their hands, threw themselves on their knees to recommend to God the soul of the victim escaping from the prison house of the body. This action was as pious as it was novel to the Gentiles, and gave them occasion to murmur, and to say that the Christians worshipped malefactors: and so they reported it to the King as a manifest crime."

These extracts will serve to elucidate the references in one or two of the paragraphs of Iyeyasu's anti-Christian Edict of July 27th, 1614, which will be found fully translated by Sir E. M. Satow in Vol. VI. of the *Transactions of the Asiatic Society of Japan*. The language of this proclamation is remarkable as indicating the difference between Hideyoshi's and Iyeyasu's views regarding the religious needs of the Empire. Of this Hideyoshi had given a tolerably full and lucid exposition in his letter to the Viceroy of the Indies (1591) and in his dispatch to the Governor-General of the Philippines (1597). In these documents nothing was said about Chinese philosophy, and little about Buddhism. In them autochthonous Shintō was pronounced to be the proper cult for Japan. Now in Iyeyasu's proclamation the change of view is very great. Shintō is indeed alluded to, but the old gods of Japan seem to be regarded as swept into the Buddhist pantheon, and rightly appropriated as the belongings of the Buddhist priests. "Abroad we have manifested the perfection of the Five Cardinal

twelve of them did so, *leaving the other three behind them in hiding*. The twelve (together with a convoy from Fushimi, Ōsaka, and elsewhere) reached Nagasaki on March 11th, to find the city rapidly filling with the *religieux* sent from the other quarters of the empire, but as there was no shipping then available they were allowed to remain till the arrival of the "ship from Macao."

The vessel arrived in June. The captain sent seven representatives to Shidzuoka with exceedingly valuable presents. However, at the audience the head of the deputation found Iyeyasu immovable in his determination regarding Christianity; after repeating all the former accusations against the "religion," he added that if this faith spread, his subjects would soon be in revolt, and that to nip the mischief in the bud he was resolved that no Father should remain in his domains henceforth.

From this account it becomes plain that while still prepared to accord foreign traders a hospitable welcome to Japan, the old statesman was thoroughly bent upon being master in his own house, and upon seeing to it that his hospitality was not abused by his guests. So much also appears from his reply to Domingos Francisco, who had appeared a second time at Court as envoy from the Governor of the Philippines in the previous year, 1613. Francisco came to request that all the Portuguese and Spaniards who were in Japan without

Virtues, *while at home we have returned to the doctrine of the Scriptures*. For these reasons the country prospers, the people enjoy peace." Buddh'sm had again become the State religion, as far as there was a State religion. But, in addition to that, there is much in the language of the proclamation that does not belong to Buddhism at all. The Positive Principle, the Negative Principle, the Five Cardinal Virtues, Heaven—all these are conceptions drawn from Chinese philosophy. Since the beginning of the century there had been a great revival of the study of that philosophy, which had been almost utterly neglected during the turmoil of the long civil wars. It was now that Japan made her first acquaintance with the system of the Sung schoolmen; and within a century this system was destined to strip Buddhism of all its power and all its prestige among the educated classes. As yet this Chinese philosophy had to shelter itself under the wing of Buddhism, for its professors had to accept the tonsure down to about 1690 A.D. Its foremost exponent in Japan at this time was Hayashi Razan, who had entered Iyeyasu's service about 1602; and by 1614, we are told, "there was no proclamation or Government document which did not pass through his hands." Hence in all probability it was he who drafted this Anti-Christian Edict of 1614; and hence the prominence assigned in it to the ideas of the schoolmen of China. In the set of rules for the guidance of priests who were to act as inquisitors, by which this proclamation was accompanied, all conceptions from Chinese philosophy are conspicuous by their absence. This lends support to Professor Riess's supposition that these rules were drafted not in Iyeyasu's secretariat, but by Buddhist monks, who had but little knowledge of Christianity and were inclined to identify it with some of their own obnoxious sects.

permission from the King of Spain should be handed over to him to be taken to Manila, the reason being that there was a great lack of men for the maintenance of the Moluccas against the Dutch. To this request—after a long interval, in the course of which the Englishman, Captain Saris, arrived and was promptly received by Iyeyasu—it was coldly and curtly made answer that "Japan was a free country, and that no one could be forced to leave it." In September, 1614, a special messenger was sent to Nagasaki to urge on the departure of the missionaries, and at last, on the 7th and 8th November, the "great ship" and a smaller one set sail with sixty-three Jesuits, besides catechists and a number of Japanese Christians, for Macao, while at the same time a small and crazy craft departed with the Spanish *religieux*, twenty-three Jesuits, and several distinguished Japanese exiles, for Manila.[26]

Although on this occasion the "innocent stratagem" of packing the deck of the ships with sailors in priestly garb was not resorted to as it was in 1597, yet as soon as the vessels had passed six miles out of the harbour, and the guards had returned, three boats put off from the shore and took off two Dominicans, two Franciscans, and all the secular priests, while some of the Jesuits bound for Macao also found means to re-land. "There would have been more of them, if several boats had not failed to appear, in consequence of a mistake." Altogether eighteen Fathers, most of them "professed of the four vows," and nine Brothers of the "Company of Jesus," seven Dominican Fathers, as many of the Franciscans, one Augustin Father, and five secular priests evaded the Edict of expulsion; that is, altogether, another edition of the famous Forty-seven Rōnin.

And by the beginning of next year the exiled priests were re-entering Japan in various disguises—some of them as slaves! This zeal, from the point of view of the Church, was no doubt most meritorious. But what fate would have been meted out to these *religieux* if they had similarly ventured to brave the edicts of James I. of England, or of any other contemporary Protestant sovereign? And how would the King

---

26 In the previous year, 1613, there had been 118 Jesuits (63 priests) and some 33 Philippine *religieux*, besides some secular priests, in Japan.

of Spain and Portugal or the Pope have dealt either with
Protestant or Buddhist or Mahomedan missionaries, who, after
being mercifully deported, still insisted on lurking in, or on
returning to, their dominions?

It was just immediately before their departure that the
missionaries thought fit to engage in one of their miserable
internal squabbles that tended so much to bring their cause
into disfavour and disrepute. Bishop Çerqueyra had died on
February 20th, 1614, and difficulties soon arose among the
various Orders on the subject of the administration of the
Bishopric. Carvailho, the Jesuit Provincial, was elected by the
seven Japanese secular priests to be Vicar-General and Administrator until the Archbishop of Goa could provide canonically for
the administration. However, on October 21st (*i.e.* eighteen days
before the general deportation!), four of the Philippine *religieux*
got a notary to draw up a decree declaring the deposition of
Carvailho from his functions of Vicar-General! Carvailho
retorted by issuing censures against the *religieux*, by excom-
municating the unhappy notary, and by affixing his decree
to the church gate—the said church being just about to be
pulled down by the evicting heathen! The immediate matter
was compromised; but, as M. Léon Pagés plaintively remarks,
"nevertheless in the midst of the preparations for exile, and
after the departure of most of the missionaries, the dissensions
continued."

Among the "distinguished" Japanese so summarily sent
abroad for their country's supposed good—women-folk, what
not, and all—are some old acquaintances of ours. Twenty-one or
twenty-two years ago we have seen John Naitō (Hida-no-Kami)
and his son Thomas following Konishi to the Korean wars,
not as commanders of divisions or even of battalions, but as
"simple volunteers"; and a little later on we have found Naitō
at Peking as Konishi's representative solemnly imparting to
the Chinese Court the astonishing information that the
Emperor and Shōgun of Japan were (or was) one and the
same person. Then, still twenty more years before this, we
have seen this Naitō, Hida-no-Kami, then a veritable prince
with a real principality of his own, come gallantly and gaily
prancing down from Tamba, with a grand *Jesus·d'Or* on his
casque, at the head of his 2,000 troops, "whose banners all

had beautiful crosses," to support—the losing side, as it happened (1573). From that date Hida-no-Kami has been a prince without a principality! After God-and-Mammon-rewarded Sumitada of Ōmura, Naitō, Prince of Tamba, the first Japanese Daimyō to be won to profess the faith (1565), is now, after nine-and-forty years of unfeigned devotion to it, to meet his reward. Together with his sister Julia and his son Thomas, John Naitō, Hida-no-Kami, now finds that in spite of his more than three-score years and ten it is for him written *exit*—to die a stranger in a strange land. Respect for John Naitō! In spite of his little vagaries as a diplomatist, he was yet man enough to stand firm in the faith he really believed when the world went with him quite otherwise than its fashion was with Sumitada of Ōmura.

A still more illustrious exile was Don Justo Ucondono, who erstwhile offered to his subjects, not Death or the Koran, but Christianity or Eviction. A mighty man of war, Takayama, Don Justo Ucondono, undoubtedly was; and had it not been that Hideyoshi felt that his fanatical zeal as a propagandist neutralised the value to him of his great qualities, Takayama might have been a grand figure in the political history of his times. For the last seven-and-twenty years of his life he had lived in Kaga on decently good terms with Mayeda Toshiiye and his fox-shooting successor, Toshinaga. Thanks to Don Justo's influence with Toshinaga, missionaries had been welcome in the three provinces (Kaga, Noto, Etchiu) that, after Sekigahara, formed the largest non-Tokugawa fief in Japan. When Iyeyasu's Edict of January 27th, 1614, was received by Mayeda Toshinaga, it was found that Don Justo had to be sent to Nagasaki. Now let us listen to the missionaries, as epitomised by M. Pagés:—

"Don Justo [Takayama] on the point of his departure sent sixty gold ingots to Chikuzen-no-Kami, the younger brother and heir to the estates of Toshinaga [shooter of foxes], telling him that that was the revenue of the domains he had held of him, and that having had no occasion to serve him in war, he begged him to take this gold (which represented about 3,000 crowns in Europe). Besides, he sent to Toshinaga a gold tea-pot of the weight of thirty ingots. Toshinaga refused the tea-pot, but Chikuzen-no-Kami accepted the gold. In passing Kanazawa [the capital of the Mayeda fief] Don Justo [Takayama] learned that Toshinaga had shut himself up in his citadel with the *élite* of his *samurai*; in reality this Prince [Toshinaga] was not ignorant of the relations and of the influence of the exile, and he apprehended a revolt. Don Justo caused him to be reassured. Likewise in passing Sakamoto, which was only three leagues from Kyôto, they feared for the capital." . . . "Iyeyasu, to whom Don Justo might have become a redoubtable adversary, not comprehending the philosophy of this great man, wished to oppose his departure, and had the ship pursued. But it was too late; the bird had flown."

Charlevoix supplies us with the key to these hard passages. Hideyori, who in Ōsaka was then strengthening himself for the final struggle with Iyeyasu, had either gone himself or sent emissaries to Sakamoto to meet Don Justo and his companions to urge them to settle with him in his stronghold. But Don Justo had passed just a little before. This circumstance had doubtless come to Iyeyasu's knowledge.[27] The missionaries tell us that Hideyori was eagerly striving to make Ōsaka into a veritable Cave of Adullam for all the discontented and fugitive warriors of Japan, assigning them revenues without any present obligation on their part, but with an undertaking to arm and fight for his cause when need might be.

To make clear the subsequent, and even in a measure the contemporary, course of the relations of Japan with foreigners, it is now necessary to devote our attention to a consideration of the great Ōsaka struggle between Hideyori and Iyeyasu that finally, and once for all, made the Tokugawas undisputed masters of the empire for two centuries and a half. The events of 1614–15 are really of much greater importance than those of 1600 A.D., for if Sekigahara was Iyeyasu's Dunbar, Ōsaka was a *very great deal more* than his crowning mercy of Worcester.

---

[27] Don Justo died in Manila February 3rd, 1615. "At his death there was a great concourse; they kissed his feet as a saint, and some *religieux* rendered him this honour."

CHAPTER XVII.

THE GREAT ŌSAKA STRUGGLE.

IN the preceding chapter but one, dealing with internal affairs after the battle of Sekigahara, attention was almost solely confined to Iyeyasu and the measures he adopted to consolidate his power and resources in his own special domains and in Eastern and Central Japan generally. It is true that in that chapter a brief glance was cast at the feudal map of Japan as remodified by the victor in the great struggle of 1600 A.D.; but, apart from that, little or nothing was therein said about the position of Iyeyasu towards the Emperor of Japan, towards Hideyori's Court in Ōsaka, or towards the great independent feudatories like Shimadzu and Mayeda. Beyond alluding to the fact that Iyeyasu was invested with the title of Shōgun in the year of the union of the Scotch and English crowns (1603), nothing was given of the history of Japan to the West of Lake Biwa. It will therefore be well to resume the thread of the narrative of events in these Western quarters at the point where it was dropped—at the consultation between Iyeyasu and Hidetada in Ōsaka—as to whether the chief seat of their power should be established in the West or in the East.

Before leaving Ōsaka, Iyeyasu fixed the revenue of Hideyori at 657,400 *koku*, to be raised from Settsu, Kawachi, and Idzumi, from which provinces several small Daimyō were, at the same time, removed to fiefs in Yamato and elsewhere. Among these princelets was Katagiri Katsumoto, the Ichi-no-Kami of the Jesuits,[1] who was shifted from Ibaraki in Settsu (12,000 *koku*), with an increase of 16,000 *koku*, to Tatsuta in Yamato. This Katagiri at the age of nineteen had rendered brilliant services at the fight of Shizugatake in Echizen, the great

---

[1] It must be carefully borne in mind that this Ichi-no-Kami was not the Iki-no-Kami of the Korean expedition, with whom Charlevoix seems to confuse him. The latter was Mōri Katsunobu, Lord of Kokura in Buzen (60,000 *koku*), who was stripped of his fief after Sekigahara in 1600 A.D.

battle in which Hideyoshi had broken the power of Shibata
and the others of his former fellow-captains who had presumed
to dispute the supremacy with him (1583). On his death-bed
the Taikō had charged Katagiri to "care well for Hideyori,
and to be prudent so as not to cause any breach between him
and Iyeyasu." On the death of Mayeda Toshiiye, in 1599,
Katagiri became Hideyori's personal guardian; and it is
generally supposed that it was as a recognition of the new
guardian's efforts to withhold Hideyori and Yodogimi from
supporting Ishida that his revenue was now more than doubled
by Iyeyasu.

After making these arrangements in Ōsaka, Iyeyasu removed
to Fushimi, where he had the castle rebuilt and occupied by
a permanent garrison much stronger than before. Thence,
after his appointment as Shōgun, he returned to Yedo towards
the end of 1603. Before doing so, however, he had taken
effectual measures to establish his power on a strong and
stable base in Kyōto, the capital of the Empire. Of course,
from Fushimi on the south and from Zeze on the north-east
he dominated the city by the garrisons in these fortresses.
But that was not enough; he needed a *pied-à-terre* in Kyōto
itself. On the site of that palace erected by Nobunaga for the
last Ashikaga Shōgun in 1569 he built the castle of Nijō in
1601; and Nijō henceforth continued to be the headquarters
of the Shoshidai, as the Tokugawa Governor of Kyōto was
called. The Shoshidai, we are told in the so-called Legacy
of Iyeyasu, "must be a Fudai and a General, because he is
the head of the executive in Kyōto and has the direction of
the thirty-three Western provinces." As a matter of fact,
the Shoshidai's chief duty was to act as a sort of jailer for
the Imperial Court and the Court nobles, and to restrain
them from all interference in the real administration of the
country. The Shoshidai's spies were soon everywhere in
Kyōto, especially in the Imperial Court, where, among other
offices, the Shōgun's vassals had to keep watch and ward at
the palace gates.

As the Japanese historian says: "It was the policy of
the Tokugawas to revere the Emperor very highly as far as
mere appearances went, but to make his Imperial Majesty's
influence as weak as possible." Yet the Sovereign and his

Court had their immediate position somewhat bettered by Iyeyasu. Hideyoshi had fixed the revenue of the Sovereign at 5,530 *ryō*, to be raised from the land-tax in Kyōto, while besides this an allowance of 8,800 *koku* of rice was assigned for the support of the Emperor's relatives and the Court nobles. After Sekigahara, Iyeyasu fixed the Imperial revenue at 39,000 *koku* in rice and 2,000 *ryō* in cash, and in addition to this 80,230 *koku* were appropriated for the support of the Princes of the Blood and of the Court nobles. This sum of 2,000 *ryō* and 119,230 *koku* of rice represented only some tithe of the resources devoted to the maintenance of the Court in the fifteenth century. And that, too, on the supposition that the rice then assigned was really obtainable. For in Japan assessment and actual revenue were often very far from being mutually convertible terms. In the remoter portions of the Empire—in Kyūshū, and still more so in Eastern and Northern Japan, where the surveys had been imperfect, where population was sparse and did not as yet press upon the limits of subsistence, and where new land was constantly being added to the acreage under cultivation—the actual annual returns of the fiefs were frequently much greater than the figures at which they stood rated in the official lists. But in the neighbourhood of Kyōto and in the Home Province it was quite otherwise. There there had been frequent surveys, and not even the smallest nook of land had escaped notice. Besides, population there was dense; and while the soil was not remarkable for natural fertility, it had been more or less exhausted by centuries of tillage. There, then, the actual yield was wont to fall seriously short of the assessed value. Even at Mina-kuchi, in Ōmi, where conditions were more favourable than they were immediately around Kyōto, a *samurai* with an official income of 100 *koku* had to be content with 79 *koku*. Now, it was the district in the immediate vicinity of the capital which had been charged with the payment in kind that had been assigned as a Civil List. At the best of times the returns would fall short; in years of drought or famine, or when visited by the not infrequent calamities of floods and earth-quakes, they would fall seriously short. In thus limiting the resources of the Court, Iyeyasu was simply acting in accordance with his general policy of trusting to the efficiency of material resources as a means of ensuring the stability of his power and of his own House. The old statesman ever evinced a profound distrust of wealth in other hands than his own, or in those of the members of his own family. While thus crippling the Court of Kyōto by assigning it the most modest of Civil Lists, he still further restrained its influence by the issue of some seventeen Articles for its regulation which must have been more than mortifying to the more intelligent and the more ambitious among the princes and *kugé* (Court nobles). At the same time, a systematic and sustained effort was made to induce the Emperor and all his *entourage* to devote their attention to poetry, music, and the fine arts and polite accomplishments generally—to anything, in fact, except to politics and the administration of the Empire. Such were the dispositions of Iyeyasu in Kyōto that the Imperial Court there was almost entirely isolated from all contact with the rest of the nation. As regards the great feudatories, all their comings and goings were noted by the Shoshidai and his subordinates, who made all access to the Emperor's presence almost impossible —all secret access to it entirely impossible. Accordingly the opportunity left the great feudal chiefs for intrigue in the old Western capital was exceedingly slight,—virtually there was none.

Nor was this all. While thus reducing the Imperial Court of Japan to an empty simulacrum, in his own Eastern capital of Yedo, now springing up with the rapidity of the mushroom, but with the vigour and vitality of the oak, he established and organised a Court which was to be no phantom, but a very substantial and a very formidable reality. The magnificence of the palace reared on the site of Ōta Dokwan's old stockade,—in lieu of the dilapidated structure that had made the worthy Honda Masanobu hold up his hands in horror in 1590—was in wonderful contrast with the modesty of the quarters then inhabited by the Emperor of Japan. Father Paez, the Jesuit Vice-Provincial, was conducted over it—or rather over them, for there were two palaces within the Yedo *enceinte*—in 1607. "The palaces were not less magnificent than those of the Coubo [at Shidzuoka,[2] where Paez had just seen Iyeyasu], and

2 Iyeyasu seems to have just taken up his quarters there. The date assigned by the Japanese for his retirement from Yedo to Shidzuoka is the seventh month of 1607. However, Paez had an interview with him in Shidzuoka late in May or early in June that very year.

decorated with an immense profusion of gold and of paintings by the hands of the greatest artists; the work of each of the panels, less than two Portuguese *palms* square, being valued at a bar of gold [*ōban*] or eight hundred cruzados [Cocks in his Diary puts the bar of gold (*ōban*) at a value of £13 10s.]; and those who had seen the Taikō's palace of the Jūraku in Kyōto did not think that it was in any way superior to those of the Shōgun. The principal Lords had also built sumptuous residences, and these immense and numerous edifices formed another city by the side of that inhabited by the merchants and the people." Two years later on (in 1609) Vivero, who had a most honourable reception from Hidetada, found "the palace of the Prince magnificent, and decorated with an extraordinary luxury. More than 20,000 people were employed there."

As early as the spring of 1603, the Daimyō of the Western provinces had come up to the new Court to pay their respects to Hidetada there—Iyeyasu being then still at Fushimi. In the following year, Tōdō, Daimyō of Imabaru in Iyo (whose revenue had been raised from 83,000 to 203,000 *koku* in consequence of Sekigahara), either in thankfulness for mercies received or prompted by that species of gratitude which consists in a lively sense of favours to come, proposed that every Daimyō should be called upon to establish a residence in Yedo. Daté Masamune supported the proposal, and it was adopted, as we can see from Father Paez's account. A little later on all the Daimyō—to whom Tōdō and Asano Nagamasa of Kishiu set the example in this respect—brought their wives and children to Yedo; and in 1608, Tōdō, unwearied and indefatigable in his subserviency, urged that the sons of the chief retainers of various Daimyō should be kept in Yedo as hostages. Tōdō's plan was again adopted, and in 1614 we find him established as Lord of Tsu in Ise (243,000 *koku*), with an increase of 40,000 *koku* in his assessment.[3]

It will thus become plain how it was that Vivero on his shipwreck at " Yubanda," ten leagues from Ōtaki in Kadzusa, received succour from the Prince of Satsuma! Satsuma, like

---

[3] It will be remembered that Hosokawa's son and Mayeda Toshinaga's mother (sent in 1599 or 1600) were the first hostages sent by independent Daimyō to Yedo.

the other great feudatories, had by this date (1609) built
himself a *yashiki* in the Tokugawa metropolis. And yet
Satsuma was the only great feudatory of which Iyeyasu had
really stood in dread after Sekigahara. A strong expedition
for the reduction of the great Southern principality had been
set on foot in 1601 (Arima and Ōmura were to take part
in it); but Iyeyasu had deemed it better to exhaust all the
means of conciliation before actually proceeding to extremities.
The result was that the young Prince, Shimadzu Tadatsune,
appeared at Fushimi in 1602, and was there received with
the greatest consideration by Iyeyasu, who, among other
marks of favour, bestowed upon him one character (*Iye*) of
his own name, Tadatsune thenceforth appearing in history as
" Iyehisa." From this time onward, to the death of Iyeyasu
at least, relations between the Houses of Tokugawa and of
Shimadzu continued to be friendly. The Lūchū Islands,
which were tributary to China, had also from 1451 A.D. sent
tribute to the Shōgun of Japan; but of late years the island
prince had neglected to perform this courtesy. Taking advantage of this circumstance, Iyehisa obtained permission
from Iyeyasu to send a punitive force of 3,000 men into
the little archipelago, whose capital was taken and the " King,"
Chang-ning, brought a prisoner to Japan.[4] The Lūchūs thence-
forward counted as a Satsuma appanage, with the result that
the assessed revenue of the clan was advanced from 605,800
to 729,500 *koku*. This conquest, apart from mere territorial
value, was a most important one. As has been repeatedly
stated, although the Japanese were eager for commercial
intercourse with the Middle Kingdom, no direct trade with
China was possible until the overthrow of the Ming dynasty
in 1643. But an active trade between China and the Lūchūs
was carried on, and thus the Satsuma conquest of the islands

---

[4] "In his captivity Chang-ning displayed a most noble character. His
conquerors, admiring his firmness, sent him back to his estates with honour at
the end of two years." "About the same time Iyeyasu endeavoured to establish
relations with Formosa, an island of great importance to navigation, situated
between Japan on the one side and Macao and China on the other. With
a view of acquiring a harbour of refuge there, Iyeyasu sent vessels with men
of intelligence to learn the language and to assure themselves of the disposition
of the inhabitants. But the Formosans maltreated the strangers and slew
several of them. The survivors returned to Japan, taking some natives with
them as prisoners. Iyeyasu had himself been informed of these events, but,
far from showing harshness to the prisoners, he supplied them abundantly
with everything, and sent them back to their country."

enabled the Japanese to establish indirect commercial relations with the continental empire. We shall find Iyeyasu doing all in his power to encourage the Satsumese in the prosecution of over-sea trade. Patents were issued to the English in Hirado, giving them access both to Satsuma and to the Lûchûs.

Doubtless one of the considerations that prompted Iyeyasu's very conciliatory attitude towards Satsuma was the fact that the great fief of Higo (520,000 *koku*) on its northern frontiers was held by Katō Kiyomasa, who was unfeignedly devoted to the interests and the fortunes of the House of Toyotomi. Kiyomasa, although he had not fought at Sekigahara, had yet espoused Iyeyasu's cause against Ishida; but it may shrewdly be suspected that in doing so he was influenced not so much by love for the Tokugawa as by hatred of his old rival and neighbour, Konishi of Udo, whose fief he now conquered and incorporated with his own. As Katō Kiyomasa's name was one to conjure with among Japanese *samurai*—many of whom were now *rōnin*, or lordless men—an alliance between him and the great Satsuma clan, reinforced as it might be by Tanaka (325,000 *koku*) of Chikugo, another devoted Toyotomi partisan, would have been a formidable matter. It is significant that it was not till Katō—whose death by poison Iyeyasu (on no sufficient evidence, however) is accused of having prompted—and most of the other great captains of the Taikō had passed away, that Iyeyasu ventured to provoke an open breach with Hideyori. Asano Nagamasa (65) and Katō Kiyomasa (53) both died in 1611; Ikeda Terumasa (50) and Asano Yukinaga (38) in 1613; and Mayeda Toshinaga in June or July 1614; while from 1611 Fukushima of Aki (498,200 *koku*) had been virtually a prisoner in Yedo.

It will now be well to devote our attention to the immediate relations of the Houses of Toyotomi and of Tokugawa. The marriage of Hideyori to Hidetada's daughter in 1603[5] was the third such alliance between the families, for Iyeyasu's last consort had been Hideyoshi's sister, while Hidetada's wife was a sister of Yodogimi, Hideyori's mother. Yet in spite of all this, Yodogimi was far from brooking with patience

---

[5] The missionaries say in September, 1602.

K K

the rapidly rising ascendency of her Tokugawa relatives. In
1605 she gave forcible expression to her real and innermost
feelings. In that year the aged Iyeyasu resigned the office
of Shōgun, and obtained the appointment for Hidetada (26)
in his stead. Of this event the missionaries, as summarised
both by Charlevoix and Pagés, have a good deal to say. The
latter writes:—

"Hidetada, with an army of 70,000 men, came to Fushimi,
the residence of his father; and a few days afterwards the latter
sent him to Kyōto to receive the title of Shōgun from the
Dairi. On this occasion there were magnificent *fêtes*. It
was wished to renew the ceremonial of the journey of a former
Shōgun, Yoritomo (1192–1199), when he proceeded from the
provinces of the Kwantō to Kyōto to receive investiture. At
the same time, Iyeyasu exerted himself to draw Hideyori out
of Ōsaka. He invited this young prince to visit the Shōgun
(Hidetada), who was his father-in-law. But Mandocorosama,
the mother of Hideyori, foresaw the danger, and saved her son
from it. She alleged excuses, and after various *pourparlers* she
ended by saying that she herself and her son (13) would disembowel themselves rather than quit the fortress. Iyeyasu was
greatly irritated; but he did not venture to have recourse to
force. However, the prince Hideyori from then found his influence
much weakened: but his father had acted in the same fashion
towards Nobunaga's heir, and he himself was undergoing the just
punishment for that."[6]

According to the Japanese account, Iyeyasu, through Oda
Yuraku, Yodogimi's uncle, intimated his wish that Hideyori
should come to Kyōto to congratulate Hidetada on his promotion. Yodogimi, however, positively refused to send Hideyori
to Kyōto, holding it to be a disgrace that the son of the great
Taikō should be obliged to congratulate an erstwhile subordinate on any promotion of his.

However, with lapse of time Tokugawa power and prestige
increased apace, and Yodogimi found herself constrained to
abase her pride and to dissemble her resentment. In the
eighth month of 1608, when the castle of Shidzuoka was
completed,—and again in the spring of the following year,
when Yoshinao, Iyeyasu's eighth son (then eight years of age),

<hr/>

6 M. Pagés here has not used his authorities as he might have done.
Yodogimi and Mandocorosama were different personages. The latter, called by
the writers of the Annual Letter "Kita Mandocoro, the best and most beloved
spouse of the Taikō," was his legitimate wife, *née* Sugihara. Kita-no-Mandokoro
was a title for the wife of the *Kwampaku* or of the Shōgun; Ōmandokoro, for
the mother of either one or the other of these dignitaries. Yodogimi's real
threat, as given in the letters wrongly summarised by M. Pagés, was that she
would "cut her son's belly with her own hand, rather than let him leave Ōsaka."

was invested with the fief of Owari,[7]—Hideyori dispatched (reluctantly, no doubt) congratulatory messengers; and from 1610 similar messengers were sent from Ōsaka to Shidzuoka every New Year.

Nor was this all. Under the year 1611 we meet with the following in M. Pagés:—

"Iyeyasu, at the head of an army of 60,000 or 70,000 men, had come from Suruga to Kyōto, and was followed thither by several princes with their troops. The old Prince sent to ask Hideyori to visit him, saying that he wished to see him again a last time before he (Iyeyasu) died. Hideyori, who still cherished a feeble hope of recovering the empire, based this hope upon the ramparts of Ōsaka; if he allowed himself to be enticed beyond them, he might lose his treasures and find himself at the mercy of the usurper. At first he excused himself; and, keenly pressed, he declared that he would kill himself rather than go out. However, in accordance with the counsels of his most devoted partisans, who foresaw a baneful issue if war should be declared, and who exerted themselves to guarantee the safety of the young prince, Hideyori betook himself to Kyōto. When he arrived near the capital he was met by two young sons of Iyeyasu. Iyeyasu received him with great honours, treated him on a footing of equality, and recalled at length the benefits which he himself had received from Taikōsama. Magnificent presents were then exchanged, and Hideyori returned to his fortress, to his own great joy, and still more to that of his mother. Iyeyasu charged his sons to return the visit in his own name. Peace then appeared to be assured for some time to come."

Siebold writes at much greater length of this incident, but his account is by no means so clear as that of the Japanese historians. According to them, Iyeyasu in the third month of 1611 went up to Kyōto and stayed in the castle of Nijō. Shortly after his arrival, through Oda Yuraku, the uncle of Yodogimi, he conveyed his desire to see Hideyori, and although Yodogimi was extremely reluctant to allow her son to quit Ōsaka, yet on the advice of Katō Kiyomasa and Asano Yukinaga, Hideyori repaired to Kyōto, escorted by Katagiri, Oda Yuraku, Ōno Harunaga, and several others of his own captains. Iyeyasu entrusted his sons Yoshinao (æt. 12) and Yorinobu (9) to the care of Katō and Asano as hostages, and through them welcomed Hideyori at the Tōji temple, whence on the following day he (Hideyori) was conducted to the castle of Nijō. Here a feast was given by Iyeyasu, and after a stay of some two hours Hideyori took leave of his grandfather-in-

---

[7] The former Lord, his brother Tadayoshi, Iyeyasu's fourth son, had died in 1607, æt. 27.

law; Katō Kiyomasa escorted him back to Ōsaka, and so the interview ended without any mishap. It proved, however, to be the last meeting between the two men. It is said *that at this interview Iyeyasu was greatly struck by the sagacity displayed by Hideyori!*

The last sentence is very significant; and in the light of subsequent developments it tends, if not to inspire the belief, at all events to raise a suspicion, that it was this interview (harmless as it was in its immediate results) that really sealed Hideyori's doom. Iyeyasu was then sixty-nine years of age, and so could not hope for many more years of life. His son and successor in the Shōgunate, though a man of solid parts enough, had nothing like his own ability as a statesman, while as a military man he had shown something very near akin to incapacity in the great campaign of 1600. Down to this point Iyeyasu may have continued to repose his trust for the safety of his own House on the imbecility and unworthiness of the representatives of the House of Toyotomi. Katagiri, Hideyori's guardian, had for years sedulously set on foot and propagated tales of the extreme effeminacy and stupidity of his ward. Accordingly, the Kyōto interview of 1611 may have furnished a very unpleasant surprise to Iyeyasu. A brilliant young chief with the potent Hideyoshi legend behind him might indeed in time easily raise a storm of war that might wreck the laboriously reared Tokugawa fabric of greatness. Therefore, Iyeyasu may have reasoned, this growing menace must be dealt with promptly and effectually!

Already, however, the old statesman, whose trust in money and material resources as political means was profound, had been occupied in a long and not unsuccessful effort to engage Hideyori and his Court in a lavish expenditure of the immense hoards of bullion and coin left by the Taikō. In 1602, through Katagiri, Iyeyasu represented to Yodogimi and Hideyori that the re-erection of the Daibutsu destroyed by the great earthquake of 1596 had been a cherished desire of the Taikō, and that now for the repose of his spirit the work ought to be again taken in hand. "By the labour of several hundred workmen and artisans a huge image was completed up to the neck, but as they were engaged in casting its head (January 15th, 1603) the scaffolding accidentally took fire, and all efforts to extinguish the flames, fanned by a gale then blowing, being ineffectual, they spread to the temple and rapidly reduced it to ashes." Nothing was then done until 1608, when the work was resumed under the superintendence of Katagiri. When Vivero visited Kyōto in the following year, he found 100,000 men at work on this "Daibu" temple, being erected in memory of "Taikōsama, whose soul is in hell to all eternity." The expenses of the image and its temple were extraordinary, and consumed a great amount of the gold bullion in the vaults of Ōsaka keep. Many of the Daimyō of the Western and Northern provinces sent contributions in rice to assist the work, but Iyeyasu, when privately invited to contribute, positively refused to do so. At the same time the old statesman had induced Hideyori and his mother to undertake the repair or the reconstruction of several other shrines and temples. "In fact," write the missionaries sadly, "Hideyori and his mother were erecting new temples every day, and were consuming excessive sums in processions and idolatrous *fêtes.*"

Yet withal, though all this did much to put Hideyori's hoard of bullion into circulation as duly minted coin, it by no means sufficed to reduce him to indigence. Kyōto was then the largest city in Japan—Vivero pronounced it to be the largest city in the world at the time—and most of its supplies and of its trade came through Ōsaka and Sakai, which both belonged to Hideyori. The wealth and the commerce of these two great towns were immense, and in case of need these would supply him with the sinews of war in abundance.

In 1612 the Daibutsu was completed, and all its immense expenses liquidated. The only thing that remained to be done before proceeding to the formal dedication of the temple and its idol was the casting of a bell. This task was begun in the fourth month of 1614. We are told that altogether 3,100 founders and workmen were engaged under the supervision of Katagiri, and that the copper used amounted to 19,000 *kwamme* (72 tons). The casting was successful; and a magnificent bell, more than 14 feet in height and over 63 tons in weight, stood ready to receive its inscription. This—the source of woe to the House of Toyotomi—was an elaborate Chinese composition from the pen of his reverence Seikan of

the Nanzenji, summarising the story of the erection of the
temple, and extolling the merits of the bell. Everything was
at last ready for the solemn dedication of the fane. Hideyori
had consulted Iyeyasu, and obtained his permission to superintend the function, while Hidetada had promised to honour the
occasion with his presence. So far all accounts are in harmony;
the exact details of the immediate sequel are variously related.
Sir Ernest Satow summarises the authorities on the matter
thus :—

"By the spring of 1614 both image and temple had been
successfully completed, and the population of the capital and
surrounding provinces flocked in crowds to witness the opening
ceremony. But the High Priests who, with the aid of a thousand
bonzes of inferior grade, were to perform the dedicatory service,
had hardly taken their places and commenced to repeat their liturgies
when two mounted messengers suddenly arrived from the Shōgun's
Resident (Itakura, the *Shoshidai*) with orders to interrupt the proceedings and forbid the consecration. The disorder that ensued among
the assemblage, balked of the sight for which many of them had
come a long distance, and ignorant of the cause of this unexpected
termination of their holiday, ended in a riot, which the police were
unable to repress, and the city is said to have been actually sacked
by the infuriated crowd of country people. It afterwards became
known that Iyeyasu had taken offence at the wording of the
inscription of the great bell, into which the characters forming
his name were introduced, by way of mockery as he pretended to
think, in the phrase *Kokka ankō*, 'May the State be peaceful and
prosperous' (*ka* and *kō* being the Chinese for *iye* and *yasu*); while
in another sentence which ran, 'On the east it welcomes the bright
moon, and on the west bids farewell to the setting sun,' he chose
to discover a comparison of himself to the lesser, and of Hideyori
to the greater luminary, from which he then inferred an intention
on the part of Hideyori to attempt his destruction."

Although this summary is substantially correct, it appears
that there is room for doubt as to whether the exact circumstances of the interposition of Iyeyasu's veto were really so
dramatic as here represented. It seems that Katagiri was
informed that the dedication ceremony must be abandoned
several days before the date appointed for it; and that he
then went to the *Shoshidai*, Itakura, and earnestly besought
him to appease the wrath of Iyeyasu, "so that the *fête* might
be celebrated on the appointed day." Hideyori, he pointed
out, was not responsible for the inscription; and he staked
his own life that after the dedication service had been duly
performed the inscription should be effaced. But it was all
to no purpose; and the *fête* had to be abandoned.

On September 16th, 1614, summoned by Iyeyasu, and also with instructions from Hideyori, Katagiri started for Shidzuoka to clear up the misunderstanding. Accompanied by Seikan, the author of the legend, he arrived at Mariko, near Shidzuoka, and from there sent notice to Honda Masazumi of the fact. Previous to this, Itakura in Kyōto had sought the opinions of the Abbots of five of the chief temples in the capital on the inscription. These dignitaries were jealous of the favour and regard Seikan received from Hideyori on account of his scholarship and skill in composition, and so, glad of an opportunity to injure him, four of them not only pronounced the sentence in question ill-omened, but asserted that several others also were more or less obnoxious. This criticism had been conveyed to Iyeyasu by Itakura's son; while at Shidzuoka, Hayashi Nobukatsu, a great Chinese scholar in the employ of Iyeyasu, also joined in the condemnation of the legend on the bell. In consequence of all this Iyeyasu showed more anger than before—anger intensified by the rumours that Hideyori was now enticing rōnin (lordless men) to Ōsaka in great numbers, and was making preparations for war. Already in April, 1614, Oda Yuraku, Yodogimi's uncle, and Omoshiri Shi had written to Mayeda of Kaga reminding him of the fact that Hideyori had come of age, telling him of the large stock of rice heaping up in the castle, and asking him to come to Ōsaka and contribute 1,000 koban for buying munitions of war; and Mayeda, instead of complying with the request, had forwarded the letter to Iyeyasu. It is probable, however, that this letter was sent to Mayeda without Hideyori's knowledge.

On September 23rd Katagiri was summoned from Mariko to Shidzuoka; and there Honda, according to orders, informed him of Iyeyasu's profound dissatisfaction with the inscription and also with Hideyori's suspicious behaviour. Katagiri was at the same time ordered to undertake the speedy effacement of the legend and the task of effecting a reconciliation between Hideyori and Iyeyasu.

Meanwhile Yodogimi, on hearing of Iyeyasu's resentment, had sent two of her Court ladies to Shidzuoka to express her sincere regrets. They were at once admitted into Iyeyasu's presence, and met with a very cordial reception. Iyeyasu asked them about the health of Yodogimi and of Hideyori, and went on to say that he regarded Hideyori, the husband of his grand-daughter, with as much affection as if he were his own son; that if Hideyori would only show his sincerity towards him, all the troubles would cease, and the two Houses of Tokugawa and Toyotomi would stand fast together; but that there were bad men about Hideyori, who instigated him to hostile acts against his wife's relations. "Therefore," continued Iyeyasu, "let Hideyori dismiss all bad men from his *entourage*, drive out all the *rōnin* [lordless men] who have congregated in Ōsaka, stop all preparations for war, and thus show his fidelity." All this was said in the kindest and most friendly tone; no reference was made to the offensive inscription on the bell whatsoever. The ladies before starting had studied this thoroughly and committed it to memory, and were ready with an elaborate apology for it. Great was their relief, however, to find that Iyeyasu made no mention of it, and still greater to find him so amicably disposed towards the House of Toyotomi.

Quite different, however, was the old statesman's attitude towards Katagiri. On October 10th, Honda was again sent to request the latter to bestir himself to devise measures for effecting a reconciliation between Iyeyasu and Hideyori. Katagiri excused himself as being unequal to the task, and asked Honda to indicate what measures he should adopt. Honda would not tell him anything about Iyeyasu's wishes officially; but privately he informed him that what he supposed Iyeyasu hinted at was the removal of Hideyori from Ōsaka to some other fief; and that it would be well for him (Katagiri) to act upon this supposition. Katagiri made answer that this was a most momentous affair, involving the most far-reaching consequences to the House of Toyotomi, and that he could only reply after due consultation with Hideyori in Ōsaka. Katagiri, after an illness that confined him to bed for several days, was finally dismissed from Shidzuoka without any personal interview with Iyeyasu.

Both he and Yodogimi's ladies left Shidzuoka on October 15th, but at different hours. Four days later both parties were in Tsuchiyama, a little town on the Tōkaidō in Ōmi, and the ladies here went to Katagiri's inn, and asked his opinion on the situation. Katagiri then told them that the demand of Iyeyasu was really a puzzle to him, but that he presumed Iyeyasu wished Hideyori's transfer from Ōsaka to another fief. To consent to such a transfer, he (Katagiri) ventured to think, involving the abandonment of the strongest castle in the whole empire, was the worst thing Hideyori could do; but, on the other hand, a refusal to accede to Iyeyasu's wish would make the rupture between them complete. Under these circumstances he believed the best thing to do was to send Yodogimi as a hostage to Yedo, and, failing that, that Hideyori and his consort should go there themselves. He added that if Yodogimi would consent to proceed to Yedo, he himself would put in train a plan which had been conceived by himself and the late Katō Kiyomasa some time before.

As the ladies had been so cordially treated by Iyeyasu, their suspicions were roused by this discourse of Katagiri, and, coming to the conclusion that he was simply endeavouring to promote his own selfish interests at the expense of their mistress, they at once hurried on to Ōsaka to put Yodogimi on her guard. They reported all the incidents of the journey, and said that it appeared to them that Katagiri was aiming at making Yodogimi Iyeyasu's wife, and that an understanding on the matter had already been arrived at between Katagiri and the prospective bridegroom. This assertion tried Yodogimi's pride severely. "Although I was only a secondary wife of the Taikō's," she broke forth angrily, "yet I am the mother of Hideyori and the niece of the great Oda Nobunaga. I will die with my son here in Ōsaka rather than go to Yedo and submit to such an ignominy. As for Katagiri, his punishment shall be death."

Ōno Harunaga was at once summoned. Now, Ōno was extremely jealous of Katagiri, whose revenue—he was now back in Ibaraki with 40,000 koku—had been more than once increased on Iyeyasu's recommendation, and who had contracted a marriage that attached him to two of Iyeyasu's prominent followers. Ōno really suspected Katagiri of treachery, and it would seem that he was far from standing alone in this matter, for the missionaries assure us that long before the rupture between the two Houses, "Iohi-no-cami," as they call Katagiri, had hopelessly sold himself to the "terrible old man" of

Shidzuoka. Ōno, therefore, strongly urged that Katagiri should at once be made away with, and open war declared against the Tokugawa.

Unaware of all this, a little later Katagiri arrived in Ōsaka, and made a full report to Hideyori, before whom he laid the three plans he had already disclosed to Yodogimi's two Court ladies. No decision was then taken, but three days later (October 26th) Katagiri, on being summoned by Yodogimi to the palace, did not go, inasmuch as he had learned that an ambush had been prepared for him there. Thereupon Ōno ordered the seven captains of the guards to fall upon Katagiri with their men; but as they all had perfect trust in Katagiri's good faith they refused to do so, and one of them, Hayami Morihisa, insisted upon getting Ōno and Katagiri to understand each other.

This episode is exceedingly interesting, for on Hayami's proceeding to Katagiri's quarters, the latter made a frank *exposé* of what was behind the plans he spoke of. His sole aim, he said, was to gain time. Iyeyasu's days were numbered—he was then seventy-three years of age—and it would be best for Hideyori, in attempting to recover his power, to wait until the old man had passed away, and left nothing more than a mediocrity to deal with. If Yodogimi would consent to go to Yedo, the site for her residence would be chosen on some difficult ground, which it would take long to prepare for the purpose, and her palace should be made as sumptuous as possible, so as, Penelope-web fashion, to gain time. Some years would thus be consumed; and then elaborate preparations for her journey would have to be made, and just as they were completed Yodogimi would in all certainty be taken seriously ill. Meanwhile Iyeyasu would most likely have been gathered to his fathers, Hideyori would be approaching the prime of manhood, and with his own great and brilliant abilities, supported by the legend of his sire, the greatest man Japan had ever seen, he would find it no hard task to make that stodgy plodder, his father-in-law Hidetada, bow his head before him. Continuing, Katagiri remarked that all this had been in his mind for years, that he had purposely circulated outrageously false rumours of Hideyori's effeminacy and stupidity, and that he had been bitterly disappointed to find that Yodogimi and Ōno had rewarded him for his pains by branding him as a fawner upon the favour of the Tokugawa. Iyeyasu had been surprised at Hideyori's sagacity at the Kyōto interview in 1611; and he (Katagiri) was perfectly assured that Iyeyasu's motive in raising all this commotion over the inscription on the bell was merely to devise a pretext to enable him to crush the House of Toyotomi before he died. Now that all his three plans had been rejected, he (Katagiri) was sure that Ōsaka would soon be invested by a Tokugawa army. It was indeed unfortunate that the House of Toyotomi had been driven to an open breach with its rival while Iyeyasu was still alive. So saying, Katagiri wept bitterly; and, thoroughly moved, Hayami bade him good-bye, also in tears.

Shortly afterwards one of Hideyori's immediate attendants called upon Katagiri and urged him to make a night attack upon the castle, kill Ōno and his associates, and then shape his actions according to the attitude displayed by the Tokugawa. To this Katagiri replied that it was his misfortune to be falsely accused of disloyalty, but that to kill his accusers would be to slight his Lord; and that he was prepared to kill himself after doing battle with Ōno and his supporters if they should come to attack him. The visitor then asked whether he was willing to give an earnest of his fidelity by sending a hostage to the castle. One of Katagiri's sons was at once sent into the citadel as such, while in turn Ōno and his confederate, Oda Yuraku, each sent a son to Katagiri in exchange. A little later, however, Katagiri's son was escorted back to him by Hayami, who, at the same time, brought orders from Hideyori for Katagiri to retire to his own fief of Ibaraki and there await further instructions. On November 2nd Katagiri accordingly left Ōsaka with five hundred of his own men, and escorted by Hideyori's seven- captains. At Matsubara in Kawachi they stopped to drink a farewell cup; Katagiri handed over Ōno's and Oda's sons to be returned to their fathers; and in tears the unfortunate guardian of Hideyori and his friends parted for ever. This withdrawal of Katagiri from Ōsaka effectually disposed of all prospects of peace.[8]

---

[8] Katsumoto Katagiri seems to have been a man of remarkable ability in an age singularly prolific in men of ability. Born in 1565, we find him

Down to this point, in spite of the compromising action of Oda Yuraku and others of his subordinates, it does not appear that Hideyori had been meditating any recourse to arms. In the beginning of June, 1614, there had been no possibility of selling the English gunpowder stored in Ōsaka, and the whole of it was sent back to Hirado. On October 27th (old style) Eaton, the English factor in Ōsaka, writes:— "There is great inquiry now for gunpowder, which would sell at a good price. I wish I had all you have at Hirado here." While English gunpowder fetched no more than ten *taels* per picul in March, 1614, by October as much as sixteen *taels* was being paid for an inferior Japanese article; and when Eaton found it advisable to make Hideyori a present of fifty catties of this Japanese gunpowder in December, its price had advanced to thirty-five *taels*. In June, 1614, when English gunpowder could find no market in Ōsaka, it was eagerly bought up at Shidzuoka, when Iyeyasu also purchased five pieces of English ordnance.[9] However, now in October Hideyori, in spite of the opposition of some of the Seven

acting as one of the three master-builders of Ōsaka castle in 1583—at the age of eighteen! A year later he immortalised himself as one of the Seven Spearmen of Shizugatake. Hideyoshi had such confidence in Katagiri that on his death-bed he sent for him and gave him special instructions to endeavour to keep Hideyori and his mother out of all difficulties or misunderstandings with Iyeyasu. From this time onwards Katagiri's position was an exceedingly delicate one, although down to the autumn of 1614 the influence he wielded over the adherents of the House of Toyotomi continued to be at once strong and salutary. The missionaries paint him in black colours, since to conciliate Iyeyasu he showed himself inclined to enforce the anti-Christian Edict of January, 1614, in the domains of Hideyori. But notwithstanding that the priests accuse him of treachery, it is probable that the statement of intentions he made to Hayami was perfectly correct. Yet we find his troops acting against Hideyori in the winter campaign, while we are also told that Katagiri was summoned by Iyeyasu to Ōsaka to work for peace, and that after a good deal of urging he did so, and was then frequently consulted by Iyeyasu. In the summer campaign of 1615 Katagiri was again in the Tokugawa camp in front of Ōsaka, and on that occasion spared no effort to save Hideyori and Yodogimi. Their death at the fall of the fortress was so keenly felt by him that he fell seriously ill. At this juncture he was summoned to Shidzuoka, whither he proceeded in spite of his illness. There, it is said, a few days after his arrival he arrayed himself in his robes of ceremony, burned incense, turned towards the West, saying, "It is my great regret that I have failed to accomplish the trust committed to me by my Lord; therefore I die by my own hand," and then calmly disembowelled himself (1615).

9 Four of these pieces were long cannons called "Culverines," weighing 4,000 pounds each and throwing shot of thirteen pounds. The other was a "Saker" (3,200 pounds), casting a twenty-three-pound projectile. Professor Riess writes:—"When afterwards Honda, Kōzuke-no-suke, gave an order for six English brass falcons of large calibre, Cocks informed him that the Factory thought of having its ordnance cast in Japan. But Honda answered that he would rather have one of those cast in England than ten of such as were ever cast in Japan." The cannons brought by the *Clove* and sold to Iyeyasu had evidently given satisfaction at the siege of Ōsaka.

THE GREAT ŌSAKA STRUGGLE.

Captains, resolved to throw down the gage of battle. Besides these Seven Captains, his chief counsellors at this time were Ōno Harunaga and his brother Harufusa, Oda Yuraku, and Kimura Shigenari. Among them no man was sufficiently pre-eminent over his fellows to command their obedience, and as in the case of the confederates of 1600, the Ōsaka faction was seriously hampered by having too many commanders of co-ordinate rank with no one supreme head over them. However, they agreed in the advisability of inviting to Ōsaka all those who had suffered by the rearrangement of the fiefs after Sekigahara. The number of *samurai* thrown on the world as penniless *rōnin* (lordless men) by the confiscations and appropriations of 1600–1602 had been immense, and now after fourteen years of obscurity and misery they all at once found an opening not merely for employment and preferment, but for revenge. The response of this class, with much to gain and nothing to lose, to Hideyori's invitation was at once large and prompt. Within a week a constant stream of *rōnin* was flowing in through the gates of Ōsaka castle, and within a month 90,000 determined men were either within its ramparts or garrisoning its outposts.

Among this host were some men of distinguished military ability. In addition to Chōsokabe, the ex-Daimyō of Tosa, who had been living in obscurity in Kyōto since he had been stripped of his domains, Hideyori was now joined by Sanada Yukimura, Gotō Mototsugu, and Akashi Morishige. The first was that Sanada who, together with his father, had conducted one of the three classic sieges of Japan when Hidetada was so hopelessly foiled at Uyeda in Shinano, thus seriously dislocating his father's strategy in the great Sekigahara campaign. At that time it will be remembered young Sanada's brother had espoused the Tokugawa cause, and had been rewarded with his father's fief, increased from 27,000 to 115,000 *koku*. This Sanada, who now joined Hideyori, had then been compelled to shave his head and retire to Kōya-san—the great monastic retreat for fallen feudal greatness—and from Kōya-san he now emerged to be the hero of yet another siege. To escape with his attendants from the monastery was difficult without horses; to get them he invited some hundred rich farmers from ten to thirty miles around to a banquet; they came—as he knew they would come—on horseback; Sanada plied them with strong drink; and when his guests had been overcome with it, he and his companions seized the steeds and made off at a gallop. In soldierly reputation Sanada was but little superior to Gotō, a veteran of the Korean campaigns, where he had been a tower of strength to his young master, Kuroda Nagamasa, the Cai-no-cami of the Jesuits. Like Kuroda at one time, this Gotō seems to have been a Christian, for the missionaries now curtly dismiss him as a "renegade." However, although complaisant towards his master Kuroda in the matter of religion, Gotō did not hesitate to quit his service when he began to display a lukewarm attitude towards that House of Toyotomi to which the Kurodas owed so much. As for Akashi, his career, fully outlined by the missionary writers, is very instructive. He was a cousin of Ukida Hideiye, the commander-in-chief in the first Korean campaign, one of the regents, and Daimyō of Bizen. In 1600 the missionaries tell us "in Bizen also there was a very edifying population. The Lord of the country (Ukida Hideiye) was a pagan, but his cousin, John Acachicamandono, who governed in his place, was a zealous Christian."[10] After Sekigahara, we learn that "Don John Acachimandono, a Christian Lord, cousin of the Prince of Bizen and administrator of his estates, occupied a fortress with 3,000 Christians. All perished or were exiled. The Prince himself, who appeared to be inclined to be converted, was killed in the battle."[11]—(1602.) "Most of the officers of Cai-no-cami (young Kuroda) were also Christians, and this prince furthermore admitted among his vassals the virtuous Don John Acachicamon and three hundred persons in his suite."[12] In Chikuzen Akashi had shown himself a vigorous propagandist. As such

---

10 What follows is also of interest. "In this province there were (1600 A.D.) two thousand baptisms; and, as in Chikugo, the conversion of those condemned to death was undertaken in order to save their souls, since, in accordance with the laws and customs, it was not possible to obtain pardon for these unfortunates."

11 This last statement, as already pointed out, is quite erroneous.

12 Regarding Sekigahara we are told:—"Acachicamon, one of the chief captains in the army of the regents, commanded the left advance-guard (!). He was fighting valiantly when treachery left him alone with a handful of men in the midst of the *mêlée*. In accordance with a point of Japanese honour, in order not to fall alive into the hands of the enemy, nothing remained for him but to disembowel himself, and fall by his own hands. But he was a Christian, and he resolved to throw himself into the heart of the fight, to be crushed by numbers. But he met face to face with Cai-no-cami, his old friend, who called to him to surrender and offered him quarter. Acachicamon surrendered to him. Cai-no-cami [young Kuroda] obtained his pardon from Daifousama [Iyeyasu]."

he has received his reward from the missionaries; for if we are to believe them, it was Akashi, and neither Sanada, nor Gōtō, nor Mōri Katsunobu, that was the hero of the great Ōsaka war.

In a council of war, presided over by Hideyori himself, it was resolved to act on the defensive merely and to await the enemy's attack in Ōsaka castle. This resolution had been strongly opposed by Sanada and Gotō, who had urged an immediate occupation of Oji on the Yamato road to block any Tokugawa advance by that route, while the main army should push on to Seta in Ōmi after reducing Fushimi and seizing upon Kyōto. The possession of the person of the Emperor would impart legality to their cause, and enable them, acting in his name, to put the Tokugawas to the ban as rebels, while it might also induce the Daimyō friendly to the House of Toyotomi to join the Ōsaka army with their levies. This last would have been a consideration of the utmost importance, for as things then stood Hideyori's summons to the feudatories had been attended with the most unfortunate results. Shimadzu, Daté, Mayeda, and Asano among the others turned a deaf ear to him; his letters were promptly dispatched by them to Iyeyasu, and in several cases his messengers were killed.

A comparison of the list of the Daimyō for this year of 1614 with that of 1600 is instructive. Before Sekigahara, including Iyeyasu himself, there had been two hundred and fourteen feudatories with assessments of 10,000 *koku* or over. Now there were one hundred and ninety-seven. After Sekigahara we found that the relatives or *Fudai* of Iyeyasu held some sixty fiefs in all. The number of these had now advanced to eighty-two. Besides that, of the one hundred and fifteen *Tozama*, or outside Daimyō, thirty-four were now the avowed friends and supporters of the House of Tokugawa, sixty-seven were neutral, and but fourteen sympathetic with Ōsaka. And as all these fourteen had hostages in Yedo, and as several of these fourteen fiefs had just fallen to minors, it is perhaps not so very strange after all to find that so far from making cause with Hideyori at this crisis, their troops actually (no doubt unwillingly) joined in the assault on Ōsaka castle.

Yet another reason for the non-response to Hideyori's summons was that even in this matter Iyeyasu had anticipated him. As early as the 7th of the ninth month (October 10th), *the very day on which Honda had been sent to Katagiri again to request him to devise some plan to effect a reconciliation between Iyeyasu and Hideyori,* the old man had demanded and received written professions of fidelity from Shimadzu, from Hosokawa, and from forty-eight other Daimyōs in the Western provinces! And only eleven days later, on October 21st, two days before Katagiri's reappearance in Ōsaka, when Ikeda of Bizen had on his way from Yedo called on Iyeyasu at Shidzuoka, he had been ordered to dispatch his troops to Amagasaki at once, and, together with the Lord of that castle, be prepared for emergencies—against Ōsaka, of course. Everything points to the conclusion that the "terrible old man" was resolutely bent on war.

On November 2nd, the very day on which Katagiri withdrew from Ōsaka, an urgent messenger from Itakura, the Shoshidai of Kyōto, arrived at Shidzuoka with intelligence of the latest developments at Hideyori's Court. On hearing of them Iyeyasu is said to have exclaimed, "Out of compassion I have again endeavoured to teach Hideyori wisdom. But as he is foolish enough to grow rooted in his wicked ambition, I must now remove him by force." Instructions were at once sent to Hidetada to mobilise the Yedo troops and to order all the Daimyō to dispatch contingents to occupy various points in an irregular curve some fifteen to thirty miles distant from Ōsaka, and ringing it round on the land side from Kishiwada in Idzumi on the south to Nishinomiya in Settsu on the west. Iyeyasu himself set out on the 11th and arrived in Kyōto on the 23rd of the tenth month (November 24th), his ninth son, Yoshinao of Owari, having marched in there two days before with 15,000 Nagoya troops. Here Iyeyasu remained waiting for the Yedo army and its auxiliaries under Hidetada.

As for Hidetada, on November 5th he had dismissed nearly all the Daimyō in Yedo to their fiefs to bring up their musters. However, Katō Yoshiaki, Kuroda, and Fukushima of Aki were not allowed to quit the Tokugawa capital. The latter especially lay under very strong suspicion—so strong, indeed, that Tadateru, Iyeyasu's sixth son, left behind as commandant in Yedo, had instructions to keep the closest watch on all his movements and to make away with him if he deemed it advisable to do so. As a matter of fact, although Aki levies under Fukushima's son joined in the assaults on the castle, yet a brother of his held a command among the besieged. It was not till the 23rd of the tenth month (November 24th)—the day of Iyeyasu's arrival in Kyōto—that Hidetada left Yedo with the main Tokugawa force of 50,000. Its departure had been preceded by that of Daté with 10,000, and of Uyesugi with 5,000 men on November 22nd, while Satake had followed with 1,500 troops on the 25th. The whole force was ·at Fushimi by the 10th of the following (eleventh) month (December 10th), by which date the Western Daimyō had already arrived and occupied the positions assigned to them on the irregular curve alluded to, which, however, had meanwhile been advanced much nearer to Ōsaka. In fact, there had already been skirmishes in Sakai and also to the west of the fortress. Some troops of Katagiri, dispatched to reinforce the Tokugawa men in Sakai, had there found the Ōsaka *rōnin* in possession, and had been cut to pieces nearly a month before (November 14th), while on the 6th of the eleventh month (December 6th) the Ikeda brothers, in command of 15,000 men advancing from the West, had driven in the Ōsaka outposts on the Kanzaki river and obtained possession of Nakajima,[13] the big rhomboidal island in the centre of which Umeda Railway Station is now situated.

To follow the course of the subsequent operations it will be necessary to devote some little attention to the troublesome subject of topography. Some distance above Ōsaka the Yodogawa, which drains the basin of Lake Biwa and of the whole plain between the mountains of Tamba and those of Yamato, sends off the Kanzaki branch to the right, and a little lower down the Nakatsu, which, after compassing two sides of the rhomboid of Nakajima, again partially rejoins the main stream as it enters the sea. Nowadays the delta formed by these various mouths is quite a considerable one, for since 1614 the land here, as in the Inland Sea generally, and indeed along the greater part of the Japanese coast, has

---

[13] There were four Ikedas—Ikeda Tadatsugu of Okayama, 445,000 *koku*; Ikeda Toshitaka of Himeji, 320,000 *koku*; Ikeda Nagayuki of Tottori (Inaba), 65,000 *koku*; and Ikeda Tadao of Sumoto in Awaji, 63,000 *koku*.

been gaining on the ocean. In the year in question the salt water was several miles nearer Ōsaka castle than it is to-day. Apart from this natural change in the topographical features of the neighbourhood, there has been an artificial one of some importance. Down to a date subsequent to 1615—to 1673, in fact—the Yamato river, which now falls into the sea near Sakai, ran in a curving sweep to the north of the castle and joined the Yodo just at the point where the Sotobori, or outer moat, nearly touched the stream. This outer moat and its ramparts no longer exist; the time and occasion of their destruction we shall have to deal with presently. Within this *enceinte* again, also within *its* own moat and defences, stood the innermost citadel, with the palace of the Taikō, perhaps the most magnificent building ever reared in Japan. It will be remembered that the castle had been built by Hideyoshi between 1583 and 1585, that it had—or rather the structures within its *enceinte*—been grievously wrecked by the great earthquake of 1596, and that it—or rather they—had been immediately repaired in order that the Chinese embassy then in Japan might be suitably received in solemn audience in due time.

With so much of a general preliminary explanation, and by reference to the accompanying map, the following extracts from the General Staff's account of the Ōsaka campaigns will be readily understood:—

"The castle of Ōsaka was in fact the strongest in the whole empire. The ramparts were one hundred and twenty feet in height, while the moats were both broad and deep. On the west it faced towards the sea beyond Semba; to the north ran the river Temma (a reach of the Yodo), beyond which in Nakajima was an extensive stretch of paddy-fields; while on the east flowed three streams—the Nekoma, the Hirano, and the Yamato. To the south of the castle there was an open expanse of level ground not intersected by any watercourse. Here, therefore, a moat was hastily excavated and connected with the Nekoma stream on the one hand and with the Ikutama canal on the other, and all along this line of defence a stone wall ten feet in height was built behind it. Outposts were also stationed at Yetazaki, Bakurogafuchi, Awaza, Yosaza, Noda, Yebiye, Kiyō, and elsewhere, while Sanada took up his station at Hiranoguchi, commanding the southern approach."

The Tokugawa troops—those of Hidetada and Iyeyasu—occupied the flat expanse to the south of the city, and along with them were the levies of Daté, of Tōdō, of Matsudaira of

Echizen, of Ii of Hikone, of Mayeda, and of some small Daimyō. For a week or two these forces remained inactive while the Western Daimyō were capturing the Ōsaka outposts at Yetazaki, Awaza, Yosaza, Bakurogafuchi, and elsewhere, a task that was accomplished only after severe fighting and heavy losses. By the 29th of the eleventh month (December 29th) the last of these outposts had been evacuated by the besieged, and immediately in front of the outer ditch of the castle, and between it and the sea, the troops of Mōri, of Nabeshima, of Hachisuka, and of six other Daimyō had established their quarters, while the opposite bank of the Temma reach, the spit between the Yodo and the Yamato, and the northern bank of the Hirano stream were also in the hands of Iyeyasu's allies. The occupation of the last of these positions had proved an expensive operation. At Imafuku on the further side, and at Shigino on the Ōsaka side of the Yamato river, the outworks were exceedingly strong, and in the desperate engagements of the 26th of the eleventh month (December 26th) at these places the levies of Uyesugi and of Satake were very roughly handled by Gotō and Kimura.

At the beginning of the twelfth month Iyeyasu advanced his own headquarters from Sumiyoshi to Ohausuyama, as did Hidetada his from Hirano to Okayama; and an assault was ordered upon the southern defences of the besieged. Here Sanada was in command. He had an outpost on Sasayama, but learning from his scouts that Mayeda's troops were to attack it before daylight on the 4th of the twelfth month (January 3rd, 1615), he ordered the knoll to be evacuated, and a division of Mayeda's men seized it with a shout of triumph. This put the second Mayeda division on their mettle, and, hurrying on in the darkness, they stumbled on to the front of Sanada's position. The latter's officers urged him to sally out and fall upon this enemy, but "Sanada calmly sat against a post and appeared to be asleep." At daylight he ordered a soldier to mount the wall and to inquire of Mayeda's men what success they had in their hunting at Sasayama, ironically saying that it was to be feared that the game had all been scared away. "If you have any leisure, come on and fall upon us; we have a few country-made arrows for you." This insult had the result expected; Mayeda's troops

tried to scale the wall, and Sanada's men simply laid them
in swathes with their sustained and accurate matchlock fire.
The third division came up, only to be decimated in similar
fashion, and another general attack on Sanada's position
later on in the morning proved equally disastrous to the
assailants. Nor was this by any means the worst of it. While
Mayeda's last assault was being delivered, the troops of Ii and
of Matsudaira Tadayoshi, another Fudai Daimyō, had surprised
the Ōsaka men under Ishikawa at the gate of Hachomeguchi,
had got over the ramparts, and were pushing forward into the
enceinte when they were met by Kimura with 8,000 men,
whose matchlock fire broke them utterly. Very few of them
made good their retreat. And then the besieged assumed
the offensive to dire purpose. They sallied out upon the
stations of Terasawa and Matsukura, drove the troops there
pell-mell into the large Echizen camp, and worked terrible
havoc in it. "The battle began before dawn, and raged for
seven or eight hours. It was a decided victory for the Ōsaka
troops, who sustained very little loss, while the assailants
suffered most severely. At three o'clock in the afternoon the
besiegers withdrew with the greatest difficulty."

On the following day—January 4th—on account of an
intestine quarrel among Oda Nagayori's troops at Tanimachi-
guchi, Tōdō's command had all but entered the castle itself
when Chōsokabe appeared and beat them off after a stubborn
contest. "After this the besiegers attempted no more assaults,
but remained in their respective positions, which were quite
close to the castle moats. The Ōsaka troops poured a deadly
hail of bullets into them daily, and their casualties were
exceedingly heavy. But although the assailants also replied
with an incessant fire, it was very ineffective, the enemy being
under the shelter of a strong wall. In this way the prospect
of the capture of the castle seemed to be very remote."

The simple fact of the matter was that so long as the
defenders were united the castle was impregnable. It was
amply provisioned—200,000 *koku* of rice had been taken
from the junks moored in the river just before the siege
began, and this was only a fraction of the supplies stored
up in the granaries. The garrison of 90,000 men, commanded by some of the ablest military men in Japan and

composed of *rōnin* only too glad to have an opportunity of service, standing as it did behind the strongest ramparts in the empire, had no reason to fear all the forces Iyeyasu had brought against it. At the outside these footed up to no more than 180,000 men, and of these, if we are to believe the missionaries, some 35,000 had been put *hors de combat* before the beginning of 1615. It had already appeared that there was but scant prospect of carrying the fortress by assault; and Iyeyasu had now given strict orders that "no imprudent attack should be made, and whenever such was attempted and failed he manifested the strongest displeasure." Yet, withal, time was of much more consequence to the besieger than to the besieged. The Daimyō supposed to be really friendly to the House of Toyotomi were now among the besiegers of Ōsaka merely because they had been cowed by the belief that the Tokugawa might was invincible. The events of the last month had done much to show that this belief might very well stand in need of revision. Should there be any defection on the part of his most powerful allies—and a prolongation of the check just experienced might very easily lead to that— Iyeyasu's position would become a difficult one. In truth, at this crisis the fortunes of the House of Tokugawa stood in greater jeopardy than they did on the eve of Sekigahara.

Of this Iyeyasu himself was no doubt perfectly well aware. But to speak in a fashion sadly inconsistent with that most revered figment, the dignity of history, soldiership was merely one item in the old statesman's plethoric bag of tricks. In front of the impregnable keep of Ōsaka, held by 90,000 of the most fearless and the most desperate swashbucklers in Japan, soldiership even of the best had proved useless to advance his ends. Therefore the "terrible old man" was untiring in his efforts to attain his purpose by bribery and diplomacy. As regards the use of the former device—bribery—Iyeyasu at one moment stood on the threshold of success. A certain Nanjō Tadashige who held a subordinate command in the castle had sold himself for a very moderate price and had agreed to admit the Tokugawa troops into the stronghold, when his treachery was discovered, and his life paid for his dirty work. Iyeyasu then tried to seduce—Sanada, of all men! The proffered guerdon of the expected treachery in this case was to be a handsome one. Shinano was one of the broadest of all the six-and-sixty provinces of Japan, and the whole of this magnificent domain was offered to Sanada in fee if he would betray his trust. The gallant Sanada rejected the overture with scorn and indignation, and promptly published the incident in the castle.

Baffled in this respect, Iyeyasu now put forth all his strength and cunning to lure the impregnable besieged into peace negotiations. Even before the siege had been a fortnight old he had been making overtures in this direction, and on the 20th of the eleventh month (December 20th) he had sent a Kyōto merchant, Gotō Mitsutsugu, into the castle with a letter to Ōno and Oda Yuraku urging them to induce Hideyori to come to an arrangement with him. However, no reply had been returned to this missive, nor to those that were sent in on the following day and on subsequent occasions. At last, on the 8th of the twelfth month (January 7th, 1615), a reply was returned to one of the letters, and four days later on Ōno and Oda actually—like the fools or traitors they were—sent messengers to Iyeyasu to discuss terms of accommodation with him! Iyeyasu then offered a free pardon to all the Ōsaka troops, and the provinces of Kadzusa and Awa to Hideyori as a new fief. Hideyori, however, insisted on obtaining two provinces in the island of Shikoku, and this demand seemed likely to cause the rupture of the negotiations. Accordingly Iyeyasu (January 13th, 1615) sent to Kyōto for his chief lady-attendant, Ochanotsubone, who was intimate with Jōkōin (the Maria Kiogocou of the Jesuits), the younger sister of Yodogimi, intending in this way to establish his influence over Hideyori's mother. At the same time he set to work to bring Yodogimi to a frame of mind that would facilitate the task of her younger sister, the Christian "Maria Kiogocou," as a peacemaker. On January 15th he made the best gunners in his camp train a few pieces of ordnance upon the tower in the castle where Yodogimi's quarters were, and after some little practice they succeeded in dropping a shot—in all likelihood a thirteen-pounder from one of four long "culverines" brought out from England by the *Clove* and purchased through Adams some six months before this—in the ladies' apartments, killing two of Yodogimi's maids-of-honour there. Iyeyasu would appear to have taken the measure of Yodogimi's real moral temperament very accurately. In spite of all her pride and haughtiness, and all her proneness to indulge in fiery and heroic speeches, at bottom she was merely a vain and cowardly woman with a very fine solicitude for the safety of her own well-favoured and delicately-nurtured person. Now, to ensure that safety at present all she had to do was to remove from her luxurious rooms in the palace to some casemate where the "culverines" could make not the slightest impression. But her terror was so abject that she at once sent for Ōno and Oda, and implored them to urge Hideyori to make peace without delay. The son was of a sterner mould than the mother, however, and told her emissaries that he meant to make the castle his tomb, if need be. Just at this juncture Gotō, Sanada, Chōsokabe, and others appeared, and laughed the peace proposal to scorn. Then when they withdrew Ōno said to Hideyori that these captains wanted war, because after the conclusion of peace they would starve, and that they had no thought of Hideyori's real interests whatever. On this Hideyori sent requesting them to express their opinions in full. Gotō said that all this talk about peace was merely the result of discord among the people in the castle; that if they kept firmly united, they could laugh at all the efforts of the enemy, even if he brought a million men against the stronghold. They wanted a real commander-in-chief, however. Let Sanada be appointed such. Oda Yuraku (we shall see him desert later on), on hearing of this, said that peace could not be concluded merely because Hideyori was too careful of the interests of his new generals. To this remark Sanada made answer that if such was really the case he had no objection to a speedy conclusion of peace, and that he and his fellows would quit the castle. They had fought against the Tokugawa, and the honour of having done so would amply compensate them for the sacrifice of their lives; at the same time he was very suspicious of all this peace-talk, and trusted that they were not allowing themselves to be deceived by the cunning old man. Ōno and Oda then went to Hideyori and informed him that Sanada and the others were in favour of a temporary peace, for

Iyeyasu, being old, would die, and then the power would fall into his (Hideyori's) hands. "Why," exclaimed Hideyori angrily, "this is exactly what Katagiri proposed to me! Sanada, Gotō, and their fellows would never urge such a thing! No more of this!" Ōno and Oda, thus repulsed, went off to Yodogimi, and advised her to see her son and personally to beg him to listen to Iyeyasu's overtures. But she met with no success, in spite of all her tears.

On January 17th Iyeyasu sent Honda Masazumi—Kōdzuke-no-suke (or "Codskindono," as Cocks calls him)—with Ochanotsubone to the camp of Kyōgoku Tadataka (the son of Jōkōin, and hence the nephew of Yodogimi), whither Jōkōin, Yodogimi's younger sister, also repaired from the castle.[14] On meeting Ochanotsubone there, Jōkōin (Maria Kiogocou) was informed that Iyeyasu really bore no ill-will against Hideyori, that he was really very anxious to spare him, but that Hidetada was obstinately bent on capturing the castle, and that for that purpose he had collected thousands of miners who at that very moment were busily driving tunnels beneath the moats. Ochanotsubone asked Jōkōin to look at this work on her way back, to tell Yodogimi of what she had seen, and to urge her to make peace speedily. At the same time Honda said that Iyeyasu was minded to allow Hideyori to retain Ōsaka castle with an undiminished revenue; that if he removed from the castle his revenue would be increased; that all the captains and soldiers who had espoused his side would be free either to stay in the castle or to leave it; but that Iyeyasu would need some hostages as a token of good faith. Honda further told her *privately* that as Iyeyasu's great military reputation would be impaired if he were to withdraw his troops without some plausible excuse, "Hideyori ought, just for the sake of politeness towards him, to destroy the outermost defences of the castle and thus furnish a memento of the campaign"!

Jōkōin's (Maria Kiogocou's) report of all this—especially

---

[14] Among the hundred and twenty-one Daimyō of more than 20,000 *koku* at this time there were seven Hondas. This Honda Masazumi, Kodzuke-no-suke ("Codskindono"), held the fief of Koyama (33,000 *koku*) in Shimosa, and (as were five of the other six) was a Fudai of the Tokugawa. Kyōgoku Tadataka was a Tozama, Daimyō of Obama (92,000 *koku*) in Wakasa. It has been already mentioned in a footnote that the missionaries claim him as a Christian. Jōkōin, his mother, is the Maria Kiogocou of the Jesuits. She was confirmed by the Vice-Provincial Paez during his visit to Hideyori's Court in 1607.

of the driving of mines under the castle—increased Yodogimi's terror and frantic eagerness for peace. That very day she got Ōno, Oda, and the seven captains of the guard to approve of the conclusion of peace, and on January 18th information of this was sent to Honda. Thereupon he and Ochanotsubone again met Jōkōin in Kyōgoku's camp, when Jōkōin submitted terms which were accepted by Iyeyasu, who, however, casually added that as the war was now over the surrounding outermost moat was useless, and that therefore it should be filled up by his troops. On returning to the castle Jōkōin clearly mentioned this matter to Yodogimi, but the latter was so overjoyed at the conclusion of peace that she paid no heed to it. On the following day Ōno and Oda delivered their sons as hostages to Iyeyasu, and Hideyori sent Kimura to Chausuyama to receive Iyeyasu's agreement. The document, sealed with blood from the tip of Iyeyasu's finger,[15] ran as follows:— "That the rōnin in the castle should not be held responsible; that Hideyori's revenue should remain as of old; that Yodogimi should not be asked to live in Yedo; that if Hideyori should choose to leave Ōsaka he might select any province for his fief; that his person should be held inviolable." Hidetada also signed the document.

On the 22nd (January 21st) Iyeyasu got a solemn undertaking from Hideyori and Yodogimi to the effect that "Hideyori should not entertain ambitious designs or raise rebellion against Iyeyasu and Hidetada; that Hideyori should directly consult Iyeyasu's will to the neglect of all intermediate (or other) counsellors; and that everything should be carried on as before."

That very evening it was proposed in Ōsaka to make a sudden general night attack upon the Tokugawa camp, but after due consideration the proposal was negatived. On the following day, or at all events shortly afterwards, most of

15 Mr. Masujima writes:—"The word keppan means 'blood stamp,' because it was a mark impressed by pressing the wound made in the fore-part of the finger under the signature, so as to leave a blot of blood over it. A document confirmed by the keppan was considered to be of the most sacred character, and the violation of any words or promise made by this evidence was believed to draw down divine vengeance on the offender. It was generally used in such public documents as treaties of peace, oaths of fealty, etc. This method of confirmation was resorted to much more rarely than was the kaki-han, or 'written stamp,' as the occasions for which it was required must necessarily have been very few, even in the old ages of violence."

the Tozama levies in the Tokugawa camp were ordered to withdraw, while Shimadzu of Satsuma and various other Kyūshū Daimyō, who meanwhile had arrived at Hyōgo by sea, were requested to return.

As for Iyeyasu himself, he left for Kyōto on the 25th of the twelfth month (January 24th), and after a week's stay there he set out for the East. Hidetada remained in his quarters superintending the filling up of the moat and the demolition of the outermost rampart—a task that had been assigned to various Fudai Daimyō, among them being two of the Hondas, Tadamasa and Yasunori to wit. This work was commenced on January 22nd, 1615, the very morning after the ratification of the peace conditions, and was pushed on with the greatest energy. In a few days not only had all the outside ramparts with their moats almost entirely disappeared, but even a portion of the moat of the inner citadel had been filled in. Ōno at once remonstrated with the commissioners about this, but they merely informed him that they were simply carrying out Iyeyasu's orders, and urged the labourers to greater exertions. Ōno then sent an indignant message to Honda Masazumi (Codskindono), who had taken an important part in the peace negotiations and was thoroughly conversant with the exact conditions agreed upon. This Honda blamed the commissioners for misunderstanding their orders, and personally appeared upon the scene to stop the work on the inner moat. As soon as he had turned his back, however—which he no doubt did with the Japanese equivalent for a wink—the work was resumed as vigorously as before. Enraged at this, Yodogimi sent Ōno and one of her maids-of-honour to Kyōto to remonstrate with yet another of the seven Hondas—Honda Masanobu (Codskindono's father) about this outrageous yet serious farce. To this farce, however, Ōno and his colleague ultimately found Masanobu to be a party. This Honda said that his son Honda Masazumi was foolish in having "miscarried" Iyeyasu's order to the commissioners (two of whom were also Hondas, be it remembered), and that he would speak to him about it; but that, as he was sorry to say, at present he himself had a bad cold; as soon as he was better he would see his Lord. Dissatisfied with this, the Ōsaka embassy of assorted sexes then went to Itakura, the *Shoshidai*, or Shōgun's representative in Kyōto, and spoke to him in pretty strong terms. All the satisfaction they got from this source was to be told that "as Masanobu would soon recover, they had better wait a little longer"!

While this comedy was being carried on in Kyōto, the work of filling in the inner moat in Ōsaka was being carried on with the utmost vigour, and was rapidly nearing its completion. In course of time the reports of Honda Masanobu and of Itakura reached Iyeyasu, and he replied that Ōno and his female colleague should first return to Ōsaka, and that Honda Masanobu would then be sent there to see to the matter. Masanobu, on appearing there, played his part with all the seriousness of an ancient Roman augur or the gravity of the most impudent modern quack-doctor. His surprise at the stupidity of Masazumi was simply overwhelming. "Masazumi has really been so foolish as to do such a careless thing! But it is now too late for regrets. To dig up this inner moat would take ten times the labour that has been so idiotically employed in filling it up. But as peace is now established, there is really, if one comes to think over it, no necessity for having the moat. Therefore be good enough to pardon us"! There-upon the inner moat was completely filled in, and on that very day, the 19th of the first month (February 16th), 1615, Hidetada left Ōsaka and went to Fushimi. The work of demolition had thus gone on for twenty-six days.[16]

Of course it becomes tolerably evident that Iyeyasu looked upon the peace just concluded as merely a means to an end. His immediate object in concluding it was clearly to effect the demolition of the outer citadels and the filling in of the moats of Ōsaka castle. These two points were not mentioned in the documents exchanged between him and Hideyori at all, and Iyeyasu had verbally referred to them so lightly that the Ōsaka men, considering them to be matters of trifling import, had been completely and out-rageously hoodwinked. Naturally their resentment was keen; but the thing had been accomplished, and it is but ill work

---

16 In one dispatch from Hidetada to Iyeyasu apprising him of the progress of the work it is stated that the moat of the outer citadel was 240 feet wide and 36 feet deep, while the depth of the water in it varied from 12 to 24 feet.

girding against accomplished facts—and Iyeyasu, like the Russians of these days, had mastered that item of political philosophy long before he had attained the span of three-score years and a dozen. The way to a decisive success was now comparatively open to the Tokugawa whenever it became advisable to re-open hostilities with the House of Toyotomi. All that now was necessary was merely—a pretext.

This pretext was readily found. Hidetada had returned to Yedo on the 14th of the second month (March 13th) of 1615, and about this time Hideyori once more set to work to allure *rōnin* to Ōsaka. Now, in Ōsaka, one of the most trusted men was a certain Obata Kagenori, who had formerly been a retainer of Iyeyasu's. He had been dismissed from his service for some trickery or other, and he was now trying to return to his former position by the exercise of that gift of his for chicane that had brought about his discharge. In Ōsaka he was acting as a Tokugawa spy, and everything that was done there he at once reported to the Kyōto *Shoshidai*, Itakura, who in turn at once reported it to Iyeyasu and Hidetada. These reports proved sufficient to furnish the Toku-gawa with an excuse to act; and Iyeyasu thereupon sent an order to Hideyori to remove from Ōsaka to another fief—where situated is not chronicled.

On the 4th day of the fourth month (May 3rd) of 1615 the old man left Shidzuoka, ostensibly to attend the marriage of his ninth son, Yoshinao (*œt.* 15), at Nagoya, but in reality to proceed westwards to deal with Ōsaka—this time finally, drastically, and effectually. The old man reached Nagoya on May 9th, was present at the marriage ceremony on the 11th, and on the following day (12th) was visited by the traitor, Oda Yuraku (who had had to flee from Ōsaka shortly before), and was informed by him that there were factions in Ōsaka castle; that besides, Yodogimi often interfered; and that the councils of war there continually held con-stantly ended in—nothing.

Five days after this Iyeyasu had arrived at the castle of Nijō in Kyōto, where the Daimyō were already assembling with their contingents, and where Hidetada appeared with the bulk of the Eastern levies about the 21st or 22nd of the fourth month (20th or 21st May). As early as the middle of the preceding

month Itakura, the *Shoshidai*, had sent an urgent message to
Iyeyasu informing him that in consequence of disquieting
rumours to the effect that the Ōsaka *rōnin* were to advance
upon Kyōto and burn it, the citizens were seeking safety in a
panic-stricken flight. The missionaries, however, allege that
this disquieting · rumour had been set on foot by Tokugawa
officers in accordance with instructions from Iyeyasu. It should
also be · mentioned that on the 10th of the fourth month
(May 9th), while in Nagoya, the old man had thence dispatched
Jōkōin and Ochanotsubone to Ōsaka to say that the hostile
activity of Hideyori and of his mother was likely to prove
injurious to the interests of the House of Toyotomi, that Hideyori
should withdraw to Koriyama in Yamato, disbanding all the
rōnin he had assembled, that Iyeyasu would then repair the
castle of Ōsaka, and that after the lapse of seven years Hideyori
would be restored to it. Again at this very moment, when
Iyeyasu was prepared once more to launch all the forces of the
empire against Ōsaka, he sent the two ladies to urge Hideyori to
adopt the course suggested, and so to avoid hostilities and his
own ruin. Of course the old statesman was perfectly well
aware that after the trick of the filling-up of the moat just
.practised upon them the Ōsaka men would not be likely to
trust even his smoothest professions; and so on the 25th of the
fourth month (May 24th) he gave orders for some 35,000 men
to advance on Ōsaka from Yamato, while 121,000 men were
to threaten it from Kawachi. In this second siege of Ōsaka—
the "summer campaign" of 1615, as the Japanese call it—the
missionaries tell us that as many as 260,000 or 270,000
Tokugawa troops were engaged. Although this is nearly four
times the number of Iyeyasu's men at Sekigahara, and much
more than twice the total of the *actual* combatants there, yet
it may be doubted whether the missionaries are guilty of any
very extraordinary exaggeration. The 156,000 men we have
alluded to came from Northern, Eastern, and Central Japan
exclusively, and in addition to these there may very well have
been another 60,000· men from Shikoku, Kyūshū, Kishiu, and
the west of the main ·island.

As regards the numbers on Hideyori's side on this·
occasion the various statements differ widely. One missionary
authority puts the total of the host within the fortress at

190,000, another at 170,000, while Father Apollinario told Cocks that at the fall of the castle the defenders amounted to more than 120,000 men! [17] The statement of the Japanese Army General Staff's compilation is as follows:—" By the middle of the third month (of 1615) many thousands of *rōnin* (lordless men) flocked to the castle. The entire number was declared to be 150,000, but about 60,000 appears to have been the total. They were divided under the command of the following general officers: Ōno Harunaga, Ōno Harufusa, Ōno Doken, Kimura, Sanada, Mōri Katsunaga, Chōsokabe, Gotō, Akashi [Don John Acachicamon of the Jesuits], and the seven captains of the bodyguard." If to these 60,000 *rōnin* (lordless men) we add the household troops of Hideyori the total might very well have reached the neighbourhood of the 120,000 men Apollinario puts it at.

Of this second siege Charlevoix, Pagés, and Siebold have all given accounts which in their essentials are not seriously at variance with those of the best Japanese authorities. The narratives of Charlevoix and Pagés are based entirely upon Morejon's *Historia y Relacion de lo sucedidos en los Reinos de Japon y China* and the letters of the missionaries, six of whom were in the castle at the time of its fall.[18] Some of the details furnished by the five foreign priests who escaped are significant. " Besides Acachicamon and his command numerous

[17] "June 7th, 1615.—After dyner came a Franciskan frire called Padre Appolonario, whom I had seen 2 or 3 tymes in Firando heretofore. He was in the fortress of Osekey when it was taken, and yet had the good happ to escape. He tould me he brought nothing away with hym but the cluthes on his back, the action was soe sudden; and that he marvelled that a force of above 120,000 men (such as was that of Fidaia Samme [Hideyori]) should be so sowne overthrowne. He desired me for God's sake to geve hym something to eate, for that he had passed much misery in the space of fifteen daies, since he had departed out of the fortres of Osekey. So after he had eaten, I gave hym fifteen mas [9d.] in plate; and soe departed."—*Diary of Richard Cocks*. The entry here is according to old style. The final assault on and capture of Osaka took place on June 3rd according to the Gregorian calendar; hence Apollinario had plenty of time to reach Hirado.

[18] "At the first rumours of war Father Hernando de Saint Joseph, an Augustin, had traversed 400 miles in a fishing-boat, together with Father Pedro Baptista, to shut himself up in the camp of Hideyori. Father Apollinario Franco, also a Franciscan, shared their apostleship. During the assault on Osaka Fathers Saint Joseph and Franco found themselves on a hill, and seeing the city in ashes, they escaped through conflagration, swords, and waves, as Father Saint Joseph himself writes." Of the three other missionaries, the Japanese Father Francisco, the son of the apostate Tōan, Deputy-Governor of Nagasaki, was killed in the assault. At that moment the other two—Fathers de Torres and Porro—were in the house of Don John Acachicamon (Akashi Morishige) and had most miraculous escapes.

Christian exiles from the Home Provinces and fiefs of the North—among these latter being the former vassals of Don Justin Ucondono—had rallied to Hideyori's standard. Six great banners bore as devices, together with the Holy Cross, the images of the Saviour and of St. James—the patron Saint of Spain—while some of them even had as a legend, 'The Great Protector of Spain.'" It must not be forgotten that more than a year before this date all foreign *religieux* had been ordered to quit Japan, and that in the previous November they were all supposed to have been deported. The presence of these law-breakers, as Iyeyasu might with reason regard them to be, in the camp of the enemy might well serve to sharpen the resentment of the Tokugawa authorities against Christianity and its professors.

On this occasion Hideyori's prospects were much less satisfactory than they had been in the December of the previous year. The filling-in of the moats and the demolition of the outer ramparts had robbed the great stronghold of its impregnability. It is true that time was found to re-excavate portions of the middle moat, to raise parapets, and to fortify all the approaches to the castle. But withal, the Ōsaka leaders felt they could not repose much trust in these hastily constructed defences.

Besides this there was the greatest unrest in the castle, excited by the suspicion of the presence of traitors in the camp. The defection and flight of Oda Yuraku have already been alluded to; his desertion had been preceded by that of Oda Nagayori. Then a few nights later on (May 8th), an attempt on Ōno Harunaga's life was made. The would-be assassin, according to some Japanese authorities, was a retainer of one Narita, who was a vassal of Ōno Harunaga's brother, Harufusa, who, the same authorities allege, was highly displeased with Harunaga's weak and vacillating measures. " Narita, on being summoned to furnish an explanation of his subordinate's attempt, set fire to his house and killed himself. Men began to suspect each other, and the state of things in the castle was anything but composed."[19]

---

[19] The missionaries accuse Iyeyasu of having instigated this crime. "The culprit, being put to the torture, did not disclose who had armed him; but the common voice accused the Kubo [Iyeyasu]. Later on no doubts of this were entertained, and stern justice was done upon several other assassins paid by the enemy."

In this "summer campaign" of 1615 the Ōsaka men resolved to assume the offensive. On the 26th of the fourth month (May 28th) 2,000 troops under Ōno Harufusa made a rapid advance into Yamato, burning Kōriya, Hōriuji, Tatsuta, and several other places, and threatening the town of Nara. Driven back from here, Ōno Harufusa, on May 28th, again sallied out of Ōsaka, this time with 3,000 men, to check Asano, Daimyō of Kishiu, who was advancing from Wakayama with 5,000 troops to join the Eastern army. In the course of this expedition Sakai was fired and burned to the ground by Ōno Doken, in command of Harufusa's rear-guard.

So far all this was merely preliminary skirmishing. But on the 6th of the following (fifth) month (June 1st) there was really serious fighting at Dōmyōji in Kawachi, some twelve miles from Ōsaka, and at Yao and Wakaye, about half that distance to the south of the castle. To Dōmyōji the Ōsaka men proposed to throw forward 18,400 men to block the Tokugawa advance from Nara in the passes there. The advance-guard of 6,400 men—or, at all events, 2,800 of them under Gotō—did reach the defiles in time, but they proved altogether insufficient to hold them against the vastly superior numbers of the Easterners. The main body of 12,000 men under Sanada, which was to march by a different and difficult route, had been delayed by a dense fog, and when it did arrive it was too late to retrieve the situation, for Gotō had fallen and his command had been cut to pieces.[20] Sanada, however, managed to fight a stubborn and indecisive action with Daté's troops (who were in the Tokugawa van), and to withdraw safely as evening fell. This much he could not have effected but for the misbehaviour of one of the Tokugawa commanders. Matsudaira Tadateru, Iyeyasu's sixth son, in command of the fifth division, had arrived at Katayama early in the afternoon, after a forced march from Nara, which he had left that morning. At Katayama he was urged by some of his officers to pursue Sanada's retreat, but he obstinately refused to do so—a refusal that subsequently cost him dear.

Meanwhile at Yao and Wakaye the fighting had been

20 Just before the battle it is said he had been offered the whole province of Harima if he would carry his troops over to Iyeyasu's side.

equally hot. Here Chōsokabe and Kimura, with 10,000 Ōsaka troops, threw themselves in the way of the advance of the Easterners under Tōdō and Ii. After an engagement of several hours, in which the Ōsaka men lost some six hundred, together with their leader Kimura, they broke, and in the retreat—or the flight—they lost nearly three hundred more.[21]

Although thus baffled in their attempts to check the Tokugawa advance at Dōmyōji and at Yao, the Ōsaka leaders were by no means minded to give up the struggle in the open as hopeless, and to throw their trust upon the imperfectly reconstructed defences of the castle. In a council of war held on the evening of June 2nd, 1615, it was resolved to fight a great battle on the following day on the open ground to the south of the fortress. As this, apart from the Shimabara affair of 1638, was really what Sekigahara is usually mistakenly pronounced to be—the last great battle fought on Japanese soil for two centuries and a half—it may be well to sketch its salient points of interest in some detail.[22] In doing so,

---

[21] In mediæval Japanese battles in the open the percentage of casualties does not appear to have been extraordinarily high. Here the Ōsaka men lost nine per cent. merely, for all the wounded that fell into the hands of the enemy would have their heads promptly struck off, and so counted among the killed. This goes to account for the high rates of killed to wounded in the casualty returns of the battles of those days. Another factor to be taken into account is that prisoners were rarely or ever made in those times. To avoid capture, where flight was impossible, the defeated had recourse to *hara-kiri*. In this battle of Yao, Tōdō lost three hundred killed in his command of 5,000 and Ii one hundred in his of 3,200. And yet in connection with the great battle of the following day—June 3rd—we are told:—"*Tōdō having declined to lead the van on account of the great loss (six per cent. of dead) he had sustained on the previous day*, Mayeda (of Kaga) was put in his place with orders to march on Okayamaguchi, while Honda Tadatomo, *relieving Ii* (less than three per cent. of dead on the previous day), was to advance on Tennōjiguchi." In Sanada's drawn battle with Daté on June 2nd at Dōmyōji, out of 12,000 Ōsaka troops only one hundred and eighty were killed and two hundred and thirty wounded—a casualty percentage of between three and four! A siege, of course, was a very different matter from a battle in the open. Here it was frequently extermination for the vanquished side, and in that case the casualties were apt to be a good deal more than heavy—as they were at Tredah in Ireland in 1649. At Sekigahara—often quoted as the decisive battle in Japanese history—they were comparatively moderate, as we have already seen. In this connection it is but just that the painstaking accuracy of the work of the Japanese Army General Staff should be acknowledged. The Japanese military authorities in the Chinese war of 1894-95, and in the campaign of 1900, have made a point of abstaining from all exaggeration in the important matter of figures, as well as in other respects. And their publications on the campaign of Sekigahara and of Ōsaka, compiled for the instruction of their own officers and not in any way to appeal for foreign admiration—a failing conspicuous among those Japanese whose notion of patriotism is merely the lusty banging of the tribal tom-tom—must be admitted to be remarkable for the strenuous and indefatigable efforts of their authors to arrive at the sober truth.

[22] In the siege of Hara castle, in the so-called Shimabara Rebellion, between 120,000 and 150,000 men are said to have been involved. In 1865-66 and 1867-68, although the fighting was stubborn enough, the contending forces were numerically insignificant. The Satsuma Rebellion of 1877, although a much more

the *Nihon Senshi's* account will chiefly be followed, and in order to understand the narrative the reader is respectfully requested to study the accompanying map very carefully.

The great battle of June 3rd, 1615, began at noon, and at that hour the respective positions of the opposing forces were as given in the accompanying plan. The wide expanse of open·ground to the south of the castle, between the Hirano stream on the east and the sea on the west, was the scene of the strife. The Tokugawa advance was from the south. The extreme right front was formed of Mayeda's 15,000 men, supported by the retainers of Katagiri and of Honda Yasunori. In the centre Akita, Asano Nagashige (a Fudai Daimyō— not the great Asano from Wakayama), Honda Tadatomo, and Sanada Nobuyuki (the brother of Sanada, the Ōsaka commander) were in the van, and behind them were 15,000 Echizen levies under Matsudaira Tadanao (Iyeyasu's grandson), and about half as many under various smaller Daimyō. On the left, next the sea, Daté led the column, and Matsudaira Tadateru, Iyeyasu's sixth son, with Mizuno and Murakami, were behind him. Still further to the rear in this direction, and quite close to the sea, was Asano from Wakayama with 5,000 troops. (An unexpected movement on the part of these latter at a critical moment of the battle was to threaten Iyeyasu with something like disaster.) As for Iyeyasu and Hidetada, they both crossed the Hirano stream at the same point, but while Hidetada's division, led by Tōdō, Hosokawa, and Ii, advanced to the support of Mayeda on the right wing, Iyeyasu pushed on to act as a reserve for the centre.

As regards the Ōsaka men, whose numerical inferiority— they now amounted to only 54,000 according to the *Nihon Senshi*—was serious, they had thrown the bulk of their troops forward beyond Tennōji to oppose the Tokugawa centre. Here Sanada and Mōri Katsunaga held command. Behind these, at various distances, reserves were posted, while Ōno took up his position immediately in front of the eastern extremity of the outside castle rampart and not far from the Hirano

---

business-like affair, involved at the outside only 100,000 combatants, and at Tawarasaka, the greatest of all its engagements, no more than 40,000 men on both sides were engaged. Even in the Korean and North China campaign of 1894-95 the Japanese had never more than 80,000 troops in the field, of whom they lost a little over 3,000 men.

brook. It had been arranged that while Sanada and his fellow commanders barred the Tokugawa advance, Akashi, with a strong body of troops, was to push round from Semba through the city lanes, get upon the rear of the enemy, and assail him from that quarter, and at the same time Chōsokabe with some flying columns was to watch keenly for any opportunity for an unexpected flank attack that might offer. Until Akashi had accomplished his purpose, and until his rear attack had thrown the Easterners into confusion, the Ōsaka main body at Tennōji was, if possible, to remain inactive. Then when the confusion was at its height Hideyori was to sally out with his household troops and push matters home.

However, these dispositions were not carried out. Akashi was discovered and checked before he had emerged from the lanes, and the impetuosity of the *rōnin* in Mōri Katsunaga's command in front of Tennōji precipitated the general engagement. Mōri's men at once opened a deadly small-arm fire upon the Tokugawas, and when ordered to desist both by Sanada and by their own leader they only redoubled their fire. Seeing this, Mōri thought it as well to take full advantage of the ardour of his troops, and, dividing his command into two columns, threw them forward on the huge Tokugawa centre. Here Akita, Asano Nagashige, Sanada Nobuyuki, and Honda were at once broken, while the troops of the smaller Daimyō on the Echizen right were beaten tempestuously back. As regards the big Echizen division of 15,000 men, it was meanwhile staggering under the onset of Sanada's own command. The latter, seeing that all his plans were likely to be ruined by the impetuosity of Mōri's men, sent his son Sanada Yukitsuna to the castle to urge Hideyori to sally out with his troops at once, and then he himself fell upon the Echizen men. As these were beginning to give way, Iyeyasu came up behind them, and would likely have steadied them at once but for a most unexpected development. Just at this moment Asano of Wakayama, with his 5,000 men, came up from the extreme left-rear, swung round the Echizen left flank, and marched forward on Imamiya. This movement was strange, not to say suspicious; it looked like desertion. A cry of treason was raised, and a serious panic ensued in the Tokugawa centre, many of the Echizen men and the broken minor bodies rushing pell-mell into the ranks of Iyeyasu's body-guards. Even when the latter, clearing themselves from the confusion, came into action the situation was highly critical. However, sheer force of numbers prevailed, and the death of the gallant Sanada, who fell just at this moment, was the signal for the retreat of his men that survived. Thus relieved, the Echizen division, as well as Iyeyasu's guards, were enabled to throw themselves upon Mōri's wild-cat *rōnin*, who, after bearing down everything directly in front of them, had been meanwhile assailed on their left flank by the troops of Ii and Tōdō, who had pushed across from the van of Hidetada's column. The result was that the Tokugawa centre, thus reinforced by Ii and Tōdō, had by 2 P.M. been able to hurl their opponents back into the castle. Here Akashi, foiled in his attempt to get upon the Tokugawa rear; was able to make vigorous head against them for a time; but again weight of numbers told, and while Akashi and the remnants of Sanada's and Mōri's commands were still bearing up against Echizen (now supported by Daté and the left Tokugawa wing generally), Midzuno, a small Fudai Daimyō (Kariya, Mikawa, 30,000 *koku*), who had been in the rear of the Tokugawa centre, pushed on to the front, traversed the third castle *enceinte*, and then the second, and actually planted his flag at the Sakura gate, the southern approach to the innermost citadel of the fortress.

While all this was going on in the Tokugawa centre and on the left (which scarcely at all came into action), the Tokugawa right had been exceedingly roughly handled. Here it will be remembered Mayeda, with 15,000 men, was in the van, and behind him came Hidetada's big division, minus Ii and Tōdō, dispatched to deal with Mōri's wild-cat *rōnin*. At one time the Ōsaka men, who, like the rebels in the Shimabara affair of 1638, seem to have relied greatly upon fire-arms, were on the point of making short work of the Tokugawa right. Mayeda's 15,000 men, supported even by Hidetada's own still larger command, were so fiercely received by the troops of the Ōnos (Harunaga and Dōken) and of Naitō that Hidetada seems to have all but lost his head. However, after overthrowing Mōri's wild-cats, Ii's troops came back in time to deliver a flank attack that relieved the situation, and by 3 P.M. the Tokugawa right had been enabled to drive their opponents back into the fortress. By this time, also, Ikeda, who, it ought to have been said, had come up by sea and had seized upon Nakanoshima, was pressing upon the castle from the Temma reach of the river Yodo, while the two Kyōgoku and Ishikawa, who had marched by a circuitous route from the main Tokugawa army in the previous evening, were threatening it from the north-east.

From this account it will be readily apparent that apart from the non-appearance of Akashi and his command on the Tokugawa rear, there had been a serious dislocation in the arrangements projected by the Ōsaka leaders. At the critical point of the struggle in the open it had been arranged that Hideyori was to sally forth from the castle at the head of the Household troops and complete the havoc already worked by the *rōnin* among the Tokugawa. If this part of Sanada's plan—Sanada, it may be said, was responsible for the strategy, or rather for the tactics, in this great fight—had been executed, Akashi's failure and Mōri Katsunaga's precipitate impetuosity and the fortunes of the day might very well have been retrieved. But even when summoned by Yukitsuna, Sanada's son, Hideyori failed to appear on the field. Rumours of treachery in the castle were afloat; as soon as Hideyori left it, it was to be fired by traitors. Accordingly, Hideyori did not move, or at all events went no further than the gate; and his hesitation enabled both the Tokugawa centre and the Tokugawa right to recover from the panic and confusion, and by sheer weight of numbers to hurl the Ōsaka *rōnin* back upon their base. According to the *Nihon Senshi*, "Hideyori, when he received intelligence of the defeat of his *rōnin*, said, ᵗDeath is what I have been ready to meet for long,' and was about to sally from the castle in order to fight his very last battle when he was stopped by Hayami, one of his seven captains, who urged that a commander-in-chief should not expose his person among the promiscuous dead. Let Hideyori defend the castle to the last; when it fell, it would then be time to take a decision"! Shortly after this, Ōsumi, Hideyori's chief cook(!), turned traitor and set his kitchen on fire. The strong wind then blowing fanned the flames and carried the sparks far and wide, and soon the conflagration became unmanageable. In the midst of the confusion thus occasioned the assailants at the gates redoubled their efforts and made good their entrance into the second *enceinte*. By 5 P.M. the whole of the fortifications within this circuit were in their hands. Many of Hideyori's officers now had recourse to *hara-kiri*, while two of the Ōnos (Harufusa and Dōken) had recourse to flight. Hideyori, accompanied by his wife and by Yodogimi, took refuge in the donjon of the innermost citadel, intending to put an end to himself there, but Hayami again interposed and conducted the party to a fire-proof storehouse in Ashida-guruwa. Thence Ōno Harunaga dispatched Hideyori's wife to her father (Hidetada) and to her grandfather (Iyeyasu) to beg them to spare her husband's life and that of Yodogimi. "All this while the main citadel was burning, and the survivors of the Ōsaka troops were either killed or committed suicide or fled."

On the morning of June 4th Hideyori, in his fire-proof refuge, not receiving any favourable reply from Iyeyasu, and being fired on by the troops of Ii and of Andō, concluded that there was no intention to spare him, and so committed suicide, while Yodogimi was killed by one of his retainers. At the same time Hayami and the thirty men and women who had accompanied Hideyori into his place of refuge set fire to the building, disembowelled themselves, and perished in the flames. "And so fell Ōsaka castle, and so was the House of Toyotomi destroyed." [23]

---

[23] Such is the gist of the account of this all-important episode in the history of the Houses of Tokugawa and of Toyotomi—and even of Japan—given by painstaking Japanese experts after a collation of all available documents. That it is correct in every detail cannot for a moment be expected. Even in these days of ours, when readiness with the pen is exceedingly common, and when every army is followed by a crowd of war correspondents, it is by no means easy to arrive at the truth, the whole truth, and nothing but the truth in connection with engagements of much smaller magnitude than the five hours' fighting in front of and in Ōsaka castle on the afternoon of June 3rd, 1615. And in those days writers in Japan were by no means so plentiful as they are now. The documents dealing with the struggle of 1614–15 must leave many matters of moment in it untouched, while—a consideration that is now and then apt to be forgotten—the mere circumstance of a statement being committed to paper is no absolute guarantee either of its absolute accuracy or even of its general truthfulness. Three centuries ago falsehoods not infrequently got set down in black on white, just as they occasionally do to-day. Yet, withal, the preceding narrative seems to be fairly accurate in its general outlines at least.

Siebold, who follows and summarises the commonly current Japanese accounts, makes one or two interesting assertions. He says, among other things, that just when the Tokugawa troops were reeling (under Mōri Katsunaga's and Sanada's desperate onset) Iyeyasu sent the son of Ōno Harunaga, whom he held as a hostage, with a letter to his father, saying, "Do not let Hideyori leave the castle. In the castle is a conspiracy, and as soon as he leaves it he will be attacked from the rear," and that it was Ōno Harunaga who, on a perusal of this missive (and not Hayami as stated in the text) stopped Hideyori's exit at the head of his guards. Almost at the same time Iyeyasu sent an offer of peace to Yodogimi, and Yodogimi at once summoned Hideyori, Ōno Harunaga, and several of the officers stationed in front of the castle (near the Hirano stream) to consider the matter. Their retreat (with their standards) into the castle for this purpose alarmed the Ōsaka van, then making vigorous head in the open. Fancying there had been a revolt in the castle, these Ōsaka men gave way and rushed in headlong through the gates, closely followed by the enemy, who disposed of some 15,000 of them in this débâcle. (From the missionaries' accounts—Porro's and de Torres's—it seems tolerably plain that such a débâcle did take place, and that the fortunes of the day were practically decided by the incident.) When Hideyori's wife reached her father, Hidetada, the latter indignantly asked, "Why don't you die with your husband?" Iyeyasu, on the contrary, declared himself ready to protect Hideyori and Yodogimi, "bearing in mind the benefits he had received from the Taikō." On the following day Ii, "who had been detailed to guard Hideyori in his retreat," exceeded his instructions and fired upon the storehouse where Hideyori had taken refuge. After the death of Hideyori and Yodogimi, Ii reported the circumstances to Iyeyasu, "requesting to be punished for his arbitrary action. Iyeyasu merely nodded." (A few weeks later on Ii's revenue at Hikone, in Ōmi, was raised from 180,000 to 230,000 koku, and still later on, in 1617, to 280,000 koku.)

As has been said, Charlevoix's and Pagés' narratives are based entirely upon missionary accounts. Ureman, who wrote the "Annual Letter" of 1615, of course had Porro's and de Torres' statements before him. Both these (Jesuits) have left long letters dealing with the event. It is to be remembered, however, that they were too busily occupied in effecting their own escape to have been able to devote attention to the immediate fortunes of Hideyori. About some features in their reports more will be said in a subsequent chapter. Here, as much as a curiosity as anything else, we reproduce M. Pagés' narrative:—

"Iyeyasu's army of 300,000 men was the most numerous and the best disciplined ever seen in Japan. [As a matter of fact, after the battle many of Iyeyasu's troops had to be punished either for cowardice or for misconduct!] Hideyori's army, less numerous but equally warlike, had been waiting for two days, drawn up in fine order and ready for the battle. The general mélée took place on June 9th [really June 3rd], and after bloody vicissitudes Iyeyasu's military science assured him of the victory. The generals of Hideyori, notably Acachicamon [Akashi Morishige], had done prodigies, and on four occasions the Shōgun's corps d'armée had been broken. The Shōgun [Hidetada], who wished to flee, had been restrained by his officers [!]. [The truth seems to be that Hidetada—who, although no genius, was no coward—was restrained by Kuroda and Katō and others from heading his troops and fighting sword in hand when they were reeling under the onset of Ōno Harunaga, Ōno Dōken, and Naitō.] Iyeyasu himself—and this fact seems to be fully established—for some time despaired of victory, and was on the point of opening his bowels when an imprudence of his adversaries, from which he knew how to profit, re-established and determined fortune in his favour. Wonochouri [Ōno Harunaga], commander of Hideyori's principal corps, and also his standard-bearer, desired that his master, who had remained in the fortress, should sally out to reap the honours of victory or to perish with glory. A movement of retreat, effected by this general in order to protect the exit of the Prince (Hideyori), had the appearance of flight, and terror seized upon the whole army. Iyeyasu perceived the turn of fortune, and from that moment he was master of the battle. Less than an hour [!] had sufficed to decide the issue between two such formidable armies. Hideyori's troops on all sides took to flight, and the victors penetrated into the town [what M. Pagés means is the castle; the town was defenceless and counted for nothing], massacring without mercy, sacking and burning everywhere. After two hours of carnage, Iyeyasu, fearing a desperate rally on the part of the vanquished, gave orders to leave an open passage in the direction of Kyōto. Some, principally the chiefs, sought safety by this way, but the great part of the soldiers perished isolately, and the road was literally covered with their corpses. In this war, between the two factions ~100,000 men perished. [At Sekigahara 15,000 men at the outside.] Hideyori apparently perished in the town [castle] by an unknown death in the midst of the general massacre. The end of this prince, buried in the shade, was also the end of the infinite hopes of Taikōsama, by a just chastisement for his impious pride. [Hoity-toity!] But to complete this huge disaster, and to consummate the justice of God [!], the city of Osaca, so dear to Taikōsama, whose imperial residence it had been, was to cease to exist; the inhabitants by their crimes had really provoked the divine vengeance [!]. Some of Hideyori's partisans, shutting themselves up in the citadel, fired the powder-magazines and caused the conflagration of the whole city. The wind multiplied and fanned the flames. This city of palaces and of temples—as did Sakai—disappeared in the space of a night, and presented nothing but ruins, half-burned corpses, and here and there stray fugitives covered with wounds and aimlessly wandering. Thus fell this Babylon, slave to its idols, which refused the light divine. Since an abominable bonze, author of the impious doctrine of the Icocbus [i.e. one of the Monto sect, the Protestants among Japanese Buddhists, and at the present day by far the greatest religious force in Japan], had made of it the headquarters of his sect, and there had himself worshipped as an incarnation of Amida, the torrent of superstitions had completely infected it [What about the miraculous crosses of Kori in Hizen, and of Higo in 1618?], and the Christian truth offered to its inhabitants had left them voluntarily blind, amidst darkness, tous les jours plus épaisses [!]. The Osaka war had caused, as we have said, the death of 100,000 men, and, according to the accounts of trustworthy witnesses, the field of battle disappeared covered with dead; the heaped-up corpses in the river there formed a dyke which could be crossed dry-shod.

"Iyeyasu returned to Suruga (Shidzuoka) towards the end of July and ordered the era or nengo, which had lasted nearly twenty years and which bore the name of Keicho, to be changed and called Genna. Become undisputed master of the empire, and the possessor of the treasures of Hideyori, the old man was not yet satiated; it remained for him to consummate his revenge. He gave orders for all his surviving adversaries to be conducted into his presence. His decrees were obeyed; and all who could be discovered were seized and conducted to his feet; troops of men were dragged to the capital in order to be dispatched before the eyes of this prince; even such an excess of horror was seen as that a child of seven years, a natural son of Hideyori's, was infamously promenaded in the principal streets of Kyōto and beheaded in Iyeyasu's presence. And it is reported that at this last moment this fearless child dared to reproach Iyeyasu with his treason towards Taikōsama and Hideyori, and boldly presented his throat to the executioner. Iyeyasu caused the heads to be exposed on planks reared along the highway between Kyōto and Fushimi; there were eighteen rows of three planks, and on certain rows more than a thousand heads were counted. Iyeyasu issued orders for the immediate rebuilding of the cities of Sakai and of Osaka. [Thus, as a punishment for their rejection of "Religion," they were not to disappear from the face of the earth after all! And from 1615 onwards they were certainly more flourishing and much less Christian than they had been before. It is to be feared that M. Pagès, in the fervency of his zeal for Christianity, has penned not a few paragraphs that afford the enemy only too good reason not so much to revile as to smile.] At the same time, and to disconcert the Lords and to render them impotent, he issued orders that all fortresses should be rased, with the exception of a single residence for each of the princes; four hundred citadels disappeared in a few days. Finally he stripped Catzousadono [Matsudaira Tadateru, Kadzusa-no-suke, Daimyō of Takata in Echigo, 480,000 koku] of his principality, made him shave his head, and shut himself up in a monastery of the bonzes [in Kōya-san].

"Then only the terrible old man believed that he had made sure of his empire and had reaped the fruits of his statecraft. He went to seek repose in his residence at Suruga; the Shōgun, his son, always resided at Yedo. If one considers, says an author, the results of this war from the point of view of religion, one cannot regret that Hideyori did not have the advantage by reason of his unbridled superstition. In reality this prince and his mother were daily erecting new temples and consuming enormous sums in processions and in idolatrous rites. Hideyori reposed all his hopes on his false gods, and allowed himself to be directed by their oracles; soon undoubtedly, on the advice of the bonzes, he would have sacrificed the Christian religion, its ministers, and its confessors. [In connection with this it is curious to find that the English and Dutch write that if Hideyori had been victorious the Spanish and Portuguese priests would have been re-established in Japan, and that they, the northern heretics, would assuredly have been expelled. Also on page 298 of M. Pagès' very own book, we read: "All the (Christian) inhabitants (of Nagasaki) desired the triumph of Hideyori by reason of his promises"!   M. Pagés for the moment seems to have forgotten about the numerous Christians in Hideyori's army. And in view of his sequent paragraphs his tacit adoption of the foregoing assertion is strange.]   Thus it may be said generally that Hideyori had fought for the cult of the idols much more than for the empire [a few pages before the author accuses Hideyori's adversary, Iyeyasu, of superstition], and Iyeyasu often repeated that Taikōsama, the God of Battles, had protected his son badly ! [In the matter of Buddhism, or of non-Christianity, M. Pagés seems to think any stick is good enough to beat a dog with. But what would the Founder of the Christian religion himself have said to this sort of thing?   Justice, if not the basis of all morality, is certainly by far the most important item in morality.   And when we come to Religion, are we to sacrifice the most important part of morality ?]   Thus were the idols of the sects discredited.   An infinite number of temples were annihilated.   In Ōsaka alone a complete street of magnificent temples was reduced to ashes; in Sakai and its suburbs were over-thrown two hundred temples, among which were three of the most ancient and the most famous in the empire; the Tennōji, which counted a thousand years of existence and was the first monument of the cult of the Hotokes [a mistake, by the way]; the Tenjin, dedicated to the tutelary *Kami* of Hideyori; finally the Sumiyoshi, built ninety years before.   All these edifices were destroyed by John Acachicamon, one of Hideyori's generals."

Acachicamon—Akashi Morishige—is the Christian commander to whom M. Pagés elsewhere in various passages assigns such an extravagant importance. Both the Jesuit priests were in his house at the moment of the final assault in the castle. Akashi, in sober truth, seems to have been a good and an able soldier.   But then good and able soldiers were tolerably common in the Japan of those days.   The mere fact of his having destroyed the Tennōji and the temples of Tenjin and of Sumiyoshi would seem sufficient to give M. Pagés a high idea of his merits.   But vandalism of this sort can have done little to attract the favourable regard of the bulk of Akashi's compatriots, who, whatever may have been their faults, did not as a rule carry bigotry to such outrageously aggressive lengths.   Can we wonder at the Tokugawa administra-tion if it regarded the propagation of Christianity as inconsistent with the domestic peace of the country when its votaries made a merit of wrecking and burning the religious edifices of those of their fellow-subjects who refused to adopt their cult?

Charlevoix, by the way, in connection with one reported incident in this great struggle, writes in a fashion that excites surprise.   Iyeyasu, he says, was stated to have charged some of his immediate attendants to kill him in case his troops gave way in the final shock, and on this ground he accuses Iyeyasu of—cowardice!   Iyeyasu was then seventy-three years of age; he was then fighting his ninetieth battle, and already before this in his long career he had stood in imminent jeopardy of his life on eighteen occasions!   The accusation of cowardice on his part at this late time of day is, all things considered, simply ludicrous.

CHAPTER XVIII.

THE TOKUGAWA ADMINISTRATIVE MACHINE.

DEALING with the battle of Sekigahara (1600 A.D.) an American historian writes as follows:—

"By this battle was decided the condition of Japan for over two centuries, the extinction of the claims of the line of Nobunaga and Hideyoshi, the settlement of the Tokugawa family in hereditary succession to the Shōgunate, the fate of Christianity, the isolation of Japan from the world, the fixing into permanency of the dual system and of feudalism, the glory and greatness of Yedo, and peace in Japan for two hundred and sixty-eight years."

In the light of the story told in the previous four or five chapters, it will appear that the correctness of this view of the matter may be seriously called into question in several respects. The last assertion of all is notoriously wrong, for while at Sekigahara itself no more than 15,000 men fell, at least six times that number—probably many more—perished in the great Ōsaka struggle of 1614-15—not two hundred and sixty-eight years, but less than fifteen years after the battle on the Moor of the Barrier. And one or two of the other propositions, while not notoriously wrong, are yet somewhat misleading.

The truth seems to be that the immediate importance of Sekigahara has been seriously over-estimated by Japanese as well as by foreign historians. That the great battle of 1600 A.D. was decisive of much is perfectly true; but that by it, and by it alone, was decided the condition of Japan for over two centuries is a proposition difficult to maintain. Sekigahara was merely a very important link in a chain whose main strength was supplied by Iyeyasu's supreme political and administrative ability and by his consummate statecraft. As a military chief Iyeyasu must be assigned exceedingly high rank; besides his general dispositions for the great struggle of 1600, there were several preceding campaigns that gave evidence of his genius as a strategist. However, it must not be forgotten that his victory at Sekigahara was no mere triumph of soldiership. The fortunes of the day on that occasion were in no small measure decided by diplomacy or—by intrigue; by Iyeyasu's secret negotiations with and his seduction of Kikkawa and of Kobayakawa. A defeat on October 21st, 1600, would not necessarily have proved fatal to Iyeyasu; Hidetada's *corps d'armée* of nearly forty thousand was even then coming up to his support; Mayeda of Kaga, having cleared himself from the assaults of his neighbours, was on the point of advancing to join the Eastern host; the whole country from Utsunomiya to Gifu was held by Tokugawa garrisons; while in the North the tide of war was not running strong in favour of Uyesugi. Neither need Sekigahara have proved fatal for the confederates. Had it not been for Iyeyasu's clever diplomacy—his message to Hideyori and Yodogimi, and his cunning negotiations with Mōri—it would not likely have done so. Death and desertion had weakened their ranks by less than 20,000 men; they had still 70,000 or 80,000 troops in the strongest fortress in Japan—in Ōsaka, which the winter campaign of 1614 afterwards showed to be virtually impregnable. For eleven years (1569–1580) the great Nobunaga had besieged and assaulted Ōsaka in vain, and since his day the fortress had been strengthened tenfold perhaps. By mere force of arms Iyeyasu could never have made himself master of Ōsaka in 1600, and until Ōsaka was in his hands Sekigahara could not be reckoned as a decisive battle. How Ōsaka did open its gates to him at that time has already been told; he had to make it perfectly clear to all that he had been fighting not against the House of Toyotomi, but against Ishida and his confederates. Sekigahara, where 110,000 men or so came into action, and where about 15,000 men fell, *was no decisive battle in itself; what made it so was the subsequent exercise of Iyeyasu's diplomatic ability.*

The real contest with the House of Toyotomi in 1614–15 was a very different matter. In this struggle—or rather series of struggles—the contending forces were thrice as numerous as they had been fifteen years before, and the losses were sixfold—possibly tenfold—greater than they had been at Sekigahara. And without the aid of any subsequent diplomacy the result of this strife was really final and decisive. Iyeyasu and most of the confederates of Ishida could continue to co-exist; as Hideyori grew to manhood and Iyeyasu sank into the grave, a peaceful continued co-existence of the Houses of Toyotomi and of Tokugawa was impossible. So much would appear from Katagiri's *exposé* of the political situation, and of so much Iyeyasu was perfectly aware; doubtless he thoroughly divined what was passing in Katagiri's mind. The old statesman seems to have been fully alive to the fact that in 1614-15 the fortunes of his House, in spite of all its apparent power and prosperity, were in far greater jeopardy than they had been in 1600. What blinds the average student to this fact—for fact it is—is the apparent disparity in the strength of the rival Houses.

But the disparity of strength will be found apparent only. It is true that no great Daimyō fought on Hideyori's side, and it is also true that nearly all the great Daimyō either led or sent contingents against him. But it is equally true that, notwithstanding all this, in the winter campaign of 1614 Iyeyasu, with all his forces, was utterly, completely, and hopelessly foiled before Ōsaka. And it is equally true that nothing succeeds like success. Prestige in Japan, as elsewhere, has always counted for much; and during the month of December, 1614, the prestige of the Tokugawa had received a serious blow. Among the besiegers were the levies of six great feudatories, representing a third of the resources of the empire, who were all in sympathy with the House of Toyotomi, and now acting against it merely out of dread of its seemingly all-powerful rival.. As the prestige of the young chief rose and recalled the glories of the Taikō, all these feudatories might very well deem it safe to cast off the constraining yoke of the Tokugawa and to pass to the side of Hideyori's heir; and such an example would promptly be followed by other chiefs whose chafing under the Tokugawa supremacy was none the less bitter because it was secret. The proximate result would be that Hideyori would soon find himself not merely secure in his impregnable stronghold, but in a position to issue from it and to march upon Fushimi, Kyōto, and perhaps ultimately upon Yedo, with more than half the *samurai* in Japan under his standard. Therefore, as all his assaults on the rampart of the outermost of the *enceintes* of Ōsaka castle proved disastrous, and as the winter campaign of 1614 prolonged itself ominously and to no good purpose, it is easy to understand why it was that Iyeyasu was so anxious, like Lysander, to eke out the lion's skin with the fox's—or, in other words, to have recourse to diplomacy and trickery where soldiership had failed so signally. The fable of the Trojan horse is poor reading compared with the "ower true tale" of the filling-in of the Ōsaka moats. Even in the second and final campaign, when through his very convenient Hondas he had, as he fancied, thoroughly paved his way to victory, at one moment the fate of Iyeyasu had stood upon the "very razor's edge." If Hideyori had really sallied out with his guards at the time the Echizen troops, Iyeyasu's bodyguard, and Hidetada's *corps d'armée* were reeling under the fierce onslaught of Sanada and Mōri's *rōnins* and Ōno's Household troops, there would doubtless have been defections on the side of the Tokugawa, and a rout might very well have been the result. Even as it was, after the action Iyeyasu saw reason to order Furuta, a small Daimyō who had ostensibly supported him, to commit *hara-kiri* together with his sons, while some of his leading retainers were actually crucified. In the last and really decisive battle—really decisive in so far as it was it that decided the "condition of Japan for two centuries and a half"—the supposed defection of Asano of Wakayama had caused an almost fatal panic. Everything points to the conclusion that at this crisis Iyeyasu and his counsellors regarded such defections as much more than mere possibilities; if they had occurred the subsequent history of Japan might have been very different from what it has been. In short, the battle which decided the "condition of Japan for two hundred and fifty years or so" was fought, *not* at Sekigahara on October 21st, 1600, but in front of Ōsaka castle on June 3rd, 1615.

One point worthy of remark is the contrast of Iyeyasu's attitude towards the vanquished of 1600 and those of 1614–15. In the former case nothing was so conspicuous as his clemency. Only three of his antagonists lost their lives at the hands of the public executioner, and only a few—a very few indeed— had to sacrifice themselves by *hara-kiri*. After the fall of the great stronghold on June 3rd, 1615, the determined ferocity with which Iyeyasu pursued his adversaries was akin

to that of Marius or of Sulla in their respective hours of
triumph. Of the captured leaders the only one that was
treated with any consideration at all was Ōno Harufusa, and
in his case the consideration shown merely extended to his
being allowed to die by his own hand. As for Ōno Dōken,
who had fired Sakai at the beginning of the summer campaign, he was handed over to the enraged citizens of that
great mart, and they wreaked a cruel and fell revenge upon
him. Chōsokabe and seventy-two other captains were
decapitated and had their heads ignominiously exposed on
the public pillories. As for the rank and file who had
escaped, they were remorselessly done to death wherever and
whenever detected. Even innocent children were ruthlessly and
remorselessly made away with. Kunimatsumaro, the eight-
year-old natural son of Hideyori, was seized at Fushimi on
the 22nd of the fifth month, and beheaded in Kyōto on
the following day, while the ten-year-old child of Sengoku,
one of the Ōsaka commanders, and many more of equally
tender years met a similar fate. Surely the contrast between the clemency of 1600 and the pitiless ferocity of 1615
is pregnant with a profound significance. Sekigahara was
not in itself decisive, and Iyeyasu felt that after it it was
but true policy to conciliate; the battle of June 3rd, 1615,
was decisive, and Iyeyasu felt not only that he could afford
to exterminate, but that in the utter, complete, and unsparing
extermination of the rival House of Toyotomi and of its partisans
lay the surest and the best and the only safe guarantee for the
permanent peace of the Japanese empire.

It may well be asked how it was, with a revenue of 654,700
koku, enough for the maintenance of some 25,000 or 30,000
samurai only, Hideyori was able to bid defiance to an antagonist
who could command nearly the whole assessed revenues of the
empire. (This latter statement is no mere empty rhetoric; for
even the fourteen Tozama Daimyō who were supposed to be
partisans of the House of Toyotomi, as has been said, either
led or sent their contingents to aid Iyeyasu in his operations
against Ōsaka keep.) The answer to this query serves to disclose
several very important facts. In the first place, Ōsaka was
not only the strongest fortress, but the greatest emporium of
trade in Japan. As has been already said, Kyōto, the capital

at that time, had at least a million inhabitants—probably several hundred thousand more—and most of the supplies for this huge human hive had to pass up the Yodo through Ōsaka. There the junk traffic was immense; we have seen that when everything pointed to war in November, 1614, Hideyori was able to transport into the granaries of the fortress as much as 200,000 *koku* of rice from the craft then moored in the stream. This indicates that not only was it an easy matter for him fully to provision the stronghold at any time at the shortest notice, but that the city of Ōsaka itself must have furnished him with ·a constant revenue, more considerable, perhaps, than that which he drew from the somewhat circumscribed landed estates assigned for his support after Sekigahara. Nor was this all. The Taikō, although maintaining a most sumptuous Court and keeping up a continual succession of *fêtes* and pageants that involved the pouring out of money like water, and apparently the victim of an unreasoning craze for costly colossal architectural and kindred enterprises, had been in reality the reverse of a spendthrift. For all this state, all this magnificence, and all these grandiose enterprises had cost him but little. In fact, it may be questioned whether they did not prove sources of wealth to him. Of the Daibutsu and of the building of Fushimi mention has been already made; it remains to be added that the great castle of Ōsaka itself had originally (1583–85) been reared by forced labour which the barons who then owned his supremacy had to supply. As for the *fêtes* and pageants, it was the subject feudatories who, as a rule, had to defray their expenses; witness the great water pageant at Ōsaka in October, 1596. And with the exception of the great display at Nagoya in Hizen in 1593, the scene of all these brave and costly shows had been Kyōto or Ōsaka or Fushimi, with the result, of course, that the inhabitants of these cities had been as much enriched as the peasantry and traders on the domains of the feudatories had . been impoverished. Now all these three cities were in the Taikō's own possession, and through his tax-collectors it was a matter of course that a fair amount of the wealth brought to them by the Daimyō and their trains should find its way into Hideyoshi's treasury. As a consequence; the hoard of coin

and bullion he left his heir was a huge one; and during
the earlier years of Hideyori's minority this hoard appears to
have been kept practically intact. As the young chief grew
to manhood, however, Iyeyasu, who at all times evinced a
just comprehension of the potentialities of money, and who
had for long looked at this war-chest (for it might very
well become that) in Ōsaka castle with much misgiving,
made strenuous efforts to allure Yodogimi into the erection
of sumptuous temples and other costly works of piety with
a view to removing this menace. The old statesman was only
partially successful in his aim; for even at the capture of the
castle as much as £500,000 of treasure was rescued from the
flames, although the expenses of the first campaign and a
portion of those of the second had been defrayed.

What made Hideyori's possession of this possible war-
fund an object of such anxiety to Iyeyasu was a feature in
the social life of Japan that was then, if not peculiar, at all
events very marked. For centuries Japan had been a prey
to the strife of rival feudatories, who were in many cases
nothing but upstart adventurers who had prospered in land-
thieving. Desertions of their followers to chiefs who could
hold out better prospects of advancement were exceedingly
common. When Hideyoshi had brought the whole country
under his sway he took pains to eradicate this evil. A
regulation was then issued to the effect that no *samurai* who
had been banished by his lord, or who had withdrawn himself
from his lord's estates, should be admitted into any other
lord's service without the express permission of his original
superior. This regulation was re-issued and jealously enforced
by Iyeyasu.[1] Before this date there had been *rōnin* (*lit.*
wave-men) or "lordless men" in Japan; but it cannot be
doubted that the operation of this enactment must have vastly
augmented the numbers of the class. Then in 1600, after
Sekigahara, there were vast confiscations—at least four great
fiefs were partly, and some ninety fiefs totally, appropriated,
and from these many *samurai* had been thrown on the world
with little beyond their clothes and their two swords. Here,

---

[1] In the missionaries' accounts we find frequent reference to this law—
especially in connection with the persecution in Hirado in 1599, when 600
Hiradoese Christians went into voluntary exile.

again, was another great accession to the ranks of the lordless men. For more than a dozen years the dispossessed had eaten their scanty rice in bitterness of spirit, sustaining themselves with the hope that the day might come when they might obtain employment for their idle blades—and revenge. If Hideyori should make announcement that the contents of his war-chest were at the disposal of brave men who embraced the fortunes of his House, as Iyeyasu must have known, the Taikō's heir, albeit unsupported by a single great Daimyō, would soon find himself at the head of one of the most formidable hosts ever mustered in Japan. And the event was even so. The defenders of Ōsaka castle were no mere rabble of braggart Bobadils sharked up from Japanese Alsatias. The majority of them had been seasoned to war in the Taikō's campaigns and the Korean expeditions; and under chiefs of genius like Sanada, and of ability like Mōri Katsunaga and Gotō, they showed themselves not unamenable to discipline—although the impetuosity of Mōri's wild-cats was perhaps too extreme—while in *élan* they altogether outclassed the Tokugawa troops, many of whom, after the battle of June 3rd, 1615, "were punished for cowardice and misconduct."

It is, however, safe to presume that the better among these 60,000 *rōnin* that mustered to Hideyori's standard were attracted to it by something loftier than the mere prospect of fingering some of the broad gold pieces that lay stored up in the castle vaults. While all were eager for service—(for to the survivors of the men of the Taikō's time war was not merely a business, but an amusement, and since the great campaign of 1600 there had been a sad dearth of this kind of amusement in Japan)—most were inflamed with a burning desire to strike a deadly stroke at the power of the Tokugawa, who had made beggars of them. And a very fair proportion of them had rallied to Hideyori's call, prompted by nothing so much as by pure and unfeigned devotion to the heir of the Great Taikō. In the case of defeat they had nothing to lose but their lives,— and of their lives at this date many Japanese recked little or nothing, while victory, of which they had no reason to despair, meant fiefs and power and honour; and to the average Japanese *samurai* of these days fiefs and power—and above all honour—were everything.

N N

Hence, although not a single feudatory responded to Hideyori's summons, the contest was the reverse of a one-sided one. At this date the *rōnin* or "lordless man" proved to be a political factor of prime importance. This fact helps us to understand why Iyeyasu was so ruthless in his treatment of the vanquished on this occasion. So long as Japan had its tens of thousands of lordless men with nothing to lose but their lives, and setting no very high value upon them even, any bold rebel with a modicum of resources at command could always count upon rallying a considerable force at very short notice. This was a danger that had to be removed. And the proper time to remove it was at and immediately after the capture of Ōsaka; and the proper method of removing it was by a wholesale extermination of the desperadoes who had fought for Hideyori, and who could now be dealt with so very conveniently. There can be little question that Iyeyasu's ruthlessness on this occasion did a great deal to ensure the subsequent domestic peace of the country. Even notwithstanding, in little more than a score of years we shall find the *rōnin* formidable enough to constrain the authorities to mobilise as many men as had fought at Sekigahara to deal with them, when they found their opportunity in Shimabara in 1638.[2] This consideration, then, enables us in a measure to understand the relentless severity with which the victor treated the tens of thousands of lordless men who had rallied to Hideyori's standard. Their presence in the land was a continual menace to its inward tranquillity, and to dispose of them effectually was an urgent problem that called for a drastic solution. Such a solution Hideyoshi perhaps would have found in a prolongation of the Korean war, or in dispatching them to achieve the conquest of the Philippines. Iyeyasu took this opportunity of sending them not out of Japan, but out of the world.

But what is to be said about the scant measure of mercy meted out to the House of Toyotomi itself? It is bootless to

---

[2] Here it may be remarked that in the years following the arrival of Commodore Perry (1853) the *rōnin* or "lordless men" played an exceedingly important part in the history of the time. Some of the greatest figures in the modern history of Japan were among the *rōnin* about the date when the Tokugawa power and feudalism were tottering to their fall. Kidō, Yeto, Ōkuma at one time or another had all been "lordless men."

urge that Iyeyasu was really minded to spare Yodogimi and Hideyori when Hideyori's wife was sent to her father and grandfather as a suppliant in their behalf. One story has it that Iyeyasu actually sent back word to them that Yodogimi would have a revenue of 10,000 *koku* assigned for her support, that Hideyori would be allowed to withdraw to Kōyasan, and that it was only because Ii had exceeded his instructions, had fired upon a storehouse where the refugees had sought safety, and so had driven them to kill themselves, that the old man's word was not made good. There remains the fact of the cold-blooded execution, or rather murder, of Hideyori's eight-year-old son a fortnight after the fall of the castle.[3] What reason was there for immolating a mere infant who could have been in no wise responsible for recent events? Possibly the Tokugawa retainers may have recalled the circumstance that some four and a half centuries before, the Taira, in sparing the children Yoritomo and Yoshitsune in the hour of their triumph over the rival House of Minamoto (1159), had simply paved the way for the overthrow of their own House by these children when grown to man's estate, some five lustres or so later on. Now it was in virtue of their descent from the Minamoto that the Tokugawa had been able to possess themselves of the Shōgunate, and Iyeyasu or Hidetada or their followers may have now thought it well to be on their guard against repeating towards the House of Toyotomi the fatal mistake the Tairas had in their hour of triumph made with regard to the Minamoto.

---

[3] It ought to be mentioned that as Hideyori's body was not found, many people believed that he had made good his escape at the fall of Ōsaka, and that he had fled to Satsuma or the Lūchūs. In *Cocks's Diary* we have frequent references to this belief. For example, "September 18, 1616.—Capt. Adames went againe to the Cort [at Yedo] to procure our dispatch, and fownd all the Councell busyed about matters of justice of lyfe and death; and, amongst the rest, one man was brought in question about Fidaia Samme [Hideyori], as being in the castell with him to the last hower. This man was racked and tormented very much, to make hym confes where his master was, or whether he were alive or dead; but I canot heare whether he confessed any thing or no." "May 5, 1616.—The sonne of Tuan Dono of Langasaque [Nagasaki] [i.e. the brother of the Japanese Jesuit killed at the storming of Ōsaka], departed to sea with 13 barkes laden with souldiers to take the iland Taccasange, called per them soe, but by us Isla Fermosa. And it is reported he is at Gotō, staying for more succors which are to com from Miaco, and thought they mean to goe for Lequea [Loochoo], to look for Fidaia Samme [Hideyori]." "July 7, 1616.—Speeches geven out that the *Tono*, or King, of Xaxma [Satsuma] meaneth to make wars against the new Emperour [Hidetada] in right of Fidaia Samme [Hideyori], whom they report to be alive, and that he meaneth to begyn with Langasaque. This is now the common report." "October 15, 1616.—And it is said Fidaia Samme is alive; but what will com hereof I know not."

That mistake had re-plunged Japan into the bitterest of all her civil wars.

If regard be had to Iyeyasu's attitude towards, and his dealings with, the House of Toyotomi since the summer of 1614 merely, it will be no easy matter for a Tokugawa partisan to devise an apologia for the old statesman. Between that date and the fall of Ōsaka castle the record of cunning and trickery is indeed a black one. Not only the method in which the quarrel was forced, but the gross chicanery which the Tokugawa had recourse to at various points of the struggle must excite the disgust of every one troubled with the possession of a conscience. But yet withal, if a wider view of the situation be taken, the partisan apologist might readily find his task by no means a hard one.

In the spring of 1614 Hideyori's retainers had certainly been intriguing with some of the great Daimyō, and some of their letters had come into Iyeyasu's hands. It may very well have been that Hideyori was no party to these intrigues,—that they were being conducted without his knowledge. But Iyeyasu knew better than any one else that in Japan the ostensible head of a great princely House had often no more real control over its policy than the figure-head of a ship has over her course. Katagiri's intentions he no doubt divined accurately enough; and what these were Katagiri himself has explained in detail. The quarrel between the Taikō and his nephew (1595) had been to a large extent fomented by the adherents of the two separate Courts. And now, even though Hideyori were himself peacefully inclined, yet his councillors, dissatisfied with their own position of eclipse, would be sure, really for their own private advantage, but with the stereotyped profession of acting loyally in the interests of their lord, to force the young man into strife with the House that had been administering Japan wisely and successfully for the last dozen years. Now what Japan needed before all things was peace, and the only way to secure that peace was to crush and exterminate its inevitable disturbers while it was still possible to do so promptly.

That the old man of seventy-two did consult the interests of his own House in this is of course apparent. Possibly such was his leading motive. But, on the other hand, there seems to be

no reason to doubt that Iyeyasu believed that it was only the
supremacy of his House that could continue to the country that
priceless boon of tranquillity it had not known for the three
centuries preceding Sekigahara.   During the last fifty years
in Japan the mere fact of a man having been his father's
son had stood no one in any very great stead.   The young
Ashikaga Shōgun, replaced in authority by Nobunaga in 1565,
had been summarily set aside by that same Nobunaga in 1573,
and for the next nine years Nobunaga had been supreme at
the centre of authority.   His best if not his sole title to his
position had been the efficiency of his administration.   Shortly
after his death, in 1582, his former captain, Hideyoshi, had
set aside Nobunaga's sons and grandson as summarily as
Nobunaga had set aside the last Ashikaga Shōgun, and Hideyoshi's only title to supreme power had simply been—superior
efficiency.   Now Iyeyasu, whose birth entitled him to aspire
to what neither Nobunaga nor Hideyoshi could have aspired
to—the Shōgunate, to wit—had during twelve years or more
given practical proof that, as a ruler of the empire, in the
mere matter of efficiency his title was superior to Nobunaga's
and in no way inferior to that of Hideyoshi.

In those days mere technicalities counted for little; they
were appealed to and invoked frequently, it is true, but they
were simply used as pawns in the game.   Achievement and
efficiency were what really counted.   Of all this Iyeyasu, of
course, was perfectly aware.   Now, supposing Hidetada abdicated
the Shōgunate, and supposing Hideyori (who never could
become Shōgun) were put in the position of the Taikō—whose
heir, if not son, he undoubtedly was—could Hideyori give
to Japan that strong central administration without which
peace, the most important of all desiderata, was impossible?
Hideyori was the Taikō's heir; the Taikō's sole title to supreme
rule had been superior efficiency as a ruler;—had the Taikō
transmitted his superior efficiency as a ruler to Hideyori?
That a young man, even of great natural ability, in his early
twenties, under the sway of a proud and imperious yet really
cowardly and vain woman (who was in turn under the sway
of a good-looking paramour), and of a crowd of esurient and
self-seeking retainers, could really impose his will upon the
hot-blooded, high-mettled intriguing feudatories of Japan, for

his, their own, and the empire's good, was scarcely to be expected. Nobunaga had won his spurs honestly by hard work and superior achievement. Yet his sons and his grandson had been swept aside by Hideyoshi. Hideyoshi had really won (if man ever did win) *his* spurs by hard work and achievement, and he had not scrupled to set aside the untried descendants of his former Lord—(they seem to have been incapables without exception)—for the good of Japan as well as of himself. Now, in spite of all Katagiri's fine speeches, Hideyori, the Taikō's heir, was just as untried as Nobunaga's grandson had been when Hideyoshi thrust *him* aside into a small lordship of 135,000 *koku* at Gifu.

Besides all this, it must not be forgotten that, apart from the item of efficiency as a ruler, Hideyori's claims were exceedingly weak, or rather they were non-existent. The man whose heir he was had owed nothing to *his* birth; Hideyori could therefore rightfully claim but little on the score of lineage, even on the admission that he was of the seed of the Great Taikō—a thing that was seriously questioned by many. Iyeyasu, then, who certainly was not indifferent to the welfare of Japan as a whole, and whose services to the country had been quite as great as those of Hideyoshi, may very well be excused if he calmly dictated his line of action in the year 1614 in accordance with the answer to the question—"*How, under present circumstances, are the future peace and prosperity of Japan most likely to be best assured?*" Any resignation of the Shōgunate, except in favour of a son or a kinsman of his own, would have been impossible; at that date the all-powerful retainers of the House of Tokugawa would have never consented to such a step until they had been beaten out of their very last trench in the stubbornest of strifes. A great leader in those days owed his greatness in no small measure to the worth and will of the vassals he could surround himself with; and in all measures that really affected the welfare of the House, the opinions and sentiments of these, its mainstays, had to be consulted. Therefore any resignation of the Shōgunate by the Tokugawa chiefs was impossible; the councillors of the clan would have opposed such a proposal even to the death. A contest between Hidetada (or his successor) with Hideyori—or rather a contest between the Iis, the Hondas, the Matsudairas, and other great Tokugawa retainers on the one side, and the Onos, and the Odas, supported by Sanada, Gotō, Mōri Katsunaga and "Have-nots" like them on the other—was simply inevitable. Such being the outlook as it presented itself to the great old statesman, is it strange that he should have exerted all the fag-end of his vitality to bring the struggle to a head while he was reasonably sure of seeing to it that it was decided promptly and once for all—for the general good of Japan? Surely this was infinitely better than Tiberius's attitude, so often expressed by himself in the Euripidean line to the effect that when he was dead things might take their course.[4] Judged from the stand-point of the national welfare, Iyeyasu's triumph over Hideyori is no more to be regretted than his victory over Ishida and his partisans fifteen years before. What Japan needed above all things was peace, and as one result of the great Ōsaka struggle apart from the serious Shimabara revolt of 1638, the land did actually have peace for two hundred and forty-eight years.[5] And during all that long stretch of time the supremacy of Iyeyasu's descendants remained unquestioned.

This last fact is a remarkable one when we cast our eye over the records of Houses that had successively wielded the chief executive power since Yoritomo received his appointment as Shōgun in 1192. Within twenty years from his death the reins had slipped from the hands of his incapable sons, and

---

4 All this "surmising" may strike the adherents of the doctrine that "History is a Science"—(of course with a big capital S) as so much labour wasted. But softly! Nowadays, even, does every "truth," (to say nothing of mere "fact") of importance get committed to "documents"? In the Japan of that time every "truth," of importance certainly did not. At that date even "facts" of the slightest or of no earthly importance at all were painfully set forth in elaborate hieroglyphics, while "truths" of the highest value were either left to shift for themselves or consigned to the lowermost depths of the deepest wells in the empire—so far as "documents" were concerned. So much we know from a rather laborious collation of foreign with Japanese sources. Now does this not justify one in raising the question, "Can History really be called a Science," if we are to admit that the perfect form of knowledge is SCIENCE, with seven capital letters? Any real student who has honestly and valiantly essayed to grapple with all the factors in any period will, we think, be driven to the humiliating admission that Raleigh after all was right; that the attainment of absolute truth in History is an impossibility. Documents are of the highest value, of course, and there must be no flinching from the task of exploring them. But surely the student who believes that every truth of importance invariably sets forth in black on white is somewhat simple-minded.

5 Down to the fighting in Kyōto in 1863.

then the Hōjō, as Regents for the eight "shadow" or puppet
Shōguns, had really been the masters of an unquiet country
for a little over a century. It is true that the Ashikagas
nominally held the Shōgunate for two hundred and forty
years (1334–1573); but at times their authority was almost
naught, and Japan, not under them, but in their time, was little
better than a cock-pit. Nobunaga restored order in the capital
and over the central portions of the empire; but he failed to
transmit his power to his family. Hideyoshi reduced the
whole land to peace; but, as we have just seen, his efforts to
found a House had miscarried utterly. Now Iyeyasu comes
prominently forward, preserves order, effectually checks all
disorder—not merely present, but prospective—and actually
transmits his office to a line of fourteen successors of his own
blood whose sway continues to be absolute and unquestioned
for two centuries and a half, during which only one of them has
ever to draw the sword for serious business! And the strangest
feature of this unique phenomenon in the history of Japan is
that not one of all these successors could boast of anything
better than very respectable talents, while most of them were
worse than mediocrities. Iyemitsu is usually credited with
the possession of genius; it is hard to detect much evidence
of it in him. Yoshimune, the eighth Tokugawa Shōgun, a
man of ideas and of ability undoubtedly, was the most
respectable of the whole fourteen successors of Iyeyasu. Yet
put Yoshimune in the position either of Iyeyasu or of Hideyoshi,
or even of Nobunaga—could he have done their work? As
for Hidetada, what can be said of him? A hard, painstaking,
conscientious plodder—a good family man as things went in
Japan in those days,[6] a "great politician" as the English
merchants tell us; but a genius—or even a man of brilliant
parts—emphatically not! But then all his life long he had
been trained and schooled and drilled by one who *was* a

---

[6] The Rev. Arthur Hatch, parson of the *Pulsgrove*, thus writes of him and
of the sexual morality of the time:—"The Emperour [Hidetada] hath but one
wife, and it is generally reported that he keeps company with no other, but
her only; and if it be true as it is thought, he may in that respect be termed
the Phœnix of all these parts of the world: as for those within his own
dominions they are so farre either from imitating or following him, that one
is scarcely contented with a hundred women, and they are so shameless in that
kinde, that they will boast of it, and account it a glory unto them to make
relation of the multitude of women which they have had the use of. *Consuetudo
peccandi tollit sensum peccati*." (November 25th, 1623.)

genius—his own father, to wit. For the last eleven years of Iyeyasu's life, Hidetada had been nominal Shōgun, and, thanks to the old man's coaching, he had by practical experience learned how to sit firm in the saddle and to handle the reins so as to keep out of mischief at all events.

And the old man had done more. Hidetada at the age of sixteen had married, or rather had been married to (1595) a sister of Yodogimi. This lady had been adopted as a daughter by the Taikō. As the bride was some seven years senior to her spouse, it is tolerably safe to assume that the marriage was a political one entirely. It does not, however, seem to have been unhappy, although Hidetada at all times stood in salutary dread of his strong-minded consort,—so much so, indeed, that he was inclined to yield to her wish that their youngest son, Tadanaga, and not his brother Iyemitsu should be declared heir to the headship of the House. This came to the ears of Iyeyasu; and the old statesman, after carefully ascertaining the relative capacity of the two brothers, made a sudden visit to Yedo in 1613, and then in an unexpected and somewhat dramatic manner gave it to be understood that the succession was to be vested in Iyemitsu. In thus adhering to the principle of primogeniture in the case of Iyemitsu, and in departing from it in the case of Iyemitsu's father, we may find confirmation of the assertion of Japanese historians that Iyeyasu considered the plodding Hidetada to be the best of all his numerous offspring.

This brings us to a consideration of the old statesman's (sinner's, the Jesuits would say) family. His four daughters, as being of least importance, may be disposed of first. They were all married to various Daimyō to attach these feudatories still more closely to the interests of the Tokugawa. Besides his four daughters, Iyeyasu had eleven sons, and of these, with the exception of Hidetada, the most important were born after their father had passed his fifty-seventh year! His first son, Nobuyasu (of whom the English merchants give us some unpleasant details—most likely mere gossip), died in 1579 at the age of twenty. Hideyasu (the son of a concubine), born in 1574, died in 1607. He had proved himself a good soldier in the campaign of 1600; yet he was not made his father's heir to the Shōgunate. He was made Daimyō of

Echizen (751,000 *koku*), and his sons and their Echizen troops
had to bear the brunt of the great fight of Ōsaka on June 3rd,
1615. From this it would appear that Iyeyasu considered
Hideyasu's military ability to be far superior to his powers
as an administrator. Now, as has been said repeatedly,
Iyeyasu regarded war as merely one—albeit a very important—
piece in the statesman's *répertoire*. Hidetada had made a
great failure in the campaign of 1600; yet in spite of that
it would seem that his father held him to be a better all-round
man than his elder brother, the brilliant and intrepid soldier,
Hideyasu was. Tadayoshi, the fourth son, born in 1580, had
commanded the Tokugawa centre at Sekigahara in 1600, and
had then been made Lord of Owari with his seat at Kiyosu,
Nobunaga's old castle-town. However, he died childless in
the same year as his brother Hideyasu—1607. The fifth son,
born in 1583, was a physical weakling, who died in 1603,
and the seventh died in infancy. The sixth was that Tadateru
whom we have seen getting so seriously into his father's black
books by reason of his slackness on the morning preceding
the capture of Ōsaka, that the old man would never afterwards
allow him (Tadateru) into his presence. Tadateru, who was also
somewhat vaguely accused of complicity in the so-called Christian
conspiracy of Ōkubo, was twenty-five years of age when this
misbehaviour of his at Ōsaka (or rather between Nara and
Ōsaka) gave such deadly offence to Iyeyasu. He was stripped of
his fief of Takata in Echigo (480,000 *koku*) and sent to Koyasan,
where it was expected at the time he would not be very
long-lived.[7] However, in spite of all his youthful irregularities

---

[7] "Here [at Yoshida on the Tōkaidō] we had news how Calsa Samme [*i.e.*
Matsudaira Tadateru, *Kadsusa-no-suke*] hath cut his belly, being attaynted of
treason against his father and brother to have destroid them and set up Fidaia
Samme [Hideyori], his enemie. It is thought it will goe hard with Masamone
Dono [*i.e.* Daté Masamune], his father-in-law; and speeches are geven out
that the Jesuistes and other padres are the fyre brands and setters on of all this,
in provoking children against parents and subjects against their naturall
princes."—*Cocks's Diary*, August 18th, 1616.

"Here [at Hamamatsu] we had news how Calsa Samme was to passe this way
to-morrow to goe to a church near Miaco [Kyōto], called Coye [Kōyasan]; som
say to cut his bellie, others say to be shaved a prist and to remeane theare the
rest of his daies. All his owne men are taken from hym, and he sent with a
gard of the Emperour, his brother's, men. His wife he hath sent to Massa
Moneda Dono, her father. All [he] hath for his alowance in the pagon church
[is] i. *mangoca* per anno [10,000 *koku* of rice per annum]."—*Idem*, August 19th, 1616.

"It is said there goe divers other with him [Tadateru] to that church (or
pagod), where it is thought they shall all cut their bellies, som of them being
men of 40 or 50 *mangocas* per anno [400,000 or 500,000 *koku* per annum], which is
8 or 10 tymes more than the King of Firando hath."—*Idem*, August 20th, 1616,

as a wine-bibber [8] and as a plotter, the death he died was no premature one; for when he did die at Suwa in Shinano in 1683, he had attained the patriarchal age of ninety-three.

Iyeyasu's last three sons were, as has been said, all born to him after he had passed his fifty-seventh year. Yoshinao, born in the same year as Oliver Cromwell, 1599, was made Lord of Owari when his elder brother. Tadayoshi, Iyeyasu's fourth son, died in 1607. About the same time Yorinobu, born in 1602, was given a fief of 500,000 koku in Suruga and Tōtōmi, while Yorifusa, born in 1603, was made Lord of Mito, with a revenue of 250,000 koku, in 1609. Thus on the death of Iyeyasu (June 1st, 1616) the fabric of the Tokugawa greatness stood on a very wide and a very stable basis. Iyeyasu's third son, Hidetada, as Shōgun possessed the extensive family domains proper, had absolute control over the *Fudai* Daimyō who held about a third of the total revenues of Japan, and by the system of hostages in Yedo, and of espionage, exercised a very strong control over the great *Tozama* or non-*Fudai* Lords. Hidetada, too, was in the prime of life (37), and even in the case of an untimely death a successor in the person of his own son, Iyemitsu, had already been provided. Then four of the great fiefs were held by his brothers—or, rather, by his three brothers and a nephew. Echizen (670,000 koku) was in the hands of the son of his elder brother Hideyasu (died 1607), while, as has been said, his three younger brothers in Owari, Suruga, and Mito held revenues amounting to 1,290,000 koku, which, added to those of Echizen, represent a total of nearly 2,000,000 koku in the hands of Hidetada's immediate relatives. Besides all this, by marrying his daughters, his grand-daughters, his great-grand-daughters, his nieces and grand-nieces and all the numerous tribe of his female relations, natural or adopted, Iyeyasu had contrived to attach (more or less) a host of the feudatories to the interests of his House; while by bestowing his own name of Matsudaira and other judicious but inexpensive

At Shidzuoka " we understood that the ould Emperour [Iyeyasu died June 1st, 1616] had left order with Shongo Samme (now Emperour) [Hidetada, that is] not to kill his brother Calsa Samme, but to confine hym in the pagod aforesaid for 10 yeares, and in the end, fynding him conformable, to use his discretion."— *Idem*, August 21st, 1616.

8 See Dickson's *Gleanings from Japan*, pp. 183-4.

marks of honour upon others he had conciliated the goodwill of more than one potential foe.

But this was by no means all. In the course of his own long life he had surrounded himself with an array of able and devoted adherents—the Iis, the Hondas, the Sakakibaras, the Sakais, the Abes, the Ōkubos, the Dois, and others like them; and the vital interests of all these henchmen—now amply, albeit not extravagantly, rewarded with fiefs and honours—committed them to the most strenuous support of the power and prestige of the House of Tokugawa. And things had been so arranged that not one of these men could ever play towards Iyeyasu's successors the part that had been played by the Hōjōs towards the sons of Yoritomo, or by Hideyoshi towards the offspring of Nobunaga. It is but rarely that a great ruler—especially one who has had to carve his own way to place and power—leaves behind him a genius in the person of his son. Of this fact Iyeyasu took careful heed, and in addition to expending years upon the training of the solid, but by no means brilliant, Hidetada, he devoted his keenest attention to devising and bequeathing to his successors a system of administration that could be manipulated with safety even by men of merely average capacity—or of less. In fact, as we shall see, long before the fall of Feudalism in 1868, this system had become purely mechanical, and for years before the arrival of Perry the ominous creaking of its gear had been giving intimation that it was on the point of a breakdown. But in its day the machine in question was no small triumph of political engineering, and it certainly must be counted among factors that enabled Iyeyasu to accomplish what Yoritomo, Nobunaga, and Hideyoshi had alike signally failed to accomplish. This is not the place to set forth the details of the Tokugawa administration; that subject is reserved for treatment in a subsequent volume. Yet even here something must be said about Iyeyasu's constructive statesmanship.

What strikes one most in connection with Iyeyasu is his consummate judgment. If genius can be accurately defined as an infinite capacity for taking pains, then Tokugawa Iyeyasu was certainly possessed of a large measure of genius. Yet that he had the brilliant originality of Hideyoshi in coping with fresh and unexpected situations, or in the rapid devising—or rather in the improvising—of accurate solutions for new and startling problems does not by any means appear. On the other hand, where the Great Taikō might have ventured on the accomplishment of the impossible, Iyeyasu would never have done so. Both of these great men possessed that constructive imagination without which any real grand achievement is impossible; but while in Hideyoshi's unguarded moments his might have been tinged with a suspicion of grandiose megalomania, Iyeyasu's was always kept under restraint by an omnipresent and almost Sancho Panza sense of actual and prosaic realities. Another point of difference between these two great men was that while Hideyoshi trusted mainly to the fertility and resources of his brain, Iyeyasu was an adept in "picking the brains" of others—a fact that is attested by a score of anecdotes. One thing to be noted is that of these two it is Iyeyasu who is really the representative of the Japanese genius at its best. In common with the Norman as depicted by M. Taine, the average Japanese can adopt and adapt, and even systematise the original discoveries of others. But to originate or even to *discover* anything entirely new himself, he is impotent. In this respect Hideyoshi was no representative Japanese; for pitted against even an Alexander, or a Hannibal, or a Cæsar, or a Napoleon, he might well have come off on equal terms, chiefly on the ground of his incontestable originality. Against any of these great men Iyeyasu would have made in all probability but a poor appearance. At the same time, Iyeyasu was able to do what none of these great men (except Cæsar, who was especially fortunate in so far as his heir and successor, Augustus, was a man of rare ability) were or have been able to accomplish, to transmit his power and his position to his unborn descendants for more than a dozen generations. In the system of administration he devised for his successors it is difficult to discern the presence of many original items; yet the results of the patch-work mosaic he put together prove its author to have been possessed of a very high order of ability.

It will be remembered that Hideyoshi endeavoured to provide for the interests of his heir and for the government of the empire by the creation of the five *Tairō*,—a Board of Regents that was to be superior to the five *Bugyō* or Ministers who had been his executive agents since 1585, and that between these an intermediate Board of three *Chūrō*, or Mediators, was introduced. The wreck and ruin of this unfortunate administrative machine we have already recounted at length. The chief executive machinery devised by Iyeyasu, while modelled on that of the Taikō, was furnished with safeguards which the unexpected sickness of the Taikō had prevented him from providing. The supreme organ of the Tokugawa Government was to be like that of the Taikō,—a Board of five members, which was to be known as the *Gorōjū*. Below that was a junior council—afterwards known as the *Wakadoshiyori*—of five or six men who held pretty much the same position towards the *Gorōjū* that Hideyoshi's *Bugyō* were to hold towards the *Tairō* or Regents. But in the character of the components of Hideyoshi's Board of Regency and of the Tokugawa *Gorōjū* there was an important difference.

The Taikō's Board had been composed of five of the greatest and most powerful feudatories in Japan,—each with his own interests to seek and his own ambitions to follow. Hence unfeigned devotion to the cause of the House of Toyotomi was not, perhaps, to be expected from them farther than that devotion was consonant with the pursuit of their own immediate interests and their own ambitions. On the other hand, in the scheme of administration devised by Iyeyasu, not only no great outside feudatory, but no outside feudatory (*Tozama*) at all could have a place. From top to bottom every office in what was now the Central Government of Japan was to be filled by a Tokugawa vassal. To the *Gorōjū* or Council of State none but *Fudai* Daimyō were eligible. As has been said more than once, these *Fudai* Daimyō were merely retainers of the House of Tokugawa who had been invested (by Iyeyasu) with fiefs of 10,000 *koku* or upward. Of the use that was made of them after Sekigahara we have also spoken at length. Now these *Fudai* were entirely dependent upon the goodwill of the Tokugawa Shōgun (and his advisers) for their place and position. By him their revenues might be increased or diminished at will; he could remove them from one fief to another hundreds of miles distant, or he could strip them of their belongings entirely—even order them to make away with themselves. (Towards any of the great *Tozama*, none of these things could be done.) In short, their dependence upon the House of Tokugawa was absolute; with it and its welfare their interests were bound up indissolubly. Therefore a Council of State composed of the ablest among these devoted vassal lords would be a very different thing from the one organised by the Taikō just before his death. Furthermore, the personnel of this Cabinet was to be frequently changed; a ten years' tenure of office in it by any one member was to be of comparatively rare occurrence. The *Fudai* who mostly had a place on this Board were as a rule far from being the richest of their class, one of Iyeyasu's principles being that the wealthy should have but little authority in the government of the State. As a matter of fact, the members of the subordinate council known as the *Wakadoshiyori* (*i.e.* the Younger Elders) were often promoted from that Council to a seat on the superior Board, and as these "Younger Elders" were often merely *hatamoto* with revenues of less than 10,000 *koku*, they had to be invested with a Daimyō's fief at the time of their promotion. Thus at no time would any member of the Tokugawa Cabinet be in a position to play towards the Shōgun or his fellow-Ministers the part that Iyeyasu himself had been able to act towards his co-Regents and towards the heir of the Taikō. With such a machine even an imbecile ruler might be fairly safe. In the case of such incapacity, however, or in the contingency of a minority, a further safeguard was to be provided by the appointment of a Regent from one of the devoted Houses of Ii, Honda, Sakai, or Sakaki-bara, the four chief *Fudai*; while careful provisions were made against any possible abuse of his power by this most important officer.

Such was the mainspring of a most intricate and complicated system of governmental machinery, with checks and counter-checks and "regulators" innumerable. A heavy and cumbrous piece of work it was indeed; yet as an aid to the accomplishment of the general purposes of its architect it must be admitted to have proved of the very highest value and efficiency. Iyeyasu was perfectly well aware that while a genius like his great predecessor the Taikō is above all mere mechanical systems, and is a law unto himself, the appearance of such men as Hideyoshi among his own descendants was not to be counted on. That any of these descendants could ever grapple with the problems of administration with the fertility and resource of that illustrious man was not to be expected. The best that could be done was to systematise and to formulate the results of Hideyoshi's methods, supplemented and corrected in certain respects, and to have them carried out in a mechanical yet exhaustive way. In the matter of hostages, for example, Hideyoshi acted with the utmost insight and judgement; those he had reason to suspect were indeed summoned or invited to his Court, where he quietly weighed them in the balance, *and then made what efficient and effective use might be made of them.* Under the Taikō men of mettle who might have otherwise proved troublesome were thus for the most part kept out of mischief by having work found for them. Hideyoshi did indeed very unobtrusively have very efficient recourse to the device of hostages; but it was employed with such consummate tact that while after his completion of the conquest of the empire in 1590 there was not one revolt against him, the device in his hands did not (with the exception of Takayama Ukon) deprive Japan of the services of a single man of ability. Now, after Iyeyasu accepted those propositions of the obsequious Tōdō, to which full reference has been already made, this device of hostages was developed into a system that soon became indiscriminating, purely mechanical, highly vexatious, and utterly prejudicial to the best interests of Japan. The enforced residence of the feudatories in Yedo had the effect of converting many of the ablest men in the empire into worthless drones and debauchees; while the closing of all avenues of advancement to men of genius outside the favoured pale of the Fudai Daimyō and of the retainers of the House of Tokugawa involved a national loss that it is hard to estimate. No such crime—for crime this undoubtedly was—can be charged against the Taikō. With the peasant-ruler of Japan —as with the Huntingdon brewer born seven months after the peasant-ruler's death, as with Napoleon—there was always *la carrière ouverte aux talents.* With Tokugawa Iyeyasu himself, the case of Ōkubo, the Christian conspirator, and of others that

might be mentioned, seems to indicate that a man who (apart
from ancestors, trappings, wealth, and all the other *simulacra* the
silly sons of men *will* persist in worshipping) was really a man
had always a welcome—and a chance.   But with Iyeyasu's
incompetent descendants it was somewhat different, and of this
probability—for such it was in the year of grace 1616—Iyeyasu
appears to have shown himself fully conscious.   In judging
the great Iyeyasu we must always bear in mind that his was a
practical intelligence bent on doing the *best* that could be done
for the empire under present actual and probable prospective
conditions.   Neither a brilliant opportunist nor a speculative
philosopher, he would appear to have passed most of his later
days in the quiet of Shidzuoka devising a sound and satisfactory
solution for a problem which he doubtless formulated in such
terms as " *How can I provide for the lasting peace of the empire
under the rule of my descendants, few of whom are likely to
be men of any very marked ability?*"·

Looked at from this point of view, the subsequent change in
the attitude of the Japanese Government towards foreigners
becomes more comprehensible.   A genius like Hideyoshi would
never have closed the Japanese ports against foreigners.   Hideyoshi would have—did—welcome foreign intercourse as .tending
to stimulate and develop all that was best in Japan.   In this
respect he was followed by Iyeyasu.   But both of these great
men had confidence in their own ability to direct the destinies
of the empire, to extract all the benefit from foreign intercourse that could be extracted from it, and still, while
treating them fairly, to keep the aliens in the land from
doing it any real injury.   Iyeyasu, however, evidently felt
that his descendants, all of whom might likely be no better
than—if not actually inferior to—the "average man," would find
their greatest danger in the support that Europeans might
only too readily extend to local chiefs who wished to emancipate
themselves from the yoke of the House of Tokugawa,—now
invested with the Shōgunate of Japan.   It is fairly safe to say
that neither Hideyoshi nor Iyeyasu would ever have closed
Japan to Western. intercourse.   Japan was closed in the
interests of the safe workings of the administrative machine
devised by Iyeyasu to safeguard the supremacy of his stodgy
successors.

oo

CHAPTER XIX.

IN a previous chapter treating of the foreign policy of Iyeyasu
from 1598 down to the issue of the Edict against Christianity
in 1614, apart from Will Adams only incidental reference
has been made to the presence of Englishmen in Japan. Yet
in 1613, several months before the appearance of the Edict in
question, commercial relations had been opened up between
the island empire of the East and the island kingdom of the
West, and Portuguese from Macao, Spaniards from Manila,
and Spaniards from New Spain found themselves confronted
with the competition of merchants from heretic England as well
as from heretic and revolted Holland.

As the Englishmen in Japan in early Tokugawa days were
all servants of the English East India Company, it becomes
advisable to recapitulate the circumstances of the origin of
that famous corporation and its history down to the arrival of its
pioneer vessel in Japanese waters in the summer of 1613.

It will be remembered that one of the most important
considerations that stimulated the merchants of Holland and
Zealand to address themselves so vigorously to tapping the
sources of the Portuguese Oriental trade was their exclusion
from the port of Lisbon (1594) and the interruption of the
part they had played as the European distributors of the rich
freights brought home by the Lusitanian galleons. Now this
departure on their part in turn served to put the traders of
London on their mettle.

"In 1599 the Dutch, who had now firmly established their trade
in the East, having raised the price of pepper against us from 3s.
per lb. to 6s. and 8s., the merchants of London held a meeting on
the 22nd September at the Founders' Hall, with the Lord Mayor in
the chair, and agreed to form an association for the purpose of
trading directly with India. Queen Elizabeth also sent Sir John
Mildenhall by Constantinople to the Great Mughal to apply for
privileges for the English Company for whom she was then preparing
a charter; and on 31st December, 1600, the English East India
Company was incorporated by Royal charter under the title of the

Governor and Company of Merchants of London trading to the East Indies."

The original company had one hundred and twenty-five shareholders and a capital of only £70,000. The corporation was to be permitted to export goods Customs-free for four years, and also £30,000 in foreign coin each voyage, provided "they brought that sum by their trade out of foreign countries into this kingdom"—those being the days when the "mercantile system" was as much in favour as were the doctrines of the Manchester school a few years ago. The charter was exclusive; no charter was to be granted to other merchants within fifteen years; however, if found detrimental to the public, on two years' warning it was to become void,— if otherwise, to be renewed with additional favourable clauses.

To those who are acquainted with the history of this company merely in the eighteenth century, when Clive and Hastings were among its servants, it may come somewhat as a surprise to learn that this great corporation at first showed itself so timid and so unenterprising that in 1604-05 its charter was in serious danger of being annulled. The pioneer expedition of five ships under Lancaster had been sent out in 1601; and while meanwhile, year after year, ships were being dispatched from the Dutch ports in dozens, the English company passively awaited the return of its initial venture, which had employed four hundred and eighty men, £45,000 for its five vessels, and £27,000 for their cargoes. For this return they had to wait three years; and only when, after establishing one factory at Acheen and another at Bantam, and opening up intercourse with the Moluccas, Lancaster reappeared in the Thames and enabled the adventurers to declare a dividend of nearly 100 per cent., did the "Company" fit out a second expedition of three not very large ships. Disappointed at this apathy on the part of the Company, the English Government had meanwhile commissioned Sir Edward Michelborne to discover the countries of Cathaia, China, Japan, Corea and Cambaia, and to trade with the people there, *notwithstanding any grant or charter to the contrary.* This expedition, so complete a failure that the "Company" preferred to drop the suit in Admiralty it had instituted against

Michelborne, is mainly remarkable for the circumstance that it
brought about the death of one of the great seamen of Elizabeth's
time at the hands of—Japanese! When Michelborne had
sailed on December 5th, 1604, he had taken with him as his
"pilot-major" the illustrious John Davys, who had given his
name to the straits between Greenland and the American
mainland, and in the course of the piratical enterprises that
marked the course of the voyage of the *Tiger* and the *Tiger's
Whelp*, an attempt was made on a Japanese junk at Bintang,
near Singapore. Michelborne speaks of "the Japons as not
being suffered to land in any port of India with weapons, being
a people so desperate and daring that they are feared in all
places where they come;" and he now had an opportunity of
tasting their quality. The Japanese, who fought, strange to
say, in the utmost silence, did terrible execution with their
swords, and among others Davys lost his life in this grim
affair.

Meanwhile, stimulated by a return of cent. per cent. on
Lancaster's initial venture (1601–04) on the one hand, and
by this licensed poaching of Michelborne's on (what they now had
reason to believe to be) their very lucrative preserves on the
other, the Governor and the Directors of the "Company"
were suddenly seized with a spasm, or a succession of spasms,
of very virtuous activity. A second "voyage" of four ships
under Middleton (Henry), while it brought the Company into
rivalry with the Dutch, proved as remunerative as Lancaster's
had been; and a third (1606–10) of three ships under Keeling,
which reached the Moluccas and returned without the loss of a
single man, was still more so. The fourth, under Sharpey,
was more or less of a failure; but on the fifth, Middleton
(David), although excluded from Banda in the Moluccas,
' where the Dutch now (1609) began to act as masters and
had the design of seizing the Captain's ship which by good
management he prevented," yet from Puloway "obtained 139
tons of Nutmegs, the like Quantity of Mace besides Pepper
and other valuable goods;" while on the sixth "voyage" Sir
Henry Middleton in the *Trades Increase*, the *Peppercorn*, and
two other ships, fitted out at an expense of £80,000, arrived
before Cambay, resolutely fought the Portuguese and beat them
off, and obtained some important concessions from native

Powers.[1] In 1610 only a single ship, which established relations with Siam and at Patani, was sent eastwards; but in 1611 three ships under Captain John Saris were fitted out for the eighth "voyage" at an expense of £60,000, and it was this "voyage" that was to open up commercial relations between the islanders of the East and the islanders of the West.

However, it may be well to leave the special fortunes of the eighth "voyage" aside for the moment in order to follow the general fortunes and enterprises of the "Company" a little further. The ninth "voyage" was in no wise remarkable, but the tenth was so. In it Captain Best, who had sailed with four ships in 1611, was assailed at Swalley, the port of Surat, by four great Portuguese galleons, twenty-six galleys, with five thousand men and one hundred and thirty pieces of ordnance, and beat them off in four successive engagements, to the great astonishment of the natives, who had hitherto deemed the Lusitanians to be invincible. At this date a single fleet of Portuguese merchantmen sailing from Goa to Surat or Cambay would number as many as one hundred and fifty or two hundred and fifty "carracks," we are told. This victory of Best's was a sad blow to Portuguese prestige in Indian waters; and when, after Shillinge's repulse of another huge fleet in 1620, the English, in conjunction with the Persians, boldly assumed the offensive and took Ormuz from the Peninsulars in 1622, it was truly Ichabod with the Portuguese power in the Orient. From this date the contest for supremacy in the East and the Far East no longer lay between the Portuguese and

---

[1] Both the *Trades Increase* and the *Peppercorn* were, or became, noted vessels. The first, of 1,200 tons, was the first merchantman of over 1,000 tons built in an English shipyard, although in 1597 one of 800 tons had been launched therefrom. Down to 1599 all the big English traders had been built in the Hanse towns; but we are told that "Hawkins's *Jesus of Lubeck* was the last great English ship either builded or bought beyond the seas." For in spite of all Harrison's perfervid patriotic account of the matter, Englishmen were not then, as now, the leaders either in the craft of shipbuilding or in mercantile marine enterprise. The Royal English Navy then was not remarkably strong. In 1608 (the year when Iyeyasu became Shōgun, and set Will Adams a-building European-rigged ships in Japan) it consisted of forty-two ships of 17,000 tons burthen manned by 8,346 men; and of these ships only two were of a burthen of 1,000 tons. In 1610, Pett, the naval constructor of the time, laid down the *Prince Royal* of 1,400 tons, with a keel of 114 feet, and armed with sixty-four pieces of great ordnance; and Stowe assures us that this vessel was "in all respects the greatest and goodliest ship that was ever built in England"! At that date the Dutchmen were far ahead.

As for the *Peppercorn*, of 300 tons, she lay for long in Hirado roadstead; and in *Cocks's Diary* (or Letters) we meet with ten entries referring to her disorderly crew.

their heretic foes, but between the heretic Dutch and the heretic English themselves.

Down to 1612 the twelve so-called "separate voyages" of the English East India Company had, roughly speaking, returned cent. per cent. But after all, compared with the success of their rivals, the Dutch, this was no great matter; for, as has been said, down to 1612 the capital of the English adventurers was no more than £70,000, and a good deal of the resulting profits had been devoted to the construction of dockyards and of new ships. Against this the Dutch East India Company, with a strong fleet of first-class vessels in existence, had been incorporated in 1602 with a capital of 6,000,000 *livres*, or £600,000.[2] It is true that after two more of these "separate voyages"—so called because the subscribers individually bore the expenses of each voyage and reaped the whole profits—had been fitted out, voyages from 1612 were undertaken on the joint-stock account, and the capital of the Company was then increased to £400,000. But even so, the English corporation was in no condition to compete effectually with its Dutch rival, empowered as the latter was to make its territorial acquisitions "national" colonies. By the year 1612 the Dutchmen had established themselves in Java; and besides this, they had now seized the Moluccas, where six forts with standing garrisons enforced the rule established by the Banda and Molucca factories, that the whole spice-crop must be sold to them exclusively. In 1610, Both, the first Governor-General of the Dutch Indies, had arrived at Jacatra in Java; and although this continued to be the seat of the administration of affairs, yet it was the Spice Islands (Moluccas) that the Dutch traders regarded as their most valuable possession. These islands they were resolute to hold against all comers—whether Spaniards, Portuguese, or English—and it was eagerness to maintain, or to obtain a grasp on, the little archipelago that was the direct cause of the deadly animosity that led to the massacre of Amboyna on February 17th, 1623, and the warfare between the rival heretic traders in the Far East which soon drove

---

2 At that date the *livre* consisted of 188 grains of fine silver, while the pound Troy of silver (5,760 grains) was coined into 62 English shillings. Accordingly, one *livre* was worth more than two shillings.

the Englishmen to confine their attention to the peninsula of Hindostan. At the time of Saris's arrival in Japan, the English had factories at Achin and at Bantam, and a very small one at Patani; while from 1615 to 1623 they had another small one at Cambello in Amboyna. After the massacre of the English settlers and their Japanese guards there in the latter year (1623), the Moluccas remained in undisputed possession of the Dutch, and the English withdrew nearly all their enterprises from the Indian Archipelago, the Malay Peninsula, and from Siam. To anticipate events somewhat it may be well to state that "in 1640 the Hollanders took Malacca, a blow from which the Portuguese never recovered; in 1651 they founded a colony at the Cape of Good Hope as a half-way station to the East; in 1658 they captured Jaffnapatam, the last stronghold of the Portuguese in Ceylon; while in 1664 they stripped the Portuguese of all their earlier possessions on the pepper-bearing coast of Malabar." To say nothing of all the territories its admirals and captains were able to attach to the State as national colonies, the additions made by the Dutch East India Company to the resources of the United Provinces were immense. Between 1610 and 1717 it paid no less than 2,784½ per cent. in dividends, or an average of nearly 26 per cent. per annum!

To return from this long but needful digression—needful, because without approximately correct views of the general situation in Eastern waters it is impossible to have clear ideas on the special contemporary foreign relations of Japan—we will now address ourselves to Captain John Saris and the eighth "separate voyage" of the English Company.[3]

On July 22nd, 1610, the *Red Lyon*, one of the two Dutch ships that had reached Japan in 1609, arrived at the Texel with a letter from Iyeyasu to the "King of Holland," by whom, of course, we are to understand the Stadtholder, Maurice of

[3] As Professor Riess in his excellent monograph on the "History of the English Factory at Hirado" points out, the mass of original matter on early English intercourse with Japan is exceedingly large. Besides the Professor's own capital treatise, the following works may be commended to those who wish to make a special study of the subject:—(1) Purchas's *Pilgrimes*, where, besides Saris's work, we meet with letters from several others—notably from Arthur Hatch, parson of the *Palsgrove*; (2) Rundall's *Memorials of Japan*; (3) *Cocks's Diary*, edited by R. Maunde Thompson; (4) *The Voyage of John Saris to Japan*, edited by Sir Ernest Mason Satow; (5) Sainsbury's *Calendar of State Papers, Colonial Series, East Indies, China, and Japan*, vols. i., ii., iii. Nos. 2, 3, and 4, are publications of the Hakluyt Society.

Nassau. Of this the London merchants soon got intelligence, and so in the following year they ordered Saris, in command of their eighth "voyage," to proceed to Japan with one of his vessels in order to open up commercial relations with a land which the Portuguese could not claim as a possession.[4]

Accordingly we find this entry in the log of the *Clove*, Saris's flagship:—" Jan. 1613.—The 14th in the morning we weighed out of the Road of Bantam for Japan, having taken in heare for that place pepper 700 sacks for a Tryall there. My company 81 persons, viz., 74 English, one Spanyard, one Japon and 5 Swarts [negroes]." On the passage Saris endeavoured to establish commercial relations with some of the Spice Islands; but the Hollanders resented any trenching upon the monopoly they now claimed. So, when the *Clove* at last arrived at Hirado on the 11th June, 1613, the officers and merchants on board could no longer believe in the true friendship of Brouwer (the head of the Dutch factory) and his fellow-traders whom they found established in the port. While in Bantam, Saris was shown Will Adams's long letter of October 22nd, 1611, and two days before the *Clove* weighed from Bantam Roads Adams had penned another to the chief of the Factory there[5] (which of course was too late to reach Saris), in which the following passages are important:—

"You shall ('I *understand*) by the letter of Sr. Thomas Smith [Governor of E. I. C.], he hath written that he will send a ship heer in Japan to establish a Factori, of which, yf yet may be profitt I shal be most glad: of which newes I told the Emperour [Iyeyasu, *aetat.* 71], thereof, and told him yt in ye next yeer the

---

4 To quote from Professor Riess:—"'The prospects of the Chartered Company as regards the trade of the East Indies were, however, somewhat uncertain as long as the Spanish authorities protested against the intrusion of English merchants in regions where the Portuguese had first settled, and where the Spaniards were restricted by their own Government from attempting any commercial competition. From Madrid the Privy Council received again and again disquieting reports from the English ambassadors about the bad feeling created in the highest Spanish circles by the trespassing of the East India Company on the limits of the Portuguese colonial and mercantile preserve. The Spanish Minister for Foreign Affairs, Conde de Lemos, went even so far as to inform Sir Charles Cornwaleys, that 'in coercions and punishments to restrain access to those countries he had an inclination rather to cruelty than clemency.' One can well understand that the English Government greatly desired that some Englishman should establish trade beyond the Portuguese possessions.'" This passage is in connection with Michelborne's expedition of 1604 6; but even in 1611 the English were anxious to establish commercial relations in the East with countries to which Portugal could lay no claim.

5 "To my assured good frind *Augustin Spalding*, in Bantam, deliuer this, per a good frind *Thomas Hill*, whom God preserue. Laus dei: written in Japan in ye Iland of Ferrando, the 12 of Jenuari 1613.""

kinges mati. of Ingland would send his imbashador with mony and marchandiz to trad in his country; and of the certenti theerof I had receued newes. At which hee wass veery glad, and rejoyced that strange nacions had such good oppinion."

This, it may be pointed out, is only one piece of evidence among many to show that the leading men in Japan at that time were the reverse of foreign-haters. To a Briton—and still more to an American—his house is his castle; and surely no Briton or American can honestly find fault with the Japanese Government if it insisted on being master in its own house when it found that the large-hearted hospitality it was extending to strangers was being abused by some of them. Japanese then, as now, were exceedingly anxious to earn the good opinion of foreign nations, whether Asiatic or European, by fair international dealing, and down to the death of Iyeyasu, at least, the treatment accorded foreigners in Japan was far more liberal than they would have met with in any other country. And this, too, altogether apart from the fact that in the great and grand and all-important matter of religious toleration Iyeyasu was centuries ahead of Europe. Therefore, hats off to Iyeyasu—*very* respectfully.

" As the shipes [Dutch, of which till then there had been less than a half-dozen at Hirado] coum lade, so thay go away much deeper lade, for heer (? *they*) lad thear shipes with rise, fish, bisket, with diuers other prouisions, monicion (munition), marriners, sojoures and svch lyk, so that in respeckt of the warres in the Mollowcouss (Moluccas) Japan is verry profittable vnto them; and yf the warres do continew in ye Mollucous with ye traffick thay haue heer wilbe a great scourge vnto ye Spaynnards, etc."

And there is no doubt that for the prosecution of the conquest of the Moluccas the Hollanders found in Japan a most valuable base of supply.

"The charges in Japan are not great; onlly a present for ye Emperour [Iyeyasu] and a present for ye Kinge [Hidetada], and 2 or 3 other presents for the Secretaris. Other coustoumes here be nonn. Now, once, yf a ship do coum, *lett her coum for the esterly part of Japan*, lying in 35d. 10m. whear the Kinge and ye Emperour Court is: for coum our ships to Ferando [Hirado] whear the Hollanders bee, it is farr to ye Court, about 230 Leagues, a werysoum way and foul. The citti of Edo lyeth in 36, and about this esterly part of the land thear be the best harbors and a cost so cleer as theayr is no sholdes nor rokes ½ a myll from the mayn land. It is good also for sale of merchandis and security for ships, forr which cass I haue sent a pattron [chart] of Japan, for which my self I hau been all about the cost in the shipping that I have made for ye Emperour, that I hau experyence of all yt part of ye cost that lyeth in 36d., etc."

On arriving at Hirado, where the *Clove* received a most ready welcome from the House of Matsuura, then as eager for foreign trade as it had been in the days of Xavier and of Torres, Saris at once got the Daimyō to dispatch a messenger with a letter to Adams. The pilot was then at Iyeyasu's Court at Shidzuoka, but the messenger did not inquire for him there, but posted on to Uraga, and thus it was forty-eight days before Adams reached Matsuura's town.[6] Hence, accompanied by Adams and ten other Englishmen, Saris on the 7th August set out for Shidzuoka, where he arrived on the 6th of the following month—September 1613.[7]

The reception here accorded Saris cannot be better described than in Adams's own words:—

"So the next daye following being redy, the gennerall went to his [*the emperour's*] palles [*palace*]: being courteouly receued and bid welcoum by the tresvrer and others. So being in the palles set downe, the gennerall called me and byd me tell the ssecretari, that the kinge mati. letter he would delliuer it with his own handes. Vppon which I went and told ye secretari thearof: at which he awnsswered, that it was not the covstoum of the land to delliuer anny letter with the hand of anny stranger, but that he should keep the letter in his hand till he cam into the pressence of the emperor; and then he would tak it from him ovt of his handes and delliuer it to the emperour. Which awnsser I told the gennerall theearof; at which awnsswer not being contented cassed me to tell the secretari that yf he myght not delliuer it himself he would retourn agayne to his loging. Which second awnsswer I told the secretari; the which, not thinking well therof, was disconted with me in that I had nott instruckted him in the manners and coustoum of all strangers which had bein yeerly in their covntri; and made me again to go to the gennerall: the which I did; but the gennerall being verry mvch discontented, it so rested. At which

---

[6] For this mistake the messenger was banished from Hirado.

[7] Says the Captain:—"When wee approched any Towne, we saw Crosses with the dead bodies of those who had been crucified thereupon; for crucifying is heere an ordinarie punishment for most Malefactors. Comming neere Surunga [Shidzuoka], where the Emperours Court is, wee saw a Scaffold with the heads of diners (which had been executed) placed thereupon, and by were diners Crosses with the dead Corpses of those which had been executed remayning still vpon them, and the pieces of others, which after their Executions had been hewen againe and againe by the triall of others *Cattans* [swords]. All which caused a most vnsauourie passage to vs, that to enter into Surunga must needs passe by them.
"This Citie of Surunga is full as bigge as London, with all the Suburbs. [Vivero in 1610 estimated its population at between 500,000 and 600,000 souls.] The Handi-crafts men wee found dwelling in the outward parts and skirts of the Towne, because those that are of the better sort dwell in the inward part of the Citie, and will not be annoyed with the rapping, knocking, and other disturbance that artificers cannot be without."

tym, presently, the emperour came fourth, and the gennerall was brought befoor him: to whoum the emperour bid him well-covm of so weery journy, receuing his mati. letter from the gennerall by the handes of the secritary, etc."

Saris passed on to visit Hidetada in Yedo, and then, after a four days' stay with Adams on his estate at Uraga, he returned to Shidzuoka, and there received [8] the answer to his petition for privileges, which, according to instructions, he had presented. This charter, as translated by Professor Riess, runs as follows:—

(1) The ship that has now for the first time come from England over the sea to Japan may carry on trade of all kinds without hindrance. With regard to future visits [of English ships] permission will be given in regard to all matters.

(2) With regard to the cargoes of ships, requisitions will be made by list according to the requirements of the Shōgunate.

(3) [English ships] are free to visit any port in Japan. If disabled by storms, they may put into any harbour.

(4) Ground in the place in Yedo which they may desire shall be given to the English, and they may erect houses and reside and trade there. They shall be at liberty to return to their country whenever they wish to do so, and to dispose as they like of the houses they have erected.

(5) If an Englishman dies in Japan of disease, or any other cause, his effects shall be handed over without fail. [Somewhat different from the French *Droit d'Aubaine*, it may be remarked.]

(6) Forced sales of cargoes and violence shall not take place.

(7) If one of the English should commit an offence he shall be sentenced by the English General [*Taishō*] according to the gravity of the offence.

Although this charter of 1613 shows no marked advance when compared with the general "patent" of 1602 issued in consequence of the *San Espirito* affair in Tosa, it must not be forgotten that its terms were infinitely more favourable than would have been accorded by any contemporary European

8 Saris also received a present for King James I. of England—ten painted screens which he received in Kyōto on the presentation of an order from Iyeyasu. When they arrived in London the Court of Directors resolved (20th December, 1614): "Screens sent to His Majesty from Japan not being so good as some the Company have, to be exchanged."

When Valegnani got Hideyoshi's reply to the Viceroy of India (1591) he also got some most costly presents of magnificent workmanship to carry back to His Excellency. On some of his officers representing that sending articles of such finish was merely so much waste, as the Viceroy could not appreciate them, Hideyoshi burst out: "Whether he appreciates them or not is of little consequence. But my honour and dignity forbid me to offer any articles as presents except the very best!"

The missionaries are unanimous in charging Iyeyasu with stinginess and miserly avarice. He certainly had a fine sense of the value of money and was uncommonly loath to part with the "siller"—except for very good consideration received.

Government to alien traders—especially if these aliens professed
a cult in any way differing from the State religion. It will be
remembered that a dozen years before this Iyeyasu had offered
the Spanish merchants a splendid site in Yedo, but that so
far the Spaniards had failed to avail themselves of the privilege.
The old statesman, although he opposed no obstacle to their
settlement in Hirado, now gave the Englishmen a hint that
it would be well for them to be less neglectful of Eastern
Japan than the Peninsulars, in spite of all their large promises,
had proved. (Article 4.) In his efforts to get the new-comers
to make his nascent metropolis their headquarters he was
strenuously supported by Adams; but although the pilot got
Saris to examine the harbour of Uraga closely—it was found
to be excellent—and insistently dwelt upon the advantage of
establishing the factory on the Gulf of Yedo, Saris pronounced
in favour of Hirado, where the astute Matsuura had already
dined him and wined him and generally made a little god of
him.[9]

The results were disastrous, as Adams no doubt pointed out
they would be, and as Saris's own common-sense might have
told him they would be. In the matter of "Customs"—for
that is what the "presents" really amounted to—the savings
would have been not inconsiderable. In a few days at Hirado
goods to the value of 975 rials of eight had gone in presents to
the Daimyō, his relations, and a crowd of hungry underlings.
For Iyeyasu, Hidetada, their "secretaries" (Codskindono among
them), the Judge of Meaco (that is Itakura Iga-no-Kami, the
Shoshidai, who afterwards wrecked all Hideyoshi's prospects
as a god), and others, a value of £180 3s. 10d. had been set
aside; and as Iyeyasu got only 349½ rials—or £87 7s. 6d.
worth—appropriated to him, and Hidetada only 175 rials, or
£43 15s. 10d., it is not difficult to work out what the savings in
presents alone would have been if Adams's advice had been
adopted. Besides all this, the very considerable expenses of the
numerous journeys to Court would have been saved. But the
most important consideration of all would have been that in

---

[9] We get here a confirmation of the missionaries' statements about the
Spaniards frequenting Uraga at this time:—"Saris was desirous of buying a
Spanish ship riding at anchor in Uraga, but the price of £100 asked by Adams as
agent of the owners seemed to him 'very dear'; he bought only some Kyōto ware,
of which Adams kept a stock at Uraga on account of some Spaniards."

Eastern Japan no Portuguese, no Dutch, and but little Spanish competition would have had to be faced.   However, Saris, from the poor opinion he had conceived of Adams, would not listen to the pilot's advice.

After a deal of very ungenerous haggling on Saris's part, Adams *did* enter the Company's service at a salary of £100, and rendered a good deal more than sterling service.   But no thanks to Saris for that; in making that agreement with Adams he was, as his own account of the matter shows, merely making a virtue of necessity; for Adams, though neither a rich man nor a professional dollar-grinder, was yet of perfectly independent means at the time.[10]   He had trading agencies of his own at Yedo, Uraga, Shidzuoka, Kyōto, and Hirado; the Spaniards and the Dutch did employ him, the Portuguese were eager to do so, while he at the same time wore the two swords of a Japanese *samurai*, and had an estate of his own.   "Now for my service which I have

[10] In this connection it may be well to print the following from Professor Riess's valuable monograph, in which, by the way, the vindication of Adams's attitude on this occasion and general character is complete and triumphant.

"How little Saris thought of the business qualities or even of the character of the newly-appointed Adams, is clear from a 'Memorandum,' written only eleven days after signing the contract and left for the guidance of Richard Cocks in the management of the factory.   Rundall has printed a part of it, but has left out the most damaging passages.   This venomous indictment of William Adams runs:—

"'And for Mr. Adams he is only fit to be master of the junk, and to be used as linguist at court, when you have no employment for him at sea.   It is necessary you stir him, his condition being well known unto you as to myself; otherwise you shall have little service of him, the country affording great liberty, whereunto he is much affected.   The forced agreement I made with him you know could not be eschewed, the Flemings and Spaniards making false proffers of great entertainment and himself more affected to them than his own nation, we wholly destitute of language.

"'In any hand let him not have the disbursing of any money of the Company's, either for junks or otherwise; for his usual speeches is so large and his resolution so set upon getting.   I entreat you, he may always have one with him to pay out and to write the particulars of what is disbursed in all such matters as you shall employ him in.'

"'You shall not need to send for any farther order to the Emperor for the setting out of the junk, it being an article granted in the charter, as by the copy thereof in English left with you will appear.   Yet will Mr. Adams tell you that he cannot depart without a license, which will not be granted except he go up.   Believe him not; neither neglect that business: for his wish is but to have the Company bear his charges to his wife.   Yet rather than that he shall leave you and betake himself to the Spaniards or Flemings, you must make a virtue of necessity and let him go, *leaving his brother-in-law to follow his business.*'

"After a careful study of all extant materials for the history of the English factory in Japan we can only endorse Rundall's judgement: 'In all this Captain Saris was wrong and unjust.'   Adams remitted the £20 lent to his wife in England immediately after Saris's departure and proved most reliable and exact in his accounts with the Company.   Cocks had no occasion to be lenient with Adams, but felt greatly obliged to him for many services and acts of kindness, even after his engagement by the Company had expired."

doen and daily doe, being employed in the Emperours service, he hath given me a living, like unto a lordship in England, with eighty or ninety husbandmen, that be as my slaves or servants; which, or the like precedent, was never here before geven to any stranger." On February 25th, 1615, Cocks writes to the Governor of the Company: "The truth is the emperour esteemeth hym much, and he may goe and speake with hym at all tymes, when kynges and princes are kept out." And this was the man that skipper Saris in lordly wise pronounced to be fit only for a master of a junk or the post of linguist—a linguist in Japan then getting about ten shillings per week! The simple truth of the matter seems to be this—that with all his great qualities as a worker, in spite of all his deftness with the pen, Saris at bottom was not much better than a mere dollar-grinding Philistine with a taste for pornographic pictures—a good man spoiled from having had to take up the trade of a merchant skipper, whose then use and wont it was to address his subordinates in the tone of a God Almighty delivering himself to a black beetle.

The sum of the story of the Factory established by Saris (contrary to Adams's advice) in Hirado is easy to give. After a troubled and troublous existence of ten years it was finally dissolved with a loss of something between £5,000 and £10,000 [11] in the very year (1623) when the Dutch President was writing that "in one voyage to Japan above 76 per cent. may be gained; sufficient to buy up all the returns needful for Europe." We have seen that in 1609 the Great Ship from Macao had brought a freight valued at over 1,000,000 crowns. The Factory at Hirado was opened with a capital of £7,000, one-half of which was in the form of cash, while Professor Riess estimates the total value of the imports brought by the three English ships that subsequently carried cargoes to Hirado at a little over £3,000. From 1617 to 1620 the only English vessels that entered Hirado were two or three of the Company's ships *brought in as prizes by the Dutch*. From the former year the Hollanders took vigorous

---

[11] From the Court Minutes of the East India Company the loss appears to have been really less than this estimate of Professor Riess's:—"March 13th, 1633.—Mr. Governor made known with what difficulty they got out of Japan and that they had lost by that trade at least £1,700."

means to enforce their claim to the monopoly of trade with the Spice Islands; in 1618 three interloping English ships were captured in the Straits of Macassar, and after their officers had been replaced by Dutchmen, were at once employed as Dutch traders. One of these, the *Attendance*, arrived at Hirado on August 9th, 1618, where the Hollanders brought her in "in a bravado." In the following year the *Swan*, and later on another prize, was brought in in similar fashion.

Meanwhile (July and August, 1619) the "Treaty of Defence" between the English and the Dutch at home had been concluded, and two months after, news of this had arrived at Batavia (27th March), when the methods of defence were arranged in every detail. According to the Treaty, the Companies were to trade in the Moluccas as partners, two-thirds of the spices being reserved for the Dutch and the other left for the English, while each party was to maintain in the farther East Indies twelve ships in a common "Fleet of Defence." Who the enemy aimed at was appears very clearly from the instructions given the captains by the Council. "If you meet Portuguese, Spaniards, or their adherents anywhere, assault and surprise them." All prizes taken should at the fleet's arrival with them at Hirado be equally divided between the English and Dutch factories there. Japanese junks and Chinese ships bound for Japan were to be left unmolested; but Chinese ships bound to or returning from the Philippines were to be seized upon as good prize. "If any Portugal shipping shall in flying recover any road or port upon the coast of Japan, you shall nevertheless force him from his anchorage from under the land." And at this time England was supposed to be at peace with Spain (and Portugal), while the nine years' truce of 1612 between the Dutch and Peninsulars was supposed to be still in force!

From Hirado as a base two filibustering expeditions were directed against Manila Bay, as the result of which, and of some minor captures, prizes to the value of some £100,000 had to be divided between the associated freebooters before the dissolution of their alliance in the summer of 1622. This dissolution was brought about by the inability of the English to contribute their stipulated quota of ships, men, and money. A few months afterwards (February 17th, 1623) occurred the so-called massacre of Amboyna, to exact reparation for which the English were impotent till 1654 ; [12] and shortly after this all the English factories were withdrawn from the Indian Archipelago.

Previous to the Amboyna affair, however, it had been resolved by the English Company's agents in Batavia to reduce, if not to withdraw, its meagre staff in Japan ; and on May 22nd, 1623, imperative orders for its withdrawal were issued. Accordingly " on the 22nd December many of the townsmen [of Hirado] came with their wives and families to take leave of the factors, some weeping at their departure. On the 22nd the factors went on board intending to set sail. But the Dutch merchants and many Japanese friends came on board with eatables and drinkables to have a jolly leave-taking. As there was not room on board for so large a company (over one hundred) they all went to Kōchiura and spent the day there, postponing their departure till the following day. At noon of the 24th December, 1623, the *Bull* set sail for Batavia. The English Factory at Hirado was a thing of the past."

Of course, the ten years' sojourn of six or seven English merchants with their headquarters in an insignificant " fisher town" on a remote Western islet exercised little or no appreciable influence upon the history of contemporary Japan with its population of 15,000,000 or 20,000,000 souls.[13] Neither can the worthy traders be regarded as authorities on the contemporary history of Japan, in spite of the *cacoethes scribendi* with which several of them were infected. Yet withal, to them the discerning historian will readily acknowledge a debt of gratitude, for apart from the fact that they frequently confirm our Japanese and our still more valuable missionary authorities, they now and then make statements which, astounding and

---

[12] "It is agreed as above that the Lords of the States-General of the United Provinces shall take care that justice be done upon those who were partakers or accomplices in the Massacre of the English at Amboyna, as the Republick of England is pleased to term that Fact, provided any of them be living."—27th Article of Treaty of April 5th, 1654.

[13] Their chief service rendered to the country seems to have been the introduction of the common or garden potato. Cocks's Diary:—"June 19th, 1615.—I tooke a garden this day and planted it with pottatos brought from the Liquea [Luchus], *a thing not yet planted in Japan*." July 29th, 1618:—"I set 500 small potata rootes in a garden. Mr. Eaton sent me them from Liquea." Adams had brought the first lot. The Japanese call the common potato *Jagatara-imo*. Jacatra stood on the site of the modern Batavia, and hence it would seem that the Japanese regard Java as the source of one of their staples of food.

inaccurate as they may be, are yet extremely serviceable in suggesting lines of investigation that afford the richest returns when followed up by Japanese experts. As regards several of the results in the following chapter, casual remarks in Cocks's Diary or in the correspondence of the Hirado Factory have primarily supplied the clue that has led to their attainment.

CHAPTER XX.

CHRISTIANITY AND FOREIGN RELATIONS (1614–1624).

IN a previous chapter we have dealt with the general fortunes of Christianity in Japan from the death of the Taikō in 1598 down to the date of the expulsion of the missionaries in the November of 1614, just a month before the beginning of the winter campaign against Ōsaka castle. In spite of the supposed deportation of all the foreign *religieux* from Japan, yet, as we have said, there were at least five European missionaries in the great stronghold at the time of its capture on June 3rd, 1615. And, strangely enough, on that occasion all the five escaped with their lives.[1] The two Jesuits, Porro and de Torres,[2] had a series of most remarkable adventures;[3] and the letters in which they recount them as well as the events of the storming of the fortress are worthy of careful perusal. However, it is to one single passage in Porro's epistle that attention is here to be directed.

It will be remembered that Daté Masamune with 10,000 troops had formed the van of the Tokugawa left wing on the day of the grand assault. Writes Porro :—

"Finally, leaving Ōsaka behind me I traversed the army of Masamune, the father-in-law of Daifousama's second son.[4] I was observed by a soldier, who, presuming that I might be one of the Fathers, called me and very respectfully conducted me into his tent, telling me that he would never consent to my going further at such a crisis and at the very evident risk of my life. I remained all that day (4th) with him; on the next day, which was the 5th of June, my host set out for Kyōto; and I myself, again falling into extreme peril, directed myself towards Masamune's presence. I found

---

[1] The Japanese secular priest who was with them was killed by a sabre-stroke.

[2] De Torres had been for long settled in Kaga with Takayama Ukon, and Takayama's former retainers had mostly joined Hideyori.

[3] Both, fleeing in different directions, were stripped naked by the pillagers, and to that in no small degree it would appear that their safety was due. As soon as they were recognised to be non-Japanese (from their colour) they were left alone.

[4] This, of course, is a mistake. Hideyasu, Iyeyasu's second son, had died in 1607. Tadateru, Masamune's son-in-law, was Iyeyasu's sixth son.

this lord on the point of mounting to proceed to Kyōto. I briefly explained to him that I was a foreigner, of the city of Nagasaki, and that finding myself in Ōsaka during the late circumstances, I was reduced to the sad condition in which he saw me, and I begged him graciously to facilitate my passage to Muro, and thence to Nagasaki. Masamune answered me through a page that he would have granted my request without difficulty and at once, *if I had not been a Christian !* "

Now the strange thing is that at the very moment Daté Masamune made this unsympathetic remark to Father Porro, he (Daté) had an embassy of more than sixty persons in Spain, on its way to the Pope of Rome, bearing a letter from him in which His Holiness was asked to send Franciscan monks for service in Daté's domains, to appoint a "'great prelate' through whose zeal and under whose direction all the inhabitants might be converted without delay to the Christian religion," and to use the weight of his authority to aid Daté in accomplishing his ardent desire to enter into friendly relations with the King of Spain and his Christian States ! And at the very time that all the foreign missionaries with their most illustrious converts were herded together in Nagasaki for deportation from Japan as soon as "the Great Ship from Macao" should arrive, this embassy of Daté Masamune's was being fêted and feasted in royal style in Seville, one of the most bigotedly Christian cities in the world ! The reproduction of the following extract from M. Pagés will furnish the means of dealing with this most puzzling episode in Japanese foreign intercourse in the most compendious way:—

" Father Sotelo, with Hashikura, sent by Daté Masamune, Prince of Oshiu, arrived in New Spain on October 28th, 1613, and at the port of Acapulco on January 24th, 1614. The Spanish authorities gave them a splendid reception. From there they went to Mexico, where the Viceroy welcomed them with great honours. It was the time of the Holy Week, and sixty-eight persons in the suite of the ambassador [Hashikura], who had been perfectly instructed, were solemnly baptized in the church of Saint Francis, and confirmed by the Archbishop.[5] It was determined that the baptism of the ambassador

---

[5] At the very moment of this august ceremony in the church of Saint Francis, in the city of Mexico, the Christian ladies of Kyōto, the capital of Japan, were being subjected to very outrageous treatment. Says Pagés:— " Itakura, the Governor of Kyōto, not daring to disobey the Imperial order, charged Sagamidono [*i.e.* Ōkubo, to whom we have alluded in the foot-note on pp. 493–494, whence the significance of the incident will readily appear] to destroy the churches and to compel the Christians to apostatize, leaving them only the choice of a sect. He [Itakura] had secretly given orders to his Minister [Ōkubo, Sagami-no-kami] to make use of threats and harsh and ignominious treatment before all things, and in the last place to exile the refractory, *but to*

PP2

should take place only in Spain. Hashikura left Mexico on
Ascension Day; he was at Puebla da los Angeles on the Day of
Pentecost. He embarked at San Juan d'Ulloa on June 10th, 1614,
touched at Havana on July 23rd, resumed his journey on August 7th,
and arrived at the harbour of San Lucar de Barrameda in Andalusia
on October 5th. A magnificent entry into Seville was prepared for
him. The city showed itself equally proud to welcome Father Sotelo,
who had been born within its walls, and to fête in him one of the
glories of the Church and the apostle who had converted and baptized
an infinite number of pagans. The authorities of Seville received the
ambassador in solemn audience, and listened to the communication of
the dispatches addressed to the city. In reality, the Prince of Oshiu
[i.e. Daté Masamune] had written directly to the city, and had sent as
a present a sword and a dagger of great value, in token of friendship.
He expressed his desire to embrace the Christian faith as soon as
circumstances should permit him to do so, and his wish to see all his
vassals profess the same religion. At the same time he proposed
favourable arrangements for trade with the Spaniards. The letter was
dated Sendai, October 26th, 1613. It was decided that the matter
should be referred to the King of Spain. The ambassador quitted
Seville on November 25th, passed through Cordova and Toledo, and

---

deprive no one of his or her life: [This statement must not be overlooked.] Five
days only after the removal of the missionaries, Sagamidono [Okubo of
Odawara] posted an Edict to the effect that every Christian who would not
deny his faith would be burned alive, and that whoever refused to apostatise
had only to prepare the stake to which he would be bound. Many of the
Christians hastened to prepare their stake. However, the Commissioner
[Okubo of Odawara, see footnote on page 494] caused the house of the Company
at Kyōto, as well as those of the Franciscans at Fushimi, to be razed. [All
this, it will be observed, is in perfect accord with the Japanese sources.]
Some Christians then fell away from the faith, and removed their names from
the list of the faithful—that is to say, from the Book of Life. But the
greater number remained invincible, and preferred exile. . . . Several ladies
who had made the vow of chastity practised *la vie commune* under the conduct
of one of their number, Julia Naitō. [This was the sister of the Christian
diplomatist, Naitō, the first Japanese Daimyō to be baptized. She died in Manila
on March 28th, 1627, after thirteen years of exile.] They occupied themselves
with the conversion of persons of their sex to whom the missionaries could
not penetrate. These ladies offered a victorious resistance to humiliating
trials. It was proclaimed that they were to be promenaded *nude* through the
whole city! They at once caused nine of the youngest and of the most
beautiful to be concealed in places of security; the other nine betook themselves to prayer and awaited the hour of combat. Bags of rice-straw were
brought, and they were put into them; then they were suspended in pairs on
poles, and promenaded in this way, in the midst of the insults of some and
of the blessings of others. At the close of the day the exhausted satellites
deposited them in the middle of a field on the bank of a river, on the
execution-ground. There they were left until the following day. One of them
who had been set free and conducted to her father's house, returned therefrom,
carrying her straw-sack, and rejoined her noble companions. The lieutenant
of the Governor [this would seem to be Okubo of Odawara, whose
position in the matter has been explained in the footnote on p. 494],
ashamed of having been conquered by women, wished to surrender them
to the heathen as subjects for their debauchery; but he pardoned them, and
caused them to be consigned to the care of Christians as prisoners. The
persecution was acute during nine or ten days; but Sagamidono [Okubo
of Odawara] was recalled and exiled, and the Viceroy [Itakura] ordered a
pause until the receipt of a fresh order."

All this squares exceedingly well with the data in the footnote just referred
to, except only that the missionaries here make no mention of the execution
of sixty Christians by Okubo.

entered Madrid on December 20th, 1614. During all its progress through Spain the embassy had been generously maintained by the King of Spain, and at Madrid it received hospitality in the convent of Saint Francis at the expense of the same sovereign."

On January 30th, 1615, the Japanese ambassador and his colleague, Father Sotelo, had an audience with the King, Philip III., and five days later Hashikura went to pay his respects to the all-powerful Duke of Lerma, who assured him of his benevolent co-operation. Then, on February 17th (1615) Hashikura received holy baptism in the convent of the Franciscans (Descalzos) from the hands of Guzman, the chief chaplain of the King (acting as substitute for the Archbishop of Toledo, whose sickness prevented him from officiating). The godfather and the godmother were the Duke of Lerma and the Countess of Barachia. It is needless to say that in this Duke of Lerma we are dealing with one of the leading characters in Lesage's immortal narrative of *Gil Blas's* Adventures.[6] After a further stay of eight months in Spain, Hashikura and his train passed from Barcelona to Savona and thence to Genoa, where the Doge and the Senate treated them as royally as they had been treated at Seville. Thence they sailed for Civita Vecchia, and arrived in Rome towards the end of October, 1615. To the events of their stay there the historians of the Church devote page after page. We hear of the Swiss guards firing salvoes of artillery in their honour from Saint Angelo (the mole of Hadrian) and elsewhere, of the trumpets of the Senator and of the Conservators sounding fanfares, and so forth

---

6 To Hashikura, and still more to the intriguing ambitious Sotelo (the "priest-ambassador" was really angling for the creation of an Archbishopric of Japan in his own favour) the "benevolent co-operation" of the Duke must have been of no little consequence. The following passage (*Gil Blas*, viii. 5) is doubtless familiar to most of our readers:—"I likewise accompanied my lord duke when he had an audience of the king, which was usually three times a day. In the morning he went into his majesty's chamber as soon as he was awake. There he dropped down on his marrow-bones by the bedside, talked over what was to be done in the course of the day, and put into the royal mouth the speeches the royal tongue was to make. He then withdrew. After dinner he came back again; not for State affairs, but for *what, what?* and a little gossip. He was well instructed in all the tittle-tattle of Madrid, which was sold to him at the earliest of the season. Lastly, in the evening he saw the king again for the third time, put whatever colour he pleased on the transactions of the day, and, as a matter of course, requested his instructions for the morrow. While he was with the king, I kept in the ante-chamber, where people of the first quality, sinking that they might rise, threw themselves in the way of my observation, and thought the day not lost if I had deigned to exchange a few words of common civility with them. Was it to be wondered at if my self-importance fattened upon such food? There are many folks at Court who stalk about on stilts of much frailer materials."

and so forth. "It might have been fancied that one was assisting at an ancient triumph."

The delivery of Daté's letter to His Holiness must really have been a magnificent function. "The Pope [Paul V., a Borghese] was surrounded by cardinals, by archbishops and bishops, apostolic proto-notaries, the clerks of the chambers, and the chief lords of the nobility." However, the stately and imposing ceremony was not without its spice of comedy. This was supplied when, after the reading of Daté's letter, Father Petrocha of Mantua pronounced a discourse in the name of the "Prince" (Daté Masamune) and of the ambassadors; for the worthy Father then "represented the Prince as a Christian in intention, *voto christianus*, the saviour of eighteen hundred victims destined for death, and the future Defender of the Faith in Japan"! And on the previous 5th of June this future "Defender of the Faith in Japan" had curtly told Father Porro, who in the direst extremity had invoked his assistance, that the favour asked would have been accorded without difficulty and at once, *if its asker had not been a Christian!*

Thus during the nineteen months' interval between the departure of the embassy from Sendai (October 21st, 1613) and the meeting with Porro after the fall of Ōsaka, a great change must have come over Daté's feelings towards Christianity. That is, on the supposition that, unlike the Bishop of Japan—a Jesuit, by the way—we admit the original sincerity of his professions. In his letter of October 5th, 1613, Çerqueyra (the Bishop) is indeed very frank in the expression of his opinion on the matter. Inasmuch as in this communication of his (to the General of the Company) there are some very suggestive hints on the general state of the foreign relations of Japan at the time, it may not be amiss to reproduce the greater portion of it.

After mentioning the wreck of the vessel (with Sotelo on board) for New Spain at Uraga in 1612, and the construction of a new ship to proceed thither with a few Spanish passengers, he goes on :—

"Among them is a Franciscan monk called Louis Sotelo, who, it is said, is sent as ambassador to Rome by a Japanese gentleman named Masamune, a subject of the 'King' of Japan, but Lord of several provinces, with the ostensible object of requesting both His

Majesty [Philip III. of Spain] and His Holiness [Paul V.] to send over here missionaries to preach the Gospel in his dominions, but who, as a matter of fact, only does it on the expectation of great material advantages by the arrival of the Spanish ships in his ports; should the request of the said ambassador be granted, great inconvenience may be expected not only for these Christians, but for the Franciscan monks likewise for having taken a principal part in this transaction. This is the reason *why the father Jesuits out here did all they could during these last months to prevent not only the embassy, but also the voyage of Father Sotelo to New Spain, and worked hard but unsuccessfully to get him into their hands and to send him to Manila.* I am told now that, as the Superiors could not prevent his going to New Spain, they have informed the Commissioner-General to Mexico of the little foundation of the embassy, and of the dangers *which may issue, if successful,* as the Lord of the Tenka [*i.e.* Iyeyasu] and the prince his son [*i.e.* Hidetada the Shōgun] do not wish the Franciscan monks to build churches in the Kwantō; nay, that the former [*i.e.* Iyeyasu] has already written to the Viceroy of New Spain *that it is not religion but commerce he wants.* And we fear, therefore, and with good cause, that should any further mission of Franciscan monks or any other mission land here, it might greatly exasperate the 'King' against them and Masamune, whose real object in wanting the mission in his estates will then become too manifest. And as the 'King' is already very distrustful of the Spaniards for reasons we have explained to you before, *he may be led to suspect there exists some ominous alliance between them and Masamune,* and give vent to his indignation by causing the total ruin of the latter, whose estates' are entirely dependent on the 'King's' good-will, who may deprive him of them as well as of his life whenever he should think it convenient to do so. I wrote to His Majesty [Philip III. of Spain] about everything deserving prudence and reflection with regard to this embassy, and now I do the same to you [*i.e.* Acquaviva, General of the "Company of Jesus" from 1581 to 1615], so that, if needful, you may inform His Holiness, lest through lack of trustworthy information about the real import of this embassy they may send over here an expedition that might endanger the interests of the Church and the authority of the Pope." [7]

In a previous chapter Sotelo's story had been brought down to the summer of 1613, when he was arrested and condemned to death for returning to Yedo and preaching there in defiance of Hidetada's proscription of the foreign religion. However, although the members of Sotelo's congregation, mostly lepers and outcasts, were sharply dealt with,

---

[7] This is quoted from Mr. Meriwether's interesting monograph on "Daté Masamune" in Vol. XXI. of the *Transactions of the Asiatic Society of Japan.* Readers who wish to learn all about the details of the building of the ship for the embassy are referred to that monograph and to the monograph of Dr. Nachod, already referred to. Pagés, Charlevoix, and Crasset have each page upon page devoted to Sotelo. The latter two writers, being Jesuits, are none too favourably inclined towards him, any more than they are towards Collado afterwards.

yet at the time—and indeed down to the year 1617—the Shōgun was utterly averse to shedding the blood of the foreign priests; and when Daté came forward with a plea for Sotelo's life, the Franciscan was at once entrusted to his keeping. A few months later on (October, 1613) Sotelo set out as the head of Daté's embassy to the city of Seville, to Philip III. of Spain, and to Pope Paul V.

Although Sotelo had been thrown over by the Shōgun Hidetada, he yet kept the Shōgun's dispatch to the Spanish King in his possession. In view of this fact, Pagés' account of his conduct at the audience on January 30th, 1615, is amusing:—

"Then Father Sotelo, having obtained the word, expressed himself in the name of the Emperor of Japan, and said that five years previously [1610] the Emperor had chosen him to carry to His Majesty [Philip III.] words of amity and alliance, but that his failing health not having permitted him, the ambassador, to pass into Spain, Father Alonso Muñoz had been substituted for him; that, having remained in Japan, he had learned that the Dutch had dispatched an embassy from Europe to the Shōgun to oppose his projects of alliance with Spain by proposing new conditions of immense advantage. 'And I have persuaded the Emperor,' added Father Sotelo, 'that with the friendship of the King of Spain alone he may obtain results much more considerable than those promised by the Dutch. In consequence the Emperor has charged me with the present embassy, in order to solicit Your Majesty's alliance.' Then (after the King's answer) Father Sotelo delivered the Imperial letter to His Majesty."

Was ever such an equally delicious piece of comedy as this played off in the haughty and stilted Court of Spain? And what makes the incident all the more surprising is that on November 15th, 1612, Çerqueyra, the Bishop of Japan, had addressed a long letter to the King of Spain, of which this was the concluding paragraph:—

"Another unfavourable circumstance is that of the ship of more than 400 tons, which the Spaniards built for the Japanese at Yedo, and which was intended to make the voyage to New Spain in company with the small ship of the Spanish Captain [Sebastian Vizcaino] of whom I have just spoken. This *commerce was pursued contrary to the orders of the Viceroy*; and the Japanese lost several thousand taels in the venture. Actually the ship set out on the 3rd October last (1612) from Uraga, and on the 4th of the same month she was cast upon the rocks, and all her cargo was lost. On board of her was Fray Luis Sotelo, chief instigator of the voyage; and it is alleged that it was against the will of his Superiors, who for some time have been regretting in the highest degree the imprudent steps of certain *religieux*. It even appears that the

Superiors have gravely censured the Father [Sotelo] of whom I speak. It is for this reason that he has been recalled to Manila. At this date it is not known how the sovereign [Hidetada] will take the incident of the ship, for he himself had a great interest in the expedition."

And elsewhere in the same letter the Bishop says:—

"It is thus that the Franciscans have seen themselves frustrated in their original design of opening up commercial relations between Japan and New Spain, *relations so prejudicial to Manila.*"

It is to be noted that this effort to open up trade between Japan and New Spain was an effort to infringe one of the cardinal principles of Spanish colonial policy. Between the Spanish colonies and any foreign State no direct commerce was permitted, while down to 1714 the various Spanish provinces situated on the South Seas were prohibited from holding any tradal communication with each other. As a matter of fact, the only trade possible for the colonists was with the mother country, and all this trade, such as it was, was confined to one single port—Seville. (Hence, perhaps, one reason why Daté Masamune's ambassadors delivered dispatches to the authorities of that city.) Of all the Spanish possessions, one only was free from this galling restraint—Manila to wit. Robertson's exposition of the situation here is so clear and succinct that its quotation in full is not inadvisable. Says he:—

"Soon after his accession to the throne, Philip the Second formed a scheme of planting a colony in the Philippine islands, which had been neglected since the time of their discovery; and he accomplished it by means of an armament fitted out from New Spain. Manila, in the island of Luconia, was the station chosen for the capital of this new establishment. From it an active commercial intercourse began with the Chinese, and a considerable number of that industrious people, allured by the prospect of gain, settled in the Philippine islands under the Spanish protection. They supplied the colony so amply with all the valuable productions and manufactures of the East, as enabled it to open a trade with America, by a course of navigation the longest from land to land on our globe. In the infancy of this trade, it was carried on with Callao, on the coast of Peru; but experience having discovered the impropriety of fixing upon that as the port of communication with Manila, the staple of the commerce between the East and West was removed from Callao to Acapulco, on the coast of New Spain.

"After various arrangements, it has been brought into a regular form. One or two ships depart annually from Acapulco, which are permitted to carry out silver to the amount of five hundred thousand pesos, but they have hardly anything else of value on board; in return for which, they bring back spices, drugs, china, and japan wares, calicoes, chintz, muslins, silks, and every precious article with which the benignity of the climate, or the ingenuity of its people, has enabled the East to supply the rest of the world. For some time, the merchants of Peru were admitted to participate in this traffic, and might send annually a ship to Acapulco, to wait the arrival of the vessels from Manila, and receive a proportional share of the commodities which they imported. At length the Peruvians were excluded from this trade by most rigorous Edicts, and all the commodities from the East reserved solely for the consumption of New Spain.

"In consequence of this indulgence, the inhabitants of that country enjoy advantages unknown in the other Spanish colonies. The manufactures of the East are not only more suited to a warm climate, and more showy than those of Europe, but can be sold at a lower price; while, at the same time, the profits upon them are so considerable, as to enrich all those who are employed either in bringing them from Manila, or vending them in New Spain. As the interest both of the buyer and seller concurred in favouring this branch of commerce, it has continued to extend in spite of regulations concerted with the most anxious jealousy to circumscribe it. Under cover of what the laws permit to be imported, great quantities of India goods are poured into the markets of New Spain; and when the flota arrives at Vera Cruz from Europe, it often finds the wants of the people already supplied by cheaper and more acceptable commodities.

"There is not, in the commercial arrangements of Spain, any circumstances more inexplicable than the permission of this trade between New Spain and the Philippines, or more repugnant to its fundamental maxim of holding the colonies in perpetual dependence on the mother country, by prohibiting any commercial intercourse that might suggest to them the idea of receiving a supply of their wants from any other quarter. This permission must appear still more extraordinary, from considering that Spain herself carries on no direct trade with her settlements in the Philippines, and grants a privilege to one of her American colonies which she denies to her subjects in Europe. It is probable that the colonists who originally took possession of the Philippines, having been sent out from New Spain, began this intercourse with a country which they considered, in some measure, as their parent State, before the Court of Madrid was aware of its consequences, or could establish regulations in order to prevent it. Many remonstrances have been presented against this trade, as detrimental to Spain, by diverting into another channel a large portion of that treasure which ought to flow into the kingdom, as tending to give rise to a spirit of independence in the colonies, and to encourage innumerable frauds, against which it is impossible to guard, in transactions so far removed from the inspection of Government."

In view of all this, it was not to be expected that the Spanish King would be at all ready to grant Daté's request for trade with New Spain; and hence it is not strange to find Daté soliciting the Pope's assistance in the following terms:—

"I have learned that my kingdom is not far removed from the kingdoms of New Spain, which form part of the dominions of the very powerful King of Spain, Philip. It is for this reason that in the desire to enter into relation with him and with his Christian States I keenly desire his friendship; and I have no doubt of obtaining it, if you assist me with your authority, as I humbly beseech you to do, conjuring Your Highness to undertake this task, and to bring it to an end, above all because these kingdoms are the necessary route for the *religieux* sent by you into our kingdom."

It must not be forgotten that in 1613, at the date of the dispatch of Daté's embassy, Iyeyasu was already in bad humour over the poor results of the intercourse with New Spain. When Vivero had been sent thither in Will Adams's ship in 1610, Iyeyasu had entrusted him with a letter and rich presents for Philip III., and the Franciscan Muñoz went along with him to carry these from Mexico to the Spanish Court. Since then there had been embassies from New Spain, but little or no trade, while from his Spanish Majesty so far Iyeyasu had not heard. As a matter of fact, it was only on June 20th, 1613, that Philip III. dispatched three Franciscans with a letter to acknowledge Iyeyasu's presents. They did not arrive in Japan till the end of 1615; and then Iyeyasu refused to receive them, while Hidetada rejected their presents and ordered them to leave for New Spain at the first opportunity. Meanwhile, to Daté's request the Spaniards had just given a very decided, albeit indirect, answer. Writes Cooks on December 6th, 1615:—

"Also yow may understand how a shipp arived at Quanto [Uraga] in Japon this yeare, which came out of New Spaine and brought good quantety of broad cloth, kersies, perpetuanos, and raz de Millan, which they offer at a loe rate; but I thinke it is the last that ever will be brought from thence, for it is said the Spaniardes made proclemation with 8 drums at Aguapulca and other partes that, upon payne of death, their should neaver any more Japons com nor trade into New Spayne, and that both they and all other strangers of what nation soever should forthwith avoid out of all partes of New Spaine. But in requitall hereof the Emperour of Japon hath made proclemation, in payne of death, that neaver hereafter any Japon shall trade or goe into New Spaine, and comanded the fryres or padres which came in this shipp should avoid out of his dominions; for the truth is, he is noe frend nether to Spaniardes nor Portingalles."

Now although all this was perfectly correct, yet in M. Pagés we read as follows:—

"At the time when their [Philip III.'s discredited envoys'] vessel was to put to sea, some lords of the [Shōgun's] Court

wished to take part in the voyage in the interests of commerce!
One of them, named Mukai Shogen, General of the Emperor's
ships, to contrive for himself great advantages *vis-à-vis* the Spaniards,
asked for and obtained the release of Father Diego de S. Francisco,
who had been a prisoner in Yedo for a year.[8] The vessel put to

8 This priest's account of his imprisonment is valuable for the light it
throws upon the economy of a Japanese jail:—"The prison was very narrow
and dark, with no opening but a small wicket for passing in the porringers;
its area was twelve *canas* [a Catalonian measure equal to about six feet] in
length and five in breadth, while the ceiling was singularly low. A second
enceinte prevented communication with the outside. A numerous guard made
no cease night or day in calling aloud, to show that they were not asleep.
One hundred and fifty prisoners were confined in this pestilential hovel!
Among these were ten or twelve Christians. But the missionary in 18 months
baptized 70 infidels. [Here is an instance of M. Pagès' failure to co-ordinate
his data. "Eighteen months" and "a year" are not the same.] There were
two divisions, in each of which the inmates [there were one hundred and fifty
of them, be it remembered] were arranged in three rows. The place assigned
to the Father was three palms [18 in.] long, by 4½ wide. To sleep one must
support oneself on one's neighbour. Hence many quarrels about the space to
be occupied and the length of sleep, and in consequence fights were frequent.
If anyone wished to put on the least bit of clothing, the others objected,
especially during the summer-heat, for with clothes on one took up more room
and made his neighbours hot. As an exceptional favour the Father was
permitted to wear a garment of thin texture; and often he himself could not
endure it. For a year and a half the missionary never cut his hair, his beard,
or his nails! *La vermine pullulait a l'infini sur son corps.* Commonly there
were about 80 individuals, to whom nothing was given to eat, and who perished
of hunger. Another score, among whom was the Father, got mouthfuls merely.
Those generally succumbed in 40 or 50 days. The Father owed his life to
the charity of the Christians, who fee'd the guards. Vincent, a carpenter, a
very zealous believer, brought sustenance for the missionary for some days;
but the guards fearing for themselves, at last denounced him. The judge
decided that this man ought to be united with the Father and to follow him
to prison. [Vincent, the Christian carpenter, became blind, and attained
martyrdom in 1617.] Among the number of the prisoners was Laurence, the
son of the Shōgun's physician. [He also became a martyr in 1617.] Almost
all the prisoners became sick and no physician could penetrate to them; it
was feared that he might introduce poison. The sick exhaled a horrible
stench, when they were too weak to displace themselves *pour leurs besoins
naturels.* Often their neighbours killed these unfortunates in order to get rid
of them. They smashed their heads against the joists, or more frequently
they strangled them. Some of them committed suicide, preferring death to
the extremity of their sufferings, 'On en vit qui, désespérés, s'écriaient: Je fais
tout pour me donner la mort, et je n'y puis réussir.' All that was given them to
drink was a porringerful of water in the morning, and another in the evening;
a certain number died, after having become mad from thirst. Thus, when
the Father baptized any one, not a single drop of water was lost; the baptized
received the water, and drank it to appease his thirst! Thirty or forty among
the sick were always so weak that they could not raise themselves to receive
their miserable allowance. Their neighbour seized upon this pittance and
devoured it, saying that the sick ought not to eat où l'on ne se lavait pas pour
faire ses ordures; thus nobody would be either infected or inconvenienced.
Several of the sick observed this counsel of themselves. At the sight of such
cruelty the Father called upon the Christians to exercise the office of nurses.
But the most horrible detail was that the corpses of the deceased were only
removed with the permission of the Governor. These were left for seven or
eight days, and often the heat had putrified them in seven hours. From them
trickled putrid streams which flooded the surroundings, and poisoned the living.
Every individual who entered the jail there contracted frightful ulcers, and
his body became a 'hearth' of corruption. The ears became the seat of a
fluxion of humours. The knees, the feet, and the hands swelled and became
ulcerated; in most cases the extremities of the feet and of the hands mortified
and dropped off. Father Diego found himself a complete leper from the crown
of his head to the soles of his feet. And in the devouring fire of this leprosy

sea on September 30th, 1616. This voyage was unfortunate for the Japanese, most of whom died in the course of it. In the crew were only ten Spanish sailors; the rest were Japanese, to the number of two hundred, and of these only fifty reached New Spain. [Father Peter Baptiste instructed and baptized all those who died. The survivors also became Christians.] Meanwhile, after a very trying voyage of five months, Father Diego de San Francisco had arrived at Acapulco on the 23rd February, 1617, and shortly afterwards at Mexico, *where Father Sotelo then was.* The Viceroy, Don Diego Fernandez de Cordova, Marquis of Guadalaxara, received him favourably. The Father asked him firstly *for the remission of the capital penalty, lawfully incurred by the Spaniards for having conducted the vessel directly from Japan to New Spain;* and, secondly, for the prompt dispatch of the commercial affairs of the Japanese officer, Mukai Shogen; and he obtained all that he asked."

Now, after collating a good many documents on this episode one cannot help feeling that Charlevoix, who has followed Father Marianus, treats the matter with greater accuracy than M. Pagés has done. He tells us that in 1617 Sotelo and Hashikura found Daté's vessel at Acapulco, and that a new Governor, then proceeding to the Philippines, finding the Spanish shipping then in harbour insufficient for the accommodation of his suite, chartered the Japanese vessel to accompany him to Manila. Of course one object in this manœuvre was to prevent direct communication between New Spain and Japan; and as a cargo of silk from Manila would be far more valuable than any cargo from New Spain (where the Japanese ship had disposed of her lading for ready money at a great profit), the Japanese captain was only too glad to have his ship thus chartered. On board went Sotelo and Hashikura and the survivors of their train. They reached Manila in June, 1618; and here shortly afterwards, in accordance with instructions from the Council of the Indies, Sotelo had all his papers seized, while he himself, eighteen months later on, was shipped off to New Spain. The authorities of Manila had written to the King of Spain in terms exceedingly hostile to Sotelo and Daté's embassy as soon as they had heard of it; and the Spanish King had been offended because a subject of his had been appointed Bishop of Northern Japan and Papal

he involuntarily tore himself day and night; *see plaies enormes du siège, des cuisses et des mollets ruisselaient de sang et de pus.* In the midst of such trials six of the most vigorous and most wicked prisoners exercised a tyranny without limits over their companions; their outrages caused furious howls and despairing curses in this hell. For a time the Father had been able to practise the holy exercises with Louis, Thomas, and Vincent. It was in the first times that the 66 infidels were baptized. But the prisoners that came in afterwards, veritable wild beasts, stopped preaching and the performance of any sacred ministry."

Legate there without his assent being asked. As Protector of the Church he caused the Pope to withdraw the Bulls making the appointments, while the Council of the Indies took sharp measures against Sotelo. How long Daté's ship lay in Manila Bay is not known, but Mr. Meriwether tells us she again reached Sendai only in August, 1620, with Hashikura and his suite reduced to eleven persons. And this was the end of the ten years' efforts to open up a Japanese trade with New Spain.

That Iyeyasu was perfectly cognisant of the dispatch of Daté's embassy is incontestable, for it was under the superintendence of Mukai Shogen, Iyeyasu's own "Admiral," that Daté's vessel was fitted out for the voyage. Whether the old statesman was conversant with the tenor of Daté's missives to the King of Spain and to the Pope is a very different matter, however. At all events, shortly after the death of Iyeyasu in 1616, Cocks (then on the Tōkaidō) tells us in one passage that it was said the Shōgun was to raise troops for a war with Daté, and in another that Daté was to be put to death. At that time Tadateru (Iyeyasu's sixth son), Daté's son-in-law, was being punished, nominally for his slackness at the battle of Dōmyōji, where Daté had also refused to follow up the retreat of the beaten Ōsaka troops. Tadateru's name was mixed up with Ōkubo's alleged plot; and by the end of 1616 news of the doings of Daté's envoys in Spain may very well have reached Japan. In 1618 Araki, a Japanese Jesuit ordained in Rome, openly apostatised, and Charlevoix tells us that some time before this, on his return to Japan, Araki complained bitterly that while in Madrid he had learned that the *religieux* of a "certain Order" were exerting all their efforts to induce the King of Spain to undertake the conquest of Japan.

However, the Shōgun neither attacked Daté, nor was Daté put to death, for he died peacefully in his bed at the age of 70, twenty years later on (1636). Nor, in spite of his attitude towards Porro at Ōsaka on June 5th, 1615, did Daté show any special hostility towards Christians until 1620. Three days after Sotelo's arrival in Manila seven Spanish *religieux* left it for Nagasaki, where they arrived on August 12th, 1618. Among them was that Diego de San Francisco whom Mukai Shogen had rescued from the Yedo prison in 1615; and on arriving in Nagasaki this priest at once sent on Father Galvez (who had returned to Japan a few weeks after his deportation in 1614) with a message for Daté from Sotelo. Galvez was not only well received by Daté, but he actually obtained permission from him to preach in his capital of Sendai. However, two years later (1620), under pressure from the Yedo Government, "Daté, whom his embassy had rendered suspected, and to whom was attributed an effort to secure the alliance of the King of Spain in order to dethrone the Kubosama [Iyeyasu]," was constrained to issue three anti-Christian Edicts. Those who had become Christians "contrary to the will of the Shōgun" had to abjure their faith, the penalties for refusal being confiscation of property for the rich, and death for the poor; rewards were offered to informers; and all the ministers of the Gospel were to be banished unless they renounced their faith. About this time Hashikura, the envoy, returned after seven years' wanderings in Christian countries, and declared that Christianity was only a "vain show."

These Edicts of Daté's were not particularly severe, and such as they were they seem to have been enforced in a somewhat half-hearted way; for down to 1624 Gotō, one of his chief vassals, was permitted to profess his Christianity publicly together with all his own retainers, while until then Daté, who was blind of one eye, shut the other to the presence of foreign priests in his capital. Nor was his case at all singular among the feudatories. Many of them were utterly averse to interfering with the Christianity of their subjects, for freedom of conscience was highly regarded by the best Japanese of the time. Kuroda of Chikuzen (the young Kuroda who showed himself a gentleman towards Ishida, sitting bound with a rope on a mat in front of Iyeyasu's tent at Ōtsu in October, 1600) was only driven to persecute his Christian subjects by pressure from the Shōgunate. (Cocks tell us that Kuroda also was to be put to death in 1616.) His first victim was "John Akashi Jirobioye, a valiant man of war" (40), the son of his old friend Akashi, whom he had saved at Sekigahara, and who afterwards had commanded a brigade of Christians in Hideyori's service in the great

Ōsaka struggle. At this time Kuroda was virtually a prisoner in Yedo; and if left to himself, it is safe to say the son of his old friend would never have been shortened by the length of his head, despite all his fanatical Christianity. Hosokawa (the Jecundono of the Jesuits) was forced into anti-Christian action only in 1618; and it was not till October 15th, 1619, that he had any of his vassals killed for their Christianity.[9] As regards the great Fukushima of Aki, who Cocks tells us was much respected all through Western Japan, the missionaries inform us that "at the beginning of the year, the Prince of Hiroshima, a great man of war, lord of two provinces, whose revenues amounted to 500,000 sacks of rice (really 498,200 koku), was dispossessed by the Emperor and sent into exile for having been too favourable towards the Christians."[10]

Another great feudatory, Uyesugi Kagekatsu (300,000 koku), who had begun the great war of 1600 against Iyeyasu, down to the year of his death (1628) regularly made report to the Shōgun's Council that there was not a single Christian in his domains, although there were thousands of them; and it was only when his son succeeded to the fief that a persecution was instituted in Yonezawa and the province generally. And even the Governors of the Imperial cities of Kyōto and Nagasaki showed themselves most reluctant to enforce the anti-Christian decrees of the central authorities with any stringency, while we find that Matsukura Bungo-no-Kami, at first Lord of Shimabara, and after 1627 Daimyō of Arima, and whose death (1630) is so luridly described by Charlevoix, did everything he possibly could to protect the foreign priests and their converts from the consequences

---

[9] There is a grim comicality in a note of M. Pagès here. "Diego [the martyr on this occasion] one day said to his prince [Hosokawa]: 'You would not wish me to go to Hell.' 'Why,' answered Hosokawa, 'If I go there, would you not go there with me? Act like a loyal servant and for the love of me.'"

[10] It is interesting to compare this with the account of the matter given in the Nihon Senshi's volume on the Ōsaka campaigns:—"Fukushima had his fief of Aki (498,200 koku) confiscated, and was removed to a fief of 45,000 koku in Shinano and Echigo, in the fifth year of Genwa [1619]. Although other reasons were alleged for this, yet what led to it was the Ōsaka affair of 1614–15." Fukushima in spite of all his faults seems to have been a great champion of the cause of toleration, as appears from the letters of the missionaries. He was no Christian himself; but because he believed the foreign priests were really doing good humanitarian work he subsidised them liberally year after year. He refused to persecute himself, and he did everything he could to get his neighbours to refrain from doing so, always appealing to their best and most liberal instincts. From what the missionaries and Cocks say, the moral influence exercised by Fukushima of Aki must have been very great.

of their fanaticism before he began his career as the bitterest persecutor of his times.

As regards the central administration, after the (supposed) deportation of all the Christian *religieux* and their most dangerous converts in November, 1614, its attitude towards the proscribed religion and its professors for some two years can scarcely be described as a sternly resolute one. The reason for this is to be sought in the contemporary internal politics of Japan. Just a month after the expulsion of the missionaries the winter campaign against Ōsaka began, and, until the end of the summer campaign in June, 1615, Iyeyasu had to devote all his energies and attention to that life-and-death struggle. Besides, among the most influential retainers of many of the Daimyō whose contingents supported him were many Christians, while some of these Daimyō, such as Fukushima, Uyesugi, Daté, Kuroda, and Hosokawa, were themselves utterly averse to any persecution. As regards the Expulsion Edict of January 27th, 1614, Tanaka of Kurumé had actually refused to enforce it in his fief, and "Iyeyasu had closed his eyes." Even some of his own officers were inclined to make it a dead letter. Itakura, the *Shoshidai* of Kyōto, exerted himself to keep the brief persecution instituted in the capital a bloodless one ; while Tōan, Deputy-Governor of Nagasaki, with his family, openly took part in one of the processions conducted by the foreign priests just before their deportation. Nagasaki was then a town of 50,000 inhabitants, all Christians, and "all the inhabitants hoped for the triumph of Hideyori by reason of his promises." Tōan, the Deputy-Governor, who apostatised in 1615, was executed in Yedo in November, 1619, mainly on the grounds that the Japanese secular priest, his son, who was killed at the capture of Ōsaka, had actually led four hundred Christian troops to the support of Hideyori. And that the average Japanese was no Christian-hater at this time is evidenced by the miraculous escape of all the five foreign priests in Ōsaka in the general massacre that followed the capture of Hideyori's stronghold.

One man who was emphatically no average Japanese in this respect was Hasegawa Fujihiro (the Safioye of the missionaries), Governor of Nagasaki from 1606 to 1614. From data in "Cocks's Diary" it would appear that this Hasegawa

was not merely violently anti-Christian, but anti-foreign
generally. It was chiefly through him that the old Christian
Prince of Arima had been ruined in 1611–12, for Hasegawa
had for long cast covetous eyes upon this fief. When the
young prince apostatised and began the persecution of his
Christian subjects in 1612, Hasegawa was entrusted with
the task of seeing that there should be no lack of zeal on
the young turncoat's part. One result of this was that Arima
was removed to Nobeoka in Hiūga (53,000 *koku*) about 1614,
and Hasegawa became Lord of Arima. The persecution he
carried on was so atrocious that many heathens even were filled
with disgust. In November, 1614, he had a mixed force of
some 10,000 Satsuma and Hizen *samurai* detailed to help him
to make an end of the business.

"While the inquest went on at Arima, the Satsuma men
followed the coast towards the east, and proceeded to Ariye, to
Shimabara, and to the villages. These men of war, accustomed to
shed blood only in the midst of combats, sent word in advance to
the Christians to withdraw for a time; and most betook themselves
to the mountains. The Satsuma men feigned to have executed their
orders, and made report that there were no Christians in the country."

Just at this point Hasegawa and his auxiliaries were
hastily summoned away to co-operate in the great siege of
Ōsaka, and the persecuted Christians of Arima had a respite, as
had Christianity in general.

"During all these wars," writes M. Pagès, "and down to the death
of Iyeyasu [June 1st, 1616], Christianity enjoyed a tolerable tranquillity. Most of the Lords, engaged in one cause or the other
[they were all on Iyeyasu's side], found themselves always in the
field; those who remained at home reserved themselves to act after
the example of the victor, and shut their eyes as regarded Christians.
The prudence of the missionaries [at the end of 1615 there were
fifty-three of them in Japan] and of the Christians themselves
knew how to accommodate itself to the times, while repairing
the disasters of religion and of worship."[11]

Now at this time the Yedo Government was still averse to
taking the life of any foreign priest. Diego de S. Francisco, as
soon as the roads were clear after the fall of Ōsaka, had disguised himself as a soldier, and, mingling in the ranks of
Hidetada's army, had entered Yedo, where he at once began to

---

[11] Charlevoix, it ought to be remarked, writes in a somewhat different
strain. He roundly blames some of the missionaries for imprudence, while
the ill-considered zeal of many of their converts he pronounces to have been
very detrimental to the real interests of the Church.

propagandise. When detected he was not killed; he was cast into that terrible hell of a prison from which the Admiral, Mukai Shogen, rescued him in September, 1616—in the interests of Japanese trade with New Spain. Pagés writes with perfect accuracy:—

"The Shōgun [Hidetada], as well as his father [Iyeyasu], no longer wished to have priests in his Empire, but he contented himself with exiling them without putting them to death, hoping that, the ministers being wanting, the Christians would forget the faith."

As has been said before, *under Iyeyasu not one single foreign missionary was put to death.*

It is perhaps not unprofitable here to review all the anti-Christian Edicts of Iyeyasu. The first, issued in 1606, was issued merely to humour a capricious woman's whim and to please Yodogimi, Hideyori's mother. It was for strictly local consumption in Ōsaka, and even there it was enforced with discretion. At all events, a few months later on (1607), Yodogimi and Hideyori received the Jesuit Vice-Provincial Paez and his suite with the greatest kindness, and on that occasion Yodogimi's own sister, Jōkōin (the Maria Kiogocou of the missionaries), was confirmed by the Vice-Provincial.

Besides this mere make-believe, three anti-Christian Decrees were published by Iyeyasu before his death on June 1st, 1616. The first of these is found in an article issued on September 13th, 1611:—"The conversion to the Bateren religion is prohibited. Those who violate this prohibition shall not escape due punishment." This, however, would seem to have been an instruction addressed to Iyeyasu's own officers solely. The next, issued on April 22nd, 1612, immediately after the detection of Arima's intrigue with "Codskindono's" secretary, was published throughout the whole country, and stated that "the religion of Kirishitan is proscribed under heaven." Then, on January 27th, 1614, appeared (under Hidetada's name) the long Decree with which Sir Ernest Satow has dealt so exhaustively in Vol. IV. of the *Transactions of the Asiatic Society.*

The missionaries are very emphatic in charging Hasegawa, the Governor of Nagasaki, with the responsibility for these last two Edicts, and there is not the slightest doubt that he did much to prompt those of the eighth month of 1616, for Cocks corroborates this charge strongly, being in a position (all unknown to

QQ 2

himself) to give chapter and verse. On the death of Iyeyasu the "Cape merchant" had gone up to Yedo to get the English privileges confirmed by Hidetada. After a good deal of waiting, Cocks had had an interview with the Shōgun,—had received, as he thought, a confirmation of the privileges,—and was staying at Adams's house near Uraga on his way back, when on September 30th, 1616 (old style), "towardes night arived a man of Capt. Adames expres, sent from Mr. Wickham with letters and others from Firando [Hirado], Mr. Wickham advising that by proclemation at Miaco, Osakay, and Sackay, it was defended that no Japon should buy any merchandize of strangers. Whereupon he could make no sales of our comodeties, and therefore did wish me, yf I met the expres on the way, to retorne to Edo to redrese it, yf I could."

Now this report of Wickham's was perfectly correct. On the 20th day of the eighth month of the second year of Genwa (1st October, 1616, new style) the following Edict had been issued by the Gorōjū, or Shōgun's Cabinet:—

> "Be it strictly instructed that according to the command of the Shokoku [Premier], issued some years ago, to the effect that the conversion of the Japanese to Christianity is strictly prohibited, the Lords of all the provinces shall take special care to guard [keep] all people *down to farmers* from joining that religion. Also as the black ships, namely the English ships, belong to that religion, the provincial Lords [*i.e.* the Daimyō] should send any of those ships to Nagasaki or Hirado, in case they happen to put in to the ports of their dominions, and no trade shall be carried on therein. This is proclaimed in respectful accordance with the will of our Lord.
>
> "ANDŌ TSUSHIMA-NO-KAMI.
> "DOI ŌI-NO-KAMI. ["Oyen Dono."]
> "SAKAI BINGO-NO-KAMI.
> "HONDA KŌDZUKE-NO-SUKÉ.
> ["Codskindono."]
> "SAKAI UTA-NO-KAMI.

"20th of 8th month, the 2nd year of Genwa."

Poor Cocks, on getting Wickham's letter, hurried back to Yedo to find that Wickham had spoken but the truth. After having been kept kicking his heels in the ante-chambers of the councillors and of their underlings for more than a fortnight he had to depart on the 17th October (old style) *re infectd.* In his "Diary," October 3rd, 1616, we read as follows:—

> "Jno. Yoosen [one of Will Adams's companions in the *Liefde,* after whom the Yaoyasu Gate of the Yedo castle was named] came to vizet me, and tould me he howrly expected the Hollanders, and that,

tuching the cortalling of our prevelegesse, it was *not* to be suffered it being wrought per Safian Dono [Hasegawa Sahyōye, Governor of Nagasaki] and other his associates to have us pend up at Firando [Hirado], to the entent to work upon us as they did on the Portingals and Spaniardes at Langasaque [Nagasaki]; but (said he) the Hollanders will forsake Japon before they will be bownd to do it." October 8th, 1616 (old style):—"We went to vizet the counsellars againe, to have our dispach in remembrance. And first to Oyen Dono [*i.e.* Doi, Ōi-no-Kami], the secretary, whoe tould us that we should speake to Codgskin Dono [*i.e.* that Honda Masazumi who had played such a prominent part in the filling-in of the Usaka moats some eighteen months before], for that he could do nothing of hym selfe. [Ōi was a real diplomatist, in the worst sense of the word.] Unto which I answerd that the rest did refer us to hym, and therefore I besought his Lordship to procure our dispach; for I stood in dowbt my long staying and want of sales of our goodes per meanes of this edict would be an occation I should not send away our 2 shipps and junck this yeare, which would be a borthen to hevie for us to beare or to answer to our employers. He said he would doe what he could and take councell with the rest what might be donne. So from thence we went to Codgskin Dono, whome the servantes tould us was in the house. Yet could I not come to speech of hym, but lost my errant with his cheefe men. *I forgot to note downe that Safian Dono* [Hasegawa, Governor of Nagasaki] *was at the secretaries* [Ōi, Doi-no-Kami] *howse, siting in a darke corner, I being cald in and apointed to syt on the better hand of hym, not knowing whoe he was till Capt. Adames tould me, which then I went on the other side and craved pardon as not knowing hym.* In fyne, every one complayneth that matters are worse than in the ould mans [Iyeyasu's] daies, and that this man [Hidetada] doth nothing but change offecers and displace *tonos* [Daimyō], sending and changing one into an others contrey; so that much grudging is at it and all in law and plitos on with an other, so that what will com of it God knoweth, for, as the comon report is, no man dare speake to the Emperour [Hidetada] of any matter they think is to his discontent, he is so furious, and no meanes but death or distruction. So that what will come of us or our sute I know not, for I tell them it were as good for the Emperour to banish us all out of Japon as to shut us up in Firando, it being a place of no sales."

On the same 8th October, 1616:—"After nowne Capt. Adams and our *jurebasso* [interpreter] staid wayting at Court gate to speake with the councellers, who still geve good words." Bacon, indeed, assures us that "by indignities men come to dignities"! But, good heavens! is the game worth the candle? Adams's loyalty towards the money-grubbing ungrateful Company is fine; but at the same time one cannot help feeling sorry for Captain Will Adams on this 8th October, 1616. To go bonnet-in-hand to any of the sinful sons of men, booin', booin', is about the saddest lot that well can fall to any self-respecting mortal—and such grand old Will Adams undoubtedly was. It would appear that Adams's friendship for the Spaniards who frequented Uraga had rendered him suspect. On September 11th, 1616, Cocks writes :—

"Oyen Donos secretary came to vizet me, and tould me he suspected that our delay grew per meanes of the looking out for. padres, which weare much sought after by the Emperour, and reportes geven out that som were at Capt. Adames howses at Orangaua [Uraga] and Phebe [Hemi]. So Capt. Adames wrot againe to his folkes, to look out that no such matter were proved against them, as they tendered their lives."

Cocks's letter of January 1st, 1617, to the East India Company throws so much light upon the general political situation at this time that it is advisable to reproduce the major portion of it :—

"It was generally thought fit that I made a journey to the court of the new Emperour Shungo Samme [Hidetada], to renew our privelegese (as the Hollanders ment to do the lyke), in which voyage I was 4 monethes and 5 daies before I retorned to Firando [Hirado], and the Hollanders are not yet retorned. Yet the 5th day after I arived at court our present was deliverd, and had audience with many favorable wordes, but could not get my dispach in above a month after; so that once I thought we should have lost all our privelegese, for the *Councell sent unto us I think above twenty tymes to know whether the English nation were Christians or no.* I answerd we were, and that they knew that before by our Kinges Maties. letter sent to the Emperour his father [Iyeyasu] (and hym selfe) [Hidetada], wherein it apeared he was defender of the Christian faith. 'But,' said they, 'are not the Jesuits and the fryres Christians two?' Unto which I answerd they were, but not such as we were, for that all Jesuists and fryres were banished out of England before I was borne, the English nation not houlding with the pope, nor his doctryne, whose followers these padres [*Bateren*] (as they cald them) weare. Yt is strang to see how often they sent to me about this matter, and in the end gave us waynyng that we did not comunecate, confesse, nor baptiz with them, for then they should hold us to be all of one sect. . . .

"Soe, in the end, they gave me our new privelegese with the Emperours ferme, telling me they were conformable to the former. So herewith I departed, and, being 2 daies journey on my way, met an expres from Mr. Wickham, wherin he wrot me from Miaco [Kyoto] that the justice [*i.e.* Itakura, Iga-no-Kami, the Shōgun's *Shoshidai*] (per the Emperours comand) had geven order that all strangers should be sent downe to Firando or Langasaque, and forthwith departe and carry all their merchandiz with them and not stay to sell any, so that he was forced to keepe within howse, and our hostes durst sell nothing. Which news from Mr. Wickham seemed very strang unto me. Whereupon I sought one to read over our privelegise, which with much a do at last I fownd a *bos* (or pagon prist) which did it, *and was that we were restrayned to have our shiping to goe to no other place in Japon but Firando, and there to make sales.* Whereupon I retorned back againe to the court, where I staid 18 or 20 daies more, still suing and puting up suplecations to have our privelegese enlarged as before, aledging that yf it were not soe, that my soveraigne lord King James would think it to be our misbehaviours that cauced our privelegese to be taken from us, they having so lately before byn geven us by his Matis. father [Iyeyasu] of famous memory, and that it stood me upon as much as my life was worth to get it amended, otherwais I knew not how to shew my face in England. *Yet, for all this, I could get nothing but wordes.* Whereupon I desyred to have the ould privelegese retorned and to render back the new, with condition they would geve us 3 yeares respite to write into England and have answer whether our Kinges Matie. would be content our privelegese should be so shortned or no. Yet they would not grant me that. And then I desird we might have leave to sell such merchandiz as we had now at Miaco, Osakay, Sackay, and Edo; otherwais I knew not what to do, in respect Firando was but a fysher towne, haveing no marchantes dwelling in it, and that it was tyme now to send back our shipps and junckes, and nothing yet sould. *Yet this I could not have granted nether.* So that with much a doe in the end they gave me leave, as I past, to sell my goodes to any one would presently buy it, or else leave it to be sould with any Japon I thought good to trust with it. Which restrant hath much hindered our sales and put me to my shiftes, the rather for that the order of Japon is that no stranger may sell any thing at arivall of their shipps till it be knowne what the Emperour will take; so that it is allwais above a month or 6 wickes before a post can run to and fro to have lycence.[12]

"At my coming away Oyen Dono and Codsquin Dono [*i.e.* Doi, Ōi-no-Kami, and Honda Kōdzuke-no-suke], the Emperours secretarys, tould me that they were sory they could not remedy this matter of our privelegese at present, the reason being for that an Emperours edict *per act of parliament* (!) being soe lately set out could not so sowne be recalled without scandalle, but the next yeare, yf I renewed my sute, my demandes being so substantiated, they did verely think it might be amended, in respect Firando was well knowne to be but a fisher towne. So that I aledged the Emperour might as well take away all our privelegese and banish us out of Japon as to shut us up in such a corner as Firando, where no marchantes dwell. . . ."

At Miaco "I would have left Richard Hudson, a boy, your Wor. servant, to have learnd to write the Japans; but might not be suffered to doe it, the Emperour haveing geven order to the contrary. Soe we withdrew all our factors from Edo, Miaco, Osakay, and Sackay to Firando. . . .

"And I had allmost forgotten to adviz your Wors. of a Spaniard, which was at the Emperours court at Edo when I was theare. He went out of a ship of theirs from Xaxma [Satsuma], where 2 greate shipps of theirs arived out of New Spaine, bound, as they said, for the Phillippinas, but driven into that place per contrary wynd, both shipps being full of souldiers, with greate store of treasure, as it is said, above 5 millions of *pezos.* Soe they sent this man to kis the Emperours hand; but he never might be suffered to com in his sight, allthough he staid theare above a month; which vexed hym to see we had axcesse to the Emperour and he could not. So that he gave it out that our shipps and the Hollanders which were at Firando had taken and robbed all the China junckes, which was the occation that very few or non came into Japon this yeare. And som greate men in the court did not want [omit] to aske me the question whether it were true or no, Mr.

---

[12] It would have been better for the East India Company if Saris had taken Adams's advice and established their factory on the shores of Yedo Bay.

Wm. Adames being present.   Which we gave them to understand that, concernynge the Englishe, it was most falce.   And withall I enformed the two secretaries, Oyen Dono and Codsquin Dono, that, yf they lookt out well about these 2 Spanish shipps arived in Xaxma full of men and treasure, *they would fynd that they were sent of purpose by the King of Spaine, haveing knowledg of the death of the ould Emperour* [Iyeyasu], *thinking som papisticall tono might rise and rebell and so draw all the papistes to flock to them and take part, by which meanes they might on a sudden seas upon som strong place and keepe it till more succors came, they not wanting money nor men for thackomplishing such a strattagim.*   Which speeches of myne wrought so far that the Emperour sent to stay them, and, had not the greate shipp cut her cable in the howse so to escape, she had byn arested, yet with her hast she left som of her men behind; and the other shipp being of som 300 tons was cast away in a storme and driven on shore, but all the people saved.   So in this sort I crid quittance with the Spaniardes for geveing out falce reportes of us, *yet since verely thought to be true which I reported of them.*

"Also may it please your Wors. that, at our being at themperours court, the amerall of the sea [*i.e.* Mukai Shogen] was very ernest with Mr. Wm. Adames to have byn pilot of a voyage they pretended to the northward to make conquest of certen ilands, as he said, rich in gould; but Mr. Adames exskewced hym selfe in that he was in your Wors. service and soe put hym afe.   And as I am enformed, they verely think that our pretence to discover to the northward is to fynd out som such rich ilandes and not for any passage.[18]   Yet I tould the admerall to the contrary, and tould hym that my opinion was he might doe better to put it into the Emperours mynd to make a conquest of the Manillias, and drive those small crew of Spaniardes from thence, it being so neare unto Japon; they haveing conquered the Liqueas allready.   He was not unwilling to listen heareunto, and said he would comunecate the matter to the Emperour [Hidetada].   And out of dowbt yt would be an easy matter for the Emperour to doe it, yf he take it in hand, and a good occation to set the Japons heades awork, to put the remembrance of Ticus Samme and his sonne Fidaia Samme [Hideyori], so lately slaine and disinhereted, out of their minds."

A careful reading between the lines of the foregoing will enable us to understand the following extract from M. Pagés more clearly :—

"In the month of September, 1616, the new Sovereign [Hidetada] issued an Edict to renew that of 1614.   In the sentence of exile were

---

18 This is interesting. The maritime enterprise of the English of those days was mainly directed towards the discovery of a North-west passage. When Saris had had his interview with Iyeyasu (1613), Adams was afterwards called in privately, and asked whether the arrival of the *Clove* was not to some extent connected with the discovery of "other countries further to the northwest and north." Adams's answer, "Our country still continues to spend much money in the discovery thereof," was perfectly true, for as late as 1611 the East India Company had voted an annual grant of £300 for encouraging attempts for the discovery of this North-west passage (RIPON). But about this time (1611-13) Sebastian Viscaino was searching for the island El Dorado in the Pacific off the coasts of Japan, and the real purpose of his voyage had leaked out. Iyeyasu, perhaps, was really then thinking of the Island of Gold and the Island of Silver more than of any North-west passage.

comprehended all priests and *religieux* without exception—even those who had been granted to the Portuguese to assist them spiritually. It was forbidden to the Japanese, under the penalty of being burned alive and of having all their property confiscated, to have any connection with the ministers of 'religion,' and with their co-operators or servants, and, above all, to give them hospitality. The same penalties were extended to women and children, and to their five nearest neighbours on both sides of their abodes, unless these became informers. *It was forbidden to any prince or lord to keep Christians in his service, or even on his estates.* The promulgation of the edict was made *solennellement.* Commonly in Japan the tenor of an edict was verbally expressed by the governor of a town, or announced by the officers of justice; besides this there was no other promulgation. In this case placards were posted containing the Imperial decree. The universal inquest on religion was deferred to the next year on account of the preparations for the apotheosis [of Iyeyasu] and the first cares of the reign."

However, some months before the dedication of Iyeyasu's shrine at Nikkō (May, 1617), Hidetada had shown himself in earnest about the enforcement of this anti-Christian Edict. The Prince of Ōmura (son of Don Sanche, who had apostatized in 1604, it will be remembered) had been one of the five Kyūshū Daimyō charged with the superintendence of the deportation of the *religieux* in 1614; and he had reported that the commission had been carefully and exhaustively executed. As a matter of fact, this young Daimyō, having been baptized in his infancy, and his sister being even then an ardent believer, had connived at the escape or the return of some of the priests. Hidetada, now hearing of this, caused his Ministers to censure Ōmura severely when he appeared at Court on Japanese New Year's Day (February 6th, 1617) to congratulate the Shōgun, and to dispatch him at once to Nagasaki to carry out the Edict without fail, while he received secret instructions to put the priests to death. At this date there were as many as fifty *religieux* in Japan, most of whom were in Nagasaki. Of these some ten or a dozen were now seized and sent to Macao and Cochin China; but of these, two Dominicans and several others very soon came back. Ōmura, thus finding his hand forced, all unwillingly made up his mind to have one foreign priest killed to show that he was really in earnest, and so to intimidate the others. Two, however, were arrested by his over-zealous officers. " Ōmura, however, in the hope of obtaining an attenuation of the sentence, sent his report to the Court, asking for a

decision. The reply, which was received on May 21st, 1617,
was a sentence of death "; and on that day Fathers De
l'Assumpcion and Machado were beheaded, *not by the common
executioner, but by " one of the first officers of the Prince."*
These, so far, with the exception of the six Franciscans
executed in 1597 by Hideyoshi's orders, were the only foreign
priests whose blood had been shed by the Japanese authorities.

The immediate result of the execution must have been
disappointing to Ōmura.

> "The bodies, placed in different coffins, were interred in the
> same grave. Guards were placed over it, but the concourse was
> immense. The sick were carried to the sepulchre to be restored
> to health. The Christians found new strength in this martyrdom;
> the pagans themselves were full of admiration for it. Numerous
> conversions and numerous returns of apostates took place every-
> where, and it was at first believed that the prince (Ōmura) himself
> would return to the faith."

And in the midst of all this, Navarrete, the Vice-
Provincial of the Dominicans, and Ayala, the Vice-Provincial
of the Augustins, came out of their retreat, and in full
priestly garb started upon an open propaganda in Ōmura's
domains, heralding their approach by a letter addressed to
him in the most defiant terms! Naturally, Ōmura, thus
challenged, was forced to act promptly, all the more so
as Navarrete told him that he (Navarrete) did not recognise the Emperor of Japan, but only the Emperor of
Heaven! The two fanatics—for so even Charlevoix considers
them to have been—were secretly conveyed to the island
of Takashima and there decapitated, while their coffins were
weighted with big stones and sunk in the open sea.[14] Thereupon the newly-elected Superior of the Dominicans at once
sent three of his priests to preach in Ōmura's territories, and
two of them (one of whom openly went about in his robes)
were seized and cast into the Ōmura prison, where they
remained for five years.

Some fourteen or fifteen months passed before any other
foreign priest was executed. The first victim was the
old Franciscan, Juan de Santa Martha, who had been

---

[14] "It is said two more papist priests are put to death in Ōmura; and
because the people carried away the blood in handkerchiefs and clouts of the
other two executed before, he caused these two to be cast into the sea with
stones tied about their necks (?)"—*Cocks's Diary*, June 6th, 1617.

for three years in prison in Kyōto, and whom Itakura, the *Shoshidai*, wished to release and send to New Spain. But the old man told Itakura that if released he would stay in Japan and preach there. Accordingly the staunch old fanatic was decapitated on August 16th, 1618. It is to be noted that he, unlike the victims in Ōmura, was executed like a common criminal, his body being cut into small pieces—Saris has described the custom—and his head exposed on the public pillory. After this no more foreign *religieux* were killed until 1622. However, Japanese who had given hospitality to the priests were sharply dealt with—beheaded or burned alive— a fate that also overtook the Portuguese merchant, Domingo Jorge (November 18th, 1619), for having sheltered Spinola and another Jesuit in the previous year.[15]

Now just four days before de Santa Martha was beheaded in Kyōto, about half-a-dozen Philippine *religieux* had arrived in Nagasaki, while Jesuits from Macao also had come in about the same time—a fact of which the Japanese authorities soon became apprised. In these circumstances their forbearance towards the foreign priests is something remarkable. At that date Mahometan emissaries suspected of a design to subject Most Catholic Spain to the sway of the Father of the Faithful

---

[15] Professor Riess's excellent essay on "The Causes of the Expulsion of the Portuguese" (German Far East Asiatic Society, Vol. VII., pt. i.) is worthy of careful perusal. He quotes from authentic Japanese sources (page 14):— "At Sakai a foreign ship was captured by the Dutch; it belonged to Jorchin [Domingo Jorge] and brought letters from the Portuguese. When these had been translated by the interpreters in Hirado, it was found that the Southern Barbarians [i.e. Spaniards and Portuguese] instigated the Japanese Christians to make a revolt." The sense of one letter was:—"As soon as the news arrives that the number of Japanese Christians is sufficient, men-of-war will be sent." If we remember what Cocks had told "Codskindono" and Doi, Ōi-no-Kami, about the intentions of the Spaniards, we can easily understand what an effect this must have produced upon the Shōgun's Government. In connection with this the following extract from M. Pagés is interesting:—"This year [1617] the captain of the Portuguese ship, Lope Sarmiento de Carvalho, had gone to the Court at Kyōto to greet the Shōgun. The object of his visit was to ask for the Portuguese of Nagasaki the concession of a site sufficiently extensive for the erection of a Custom-house: it was hoped that the missionaries could there be sheltered under the appearance of secular *employés*. The Portuguese and the other Christians of Nagasaki had in common contributed the expenses of the presents meant for the Shōgun. Carvalho was suitably treated; but the project of the Custom-house miscarried, by reason of the opposition of Hendrik Brouwer, Chief of the Dutch Factory; and the situation of the *religieux* became consequently more precarious." The two paragraphs that follow the above and their footnotes (p. 381-2) are also worthy of attention.

Here it may be said that Professor Riess makes short work of the story of the treasonable letter from Japanese Christians to the King of Spain found in a Portuguese ship captured by the Dutch off the Cape of Good Hope—a story that is gravely repeated in most Japanese histories. Charlevoix, as early as 1736, had really dealt with the (alleged) incident drastically enough.

would have met with short shrift. It is well to bear in mind
that at the very time this "inquest on religion" was afoot in
Japan—merely on political grounds—the Inquisition was by
no means inactive in the wide dominions of His Majesty
Philip III. of Spain. And, unlike Hidetada, the Shōgun of
Japan, Philip III. had no earthly reason to believe that
Spanish national independence was in any way threatened by
the propagation of an alien faith in the Peninsula or its
dependencies. All things considered, the measure of forbearance
extended towards the persons of the foreign *religieux* by
Hidetada was remarkable. Towards his own subjects he was
less considerate; several Japanese priests and a good many
converts were executed in the years 1618 to 1621—notably fifty-
two Japanese Christians at Kyōto (October 7th, 1619), whom
Itakura, the *Shoshidai*, had done his best to shield from the
effects of their devotion or of their fanaticism. However,
the Shōgun showed himself resolute to deal with the persistent
obstinacy of the foreign priests. In 1618 Hasegawa Gonroku,
who had succeeded his uncle "Safiandono" in the governorship
of Nagasaki, extended the penal clauses of the Edict of 1616
to Spaniards and Portuguese after the two Jesuits, Spinola
and Fernandez, had been discovered harboured in the house
of the Portuguese merchant, Domingos Jorge. And "thirty
bars of silver openly exposed in the principal square of
Nagasaki were to be the reward of the informer; a notice
posted beside them by the order of the Governor, and which
at first contained only the words, 'This sum will be given
to whosoever shall denounce a *thief*' (it is well-known how
abominable a theft is considered in Japan) soon received the
addition of 'or a *religieux.*'"

It is abundantly clear from the letters of the missionaries
themselves that some of the officials of the Shōgunate they
most malign did everything they possibly could to avert the
shedding of the blood of the foreign priests. This Hasegawa
Gonroku, Governor of Nagasaki, seems to have been a really
fine fellow, and a gentleman in the best sense of the word—
very different from his intriguing uncle, "Safiandono." His
conduct towards Zuñiga, the Dominican, abundantly testifies
to this. This Zuñiga was really a blue-blooded *hidalgo*, being
the son of that Marquis of Villamanrica who had been the

sixth Viceroy of New Spain (1585–1599). Zuñiga had become a Dominican in 1600, and had gone to the Philippines in 1610, whence he had proceeded to Japan in 1618. In 1619, we are told, "Gonroku, who had known Father de Zuñiga, and had seen him dressed as a merchant, appreciated his great qualities and respected his illustrious origin. He had given him notice to quit Japan, and even invited him to come to see him, pledging his word for his safety. He conjured him to withdraw by the first vessel." Zuñiga did withdraw to Manila for a time; but in 1620 he determined to return, and, in company with Flores, a Dominican, and two Spanish merchants, he took passage in a Japanese craft commanded by one Hirayama, a Japanese Christian. Off Formosa this craft fell in with the English cruiser *Elizabeth*, one of the "Fleet of Defence," and after a day of *pourparlers* the English finished by taking possession of the Japanese ship, and transferring its crew to their own vessel. They soon recognised the ecclesiastical character of two of the passengers—a discovery which filled them with joy, for in the terms of the Imperial Edict the Japanese ship then became good prize. On being taken to Hirado by the Dutch vessel, to whom the *Elizabeth* had handed them over, the Spaniards were entrusted to the keeping of the Dutch, and the Japanese to the English, by whom they were at once liberated—to save expenses. In spite of being put to the torture by the Dutch, in spite of the production of the compromising letters from the Archbishop of Manila found in Hirayama's craft, in spite of being identified by several Chinese and Japanese, Zuñiga for sixteen months strenuously refused to admit that he was a priest. This, of course, was merely to save the lives of Hirayama and of his Christian crew. Hasegawa Gonroku had gone down to try the matter in Hirado; and although he knew Zuñiga perfectly well, he kept on pronouncing all the evidence adduced to be insufficient. When at last, on November 30th, 1621, Zuñiga suddenly declared himself (Flores did so some time after), there was no longer any help for it, and Gonroku had to go up to Court to make report of the matter to the Shōgun.

Hidetada's wrath was great—all the more so as there were rumours to the effect that Zuñiga was a natural son of the

Spanish King, who had undertaken the task of paving the way to a conquest of Japan; and that pamphlets were being written by apostates and widely circulated maintaining that all the zeal of the foreign priests in propagating their religion was inspired by political motives only.[16]   An attempt by Father Collado and some Japanese Christians to rescue Father Flores from his imprisonment in the Dutch Factory still further inflamed the Shōgun's ire.   Accordingly, Gonroku, who was severely censured, was ordered to return to Nagasaki, and there to see to it that the two priests and Hirayama, the Japanese captain, were burned alive—or rather slowly roasted to death, while the same sentence was also passed upon all the *religieux* in prison as well as upon those who had harboured them.   " The wives and children of the hosts were to be decapitated; likewise the Christian crew and passengers of Hirayama's ship, as well as the wives and children of the martyrs immolated three years before."   Yet even so, Gonroku strenuously exerted himself to save the minor victims at least; he wished to set them free without noise; but, irritated by their marvellous persistence, he finally sent them to the stake along with the others.   Zuñiga, Flores, and Hirayama were in the flames for three-quarters of an hour before they expired, August 19th, 1622.

Three weeks later (on September 10th, 1622) occurred the " Great Martyrdom " at Nagasaki.   Then thirty Christians were beheaded, and twenty-five others, among them nine foreign priests, literally roasted to death, for their tortures lasted between two and three hours; while four other foreign priests suffered similarly before the close of the year.   " Our memoirs count for this single year, 1622, more than a hundred and twenty martyrs consumed by the sword."   Among these were sixteen priests (eight Dominicans, four Jesuits, three Franciscans, and one Augustin) and twenty Brothers of the different Orders.

The Shōgun had plainly resolved to make an end of the

---

[16] About this affair the literature is extensive.   Six or seven of the original letters published in Pagés' second volume deal with it.   Charlevoix (who was a Jesuit, it must be remembered) supplies valuable details in his " Histoire du Japon" (1736) and no less interesting comments.   In Cocks's Diary and Letters there are many references to it.   Professor Riess has treated the incident very lucidly in his " English Factory at Hirado" (pp. 90 and 91), in connection with which he gives several original documents.

matter—by extermination. "Three days after the Great Martyrdom," we are told, "by order of the Governor, all the bodies, with images, rosaries, and all the objects of religion seized among the Christians, were cast together into a great pit, as pestiferous objects. A thing unheard of hitherto, but which was to be the case at all the future martyrdoms, they threw into this pit a bed of charcoal, the *débris* of the stakes and of the ashes, a layer of the bodies of the decapitated, a layer of wood; then they piled on all the objects of religion and set fire to the mass. It burned for two days. Then they collected the ashes, and even the earth soaked with the blood shed. The ashes and this earth were put into straw sacks, and they were sent to be scattered on the open sea. Afterwards the boatmen were made to strip and bathe, to wash the bags and even the boats, so that no dust or any vestige might remain after this great holocaust."

Everything points to the conclusion that by this time Hidetada's distrust of the Spaniards was profound. The missionaries assert that he stood in apprehension of a foreign invasion, and that he looked upon the foreign priests as the *avant-couriers* and harbingers of a Spanish conquest. In 1622 an embassy from Manila was sent away without its presents being accepted; in 1624 another embassy from the Philippines —it had arrived in Japan in the previous year—was treated with the utmost indignity. Gonroku, who met the envoys on the way, gave them to understand that their mission would prove an absolute failure if it had any reference to Christianity. They replied that they came merely to arrange a convention between the two empires in the interest of commerce and to notify to the Japanese Emperor the accession of His Majesty Philip IV. (1621–1665) to the Spanish throne. In order to obviate all difficulties, the Governor of the Philippines had issued an Edict forbidding under heavy penalties (the same regulation extended to Macao) any captain proceeding to Japan to carry *religieux* thither. The Archbishop of Manila, appreciating the Governor's reasons, had joined His Excellency in interdicting the passage of the missionaries. The reply of the Court was unfavourable. The "Emperor" (Iyemitsu now, ostensibly, really Hidetada) declared that the embassy was not serious; that it was merely a device of the missionaries of Luzon; and that in any case he would not receive the ambassadors of an empire where a false and pernicious "law" was professed,—a "law" which ought to be prohibited and whose missionaries he had banished. He added that at first he had welcomed the Spaniards, as they came under the pretext of trade; but that in place of contributing any advantage to his empire they had sullied it with their diabolic religion. The ambassadors, thus rebuffed, resumed their way to Nagasaki, treated as "suspects" and subjected to a thousand humiliations. In the harbour itself they were kept under surveillance night and day, and were soon obliged to return to Manila, as was the "Royal Spanish Fleet" that arrived in Nagasaki in the following year, 1625.

The speech of the Spanish pilot in 1596, the talk of the Spaniards to Iyeyasu in 1605, the suggestions of the English and the Dutch, the intrigues of Japanese Christians in Japan with Manila, Araki's assertions, and Daté's mission might very well have sufficed to convince Hidetada that the Spaniards really meditated a conquest of Japan. But there was more than that. The following passage from an official History of Japan is striking :—

"Hidetada, desiring to have accurate information about Christianity, sent one of his subjects, named Ibi Masayoshi, to Europe to study the principles of this religion carefully. Masayoshi returned to Japan at the end of seven years, and was at once summoned to the Palace to make his report. Hidetada listened to him attentively day and night without any interval until he had finished speaking. In the course of this lecture some courtiers [superior flunkeys, really] represented to Hidetada that he was fatiguing himself to the detriment of his health. The Shōgun made answer, 'You speak of my fatigue, gentlemen; but what is that in comparison with the fatigues—I will rather say the sufferings, the privations, and the dangers—that Ibi Masayoshi has not feared to face in the faithful discharge of his mission?' After having heard everything, and after long pondering, Hidetada came to the conclusion that the Christian religion was detrimental to Japan, and he renewed the interdict against the practice of the cult."

Now from other Japanese sources we learn that this Ibi Masayoshi (or Yoyemon), to whom Hidetada listened for three consecutive days and nights, had been sent abroad in the "first years of Genwa," a year-period which began with 1615. Hence his return to Japan probably must be referred to 1622, the year when the foreign priests (who were all supposed to have been deported from the country in 1614) began to be dealt with in a heroic manner.

It will be remembered that both Iyeyasu and the Daimyō of Satsuma had previously sent abroad emissaries of a similar nature. It is needless here to repeat what we had to say of the contentions occasioned by religious differences in contemporary Europe. In addition to all that was then enumerated, this Ibi Masayoshi was in a position to report the outbreak of that Thirty Years' War—a purely religious struggle—that was to reduce the population of Germany from 20,000,000 to 7,000,000, to turn some of the fairest portions of Christendom into desert wastes, and therein to retard the advance of civilisation for more than a century. And Ibi's reports were only too well supported by the Dutch and the English. From Cocks himself we know that he had told the Shōgun's Cabinet all about the (supposed) participation of the Jesuits in the Gunpowder Plot of November 5th, 1605, and of their political intrigues generally. And in the petition of the "Fleet of Defence" to the Shōgun Hidetada (28th August, 1620) we find the following passage:—

". . . wherefore we are agreed and resolved to make spoil and havoc of all Portingalls and Spaniards wheresoever we meet them; the reason wherefore he [Philip III. of Spain] says he is Monarch of all Europe [1]. In regard whereof we intreat His Majesty [i.e. the Shōgun Hidetada] to think of the proceedings of the King of Spain and his subjects, who have already entered as firm inhabitants in Luzon and Macao. You may be pleased to the maintaining of your estate to have special regard unto their doings, as for example referring His Majesty [Hidetada] to our last Demonstration given to your Father Ungosisama [Iyeyasu] in the 15th year of Keichō [1610], and afterward to your Majesty in the third year of Ghennay [1617], as the proceedings of their friars has shewed itself, without any thinking we do it out of malice because we have had so many years wars with the King of Spain, but only (as the truth is) to the defending of His Majesty's [Hidetada's] land and state from the treacherous practice of the friars, being a sufficient warning, which if His Majesty do but overview their doings with time he shall find the same to be true."[17]

---

[17] One thing that Ibi Masayoshi may have told Hidetada was that the Jesuit Father Spinola, then in the Ōmura prison (martyred September 10th, 1622) was a relative of that Spinola who was the Spanish Commander-in-chief in the early years of the Great War of 1618–48. This Father Spinola was a very interesting personage. He was the son of that Count of Tassarolo who had been a favourite of Rudolph II., Emperor of Germany. He had become a Jesuit in 1584, and eleven years later (1595) he had " set out for Portugal in order to pass to Brazil, and thence to the Indies." " After a sojourn at Bahia [then the Brazilian capital] and at Porto Rico, in the passage to the Indies, near Terceira, the vessel had been captured by the English, and he had been taken to England. After his liberation he returned to Lisbon in 1598 [the year of the death of Philip II. and of Hideyoshi]. In

So profound was Hidetada's distrust of Spanish intentions
that, after refusing to receive the Philippine embassy in 1624,
he gave orders that all Spaniards should be deported from
Japan, leaving their Japanese wives and servants behind them.
In 1626 some of these exiled traders ventured to return, and,
being discovered, could only save their lives by apostatizing.
The two Philippine vessels that had brought them were ordered
to depart at once. At the same time (1624) it was decreed
that while no Japanese Christian should henceforth go abroad
for commerce, non-Christians and renegades were still to be
allowed to do so, with a proviso that they were not to sail
to the Philippines. And this was the end of all intercourse
between . Japan and the Philippines—and the Spaniards.
This intercourse had been opened up by the intrigues of the
ambitious Harada about the year 1592, and Manila missionaries
had been at work in Japan two years later (1594). The trade
was in contravention of one of the clauses of the Concordat
of 1580, and was legalised by Philip III. only in 1609. Iyeyasu,
as has been shown, made the most strenuous efforts to develop
this Philippine trade, as well as commerce with New Spain.
Now Hidetada made an end of it. Intercourse between Manila
and Japan lasted, then, for some thirty-two years (1592–1624),
As for the Portuguese, they had been in Japan fifty years
before the Spaniards appeared there, and they were allowed to
trade (from Macao) at Nagasaki for fifteen years after their
Spanish rivals had been expelled. It is with the events of
these fifteen years (1624–1639) that the following chapter
will be occupied.

March, 1599, he embarked with nineteen other missionaries as Superior of
those who were in the same ship. He had to make long stays at Goa, at
Malacca, and at Macao. In this last city he exercised his ministry with rich
fruits, and as he was a clever draughtsman he was commissioned to sketch
the plan of the new church dedicated to the Assumption of Our Lady which
was to replace the one that had just been burned. [This church is the one
that perished by fire in 1834.] Finally he was able to reach the term of
his desires and landed at Nagasaki in 1602." Spinola did in Japan very
much what Ricci did in China. After Hideyori had (on the occasion of Paer's
visit to Ōsaka in 1607) shown himself so much interested in cartography and
astronomy, Spinola established an "academy" in Kyōto. This "academy" was
no mere superior "finishing school"; it was a real "academy" in the Italian
sense of the term—i.e., it was an institution for research, something like the
Royal Society afterwards established in England. Some of the greatest figures
in Kyōto—among them the highest dignitaries in the Court of the Mikado—
were proud of their membership of this body. In 1612 Spinola had to give
up this effort in order to assume (at Nagasaki) the office of Procurator to the
Jesuit Province of Japan, which he held for years, "providing incessantly
for everything, with the fecund genius of sainted charity." Spinola, withal,
was a fine man.

CHAPTER XXI.

PORTUGUESE AND DUTCH.

THUS with the expulsion of the Spaniards in the spring of 1624 the only Europeans who continued to enjoy the pinched hospitality of Japan were the Portuguese and the Dutch, for the English had withdrawn from Hirado in the previous December (1623). And between Japan's remaining guests there was but little love lost.

In June, 1622, the Dutch, with seventeen vessels, had assailed Macao, when a landing party of 2,000 men—900 Hollanders and 1,100 Japanese and Malays—had to retreat with the loss of nearly half its numbers in killed and prisoners. The presence of the Japanese in this affair is remarkable, for in 1621 the Dutch (and English) in Hirado had been forbidden to carry out Japanese sailors or munition of war from that port, which the "Fleet of Defence" had been using as a naval base. The prohibition in question was dictated merely by the feeling that one of the chief points of foreign policy so consistently adhered to by Iyeyasu should not now be departed from. The great old statesman, while according a hearty welcome to law-abiding subjects of any and every foreign State, was resolutely resolved that Japan should not in any wise become embroiled in any differences these Powers might have with each other beyond the territorial waters of the country. During all the term of Iyeyasu's sway, Japan *vis-à-vis* all European nations in the Far East had been strictly neutral. Should Hirado be used as a base of Dutch and English naval operations against the Portuguese and the Spaniards, the latter would indeed have good grounds of complaint. About the same time Hidetada issued an Edict against piracy in Japanese waters—a circumstance that would seem to indicate that the Yedo Government was beginning to believe that the Portuguese after all did speak a certain measure of truth when they denounced the Hollanders as freebooters of the very worst type. However, withal, as the Dutch brought in none of the priests of the foreign religion Hidetada now looked upon as so menacing to the peace and even the independence of Japan, they, notwithstanding their piratical proclivities, contrived to maintain a more favoured position in Hirado than the Portuguese did in Nagasaki.

In 1625 we are told that "the envoys of the city of Macao had at first been not less well received than was commonly the case; but the capture of the Jesuit Provincial, Pacheco, at Kuchinotsu [December 17th, 1625] having been reported, and the Shōgun [Iyemitsu] having learned that this Father with his companions had come by the way of Macao, His Majesty became exceedingly enraged, and the Portuguese regarded themselves as lost. However, the storm passed over when the Shōgun learned that the *religieux* had arrived before the promulgation of the Edict, and he at last received the envoys in audience."[1]

To make the signification of this passage perfectly clear it may be well to resume the thread of the missionary narrative where it was dropped at the end of the year 1622. It ought to be remarked that, following the example of Iyeyasu towards himself, Hidetada early in 1623 retired from the Shōgunate and obtained the appointment for Iyemitsu (his eldest surviving

---

[1] Pacheco had been deported in 1614, but had returned in 1615 (with several others) disguised as a merchant. He had been Provincial from 1622 to 1626 when (June 20th) he was sent to the stake at Nagasaki. He died like a brave man and a hero. One point in connection with this martyrdom is worthy of notice. Writes M. Pagès:—"There were thirteen stakes, but there were only nine victims; four Portuguese, one of Europe and three of India captured with Fathers Zuñiga and Flores [by the *Elisabeth*], had shown a few moments before that man can do nothing of himself, and had failed miserably." The point is that the Japanese authorities were always ready to spare the life of any Christian—foreign or Japanese—who gave up Christianity. The authorities of the Inquisition treated their victims in a very different manner. The Shōgun had, after much painstaking investigation, arrived at the conclusion that the propagation of Christianity in Japan would be fatal to the independence of the country. For that reason chiefly—if not for that reason alone—he determined to suppress it. But how far was the independence of Spain menaced by those Moors and Jews and heretics the Holy Office made victims of? The invectives of the Church historians—Charlevoix excepted—against the Japanese authorities at this time are really unjust. Hidetada, as we have said, was no genius—in fact, he was a stodgy mediocrity. But in many things he was highly conscientious. His father, the great Iyeyasu, had picked him out as the best all-round man of his family; and a man of genius in judging character such as Iyeyasu was would not have entrusted the fortunes of the House of Tokugawa, to say nothing of those of Japan, to the hands of a capricious tyrant. Such Hidetada was not, as one might reasonably infer from the Ibi Yoeyemon incident, at all events.

We shall find that the efforts of the Japanese officers—many of whom acted unwillingly—were, upon the missionaries' own showing, directed not towards the taking of life, but simply towards the suppression of a cult which the rulers of Japan, after long pondering, were convinced would be detrimental to the real interests of the nation.

son), although he himself really continued to wield the real authority down to his death in 1632. Accordingly the (nominal) accession of Iyemitsu caused no break in the continuity of the policy of the Yedo administration regarding Christianity.

"At Yedo the investiture of the new Shōgun was the occasion of many martyrdoms. The new master of the Tenka [*i.e.* Iyemitsu] re-issued the old anti-Christian decrees; one of these stigmatized the Christian religion as *lèsant la majesté du prince*, and interdicted it under the pain of death. The persecution which for twelve years [1611–1623] had been raging in the provinces had always spared the imperial domain [*i.e.* the Tokugawa family possessions],[2] except at Nagasaki. Terrible storms were now to succeed this shadow of peace."

Altogether in this year of 1623 some five hundred victims were immolated on the Tokugawa possessions, there being a great holocaust of fifty (including two foreign priests) on the heights of Takanawa, near Yedo, on December 4th, and another of thirty-seven on the 29th of the same month. In the following year the persecution was especially severe in Northern Japan, there being 109 victims on Satake's fief of Akita alone, while Daté Masamune now killed Father Diego de Carvalho and a large number of his converts. At Nagasaki four foreign priests perished at the stake, among them being that Father Sotelo who had gone to Spain and Rome as Daté's envoy.[3]

Next year there were only a few martyrs in Ōmura and in Northern Japan, all the efforts of the officers in Nagasaki being directed towards allowing no missionaries to enter and towards getting the native Christians to apostatize—under the pressure of a harassing surveillance. Yet in that year and the next the eighteen or twenty Jesuit Fathers still in the country performed 3,100 baptisms, while the Philippine priests were not idle.

---

[2] This statement is untrue, as a careful perusal of M. Pagés' own volumes abundantly shows. M. Pagés as a historian is something of a curiosity. His industry is simply prodigious, and the amount of original documents he has gone through is clearly immense; yet in his finished work he now and then contradicts himself in the most flagrant manner.

[3] After being deported from Manila to New Spain in 1620, he had returned to Manila in 1622, whence he passed in a Chinese junk to Satsuma. There he was almost at once arrested and was sent to Nagasaki, where in an interview with Hasegawa Gonroku, the Governor, he announced himself as Daté's ambassador returned with the replies from the Pope and the King of Spain, and requested that the Shōgun's Council should be informed of the fact. Pagés, besides six other documents of Sotelo's, gives the text of his long Latin memorial (of some 7,000 words) to the Pope, written from Ōmura prison, which Charlevoix labours hard to prove to be a forgery—possibly of Collado's. Even at this time the Jesuits were at bitter feud with the Philippine *religieux* in Japan.

And even at this date two of the four Daikwan or Sub-prefects of Nagasaki were Christians.

A suspicion of all this may have led to the supersession of Hasegawa Gonroku by Mizuno Kawachi-no-Kami in the governorship of the town in June, 1626. During the three years (to 1629) Mizuno remained in this office he exerted every possible device to extirpate the proscribed religion. The tortures that were now inflicted upon the native Christians were of diabolical ingenuity. Among others, Matsukura, now Lord of Arima, driven into persecuting in spite of himself, hit upon the device of sending his victims to be hurled into the solfataras of Mount Unzen (1627). However, Mizuno at first endeavoured to effect his purpose without the taking of life.

> "In this persecution everything had been set to work without shedding the blood or taking the life of the confessors; stripping the rich of all their property, functionaries of their employment, artizans of their trade, depriving children of the instruction of their parents, and women of the society of their husbands. All these means were without success: and we shall soon see sanguinary measures adopted."

It is to be noted, however, that Mizuno's first step on assuming office had been to preside at the martyrdom of Pacheco, the Jesuit Provincial, and two other foreign priests (June 20th, 1626). They, of course, had shown themselves perfectly fearless; and "Mizuno, penetrated with admiration for this invincible constancy, had returned quite pensive; his pride felt itself vanquished."

Mizuno failed in his attempts at extermination; so much must have seemed apparent to the Shōgun, when a list of all the Franciscans then in Japan found on a captured priest was forwarded to him in 1628. At all events, in July, 1629, Mizuno gave way to Takenaka Uneme (who held a fief in Kyūshū), with the most extensive powers. His reputation as a persecutor was such that many Christians withdrew from Nagasaki before his arrival there with his band of five hundred satellites. At Yedo he had met Matsukura of Shimabara, and had arranged with him for his Christian prisoners to be sent to Unzen. On reaching Nagasaki he prepared stakes and faggots on the execution-ground, and, proclaiming that he would tolerate no Christian, even dead, he had several bodies in the Christian cemetery exhumed and consigned to the flames. As for the living, however, he was in no hurry to burn them. Three Spanish Augustins who fell into his hands in 1629 were merely consigned to Ōmura jail, where the quarters were none too comfortable, however. The converts who refused to apostatize were, as had been arranged with Matsukura, dispatched to Unzen, where they were now no longer hurled into its seething solfataras. The object was not to kill them, but to force them to abjure the foreign religion, and the infernal ingenuity of the tortures now devised proved too strong for the obstinate courage of most. Apostasies were obtained in plenty, and Matsukura of Shimabara and Takenaka received great credit for their success in dealing with the perverse sectaries.

But they were not contented with that merely. They meditated striking at Christianity by nothing less than the capture of Manila and the conquest of the Philippines. In 1630 Takenaka, and afterwards Matsukura, sent envoys to Manila, ostensibly to discuss the reopening of trade between that port and Japan. The Spaniards took care to impress the emissaries with a notion of their military strength, so that "they might disabuse their Lord, Matsukura, of his illusions of conquest." In thus suspecting the envoys to be spies the Spaniards were not all astray. Just a few months before Matsukura had addressed a memorial to the Yedo Government representing that "Luzon is governed by the Western country [Spain], and that country in conjunction with Namban [Portugal] is ever looking for an opportunity to invade this empire. For that reason there is a fear that our country will be disturbed. All who come from Spain to Japan touch at Luzon. Therefore if I shall conquer that country with my own troops, place my own agents there, and thus destroy the base of the Westerners, this country will be secure for years to come. If I be permitted I will cross over to Luzon and conquer it. I pray that the vermilion seal of the Great Lord, giving me an estate of 100,000 *koku* there, may be granted me." Although the Yedo Government gave no reply to this representation, Matsukura, a few days before his death, dispatched two of his retainers to Manila,—disguised as merchants, the Japanese authorities say.[4]

4 In some respects it is difficult to reconcile the statements of the Japanese authorities about this Matsukura with those of the missionaries. The latter

As has been said, three Spanish priests and two Japanese *religieux* had been consigned to Ōmura jail in 1622. Towards the end of 1631 Takenaka, having found the torments of Unzen so efficacious in dealing with the converts, resolved to try what he could effect in the case of the missionaries themselves. The apostasy of a foreign priest would naturally prove a terrible blow to the proscribed cult, so difficult to suppress. These five *religieux* were accordingly sent to Unzen, and passed the month of December, 1631, there, subjected to the most atrocious tortures. However, they all proved staunch, and were brought back to Nagasaki early in 1632, and kept in the public prison there till they were sent to the stake on September 3rd. These were the first foreign priests that Takenaka, so far the most successful of all the persecutors, had killed. At the same time when he had sent the five priests to Unzen he had initiated a new departure by subjecting lay Portuguese to torture. Two Portuguese ladies had been sent with the priests, and had along with them been horribly mangled. On their return to Nagasaki, Takenaka deported them to Macao.

In the following year the indefatigable Takenaka found himself at last in the proud position of being able to boast of having compelled the apostasy not merely of a foreign priest, but of the Jesuit Provincial himself. In that year a new torture of the most devilish ingenuity was devised. This was the torment of the "fosse," or the pit. A hole six feet deep and three in diameter was dug, and by the side of it a post with a projecting arm was planted. From this arm the victim was lowered head downwards into the pit, and there left to hang till he (or she) either died or recanted. Only, before being lowered the victim was

---

are unanimous on the point that down to 1622 Matsukura, "who was mild by nature," did everything he could to save the Christians, especially Father Navarro, who had been captured in his fief. According to Japanese writers, Matsukura, originally a small Daimyō of Yamato, had distinguished himself in the advance on Osaka on June 1st and 2nd, 1615, and as a reward for this he was later on (in 1617) removed to Shimabara with 43,000 *koku*, afterwards increased to 60,000 *koku*. "He was a bold and daring man, and on that account he was specially appointed to that fief, so that he might carry out the extermination of Christianity with vigorous hands. For that purpose he was exempted from all dues and taxes. He had always 3,000 picked men armed with matchlocks ready for service." On his death, in 1630, his son Matsukura, Nagato-no-Kami, succeeded to the fief of Shimabara. "He was a weak man and a tyrant, and his oppressions constituted one of the causes of the Shimabara rebellion of 1637-38."

tightly corded so as to impede the circulation of the blood; in some cases swathed in a sack confining all the person except one hand, left free to make the sign of recantation.

"Soon blood began to ooze from the mouth, the nose, and the ears. For most death came only at the end of two, three, and even six days. Care was taken to bleed victims in the temples of the head, to prevent a too rapid congestion and to prolong the pain."[5]

The first victim, a Japanese brother of the "Company of Jesus," lived in "the pit" from 3 P.M. of July 28th to 9 A.M. July 31st, 1633—that is, for sixty-six hours. Between this date and October 10th several foreign and Japanese priests had been done to death in this horrible manner, without any flinching on their part. Then on October 18th, 1633, Ferreyra, the Jesuit Provincial, three other foreign priests, and four Japanese *religieux* were subjected to this awful torture.[6] All the others endured to the bitter end; but Ferreyra, then fifty-four years of age, very high-strung and physically sensitive, after five hours of the infernal torment, could stand no more, and gave the sign of recantation. This was perhaps the severest blow Christianity in Japan had as yet sustained; and that, too, in spite of the fact that in addition to all the martyrdoms of preceding years, in this fatal year of 1633 no fewer than thirty-four *religieux* of different Orders perished within the bounds of the Empire.[7]

---

[5] See L. Pagés, p. 786, and Father Tanner's *Die Gesellschaft Jesu* (Prague, 1683).

[6] One of these Japanese *religieux* was Father Julian Nakaura. Says M. Pagés:—"While proceeding to his martyrdom he said, 'I am the Father Julian that went to Rome.' He was sixty-six years of age, and had been forty-two years in the Company." M. Pagés, however, gives no hint that he had been one of the four members of the famous embassy to the Pope organised by Valegnani in 1582. His sickness on entering Rome had delayed the reception of the embassy somewhat. And now, forty-eight years after his reception by the Pope, he achieves the martyr's crown in the *fosse* at Nagasaki after three days' suffering (October 21st, 1633).

[7] The accounts given by the Church historians of Ferreyra's subsequent miserable indigence as a mere hanger-on of the Dutch are most likely incorrect. All the foreign priests (Chiara, Cassola, Marques, and others) who subsequently apostatised were well provided for by the Japanese authorities. For example, Brother Andrea Vieyra and Father Chiara each received ten men's allowance of rice per day, besides 1,000 *momms* [60 *momms*=1 tael=6s. 8d.] per annum. As to the story that Ferreyra repented and was *fossed* at Nagasaki in 1653 (at the age of seventy-four), there seems to be no foundation for it.

How the Japanese officials looked at all this horrible business may be gathered by the following extracts from Satow's translation from the *Kirisuto-ki*. Speaking of three priests arrested in Daté's domains and sent to Yedo in 1638, it says:— "The above three *Bateren* were examined during ten days at Chikugo-no-Kami's on the laws of Kirishtan, and after three days Chikugo-no-Kami sent his retainers to the three *Bateren* [Padres] in prison and ordered them to be tortured. They caused two of them to apostatise [*korobasu*] and to repeat the invocation to Buddha. Kibe

Yet, in spite of all this, and in spite of the efforts of the
Governor of Manila (1623) and of Macao (1620), and of the
Spanish King himself—in 1628 his Majesty had ordered that
for the next fifteen years no *religieux* should pass from the
Philippines to Japan—missionaries continued to find their way
into the country. In 1632 as many as eleven of them in four
different bands had reached Japan from Manila in Chinese
junks. The most distinguished of these was the Jesuit Father
Vieyra, Vice-Provincial of the Company, who, after a daring
propaganda of nearly a year in Kyūshū and Western Japan, was
at last captured near Ōsaka in the summer of 1633. He was
taken to Ōmura jail; and thence he was sent to Yedo to be
examined by the Shōgun's Cabinet. The Shōgun, Iyemitsu
himself, was exceedingly interested in the venerable Father, who
on instructions from him was requested to write out a sketch
of the Christian doctrines. This sketch was read by Iyemitsu
himself with close attention, but it did not save Vieyra.
After three days in the *fosse* he was finally burned to death
on June 9th, 1634. Still the fact remained that, notwithstanding the impression made by Vieyra's intrepidity and
heroism, one foreign priest, the Provincial Ferreyra, had
already been driven to apostatize.

Three years later, in 1637, five more missionaries arrived
from Manila, and in 1642 four more. But all soon fell into
the hands of the authorities, and, apart from the two or three
that apostatized, suffered the usual fate.

How it had meanwhile fared with the Japanese Christians

Beitoro [*i.e.* Father Pedro Cassoui: Pagés, page 850] did not apostatize, and was
put to death by suspension [*i.e.* in the *fosse*, or pit]. *The reason of this was that at
that time there was want of skill* [in *inducing apostasy*]! Two catechists were
suspended in the same pit with Kibe, and therefore persuaded [? the officials] to
kill Kibe. After his death both apostatized. . . . It is stated, too, that not only
the Namban *Bateren*, but the Japanese *Bateren*, after being examined as to the
merits of their sect, were all tortured into repeating the invocation to Buddha,
made to seal a declaration, and made to apostatize. Seven men's allowance of rice
was granted to the Catechists, ten men's allowance to the *Bateren*, and 1,000
momme [then about £5 in English money] in silver. They were all kept within
a stone wall and frequently subjected to interrogation; and it was
ordered *that if they did not say that Namban had designs on Japan, they were to be
tortured.*" The grounds for the ruthless extirpation of Christianity in Japan
were *political, merely.* To find fault with a nation for being determined to
maintain its political integrity and independence is at once unreasonable and
unjust; to refuse to accord our meed of respect to the Christian missionaries in
their devotion to what they conceived to be their duty would, on the other
hand, be ungenerous. This persecution was a duel to the death between
Christian priests resolved to carry out the command of the founder of their
religion, and of Japanese equally resolute to preserve the independence of their
country.

may be inferred from the curt statement "that the institution of the persecution [perhaps 1614 is meant] down to 1635 no fewer than 280,000 Japanese had been punished for accepting Christianity."8 And in the *Buke Shohatto*

8 About 1636, Caron, of the Dutch Factory, thus sums up the course of the persecution in Japan:—

"At first the believers in Christ were only beheaded and afterwards attached to a cross; which was considered as a sufficiently heavy punishment. But when many of them were seen to die with emotions of joy and pleasure, some even to go singing to the place of execution; and when although thirty, and sometimes one hundred, were put to death at a time, and it was found that their numbers did not appear to diminish, it was then determined to use every exertion to change their joy into grief and their songs into tears and groans of misery.

"To effect this they were tied to stakes and burnt alive; were broiled on wooden gridirons, and thousands were thus wretchedly destroyed. But as the number of the Christians was not perceptibly lessened by these cruel punishments, they became tired of putting them to death, and attempts were then made to make the Christians abandon their faith by the infliction of the most dreadful torments which the most diabolical invention could suggest.

"The women and girls were stripped naked, and compelled to crawl on all fours through the streets; after which they were violated in public by ruffians, and at length were thrown into tubs full of snakes, which were taught to insinuate themselves into their bodies. One's heart shrinks to hear of the many other abominable and inhuman cruelties which were committed, and the pen refuses to record them.

"The Japanese Christians, however, endured these persecutions with a great degree of steadiness and courage; very few, in comparison with those who remained steadfast in the faith, were the number of those who fainted under their trials, and abjured their religion. It is true that these people possess, on such occasions, a stoicism and intrepidity of which no examples are to be met with in the bulk of other nations. Neither men nor women are afraid of death. Yet an uncommon steadfastness in the faith must at the same time be requisite to continue in these trying circumstances.

"Once a year a General and a strict search is made throughout all the territories of the empire. All the inhabitants are assembled in the pagodas, where they must sign with their blood that they are true Japanese and not Christians; or, if they are Christians, they must abjure their faith. But this measure has not produced the effects the Emperor expected from it; as not one year elapses in which several hundred Christians are not put to death.

"All these persecutions and massacres have, in fact, considerably reduced the number of Christians; and the Court has directed, in order to discover those that remain, that if any one was found to be a Christian he should be relieved from the punishment to which he would otherwise be liable, upon making discovery of a fellow-Christian; or, if he could or would not point out another, that then he should suffer the penalty affixed to the profession of his religion, namely to be hung up with his head downward [*i.e. fossed*]. It is generally supposed that this measure will be more efficacious for the extirpation of Christianity than all the punishments that have hitherto been devised.

"An accurate register is kept of those Christians who have saved their lives by treachery of this kind; and the strictest measures of precaution are observed that they may not abscond. They are consequently all known; it is known where they are, and they can be forthcoming as often as they may be desired to appear.

"Japanese who were well informed and experienced in the affairs of State alleged that there was no doubt but the Court had in view to destroy all the Christians in one day, without sparing one individual, as soon as an assurance could be obtained that none others were to be found in the empire; in the hopes in that case of preventing Christianity from ever again rearing its head."

In this account there seem to be exaggerations. We have carefully checked Father Cardim's *Catalogus eorum qui in Japponia in odium Christianæ Fidei violentâ morte sublati sunt*, and we find that apart from those that perished in the Shimabara Revolt (1637-8), and the Portuguese Ambassadors and the crew of their vessel in 1640, he claims no more than 1,430 victims. Of these 9 perished before 1632, 87 under Hideyoshi, 72 between 1598 and 1614,

(Regulations for the Military Class) addressed to various Daimyō in the August of that year one clause lays it down that "in certain provinces and places the Christian religion shall be more resolutely proscribed than ever," while three months afterwards strict injunctions for the utter extirpation of the cult were given to *all* the Daimyō.

And shortly afterwards (June 23rd, 1636) the Shōgun's Cabinet issued instructions to the newly-appointed Governors—now two in number—of Nagasaki, which disclose very clearly how radically the Tokugawa policy had changed since the years when Iyeyasu was unsparing in his efforts to foster the development of a Tokugawa mercantile marine—a change which is to be attributed to sheer dread of the political effects of Christianity. Now,

"No Japanese vessel was to be allowed to proceed abroad; Japanese trying to go abroad secretly were to be punished with death, the vessel and her crew seized 'to await our pleasure.' Any Japanese resident abroad was to be executed if he returned to Japan. Denouncers of *Bateren* were to be rewarded with three hundred pieces of silver in the case of a Father, and two hundred in that of a Brother, and with a lesser amount for Catechists. The descendants of Namban [Portuguese] people shall not be allowed to remain. This must be fully and strictly explained to them. Whoever remains shall be punished with death, and his [or her] relatives punished according to the degree of their offence. The children of Namban people, their children, and those who may have adopted them shall be delivered to Namban [Macao]; though death is due to them all. So if any of them return to Japan, or sends correspondence to Japan, he shall of course be killed, and his relatives also shall be punished according to the degree of their offence." 9

and 1,596 between 1614 and 1640. The only years when the numbers exceeded a hundred were 1622 (117), 1624 (214), 1627 (127), 1630 (115), and 1633 (110). As Cardim reckons among these several of the exiles who died at Manila and others who died a natural death in Japan, the list is longer than it should be. As regards the number of Christians in Japan, in 1596 they are put at 300,000 in three separate letters. Six years later (1603), according to the Bishop of Japan, they had sunk to 200,000. After that date the adult baptisms by the Jesuits were as follows:—1605, 10,000; 1604, 4,500; 1606, 5,450; 1607, 7,960; 1608, not ascertained; 1609-10-11-12, 16,400; 1613, 4,888; 1614, 1,351; 1615-16-17-18, 6,500; 1619-20, 3,100; 1621, 1,948; 1625, 1,140; 1625, nearly 2,000. In addition to these, there were those by the Philippine *religieux*,—perhaps half as many. But then meanwhile apostacies were numerous.

9 In Vol. II. (Annexe 116) M. Pagès gives a translation of the Ordinance of December 7th, 1636. Several of its clauses are similar to those of the one whose chief (extra) provisions we have cited. But that Ordinance of December 7th, 1635, calls for a few remarks. Article 7 runs:—"The Spaniards, the priests, and all who are stained with those perverse names, ought during the investigation of their case to be kept prisoners at Omura." Article 14:—"The ships of foreign countries ought to be dispatched on the 20th day of the ninth month; those who arrive late, may remain for fifty days from the date of their arrival; you will not be too rigorous either with the Chinese or with the *Portuguese*."

In accordance with the last quoted clauses of the Ordinance, on October 22nd, 1636, two Portuguese galleons took away two hundred and eighty-seven persons, with their property amounting to 6,697,500 florins. From this last sentence it may be readily inferred that a Portuguese commerce between Japan and Macao was still maintained. Indeed, down to 1638 it was not inconsiderable, raw silk being the staple commodity. In 1636 the imports from Macao amounted to a value of £100,000; small, indeed, compared with those of the Dutch, which in 1638 footed up to 3,760,000 gulden, and in the following year to nearly 3,500,000, while their return cargoes for 1640 were valued at close on 4,000,000 gulden.

But such as this Portuguese trade was, it was now conducted under the most galling restrictions. Since 1623 the galleons and their cargoes were liable to be burnt and their crews executed if any foreign priest was found on board of them. An official of the Japanese Government was stationed in Macao for the purpose of inspecting all intending passengers, and of preventing any one that looked in any way suspicious from proceeding to Japan. A complete list and personal description of every one on board was drawn up by this officer, a copy of it was handed to the captain, and by him it had to be delivered to the authorities who met him at Nagasaki before he was permitted to anchor. If in the subsequent inspection any discrepancy between the list and the persons actually carried by the vessel appeared, it would prove very awkward for the captain. Then in the inspection of the vessel letters were opened, trunks and boxes ransacked, and all crosses, rosaries, or objects of religion of any kind had to be thrown overboard. Then in 1635 Portuguese were forbidden to employ Japanese to carry their umbrellas or their shoes, and only their chief man was allowed to carry arms, while they had to hire fresh servants every voyage. It was in the following year that the artificial islet of Deshima was constructed for their special reception, or rather imprisonment. It lay in front of the former Portuguese factory, with which it was connected by a bridge, and henceforth the Portuguese were to be allowed to cross this bridge twice a year,—at their arrival and their departure.

Furthermore, all their cargoes had to be sold at a fixed
price to a ring of licensed merchants from the Imperial
towns during their fifty days' stay. Times were now somewhat
different from those ante-Tokugawa days, when the Japanese
so eagerly welcomed the Portuguese to their ports, that if they
did not come they complained bitterly. Iyeyasu had given the
country peace, and so far the Yedo bureaucracy had justified
its existence by the maintenance of that peace, but it may
well be doubted whether the price the nation had to pay for
the rule of the bureaucracy in question was in every respect
a moderate one. It was certainly stiffening the population
into castes, and stifling legitimate enterprise among the nobles
and the *samurai*. In Hideyoshi's time many of the most
enterprising traders had been *samurai*, and not a few of
the merchants had then been received into the ranks
of this privileged class. Even Daimyō had been encouraged
by Iyeyasu in the early years of his rule to fit out over-
sea commercial ventures—Arima, and Matsuura of Hirado,
for example, to say nothing of Satsuma, whose Manila-
traders we find commanded by *samurai*. All that was now
brought to a stop. One of the Articles in the instructions
addressed to the Governors of Nagasaki in 1635 and 1636
forbade them to allow *samurai* to buy anything from
foreign merchants ;—"they must buy it at second-hand
from the licensed merchants." The rulers of Japan, really
distrustful of their powers to cope with men of energy, no·
doubt flattered themselves that theirs was that government by sages commended by the Chinese philosopher.[10]
Japan was now beginning to pay a heavy price for the
lack of a ruler of the commanding genius of Hideyoshi or
Iyeyasu.

At this date (1631–1636) the Dutch in Hirado were
meeting with but little better treatment than that accorded
the Portuguese in Nagasaki. In 1623, after the failure of
their attack on Macao, they had established themselves in

---

[10] "A government conducted by sages would free the hearts of the people
from inordinate desires, fill their bellies, keep their ambitions feeble, and
strengthen their bones. They would constantly keep the people without
knowledge, and free from desires, and where there were those who had
knowledge [or enterprise] they would have them so that they would not
dare to put it into practice." Laôtze, *Tuó Tı́h Kı́ng*, Chap. III.

the Pescadores, and in the following year at Fort Zelandia in North Formosa. In 1628 Peter Nuyts was the commandant of Zelandia. Now in the previous year Nuyts had gone on a mission to Yedo, and the discourteous reception then accorded him by the Shōgun's officers had made him look out for an opportunity to make himself unpleasant to the Japanese. This he now found when two of their vessels, on their way to Cochin-China, put in to Zelandia. He promptly removed their yards and rudders, and made them lose the monsoon. By a *coup de main*, however, the Japanese seized upon the person of Nuyts, and only set him free after he had made the *amende honorable* and duly indemnified them for the losses involved by their year's detention, while the five hostages they insisted upon taking with them to Japan were consigned to prison there, where two of them died in 1631. Nor did the matter end here. On their return to Japan their chief, Hamada, reported the affair to the Yedo Cabinet, with the result that several Dutch vessels were sequestrated, the trade of the Hirado factory suspended, and a demand made for the surrender of Nuyts's person.[11] When this demand was not complied with, the Japanese insisted upon Fort Zelandia in Formosa being ceded to them by the Dutch. The Hollanders, thus pressed, induced Nuyts to surrender himself to the Shōgun's

---

[11] The following (translated by Sir E. Satow) from Meylan's *Geschiedkundig Oversight van den Handel der Europeen of Japan* (Historical Review of the Trade of Europeans in Japan) is, however, worthy of attention in connection with this matter:—

"Some historians have made out that the dissatisfaction of the Supreme Indian Government with Herr Nuyts went even so far that they caused him to be carried back as a prisoner to Japan, in order to be placed at the disposition of the Japanese Government, as a State sacrifice; but this fable, which is taken from the *Recueil de Voyages au Nord*, is positively contradicted by all genuine information and records of that period. It is true, nevertheless, that Herr Nuyts, recalled from Formosa to Batavia, received a not very honourable dismissal, not only from his office of Governor, but from his rank as Councillor of India [as a matter of fact he was punished with two years' incarceration]; that he afterwards returned to Japan in 1632, not under compulsion, but of his own choice, because his enemies gave out that many things had come to light in Japan to his disadvantage; and he said he was not afraid to go to defend his cause, which he held to be justified in that country also; that he subsequently, upon his arrival at Hirado, was immediately put in prison by order of the Japanese Government, without being granted any trial or hearing; and lastly, that after his arrest the [successive] Superintendents, under repeated instructions from the Supreme Government, left nothing untried to procure his release, sparing neither representations, money, or presents, though his release was not obtained until the month of July, 1636. So much expenditure and solicitude on the part of the Supreme Government to effect the release of Herr Nuyts from Japan prove abundantly that he was not sent thither as a political victim, whatever reasons for dissatisfaction the Supreme Government may have had with the said gentleman."

officers, and the hapless ex-commandant had a taste of the quality of a Japanese jail—in Hirado or in Ōmura, for authorities differ on the point—for nearly four years (November 1632 to July 1636). Then only—although vessels had meanwhile come from Batavia in the name of individual merchants— was the Company permitted to resume its Hiradoese trade. About 1634 the Dutch had been ordered to send all their raw silk for sale to the "ring" at Nagasaki, and on the Chief of the Factory, Koeckebacker (1633–39), trying to evade the instruction, he was most severely admonished, and on October 6th had to sign a declaration to the effect that "in future the orders of the Governors would be executed at once and to the letter—that is, in their full extent—by the Hollanders; that no Japanese would be treated unjustly by them; that all the items of merchandise should be specified, and that the merchants should be designated by name without exception." And for all this the Dutch had to sign a final clause expressing their gratitude! Moreover, on November 28th, Koeckebacker was informed that "thenceforth no Japanese was to be allowed to serve the Dutch in public, but only in their house; and that when he betook himself to Batavia to inform their lordships of the state of affairs, he ought to give them to understand that they ought not to give any instructions or issue any regulations for the agents of the Company in Japan, but that they ought to leave everything subject to the laws and ordinances of Japan."

According to Carons's "Account of Japan," Hagenaar was sent from Batavia to Japan, and arrived at Nagasaki on November 1st, 1634, where "he found Melchior van Sanvoort, who had resided there thirty years, having belonged to the fleet of Mahu, one of whose ships had been lost here."[12] At the beginning of 1636 he went up to Yedo as envoy from the Company. He himself was not received in audience, but Caron, whom he left behind, managed to see the Shōgun some months later, and to obtain the release of Nuyts from prison. Brouwer (who had intrigued against Saris in 1613), then Governor-

---

[12] Of course this is a mistake. That ship, the *Liefde*—Will Adams's ship— had arrived in Bungo (April, 1600), had been sent on to Yedo, and was lost somewhere in the neighbourhood of Uraga as she entered what is now called Tōkyō Bay.

General at Batavia, had sent a report of the Governor of Macao on the ten days' ceremonies with which Vieyra's martyrdom had been celebrated in the Portuguese settlement[13] for delivery to the Japanese authorities, " in order that His Majesty may see more clearly what great honour the Portuguese pay to those he had forbidden his Realm as traitors to the State and to his Crown," and with the expressed hope that it would prove to the disadvantage of the Portuguese and to the benefit of the Dutch. Caron, however, was told (by the Daimyō of Hirado) that all this was perfectly well known to the Japanese from Christian apostates, and that " the letter cannot make the Portuguese more odious than they are, and that the service in question could not bring the Hollanders the slightest advantage." This was in March, 1636, and although annual galleons came from Macao in that and the following year, yet on October 6th, 1637, an Edict forbade " any foreigner to travel in the empire, lest Portuguese with passports bearing Dutch names might enter it." And about two months later, December 12th, 1637, broke out that Shimabara rebellion which was to be the occasion of the cessation of all communication between Macao and Deshima.

---

[13] It had been found on a Portuguese vessel captured on the voyage from Macao to Goa.

CHAPTER XXII.

THE SHIMABARA REVOLT.

IN view of the fact that between 1614 and 1635 as many as 280,000 Japanese Christians had been punished for their faith, it may well seem strange that no armed opposition was organised by the persecuted believers. One fact that must not be overlooked, however, is that of the 300,000 Japanese Christians many belonged to the outcast classes—*eta, hinin,* beggars, and lepers—towards whom, to their honour, the missionaries were especially attentive. Of the remainder the vast majority belonged to the productive classes—farmers, artisans, and traders ; and although the work of the missionaries among the *samurai* or two-sworded class had been far from ineffectual, yet its results had been minimised by the jealous surveillance that had been exercised over that privileged class by their lords—by the Daimyōs of Satsuma and of Chōshiu, for example, quite as much as by Iyeyasu himself. In a previous chapter it has been pointed out that among the two hundred daimyō of .the empire, at no time could the missionaries boast of more than seven or eight converts, and that of these three at least were of but little consequence. The regulation forbidding any daimyō to embrace Christianity was strictly enforced by Iyeyasu; and after the discovery of Arima's intrigue with Okamoto Daihachi in 1612, Iyeyasu issued strict orders that all the *samurai* in his employ should abjure their Christianity or lose their revenues. On some of the great fiefs this example was followed. But on others, notably on those of Uyesugi, Daté, Hosokawa, Kuroda, and Fukushima, down to 1618—in some cases down to 1622 or 1623—Christian *samurai* were not interfered with.

However, about that latter date all *samurai* believers were stripped of their incomes, and had either to take to trade or farming, or to become *rōnin*, or lordless men. Some of these undoubtedly found their way abroad; but in all likelihood a much greater number passed to Nagasaki and its neighbourhood, where they fancied there might be a chance of earning a living as merchants or otherwise,—where, at all events, they would be sure of the sympathy of the mass of the inhabitants, which, even as late as 1622, was largely Christian. Then, hunted and harried from Nagasaki by the growing intensity of the persecution, they withdrew to the wilds of Arima and of Amakusa, where half-a-score of years before the population had been entirely Christian.

This was not the first occasion on which Christian refugees had sought an asylum in these quarters. On Konishi's fief of Southern Higo there had been 100,000 believers in 1600 A.D., and when that fief passed into the hands of the persecuting Katō Kiyomasa (1601) many of Konishi's *samurai* had withdrawn to Amakusa and the Shimabara peninsula. The survivors of these would now (1637) be few in numbers and feeble from weight of years; yet although the children of these *samurai* exiles had had to work as farmers, it is not likely that their fathers had neglected to teach them the use of arms, or to instruct them in the art of war. Most of these retainers of Konishi's had made the great Korean campaigns with him; and it was not probable that they would fail to let their sons know all about them. In addition to all this it must be remembered that until the Yedo bureaucracy stiffened and consolidated the caste system, there was no impassable barrier between the warrior and the farmer or the trader. To say nothing of the fact that Hideyoshi himself was a peasant's son, Katō's father had been a blacksmith, Konishi's a druggist, while old Kuroda is said to have started life as a horse-dealer. The *samurai* in those days, when a man had to be the architect of his own fortunes, were by no means unacquainted with commerce and industry; while on the other hand the trader or the industrialist was far from unacquainted with the use of arms. Hence, in the earliest years of the seventeenth century the Japanese farmers, traders, artisans, and seamen were often the reverse of the submissive drudges they became when with the cessation of all internal strife and of all foreign intercourse the stiffening of the caste system made all ambition—healthy or unhealthy—not only vain, but dangerous. Furthermore it must not be forgotten that it was only about 1685 that non-*samurai* were forbidden to wear swords.

However, by 1637 the paternal government of the Yedo bureaucracy had made no small progress in its task of curbing all spirit of enterprise and of self-reliance among its subjects. The *samurai*, with their assured position no longer threatened by the competition of low-born men of ability, and with no hope of preferment by the exercise of anything except their faculty for intrigue and lick-spittle flattery, had certainly as a body deteriorated in moral fibre since the days of the Taikō—those days with *la carrière ouverte aux talents*—the Napoleonic times of Japan. Even during the brief fourteen years' peace after Sekigahara there seems to have been a certain amount of moral dry-rot among the privileged class, for after the great Ōsaka campaign a certain number of Tokugawa troops " had had to be punished for cowardice and misconduct." Now, since Ōsaka, more than a score of slothful years had passed, and when the so-called " farmers " of Shimabara and Amakusa rose in desperation (1637) the inroads that dry-rot had made upon the moral fibre of the privileged Japanese *samurai* were found to be alarming. A Hideyoshi or a Tokugawa Iyeyasu would at once have seized the import of the phenomenon, and promptly have sent the Yedo bureaucracy and its policy a-packing. What it really amounted to was that this Yedo machine of mediocrities had converted Japan from a progressive into a stationary state,—chiefly because the Tokugawa flunkeys of those days wished to preserve their own positions, and that with foreigners in the land they felt it would be difficult for them to do so. Neither Hideyoshi nor Iyeyasu would have so distrusted themselves. It is safe to say that they would have continued to welcome the foreigner to Japan—even as Athens welcomed men of ability from any State, even as England and Prussia eagerly welcomed the Huguenots, even as the United States of America used eagerly to welcome every one that could add to the prosperity of the Republic. To have a country governed by mediocrities puffed up with absurd notions of their own importance is a calamity not only for that country, but for civilisation. From this point of view it is difficult to forgive Hidetada, Iyemitsu, and their political scullions. Good and able men there still were in Japan in those days in plenty, but unfortunately for them and for the empire it was no longer *la carrière ouverte aux talents*, as it had been half a century or even a quarter of a century before. In a stagnant pool it is the scum that rises to the top; and Japan was now rapidly drifting into the state of a moral, an intellectual, and a political quagmire—a quagmire of which marsh gas was the most brilliant and most appreciated product. "The frog in the well knows not the great ocean," and now that the self-distrustful beadledom of Yedo was turning Japan into the Universe (*Tenka*), the silly and lazy and conceited and pampered and ridiculously self-important *samurai* bull-frog was beginning to croak with a vengeance. And just at this point he happened to knock up against the so-called "farmers" of Shimabara and Amakusa with results most disastrous to his absurdly overweening sense of self-importance.

The simple fact of the matter is that, to any one who can really probe below the mere surface of things, these "farmers" of Amakusa and Shimabara were in 1637 what the *rōnin* of Ōsaka had been twenty-three years before—the very best fighting men in Japan. Like the Ōsaka *rōnin* they had been tried and proved and tempered to the finest of tempers by adversity; like the Ōsaka *rōnin* they had little to lose by defeat, while many of them being Christians who held the doctrine of the immortality of the individual soul, and who were assured of Paradise if they died in defence of the faith, were perhaps of even a loftier courage than the best of Mōri Katsunaga's wild cats had been at Ōsaka in 1615. There can be no doubt that in mere *moral* the insurgent (so-called) "farmers" of 1637–38 were far—very far, indeed—superior to their adversaries. The incident would have taught a really great man, such as Hideyoshi or Iyeyasu, a salutary lesson from which he would have been glad to profit. To expect the peddling and pretentious mediocrities who then swayed the fortunes of Japan to have utilised this severe lesson for the good of the empire would perhaps have been demanding too much of them.

To understand this Shimabara and Amakusa rebellion thoroughly, it may be well to recapitulate the history of these two fiefs. As already set forth, the missionaries had been at work in both of them at an early date. In 1577 the princelet of the chief section of Amakusa (baptized in 1570, and then a feudatory of Ōtomo of Bungo) had ordered all his subjects to accept Christianity or to withdraw from the island on the following day, and thus that little fief then became entirely Christian. This bigoted princelet, on getting into difficulties with Hideyoshi some dozen years or so later on, was stripped of his possessions by an expeditionary force headed by Katō and Konishi. After Sekigahara his fief was bestowed upon Terasawa, then Governor of Nagasaki and also Daimyō of Karatsu; and although, in consequence of misbehaviour in connection with the Portuguese trade, Terasawa was deprived of his governorship, he continued to hold both Karatsu (80,000 *koku*) and Amakusa (40,000 *koku*) down to his death in 1633. This Terasawa is said to have been secretly baptized in the Taikō's days; but he soon threw his Christianity overboard. However, in 1601 or 1602, when he got into difficulties with Iyeyasu, he exerted himself to conciliate the missionaries, and promised them free entrance into his new fief of Amakusa. When the persecution broke out, it does not seem to have struck the Christianity of Amakusa at all heavily until 1629, when Miwake, a renegade, was sent as commandant by Terasawa, charged with the task of effecting the apostasy of the inhabitants. This man, Miwake, was still (1637) in office under Terasawa's son and successor, and although Correa writes that he was a man of good reputation, yet from his zeal as a persecutor he was heartily detested by the "farmers."

As regards Shimabara it was now practically synonymous with that fief of Arima about which so much has been said in the earlier chapters. In the year 1612 nearly the whole population of Arima, from the Daimyō down to the beggar, was Christian. What happened in that year has already been set forth at length; for his intrigues the old Daimyō was executed, and his son and successor not only apostatized, but promptly instituted a violent persecution, in which he was assisted, or rather supervised, by Hasegawa Sahyōye, Governor of Nagasaki. In 1614 this Hasegawa obtained the fief, when Arima was removed to Nobeoka in Hiūga, and shortly after the death of Hasegawa in 1617 the domain was bestowed upon Matsukura, Bungo-no-Kami, with a revenue of 43,000 *koku* and his seat in the castle of Shimabara. According to the

Japanese authorities, this Matsukura was transferred to Shimabara for the express purpose of exterminating Christianity in
the former Arima estates. On the other hand, the missionaries
assert that it was not till 1625, when he received imperative
instructions from the Yedo Cabinet, that Matsukura took
any very drastic measures against either the half-dozen foreign
priests lurking on his domains or his Christian subjects. Be
that as it may, at all events after 1625 he soon acquired the
reputation of being one of the two most ruthless and most
successful persecutors in Japan.[1]

When Arima had been removed to Hiuga (1614) he had
taken few or none of his *samurai* with him, and when
Matsukura entered into possession of Shimabara in 1617 he
was accompanied by all his own *samurai*. The former Arima
two-sworded men—mostly Christians—had thus been deprived
of all their revenues and offices, and had had to betake themselves to manual labour, and were furthermore heavily taxed
for the support of the new *samurai*, brought in for the suppression of Christianity. As long as Matsukura, Bungo-no-Kami,
lived, this state of affairs, as well as the persecution, was

---

[1] In 1622 Father Navarro had been arrested on his domains. Before
this Matsukura had boasted to the Shōgun that there were no Christians on
his estates; a vaunt he made with the intention of preventing any search for
Christians there, for he was really well-disposed towards them. The arrest
of Navarro was thus an exceedingly awkward event for him. "He often took
the priest out of prison under the pretext of examining him, but really to have
the pleasure of talking with him. The first conversations turned upon Religion,
upon the establishment of the Church, upon the conversion of the Roman
emperors; and Matsukura was so charmed with all he learned that he evinced
a supreme chagrin at the Shōgun's ignorance of the men he persecuted. At
the following interviews there was much said of the conquests of the Spaniards
and of the Portuguese in the Indies and the New World; *it was then the common
topic of the time in Japan, and it was almost impossible to persuade the great lords of
Japan that the missionaries were not the avant-couriers of the conquerors.* Navarro
spoke so sensibly and so convincingly on these subjects that none of his auditors
had any answer to make to him." (See also Navarro's own account reproduced
in the Annual Letter of 1623.)

Pacheco, the Jesuit Provincial, was arrested at Kuchinotsu in Arima in
1625. "Matsukura found himself then at the Shōgun's Court, and his good
fortune having rendered him more timid and more politic, he wrote to those
who had charge of his estates in his absence ordering them to spare nothing
to render an entire obedience to the Edicts of the Shōgun against the Christians."
In 1627 more *religieux* were found on his domains, and he stood in great danger
of being stripped of them. "He extricated himself from this difficulty, but
it was only by taking an oath that he would exterminate Christianity in his
fief, and the orders he at once sent to his lieutenants made it clear that he
meant to keep his word." In spite of the ruthless persecution he then
instituted he was again denounced to the Shōgun's Cabinet (this time by
Takenaka Uneme) for giving the missionaries an asylum in his domains, and
because most of those he had caused to apostatize had again become Christians.
The tortures he then devised and inflicted upon his Christian subjects were
of diabolic ingenuity, and apostacies became frequent." For his death, see
Charlevoix, Vol. VI., p. 855.

patiently borne, for Bungo-no-Kami was an able administrator, and a man of enterprise withal. We have seen that in 1630 he petitioned the Tokugawa Government to be allowed to proceed to the conquest of the Philippines with his own troops, the great number of which he seems to have perceived to have been more than the limited resources of his fief could well support. If such a petition had been preferred to the Taikō, Matsukura would undoubtedly have been told to proceed. As it was, no reply to it was ever returned by the Yedo beadledom, and in that same year (1630) Matsukura, Bungo-no-Kami, died (see Charlevoix for a bit of lurid writing), and was succeeded by his son Matsukura, Nagato-no-Kami, a man of a very different stamp. The father had been a fine fighting man, a man who had honourably won his spurs by hard work. The son was, indeed, a Matsukura also—but not likewise.

This Matsukura, Nagato-no-Kami, was indeed an illustration of the Japanese saw to the effect that "the great man has no seed." Brought up in the piping times of peace, when the mere fact of being one's father's son was itself a high claim to the pestiferous incense of intriguing sycophants, the young man seems to have succeeded to his father's seat with none of the manly faculties developed. All that he had was an inordinate appetite for servile adulation. In Yedo, where he passed most of his time, he entered into the competition in ostentatious display, into which the Yedo beadledom were making strenuous efforts to engage the feudatories for their own undoing, with the greatest zest.

As a consequence the Shimabara peasantry had to suffer. In Bungo-no-Kami's days, in order to maintain his force specially equipped for the suppression of Christianity, taxation in the former Arima domains had not been light. On his death in 1630 it had rapidly grown heavier; and by 1637 the farmers were loaded with a burden of new and unheard-of imposts that made life not merely hopeless, but virtually impossible. From Duarte Correa's account of the situation it is hard to see how the "peasants" could have found anything left to eat at all. And others besides the "farmers" had to suffer in order that the young Matsukura's fondness for display and his appetite for empty and extravagant pomp might be satiated. The very military force maintained for the extirpation of Christianity in the Arima domains had—unheard-of thing in Japan—to turn to and address itself (or themselves) to coolies' work. They had to go into the hills and forests to cut wood for fuel to keep the furnaces of the salt-works going. Naturally this sort of thing was not very much to the taste of Japanese *samurai*; and desertions from Matsukura, Nagato-no-Kami's troops, were frequent. Thus in the old Arima fief, apart from all question of religion, by 1637 the discontent engendered by misgovernment was intense.

In Amakusa it was pretty much the same; for there the renegade persecutor, Miwake, had been hard put to it to meet the financial demands of young Terasawa, Lord of Amakusa (40,000 *koku*), as well as of Karatsu (80,000 *koku*), who, detained in Yedo, had been swept into the vortex of the criminal profusion into which the Yedo authorities were then alluring the Daimyō.

Both the Dutch and the Portuguese, no less than the Church historians, labour hard to show that this rebellion of 1637–38 was not prompted by religious motives, but merely by grinding economic conditions. In short, according to heretic Hollanders and orthodox Peninsulars alike, it was a *Jacquerie*; a Wat Tyler insurrection. Writes Correa:—

"The labourers that could not pay were cruelly maltreated. Their wives were seized as hostages, and these unfortunate women were frequently put to the torture. Several of them who were pregnant were plunged into frozen ponds and some of them succumbed. In the last place the daughter of a principal labourer had been sequestrated; and young and beautiful as she was, she was exposed nude and branded all over the body with red-hot irons. The father had supposed that the girl would merely be detained as a hostage till his debt was paid, and so he had accepted the temporary separation, but on learning the barbarous treatment to which she had been subjected, he became furious with grief, and, summoning his friends, he fell upon the local governor and killed him, together with thirty of his satellites. This event, which took place on December 17th, 1637, was the signal for a general revolt. The prince's troops saw themselves besieged in the castle of Shimabara, and the town itself was delivered to the flames." [2]

---

[2] This Duarte Correa was an old Portuguese captain, a Familiar of the Holy Office, and affiliated with the Society of Jesus. At the time of the revolt he was a prisoner in Ōmura jail, which he left only to perish at the stake in August, 1639. Hence, of course, he was no actor in or eye-witness of the chief events he recounts. The letters of Koeckebacker, head of the Dutch Factory in Hirado, are very important, for Koeckebacker was engaged in the operations himself. Besides the two foreign accounts of the revolt, there are several Japanese ones of very considerable value. Professor Riess has dealt with the "sources" very thoroughly in his monograph *Der Aufstand von Shimabara* in Heft 45 of the *Mittheilungen der Deutschen Gesellschaft für Natur- und Völkerkunde Ostasiens*.

Koeckebacker's letter to Governor-General Van Diemen also attributes the outbreak of the rebellion to economic causes; the penultimate paragraph in the following extract is worthy of close attention:—

"On the 17th December, 1637, we received intelligence that the peasants in the county of Arima had revolted, taken up arms, set fire to all the habitations of the nobility and citizens, murdered some of the nobles, and driven the remaining gentlemen within the walls of the castle.

"Some years ago [1614] the prince of the county of Arima had removed, by order of His Majesty [the Shōgun], to another county with which he was endowed [by the Shōgun]. At his departure he left nearly all his retainers and nobles behind, taking only a few with him to his new post, whilst the newly-appointed prince, on the contrary, came hither with nearly all his retainers. The servants of the departed prince were then deprived of their income and obliged by poverty to become farmers, in order to procure for their wives and children the necessaries of life. Although thus becoming peasants in name, they were in reality soldiers well acquainted with the use of weapons. The newly-arrived lord, not content herewith, imposed moreover upon them and upon the other farmers more taxes, and forced them to raise such a quantity of rice as was impossible for them to do. Those who could not pay the fixed taxes were dressed, by his order, in a rough straw coat (*mino*) made of a kind of grass with long and broad leaves and called *mino* by the Japanese, such as is used by boatmen and other peasantry as a rain-coat. These mantles were tied round the neck and body, the hands being tightly bound behind their backs with ropes, after which the straw-coats were set on fire. They not only received burns, but some were burnt to death; others killed themselves by bumping their bodies violently against the ground or by drowning themselves. This tragedy is called the Mino dance (*Mino-odori*). This revengeful tyrant,[3] not content with his cruelty, ordered women to be suspended quite naked by the legs, and caused them to be scoffed at in various other ways.

"The people endured this ill-treatment of the said prince as long as he was present amongst them, but as his son, the present lord [Matsukura, Nagato-no-Kami], who resides in Yedo, feels also inclined to follow in the footsteps of his father, and forces the farmers to pay far more taxes than they are able to do, in such a manner that they languish from hunger, taking only some roots and vegetables for nourishment, the people resolved not to bear any longer the vexations, and to die one single death instead of the many slow deaths to which they were subjected. Some of the principal amongst them have killed with their own hands their wives and children, in order not to view any longer the disdain and infamy to which their relatives were subjected.

"The farmers of the island of Amakusa, situated southward of Nagasaki bay, just opposite to the district of Arima, whence the island may be reached on foot at low tide, have also revolted against their magistrate; as soon as they heard of the insurrection in Arima,

---

[3] Matsukura, Bungo-no-Kami, is meant. But the missionaries never accuse him of maladministration: they complain only of the fiendish persecution he ultimately instituted and carried on in his fief under compulsion from Yedo.

they joined their neighbours, killed their regent, shut up the nobility in the castle, and made themselves masters of the island. The reason of their discontentment was that their lord, the Prince of Karatz [Terasawa], had also inflicted many vexations upon them. The magistrates of Karatz, situated nearly fifteen miles to the north of Hirado, sent some commissioners and soldiers to Amakusa as soon as they heard of the rebellion to quell the revolt and to punish the ringleaders. On the 25th December, 1637, they passed Hirado with thirty-seven row-barges and cargo-boats on their way to Amakusa, but on their arrival there they were received in a hostile manner by their own subjects, the majority of the troops being killed, the barges burnt to ashes, and some of them kept in captivity. As yet only one single boat with two mortally wounded noblemen returned to Hirado on the 3rd January (1638).

" A few days after the outbreak of these discords, the Christians of Arima joined the farmers, who received them in a friendly manner. They burnt down all the Japanese or heathen churches, built a new church, with the image of the Virgin Mary, and their troops carried colours with a cross. They say that, whether they are victorious or defeated, it will be for the glory, and in the service, of their God; they cry out throughout the whole country that the time has now come to revenge the innocent blood of so many Christians and priests, and that they are prepared to die for their faith.

" Every day more and more persons are joining them, so that the number of farmers as well as of Christians may now be estimated at about 18C.[4] Amongst the Christians there were forty-three persons who intended to set the castle of Arima on fire and to kill the nobility who had fled within its walls. They managed to get permission to enter the castle under fine promises and friendly demands, but as the inmates of the castle had some suspicion as to the intentions of the Christians, one of the latter was put to torture. This person confessed the intentions they had of burning the castle and killing the inmates by surprise. They were then all decapitated, and the heads of these forty-three persons were exposed on long posts placed on the walls of the castle, in order that their friends outside might see them."

From both of the foregoing non-Japanese accounts it would thus appear that this Shimabara revolt was in its origin no Christian rising, but merely an economic *émeute* in which the persecuted and proscribed believers saw a last desperate chance to assert themselves. According to the Japanese narratives, however, the upheaval was Christian purely, the ringleaders being five Christian *rōnin*, formerly retainers of Konishi, who had been shifting from place to place for some time.[5] Yet

---

4 The mark " C " seems to indicate *thousand*.

5 "The above five men lived in Oyano and Chidsuka, in the district of Amakusa in Higo, but for a short time also lived concealed in Fukaiemura in Shimabara in Hisen. They having held a consultation, collected the neighbouring villagers, and privately addressed them as follows:—'Some years ago, when the sect of Jesus was prohibited, there was a priest in Kamitsura in Amakusa, who, when he was driven to foreign lands, left a book of one volume, called Hankan (Mirror of the Future). When we open this book we read as

the author of the best of these narratives informs us that the commissioner (Itakura) and his associate appointed by the Shōgun to deal with the matter fancied at first that although the name of Christian was given to the movement, it had been excited solely by reason of the misgovernment in Amakusa and Shimabara!

Whatever the movement may have been in its inception—whether economic or religious—it at all events soon became a Christian one. The rebel generalissimo—a *samurai* youth of 17, Masuda Shirō by name—was a Christian [6] who preached and

---

follows: "Hereafter when five into five [this may mean 55 or 5 by 5=25] years have passed, a remarkable youth will appear in Japan. He, without study, will acquire all knowledge. This will certainly come to pass. Then the clouds will be bright along the East and West. A wistaria flower will blossom from a dead tree. All men will wear the sign of the cross upon their heads, and white flags will flutter on the sea, on rivers, mountains, and plains. Then the time of honouring Jesus will arrive, &c." We now learn, they said, from this book that the time referred to is this present year. Many clouds are now bright in the East and West. Also a red wistaria has blossomed on a cherry tree in the garden of Oye Genyemon (one of the five conspirators). He who without study understands all sciences is a youth called Shirō, eldest son of Jimbei of Amakusa—one who, though young, is without an equal in understanding and learning. The time has then already come. Let every one, disregarding the prohibition of the Government, espouse the cause of Jesus. If we incur the displeasure of the Shōgun, is it not still our chief desire, having sacrificed our lives for our religion, to obtain the reward of heaven after death?'

"When they, with much wisdom and eloquence, had spoken thus, the villagers there present, many of whom were secretly attached to this religion, united themselves with the speakers. There was also a man called Shashi Kizaimon in Fukaiemura who had been a member of this sect for several years. He had in his possession an old picture of 'Deus,' but fearing the Government prohibition, he hid it away in a chest, and, as the picture had no border, he for a long time had been anxious to obtain a border for it. In the meantime, the picture one night was mysteriously provided with a border such as he had desired. The man Shashi greatly rejoiced, and related this fact to the people of the adjoining villages. This rumour spread, and the people assembled at the house of Shashi, where the picture being hung up, they worshipped it and were filled with wonder, and united in exalting that sect more.

"At that time a retainer of the lord of the castle of Takaji, Matsukura, Nagato-no-Kami Katsuiye, named Hayashi Hyoemon, governor of the villages, hearing of this matter, hastened to Fukaiemura on the 25th of the tenth month, and when he had entered the house of Shashi and looked around, he found a number of the villagers seated in order, conversing about Jesus. Hayashi became very angry, reproved them for the crime of violating the orders of the Government, beat some of the fellows in the company, tore down their divinity (the picture), put it into the fire and reduced it to ashes. The whole assembly was greatly enraged and beat Hayashi to death on the spot. His followers with infinite difficulty escaped death, and returned to the castle of Takaji. The villagers consulted together, and they knew that when this matter should be reported to the Lord of the land, he would, without doubt, assail them, and they knew also that preparation must be made so as not to fall into the hands of their assailants; so they returned to their homes and prepared powder and ball, and waited to be attacked."

6 "In Amakusa was a farmer called Jimbei. He was a Christian, and wandered as far as Nagasaki spreading the doctrines of the corrupt sect. His son, Shirōdayū [Says M. Pagés: "The chief of the insurgents was a young man of scarcely eighteen, Jérome Machondano Chioō, of noble origin, and a native of

celebrated Mass twice a week; all round the parapet (of the castle of Hara) were a multitude of small flags with red crosses, and many small and some large wooden crosses, while the insurgent war-cries were "Jesus," "Maria," and "St. Iago,"—the latter the battle-cry of Spain.

In the Shimabara fief the expeditionary force of four hundred men sent to punish the villagers of Fukaye were lured into an ambuscade and most of them shot down; and the "farmers," following hard upon the retreat of the survivors, assaulted the castle of Shimabara itself. As it was held by no more than seven hundred and fifty men, many of whom were more or less in sympathy with the insurgents—in fact, over one hundred were executed on that ground—the fortress was in great danger, and messengers were hurriedly dispatched to Kumamoto and to Saga to ask for assistance from the great Daimyō of Higo and of Hizen.

Meanwhile, except Shimabara castle, the whole old fief of Arima was now in the hands of the insurgents, while over the water in Amakusa the peasants had also risen and had shut the Governor, Miwake, up in the castle of Tomioka. A force sent from Karatsu in Hizen to relieve this fortress was

---

Higo"], though a youth merely, excelled all men in knowledge and skill. He was not deficient in literary acquirements, and *was accomplished in the art of war*. He could also perform singular feats. For example, he could call down a flying bird, and cause it to light upon his hand; could run over the white waves, and the like. As he deluded the farmers by various exploits, they unitedly regarded him as a superior being, nothing less than an incarnation of Deus; and thus they all reverenced him. At that time, Shirōdayū having heard of the insurrection at Shimabara, he and his father together returned to Amakusa. They found out the Christians of like mind with themselves, and secretly consulted with them, saying, 'The Christians of Shimabara have lately united together and thrown away their bodies and lives for their doctrine. They await the attack of the Shōgun, in order to gain their wishes after death. This taking up arms against the Government is, to use an illustration, as if a child should try to measure out the great sea with a shell, or as if a beetle should lift up its foot to fight against a cart-wheel. Still, when the soldiers of Matsukura, Nagato-no-Kami, attacked them, contrary to expectation the soldiers were beaten by the insurgents. For farmers to fight with soldiers and gain the victory is a thing unheard of in the past, and will be rare in the future. Now, in our opinion, this is not all owing to the courage of the farmers, but altogether to the aid of Deus. If we do not go to their aid it will be hard to escape the judgment of Heaven. And if we should altogether fail of victory, is it not yet the great desire of our sect to gain heaven after death?' In this manner they carefully exhorted their hearers, and as their hearers were all from the first favourably inclined towards the sect, and fellows who reverenced Shirōdayū, they with one mind united with him. They then collected soldiers, kept up communication with the Christians of Shimabara, and resolved to capture some suitable castle and make it their own, and fight intrepidly, resisting the forces of the Government; determined that though their bodies might decay upon the open plain, they would leave their names to future ages, and so make their fame be sounded as high as the clouds."

ambushed and beaten in three separate encounters; and it
was only by the most desperate fighting that those who had
escaped were able to maintain the very innermost *enceinte* of
the castle against the assault of the insurgents (January 7th,
1638). In these latter operations in Amakusa the 5,000
Amakusa " farmers" had been reinforced by as many more
from Shimabara, for at an early date the Shimabara insurgents
had invited Masuda Shirōdayū to assume command over them
as well as over his fellow-islanders.

A few days later (January 15th, 1638) Itakura, the Shōgun's
commissioner, arrived at Shimabara, and the forces from the
neighbouring fiefs that had hitherto been lying inactive on
the confines of Shimabara and Amakusa were now moved
against the victorious farmers. Masuda thereupon resolved to
withdraw all his men from the island and to unite them in
the defence of the ruined and deserted castle of Hara in
Arima, some twenty miles south of Shimabara. Four of his
subordinates were entrusted with the charge of repairing the
dilapidated fortress; and on the 27th of January, 1638, after
some ten days' spade work, 20,000 fighting men, with 17,000
women and children,[7] took up their positions behind its walls
and ditches. The plateau on which the old keep stood was
high and windy; on three sides it faced the open sea, which
here broke against perpendicular cliffs, a hundred feet high,
making landing impossible; while landward, in front of the
plateau, was a large swamp. The circuit of the outer ditch
and defences of the plateau are given at some mile and a half;
within that were yet two other circuits of defence, as was usual
in Japanese castles.

This fortress of Hara was of course by no manner of
means so formidable as Ōsaka had been in 1614 or even
in 1615. Apart from the mere strength of the hastily repaired
defensive works, Hara was poorly provisioned compared with
Ōsaka, while ammunition was none too plentiful; in short,
it was a lack of powder and ball that really ultimately
occasioned the fall of the place. In all this contest the
" farmers" relied not so much upon the sword as upon the match-

---

[7] Professor Riess is of opinion that this is an over-estimate, and that the
men, women, and children within the defences of Hara Castle fell short of
20,000.

lock; their victories in the open had all been won by clever
tactics and good marksmanship; and now behind the ditches of
Hara as long as ammunition lasted they were able to make
terrible havoc of their assailants fighting in the orthodox
fashion. There is no doubt that the military ability displayed
by the "farmers" was of a high order—a fact not to be
wondered at when many of these "farmers" had been *samurai*,
or were the sons of *samurai*, and when "several banished
noblemen and officers had joined the farmers." Koeckebacker,
besides making that assertion, also informs us that "it was
thought by everybody that this rebellion of the peasants and
Christians would cause more difficulties and have far more
important consequences than the siege and conquest of Ōsaka
had produced in former times." Having thus followed the
insurgents from the outbreak of the revolt down to January
24th, 1638, when they had entrenched themselves on the
steep and windy heights of Hara in Arima-no-ura, we will
now pass to the side of the authorities.

It will be remembered that at an early date urgent
messengers from Shimabara castle had been dispatched to
Saga and to Kumamoto to request relief.[8] But, in common
with the other Kyūshū Daimyō, the Lords of Saga and of
Kumamoto were then in enforced residence in Yedo, and their
officers at home were in a quandary when the messengers from
Shimabara appeared. However, Isahaya, the Saga councillor,
mustered 3,000 *samurai*, and led them to the point of the
Saga confines nearest to Shimabara, and there halted; while
a Kumamoto officer with 4,000 men advanced to the boundary
of the fief and there stopped. Says the Japanese historian:—

"According to the regulations of the Yedo Government, no one
but the appointed officer could go forth to inflict punishment in
any country whatsoever. The matter must first be referred to the
commissioner of the general Government. Sending aid rashly was
calculated to bring one into difficulty; hence the forces of both fiefs
remained in camp, while messengers were sent to the two com-

8 Saga was still held by Nabeshima, as it was indeed down to the end
of Japanese feudalism. But Kumamoto (Higo) had passed from the family
of Katō Kiyomasa. In 1632 the Katō that then held it offended the Shōgun,
with the result that Tokugawa troops were sent to occupy Kumamoto and
that Katō was stripped of his fief. A little later on it was bestowed upon
Hosokawa of Buzen; the son of "Jecundono" of the Jesuits and of Doña
Gracia. (This young Hosokawa had been very friendly towards the Christians.)
Buzen was then portioned out among *Fudai* Daimyō.

missioners for Kyūshū,[9] who then resided at Funai in Bungo. These two men having heard, sent a messenger to Yedo, and sent back word that they would give further orders as soon as instructions came from the seat of government. Thus the aid promised to the castle of Shimabara by the two fiefs was delayed till these instructions were received."

Though speedy messengers were sent one after another, some by sea in swift vessels, and some on swift horses by land, and though these hastened day and night, the news of the insurrection did not reach Yedo till the 9th day of the eleventh month (December 25th, 1637). That same evening Itakura Naizen-no-sho was sent off as commissioner to deal with the rebels; but he did not arrive at Shimabara until the 30th of the same month (January 15th, 1638). At first it was intended to make the Lords of Shimabara and of Amakusa wholly responsible for the suppression of the rebellion, but the Yedo Cabinet, on perceiving that the revolt was really a serious matter, ordered all the Kyūshū Daimyō then in the capital to hurry back to their fiefs and lead their musters to Shimabara. By the beginning of February, Itakura, who had already invested the castle of Hara, felt his force to be strong enough for a general assault on the rebel stronghold, and before daylight on the 3rd such an assault was delivered. The result was a repulse with a loss of over six hundred men, while not one single insurgent fell. Itakura, fearing to be recalled in disgrace when news of this miscarriage should reach Yedo, gave orders for another assault on the Japanese New Year's Day, eleven days later (February 14th, 1638). This proved even a greater disaster than the first; on the side of the rebels there were some ninety casualties, but Itakura himself was shot dead when trying to rally the assailants, who were beaten off with a loss of some 5,000 men. Soon after, the new commissioner, Matsudaira, Idzu-no-Kami, arrived to take command, and by the middle of March 100,600 men, led by twenty-five Kyūshū Daimyō and their sons, were camped or entrenched around the insurgents.[10]

---

9 By these are meant two *Ometsuké*, or "Overseers," who were residing in Bungo charged with the care of a distinguished State prisoner, Matsudaira Tadanao, Iyeyasu's sixth son.

10 As usual, it is not easy to arrive at absolute accuracy in the matter of numbers. Correa puts the full strength of the besiegers at 200,000 men; Koeckebacker, who was on the scene from February 24th to March 12th, tells us that down to that latter date the besiegers had lost 5,712 men killed, and

The new commissioner had instructions to reduce the castle with the least possible cost of life; and so he was in no hurry to repeat Itakura's attempts. He ordered his commanders to entrench themselves, to keep up an incessant fire upon the besieged from under cover, and to wait till the pinch of hunger began to work its effect upon the rebel garrison. Fifty junks from Higo and Chikuzen and five large junks from Nagasaki patrolled the sea off the castle, and kept throwing shot into it. However, the pieces were too light to effect much; and the Dutch Factor (Koeckebacker) at Hirado was "requested" to send round five heavy guns with ammunition; and a little later was first *advised* by the Daikwan of Nagasaki,[11] and then *ordered* by the Daimyō of Hirado, to send the Dutch ships at that time in the roadstead to Shimabara for service there. Koeckebacker promptly hurried off one of the two vessels to Formosa; and, making his best excuses, proceeded in the other (*de Ryp*, of twenty guns) to Arima, where he arrived off Hara castle on February 24th, 1638. "There," writes he, "after we had inspected the situation on shore as well as at sea, we saw clearly that we could do nothing important with our guns, as the houses are merely made of straw and matting, the parapets of the lower works of defence being made of clay and the uppermost fortress being surrounded by a good high wall, built with heavy stones. . . . It was evident that it was not much use to fire guns from the batteries of the Imperial army, nor from our batteries." However, during the fifteen days (February 24th to March 12th, 1638) the Dutch were before Hara castle they threw 426 shot into it, and, according to the best Japanese narrative, drove the besieged "to build places like cellars, into which they crowded." Then suddenly, on March 12th, the Dutchmen were heartily thanked, and told that they might withdraw.

From deserters who had been swept into the vortex of the

---

that " the army consists now of 80,000 soldiers, servants and 'berckiers' (of whom there were a great many) excepted." The figures given by the Japanese authorities (100,619) are very detailed, and seem to be trustworthy. At all events, more men were engaged in this affair than actually came into action at Sekigahara, while the casualties here were heavier than they had been on October 21st, 1600.

[11] Phesedonno, Koeckebacker calls him—that is, Sukesada *Heizo*, the son of that "Feizo" the apostate against whom the missionaries write so strongly.

revolt against their will, the commissioner had learned that hunger was beginning to do its work, and that the expenditure of Dutch gunpowder could very well be saved. " The landscape on all sides was serene, but the villagers in the castle began to be in want of food. They were wearied by the long days, and appeared disheartened and like caged birds longing after the clouds." Accordingly, with a view to capturing supplies from the besiegers, a *sortie* of 3,000 men was arranged for the night of April 4th–5th, 1638, and a determined onslaught was made on the positions of Nabeshima, Kuroda, and Terasawa, with the result that those camps were fired, but no provisions obtained, while the " farmers," after inflicting a loss of some 500 men upon the enemy, had to retire, leaving about 400 dead or prisoners behind them. Thus, although coming off on equal terms with their *samurai* antagonists, the " farmers" had failed to achieve the main purpose of the *sortie.* Nor was this the most depressing part of the situation; not merely provisions, but ammunition had given out! The new commissioner from Yedo had in a council of war expressed himself to the effect that " this is not an ordinary conflict. In this there is no difference between soldiers and farmers, *because fire-arms are used."* And now in Hara castle there is no more powder and ball; and of fighting men, all suffering from the pinch of hunger, now possibly no more than 15,000 to cope with the onset of 100,000 well-fed *samurai,* all hungry for honour and fame, each clan being bitterly jealous and envious of the others.

Nabeshima's troops—the Hizen clan—who had received such a severe mauling on the occasion of the night *sortie* of April 4th–5th, had been keenly on the alert to descry an opportunity to retrieve their honour, and, if possible, to make an end of the business unaided and alone. So five days afterwards Nabeshima summoned his officers, and remarked to them: " When we look at the part of the castle opposite to us, it appears that the garrison have ceased to pass by there. That is because of the heavy fire kept up from our mounds and towers. Let us then seize this outer wall, establish pickets, and keep up a fire. If we do so, the 'farmers,' unable to endure it, will certainly make a *sortie* upon our camp, and then we can hurl them back, enter the castle with them, and take it." Accordingly, although it was in contravention of the general orders of the Yedo commissioner, he arranged for an assault at noon on February 11th, 1638. At that hour the Hizen troops, themselves alone far superior to the whole of the defenders in number, moved close up to the outer rampart, and after a heavy fire, to which the "farmers" could no longer reply, succeeded in clutching that section of it immediately in front of them, and then swiftly pressed on to the second *enceinte*, where after a desperate conflict they established themselves. Seeing this unexpected movement on Nabeshima's part, Hosokawa's troops, who were stationed next to the sea, also made a sudden dash, cut down or drove in all the "farmers" in the outer *enceinte* in that quarter, and poured over the second line of defences almost at the same moment as Nabeshima's troops. According to some authorities, the Higo men and the Hizen men were so jealous of each other that they now began a pitched battle between themselves within the castle! However, the central part of the fortress had yet to be stormed, although Nabeshima's men had managed to seize one of its outworks before sunset and to establish themselves there. Meanwhile Kuroda's Chikuzen *samurai* had been exceedingly annoyed at being thus forestalled by their rivals of Higo and Hizen, and so before daylight on the 12th they came up and assailed the innermost wall before Nabeshima's and Hosokawa's troops were astir, and carried it, albeit with tremendous loss. Thereupon not merely Hosokawa and Nabeshima's men, but the whole investing army swarmed into the innermost keep, and the poor band of hunger-pinched farmers, with no ammunition, fighting with stones, beams, their rice-pots—with anything in short—were massacred incontinently, only 105 of them being made prisoners.

This Japanese *Jacquerie* of 1637–8 proved much more costly in life and limb than the great campaign of Sekigahara had. Of course the rebels—37,000 of them, 20,000 fighting men[12]—were exterminated. What the exact losses sustained

---

[12] In spite of the fact that these figures appear in several contemporary records, Professor Riess gives reasons for believing that not more than half that number actually perished. Thirty-seven thousand was the total number involved in the insurrection from first to last, and there had been many deserters who were admitted to mercy. Duarte Correa, however, puts the number much higher—"Este foi o lastimoso fim de trinta e cinco mil homes, outros dizem que forão 37,000, afora molheres et meninos." Professor Riess makes very summary work of the absurd tale about Pappenberg, the so-called Tarpeian Rock of Japan.

by the investing force amounted to can be stated with accuracy. Koeckebacker puts it at 40,000 and Pagés at 70,000 men, but we know for certain that, from the lists of casualties sent in to the Bakufu by the Daimyō engaged, the Yedo Government computed the killed and wounded to amount to 13,000. From his prison in Ōmura, Correa saw the road from Shimabara filled with weeping serving-men leading the riderless horses of their masters by the bridle, most of them having their queues cut off as a sign of mourning, while the wounded that were borne along in litters were innumerable.

As has been said, this rebellion, if not Christian in origin, soon became a professedly Christian movement. On February 7th a letter attached to an arrow was shot from the fortress into Itakura's camp informing the commissioner that the rebels were acting so "only because our religion is one for which it is difficult to thank Heaven sufficiently"; and three days after the fall of Itakura in the assault of February 14th, yet another letter was shot into the lines of the besiegers, again stating that the revolt was a purely religious one.[18] However, the incident of Yamada's attempted treachery serves to show that the defenders of Hara were not all of one mind on this point. This Yamada, who commanded some eight hundred men, tried to open up communication with the besiegers for the purpose of introducing them into the castle; but the attempt was detected, and his wife and children were killed and he was imprisoned until the matter could be sifted. On the fall of the castle he was set free and pardoned by the Shōgun's

---

[18] "For the sake of our people we have now resorted to this castle. You will, no doubt, think that for the sake of conquering countries and acquiring houses we have done this; but such is by no means the case. It is simply because the Christian sect is not tolerated as a distinct sect, as you know. Frequent prohibitions have been published by the Shōgun, which have greatly distressed us. Some among us there are who consider the hope of future life as of the highest importance. For these there is no escape. Because they will not change their religion, they incur various kinds of severe punishments, being inhumanly subjected to shame and extreme suffering, till at last, for their devotion to the Lord of Heaven, they are tortured to death. Others, men of resolution even, solicitous for the sensitive body, and dreading the torture, have, while hiding their grief, obeyed the royal will and recanted. Things continuing in this state, all the people have united in an uprising in an unaccountable and miraculous manner. Should we continue to live as hitherto, and the above laws not be repealed, we must incur all sorts of punishments hard to be endured; we must, our bodies being weak and sensitive, sin against the infinite Lord of Heaven; and from solicitude for our brief lives incur the loss of what we highly esteem. These things fill us with grief beyond our capacity. Hence we are in our present condition. It is not the result of a corrupt doctrine.—4th of 1st month of 15th year of Kanyei (February 17th, 1638). Addressed to the attendants on the Imperial Commissioner."

commissioners. On the 5th of February he threw the following letter into the camp of the besiegers:—

"Yamada Emonsaku addresses you with true reverence and respect. I desire to obtain your forgiveness, and restore tranquillity to the empire, by delivering up Shirōdayū and his followers to be punished. We find that, in ancient times, famous rulers ruled beneficently, proportioning their rewards to the merit of the receiver, and the punishments to the demerit of the offender. When they departed from this course, for any purpose soever, they were unable to keep the control of their countries. This has been the case with hereditary lords; much more will it be the case with villagers who rebel against the Government. How will they escape the judgment of Heaven? I have revolved these truths in my mind, and *imparted them to the eight hundred men under my command.*

"*These men, from the first, were not sincere Christians; but when the conspiracy first broke out they were beset by a great multitude and compelled to support the cause.* These eight hundred men all have a sincere respect for the armed class. Therefore speedily attack the castle, and we having received your answer, without fail, as to time, will make a show of resisting you, but will set fire to the houses in the castle, and escape to your camp. Only I will run to the house of Shirōdayū and make as if all were lost; and having induced him to embark with me in a small boat, will take him alive, bring him to you, and thus manifest to you the sincerity of my intentions. For this purpose I have prepared several boats already, having revolved the matter in my mind from the time I entered the castle. Please give me your approval immediately, and I will overthrow the evil race, give tranquillity to the empire, and, I trust, escape with my own life. I am extremely anxious to receive your orders. Yamada Emonsaku thus addresses you with true regard. 20th of 1st month. To the commanders of the royal army."

The stern and stubborn resolution displayed by the downtrodden and despised "farmers" came as a startling surprise to the Shōgun's officers and to the arrogant privileged *samurai*, none of whom had seen any real fighting since the great Ōsaka war of 1614–15, and most of whom had never seen any real fighting at all. Itakura, the commissioner, on starting from Yedo had made so light of the matter that he spent three weeks on his journey down to the seat of the disturbance. However, when he found the country full of pasquinades ridiculing the *samurai* as cowards ignorant of the art of arms, men who were good only for handling the abacus and for casting-up taxation accounts, and who had abandoned the trade of war to farmers, he began to apprehend a general revolt, and promptly issued orders for all non-*samurai* in Nagasaki, Ōmura, and the neighbourhood generally to be deprived of every match-lock and all the ammunition in their possession. If a moderately strong fleet from Manila had appeared in Shimabara Gulf with supplies and munition of war for the insurgents, this rebellion of 1637–38 would undoubtedly have proved a most serious affair.

Whether the insurrection was Christian in origin or not, its ultimate effect was to make it possible for the Tokugawa Government to deal with the Christian leaders even as Iyeyasu had dealt with the *rōnin* at Ōsaka in 1615. Nearly all the ex-*samurai* believers in Japan had been behind the ditches and bastions of Hara, even as all the two-sworded men disaffected towards the dominant House had been massed together in Ōsaka three-and-twenty years before. In both cases all the dangerous spirits in the country were entrapped into a *oul-de-sao*, and (at a great cost to the ruling powers, indeed) therein exterminated. From this time onward there was a great decrease in the annual roll of martyrs in Japan. Between 1639 and 1658 possibly not a thousand persons had to be dealt with for their Christianity; while between 1614 and 1635 as many as 280,000 are said to have been punished for their devotion to the foreign religion. And among these hypothetical thousand no more than seventy or eighty were *samurai* or ex-*samurai*, while among them there were at least one hundred and fifty outcasts or beggars—a class, or rather no-class which had never (to their honour) been neglected by the missionaries, which had become entirely Christian in some districts, largely so in others, and which in the most flourishing days of Japanese Christianity had probably furnished some tens of thousands of converts. The massacre of April 12th, 1638, practically extirpated Christianity in Japan for more than two centuries. The incident had also the effect of prompting the Japanese authorities to close the ports of the country to all intercourse with Europeans—with the exception of the subservient Hollanders.

CHAPTER XXIII.

THERE can be little doubt that this Shimabara revolt was an exceedingly important incident in the history of Japan, inasmuch as it was it that decided the Yedo Government in its resolution to close the ports of Japan to the Portuguese, and to all European nations except the Dutch. Before this Christian revolt of 1637–38 severe restrictions had indeed been imposed upon the traders from Macao. But notwithstanding, the Japanese authorities, if according but scant hospitality to the Portuguese themselves, were still anxious to obtain the foreign commodities the Macaoese vessels brought. It will be remembered that one Article in the severe instructions addressed to the Governors of Nagasaki in 1635 asserted that as regards the enforcement of the regulation for the dispatch of all foreign vessels on the 20th day of the ninth month, or fifty days after their arrival, "they were not to be too rigorous with the Chinese or with the Portuguese." Hence, on the occasion of the martyrdom of the Neapolitan Jesuit, Mastrilli, we find that the crews of as many as six Portuguese ships were staying on shore at Nagasaki on October 14th, 1637, just two months before the Shimabara outbreak. All these vessels had sailed shortly afterwards, before the insurrection began. Yet the Portuguese were suspected of having fomented the revolt. Shortly after its suppression, an Edict forbade any of the subjects of the Spanish King to set foot on Japanese soil or to enter any Japanese harbour on any pretext whatsoever. Strict investigation was to be made to discover the authors of the Shimabara insurrection, and Castel Blanco, who had been commandant of the Portuguese in Nagasaki in the preceding year, and Pereyra, who then (1638) occupied that position, were to be judicially examined in connection with the matter. This fact, as Charlevoix points out, goes to show that the previous Edicts had not been fully enforced, and that time had been granted the Portuguese to complete the sale of the merchandise their last ships had brought from Macao. Next year, however, the Edict of 1638 was confirmed and formally published, and when Almeyda with two vessels arrived in 1639, he was allowed to do no trade, ordered to sail with the first fair wind, and to carry with him to Macao a copy of the Edict which put an end to all Portuguese intercourse with Japan. *Henceforth, in terms of it, all Portuguese ships coming to Japan were to be burned, together with their cargoes, and every one on board of them to be executed.* The reasons assigned for this complete rupture of that intercourse the Portuguese had been allowed to maintain with Japan for ninety-seven years were mainly that the Portuguese, in defiance of the orders to bring no missionaries to Japan, had always continued to bring missionaries; that they had succoured these missionaries with provisions and everything else; and that they had fomented the Christian rebellion in Arima.

The return to Macao of Almeyda with all his cargoes and a copy of this Edict excited the greatest consternation there. It was mainly to the rich profits of the Japanese trade between 1560 and 1600 that the Portuguese settlement in the Canton river owed all its splendour and magnificence. From that latter date down to 1624 Spanish competition from Manila, and between 1613 and 1623 an insignificant English tradal competition, had to be faced. Now, in 1639, however, the sole European rivals of the Macaoese traders in Japan were the Dutch. These Hollander heretics had indeed proved by far the most formidable of all the Western competitors they had had to meet, and in 1639 their imports and exports had far exceeded those of the Portuguese. It was also true that a great Chinese trade had sprung up *viâ* Formosa. But, on the other hand, the Edict of 1635, crushing most effectually the efforts of that Japanese mercantile marine Iyeyasu had done so much to foster and to develop, and which at one time had actually engrossed the bulk of the lucrative silk-trade, had seemed to be a veritable godsend for the Macaoese. At all events, the Portuguese exports to Nagasaki had immediately gone up from 300,000 séraphins in 1635 to 400,000 séraphins in the following year. Even as things stood in 1639, the commerce with Japan, although not the sole, was yet the chief prop of Macao's prosperity. If that commerce were now to cease, the blow would be a severe one. Accordingly the excitement in Macao was great, and consultations as to how the Japanese Edict brought by Almeyda was to be met were numerous. At last it was resolved to send a vessel with no cargo, but with four ambassadors (and rich presents) to present a petition setting forth that for years no missionaries had entered Japan from Macao, that the Portuguese had in no way been compromised in the Shimabara revolt, and that it was as much for the advantage of Japan as of Macao that the trade between them should not be interrupted. The envoys were the four most respected men in the settlement; all had held the highest office in the Portuguese colonial administration. All were old men—one of them, Pacheco, was sixty-eight years of age—and all were fully conscious of the nature of the mission on which they volunteered to proceed. These, as well as the other seventy men who accompanied them either as crew or as suite, "prepared themselves by the reception of the Sacraments." "No one was admitted on board without a certificate of having made confession. Public prayers were offered by the religious Orders and by the whole city of Macao, and the Holy Sacrament was exposed in all the churches." [1]

On arriving at Nagasaki on July 6th, 1640, the vessel was at once surrounded by Japanese guard-boats; the rudder and sails, and afterwards the guns and ammunition, removed, and the envoys and all the ship's company, except a few negroes, placed in ward in Deshima, while the Governor of Nagasaki at once dispatched the ambassadors' memorial and his own report to the Shōgun in Yedo. In eleven days these documents reached the capital; and on the 1st August, 1640, two junior members of the Yedo Cabinet arrived in Nagasaki. "They brought with them a number of executioners equal to the number of the Europeans." This was perhaps the quickest journey ever accomplished between Yedo and Nagasaki under the old *régime*.

It was plain that the Japanese authorities had now really made up their minds. The two members of the Cabinet had reached Nagasaki late on the night of August 1st, 1640; yet

---

[1] The chief original authorities for this episode are Father Cardim, a Jesuit then in Macao, and the Spaniard Magisu, then in Manila. Both Charlevoix and Pagés have utilised them freely.

early on the morning of the following day they "summoned
the envoys to appear before them in order to interrogate
them and to notify to them the Imperial decision" which
they brought with them, drawn up and signed by all the
senior members of the Shōgun's Government on July 21st.
This audience was conducted with great circumstance and
ceremony. In it the envoys were asked how they had dared
to enter Japan in defiance of the late Edict, which pronounced
this to be a capital offence. To this they made reply that
trade and diplomatic missions were different things; that the
Edict applied to traders only—not to ambassadors, who were
under the protection of international law. The commissioners
thereupon told them that their alleged mission could not save
them; that as their own *vivd-voce* representations were at
variance with the alleged dispatches from the city of Macao in
important respects, they could not be regarded as ambassadors.
And then the chief commissioner called upon an interpreter
to read the sentence of doom signed in Yedo thirteen days
before :—

"The crimes committed by these men during a long series of
years in promulgating the Christian faith contrary to the decrees
of the Shōgun are very numerous, and exceedingly serious; last
year [1639] the Shōgun has, under the gravest penalties, forbidden
any one to sail from Macao to Japan, and he has decreed that in
case any vessel disregard this prohibition, the said vessel shall be
burned, and all her crew and passengers put to death without
exception. All the points have been foreseen, provided for, and
drawn up in Articles which have been published in due form. Yet,
by coming in this ship, these men have flouted the Edict, and,
moreover, they have grossly prevaricated. *Besides, although they assert
in words that henceforth they will send no doctor of the Christian
religion to Japan, it is certain that the dispatches from Macao nowhere
make any such promise.*[2] In view of the fact that the Shōgun has
rigorously forbidden this navigation, *exclusively on account of the
Christian religion*, and of the fact that in the dispatches from Macao
the above-mentioned assertion is not made, it is established that
the whole embassy is nothing but a pure lie. Consequently, all
who have come in this ship merit the extreme penalty, and not even
one should be left to announce the catastrophe. It is decreed that
the vessel shall be burned, and that the chiefs of the embassy with
all their suite shall be put to death, in order that the bruit of this
example may reach Macao and even the country of Europe, and
that the whole universe may learn to venerate the majesty of the

---

[2] It is to be noted that at this date the Senate of Macao had merely invoked
the Governor of Manila to moderate the zeal of the *religieux* until the Imperial
wrath abated.

'Emperor.' We mean, however, that the lowest among the crew be spared and sent back to Macao. If by any chance whatsoever—from stress of weather or from any other cause—any Portuguese vessel put into a Japanese harbour, no matter where, all on board of her shall be put to death to the last man."

When the interpreter ceased reading there was deep and solemn silence throughout the crowded hall of audience. At last, at a sign from one of the commissioners, the executioners they had brought with them from Yedo threw themselves upon the envoys, seized them and bound them as ordinary Japanese criminals were bound, and hurried them off to prison, with halberts resting on their necks. Early next morning they were offered their lives if they would renounce Christianity, but every one rejected the offer. At seven o'clock they left the prison for the Martyrs' Mount, the scene of so many tragedies, and there the heads of the envoys and of fifty-seven of their companions fell (August 3rd, 1640). The thirteen selected to carry the news to Macao, after witnessing the execution of their superiors, were then taken to witness the burning of the vessel, and on the following day they were summoned to the Governor's palace, and were formally asked by him if they had seen their vessel burned. "Then," he went on, "do not fail to inform the inhabitants of Macao that the Japanese wish to receive from them neither gold nor silver, nor any kind of presents or merchandise; in a word, absolutely nothing which comes from them. You are witnesses that I have even caused the clothes of those who were executed yesterday to be burned; let them do the same with respect to us if they find occasion so to do; we consent to it without difficulty. Let them think no more of us; just as if we were no longer in the world." Then the survivors were again taken to the scene of the tragedy and requested to identify the heads of the victims, which were fixed on planks arranged in three rows; and their attention was then directed to a tablet posted up beside them, which, after recounting the story of the embassy and the reason for the execution of the alleged envoys and their companions, wound up: "So long as the sun warms the earth, let no Christian be so bold as to come to Japan, and let all know that if King Philip himself, or even the very God of the Christians, or the great Shaka contravene this prohibition, they shall pay for it with their heads!"

Then, after rejecting the offer of a passage on a Dutch vessel, the twelve (or thirteen) survivors set out to Macao in a crazy little craft, and reached the settlement after a three weeks' voyage (September 20th, 1640).

"The whole city received their message with the most admirable sentiments, and rendered God thanks for having made of their earthly ambassadors, ambassadors of Heaven. The families of the victims occupied the places of honour at the *fêtes.* To the pealing of bells and the sound of artillery the hymn of glory broke forth upon the air, and wafted to the feet of the Almighty the Christian joy of this people and its resigned and grateful reverence."

Yet even after this tragedy the Macaoese were by no manner of means minded to abandon the trade with Japan. And that, too, although as things then stood the Japanese had virtually paid them an indemnity on account of its cessation, for, according to Magisa's account, the Japanese merchants had to surrender all claims to the moneys then owing to them by the Portuguese, and these sums amounted to more than 700,000 *taels.*[3] The Macaoese knew that if this commerce with Japan, so far from being restored to its original high condition, were to be annihilated, it would be Ichabod with their city.

The Portuguese traders were convinced that what at bottom the Japanese really were afraid of was what they themselves had suffered from—Spanish domination. That the Portuguese had suffered severely from their union with Spain (1580-1640) there cannot be the slightest question. They had been brought into antagonism with the Dutch in the Far East mainly because Philip II. had closed the port of Lisbon to the Hollanders (1594), and the rivalry of the Dutch in the Far East, especially in Japanese and Macaoese waters, had been fraught with the direst calamities to the rival interests of Portugal. Then this union with Spain had involved them in hostilities with England (the Great Armada of 1588 actually started from Lisbon), and English captains had ravaged their Brazilian settlements, and the English East India Company had also done them exceeding great damage from

---

[3] Some £230,000. The English Factory at Hirado had been started with a capital of £7,000, and after a loss of perhaps £1,700 it had been closed at the end of ten years (1613-1623). These figures may possibly serve to indicate the difference of the scales on which the Portuguese and English traded in Japan.

Ormuz even unto Japan. Philip II.'s quarrels with France had precipitated French inroads into Brazil and into their West African settlements, while even the Danes, in their opposition to Spain, had assailed the erstwhile Portuguese monopoly of Eastern trade by establishing a factory at Tranquebar. And against all these losses, what gains had Portugal made by its union with Spain? Every one of the promises made to the Cortes at Thomar had been broken. Since that date (1580) the Portuguese Cortes had been summoned only once (in 1619), and that was only for the purpose of recognising Philip, the eldest son of Philip III., as the heir to the Portuguese throne on the occasion of his only visit to Lisbon. In defiance of one of the most important of the provisions of the Concordat of 1580 (Cortes of Thomar), Lerma[4] and Olivares had appropriated to themselves large territories within the realm of Portugal. Whenever it had been possible, Spaniards had been installed in Portuguese bishoprics and in Portuguese civil offices.

Now, at least, after the sixty years' "captivity," thanks to quarrels between France and Spain, and a revolt in Catalonia which Richelieu supported, the Portuguese were able to rise, to shake off the Spanish yoke, and to instal their own Duke of Braganza as John IV. of Portugal (December 13th, 1640). In this effort they were supported by France and by Holland, while they had the moral support, such as it was, of Charles I. of England, then quarrelling with his Parliament— unfortunately for himself. When in course of time intelligence of this reached Macao, the Senate of the city fancied in the altered circumstances there might be a possibility of re-opening communication with Japan. An envoy was dispatched to congratulate the Portuguese King (John IV.) on his succession, to assure him of the devoted loyalty of the city of Macao, and, in view of the importance of the Japan trade to its prosperity, to request his Majesty to send an ambassador from Lisbon to the "Emperor" of Japan. This step was actually adopted (1644), and, in spite of the fate that had overtaken the Macaoese mission of 1640, two Portuguese vessels, with the ambassador from Lisbon on board, appeared in Nagasaki haven on July 16th, 1647.

---

4 The god-father of Daté's envoy, and a leading character in *Gil Blas*.

The envoy Don Gonzalo de Siqueira's ostensible purpose was to notify the "Emperor" of Japan of the accession of the House of Braganza to the throne of Portugal, and of the separation of that country from Spain. In His Majesty's letter it was stated that among the disadvantages that had been imposed upon Portugal from her so-called union with Spain— a union that practically reduced her to the condition of a Spanish province—the interruption of her trade with Japan was a serious and very regrettable one. Generally the tone of the dispatch conveyed the impression that the King believed that what had really led the Japanese to close their country against the Portuguese was dread of Spanish aggression—an aggression in which the Spaniards would doubtless be supported by their fellow-subjects, the Portuguese. But now that Portugal, which had herself suffered from Spanish aggression during the preceding sixty years (1580–1640), was again an independent country, actually at war with Spain, there was no longer any real basis for the former not unreasonable suspicion under which she lay in the minds of the Japanese authorities, by reason of her unwilling and unfortunate union with her more powerful neighbour.

The two vessels refused to surrender their rudders, their arms, and their ammunition to the Japanese, and thereupon urgent messages were sent to the various Kyūshū Daimyō, and in less than a month the Portuguese found themselves blockaded by a force of 50,000 men.

"Never before in Japan had such an array of men gathered to guard their country against foreigners. All the roads leading to Nagasaki were guarded. On the 28th August, Inouye, Chikugo-no-Kami [a member of the Yedo Cabinet], and the Governor of Nagasaki arrived from Yedo and presented Matsudaira [commander of the force] with a letter from the Government recommending a lenient policy. The ships were accordingly suffered to leave on September 4th, and after a few days the troops dispersed." [5]

Although there was no repetition of the *Madre de Dios* tragedy of 1610 on this occasion, and although the Portuguese were not put to death as the decree of 1640 imported they would be, yet the reception now accorded the new King's envoy at last convinced the Macaoese that all efforts to placate the Japanese authorities and to re-open the Japan trade were useless. The Yedo Government was now inflexible in its

---

[5] Woolley—*Historical Notes of Nagasaki.*

resolve to debar all Christians of the Roman Catholic faith from access to Japan. A strange illustration of this truth is afforded in connection with the attempt of the English East India Company to re-open its Japanese trade in 1673. In that year the Indiaman *Return* appeared in Nagasaki harbour, and, presenting a copy of the old "privileges" which had been returned to the authorities when the Hirado Factory had been abandoned in December, 1623, asked for permission to resume the old tradal intercourse. It will be remembered that the English had never been expelled from Japan, as the Spaniards had been in 1624 and the Portuguese fifteen years later on (1639). To quote Professor Riess:—

"As they [the English, in 1623] desired to leave Japan in friendship and facilitate a possible return, they proceeded very slowly and cautiously. Two letters were dispatched to Kyōto, where the Shōgun and the Daimyō were then staying, in order to take leave of them. The interpreter of the Factory, who was sent as bearer of these messages, had orders first to take the advice of the Daimyō of Hirado, and not to deliver the letter to the Shōgun [Hidetada] if he dissuaded him. But only a week later it was resolved, at the suggestion of the highest authorities of Hirado, to send by Hudson, an assistant in the Factory, presents to the Shōgun and his principal councillors. . . . This English messenger delivered also the Charter of Privileges of 1616 into the hands of the Daimyō of Hirado, asking him, if possible, not to return it to the Admiralty, but to keep it for them in case the Company might wish to re-open its Japan Factory. They also did not sell their houses and godowns at Hirado, but left them in trust with the Daimyō until there should be an occasion of using them for the East India Company. . . . Several times it was proposed in London to re-occupy the Factory houses in Japan. Already four years after their abandonment [1627], then again six years, and then eight years later, the thought of re-opening trade with Japan was discussed. But a serious attempt at reaching the country of the Rising Sun was only made fifty years after the dissolution of the Hirado Factory."

The English vessel was not treated as the Portuguese had been in 1647; her ammunition was indeed removed, and no one of her company was permitted to land, but the Nagasaki authorities on the whole behaved courteously towards her. The following extract from the "Japan Diary" on the *Return* tells why the English overtures miscarried :—

July 28th, 1673 (the *Return* had then been a month in Nagasaki harbour).—" In the morning about ten o'clock came on board our ship with three boats the chief secretaries and their banjoise [*Bugyō*], with seven interpreters, and our attendants. They told us that they had received letters from the Emperor, whom they had acquainted with our being here, and with the intent of our coming to trade upon

account of our former friendship (all which, as they were advised, had
been considered), *but in regard our King was married with the daughter
of Portugal, their enemy, they could not admit us to have any trade, and
for no other reason.* This, they said, was the Emperor's pleasure and
express order, and therefore they could make no alteration in it." [6]

After another month in Nagasaki harbour, where there were
six Dutch vessels at the time, the *Return* at last set sail on
August 28th, 1673.

The preceding paragraph serves to indicate that even
more than a generation after the expulsion of the Portuguese
(in 1639) the prejudice of the Yedo Government against
them was intense. It also serves to indicate that the
Dutch trade with Japan was still not inconsiderable, and
that this trade was then carried on at Nagasaki, and
not Hirado, as it had been in the earlier half of the
century. Although the discussion of the situation of the
Hollanders in Nagasaki during the Tokugawa *régime* is
reserved for a subsequent volume, it is yet advisable
to deal here with the circumstances which led to their
transference from Hirado to what was virtually the prison
of Deshima.

It will be remembered that during the Shimabara rebellion
of 1637–38, Koeckebacker, with eighty Hollanders, had joined
in the bombardment of the insurgents' stronghold of Hara
for fifteen days (February 24th to March 12th, 1638). On
getting leave to withdraw, Koeckebacker had an interview with
the Shōgun's councillors, and "they admitted that I had
myself taken much trouble and rendered good service to the
Emperor; special mention had been made of all that had
been done by us, and these reports had been forwarded daily
to His Majesty with the coming and going post. . . . We
believe firmly that the kind manner in which we were
treated was proof of their lordships' satisfaction with
what had been done by us." At that date, the Hollanders[7]
had every reason to believe that their prospects were highly
satisfactory. In the following year Caron, who had succeeded Koeckebacker as Head of the Factory, made the
journey to Court. Here he was not received by the Shōgun,

---

6 Charles II. of England had married Catherine of Braganza, the sister of
the Portuguese King, Alfonso VI., in 1662.

7 There were then two Dutchmen superintending a cannon-foundry in Yedo.

who was said to be ill, nor were his presents accepted. On the other hand, he was well received by *certain* members of the Yedo Cabinet, and was asked if the Dutch could promise to furnish Japan with all the foreign supplies that might be needed. Caron, of course, made the promise readily enough, and returned to Hirado very well satisfied with the results of his visit to the capital. Shortly afterwards, in the same year, however, at the date of the expulsion of the Portuguese, the Dutch (in common with the Chinese) received an intimation, couched in haughty terms, that if their ships brought in priests or their companions, or objects of religion, or Christian writings, the punishment would be swift and stern.

From an examination of various authorities, and a co-ordination of the facts they record, it seems very probable that the Yedo Cabinet was divided in its counsels as regards its attitude towards the Dutch. One party in it was for a general and sweeping expulsion of all Europeans from Japan: they were all Christians alike, in spite of minor differences in dogma and ritual, and as such were a menace to the peace of the country. Another faction, headed by Sanuki-no-Kami, was inclined to set much weight upon the distinction drawn by the Hollanders between their religion and that professed by the Spaniards and the Portuguese from the political point of view. Between the courses advocated by these two several parties in his Cabinet, the Shōgun Iyemitsu appears to have found it not easy to make up his mind.

Soon, however, the Macaoese envoys arrived, and of this episode the anti-Dutch faction took full advantage. Caron, it is said, on his previous visit to Yedo had not shown sufficient respect towards the *Shoshidai* or Governor of Kyōto. Now this Governor was a great friend of Inouye, Chikugo-no-Kami, who since 1632 or 1633 had been head of the commission for the suppression of Christianity in Japan,[8] and now an influential member of the anti-Dutch party. The two waited for an opportunity to gain the Shōgun's ear, and the opportunity was afforded by the Dutch in Hirado about the time of the execution of the Macaoese envoys in August, 1640. The

---

8 This Inouye is said to have been the first to cause a foreign priest to apostatize. It was probably he who devised the terrible torture of "suspension in the pit"—the *fossa*.

U U

Hollanders had just erected fine new warehouses in Hirado, and on the gables they had inscribed the date according to the Christian era. It was a small thing, but it was quite enough to serve the purpose of Inouye and of the *Shoshidai* of Kyōto. They got access to the Shōgun Iyemitsu, and he, without ever consulting his Cabinet, dispatched Inouye on a secret mission to Hirado with full instructions.

Arrived at Hirado, Inouye found the two Governors of Nagasaki with a strong armed retinue waiting for him, and all three dignitaries, together with the local Daimyō, were most lavishly entertained by Caron both on one of the Dutch ships then in the roadstead and also on shore. Then on one pretence or another they asked to be conducted over the new warehouses; and here, while pretending to be interested in European novelties, their suite turned over all the goods in the buildings opened for their inspection. *All the while they were merely searching for " objects of religion,"* or for anything that might serve to inculpate the Hollanders in a contravention of the anti-Christian instructions addressed to them on August 4th, 1639. Nothing of this sort, however, was found.

Then on the following day Inouye summoned Caron to a formal public audience, and there raised the mask. Meanwhile, acting under instructions, the neighbouring Daimyō of Kyūshū had sent strong contingents of troops to the vicinity of Hirado, where they were kept concealed in readiness to act. What Inouye evidently aimed at was a massacre of the Dutch if Caron should afford the slightest pretext to justify such a barbarity. Charlevoix's account of the matter is wonderfully lucid and clear, and well in accord with Japanese authorities, although, naturally enough, he had no notion of the real state of affairs in the councils of the Shōgun. Pagés' *précis*, as usual, as being terser (while not very inaccurate), is more suitable for quotation.[9] After speaking of the commissioner (*i.e.* Inouye) "announcing to Caron the order emanated from the Court," he goes on :—

"This order set forth that the Factors of the United Provinces and those of Portugal were *co-religionaires,* and contained several injunctions, the chief of which was to demolish the new warehouses

----

9 Pagés seems to base his *précis* on Siebold's account of the affair.

and all the houses whose pediments bore the date expressed in the years of the Christian era. Caron answered: 'Everything that his Imperial Majesty has ordered will be executed to the letter and without delay.'"

Two hundred men from the Dutch ships in the roadstead and two hundred coolies were set to work to pull down all the buildings (on the northern side) inscribed with the obnoxious chronology; and Inouye, the Grand Inquisitor of Japan, had to retire sadly disappointed that the Dutch had proved clever enough to evade the trap he had set for their destruction—sadly disappointed, in spite of all the fine speeches he felt constrained to make to François Caron by way of apology. These fine speeches were of the same tenor as the stereotyped address of an old Scotch Dominie about to flog a misguided pupil: "Believe me, my dear boy, having thus to punish you gives *me* much greater pain than it gives you!" (The snuffy old canter!)

As a matter of fact, if Caron[10] had shown the slightest reluctance to comply with this most arbitrary injunction to pull down the fine new buildings in Hirado, there would have been a massacre; for Inouye had actually instructed the numerous guard in attendance to cut the Hollanders down at a given signal! It was exceedingly lucky for the Dutchmen that they then had a chief who could penetrate below the surface of things. From his command over the Japanese language, and from his consequent knowledge of the devious Court intrigues in Yedo, Caron was able to avert a catastrophe—at some slight sacrifice, it must be admitted. Inouye, Chikugo-no-Kami, had to content himself with forbidding the Dutch in Hirado to observe the Sabbath, and with instructing them to reckon time henceforth by-

---

10 This François Caron was altogether a very able man. He began life as a cook's apprentice on a Dutch East Indiaman. From that humble but useful office by sheer ability he raised himself to the position of the Chief of the Dutch trade in Japan, and in that situation he showed remarkable fertility of resource. He was the first European servant of the Dutch East India Company who mastered the Japanese language. His two accounts of Japan are really works of merit; and to them Kaempfer owes a good deal more than he acknowledges. Later on the Dutchmen treated Caron somewhat harshly; and he (as any man of mettle would have done) resented such treatment from mere dollar-grubbers, resigned his position, and found himself appreciated by one of the greatest Frenchmen France has ever produced—by Colbert. In the French service Caron went to the East Indies, and died in the Tagus in sight of Lisbon on his return therefrom in 1674. Naturally the Dutch, after he had left them, found many hard things to say of him.

anything but by the Christian era. However, on his return
to Yedo, Inouye found means to prompt (January, 1641) an
Edict compelling the Hollanders to sell all their imports in
the year of arrival, without any choice of taking them
away in case of prices being too low. Of course this did
much to put them at the mercy of the Japanese mercantile
ring. Then, under pain of death, they were forbidden to
slaughter cattle or to carry arms, to say nothing of many
other vexatious and humiliating regulations imposed upon
them. The leaders of the Yedo anti-Dutch faction, baulked
in their attempt to find an excuse for extermination, were now
having recourse to a policy of pin-pricks—a policy sufficiently
annoying to exasperate even Hebraic sufferance.

Caron immediately hurried off to Batavia to lay the situation
before Governor-General Van Diemen; and Le Maire appeared
as the envoy of the Company, bringing with him the
original charter by Iyeyasu nearly a third of a century
before. This charter he presented in Yedo (where the Shōgun
refused to see him), and in reply to his representations the
Cabinet reported that "His Majesty charges us to inform you
that it is of but slight importance to the empire of Japan
whether foreigners come or do not come to trade; but in
consideration of the charter granted them by Iyeyasu, he
is pleased to allow the Hollanders to continue their operations,
and to leave them their commercial and other privileges, on
the condition that they evacuate Hirado and establish themselves with their vessels in the port of Nagasaki."

It is easy to understand that this reply was the result
of a compromise between the pro-Dutch and the anti-foreign
parties in the councils of the Shōgun. Even at this late
date the more liberal-minded Japanese were keenly alive to
the benefits that were to be drawn from European intercourse, provided reasonable precautions were taken to safeguard
Japan from all risks of foreign aggression. But self-seekers
like Inouye Chikugo-no-Kami (who had risen to eminence
by reason of the skill he had showed as a persecutor) saw
their account in reducing the Dutchmen to the status of *Eta*,
or of outcasts.

The traders were at first far from loth to shift their quarters
from Hirado to Nagasaki. The contrast between the fisher-

town with its small and inconvenient anchorage and the magnificent land-locked haven of the southernmost of the five Imperial towns is fully set forth in a letter of Cocks's.[11] In addition to superior shipping facilities, the Hollanders also saw great prospective advantage in the concourse of merchants that flocked to Nagasaki—many of them had establishments there—from the other Imperial cities of Yedo, Kyōto, Ōsaka, and Sakai. Indeed, some time before, the Company had been discussing the advisability of endeavouring to effect that very change in the seat of their Factory that had now been imposed upon it by the Yedo Government as the condition under which its agents might remain in Japan.

However, when on May 21st, 1641, in pursuance of the order received ten days previously, the Hollanders bade good-bye to Hirado, where they had fared well for nearly a third of a century, they found that the favourable expectations they had formed of Nagasaki were not to be realised. In the first place, they were not allowed to enter, much less to settle in Nagasaki. They found that they were to be penned up in Deshima, the island prison-house built for the reception of the Portuguese in 1636, and which had been unoccupied for the preceding three years. And for this prison-house they were told they would have to pay a yearly rent of 5,500 taels—a very great deal more than the freehold of the mud-speck was worth. Very soon, too, they discovered that their social position had altered in a striking fashion. In Hirado they had enjoyed a great measure of freedom; they had been friendly with and had exchanged courtesies with the Daimyō and his highest officers on a footing of mutual respect. In the old Hirado records we constantly read of the number of "guns" given when any guest visited or left the Dutch vessels in the harbour, while artillery salutes from the "Dutch house" itself were frequent. At the funerals of those Hollanders who had been laid to rest in the Hirado cemetery the Japanese had been sympathetic attendants.

Now in Deshima (with none of its four sides 300 paces in extent) the Hollanders found all this changed.

"A guard at the gate prevented all communication with the city of Nagasaki; no Dutchman without weighty reasons and without

---

[11] Quoted in Chap. III., note 12.

the permission of the Governor might pass the gate; no Japanese (unless public women) might live in a Dutchman's house. As if this were not enough, even within Deshima itself our State prisoners were keenly watched. No Japanese might speak with them in his own language unless in the presence of a witness (a Government spy), or visit them in their houses; the creatures of the Governor had the warehouses under key, and the Dutch traders ceased to be masters of their own property."[12]

But this was not the measure of the lowest deep in the depth of the Hollander's abasement. No Dutchman could any longer find a grave in Japanese earth. Every one that died either in Deshima or on board any Dutch ship in Nagasaki haven had to be committed to the waters of the bay. Then from all Dutch ships that entered the port the guns, the ammunition, and the rudder were removed; the sails were put under seal, while the ship was ransacked from stem to stern by the hirelings of the Governor. Of course any religious service either in Deshima itself or on board the merchantmen was impossible. Even from one Dutch ship to another no one could pass without the express permission of the Governor's jacks-in-office placed on board. And "while our vessels are being inspected and their armaments and cargoes discharged, without any reason whatsoever our ship's companies—even the chief officers—are beaten with sticks by the inspectors, as if they were dogs."[13]

Of course, from "international intercourse" of this description, conducted according to such highly civilised and cultivated amenities, apart from mere vulgar financial considerations neither party could draw very much advantage. On the whole the Batavians had perhaps the best of it; for it must not be overlooked that the servants of the Company who had the patience—not to say the moral courage—to submit to all this outrageous insolence from Japanese beadledom submitted to it in the interests of the United Provinces. In those days the very existence and independence of these provinces were based upon

---

[12] Siebold.

[13] What this meant may be inferred from the following extract from Mr. Thompson's introduction to *Cocks's Diary*:—"The difference in European and Japanese ideas of justice was well exemplified when the Dutch Factor (at Hirado), complaining of an assault on one of his countrymen, demanded that 'the parties which offered the abuse might be brought to the place where they did it and be beaten with cudgels.' At which the King [*i.e.* the Daimyō of Hirado] smiled and said it could not be, but, if he would have them cut in pieces, he would do it."

their material resources, and these material resources again
depended largely upon the successful prosecution of foreign
trade by the East India Company. It may seem wild to assert
that the Dutch traders in Deshima were really patriots; but, if
we take any large view of the situation, we shall find that the
assertion is in a measure correct. The small fry of Japanese
officialdom who inflicted all these needless indignities upon
men infinitely their superiors in intellect and enterprise were
no patriots. They were all creatures of the Harada type,—
with the difference that Harada was really a capable rogue and
a man of enterprise, while they were merely so many lazy
flunkey rice-eaters, inflating themselves, like the frog in the
fable, simply because they could safely venture to treat the
Dutch like so many *Eta*, or outcasts. It is pretty safe to say
that not one of these small Japanese officials could have
designed a Dutch merchantman, or have built her, or have
navigated her around the world; not one of them, perhaps, could
have arranged all the multiplex details in connection with
her profitable lading; none of them knew as much of the
great world as the lowest employé in the Deshima prison
knew; and yet, in spite of all that, we have these empty-
headed, ignorant, conceited Tokugawa *yakunin-sama* thrashing
the Dutchmen—infinitely their betters—like so many dogs.
*What would Hideyoshi or Iyeyasu have said to this sort of
thing?* Iyeyasu had actually promised in writing that if the
Hollanders established themselves in Japan " no man should do
them any wrong, and that he would maintain and defend them
as his own subjects"! In the Charter of Privileges granted
(1611) to the Dutch traders by the founder of the Tokugawa
Shōgunate, Kaempfer tells us it had run that " all Dutch
ships that come into my Empire of Japan, whatever port or
place they put into, We do hereby command all and every
one of our subjects not to molest them in any way, nor to
be a hindrance to them; but, on the contrary, to show them all
manner of help, favour, and assistance. Every one shall beware
to maintain the friendship, *in assurance of which we have given
our Imperial word* to these people; and every one shall take care
that our commands and promises be inviolably kept." The
presentation of this document by Le Maire, the Dutch Factor,
to the Shōgun's Council in 1641 sufficed to prevent Inouye

and his partisans from effecting the end on which they were bent—the expulsion of all Europeans from Japan.

It must be clearly grasped that this Inouye was an ambitious man, eagerly bent on rising to power; and that his elevation depended almost entirely on the efficiency of his services as Christian *Bugyō*, or the Torquemada of Japan. His success in this office had won him the favour of the Shōgun Iyemitsu, who was imperiously resolved to extirpate Christianity in Japan, and who had expressed himself to the effect that "Christianity was mixed with the merchandise of Europe." Inouye, on hearing this remark, doubtless came to the conclusion that his own personal advancement would not be seriously impeded if he succeeded in precipitating a massacre of all Europeans in Japan and in cutting off the Empire from all communication with the outside world. Now, like most other sycophantish intriguers, Inouye had his own ring of satellites; and among them seems to have been Baba, one of the Governors of Nagasaki present at the demolition of the northern section of the Dutch warehouses in 1640. So, baffled in his efforts to evict the Hollanders from Japan by reason of Le Maire having presented the great Iyeyasu's original charter, Inouye contrived their removal to Nagasaki, where they would be entirely at the mercy of his friend Baba and his underlings—all finding their account in, and vastly pleased with, the chance of making themselves "important" by baiting the helpless foreign traders.

However, they proceeded just a trifle too fast. Caron, who was then at Batavia, and who had divined the situation with a fair amount of accuracy, gave the Governor-General, Van Diemen, an approximately accurate idea of what was really toward in Japan; and Van Diemen, while keeping punctiliously polite, contrived to put His Excellency Baba, the Governor of Nagasaki, into a serious quandary. The Governor-General sent in a dispatch to Baba an address to the Yedo Cabinet, which the great and illustrious Baba was to withhold or to forward as he deemed fit. The "address," after recapitulating all the outrageous indignities to which the Dutch had been subjected since their removal to Deshima, and incidentally mentioning that in 1640–41 they had sustained serious financial losses, set forth that the Company (if agreeable) would send an envoy of high rank to the Shōgun in order either to

withdraw the Dutch Factory from Japan and to thank
His Majesty for all past kindnesses—or, to thank His Majesty
and to ask him for a continuation of his favours. Baba took
care to get the address kept back, and promptly promised the
Dutchmen better treatment.

The presentation of that address to the Yedo Cabinet would
have produced a keen conflict among its members, some of whom
appear to have been even then anxious to see European traders
in Japan, provided all Christian propaganda could be effectually
prevented. Although the Dutch were Christians, they had never
brought in any missionaries, nor had they evinced the slightest
sympathy with missionary effort. Besides, now confined to
Deshima and well watched there, even if so minded, they could
cause no trouble on religious or political grounds, while the
material benefits they might confer by bringing new products,
new inventions, and new sciences into the Empire might be
expected to prove considerable. Therefore their continued
presence in Japan was not undesirable.

That such was the view of some of the most intelligent men
in the Shōgun's Councils, Baba, the Governor of Nagasaki,
appears to have been convinced ; consequently the presentation
of the address would have led to an investigation, and any such
investigation would have been pretty sure to disclose the fact
that not only had he exceeded his instructions, but that he had
allowed his underlings to get seriously out of hand. And this
might have proved very awkward for Baba, who had evidently
been acting, if not on the private instruction of, at all events in
full understanding with, the anti-foreign councillors, whose
power he had reason to believe was rapidly on the increase.
Meanwhile, however, as these foreign-haters were as yet far from
omnipotent, it would be wise to give the Dutch good words
for the present, and to temporise till he was sure of his ground.
And so in the following year, 1643, the Hollanders had the
best season they had, or were to have of it, during all their
two hundred and seventeen years in their Deshima prison.
After that year things became nearly as unsatisfactory as
they had been in 1641–42, until in 1652 we find the authorities
at Batavia submitting to the governing body in Amsterdam
the question whether the Factory of Deshima ought not to
be abandoned "in order to preserve the national honour."

From the date the Dutch were cooped up in Deshima (May 21-22, 1641) all European intercourse with Japan may be said to have ceased for two hundred and twelve years,—for longer, indeed, inasmuch as the great nation that was once more to lead Japan into the comity of nations with a progressive civilisation was not European, but American.

That Japan had to pay a price for thus cutting herself off from all contact with the life and stir of the outside world is, of course, incontestable. Whether, however, this price has been as great as is commonly asserted is open both to doubt and discussion. Although that discussion can be undertaken with profit only when the history of the Tokugawa Shōgunate has been set forth, and the condition of Japan and of the Japanese under its rule compared with that of the peoples of contemporary Europe, it may not be amiss to recall one or two broad general facts bearing on the question.

In the very year in which the Dutch were penned up in Deshima, there was scarcely one country in Christendom that enjoyed the peace that Japan then did. The Thirty Years' War had then been in progress for three-and-twenty years, and in this struggle nearly all the Continental States were involved. It reduced the population of Germany from 20,000,000 to 7,000,000—some authorities say to 4,000,000— and turned the fairest parts of Central Europe into deserts. It took Germany at least a hundred years to recover from its effects. And Sweden, Denmark, Spain—even France and Poland—were more or less exhausted by it. And this Thirty Years' War was mainly a religious struggle. At the same date (1641) in the British Islands the Great Civil War had broken out, and in that, too, religion certainly played a part. Then in France, Richelieu (died 1643) was finishing his task of crushing all Huguenot opinions, of making the Church subservient, of humiliating the lawyers in the parliaments, of stripping the nobles of all their independence and the towns of all their self-governing powers, of silencing the States-General, of giving the Crown complete command over the purses and persons of its subjects—in fact, of establishing that centralised tyranny and that condition of things that needed the Great Revolution of 1789 to remedy them. Richelieu had unified France, just as Hideyoshi and Iyeyasu had unified

Japan. But the centralisation of power in France increased at once her aggressive power (and also her burdens), and the result was a succession of dynastic wars that more than once reduced a third of her population to starvation. For aggressive wars—or for wars of any kind—no Japanese peasant was called upon to pay taxes for more than two centuries. From 1641 down to 1789 it is pretty safe to assume that the lot of the "average man" in Japan was, if not better, at all events less wretched, than it was in France. And it is also pretty safe to assume that the general level of culture and of taste was quite as high in Yedo as in Paris or Versailles or in London or Vienna during all that period. Only, unfortunately for her, Japan produced no Pascal, no Newton, no Leibnitz,[14] and still more unfortunately, no Watt, for, fantastic and absurd as the statement may sound, it was only from the date of the utilisation of steam as a motive power that Japan began to pay a really serious price for the luxury of indulging in the seclusion of a hermit among the nations.

As regards Spain, dread of whom really occasioned the Japanese distrust of Europeans—(and this dread of Spain was by no means peculiar to the Japanese, for in 1629 we find the Pope, the Duke of Mantua, and the Republic of Switzerland all appealing to Richelieu to save them from Spanish domination)— that erstwhile Great World Power had already begun its Avernian descent. Its expulsion of the Moriscoes in 1609 had really dealt it a greater wound than the successful revolt of the Hollanders against it had inflicted. In 1640, after a "captivity" of sixty years, the Portuguese succeeded in shaking off the Spanish yoke. Although it was Spain that had subsidised the House of Austria in the Thirty Years' War, and although at the end of the sixteenth and during the early part of the seventeenth century Spain was—what England was to become in the eighteenth century—the great subsidising Power in Europe, yet by 1650 the resources of Spain were rapidly approaching exhaustion. At the beginning of the sixteenth century—just before the death of Columbus—the population of the country had amounted to more than 12,000,000; under Charles II. (1665-1700) it had sunk to less

---

14 Seki, a contemporary of Newton and Leibnitz, is said to have devised a Differential Calculus, however.

than 6,000,000. By that time the proud nation that had sent a hundred vessels to Lepanto in 1570, and that had dispatched the Great Armada against England in 1588, was actually reduced. to borrowing Genoese vessels to maintain its connection with the New World, while the army which had been the terror of Europe had sunk to a starved and rarely-paid force of some 20,000 men! "During the latter half of the seventeenth century," we are told, "the poverty and wretchedness of the Spanish people surpass all description." In any comparison between Japanese and Spanish civilisation at this epoch, the advantage will be found entirely on the side of Japan. For the civilisation to which Japan, by closing her ports, had now committed herself was a stationary one. Contemporary Spanish civilisation, in spite of its supposed contact with the culture of neighbouring nations, was neither stationary *nor* progressive, but most pronouncedly *retrogressive.* One of the chief factors in causing this strange phenomenon was the success of the effort to make residence in Spain impossible to all except the most orthodox Roman Catholic. Religious unity was indeed attained; but at what a price! In Japan, on the other hand, the Christian cult alone had been suppressed on purely political grounds; but, apart from that, the religious freedom enjoyed by the Japanese people was almost complete, and in startling contrast to the state of affairs in contemporary Europe generally, and in contemporary Spain in particular. Apart from the loss of perhaps a hundred thousand lives, and the ruin of her mercantile marine, the suppression of Christianity within her bounds did not entail any very considerable amount of loss or suffering upon Japan. The extirpation of all forms of cult except the Roman Catholic, besides costing Spain literally millions of citizens, involved her in the greatest calamities.

By the end of the seventeenth century the Spaniards were impotent in manufacturing, in mining, and in shipbuilding. Even in 1656, when it was proposed to fit out a small fleet, "it was found that the fisheries on the coast had so declined that it was impossible to procure sailors enough to man the few ships required. The charts which had been made were either lost or neglected; and the ignorance of the Spanish pilots became so notorious that no one was willing to trust them."

In view of all this, it may well be questioned whether Japan lost so very much from the cessation of her intercourse with the Spanish colonies that had gone on from 1592 to 1624. What Hideyoshi had wanted had been trade; what Iyeyasu had wanted had been trade and assistance and instruction for his subjects in the development of mines and in shipbuilding. The Japanese-Spanish trade in Spanish bottoms had never been considerable; the Spaniards had, indeed, built one or two foreign-rigged vessels in Japanese dockyards; but towards the development of Japanese mines they had furnished no assistance whatsoever. Now, strangely enough, while down to 1609 this Spanish intercourse with Japan had been illicit and a flagrant violation of the Concordat of 1580, after 1609, when Philip III. arbitrarily legalised it, the Spaniards no longer were in a position to teach the Japanese any new art or industry. All the industrial, the economic, and even all the scientific strength of Spain had lain in the Moriscoes; and these were all driven from the country in this year of 1609. The haughty Spaniard himself knew nothing of anything except war and theology; and in the art of war and in theology Japan could benefit but little by instruction from Spanish soldiers or Spanish priests. And then the memory of the frank declaration of the pilot of the *San Felipe* (1596) had by no means passed away; while apart from the "calumnies" of the English and the Dutch, the reports of Ibi Yoeyemon and fellow-Tokugawa emissaries to Europe (to say nothing of Araki and other apostate Japanese priests "ordained in Rome" and sometime resident in Madrid) had made Spanish soldiership and Spanish priestcraft objects of the deepest suspicion. It is pretty safe to assume that from any prolongation of the intercourse with the Spaniards Japan could have learned nothing, and could have derived but very little advantage.

The same remark applies also to her intercourse with Portugal *via* Macao. In the fifteenth and sixteenth centuries Portugal, in spite of the incubus of priestcraft and superstition that pressed heavily upon her, had really had a progressive civilisation. The maritime enterprise of the little kingdom had then been splendid, and worthy of the highest admiration. But her union with Spain from 1580 to 1640 had been fatal to all the elements of progress in the nation. From 1580 down to the

French Revolution—perhaps down to the present day'—it may well be doubted whether one invention or discovery of any consequence, or even one single new idea, has emanated from the kingdom that held the very first rank among the progressive nations of Europe in the fifteenth century. That fact considered, it is really difficult to perceive what the Japanese lost by their expulsion of the Lusitanians. All that the Portuguese really had to teach—except theology and the husks of scholastic philosophy, and in early times maritime enterprise—the Japanese had mastered. The use of fire-arms they certainly had learned from the Portuguese—and possibly also something of that new fashion of fortification and castle-building, of which the earliest example, after Nobunaga's Paradise of Azuchi (1576), had been Hideyoshi's keep of Himeji (1580 or 1581). From some of the Jesuits, who worked in combination with the Portuguese traders, and who had a much finer culture than the Spanish monks from the Philippines, they had also been able to make acquaintance with something beyond the Catechism and the Latin and Portuguese languages. Spinola, the Italian, for example, had taught them a good deal about astronomy and mathematics. But all things considered, Japan could have derived very little material or intellectual advantages from any intercourse with Portugal after the year 1640.[15]

---

15 It was in 1543—the year following the arrival of the Portuguese in Japan—that a copy of Copernicus' "Revolution of the Heavenly Bodies" had been placed in the hands of its author only a few hours before his death. "This 'upstart astrologer'; this 'fool who wishes to reverse the entire science of astronomy,' for 'sacred Scripture tells us that Joshua commanded the sun to stand still and not the earth'—these are Luther's words—was beyond the grip of the Holy Inquisition. But a substitute was forthcoming. Giordano Bruno, a Dominican monk, had added to certain orthodox beliefs the heresy of Copernicanism, which he publicly taught from Oxford to Venice. For these cumulative crimes he was imprisoned [in 1598, the year of the death of Hideyoshi], and after two years, condemned to be put to death,' as mercifully as possible and without the shedding of blood.'—a Catholic euphemism for burning a man alive. The murder was committed in Rome on the 17th February, 1600,'—that is, two months before Will Adams appeared in Japan, and eight months before Sekigahara. And it was men of the kidney who murdered Bruno that were to 'civilise' Japan!

At one time in Japan there was also a short-lived so-called "Namban" (i.e. Portuguese) school of surgery. But of any real knowledge of anatomy the Peninsulars were guiltless. Pope Boniface VIII. (1294-1303) had issued a Bull of major excommunication against any who should dissect the human body, and about 1660 the Holy Inquisition laid hold of the great Vesalius on some baseless charge of attempting the dissection of a living subject and imprisoned him. In the Peninsula the circulation of the blood was denied one hundred and fifty years after Harvey had proved it. It was, perhaps, on the whole no very great calamity for Japan that Portuguese medicine and Portuguese surgery never established any real footing in the country.

The chief loss entailed upon the Empire by its policy of seclusion from the world was the sacrifice of that Tokugawa mercantile marine Iyeyasu had done so much to foster. It is pretty safe to say that if Hideyoshi had been ruler of Japan between 1630 and 1640 a *Japanese* mercantile marine would not have been sacrificed, foreigners would not have been excluded from Japan, and a remedy for the persistent intrusion of foreign *religieux* where they had been warned they were not wanted would have been found in an attack upon Manila and Macao. To Matsukura Bungo-no-Kami's project of 1630 we have already alluded. No reply to his memorial was ever returned by the Yedo bureaucracy. Hideyoshi would not only have permitted Matsukura to proceed to the conquest of the base of the Christian propagandists, but he would probably have furthermore engaged a strong Dutch fleet in support of the effort, and Manila would assuredly have fallen. It is needless to say that the effects of such a conquest would have had the most far-reaching consequences upon the history of the Far East.

And if Iyeyasu had been the ruler of Japan when Matsukura presented his memorial in 1630, it is possible that the conquest of the Philippines might then have been attempted. It is true that under Iyeyasu Japan had ceased to be the aggressive Power she had been under the sway of the Taikō. It is also true (as a perusal of the foregoing chapters will abundantly disclose) that the measure of hospitality and consideration extended to non-clerical aliens by Japan under Iyeyasu (1598–1616) was far greater than that accorded by any other contemporary Power on the face of the globe. All foreigners of whatsoever nationality were accorded the heartiest of welcomes, provided they could contribute to the development and progress of the Tokugawa estates, and provided they did not abuse the Shōgun's hospitality. The liberal yet strict and impartial manner in which Iyeyasu, while maintaining the national dignity, fulfilled the international duties of the Empire was admirable and worthy of the highest praise, for in this respect the Japan of 1598–1616 was far in advance of any State in contemporary Christendom. Yet, true as all this is, it must not be forgotten that Iyeyasu was at once keen to resent any injustice or any slight to the prestige of Japan, and also, down to 1609, at least, exceedingly eager to establish Japanese settlements in over-sea lands where a Japanese trade could be developed. In connection with the former proposition it is only necessary to cite the *Madre de Dios* incident of 1610; in connection with the latter the conquest of the Lūchū Islands by Satsuma in 1609, and Iyeyasu's endeavour to obtain a tradal foothold in Formosa shortly afterwards. Now, if Iyeyasu had been the recipient of Ibi Yoeyemon's exhaustive report upon contemporary European Christianity, and upon the manner in which the Spaniards had possessed themselves of Mexico and of Peru, with an account of their pious murder of Athualpa, and the manifold atrocities they had committed in the name of religion, he might have been induced to adopt Matsukura's proposal to strike at the root of the standing menace to Japan. Only others besides Matsukura would have been sent on the errand. Kyūshū was the section of the Empire where the Tokugawa hold was weakest; before 1630 the *Fudai* Daimyō had scarcely obtained a foothold there. In all likelihood, then, Iyeyasu would have engaged the great Kyūshū feudatories— Shimadzu, Katō, Kuroda, Nabeshima, Tanaka, and Hosokawa— in this Philippine venture; and on their reduction of the Spanish colony he would then have assigned them new and more extensive fiefs in Luzon, and, appropriating their lands in Kyūshū, would partly have incorporated them in the Tokugawa family domains, and partly portioned them out among his most trusted *Fudai*.

It must not be overlooked that if Iyeyasu had been ruler of Japan in 1630 the Japanese would most probably have been in a position to assume the offensive against Manila with the greatest prospects of success. During his sway the old statesman had been unwearied in his efforts to foster Tokugawa marine enterprise. The presence of the Dutch in Japan would have enabled him to achieve a great measure of success in these efforts. Shipwrights could have been employed as easily as cannon-founders had been engaged; and if Iyeyasu's endeavours in this direction had been vigorously followed up by Hidetada and Iyemitsu, the Yedo Government might very well have had a fleet equal, if not superior, in tonnage and armament to any squadron the Manila authorities could then muster. But on the death of Iyeyasu in 1616 Hidetada and his

Cabinet lost all interest in naval matters, and before ten years had passed they had actually begun to strangle not only Japanese, but Tokugawa maritime enterprise. Ventures such as that of Daté Masamune's had filled the Yedo councillors with apprehension. If great feudatories like Daté or Shimadzu were to construct European-rigged and armed vessels, and to establish relations with over-sea Powers, it might well be that the Tokugawa supremacy might find itself menaced before the lapse of any very great number of years. Accordingly, from the death of Iyeyasu there was to be no more foreign trade except at the Imperial town of Nagasaki, or at Hirado, whose Daimyō of 63,000 *koku* was too insignificant to occasion the Shōgun's advisers the slightest anxiety. Besides, after 1616 the conditions of trade at Hirado were such that Dutch, English, Daimyō and all were hopelessly at the beck and call of the central authorities.

In short, between the self-confidence of the Taikō and of Iyeyasu down to 1609, and their trust in their ability to safeguard their own positions and the destinies of Japan in full and free intercourse with foreign nations on the one hand, and the timid distrust of their own faculties by Iyeyasu's successors and their councillors on the other, there is the greatest possible contrast. In 1639, for example, we find the Yedo Cabinet summarily deporting all the offspring of Dutchmen by Japanese women, as well as all the Dutchmen with Japanese wives, from Hirado to Batavia, alleging that " the Japanese desire no such intermixture of races, and will not incur the danger that, in course of time, any one of such descent should rule over them " ! We can readily imagine how either the Taikō or Iyeyasu would have smiled with mingled pity and contempt at this precious exhibition of small-minded jealousy and prejudice.

Since the entry of Japan into the comity of modern nations within the memory of many still living, nothing perhaps has been more remarkable than her rapid ascent to the position of a great Naval Power, the wonderful development of her mercantile marine, and the fondness of the Mikado's subjects for travel in foreign lands. Now, as a matter of fact, before 1616, the year of the death of Iyeyasu, strenuous efforts had been made to entice foreign shipwrights

v v

to the Tokugawa ports and to develop a Tokugawa mercantile marine, while during the sixty years before that date the Japanese had been indulging their fondness for travel and adventure in foreign lands to the full. About the embassy to Rome, organised by Valegnani in 1582, and about the embassy of Daté Masamune to Spain and Rome, organised and piloted by Sotelo in 1613, full mention has been made. But in addition to these episodes there were others. The Portuguese traders had arrived in Japan (probably) in 1542; the missionaries in 1549. Six years after that later date—in 1554–55—from a letter of Loyola's we hear of the arrival of a Japanese in Rome![16] In 1611 a Japanese Augustin monk was martyred at Moscow, of all places in the world. Then we have the Japanese Jesuit Araki, who had remained a long time at Rome, where he had been ordained, and with whom Cardinal Bellarmine had been fond of reciting *les Heures*, and who on going to Madrid had been incensed by hearing the statesmen and monks there calmly discussing the subjection of Japan to the King of Spain and to the Pope of Rome. On returning to Japan he preferred the claims of patriotism to those of religion,[17] and plainly told the Tokugawa authorities of what was really toward in the councils of Spain. Another enterprising traveller was the Jesuit Cassoui, who was martyred in Yedo in 1639. On being deported from Japan in 1614 he travelled across India and Persia to the Holy Places of Jerusalem, and from there he passed on to Rome and afterwards to Portugal; and on his way back he actually spent two years as an oarsman in a Siamese vessel, and finally re-entered Japan as a slave. Then the Japanese that fared abroad either for trade or war or piracy were not innumerous. Mention has been made of Michelborne's grim encounter with the Japanese craft near Singapore in 1604, of the fact that the garrison of Malacca that beat off the Dutch attack two years later contained not a few Japanese, that by 1608 or 1609 there were as many

---

[16] This was the Satsuma man Bernard, who had been Xavier's body-servant during his sojourn in Japan.

[17] See Charlevoix's dispassionate account of the affair. Pagés (page 378) tells us that Araki apostatized in 1627, but recovered himself later on, and died a martyr. For the erroneousness of this assertion see pp. 409, 465, 746, and 823 of Pagés' own book.

as 15,000 Japanese settled in Luzon, that shortly afterwards Japanese were employed by the Dutch to garrison the Moluccas, and that at the massacre of Amboyna in 1623 thirty Japanese soldiers were then seized together with the Englishmen.

Nor were these latter the only Japanese who had taken service with the English East India Company. On the return of the *Clove* from Hirado in 1613 Captain Saris took twelve Japanese sailors with him, and, after seeing the Thames and London, they came back to Hirado to cause poor old Cocks an infinite deal of trouble over money matters, and even to lay violent hands upon Will Adams himself.[18] Then, even by the end of the sixteenth century, we find Japanese traders established at Acapulco and elsewhere in New Spain, which they had doubtless reached by the galleons from Manila. One of the best known tales in Japan is the account of Yamada's (died 1633) adventure in Siam, where he rose to be Prime Minister of the kingdom mainly by reason of the services he and his brigade of compatriots had there rendered in the field. From the missionaries we learn that in 1625 there had been four hundred Japanese exiles in Siam, many in Cambodia, and that between Japanese settlements in Tongking and Cochin-China a flourishing trade with the mother-land went on down to the restrictive edicts of the third Shōgun. What Carvailho, the Jesuit Provincial, has said about the wonderful development of the Japanese mercantile marine between 1602 and 1612 has already been quoted.

At the date Perry's squadron appeared in Japanese waters (1853), except the *Eta* and their fellow-outcasts there was no class so much despised in Japan as the traders. In the sixteenth and (early) seventeenth centuries things were very different in this respect. Neither by the Taikō, nor by Iyeyasu, nor by the feudatories of the time, were commerce and industry

---

[18] "We had much a doe with the brabling Japons which came out of England, they demanding more then their due, as 10 *taies* for 3 mo., when per my book most of them had but 7½ *tais* per 3 mo., and the most (which was but one) had but 29 *mas* [*i.e.* 14s. 6d.] per month, and demanded 350 *tais* for their losses in England; and, had not Mr. Wickham brought a writing from Bantam of 150 Rs. of 8 rec. per them there, in consideration of the said losses, with all their ferms at it, they would have put us to much trouble. And one of them took Capt. Adames by the throte in his owne lodging, because he would not stand out for them that all the money they receved impres, at Capt. Saris being heare, was geven them gratis; and thought to have laid violent handes one Mancho, the *jurebasso* [interpreter], because he witnessed the truth. I had much a doe to hold my handes that I did not cut affe one or two of their heades, which I make no dowbt but I might well have answered."— *Cocks's Diary*, August 18th, 1617.

held in contempt. By reason of his ability in mining matters, Ōkubo, the Christian conspirator, who had originally been an actor—a profession held in the utmost disdain in those days—had been made not merely a *samurai*, but a Daimyō with a revenue of 30,000 *koku*, and so a greater man than Ōmura, himself a keen trader. In those days, from the successful prosecution of commerce and industry an enterprising man often reaped honour as well as wealth, and accordingly we find some of the ablest men in the country engaged in mercantile pursuits. However, a few years after the death of Iyeyasu this began to change; and when in 1635 all Japanese were forbidden to go abroad under pain of death, and no *samurai* was thenceforth to be allowed to purchase anything from the foreign traders, a deadly blow was dealt, not merely to the useful enterprise of the *samurai*, but to the respectability, if not the dignity, of the merchant—a blow from the effects of which modern Japan is suffering even to-day.

That it was dread of Spanish aggression, proceeding along the lines indicated by the pilot of the *San Felipe* in 1596, that chiefly constrained Iyeyasu's successors to break off practically all communication between Japan and the outside world appears from the language of the Edicts as well as from other circumstances. But it may be shrewdly suspected that that dread was not the only factor at work. Japan was now governed not so much by a Tokugawa Shōgun as by a Tokugawa clique—a widely ramified and numerous clique, it is true, but still a clique. Of the administrative machine devised by Iyeyasu in the interests of his descendants we have already spoken briefly. It is only here necessary to recall the fact that none but a Tokugawa adherent in the person either of a *Fudai* Daimyō or of a *Hatamoto* could have a place in the supreme councils of the Empire, it being an accepted maxim that no outside feudatory (*Tozama*), *however able*, could find admission to them. This phrase "*however able*" is suggestive, for among the Tokugawa bureaucrats the dread of men of ability outside their own favoured pale was almost as great, if not really quite as great, as their dread of Spanish aggression. They were untiring in their efforts to depress the feudatories (and so to render them harmless) in countless insidious ways, especially by engaging them in the wasteful

dissipation of their resources, and also by seeing to it that
these resources received as little augmentation as possible.
Now, by the prosecution of foreign trade several of the Kyūshū
Daimyō had formerly become wealthy; and if this trade, now
mostly conducted in Japanese bottoms, were to continue to
develop, Shimadzu of Satsuma, for example, could easily
laugh to scorn all their attempts to reduce him to poverty and
impotence. Supposing Shimadzu were able to hire Dutch
shipwrights to build him foreign-rigged and armed vessels,
and Dutch cannon-founders to organise an arsenal for him—
able, perhaps, to purchase the splendidly equipped Dutch
vessels that then came to Hirado, and to equip his *samurai*
with the latest European engines of destruction, and, raising
the standard of revolt and summoning to his side the greater
part of Japan, then chafing under the beadledom of Yedo—
how would it be likely to fare with the said beadledom and
its interests? That this consideration was from an early date
a very weighty one with the Yedo councillors may be inferred
from the abrupt curtailment of the "privileges" of the English
in Japan less than six months after the death of Iyeyasu.
The Daimyō of Satsuma had not been slow to assure the East
India Co.'s agents of a hearty welcome to his domains, and
it is not at all unlikely that a permanent English agency would
have been established at Kagoshima. As it was, an English
factor made several junk trips between Satsuma and its
appanage of the Lūchūs, where he was received with the
greatest kindness and the most profuse hospitality. Then in
the autumn of 1616 the Englishmen found themselves forbidden
to trade anywhere in Japan except in Hirado (afterwards at
Hirado and Nagasaki), and in 1620 Cocks wrote to the Company
in the following terms:—

"But that which cheefly spoileth the Japon trade is a company
of ruch usurers whoe have gotten all the trade of Japon into their
owne handes; soe that heretofore by theare meanes we lost our pre-
veleges geven us per Ogosho Samma [*i.e.* Iyeyasu], themperour,
wherin he permitted us to trade into all partes of Japon not
excepted, and now per this Emperour Shongo Samma [*i.e.* Hidetada]
we are pend up in Firando [Hirado] and Nangasaque [Nagasaki]
only, all other places forbidden us. For they have soe charmed
thémperour and his councell, that it is in vayne to seeke for remedy.
Aud these fellowes are nott content to have all at their owne
disposing above, but they com down to Firando and Nangasaque,
where they joyne together in seting out of junks for Syam, Cochin-

china, Tonkin, Camboja, or any other place where they understand that good is to be donne, and soe furnish Japon with all sortes of comodeties which any other stranger can bring, and then stand upon their puntos, offering others what they list them selves, knowing no man will buy it but them selves or such as they please to joyne in company with them, *nether that any stranger can be suffered to transport it into any other parts of Japon.* Which maketh me alltogether aweary of Japon."[19]

Although both the English and the Dutch suffered severely from this band of "rich usurers," it was not so much the foreigners as the commercial enterprise of the outside feudatories that this "ring" was organised to cripple. On the fall of Ōsaka in 1615, that great mart had been added to the number of the "Imperial cities"—that is, cities belonging to the Tokugawa and administered by Tokugawa officials. These cities, as has been said, now were Yedo, Kyōto, Ōsaka, Sakai, and Nagasaki. Now, this "ring" was mainly an Ōsaka one, with a few Kyōto and Sakai members. If we recognise that fact, we can perceive from the foregoing statement of Cocks's that by 1620 practically the whole foreign trade of Japan had been very adroitly monopolised by the Shōgun's own immediate subjects, to the exclusion of those of the Kyūshū Daimyō. Thirteen years later (1633) we find that no Japanese vessel might go on a foreign voyage, except the nine vessels called *Goshuin-bune,* from the circumstance that they had special permits bearing the vermilion seal of the Shōgun.

It ought, however, to have been remarked that seven years before his death, in 1616, at the very time he was exerting

---

19 A further extract from this same letter of March 10th, 1620, is valuable as showing the importance of Hirado to the Dutch as a base of operations against the Spaniards and the Portuguese in the Far East, and also as incidentally disclosing the facilities for shipbuilding in Japan:—" But, yf it please God that your Wor. lay hould or determen to sett foote in the Molucas, then Japon must be your store howse, as it is the Hollanders. For from hence they make their provision in aboundance, viz. great ordinance both of brasse and iron, with powder and shott good cheape; *beefs and pork in great quantetie;* meale and bisquite, as much as they will; garvances [*i.e.* garbanzos], or small pease or beanes, in abondance; and dried fish lyke a breame, called heare *tay,* in aboundance; tunnie fish salted, in greate quantetie; rack or aquavite, of any sort, in aboundance; rice, in what quantetie they will; with other sortes of Japon wine made of rise, what they will; and pilchardes, in great quantetie, either pickled or otherwais. And for provision of shiping, either tymber or plankes, with mastes, yardes, or what else to make a shipp, with good carpenters to work it, as also rozen or pitch enough, *but no tarr.* Also ther is hempe indifferent to make cables, and them which can reasonably well work it. And for iron work, neales, and such lyke, there is noe want, and smiths that can make ancors of hamer work of 20 or 30 C. wight, yf need be; for such have byn made for carickes which came from Amacou to Nangasaque," etc.

all his efforts to entice Spanish shipwrights to the Tokugawa ports, Iyeyasu had begun to look upon the maritime enterprise of the Kyūshū Daimyō with a certain amount of apprehension. In 1609 (the year Vivero was in the country) Mukai Tadakatsu (Cocks's "old" Admiral), with two fellow-commissioners, had been sent down to Western Japan to seize and confiscate all war-ships of over 500 *koku* burthen, and to bring them round to Shidzuoka and Yedo Gulf. Now, in 1636 a set of regulations was issued forbidding the construction of any ship of over 500 *koku*, and prescribing the exact fashion in which every one of these small vessels was to be built and rigged. The intended effect of all this was to render the vessels at once so cumbrous and so crazy that facing the fortunes of an over-sea voyage in them would be at once profitless and foolhardy. And thus in the interests of the peace and ease of the Tokugawa Shōgunate, or, to speak more correctly, of the Yedo ring, was the mercantile marine of Japan regulated off the face of the deep.[20]

---

[20] One clause in a subsequent set of regulations (1638) is worthy of notice:—"It has been ordered before that no vessels of over 500 *koku* shall be constructed. That regulation remains in force; only it should be understood that merchant ships are allowed." This was no doubt in the interests of the provisioning of Yedo with rice from Kyūshū, Osaka, Niigata, and Sendai. Towards the end of the century we find a good many rice-boats of over 1,000 *koku* trading between Osaka and Yedo.

CHAPTER XXII.

INTERNAL AFFAIRS AFTER 1616.

IN the introductory chapter it was remarked that in this volume there are two main although commingling streams of narrative—the first following the course of the fortunes of the Europeans in Japan from the arrival of the Portuguese to the penning-up of the Dutchmen in Deshima; the second pursuing the course of events that led to the re-establishment of a strong centralised government in the Empire. With the preceding chapter the first of these currents reaches its term; but, apart from incidental allusions, not much has hitherto been said about the domestic politics of Japan since the death of Iyeyasu in 1616. In this final chapter, then, we purpose to devote some brief attention to the internal policy of the Tokugawa administration under Iyeyasu's two immediate successors, Hidetada and Iyemitsu, down to the retirement of the latter in 1651.

Any menace to the supremacy of the Tokugawa was to be apprehended from two sources chiefly. The *Tozama* Daimyō, the non-Tokugawa feudatories, who were jealously excluded from all share in the central administration, might, if not carefully watched and kept to heel, conspire to cast off the yoke Iyeyasu had contrived to impose upon them. This danger, at times no inconsiderable one, would become exceedingly serious in the event of the throne of Japan being occupied by an Emperor of keen intelligence and vigorous will, especially if his Court nobles were men of ability. Such a sovereign might very well be expected to endeavour to free himself from the galling restraints placed upon him by his servant (?) the Shōgun—his Mayor of the Palace, whose creature, the *Shoshidai* of Kyōto, was practically the jailer of the Imperial person. The Tokugawa were perfectly well aware that an Emperor of parts, who refused to be a puppet, might be not at all unlikely to re-enact the *rôle* played by Go-Daigo some three centuries before. In such a case it might fare but ill with the fortunes of the House of Tokugawa, for if the sovereign aspired to play any such part, he could surely count upon the great feudatories of the South and West rallying to his call; while, in the North, Sataké, Uyesugi, Daté, Mogami, and perhaps Gamō in Aidzu, might rise and menace the Tokugawa rear even as it had been menaced by Uyesugi and Sataké in 1600 A.D. Accordingly, to the Yedo bureaucracy it was an object of the utmost importance to see to it that the throne of Japan should not be occupied by any sovereign who could think for himself or who had a real will of his own. In spite of all his numerous lip professions of devotion, Iyeyasu himself was no real friend of the Emperor Go-Yōzei (1587-1611), mainly for the reason that His Majesty now and then evinced a disposition to rule as well as to reign. On several occasions the first Tokugawa Shōgun, through the mouth of Itakura, the *Shoshidai* of Kyōto, hinted to Go-Yōzei that it would not be well for him to attempt to thwart the Kwantō Administration; and at last, in 1611, if we are to believe the missionaries, Iyeyasu marched to Kyōto with a strong army and deposed the *Dairi*! At all events, in this year, Go-Yōzei, then in the very prime of manhood (forty-one), abdicated in favour of Go-Midzuno-o, a youth of sixteen.

Everything, however, goes to indicate that this Go-Midzuno-o was something more than a mere puppet-Emperor. Four years later on, shortly after the capture of Ōsaka, and in the very hour of Iyeyasu's supreme triumph, he made the great Tokugawa understand that he must not presume to go too far. We have already spoken of Hide-yoshi's (Shintō) shrine, the Hōkoku, which must be sharply defined from the neighbouring Hōkōji, or Buddhist temple, which contained his Daibutsu.[1] Shortly after the fall of Ōsaka (1615) it was rumoured that some unknown persons had contributed a large sum of money to this Hōkoku shrine of Hideyoshi's. The report turned out to be well-founded, and thereupon Iyeyasu, determined to raze the Hōkoku shrine, sent Honda Masanobu (" Codskin Dono's ") father) to request the permission of the Imperial Court to do so, pointing out that the Great Deity of the Hōkoku had been the tutelary god of Ōsaka castle, and now that Ōsaka had fallen, and the House of

---

1 For this see *Cook's Diary*, vol. i., pages 200 to 202.

Toyotomi had perished, there was no longer any *raison d'être* for the shrine (Hōkoku) in question. Go-Midzuno-o, however, met the request with a prompt refusal; all that His Majesty would consent to was that the shrine should be converted into a Buddhist temple. After consultation with the two Buddhist priests that accompanied him, not so much as ghostly but as worldly advisers (Shūden, who conducted nearly all his foreign correspondence, and the still more astute Tenkai[2]), "the terrible old man" of Shidzuoka decided that it would be wise to abide by the Imperial decision. The Shintō priest in charge of the Hōkoku shrine (*not* the Hōkōji) was discharged; its revenues were confiscated, the image of the Taikō (Hideyoshi) removed to the corridor of the Hōkōji to be made the guardian deity of the Daibutsu, while the Shintō shrine of the new War-god was to be left to decay from the assaults of the elements and of the worms. To anticipate events somewhat, we may remark that on October 24th, 1619, Itakura, the *Shoshidai* of Kyōto, contrived to score a point in the favour of his master, the Shōgun Hidetada, by suddenly razing the Hōkoku shrine from off the face of the earth, and thus summarily wrecking all the great Hideyoshi's prospects as the new War-god of Japan.

Shortly after the death of Iyeyasu the young Emperor (Go-Midzuno-o) evinced other signs of a tendency to assert himself, and the Yedo councillors became convinced that he was a dangerous man that needed to be curbed. So to fetter him recourse was had to the threadbare but effectual Tokugawa device of a political marriage; and in the summer of 1620

---

[2] Tenkai, canonised as Jigen Daishi, "born during the troublous times that preceded the centralisation of the government of Japan under the rule of the Tokugawa dynasty of Shōguns, lived to see that rule firmly established, and during his long and active life was the favourite alike of the turbulent mediæval chieftain Takeda Shingen, and of the polite third Shōgun, Iyemitsu. Though a shining light in his own sect, he had studied all the varieties of Buddhist doctrine that had been brought to Japan, and did not disdain to inquire even into the old national Shintō religion, and into the philosophical tenets of Confucius and Lao-tsze. He died in 1643 A.D., his portrait having been taken a few days previously at the Shōgun's request by the celebrated artist Kano Tan-yu, and thence transferred to wood. He is said to have attained the great age of one hundred and thirty-four years, but the authority for this statement is doubtful."

In December, 1625, this Tenkai obtained a grant of land at Uyeno, in Yedo, and of a sum of 50,000 ryō to found a Buddhist temple there, and in 1626 the building was completed. In connection with this temple and with that of Iyeyasu's mortuary chapel at Nikko, this *rusé* old ecclesiastic contrived a very cunning political device in favour of the Tokugawa Shōguns at the expense of the Imperial House of Japan. To that reference is made in the text a little later on.

Hidetada's youngest daughter was imposed upon his Majesty as his legitimate consort. Without believing the almost incredible story to the effect that all the children of the Imperial concubines were made away with either before or at their birth, we can see from this and from what followed that the Tokugawa aimed at nothing less than filling the throne of Japan with a relative of their own.

In no long time the Emperor's Tokugawa consort gave birth to a prince, and later on, in 1623, to a princess; and soon, with a view of driving the Emperor to abdicate, his Majesty was subjected to a series of petty and vexatious humiliations. The civil list was a very modest one; but even such as it was, it was not left at the free disposal of the sovereign. The Shōgun's Kyōto officials actually went so far as to make loans of rice and money at interest from it; and people were getting to talk about so much of a rice-loan or a money-loan from the Emperor—"a thing never heard of before." It is easy enough to believe that "His Majesty thought this very derogatory to his dignity." Again, even in the Imperial prerogative of granting titles and honours the sovereign found himself interfered with. In 1627 he had conceded to a number of priests of the Daitokuji and of the Myōshinji the privilege of wearing purple robes. What must have been his astonishment and indignation when the Tokugawa authorities pronounced this to be illegal and stripped the priests of their new finery. Go-Midzuno-o was so chagrined at all this that he proposed to take the very step the Yedo administration had been all the while endeavouring to force him into—to abdicate in favour of Takahito, his son by Hidetada's daughter! In 1628, however, this young prince suddenly died. Yet, in spite of this, the Tokugawa councillors were resolved not to be baulked in their project. Four of the priests already alluded to had dared to protest against the arbitrary action of the Shōgun; and now these four reverend gentlemen were suddenly seized and banished to distant provinces as political exiles. A little later, Kasuga-no-tsubone, Iyemitsu's former wet-nurse, came to Kyōto, and obtained an audience of the Emperor *by force*— "an unprecedented thing this, that a female servant of the *Buké* (military class) should be granted an Imperial audience"!

Thereupon the Emperor communicated to Hidetada his

intention to retire in favour of Okiko, his daughter by his
Tokugawa spouse. Okiko at that time was of the mature
age of seven years, and for the eight hundred and sixty years
previous to that date (1630) there had been no female sovereign
in Japan. The only reply that came from Hidetada was that
he "thought it might not be too late"! In 1630, then,
Hidetada's grand-daughter became sovereign of the Empire,
while Go-Midzuno-o, then only thirty-four years of age, went
into a retirement which lasted just half a century—till his
death in 1680.

Shortly after Go-Midzuno-o's abdication, his Tokugawa
consort gave birth to another prince. Just as his sister, the
Empress Myoshō (1630–1643) was reaching years of discretion,
this young brother of hers was declared Crown Prince in 1641,
and two years later Emperor at the age of eleven. Then,
when in turn this Emperor, Go-Kōmiō, began to show a will of
his own, he died suddenly—not without suspicion of poison—
in 1654, and his younger brother, Go-sai-in, ascended the throne
and occupied it until 1663, when he either abdicated or had
to abdicate in favour of his sister Reigen, then ten years of age !

Thus upon the ill-starred Go-Midzuno-o and his children the
hand of the Yedo administration pressed heavily indeed. Nor
was this all. In the *Buké Hyaku Kajō*, the so-called "Legacy
of Iyeyasu," we find the following Article :—

"In *Bufu* [the Military Office, *i.e.* Yedo] I built the Temple of
Tōyeisan [*i.e.* Uyeno] and requested the Mikado to install as chief
priest a Shinnō [*i.e.* an Imperial Prince] to pray that evil influences
may be warded off, and that peace and prosperity may prevail
over Japan. And also in order that, if the Mikado should be
induced to side with traitors, and these concert with or gain possession
of the person of the Mikado, then the Dai-Shōgun shall install the
Uyeno-no-miya [*i.e.* the Imperial Prince, Abbot of Tōyei-san] as
Mikado and punish the rebels."[3]

---

[3] This Article alone suffices to cast grave doubts upon the authenticity of
the so-called "Legacy of Iyeyasu." Iyeyasu died in 1616, Toyei-san was built
ten years afterwards, in 1626; and the first Imperial Abbot took up his quarters
there in 1646 according to some authorities, in 1654 according to others, the
latter date seeming the more probable one.

Again, Iyeyasu is represented as saying: "The President of the Hyōjōsho
[Supreme Court] must be selected as being a man of the clearest mind and
best disposition." Now the first meeting of this Hyōjōsho took place in 1631
fifteen years after the death of Iyeyasu; and its full organisation did not take
place until 1657!

Once more, in the "Legacy" reference is made to the *Wakadoshiyori*, the
Junior Council, officially organised only in 1633! And there are other clauses
which, if actually penned by Iyeyasu, must have come from Iyeyasu when no
longer in the flesh.

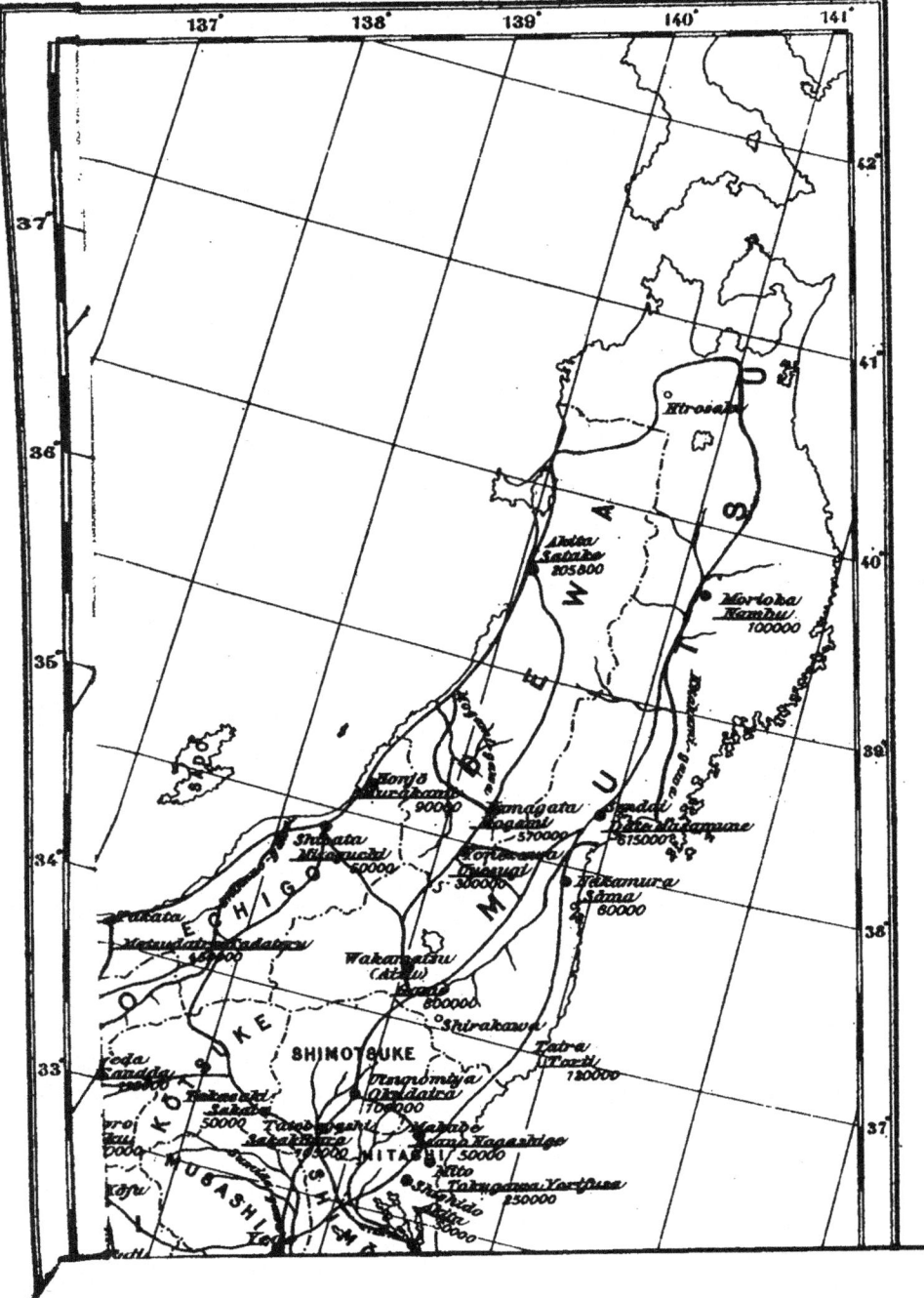

This is a correct exposition of one article of Tokugawa policy contrived by that terribly learned and still more astute shaven-pated Japanese Nestor, the priest Tenkai.

Before his death in 1616 Iyeyasu had given instructions that he should be interred at Nikkō, of which Tenkai was then Abbot; and there in 1617, after the erection of a sumptuous mortuary temple, the old statesman was buried—and apotheosized with the most splendid pomp and circumstance. As has been said, nine years later Tenkai received a grant of Uyeno, and there in 1626 another shrine was reared to Iyeyasu under the name of Tō-shō-gū. Even in the time of Hidetada (died 1632) Tenkai had represented that in the interests of the Tokugawa line an Imperial Prince should be installed as Abbot of these temples. However, it was not till 1654—ten years after Tenkai's death (1644)—that this advice was acted upon. Then Morizumi, fifth son of the ill-fated Go-Midzuno-o, was brought from Kyōto and made Abbot of Nikkō and of Tōyei-san (Uyeno), with the title of Rinnōji-no-miya. From this time down to the Revolution of 1868 the Abbot of Nikkō and of Uyeno was always a Prince of the Imperial Blood. Of course his *raison d'être* was merely that he might be an under-study ready to assume the *rôle* of a puppet-Emperor in case the jealously-guarded exponent of the part in Kyōto should not afford satisfaction to his Tokugawa masters, or should pass under the influence of evil counsellors and traitors who might presume to remind him that at one time his ancestors and predecessors had not merely reigned, but actually ruled, in the Empire of Japan. From all this it will readily appear that the Tokugawa Shōguns (and councillors) had contrived to safeguard themselves against all danger from the Imperial line of Japan so far as cunning and statecraft, professing a contemptibly hypocritical lip-loyalty, could safeguard it.

Having thus dealt with the attitude of the early Tokugawa Shōgunate towards the rightful sovereigns of Japan, we will now consider its relations towards the non-*Fudai* feudatories—the *Tozama* or "outside" Daimyō. Even before the fall of Ōsaka, Iyeyasu had so far cowed them that almost all either had led or had sent contingents to aid him in his great struggle with Hideyori. Yet, as we have seen in the case of that

Tanaka of Kurumé who refused to enforce Iyeyasu's anti-
Christian Edict of 1614, there were instances where the
"outside" feudatories paid but scant heed to the Tokugawa
ordinances within their domains.   But in spite of the reluctance
shown by Daté, Uyesugi, Fukushima, Hosokawa, and Kuroda
to begin a persecution of their Christian subjects even down
to 1622, the fall of Ōsaka in 1615 made the non-*Fudai* Daimyō
very much more heedful of the behests of the Yedo Government
than they had been before.   A curious example of this is
afforded by the early Tokugawa proclamations against the use
of tobacco.   As an article of commerce the "weed" had been
brought to Japan by the Portuguese traders some time under
Hideyoshi's administration (1582–1598); but it was only in
1605 that it was first planted and cultivated in the empire.
In 1612 Iyeyasu had issued an ineffectual Edict against its use;
and several others of a similar import had been subsequently
issued with no more effect.[4]   Then in Cocks's Diary, August 7th,
1615, seventy-five days after the fall of Ōsaka castle, we meet
with the following entry:—

"Gonosco Dono came to the English howse, and amongst other
talk tould me that the King [*i.e.* the Daimyō of Hirado, assessment
63,000 *koku*] had sent hym word to burne all the tobaco, and to suffer
non to be drunk [that is even now the Japanese word for "smoked"]
in his government, it being the Emperours pleasure it should be so;
and the like order geven thorowghout all Japon.   And that he, for
to begen, had burned 4 *piculls* or C. wight this day, and cost him 20
taies pico; and had geven orders to all others to doe the like, and
to pluck up all which was planted.   It is strange to see how these
Japons—men, women and children—are besotted in drinking that
herb; and not ten yeares since it was in use first."

A year after this (in 1616) the Yedo administration felt
itself sufficiently strong to venture upon appropriating the
whole of the European trade with Japan; and so the Portuguese
and Spaniards were confined to Nagasaki, and the English and
Dutch to Hirado, whose little lordling, Matsuura, "outside"
Daimyō as he was, could be whistled to heel if need be with a
very small expenditure of Yedo wind.   From this date the
Tokugawa Shōguns had undisputed control over all the foreign
relations of the Empire down to a time within the memory of
many now living.

---

4 King James I.'s *Counterblast to Tobacco* was published in 1616 A.D., the
year of Iyeyasu's death.

Shortly after the capture of Ōsaka (1615) a set of *Buke Shohatto* (Regulations for the Military Class), penned by the Chinese scholar, Hayashi Razan, was communicated to the Daimyō in Fushimi castle, Honda Masazumi ("Codskindono") on that occasion commenting on and expounding each one of the thirteen Articles as they were read out. As this document is the model on which many other similar ones were subsequently framed, it may not be amiss to reproduce it in full. It sets forth :—

1.—That the study of literature and of the art of war, archery, and horsemanship should be strenuously prosecuted or practised.

2.—That excessive drinking and licentious amusements should be prohibited.

3.—That [national] law-breakers should not be harboured in the various fiefs.

4.—That in engaging men and soldiers, the great and little lords and the various salaried men should summarily reject those who might be denounced as traitors and murderers.

5.—That thenceforth only the native-born, to the exclusion of all men from other fiefs, should be permitted to reside in a fief.

6.—That even the repair of the castles in the various fiefs should be notified; much more are new constructions prohibited.

7.—That should there be in neighbouring fiefs men who scheme for a new order of things, raising factions and parties, they should be speedily denounced.

8.—That marriages should not be privately contracted.

9.—That the retinues of various Daimyō, in going up to and during their residence in Yedo, should be properly limited in number.

10.—That the articles of dress should not be arbitrarily and promiscuously selected.

11.—That private persons should not use palanquins.

12.—That the *samurai* of the various fiefs should be frugal in their livelihood.

13.—That the heads of fiefs should choose capable persons as their ministers and advisers.

Several of these Articles—notably the fifth, sixth, and seventh—were clearly intended to put a curb upon the great feudatories. To ensure their due observance a most elaborate system of espionage was organised—so elaborate and so widely ramified that by the end of the century the secret agents of the Tokugawa were everywhere—expect, perhaps, in Satsuma.

A still more effective measure was the enforced residence of the Daimyō in Yedo from time to time. To the origin of that practice allusion has already been made. But the hard and fast regulations that were in force in connection with this in the early half of the present century were not the work of Iyeyasu or of Hidetada. In their days, Daimyō they had reason to suspect might, as in the cases of Kuroda and of Fukushima, be kept virtual prisoners in the Tokugawa capital for years; while, on the other hand, certain Daimyō were not called upon to quit their own fiefs. In Hidetada's time (1616–1623) often a brief visit sufficed, although that was usually very expensive, in spite of the ninth Article of the Regulations just quoted.[5] A special order was given that the two Daimyō of Kaga and of Echigo should come up to and return from Yedo alternately, and that the lords of other provinces having their castles in positions of strategic importance should also be in and absent from Yedo in alternate years. Care was also taken that there should be no communication between the feudatories and the Imperial Court, it being laid down that on their journeys the Daimyō should not pass through Kyōto, but should proceed from Fushimi, which was held by one Tokugawa *Fudai*, straight on to Zeze, which was in the hands of another.

Meanwhile several of these *Fudai* Daimyō (whose estates could be increased or curtailed at will, and who were con-

[5] So much we learn from Cocks, who was continually pestered with applications for loans from the Daimyō of Hirado to help to defray the expenses of his Yedo journey. And, furthermore, we incidentally learn that this princelet was also heavily indebted to certain Ōsaka usurers. In Caron's time we find that on these journeys the Hirado chief was accompanied by a train of 1,000 men! Tōdō Takatora, in Iyeyasu's days, had proposed that the wives and children of the feudatories should constantly reside in Yedo, and although the proposition was adopted, it had not been universally acted upon. In 1624 or 1625, when Shimadzu Iyehisa of Satsuma revived the proposal, the Shōgun adopted it, and from this time onwards it was a custom that had really to be observed. Some ten years later on the so-called Law of *Sankin* was promulgated, in terms of which neighbouring feudatories were to come to Yedo in the fourth month of every year alternately. In accordance with that law, in July, 1635, Mayeda of Kaga and twenty-five other Daimyō were allowed to return to their fiefs, while Shimadzu of Satsuma and fifty-five others were ordered to remain in the capital. In 1642 extra regulations in connection with *Sankin-Kōtai* (Taking turns to come and reside in Yedo) were issued, but they were not of much importance.

Incidentally we here find reference to the suppression of Christianity. "The following instructions were [1642] given to the Daimyō, then permitted to return to their fiefs:—(1) The Kirishtan inquisition in the respective fiefs should be carried on with increasing vigour. (2) It is reported that at various places in the respective fiefs, guards are posted in the name of the Kirishtan inquisition, causing much trouble to travellers. Henceforth travelling should be made free."

stantly being removed from one fief to another) had, between
1615 and 1642, been established in Northern and Western
Japan, in Shikoku, and even in Kyūshū, at the expense of
certain of the non-Tokugawa feudatories. In the west of the
main island Midzunō had (1620) been established at Fukuyama
in Bingo with an assessment of 100,000 *koku*; Matsudaira
Tadaaki (1639) at Himeji in Harima with 180,000 *koku*; and
Matsudaira Naomasa, Hideyasu's son and Iyeyasu's grandson,
at Matsuye in Idzumo with 190,000 *koku*; while Sakai had
been seated at Obama in Wakasa with 123,500 *koku* in 1634.
Besides these, lesser *Fudai* had also been installed in other
situations; so that altogether, in the west of the main island,
the Tokugawa had contrived to appropriate an assessed revenue
of some 700,000 *koku* at the expense of the outside feudatories—
Kyōgoku, Horio, the Ikedas and others.

In the extreme North they had pushed their encroachments
to a still greater extent. There in 1615 there were five great
Houses—Daté of Sendai, with 615,000 *koku*; Gamō of Aidzu
(Iyeyasu's grandson), with 600,000 *koku*; Mogami of Yamagata,
with 570,000 *koku*; Uyesugi of Yonezawa, with 300,000 *koku*;
and Sataké of Akita, with 205,800 *koku*. The greatest of these
feudatories, Daté Masamune, by a very pliant and adroit
policy contrived to retain his domains intact, but the Houses
of Gamō and Mogami were not so fortunate. On one ground
or another, before 1638 both had either been extinguished or
reduced to obscurity, and their combined estates of nearly
1,200,000 *koku* had been appropriated by the Tokugawa, either
through their *Fudai* or the members of their own House.
The history of this precious piece of jobbery, as given in the
Hankampu, is long and intricate, not to say somewhat tedious,
and is scarcely worth the trouble of recapitulation in detail.
Suffice it to say that the result was that the Mogami fief was
partly partitioned among *Fudai* Daimyō, partly incorporated with
the Shōgunal estates, while Gamō's domains in Aidzu (greatly
curtailed) were bestowed on Iyemitsu's illegitimate half-brother
Hoshina, the founder of that House of Aidzu which was to
prove the most staunch and the most intrepid supporter of the
Tokugawa power when it was tottering to its fall in 1867–68.[6]

_____

6 In a previous foot-note a somewhat amusing account of Hidetada as a
family man was reproduced from the Rev. Arthur Hatch, "parson of the

Then in the north of the island of Shikoku three *Fudai* were settled (between 1634 and 1639) at the expense of Katō Yoshiaki of Matsuyama, and of Ikoma in Sanuki, whose united assessments of 373,000 *koku* had made a good deal more than

---

Pulgrove." In a measure the account was accurate, for Hidetada's wife was a strong-minded woman, and the second Tokugawa Shōgun was, if not hen-pecked, at all events under a very salutary modicum of petticoat government. His strong-minded spouse was a sister of Yodogimi, daughter of Asai of Ōmi, a secondary wife of Hideyoshi and the mother of Hideyori. Hideyoshi, after adopting this termagant as his daughter, had bestowed her on Hidetada in marriage in 1595, when the bridegroom was sixteen and she twenty-three years of age. Altogether they had eight children, five daughters (the eldest of whom married Hideyori, and the youngest the Emperor Go-Midzuno-o) and three sons, the eldest of whom died in infancy. The second son was Iyemitsu, born in 1604, and the third, Tadanaga, in 1605. To quote the Japanese authorities:—

"This Tadanaga was the favourite of his parents, especially of his mother. So much was he petted by them that it appeared as if he was to be made heir to Hidetada. Kasuga-no-tsubone, wet-nurse of Iyemitsu, thought this a thing not to be overlooked. She was the daughter of Saitō Toshimitsu, a captain of Akechi Mitsuhide, and had been married to a Daimyō called Inaba Masanari. For some reason or other she had been divorced by him after giving birth to a son, and was then made wet-nurse to Hidetada's eldest son. Being a courageous woman, she did not look in silence on a state of things that might prove disadvantageous to the prince she was trusted with. Through Okaji-no-tsubone, one of the concubines of Iyeyasu, she informed Iyeyasu about the matter, and solicited his interference. At first Iyeyasu thought that it was only a trouble arising from feminine jealousy, and paid no attention to her; but as he was constantly appealed to, he began to think of it seriously. In 1613 he went up to Yedo, saw Hidetada, and warned him of the danger that might accrue from such a step as disinheriting the eldest son. At the same time he showed his resolution on the question by treating Iyemitsu with great consideration, and Tadanaga coldly. It is stated that when he saw the two young princes, he allowed the elder to dine with him, but sternly denied that honour to the younger. This decided the question of succession, and Iyemitsu's position as the heir was made secure.

"In 1618 Hidetada's wife died. Tadanaga thus lost the chief friend he had, and for certain misdeeds he also lost the favour of his father. In 1617 he had been made lord of three provinces—Suruga, Tōtōmi, and Kai—but he was not contented with his lot. He became reckless and desperate. He killed many of his attendants with his own hand in moments of anger. He incurred the anger of Hidetada more and more, and was not even allowed to visit his father when he fell ill in the autumn of 1631 and died in the first month of the next year (1632).

"Tadanaga now harboured evil designs against Iyemitsu. He plotted to rise against him and to take the power into his own hands. For this purpose he associated with him some powerful Daimyō as his allies, or rather forced them by intriguing to sign a document professing devotion to his cause. Kuroda and Katō were among those Daimyō. But Kuroda secretly gave information of it to Iyemitsu's premier, Sakai Tadakatsu. In 1633 Tadanaga was dispossessed of his fief by the order of the Shōgun, and subsequently removed to Takasaki, Kōdzuke, where he was practically kept a prisoner. In the twelfth month of the next year [January, 1635] a messenger of the Shōgun came to him, and he committed suicide. [Katō Tadahiro, son of Kiyomasa, was dispossessed of his fief in the sixth month of the ninth year of Kanyei (1632). The reasons for this are not definitely known, but his complicity in Tadanaga's plot appears to have been one of the chief.]

"Hidetada had another son by his only concubine, but, afraid of his wife's jealousy, he kept the fact a profound secret from her. This son was adopted by Hoshina Masamitsu, and assumed the name of Hoshina Masayuki. In 1636 Iyemitsu gave him a fief of 200,000 *koku* at Yamagata in Dewa, whence he was removed to Aidzu in 1644, his assessed revenue being raised to 230,000 *koku*. After the death of Iyemitsu in the fourth year of Keian [1651], according to his will, Hoshina acted as Regent during the next Shōgun's minority."

one-third of that of the whole island. Kyūshū had always been that portion of the Empire on which the Tokugawa hold was weakest. At the date of the fall of Ōsaka there had not been one single *Fudai* in that great island; while the only *pied-à-terre* the Shōgun had there had been the town of Nagasaki. However, before the death of Iyemitsu in 1651, even in Kyūshū the Tokugawas had contrived to make considerable appropriations. A small *Fudai* of 60,000 *koku* had been installed at Hida in Bungo in 1617; and on Hosokawa being removed to Kumamoto, of which the Katō family had been stripped in 1632, the whole of the Kyūshū coast of the Inland Sea had been portioned out among three Ogasawara (*Fudai*), whose joint assessments ran up to 275,000 *koku*. Then, as a result of the rebellion of 1637–38, a *Fudai* (70,000 *koku*) was seated at Shimabara, while the island of Amakusa (40,000 *koku*) had then been incorporated with the Tokugawa family domains. And in 1649 Karatsu (83,000 *koku*), in Hizen, was assigned to a *Fudai*.

Thus between the death of Iyeyasu (1616) and the death of Iyemitsu (1651) the Tokugawas had contrived to strip the "outside" feudal Houses in the north and west of the main island and in Shikoku and Kyūshū of lands of an assessed annual value of some 3,000,000 *koku*. What that exactly means will perhaps be more easily grasped if it be translated into *men*.

In 1616 Hidetada had issued an ordinance dealing with the military contingent each feudal chief had to maintain and furnish in case of need; and in 1633 this ordinance was modified by his successor Iyemitsu. The details are somewhat complicated; but it will serve our purpose to say that a fief of 100,000 *koku* was charged with the support of a force of 2,805 men, of whom 350 were matchlock men and 170 cavalry. Thus between 1616 and 1651 the Shōguns had contrived to diminish the musters of the "outside" feudatories, and to increase their own or those of their immediate and devoted dependents, by a force of some 80,000 or 85,000 men. In a previous chapter some pains were taken to mark the distinction between Iyeyasu's dependents and his allies in the great Sekigahara campaign of 1600 A.D. By 1651 the Houses of some of the most conspicuous of these allies had either been

XX 2

extinguished or had been swept into obscurity by the successors
of the equal they had then aided against his rivals. Among
the victims had been Fukushima of Aki (498,000 *koku*), Katō
of Kumamoto (520,000 *koku*), Katō of Matsuyama (200,000
koku), Gamō of Aidzu (600,000 *koku*), Mogami of Yamagata
(570,000 *koku*), Kobayakawa of Okayama (574,000 *koku*), Tanaka
of Kurume (325,000 *koku*), Terasawa of Karatsu (120,000 *koku*),
and the Kyōgokus. At the time of Sekigahara all these had
been honoured allies, and were treated as trusty confederates in a
common cause should be treated. Now in 1651 the position of
the "outside" lords was a very different one.

On the death of Hidetada in 1632—as has been said, he
nominally resigned and procured the appointment of Iyemitsu
as Shōgun nine years before (1623)—Iyemitsu suddenly
summoned the "outside" Daimyō then in Yedo to the Palace.
What then happened we give in the words of a Japanese
authority. The account may be somewhat embellished—at
all events it is distinctly melodramatic, yet it is essentially
corroborated by various other writers:—

"The Daimyō obeyed the summons, but Iyemitsu would not hurry
to see them, saying that he was ill. They had therefore to wait for
a long time. It was cold then, but no food was offered to them, and
when the evening came no light was brought in. The Daimyō began
to be frightened, and wondered what was the matter. At last, late in
the night, Iyemitsu made his appearance, and thus addressed them:
'That my grandfather and father were able to pacify the disturbance
in the Empire, although due to Providence, is nevertheless owing to
the united help rendered them by various Daimyō. In consequence
my grandfather and father regarded the (outside) Daimyō as friends,
and, treating them as cordially as possible, did not establish the
relation of master and subjects. But I have been in the position of a
superior and a master from my birth, and my case cannot be compared
to that of my predecessors. I shall henceforth treat all Daimyō,
even the lords possessing large fiefs, as my subjects. Those of you
who may be minded to disobey me in this may quickly return to your
provinces, repair your castles, and prepare your arms. I shall act
accordingly.' Thus addressed, the Daimyō were struck with awe, and
none of them dared to raise their eyes. For a while dead silence
reigned in the hall, but presently Daté Masamune spoke. 'It is our
fault that the Shōgun has thought it proper to speak thus. Even
towards the late Taikō, who had risen from the position of a humble
peasant to be the ruler of the country, the Daimyō behaved as his
subjects. Much more so is it proper that we should act as subjects
towards the Tokugawas, who are the descendants of the Emperor
Seiwa, and have already ruled the country for three successive
generations. I, Masamune, respectfully obey your command, and
I believe all will do as I do. Henceforth we shall behave as subjects
towards you and make it a rule to later ages.' Then all the other

Daimyō unanimously said: 'We are of the same mind as Masamune.' Thereupon, Iyemitsu retired to a room and summoned the individual Daimyō in turn. When one went into his presence, Iyemitsu took a sword in his hand, and gave it to him, saying: 'Unsheathe it and inspect the blade.'   In this way every Daimyō was called in, and there was none who was not awe-stricken and who did not perspire on his back. They said to each other: 'The work of the Tokugawa has been assuredly established by the third Shōgun.'" [7]

Down to this date (1632 or 1633) it had been customary for the members of the Go-rōjū, or Yedo Cabinet, to go out to Senji and to Goten-yama, behind Shinagawa, to meet and welcome the outside Daimyō on their visits to the capital. This practice was now done away with; Goten-yama, where a fine reception pavilion had stood, was turned into a pleasure resort for the citizens of Yedo, and the Daimyō had to push on into the city, there to pay their humble respects, not to the Shōgun, but to the Shōgun's Ministers, before taking up their quarters in their own *yashiki* (city mansions) !

And it is for the adoption of measures of this nature that Iyemitsu has been glorified as a genius! *But could Iyemitsu have done the work of his illustrious grandfather or of the illustrious Taikō, if placed in their positions?* Or even that of a smaller man,—of Nobunaga, the pioneer in the task of re-establishing a central government in Japan? With Nobunaga, it is true, Iyemitsu had traits in common, notably a haughty overbearing arrogance and an overweening sense of his own personal importance. But while Nobunaga had been a man of war from his youth upwards, Iyemitsu's military glory was that of the carpet-knight merely, and it is pretty safe to assume that his not very brilliant administrative measures were mostly prompted by the very shrewd and very cunning politicians in the Go-rōjū. And to these worthy Poloniuses it must have

---

[7] Another story (which is redeemed from incredibility by the Satsuma men's practical protest against the custom within the memory of the living) going to show the rapidly developed overbearing insolence of the Tokugawas is ridiculous enough for opera-bouffe. The august Shōgunal palate, of course, had to be tickled by viands and beverages of the choicest only. Now, the finest tea in Japan was then, as now, produced at Uji, not far from Kyōto; and accordingly it was from Uji that the Barbarian-Subduing-Great-General's equivalent for a tea-pot had to be supplied. The leaf was packed in *cha-tsubo*, or tea-jars adorned with the Tokugawa family crest. Now the Go-rōjū in Iyemitsu's time, wishing to test the power of their administration, gave orders that all—Daimyō included—meeting this sacrosanct Shōgunal tea-jar on its progress from Uji to Yedo should treat it with the same reverential ceremonies as they would the Shōgun himself! It was then found that the Shōgun's power was so strong that nobody dared to show defiance to this absurd requirement, and it then became customary to transport the "august" tea-jar from Uji to Yedo with all the circumstance of the Holy Sacrament.

proved a pretty hard task to keep the spoiled child their master, the third Shōgun, out of serious mischief at all times,— if we are to believe Caron's account of the matter. In 1638 he writes:—

"No one dares to attempt any opposition to the will of the Shōgun; and when he has positively stated his opinion, no one ever dares to utter anything by way of persuading him to change it. The least punishment that would await a temerity of this kind would be banishment. The placemen are chosen from amongst the lords and nobles who are educated for the particular service of the Emperor, who selects from amongst them those who please him most. Hence, in the hope of favour, in which they all live, each pays his court to the Sovereign, and is ready to fulfil his desires even before his lips are opened to express them. Whatever injustice the Emperor may commit, or into whatever extravagance of excesses he may plunge, they praise or approve of all."[8]

Things then were somewhat otherwise than they had been in the days of Iyeyasu, for there are scores of stories going to show how eager that truly great man ever was to profit by faithful, albeit unpleasant, counsel.[9]

---

[8] In view of this statement, which is corroborated from other sources, the following article from the so-called "Legacy of Iyeyasu" (penned several decades after Iyeyasu had become a god) is really comical reading:—"There are men who always say 'Yes' [i.e. agree with me], and there are others who sometimes say 'No' [i.e. express a different opinion from me]. Now the former I wish to put away from me, and the latter I wish to be near me. The Go-rōjū are to examine and see to it that men do not do such business only as is agreeable to them, and avoid all that is the reverse. *I wish to have about me men of all opinions, both those who differ from me and those who agree with me.*"

[9] To cite what Kyūso, the philosopher (1648–1734), says (as translated by Dr. Knox) on this matter may suffice, however:—

"Iyeyasu excelled all, but was not vain of his wisdom. On the contrary, he approved the honest remonstrance of his inferiors. And indeed remonstrance may be put as the foundation of the wisdom of the ruler. Only the Sage does not err. If a man listen to reproof, though he err, he is like a sick man who takes medicine and regains his strength. But however wise a man may be, if he will not listen to remonstrance he is like one who will take no medicine because his illness is slight, and so the danger remains. But most strong rulers hate reproof and insist upon their own way. In China is the office of Censor, but it is of little use. It is only a name, for honest men are readily removed and flatterers given office. When there is error there is no reform, nor remonstrance when the government is bad, a grief that lasts from ancient days until now. It is still worse in Japan with its feudal government; the rulers govern by force of arms, and inferiors must obey. Remonstrance ceases, and sympathy with the people ends. Daily the evil grows, but those who know its cause are few.

"Iyeyasu was born in the midst of war and turmoil. He was sympathetic to inferiors, and ever opened the way of words. Most admirable of men! Once in his castle, Honda Sado-no-Kami was present with some others. At the end of their business all withdrew save Honda and one other. The latter presented a writing to Iyeyasu, who took it, asking, 'What is this?' 'Matters I have thought of much,' was the reply, 'and venture respectfully to suggest, thinking possibly one in ten thousand may be of use.' 'Thanks,' said Iyeyasu; 'read it. There is no reason why Honda should not hear.' So he began, and Iyeyasu assented to each of the many particulars, and finally took the paper, saying, 'Always be free to say what you think necessary.' Afterwards, when Honda only remained, he said, 'It was rudely done, and not a suggestion of value in it all.' But Iyeyasu waved his hand dissentingly. 'Though it is not of great

The simple fact of the matter is that Iyemitsu was more than exceedingly lucky in having had Iyeyasu for his grandfather. Most of the real work of re-centralising the Empire had been done by the peasant ruler, Hideyoshi, who, in spite of all his foibles, must be regarded as the greatest and the ablest *man* that Japan has ever produced. In the great and the illustrious Iyeyasu he found no unworthy Elisha in the sphere of statecraft. Iyeyasu's astute statesmanship after Sekigahara, his organisation of a safe and efficient and easily manipulated—almost self-running—administrative machinery for his successors, and his "crowning mercy" of Ōsaka (1615) had in effect practically consolidated the work of the great Taikō. But in common with that of Nobunaga and with that of Hideyoshi, the case of Iyeyasu may be cited as one more illustration of the Japanese adage to the effect that "the great man has no seed." What really governed Japan from the death of Iyeyasu (1616) down to the Revolution of 1868 was not so much the *fainéant* and ludicrously puffed up but ludicrously commonplace descendants of Iyeyasu (Yoshimune always honourably excepted) as Iyeyasu's system—a system deliberately devised to safeguard the interests of (possible) brainless figure-heads,—and also, let it be honestly admitted, from the great Iyeyasu's point of view, the tranquillity and

---

value, still he had thought it over carefully and wrote it in secret for my eye. His spirit should be praised. If he suggests anything of value I'll adopt it; if not, I'll let it alone. We should not call such remonstrance rude. Men do not know their own faults, but common folks have friends who reprove and criticise. They have opportunity for reform. This is their advantage. But rulers have no friends, but constantly meet with their inferiors, who assent respectfully to every word. So they cannot know and reform, to their great loss. They lose their power and destroy their house because no one will remonstrate, and all they do is approved as right. Most essential is it that they be told their faults.'

"Honda remembered this and told it to his son weeping, as he spoke of the Shōgun's deep heart and broad humanity. And when the young man asked the name of the man and the purport of his paper, thinking to ridicule him, Honda reproved him sharply: 'What have you to do with the man and his suggestions? Think of your lord's fine spirit!'

"Afterwards, said Iyeyasu to his *samurai*:—'A ruler must have faithful Ministers. He who sees the error of his lord and remonstrates, not fearing his wrath, is braver than he who bears the foremost spear in battle. In the fight body and life are risked, but it is not certain death. Even if killed there is deathless fame, and his lord laments. If there is victory great reward and glory are won, and the inheritance goes down to son and grandson. But to grieve over his lord's faults and faithfully remonstrate when the words do not pass the ears and touch the heart is hard indeed. Disliked, distantly received, displaced by flatterers, his advice not taken, however loyal he may be, at last he gives up the task, professes illness, or retires into the quiet of old age. If he dares to risk his lord's displeasure in his faithfulness he may be imprisoned or even killed. He who fears not all this, but gives up even life to benefit his country, is highly to be praised. Compared with him the foremost spear is an easy post."

(therefore) the best interests of the Empire of Japan. The changes made in this machinery by Iyemitsu were exceedingly few and unimportant; in fact, apart from the organisation of the Hyōjōsho or Supreme Court (1631, 1635, and finally 1657), they were nominal only, extending chiefly to altering the name of the Junior Council from *Shutto-nin* to *Waka-doshiyori*.10

As for Iyemitsu's great achievement of bridling the "outside" feudatories, it was a comparatively cheap one. In 1632 the heads of several of these Houses were minors, while others of them, grown to manhood since the great wars, had become enervated by sloth and self-indulgence. As regards the greatest feudatory in the extreme South, Shimadzu of Satsuma, the Tokugawa had always been careful to keep on good terms with him—he alone among the leading "outside" Daimyō had had his fief enlarged since Sekigahara (from 605,000 to 729,500 *koku*)—and Shimadzu was then (1632) very well disposed towards the Shōgun. On the other hand, the greatest feudatory in the extreme North, Daté of Sendai, had been very careful to keep on very good terms with the Yedo Cabinet; and it is just possible that Daté's part in the cold and hungry melodrama of March 18th, 1632, had been duly rehearsed by that very astute and sharp-sighted, although one-eyed, politician. It was, then, all things considered, a tolerably safe thing for Iyemitsu to catch the *Tozama* upon empty stomachs, to summon them into his presence one by one, to request them to smell his sword, and then inform them that if they did not like the scent of the blade they might return to their fiefs and prepare their castles for a siege! Ever since 1615 castle-building in all the fiefs had been jealously watched and regulated by the Yedo authorities; and, furthermore, any

10 "The highest officials in the original Government organisation of the Tokugawa were called 'Buke Shitsuyaku.' Ii Naomasa, Sakakibara Yasumasa, and Honda Tadakatsu were first installed in this office. Next to 'Shitsuyaku' were 'Toshiyori,' [afterwards changed to Go-rōjū]. To this office the first appointed were Honda Masanobu and Okubo Tadachika [in Yedo], and Honda Masazumi, Naruse Masanari, and Andō Naotsugu [in Sumpu]. Below the Go-rōjū were 'Kinju Shutto-nin,' the earliest of whom were Matsudaira Masatsuna, Itakura Katsushige, and Akimoto Yasutomo [in Sumpu], and Mizuno Tadamoto, Ii Masanari, and Morikawa Shigetoshi [in Yedo]. In Iyemitsu's time the name of this Board of Kinju Shutto-nin was changed to that of Wakadoshiyori. After Iyeyasu's death the Go-rōjū and the Kinju Shutto-nin of Sumpu were abolished. Iyemitsu appointed Sakai Utanokami Tadayo the first Tairō in the spring of 1635."

one of the "outside" lords inclined to avail himself of Iyemitsu's gracious permission knew perfectly well that in order to curry favour with the overwhelming might of the Tokugawa, his fellow *Tozama* in his immediate neighbourhood would be the first to assail him.

Thus in 1651, with the whole of the main island, from Himeji in Harima on to the Nikkō mountains and the sea-board of the Pacific beyond, in the hands either of the Tokugawa or of the *Fudai*, their immediate dependents; with these *Fudai* in strong strategic positions in the extreme North, in the West, and in Shikoku, and with a fairly strong foothold in Kyūshū; with the wives and children of the "outside" lords at all times in Yedo as hostages, and the *Sankin-kōtai* making hostages of these lords themselves from time to time and effectually preventing them from conspiring and combining when not in the capital,—the Shōgun had no great reason to apprehend any rising against his authority. Then the Imperial throne of Japan was occupied by a relative of his own; the meagre Imperial civil list was dribbled out by his own underlings, and the Sovereign himself and his Court were jealously and rigorously secluded from all intercourse with the "outside" lords and such as might chafe under the despotism of Yedo. The problem of being able to keep things perfectly quiet seemed to have been really solved. So far the administrative machine devised by the great Iyeyasu had proved to be a wonderful piece of efficient handicraft, and its running had been of the smoothest. What those who had successively manipulated it since 1616 had ever regarded as most likely to throw it out of gear was the possible impact of over-sea Powers. Hence one reason for the expulsion of the Spaniards in 1624, of the Portuguese in 1639, the meditated massacre and expulsion of the Dutch in 1640 and their virtual imprisonment in Deshima (236 by 82 paces, Kaempfer says) in Nagasaki harbour. Hence, when at the overthrow of the Ming dynasty in China (1644) the partisans of that falling House implored aid from the Shōgun of Japan, that aid was promptly refused. From this date Japan settles down into that state of seclusion which presents some of the strangest phenomena in the history of the world. The organisation of society was feudal—at least, so far as feudalism meant subjection, not to

the Sovereign of the State, but to one's over-lord; so far as
there was a chain of sub-infeudation; and so far as nearly
all the land in the country was held by military service.
And yet, from the Shimabara revolt of 1638 down to
1863, when in the streets of the ancient capital the Chōshiu
clansmen, suddenly gave practical proof that the spirit of
derring-do prevalent in Japan in the days of the Taikō was
far from extinct,—during the long space of 225 years, in the
course of which at least seven generations of men had lived
and passed away, the conditions continued to be such that
(apart from one absurd episode at Nagasaki in 1808) the
feudal musters had never once to be called out for real, red-
handed war! It might very well seem that during all these 225
years—during all these seven generations—in so-called Old
Japan the tenure of lands by military service was entirely of
the *lucus a non lucendo* order. This phenomenon will be dealt
with in a future volume.

Owing to circumstances over which the " Chronicle " Office had no control, the index herewith had to be hurriedly printed in Tokyo, where the books were bound. For any errors contained therein the undersigned is alone responsible.

ISOH YAMAGATA.

INDEX.

By Isoh Yamagata.

明治三十六年十一月二十三日印刷
明治三十六年十一月三十日發行

定價金拾貳圓

著作權所有

著者　鹿兒島市清水町二十一番　ゼームス、マードック

著者　東京本郷區西片町十番地　山縣五十雄

發行者　神戸市山本通貳丁目四十三番　ロバート、ヤング

印刷者　神戸市下山手通三丁目六十五番ノ一　尾崎岩吉

印刷業
發行所　神戸市榮町一丁目七番地　神戸クロニクル社

製凾印刷　東京市神田區賀川町三番地　田村茂太郎

製本　東京市京橋區木挽町二丁目十三番地　松本治郎吉

CPSIA information can be obtained at www.ICGtesting.com
Printed in the USA
BVOW09s1328250216

437931BV00046B/34/P